EX MACHINA

BOOK FOUR

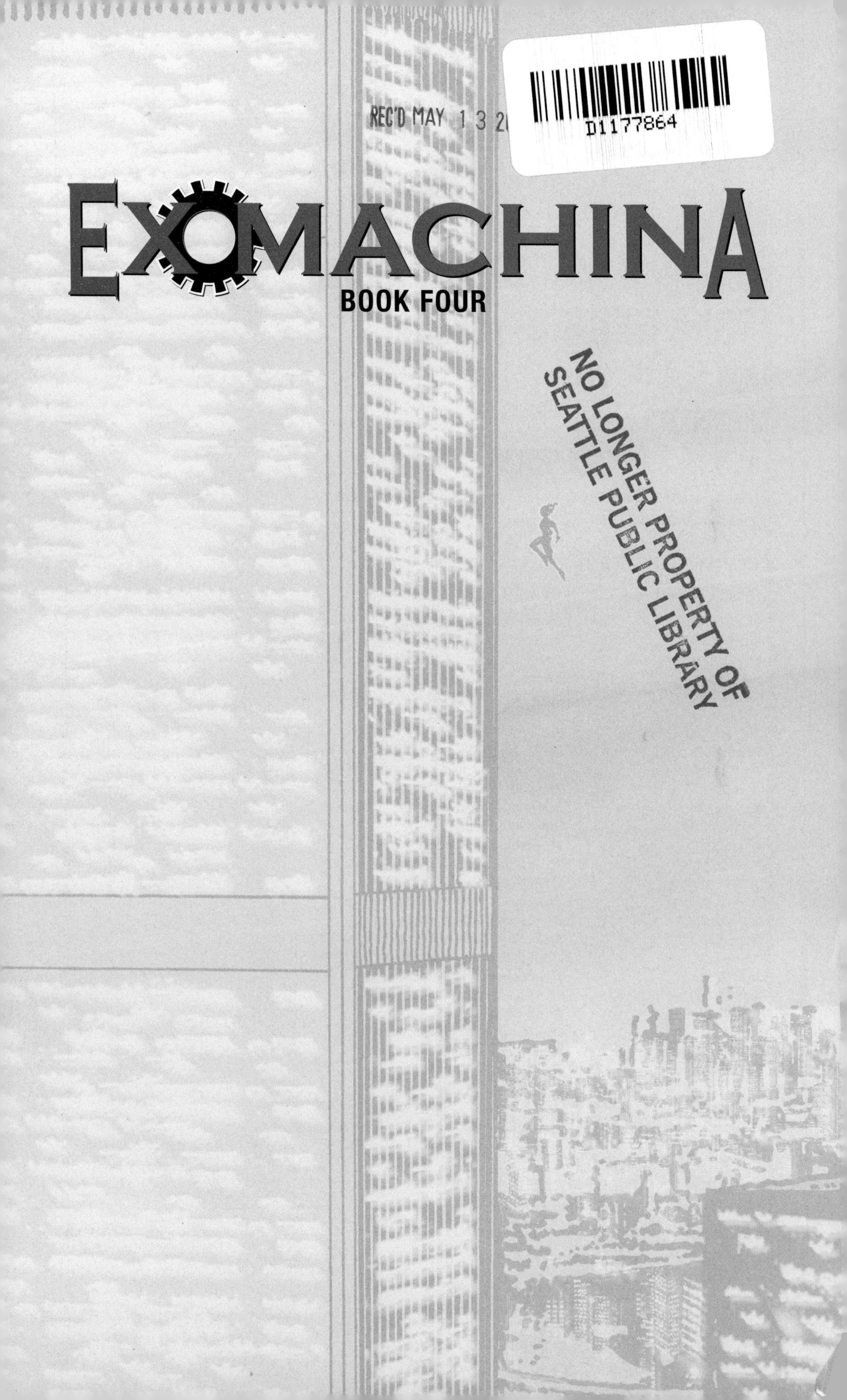

BRIAN K. VAUGHAN: WRITER
TONY HARRIS: PENCILS
JIM CLARK: INKS
JD METTLER: COLORS
JARED K. FLETCHER: LETTERS

SPECIAL THANKS TO GARTH ENNIS, JIM LEE AND RICHARD FRIEND FOR THEIR CONTRIBUTIONS TO ISSUE #40.

EX MACHINA CREATED BY VAUGHAN & HARRIS

COLLECTED EDITION COVER BY TONY HARRIS

Ben Abernathy	Editor – Original Series
Kristy Quinn	Assistant Editor – Original Series
Robbin Brosterman	Design Director – Books
Shelly Bond	Executive Editor – Vertigo
Hank Kanalz	Senior VP – Vertigo and Integrated Publishing
Diane Nelson	President
Dan DiDio and Jim Lee	Co-Publishers
Geoff Johns	Chief Creative Officer
Amit Desai	Senior VP – Marketing and Franchise Management
Amy Genkins	Senior VP – Business and Legal Affairs
Nairi Gardiner	Senior VP – Finance
Jeff Boison	VP – Publishing Planning
Mark Chiarello	VP – Art Direction and Design
John Cunningham	VP – Marketing
Terri Cunningham	VP – Editorial Administration
Larry Ganem	VP – Talent Relations and Services
Alison Gill	Senior VP – Manufacturing and Operations
Jay Kogan	VP – Business and Legal Affairs, Publishing
Jack Mahan	VP – Business Affairs, Talent
Nick Napolitano	VP – Manufacturing Administration
Sue Pohja	VP – Book Sales
Fred Ruiz	VP – Manufacturing Operationns
Courtney Simmons	Senior VP – Publicity
Bob Wayne	Senior VP – Sales

EX MACHINA BOOK FOUR
Published by DC Comics. Compilation Copyright © 2014 Brian K. Vaughan and Tony Harris. All Rights Reserved.

Originally published in single magazine form by WildStorm Productions as EX MACHINA #30-40 Copyright © 2007, 2008, 2009 Brian K. Vaughan and Tony Harris. All Rights Reserved. All characters, their distinctive likenesses and related elements featured in this publication are trademarks of Brian K. Vaughan and Tony Harris. The stories, characters and incidents featured in this publication are entirely fictional. DC Comics does not read or accept unsolicited ideas, stories or artwork.

DC Comics, 1700 Broadway, New York, NY 10019
A Warner Bros. Entertainment Company.
Printed by RR Donnelley, Owensville, MO, USA. 12/19/14.
First Printing
ISBN: 978-1-4012-5002-7

Library of Congress Cataloging-in-Publication Data

Vaughan, Brian K., author.
   Ex Machina. Book Four / Brian K. Vaughan ; illustrated by Tony Harris.
      pages cm
   Summary: "In this fourth volume, Mayor Mitchell Hundred is summoned to Rome for an audience with the Pope. But as Hundred makes his travel plans, he is unaware of the assassin who has him in his sights."-- Provided by publisher.
   ISBN 978-1-4012-5002-7 (paperback)
   1. Graphic novels. I. Harris, Tony, 1969- illustrator. II. Title.
   PN6728.E98V353 2014
   741.5'973—dc23
                                                    2014000396

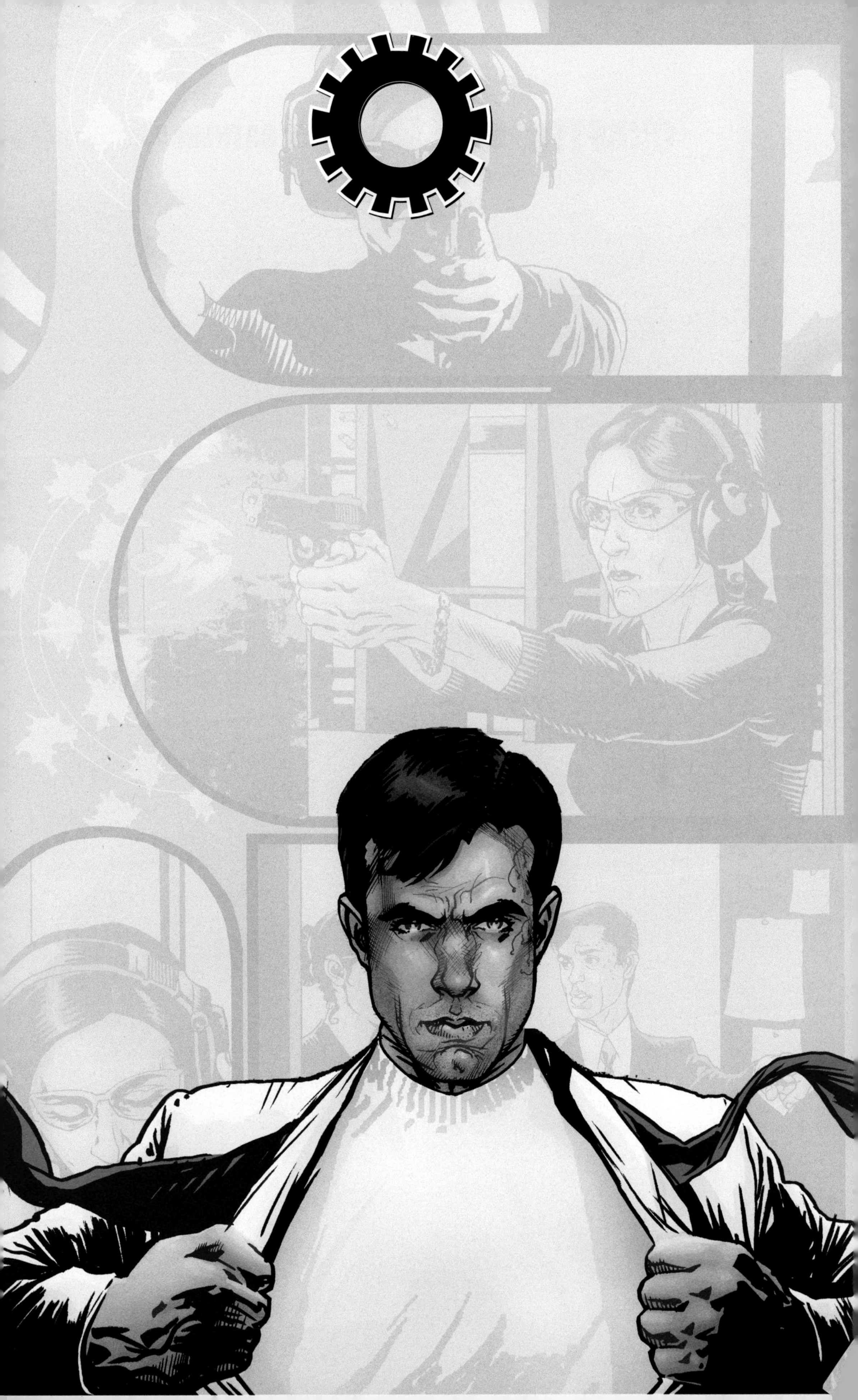

CHAPTER 1 EX CATHEDRA

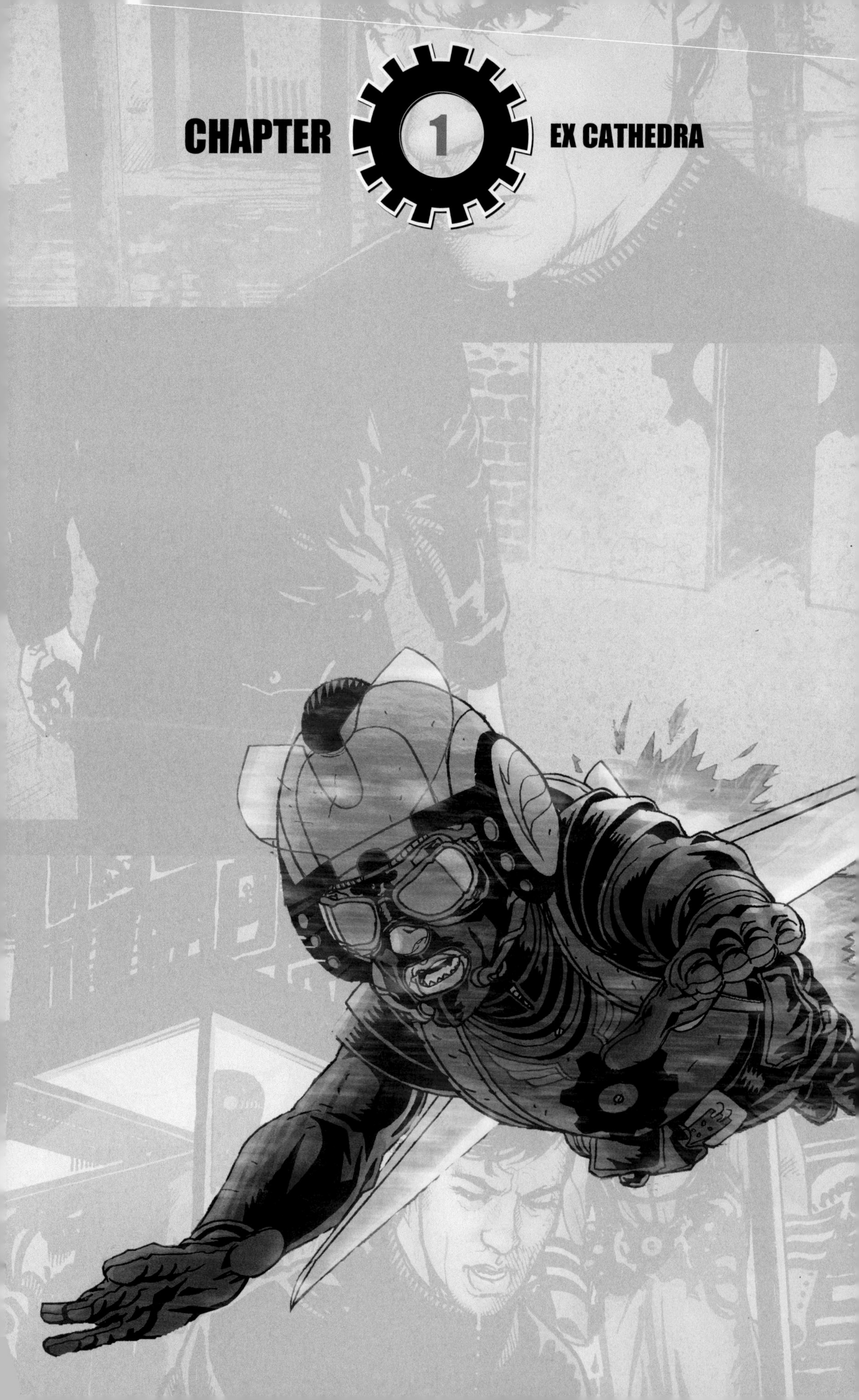

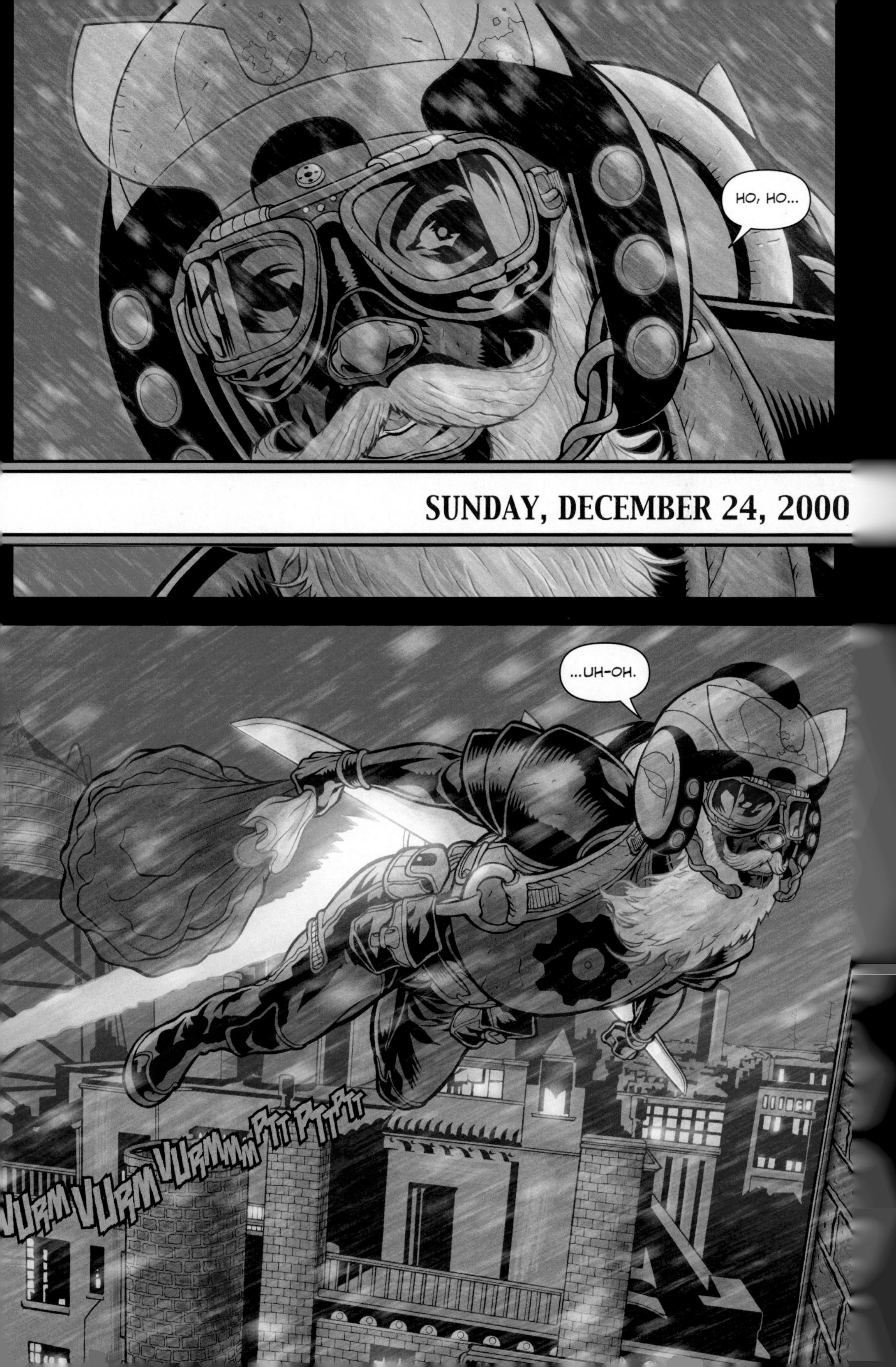
HO, HO...
SUNDAY, DECEMBER 24, 2000
...UH-OH.
VURM VURM VURMMMMPTTPTTPTT

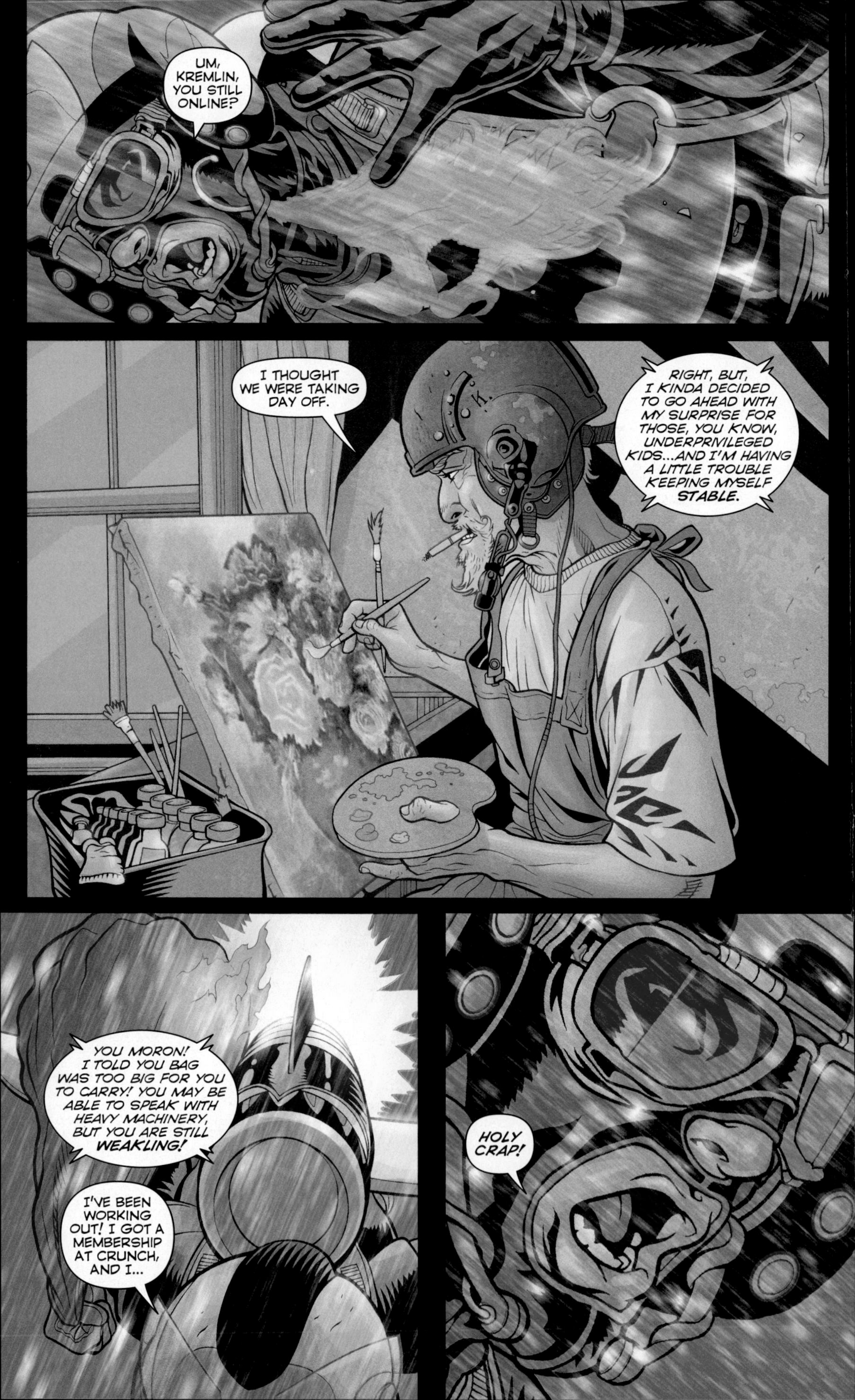
UM, KREMLIN, YOU STILL ONLINE?
I THOUGHT WE WERE TAKING DAY OFF.
RIGHT, BUT, I KINDA DECIDED TO GO AHEAD WITH MY SURPRISE FOR THOSE, YOU KNOW, UNDERPRIVILEGED KIDS...AND I'M HAVING A LITTLE TROUBLE KEEPING MYSELF STABLE.
YOU MORON! I TOLD YOU BAG WAS TOO BIG FOR YOU TO CARRY! YOU MAY BE ABLE TO SPEAK WITH HEAVY MACHINERY, BUT YOU ARE STILL WEAKLING!
I'VE BEEN WORKING OUT! I GOT A MEMBERSHIP AT CRUNCH, AND I...
HOLY CRAP!

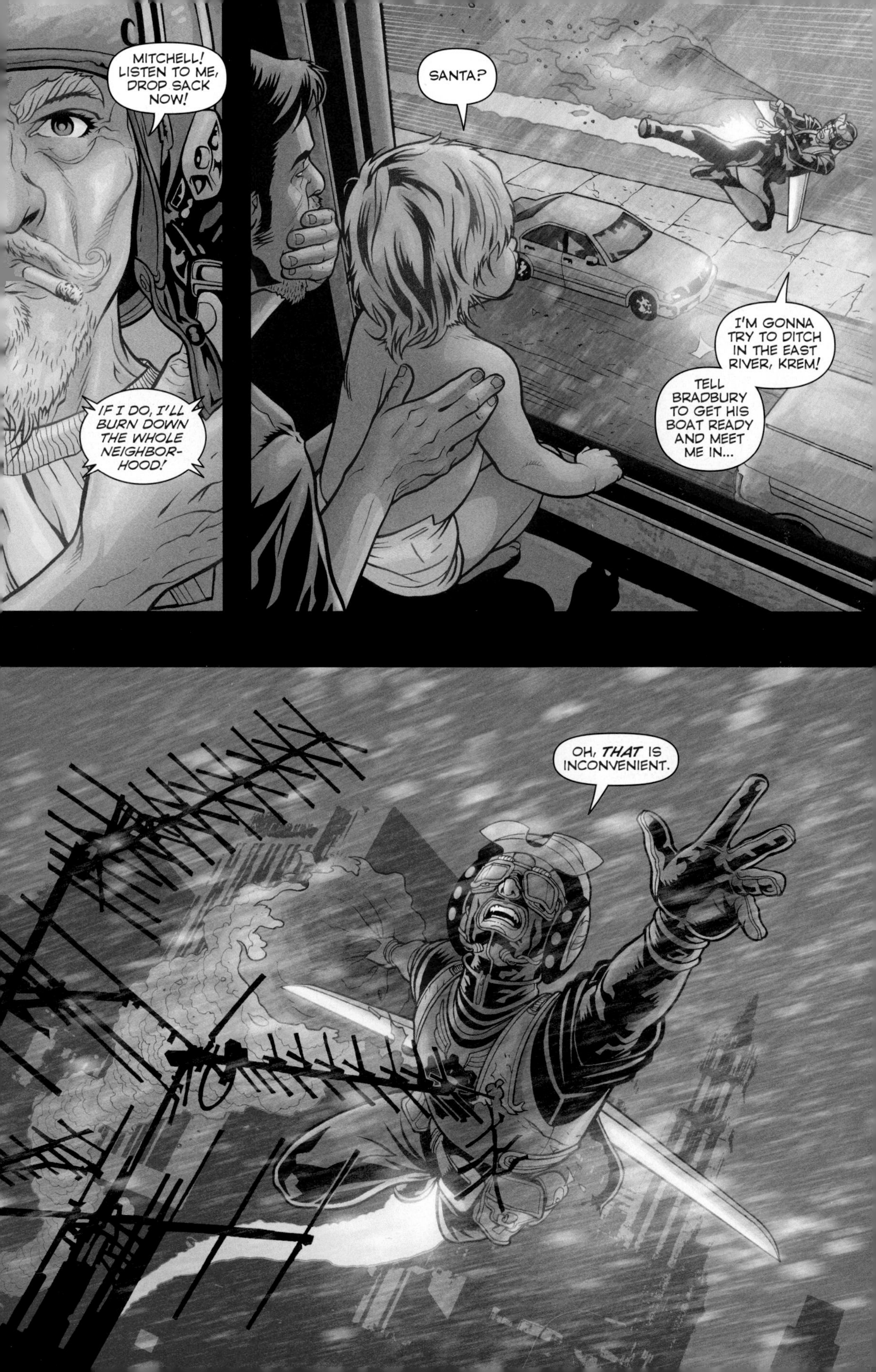

MITCHELL! LISTEN TO ME, DROP SACK NOW!
IF I DO, I'LL BURN DOWN THE WHOLE NEIGHBOR-HOOD!
SANTA?
I'M GONNA TRY TO DITCH IN THE EAST RIVER, KREM!
TELL BRADBURY TO GET HIS BOAT READY AND MEET ME IN...
OH, THAT IS INCONVENIENT.

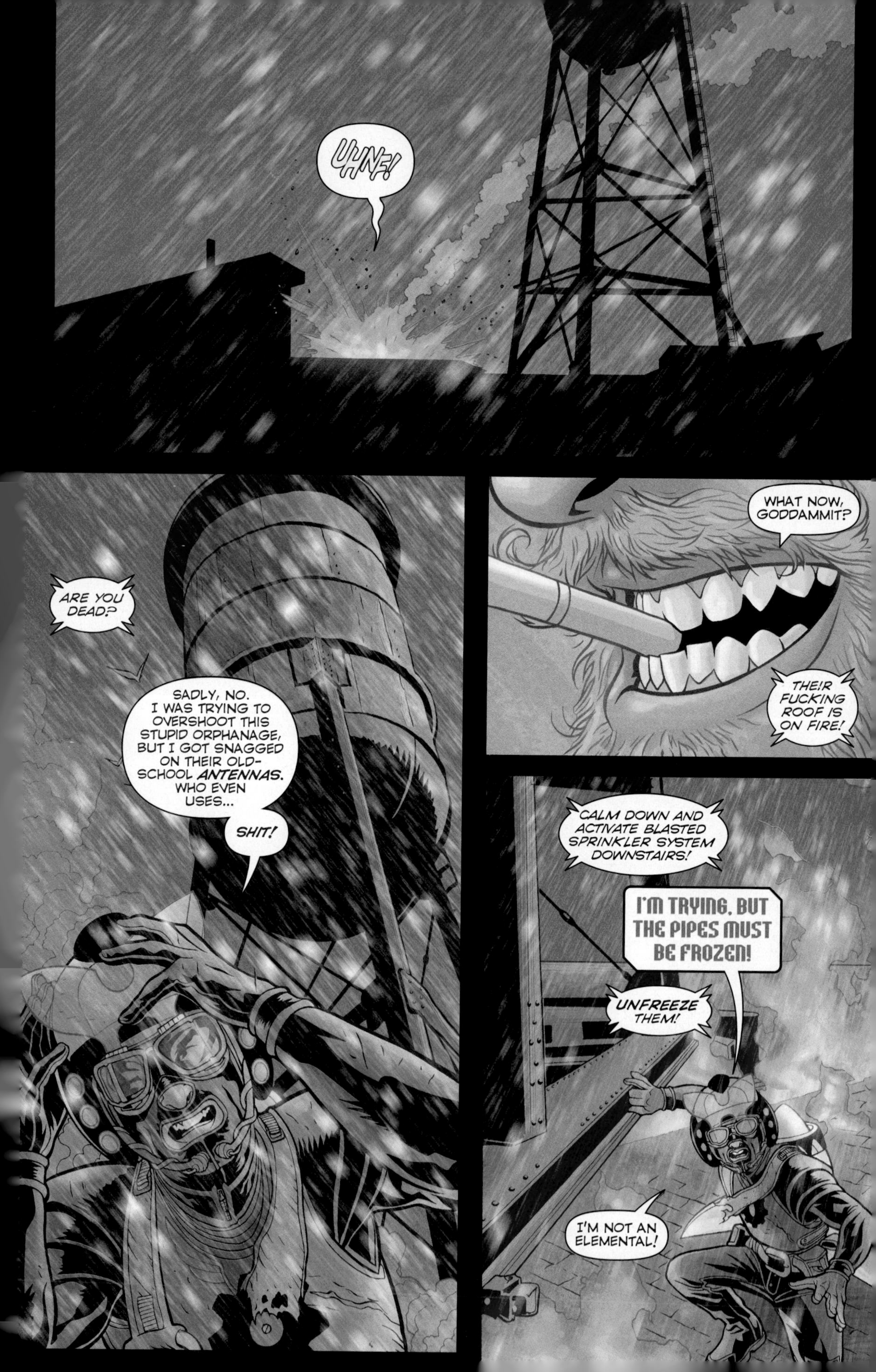
UHNF!
ARE YOU DEAD?
SADLY, NO. I WAS TRYING TO OVERSHOOT THIS STUPID ORPHANAGE, BUT I GOT SNAGGED ON THEIR OLD-SCHOOL ANTENNAS. WHO EVEN USES...
SHIT!
WHAT NOW, GODDAMMIT?
THEIR FUCKING ROOF IS ON FIRE!
CALM DOWN AND ACTIVATE BLASTED SPRINKLER SYSTEM DOWNSTAIRS!
I'M TRYING, BUT THE PIPES MUST BE FROZEN!
UNFREEZE THEM!
I'M NOT AN ELEMENTAL!

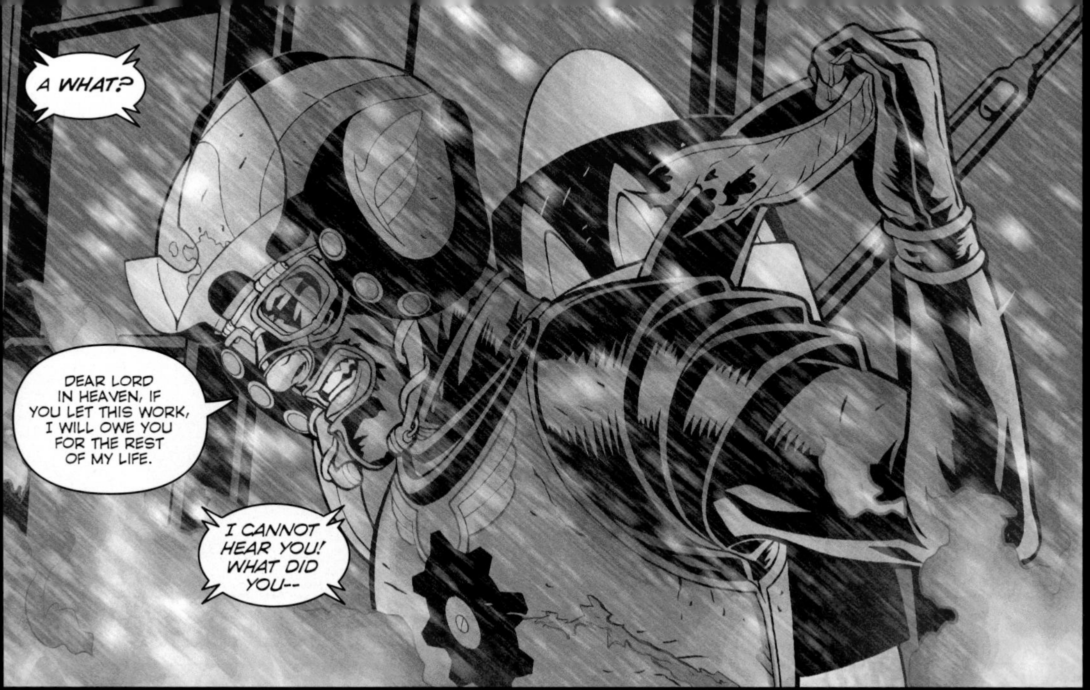
A WHAT?
DEAR LORD IN HEAVEN, IF YOU LET THIS WORK, I WILL OWE YOU FOR THE REST OF MY LIFE.
I CANNOT HEAR YOU! WHAT DID YOU--

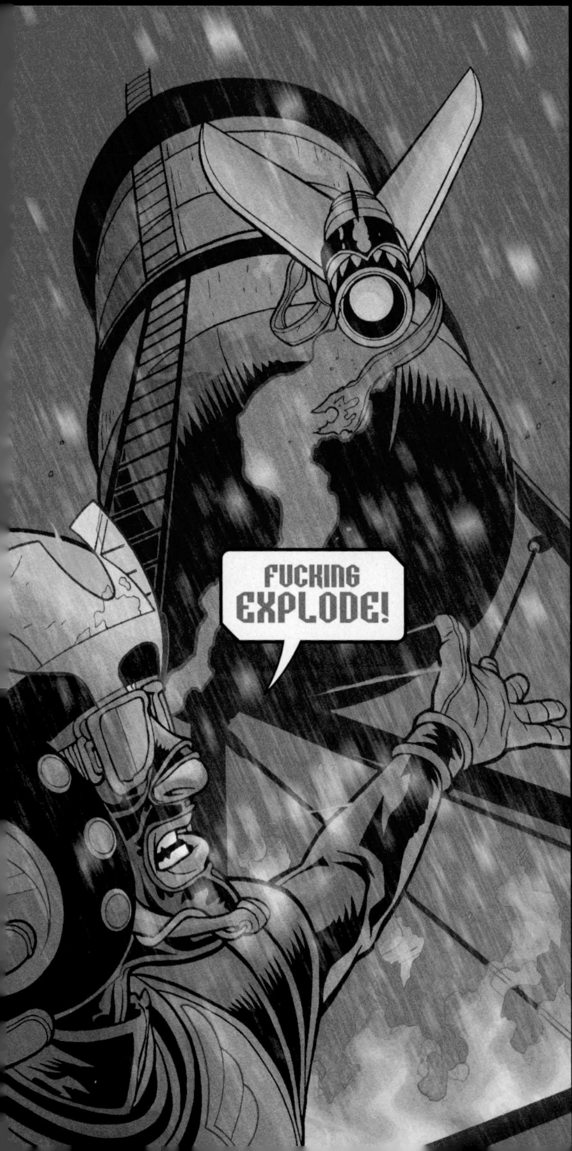
FUCKING EXPLODE!

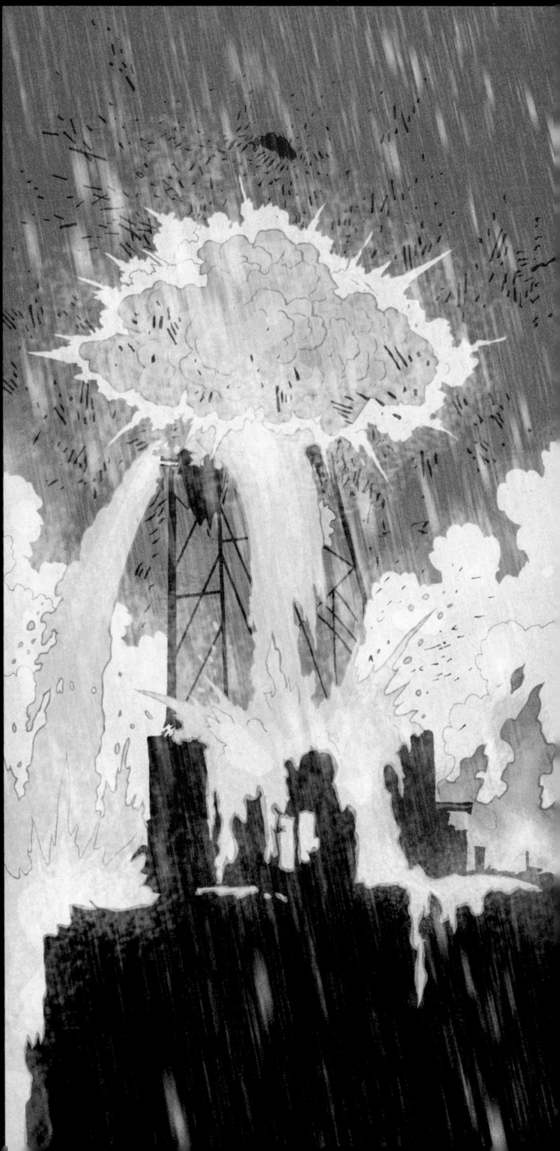

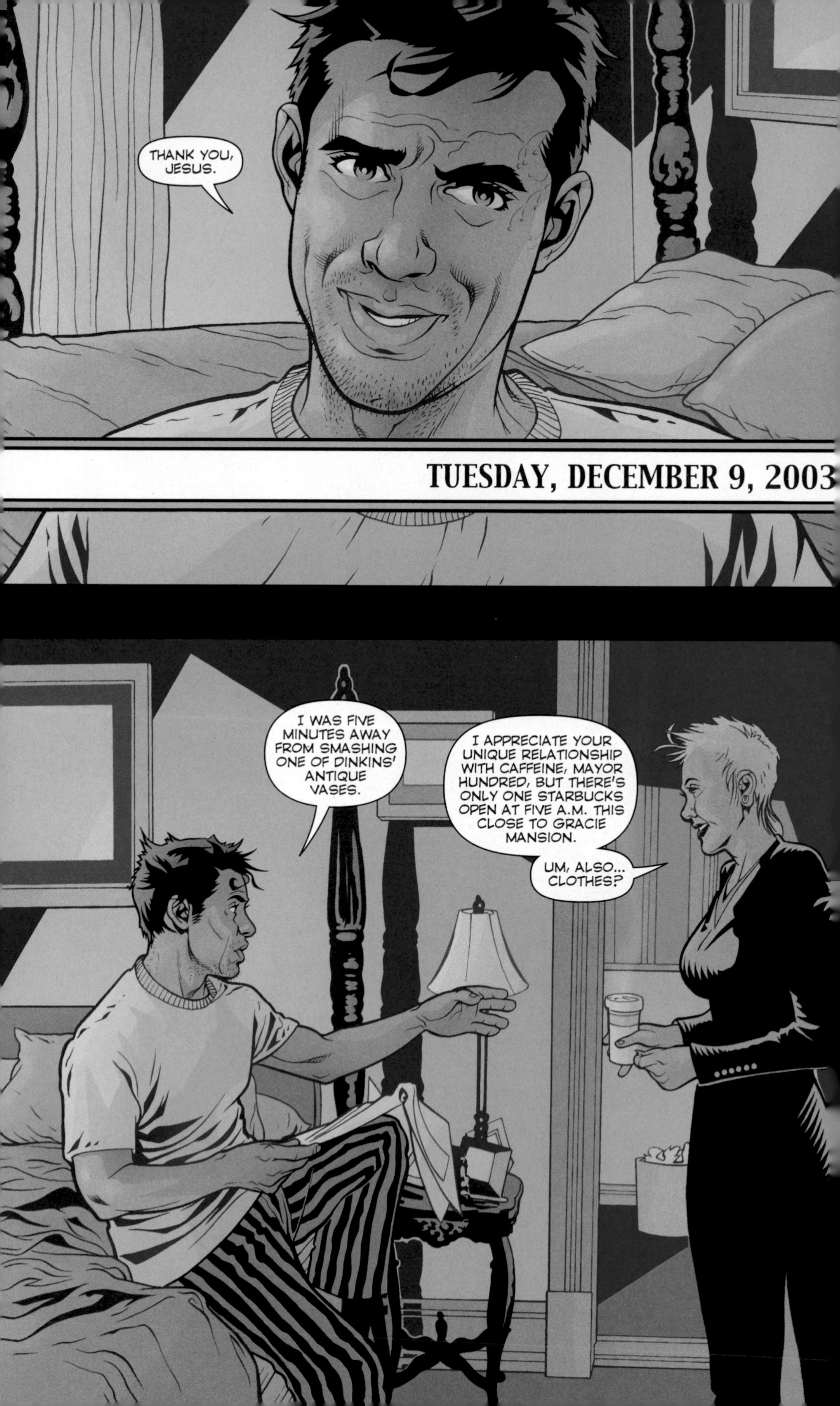
THANK YOU, JESUS.
TUESDAY, DECEMBER 9, 2003
I WAS FIVE MINUTES AWAY FROM SMASHING ONE OF DINKINS' ANTIQUE VASES.
I APPRECIATE YOUR UNIQUE RELATIONSHIP WITH CAFFEINE, MAYOR HUNDRED, BUT THERE'S ONLY ONE STARBUCKS OPEN AT FIVE A.M. THIS CLOSE TO GRACIE MANSION.
UM, ALSO... CLOTHES?

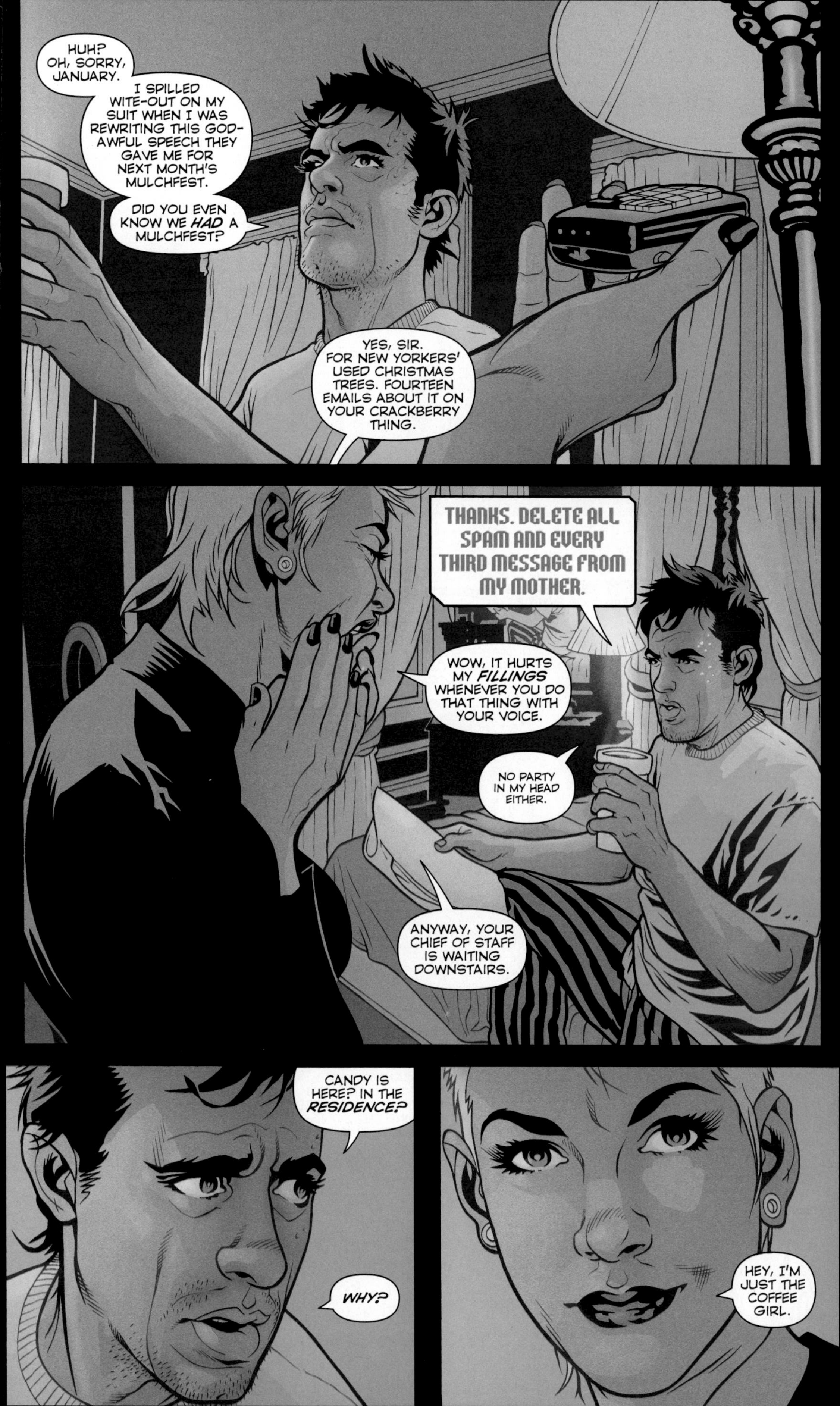
HUH? OH, SORRY, JANUARY.
I SPILLED WITE-OUT ON MY SUIT WHEN I WAS REWRITING THIS GOD-AWFUL SPEECH THEY GAVE ME FOR NEXT MONTH'S MULCHFEST.
DID YOU EVEN KNOW WE HAD A MULCHFEST?
YES, SIR. FOR NEW YORKERS' USED CHRISTMAS TREES. FOURTEEN EMAILS ABOUT IT ON YOUR CRACKBERRY THING.
THANKS. DELETE ALL SPAM AND EVERY THIRD MESSAGE FROM MY MOTHER.
WOW, IT HURTS MY FILLINGS WHENEVER YOU DO THAT THING WITH YOUR VOICE.
NO PARTY IN MY HEAD EITHER.
ANYWAY, YOUR CHIEF OF STAFF IS WAITING DOWNSTAIRS.
CANDY IS HERE? IN THE RESIDENCE?
WHY?
HEY, I'M JUST THE COFFEE GIRL.

The Zombie Pirate Padeem

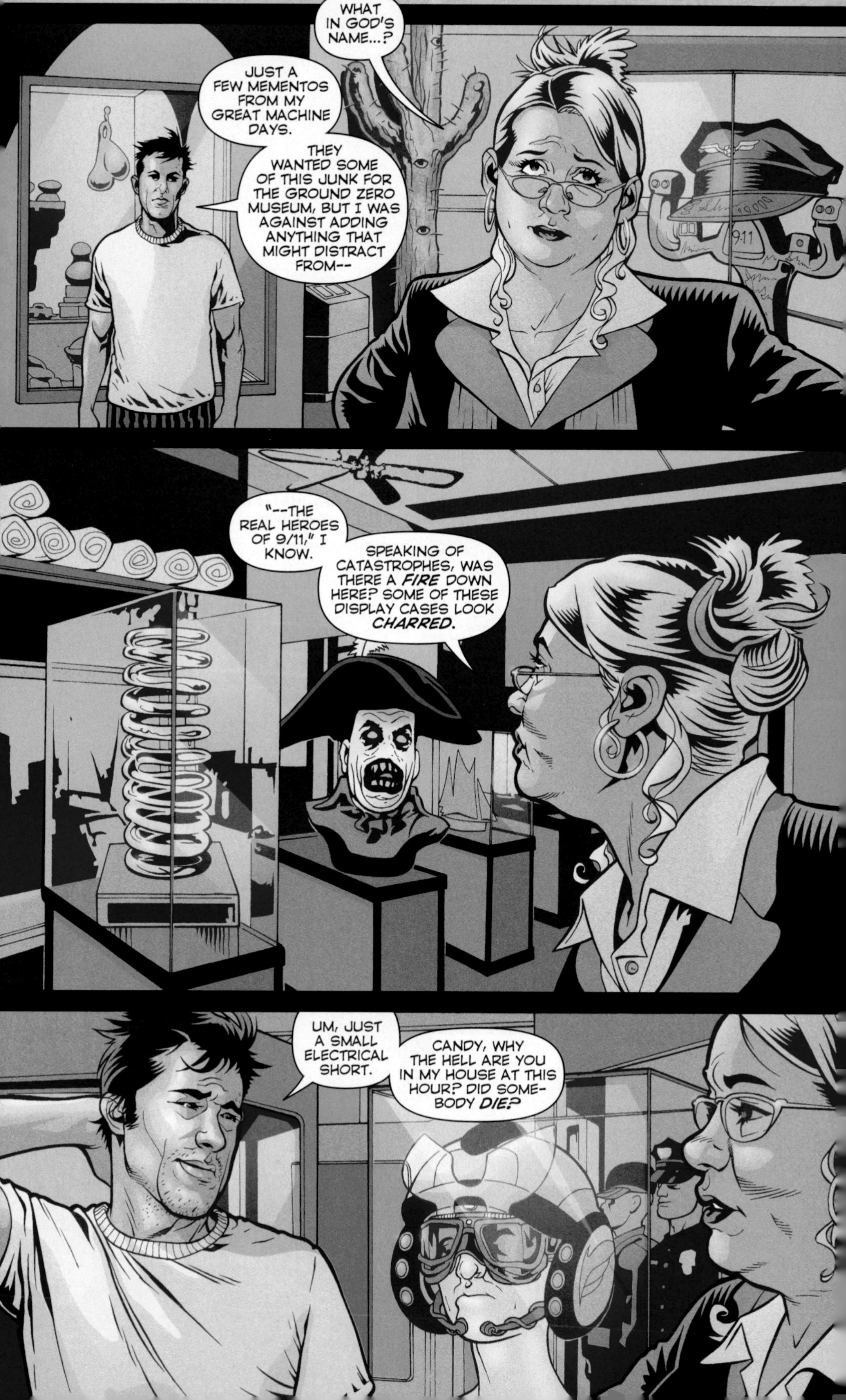
WHAT IN GOD'S NAME...?
JUST A FEW MEMENTOS FROM MY GREAT MACHINE DAYS.
THEY WANTED SOME OF THIS JUNK FOR THE GROUND ZERO MUSEUM, BUT I WAS AGAINST ADDING ANYTHING THAT MIGHT DISTRACT FROM--
"--THE REAL HEROES OF 9/11," I KNOW.
SPEAKING OF CATASTROPHES, WAS THERE A FIRE DOWN HERE? SOME OF THESE DISPLAY CASES LOOK CHARRED.
UM, JUST A SMALL ELECTRICAL SHORT.
CANDY, WHY THE HELL ARE YOU IN MY HOUSE AT THIS HOUR? DID SOMEBODY DIE?

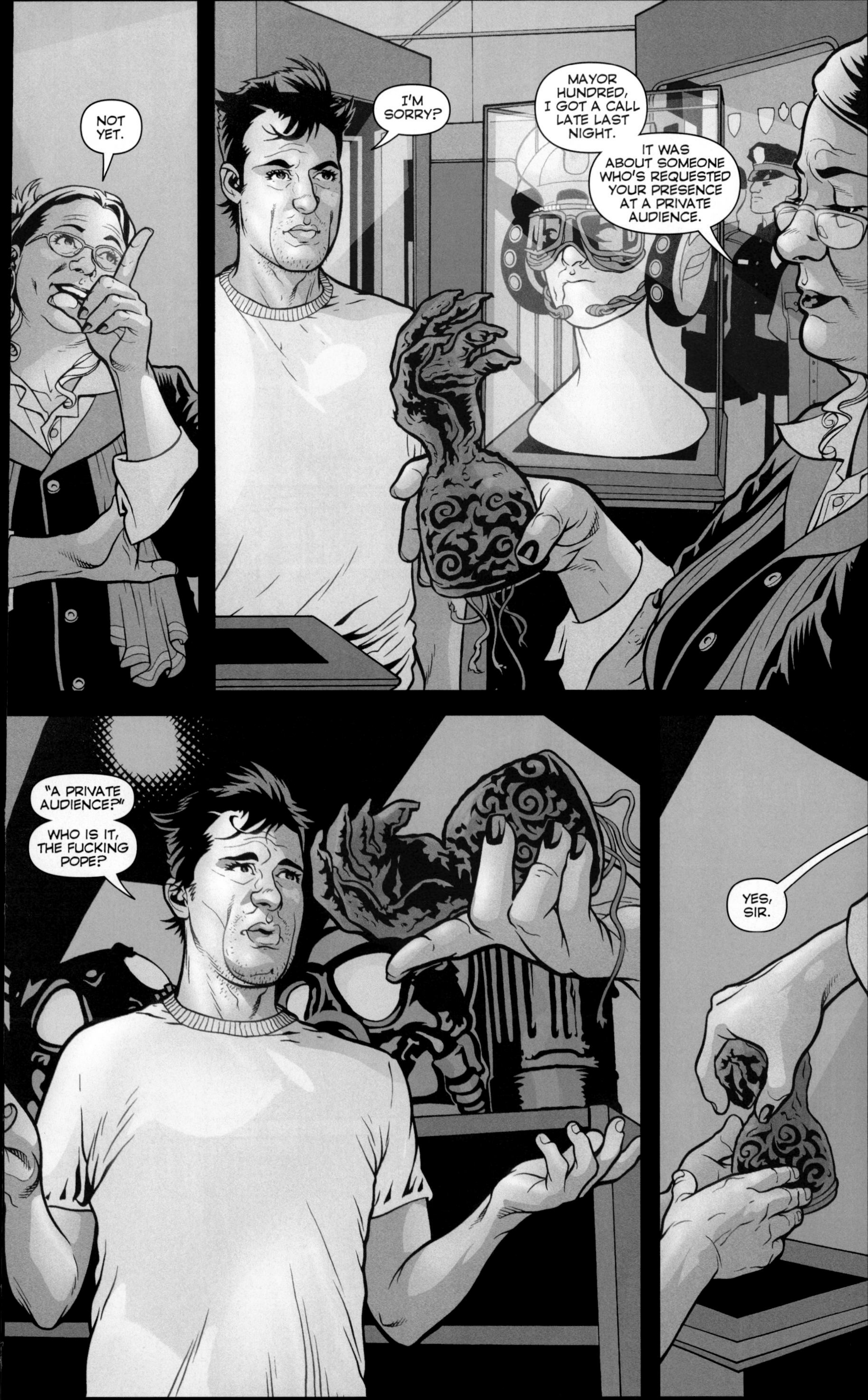
NOT YET.
I'M SORRY?
MAYOR HUNDRED, I GOT A CALL LATE LAST NIGHT.
IT WAS ABOUT SOMEONE WHO'S REQUESTED YOUR PRESENCE AT A PRIVATE AUDIENCE.
"A PRIVATE AUDIENCE?"
WHO IS IT, THE FUCKING POPE?
YES, SIR.

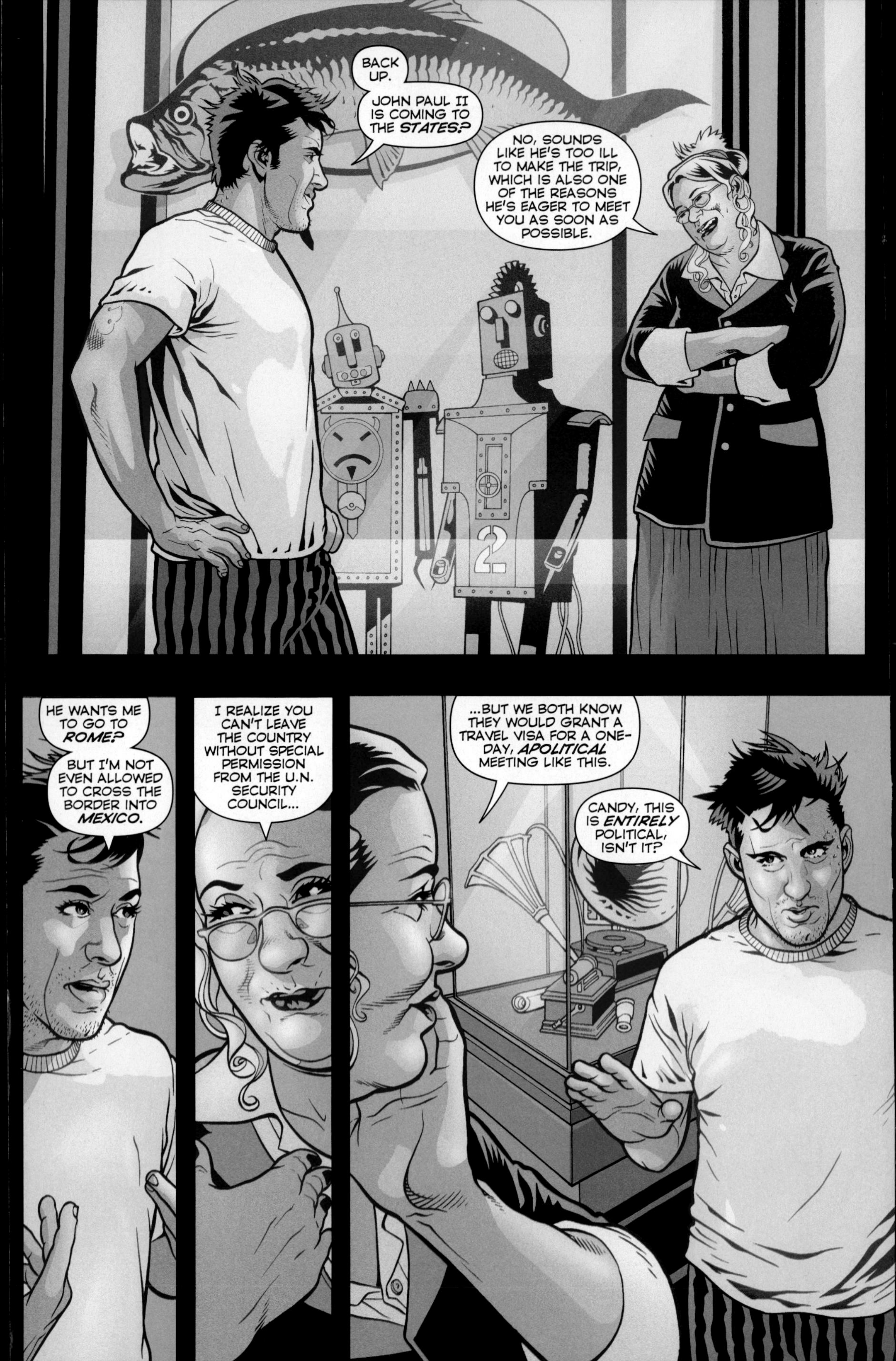

BACK UP.
JOHN PAUL II IS COMING TO THE STATES?
NO, SOUNDS LIKE HE'S TOO ILL TO MAKE THE TRIP, WHICH IS ALSO ONE OF THE REASONS HE'S EAGER TO MEET YOU AS SOON AS POSSIBLE.
HE WANTS ME TO GO TO ROME?
BUT I'M NOT EVEN ALLOWED TO CROSS THE BORDER INTO MEXICO.
I REALIZE YOU CAN'T LEAVE THE COUNTRY WITHOUT SPECIAL PERMISSION FROM THE U.N. SECURITY COUNCIL...
...BUT WE BOTH KNOW THEY WOULD GRANT A TRAVEL VISA FOR A ONE-DAY, APOLITICAL MEETING LIKE THIS.
CANDY, THIS IS ENTIRELY POLITICAL, ISN'T IT?

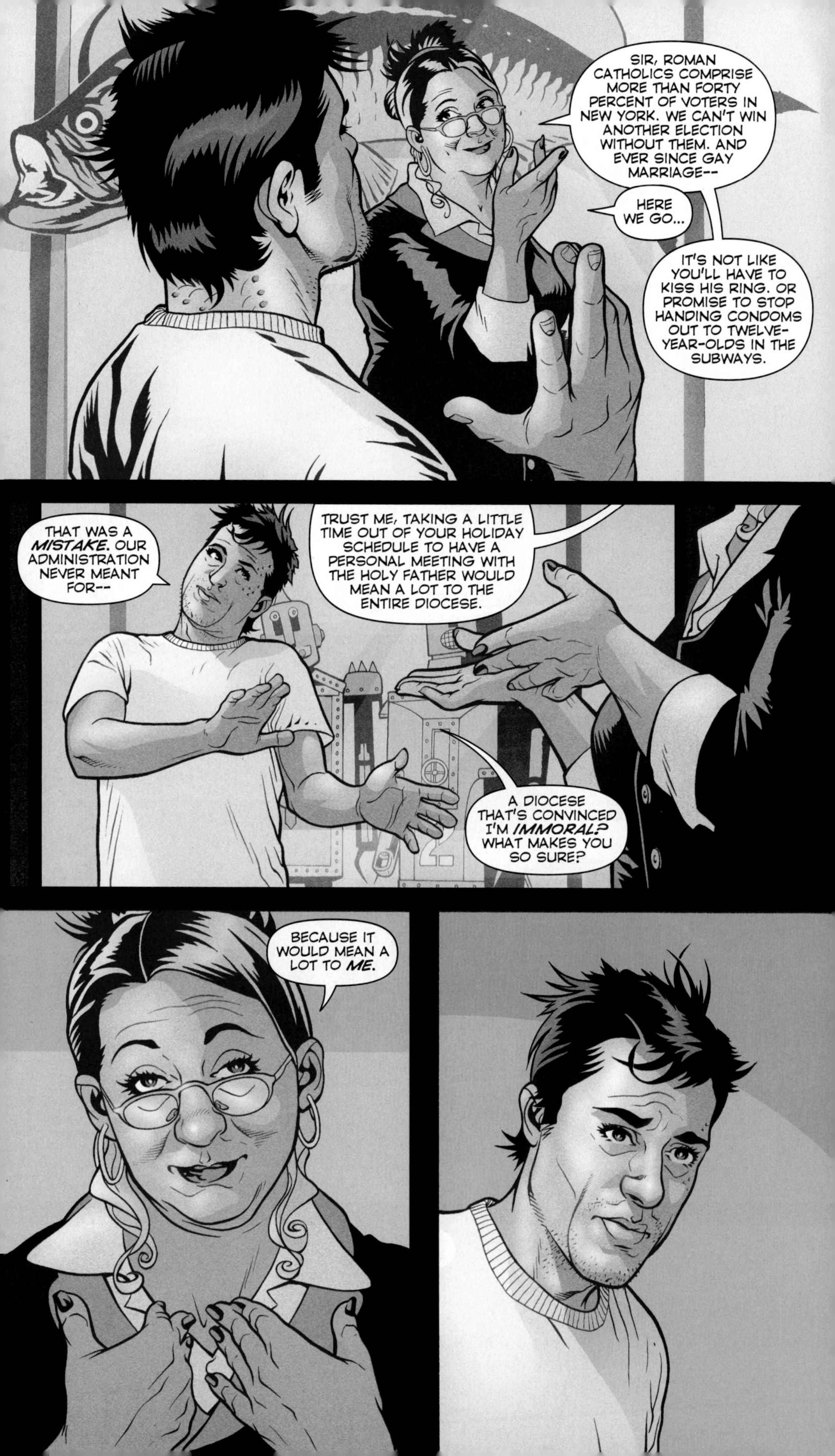
SIR, ROMAN CATHOLICS COMPRISE MORE THAN FORTY PERCENT OF VOTERS IN NEW YORK. WE CAN'T WIN ANOTHER ELECTION WITHOUT THEM. AND EVER SINCE GAY MARRIAGE--
HERE WE GO...
IT'S NOT LIKE YOU'LL HAVE TO KISS HIS RING. OR PROMISE TO STOP HANDING CONDOMS OUT TO TWELVE-YEAR-OLDS IN THE SUBWAYS.
THAT WAS A *MISTAKE*. OUR ADMINISTRATION NEVER MEANT FOR--
TRUST ME, TAKING A LITTLE TIME OUT OF YOUR HOLIDAY SCHEDULE TO HAVE A PERSONAL MEETING WITH THE HOLY FATHER WOULD MEAN A LOT TO THE ENTIRE DIOCESE.
A DIOCESE THAT'S CONVINCED I'M *IMMORAL?* WHAT MAKES YOU SO SURE?
BECAUSE IT WOULD MEAN A LOT TO *ME*.

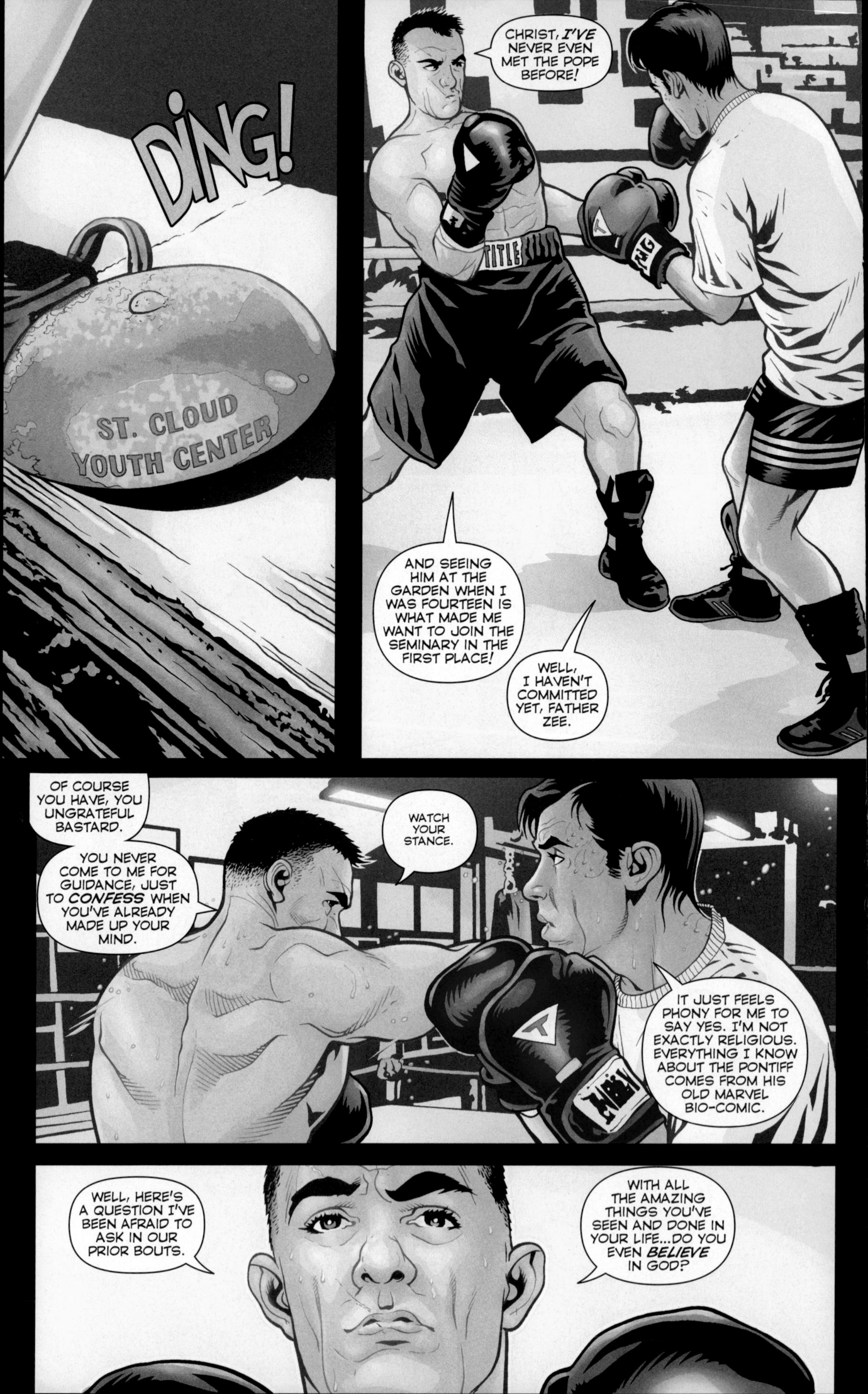
DING!
ST. CLOUD YOUTH CENTER
CHRIST, I'VE NEVER EVEN MET THE POPE BEFORE!
TITLE
AND SEEING HIM AT THE GARDEN WHEN I WAS FOURTEEN IS WHAT MADE ME WANT TO JOIN THE SEMINARY IN THE FIRST PLACE!
WELL, I HAVEN'T COMMITTED YET, FATHER ZEE.
OF COURSE YOU HAVE, YOU UNGRATEFUL BASTARD.
YOU NEVER COME TO ME FOR GUIDANCE, JUST TO CONFESS WHEN YOU'VE ALREADY MADE UP YOUR MIND.
WATCH YOUR STANCE.
IT JUST FEELS PHONY FOR ME TO SAY YES. I'M NOT EXACTLY RELIGIOUS. EVERYTHING I KNOW ABOUT THE PONTIFF COMES FROM HIS OLD MARVEL BIO-COMIC.
WELL, HERE'S A QUESTION I'VE BEEN AFRAID TO ASK IN OUR PRIOR BOUTS.
WITH ALL THE AMAZING THINGS YOU'VE SEEN AND DONE IN YOUR LIFE...DO YOU EVEN BELIEVE IN GOD?

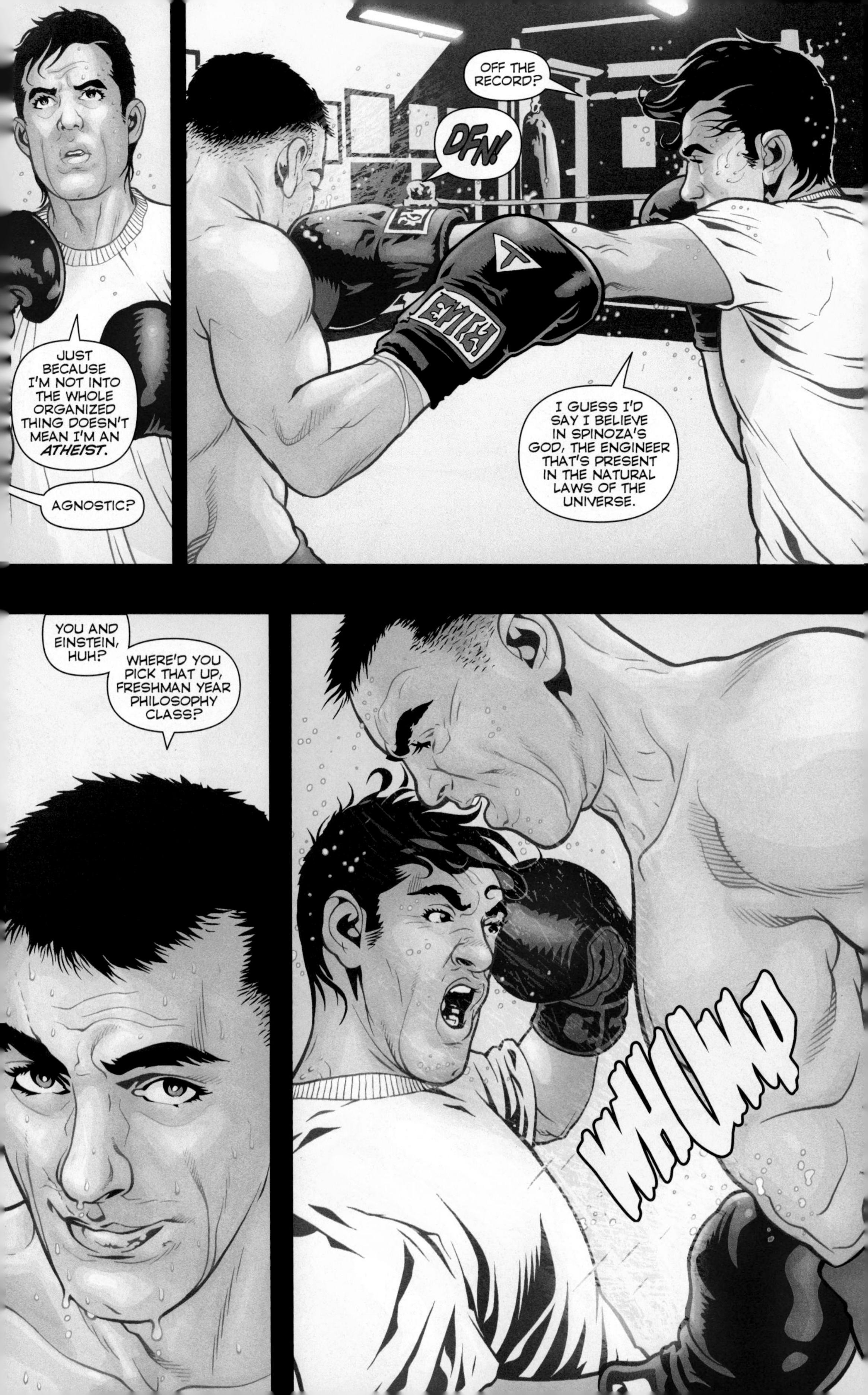
JUST BECAUSE I'M NOT INTO THE WHOLE ORGANIZED THING DOESN'T MEAN I'M AN *ATHEIST*.
AGNOSTIC?
OFF THE RECORD?
DFN!
I GUESS I'D SAY I BELIEVE IN SPINOZA'S GOD, THE ENGINEER THAT'S PRESENT IN THE NATURAL LAWS OF THE UNIVERSE.
YOU AND EINSTEIN, HUH?
WHERE'D YOU PICK THAT UP, FRESHMAN YEAR PHILOSOPHY CLASS?
WHUMP

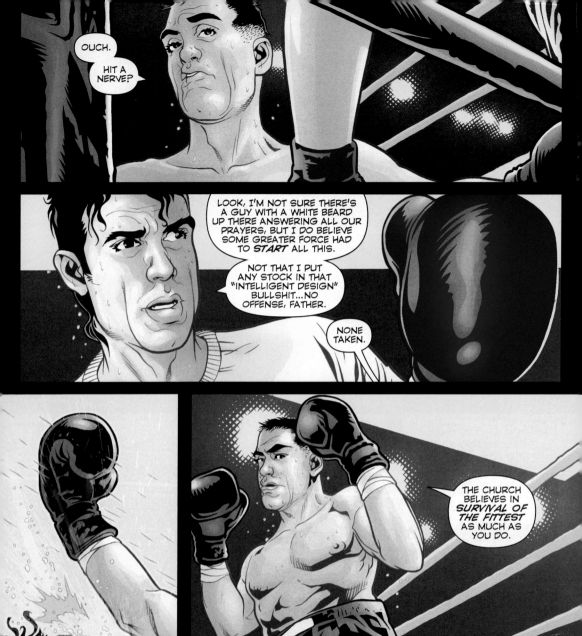

OUCH.

HIT A NERVE?

LOOK, I'M NOT SURE THERE'S A GUY WITH A WHITE BEARD UP THERE ANSWERING ALL OUR PRAYERS, BUT I DO BELIEVE SOME GREATER FORCE HAD TO *START* ALL THIS.

NOT THAT I PUT ANY STOCK IN THAT "INTELLIGENT DESIGN" BULLSHIT...NO OFFENSE, FATHER.

NONE TAKEN.

THE CHURCH BELIEVES IN *SURVIVAL OF THE FITTEST* AS MUCH AS YOU DO.

UHF!

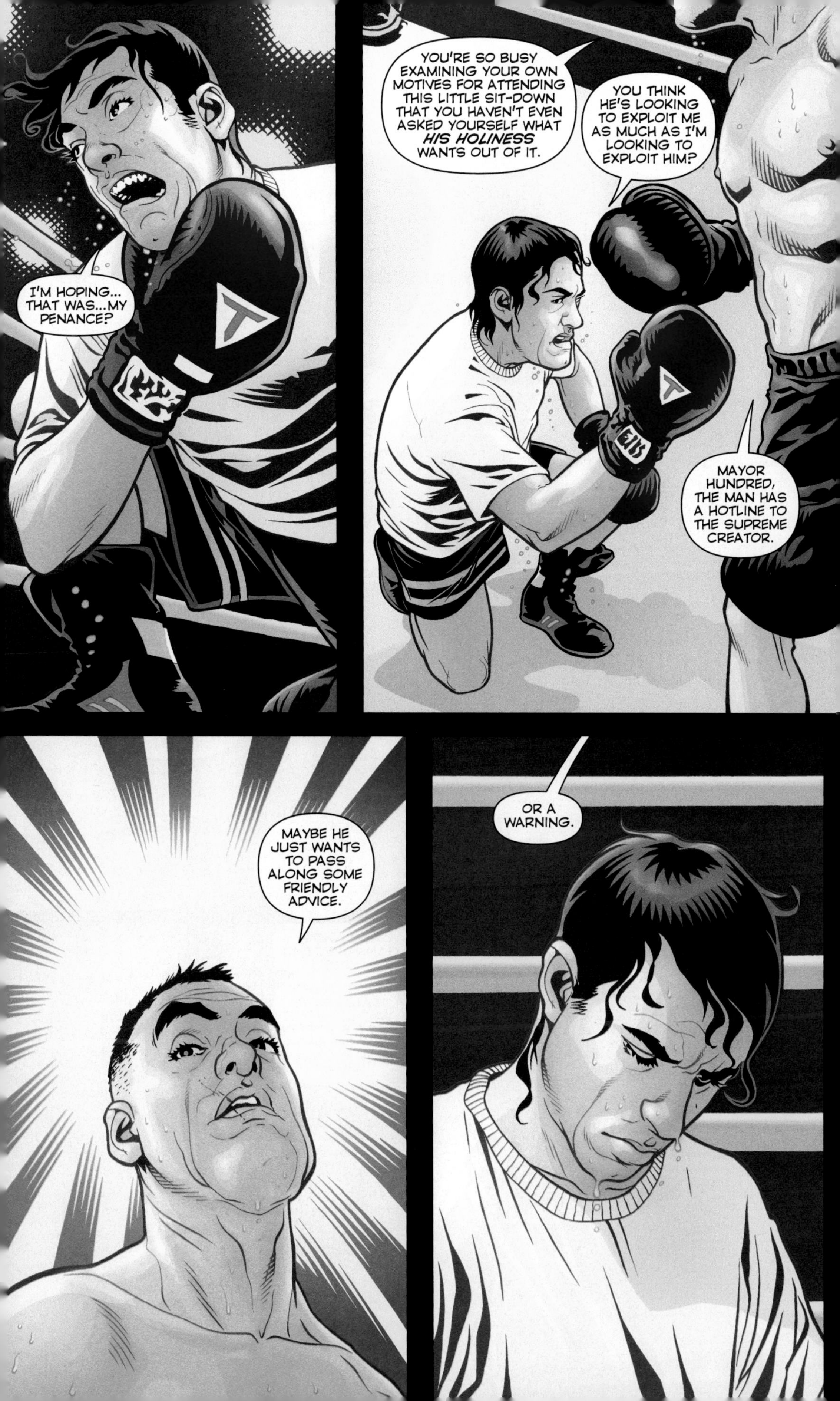
I'M HOPING... THAT WAS...MY PENANCE?
YOU'RE SO BUSY EXAMINING YOUR OWN MOTIVES FOR ATTENDING THIS LITTLE SIT-DOWN THAT YOU HAVEN'T EVEN ASKED YOURSELF WHAT HIS HOLINESS WANTS OUT OF IT.
YOU THINK HE'S LOOKING TO EXPLOIT ME AS MUCH AS I'M LOOKING TO EXPLOIT HIM?
MAYOR HUNDRED, THE MAN HAS A HOTLINE TO THE SUPREME CREATOR.
MAYBE HE JUST WANTS TO PASS ALONG SOME FRIENDLY ADVICE.
OR A WARNING.

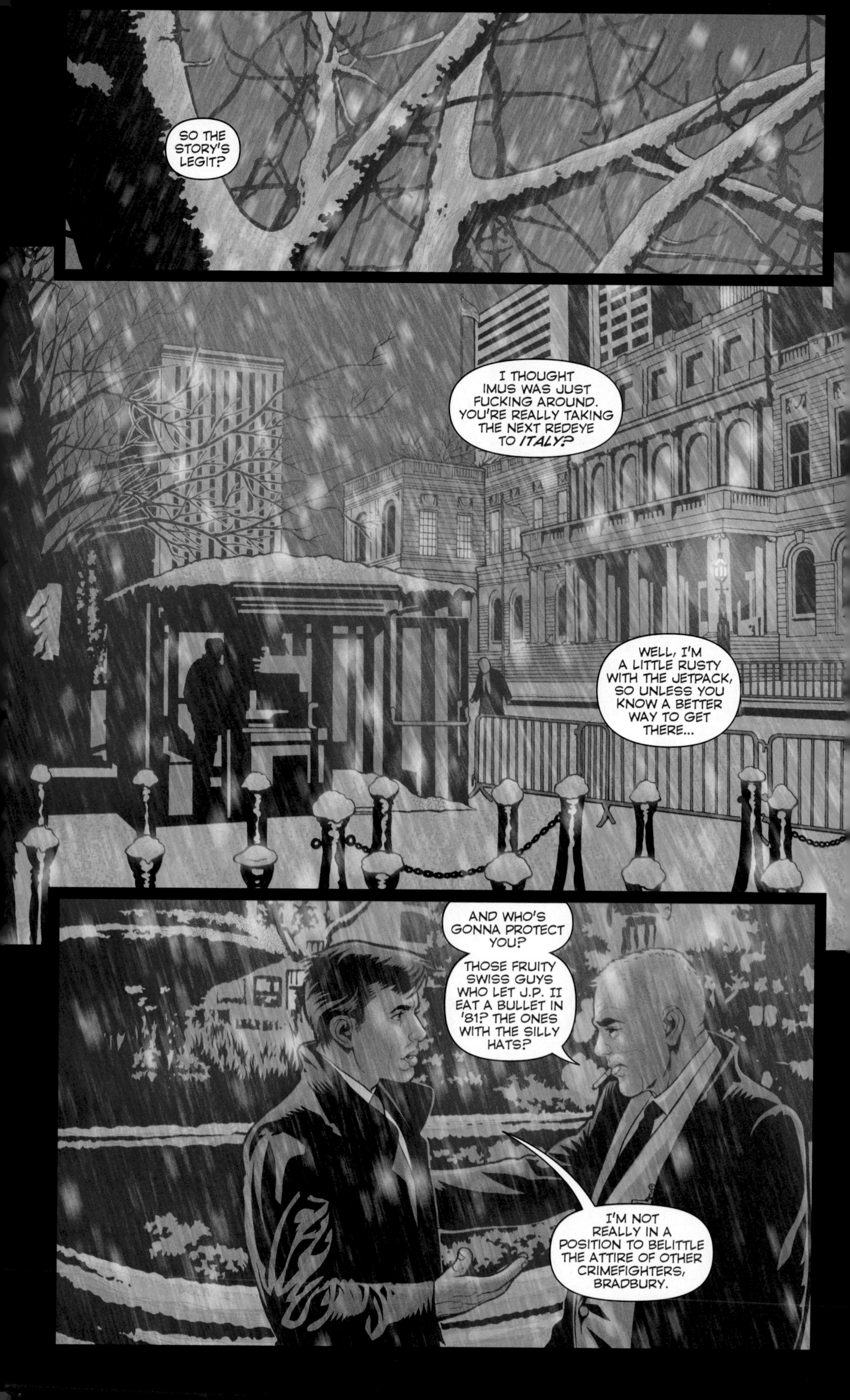
SO THE STORY'S LEGIT?
I THOUGHT IMUS WAS JUST FUCKING AROUND. YOU'RE REALLY TAKING THE NEXT REDEYE TO *ITALY?*
WELL, I'M A LITTLE RUSTY WITH THE JETPACK, SO UNLESS YOU KNOW A BETTER WAY TO GET THERE...
AND WHO'S GONNA PROTECT YOU?
THOSE FRUITY SWISS GUYS WHO LET J.P. II EAT A BULLET IN '81? THE ONES WITH THE SILLY HATS?
I'M NOT REALLY IN A POSITION TO BELITTLE THE ATTIRE OF OTHER CRIMEFIGHTERS, BRADBURY.

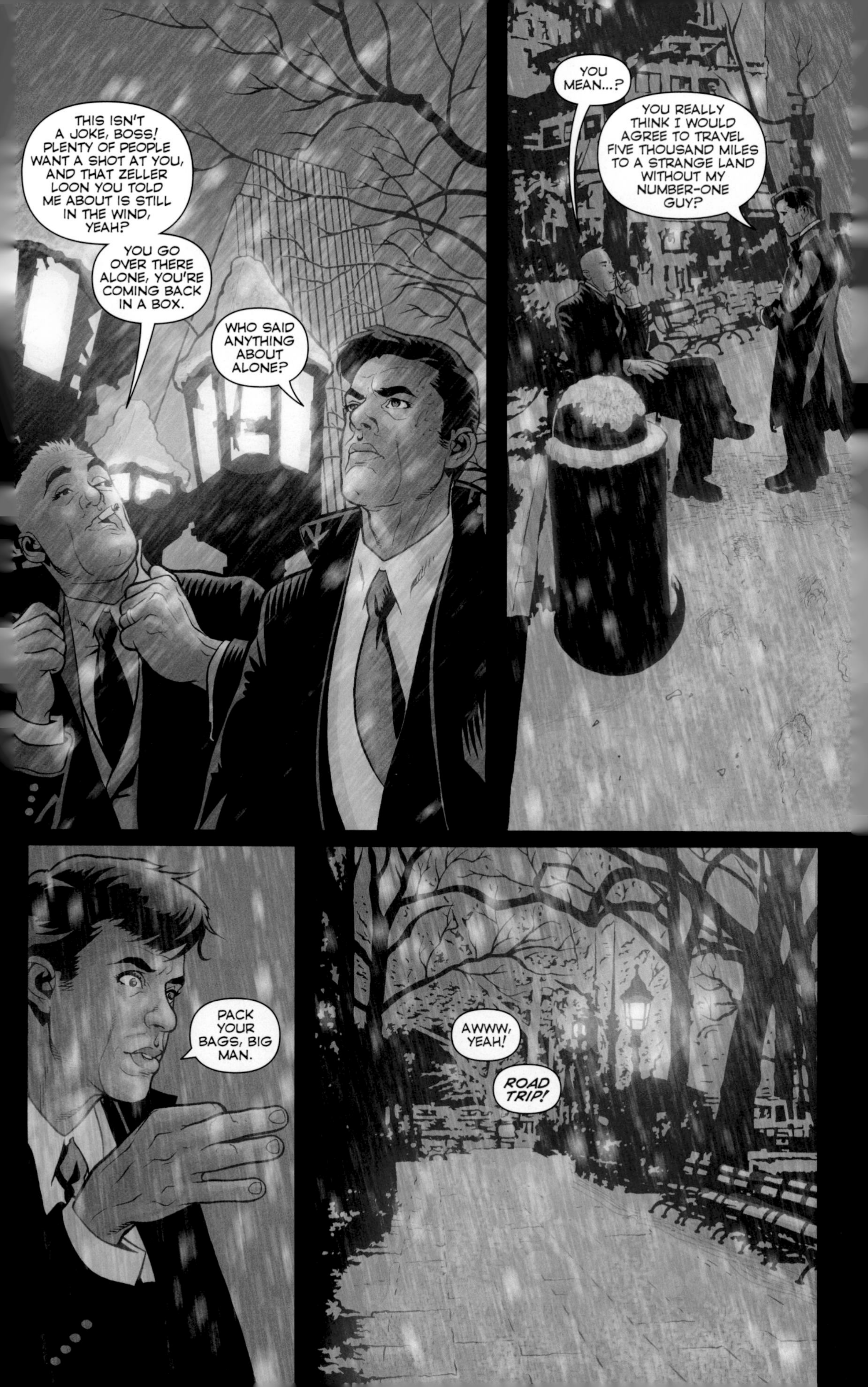
THIS ISN'T A JOKE, BOSS! PLENTY OF PEOPLE WANT A SHOT AT YOU, AND THAT ZELLER LOON YOU TOLD ME ABOUT IS STILL IN THE WIND, YEAH?
YOU GO OVER THERE ALONE, YOU'RE COMING BACK IN A BOX.
WHO SAID ANYTHING ABOUT ALONE?
YOU MEAN...?
YOU REALLY THINK I WOULD AGREE TO TRAVEL FIVE THOUSAND MILES TO A STRANGE LAND WITHOUT MY NUMBER-ONE GUY?
PACK YOUR BAGS, BIG MAN.
AWWW, YEAH!
ROAD TRIP!

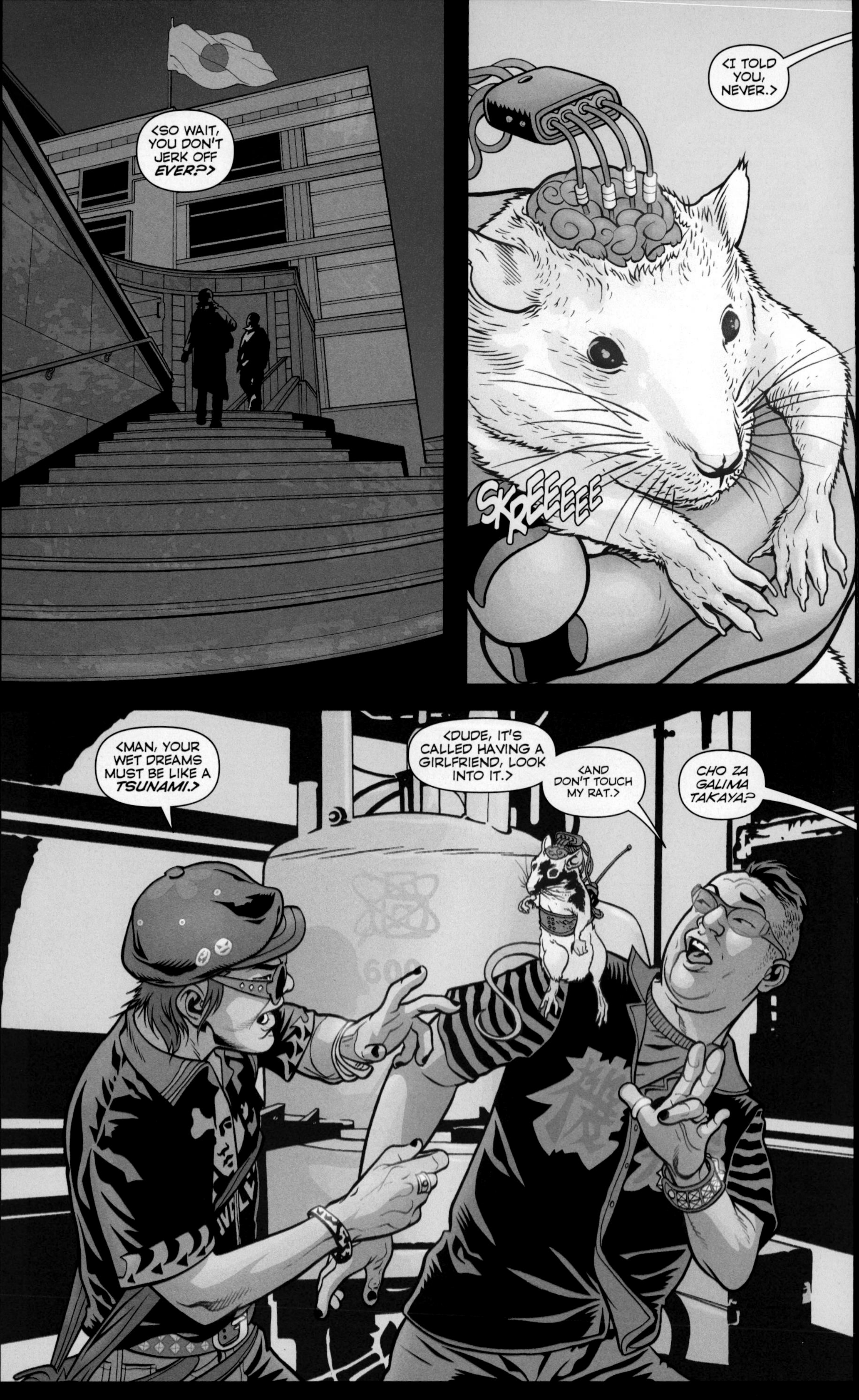
<SO WAIT, YOU DON'T JERK OFF EVER?>
<I TOLD YOU, NEVER.>
SKREEEEEE
<MAN, YOUR WET DREAMS MUST BE LIKE A TSUNAMI.>
<DUDE, IT'S CALLED HAVING A GIRLFRIEND, LOOK INTO IT.>
<AND DON'T TOUCH MY RAT.>
CHO ZA GALIMA TAKAYA?

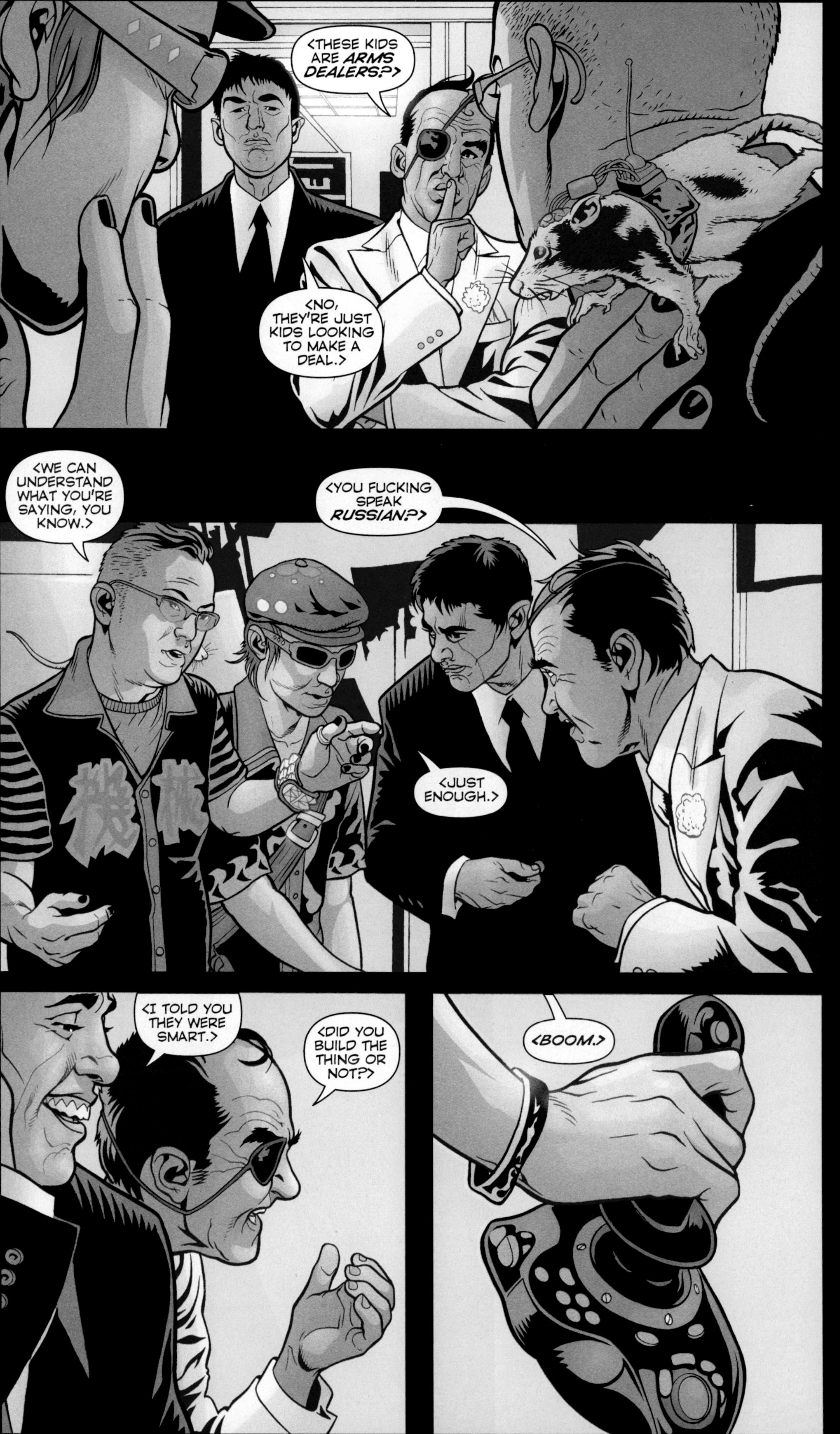
<THESE KIDS ARE ARMS DEALERS?>
<NO, THEY'RE JUST KIDS LOOKING TO MAKE A DEAL.>
<WE CAN UNDERSTAND WHAT YOU'RE SAYING, YOU KNOW.>
<YOU FUCKING SPEAK RUSSIAN?>
機械
<JUST ENOUGH.>
<I TOLD YOU THEY WERE SMART.>
<DID YOU BUILD THE THING OR NOT?>
<BOOM.>

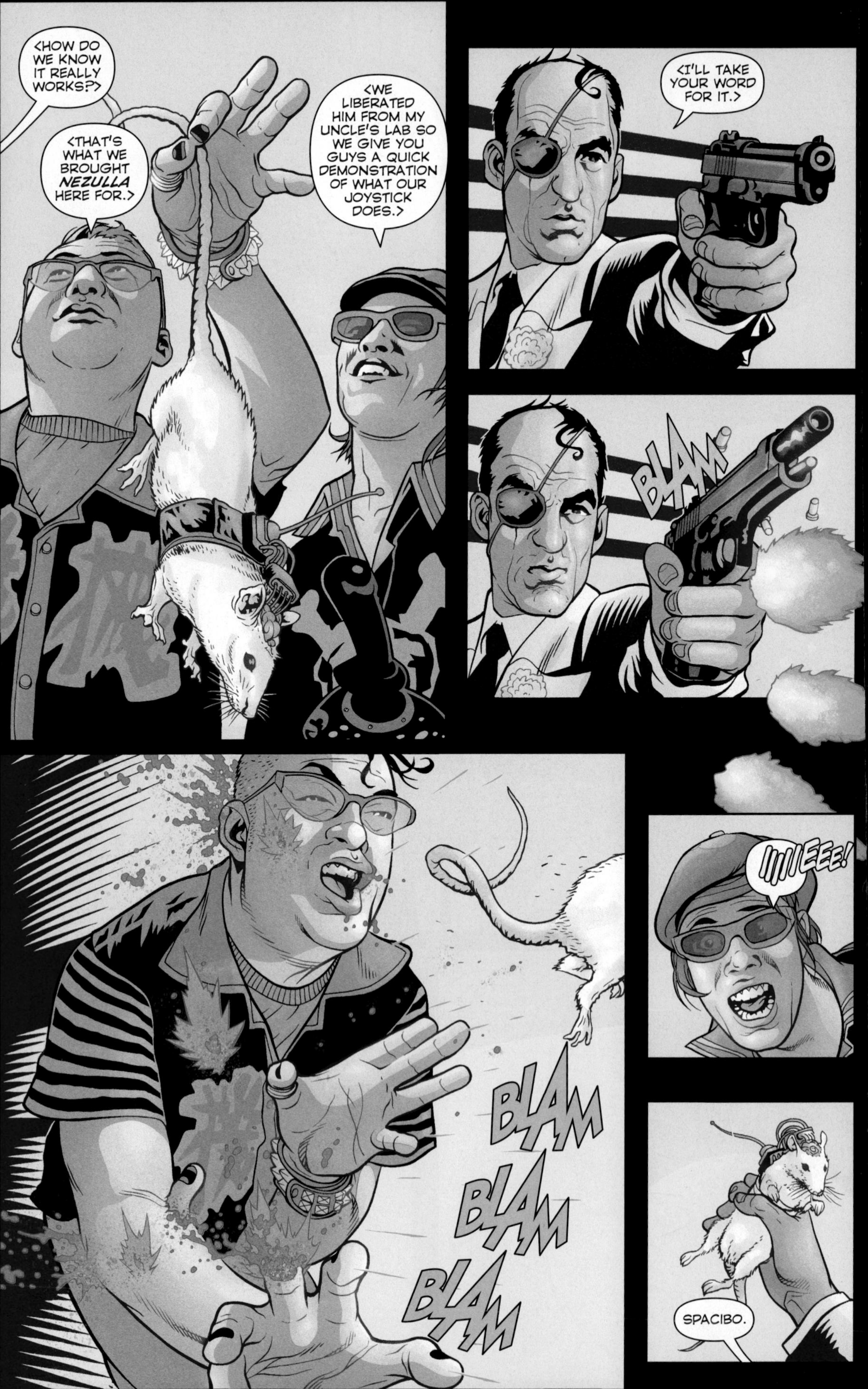

<HOW DO WE KNOW IT REALLY WORKS?>
<THAT'S WHAT WE BROUGHT *NEZULLA* HERE FOR.>
<WE LIBERATED HIM FROM MY UNCLE'S LAB SO WE GIVE YOU GUYS A QUICK DEMONSTRATION OF WHAT OUR JOYSTICK DOES.>
<I'LL TAKE YOUR WORD FOR IT.>
BLAM
BLAM
BLAM
BLAM
IIIIIEEE!
SPACIBO.

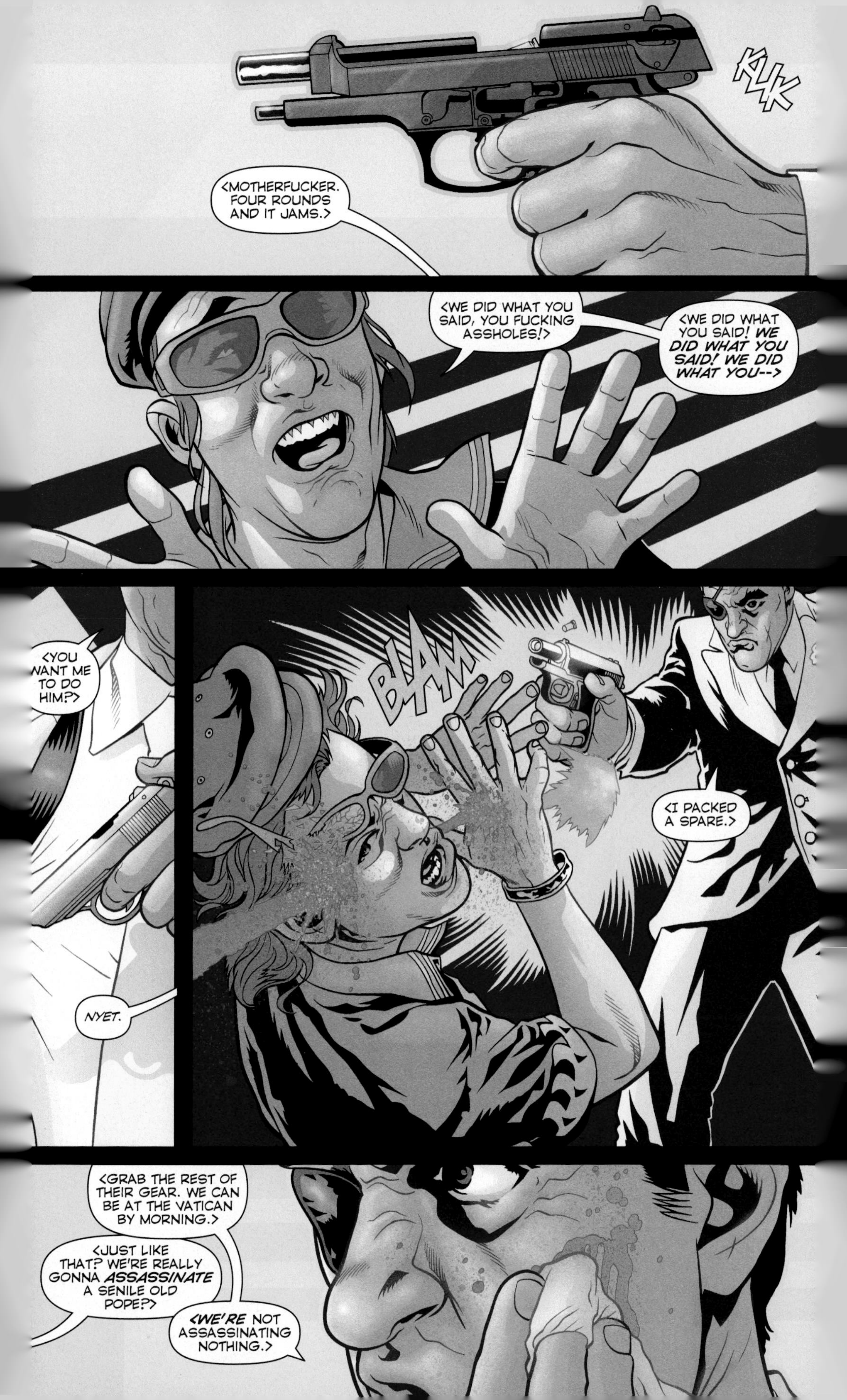
KLIK
<MOTHERFUCKER. FOUR ROUNDS AND IT JAMS.>
<WE DID WHAT YOU SAID, YOU FUCKING ASSHOLES!>
<WE DID WHAT YOU SAID! WE DID WHAT YOU SAID! WE DID WHAT YOU-->
<YOU WANT ME TO DO HIM?>
BLAM
<I PACKED A SPARE.>
NYET.
<GRAB THE REST OF THEIR GEAR. WE CAN BE AT THE VATICAN BY MORNING.>
<JUST LIKE THAT? WE'RE REALLY GONNA ASSASSINATE A SENILE OLD POPE?>
<WE'RE NOT ASSASSINATING NOTHING.>

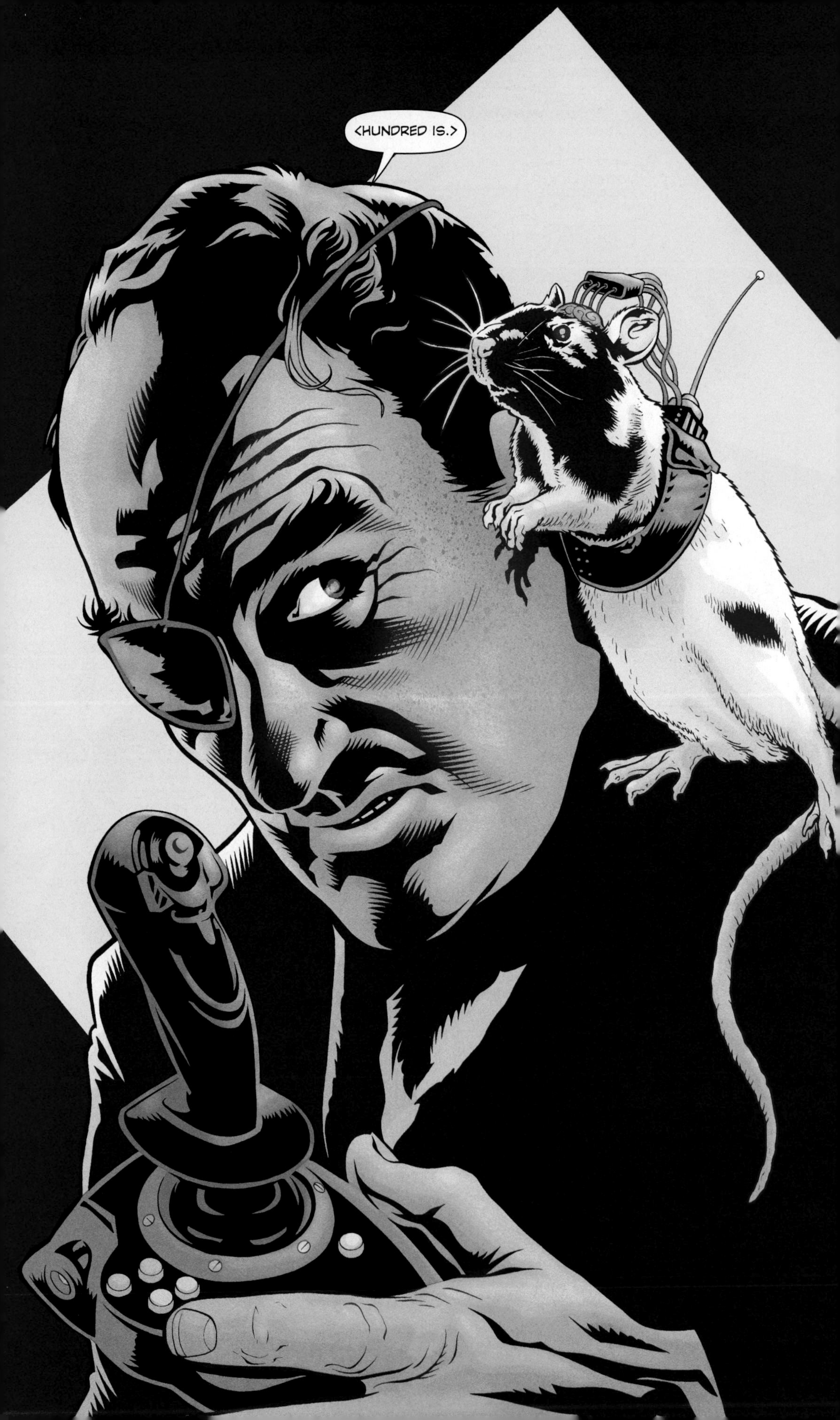
<HUNDRED IS.>

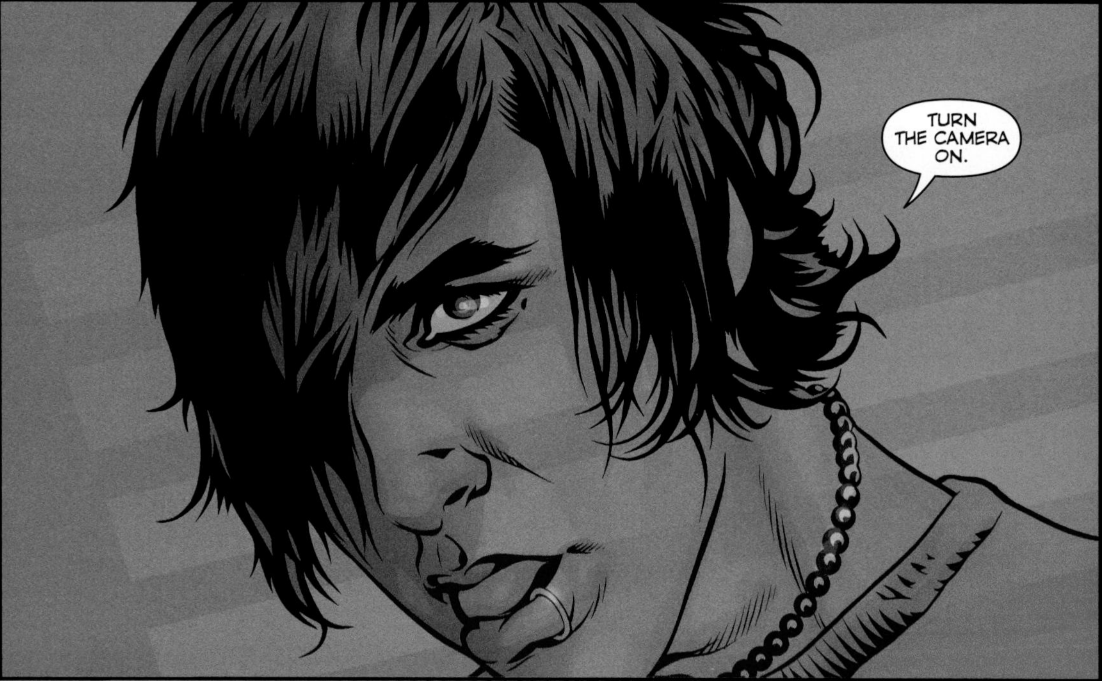
TURN THE CAMERA ON.

SATURDAY, MAY 5, 2001

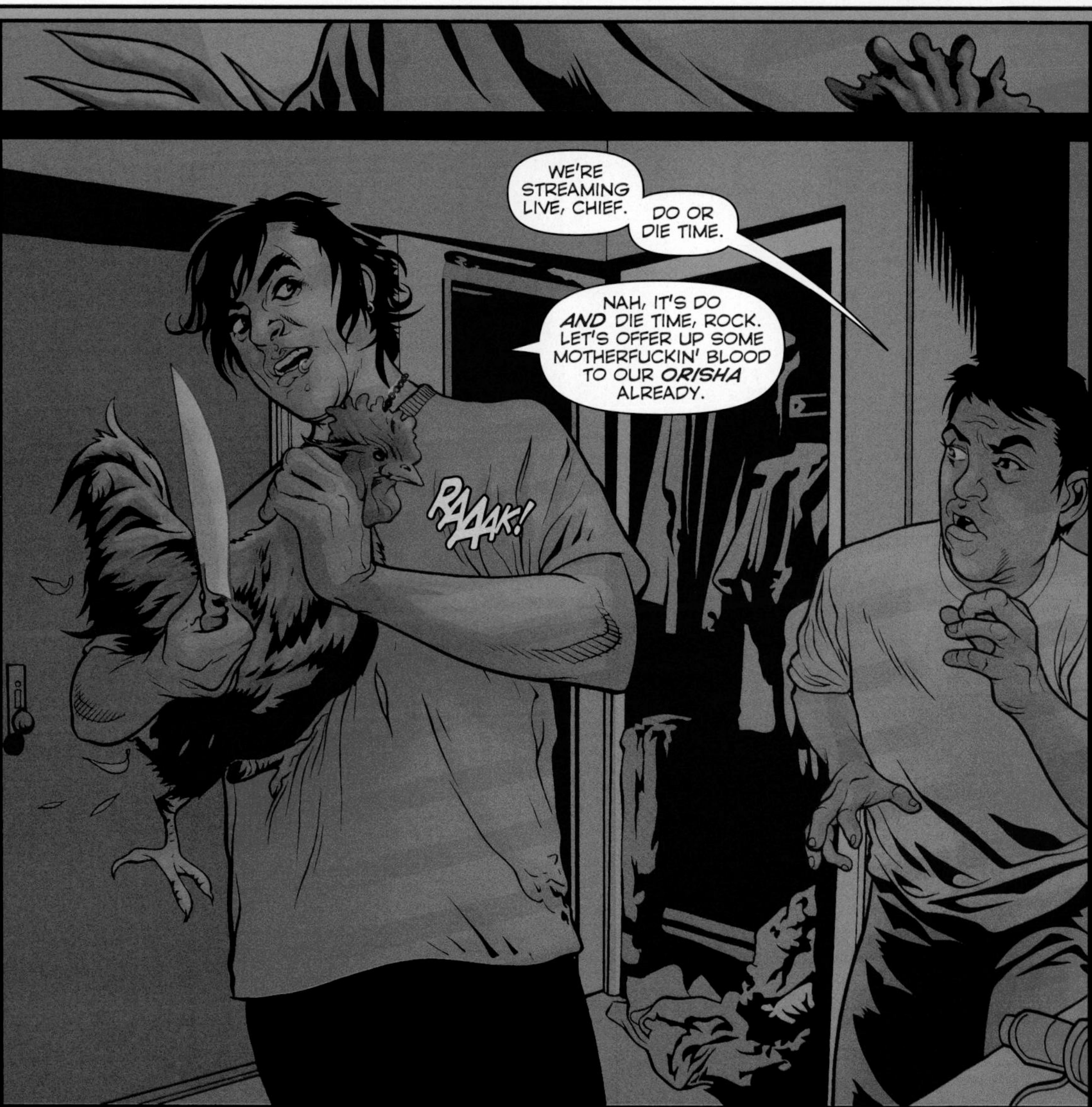
WE'RE STREAMING LIVE, CHIEF.
DO OR DIE TIME.
NAH, IT'S DO *AND* DIE TIME, ROCK. LET'S OFFER UP SOME MOTHERFUCKIN' BLOOD TO OUR *ORISHA* ALREADY.
RAAAK!

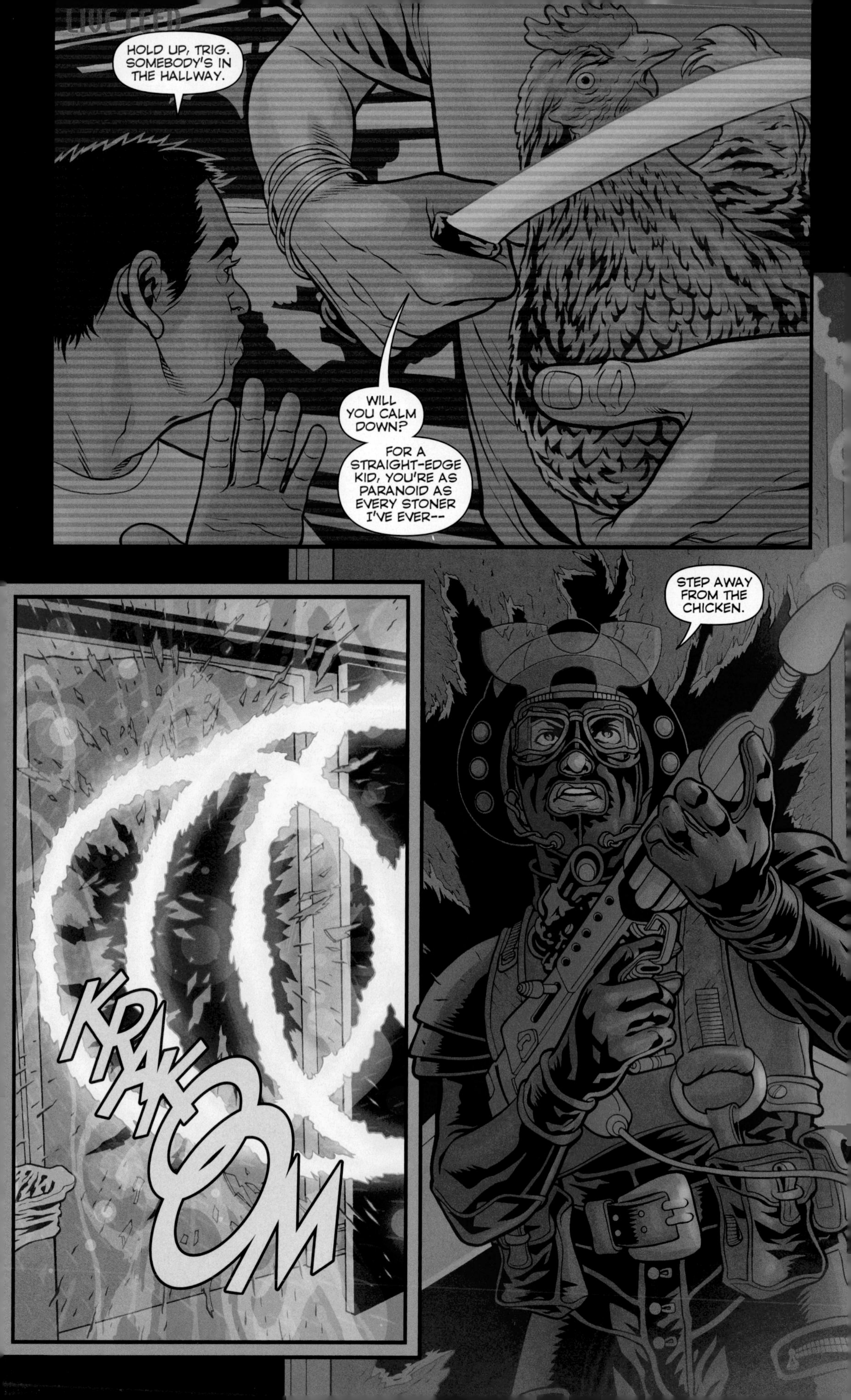
LIVE FEED
HOLD UP, TRIG. SOMEBODY'S IN THE HALLWAY.
WILL YOU CALM DOWN?
FOR A STRAIGHT-EDGE KID, YOU'RE AS PARANOID AS EVERY STONER I'VE EVER--
KRAKOOM
STEP AWAY FROM THE CHICKEN.

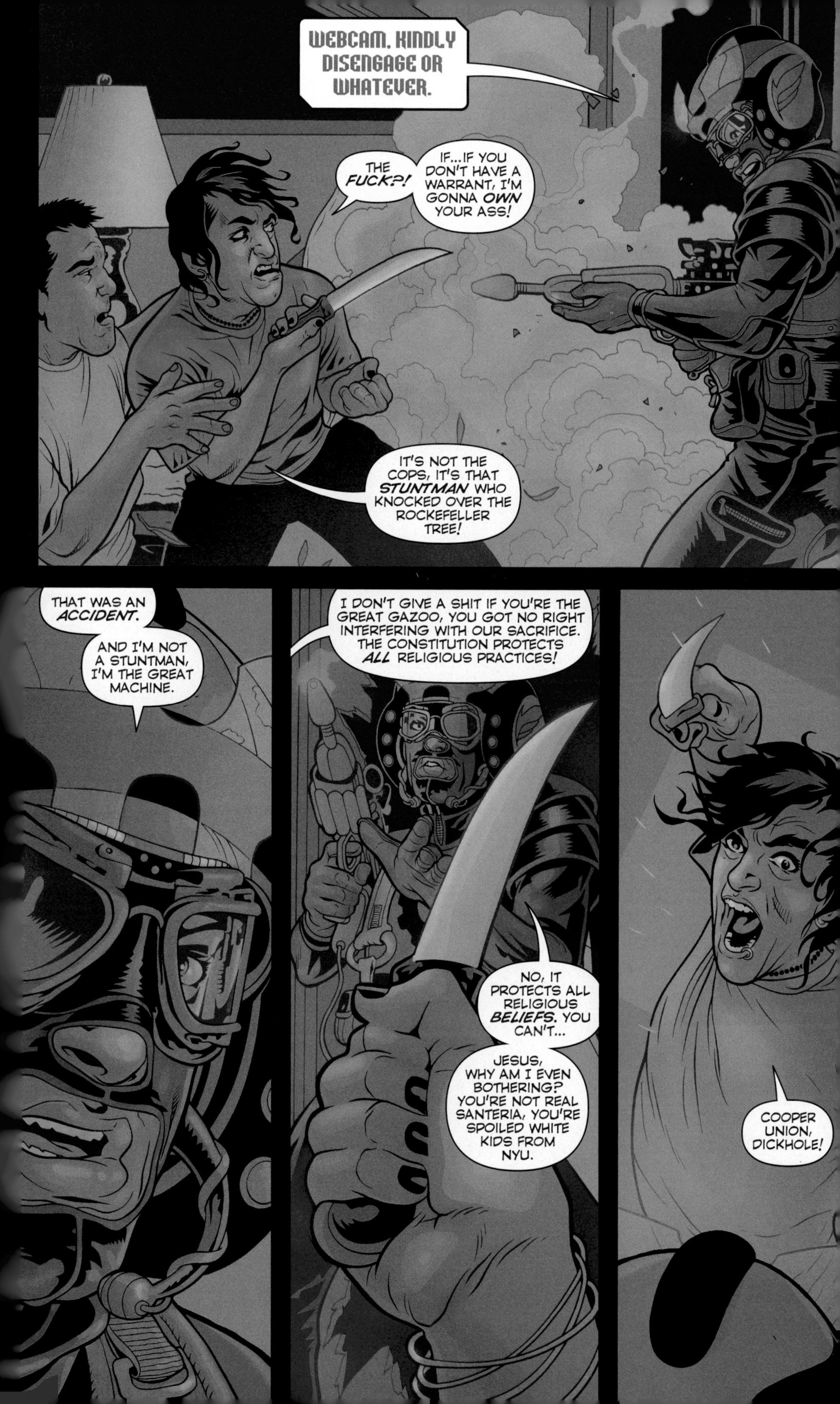
WEBCAM. KINDLY DISENGAGE OR WHATEVER.
THE FUCK?!
IF...IF YOU DON'T HAVE A WARRANT, I'M GONNA OWN YOUR ASS!
IT'S NOT THE COPS, IT'S THAT STUNTMAN WHO KNOCKED OVER THE ROCKEFELLER TREE!
THAT WAS AN ACCIDENT.
AND I'M NOT A STUNTMAN, I'M THE GREAT MACHINE.
I DON'T GIVE A SHIT IF YOU'RE THE GREAT GAZOO, YOU GOT NO RIGHT INTERFERING WITH OUR SACRIFICE. THE CONSTITUTION PROTECTS ALL RELIGIOUS PRACTICES!
NO, IT PROTECTS ALL RELIGIOUS BELIEFS. YOU CAN'T...
JESUS, WHY AM I EVEN BOTHERING? YOU'RE NOT REAL SANTERIA, YOU'RE SPOILED WHITE KIDS FROM NYU.
COOPER UNION, DICKHOLE!

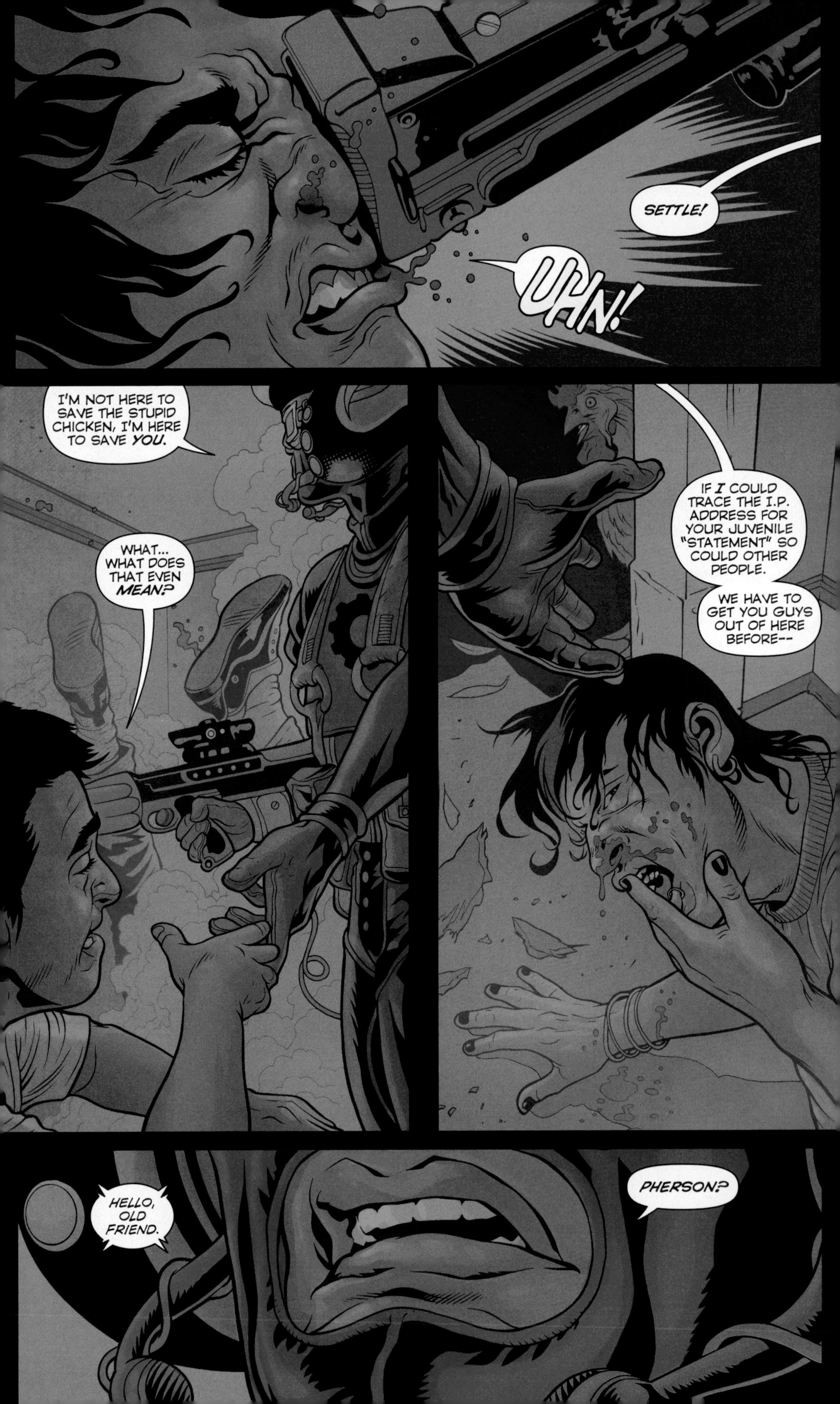
SETTLE!
UHN!
I'M NOT HERE TO SAVE THE STUPID CHICKEN, I'M HERE TO SAVE *YOU*.
WHAT... WHAT DOES THAT EVEN *MEAN?*
IF *I* COULD TRACE THE I.P. ADDRESS FOR YOUR JUVENILE "STATEMENT" SO COULD OTHER PEOPLE.
WE HAVE TO GET YOU GUYS OUT OF HERE BEFORE--
HELLO, OLD FRIEND.
PHERSON?

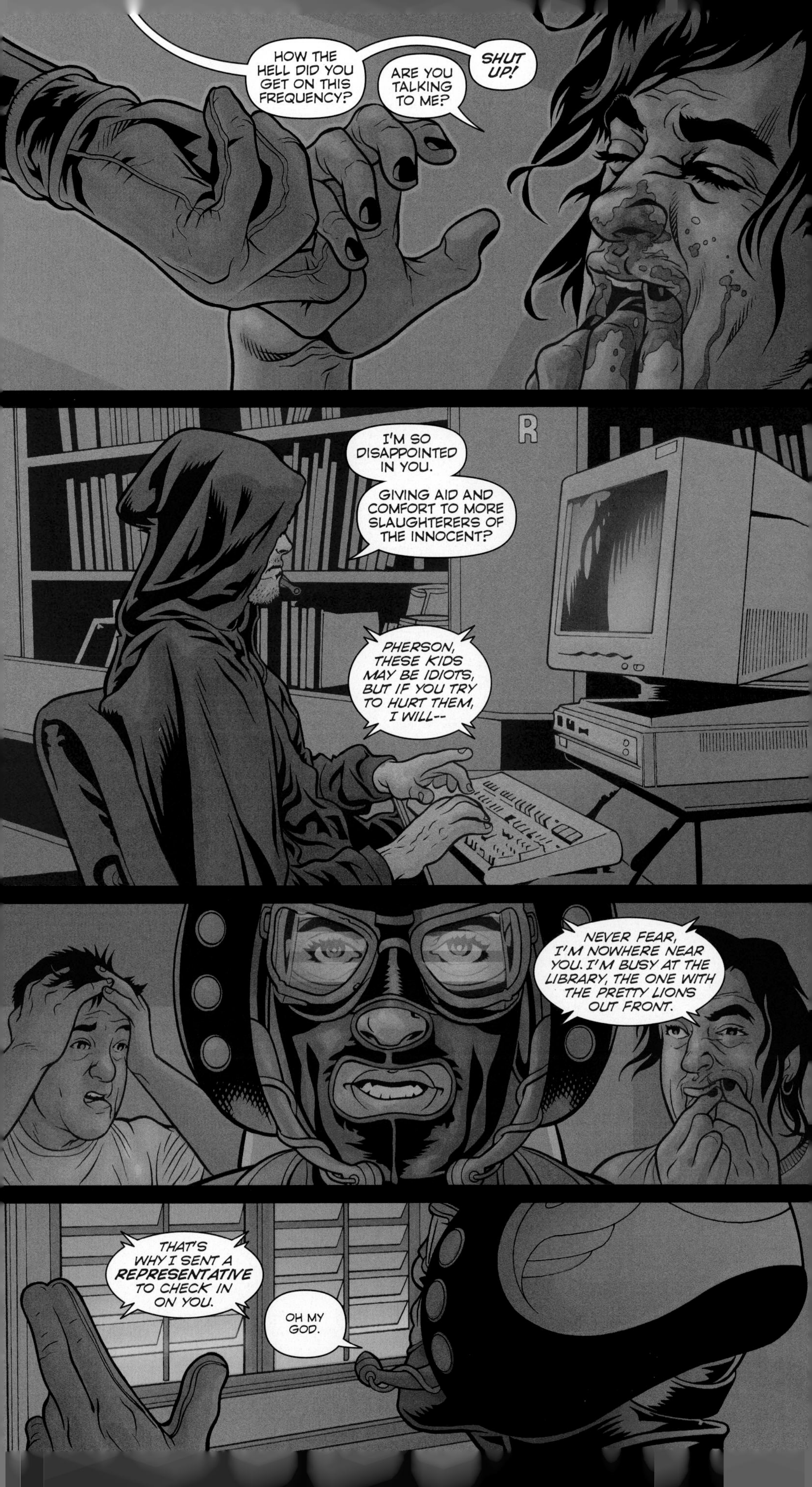
HOW THE HELL DID YOU GET ON THIS FREQUENCY?
ARE YOU TALKING TO ME?
SHUT UP!
I'M SO DISAPPOINTED IN YOU.
GIVING AID AND COMFORT TO MORE SLAUGHTERERS OF THE INNOCENT?
PHERSON, THESE KIDS MAY BE IDIOTS, BUT IF YOU TRY TO HURT THEM, I WILL--
NEVER FEAR, I'M NOWHERE NEAR YOU. I'M BUSY AT THE LIBRARY, THE ONE WITH THE PRETTY LIONS OUT FRONT.
THAT'S WHY I SENT A REPRESENTATIVE TO CHECK IN ON YOU.
OH MY GOD.

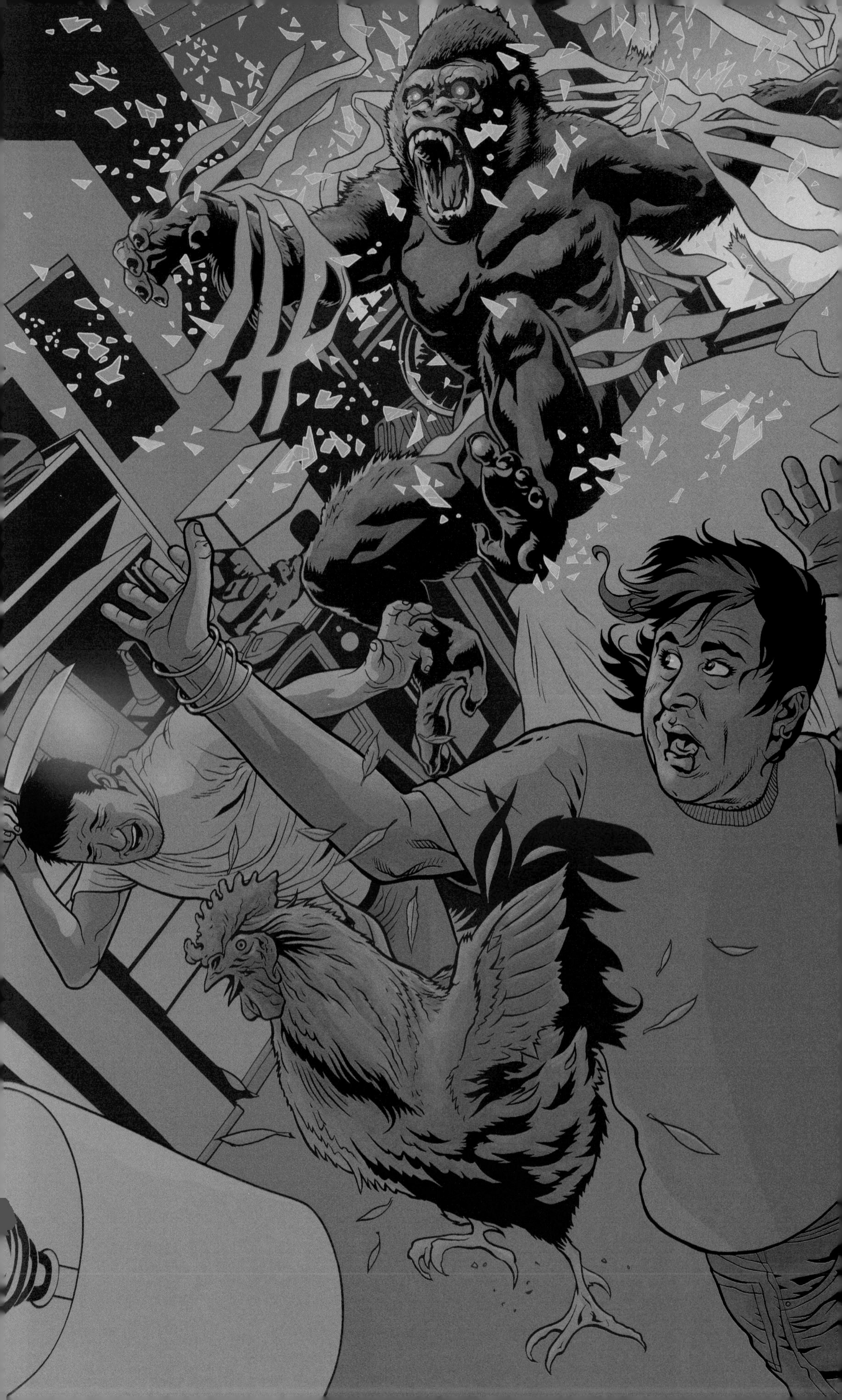

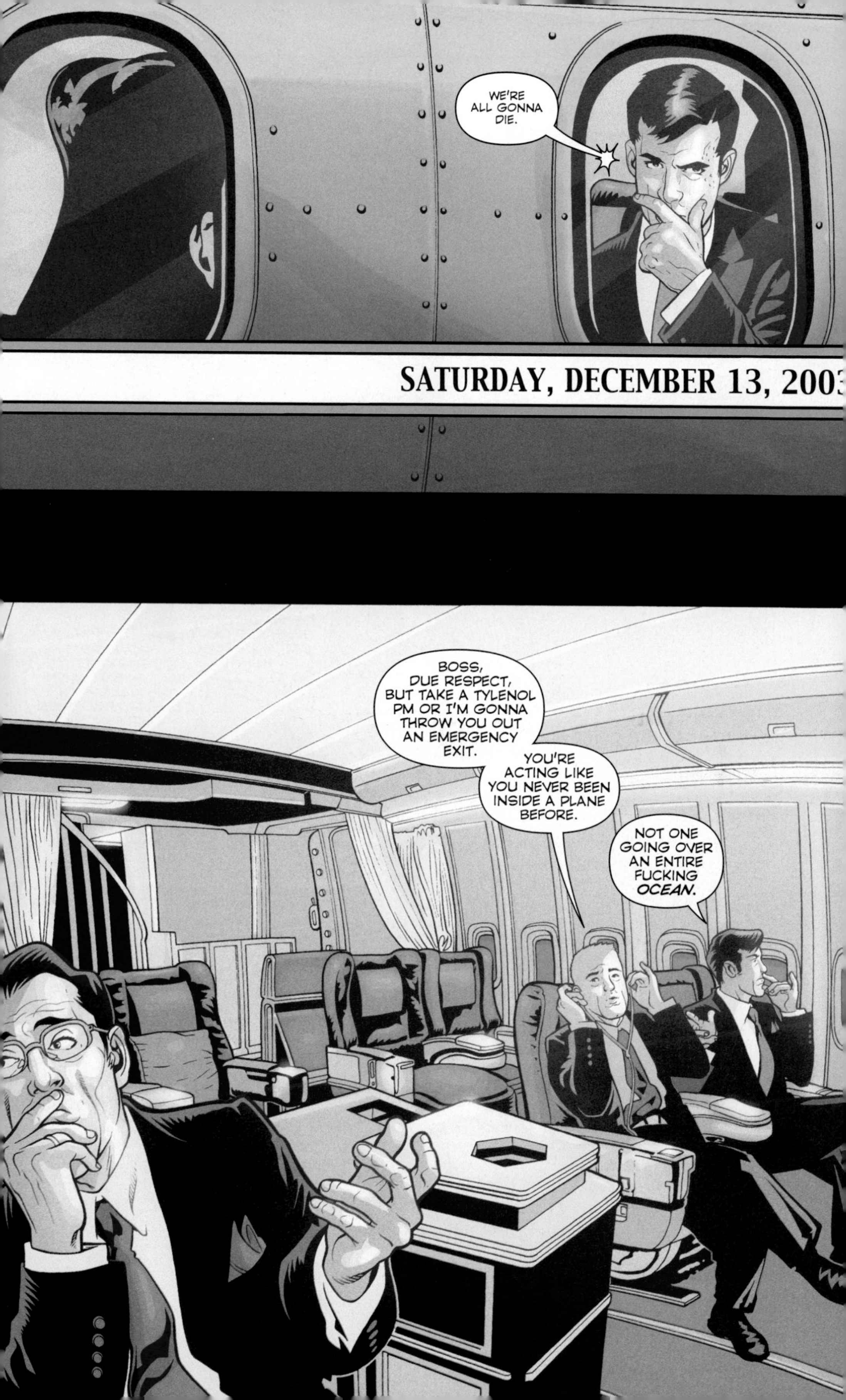
WE'RE ALL GONNA DIE.
SATURDAY, DECEMBER 13, 2003
BOSS, DUE RESPECT, BUT TAKE A TYLENOL PM OR I'M GONNA THROW YOU OUT AN EMERGENCY EXIT.
YOU'RE ACTING LIKE YOU NEVER BEEN INSIDE A PLANE BEFORE.
NOT ONE GOING OVER AN ENTIRE FUCKING *OCEAN*.

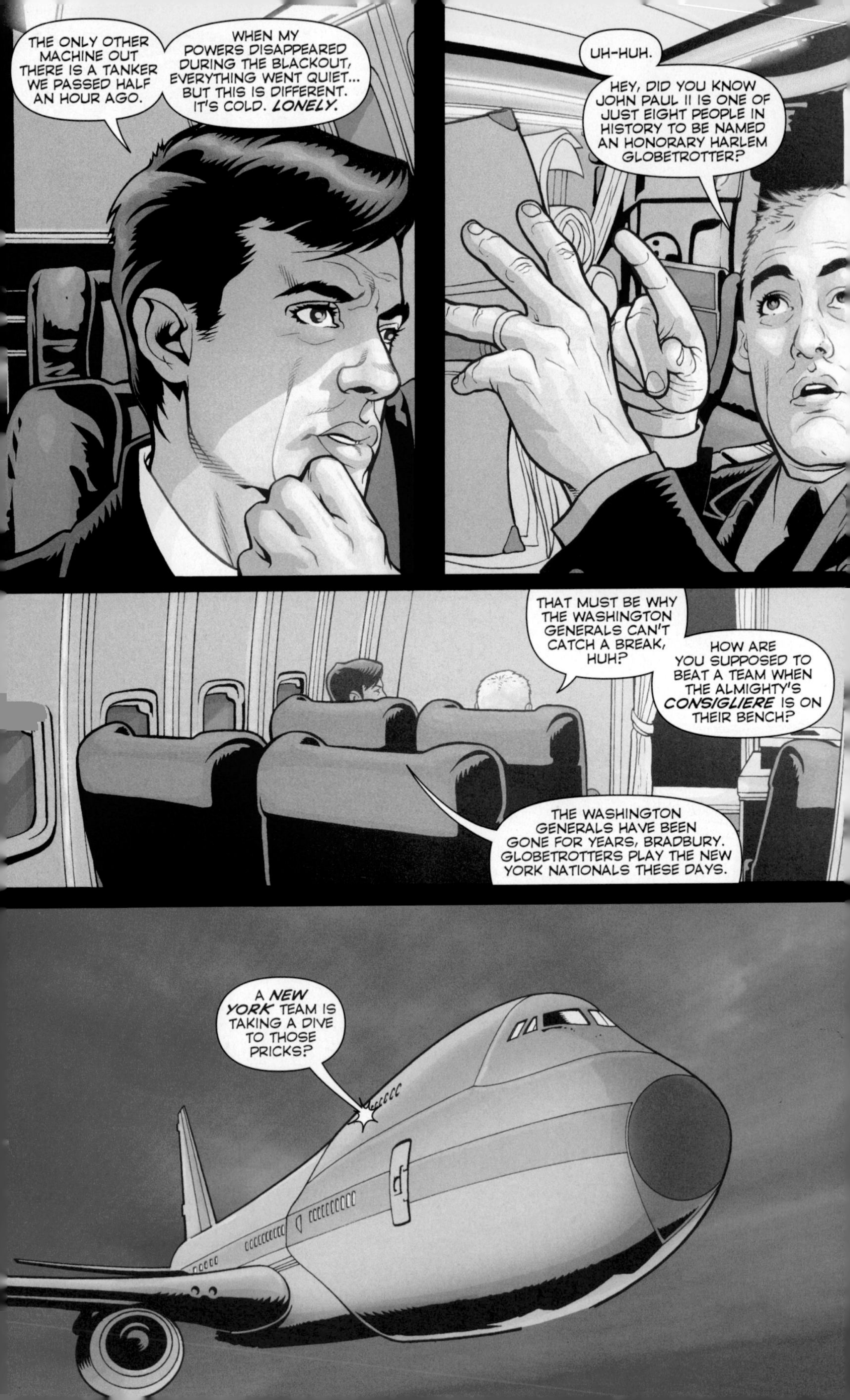
THE ONLY OTHER MACHINE OUT THERE IS A TANKER WE PASSED HALF AN HOUR AGO.
WHEN MY POWERS DISAPPEARED DURING THE BLACKOUT, EVERYTHING WENT QUIET... BUT THIS IS DIFFERENT. IT'S COLD. *LONELY.*
UH-HUH.
HEY, DID YOU KNOW JOHN PAUL II IS ONE OF JUST EIGHT PEOPLE IN HISTORY TO BE NAMED AN HONORARY HARLEM GLOBETROTTER?
THAT MUST BE WHY THE WASHINGTON GENERALS CAN'T CATCH A BREAK, HUH?
HOW ARE YOU SUPPOSED TO BEAT A TEAM WHEN THE ALMIGHTY'S *CONSIGLIERE* IS ON THEIR BENCH?
THE WASHINGTON GENERALS HAVE BEEN GONE FOR YEARS, BRADBURY. GLOBETROTTERS PLAY THE NEW YORK NATIONALS THESE DAYS.
A *NEW YORK* TEAM IS TAKING A DIVE TO THOSE PRICKS?

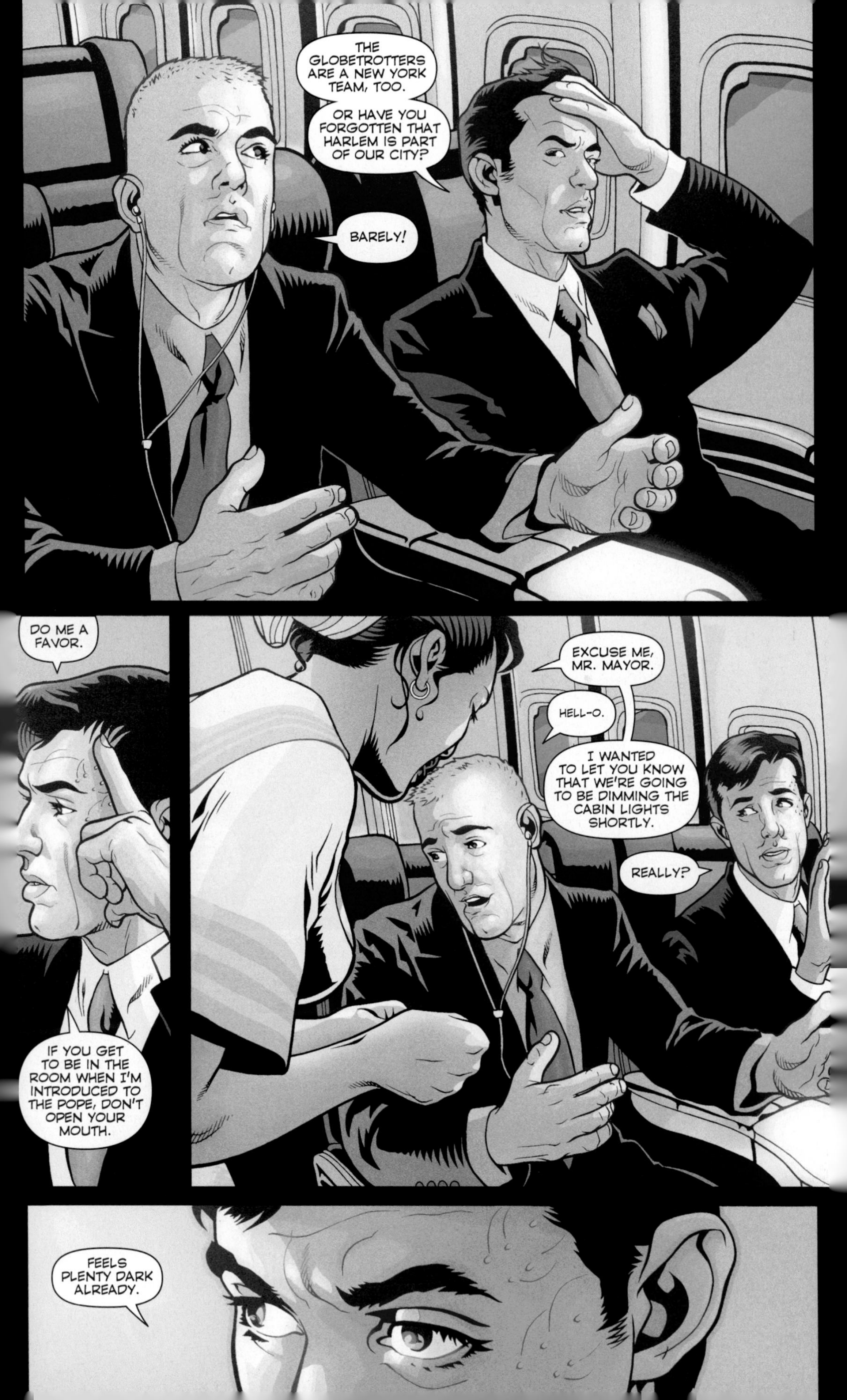
THE GLOBETROTTERS ARE A NEW YORK TEAM, TOO.
OR HAVE YOU FORGOTTEN THAT HARLEM IS PART OF OUR CITY?
BARELY!
DO ME A FAVOR.
IF YOU GET TO BE IN THE ROOM WHEN I'M INTRODUCED TO THE POPE, DON'T OPEN YOUR MOUTH.
EXCUSE ME, MR. MAYOR.
HELL-O.
I WANTED TO LET YOU KNOW THAT WE'RE GOING TO BE DIMMING THE CABIN LIGHTS SHORTLY.
REALLY?
FEELS PLENTY DARK ALREADY.

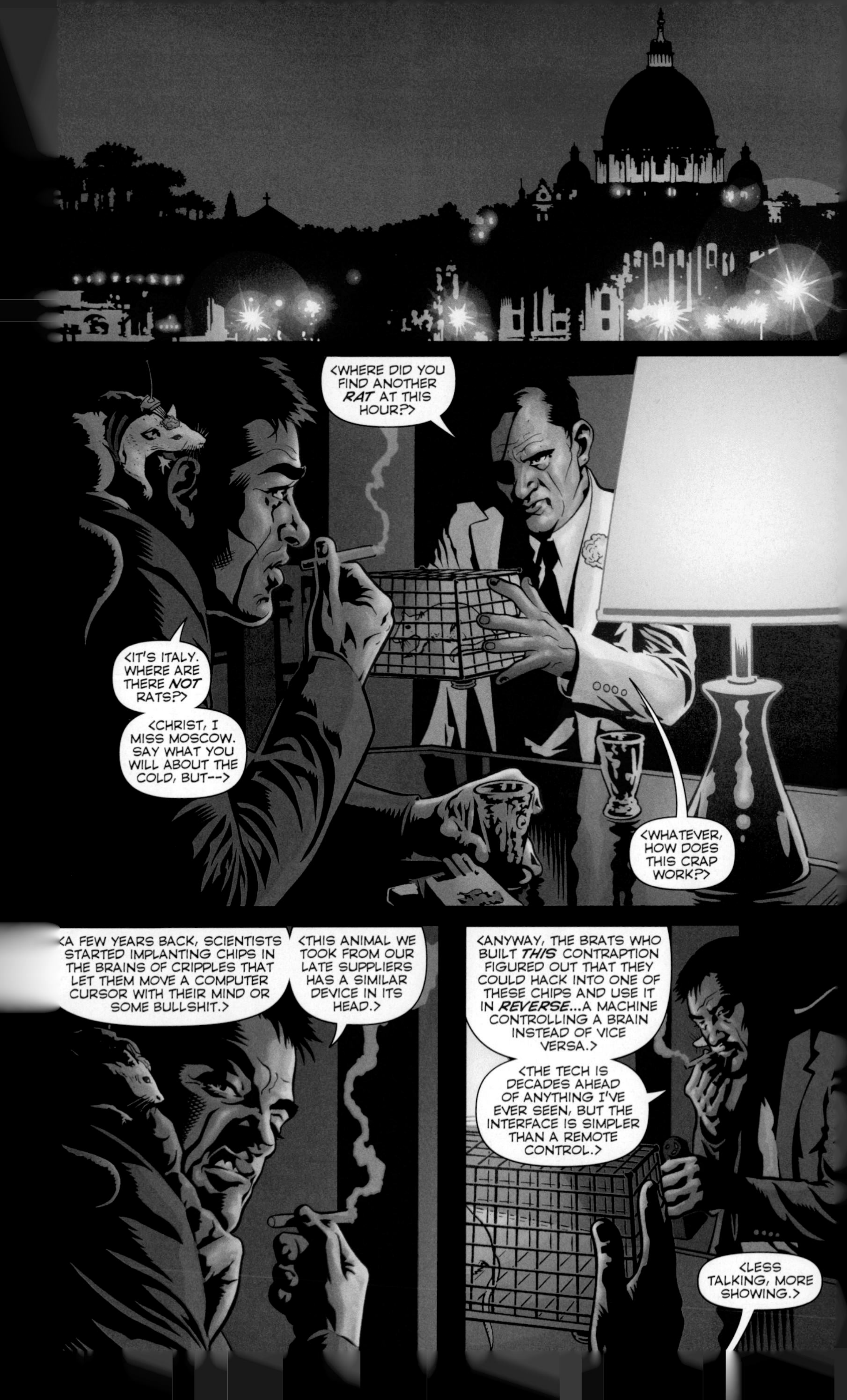
<WHERE DID YOU FIND ANOTHER *RAT* AT THIS HOUR?>
<IT'S ITALY. WHERE ARE THERE *NOT* RATS?>
<CHRIST, I MISS MOSCOW. SAY WHAT YOU WILL ABOUT THE COLD, BUT-->
<WHATEVER, HOW DOES THIS CRAP WORK?>
<A FEW YEARS BACK, SCIENTISTS STARTED IMPLANTING CHIPS IN THE BRAINS OF CRIPPLES THAT LET THEM MOVE A COMPUTER CURSOR WITH THEIR MIND OR SOME BULLSHIT.>
<THIS ANIMAL WE TOOK FROM OUR LATE SUPPLIERS HAS A SIMILAR DEVICE IN ITS HEAD.>
<ANYWAY, THE BRATS WHO BUILT *THIS* CONTRAPTION FIGURED OUT THAT THEY COULD HACK INTO ONE OF THESE CHIPS AND USE IT IN *REVERSE*...A MACHINE CONTROLLING A BRAIN INSTEAD OF VICE VERSA.>
<THE TECH IS DECADES AHEAD OF ANYTHING I'VE EVER SEEN, BUT THE INTERFACE IS SIMPLER THAN A REMOTE CONTROL.>
<LESS TALKING, MORE SHOWING.>

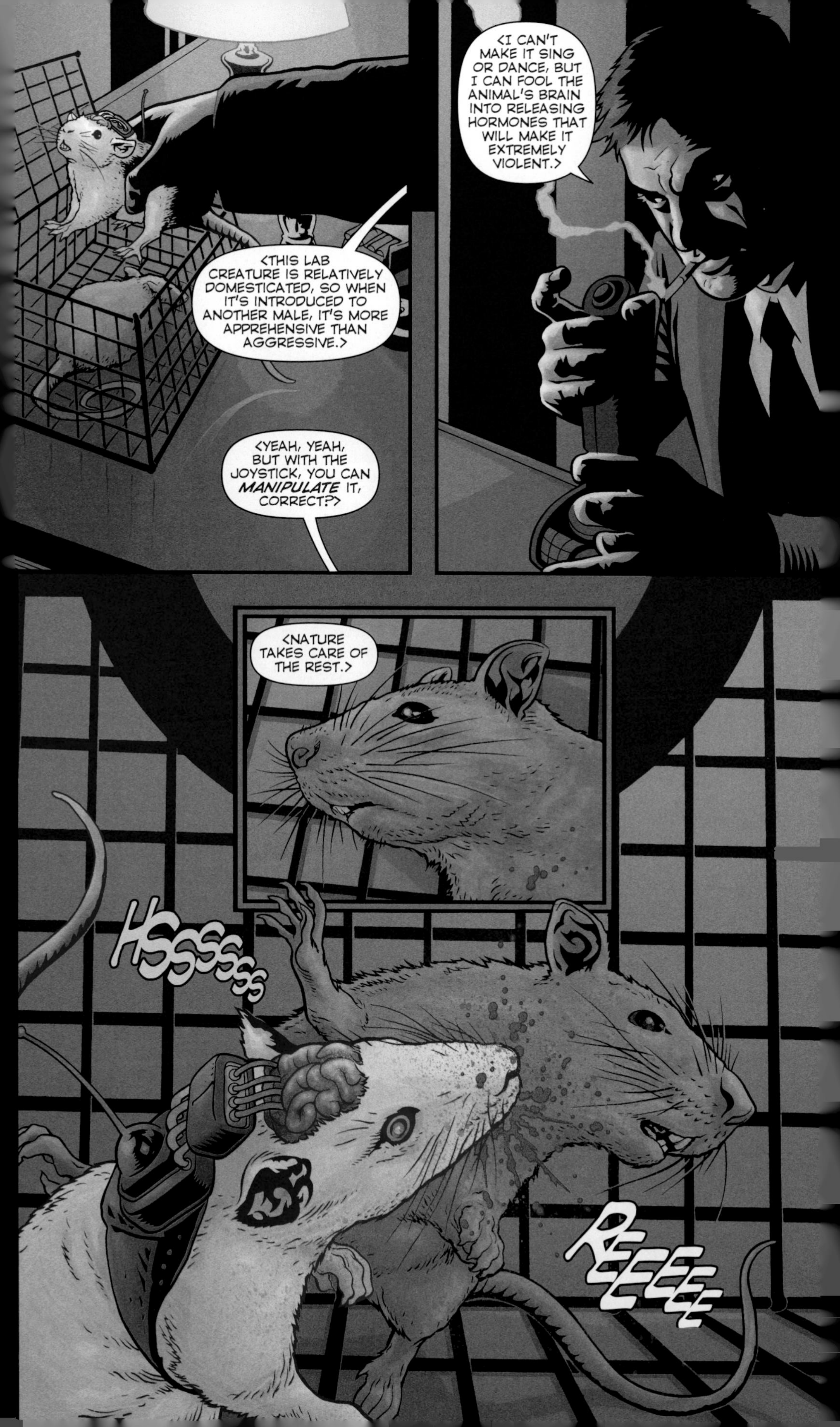

<THIS LAB CREATURE IS RELATIVELY DOMESTICATED, SO WHEN IT'S INTRODUCED TO ANOTHER MALE, IT'S MORE APPREHENSIVE THAN AGGRESSIVE.>
<YEAH, YEAH, BUT WITH THE JOYSTICK, YOU CAN *MANIPULATE* IT, CORRECT?>
<I CAN'T MAKE IT SING OR DANCE, BUT I CAN FOOL THE ANIMAL'S BRAIN INTO RELEASING HORMONES THAT WILL MAKE IT EXTREMELY VIOLENT.>
<NATURE TAKES CARE OF THE REST.>
HSSSSSS
REEEEEE

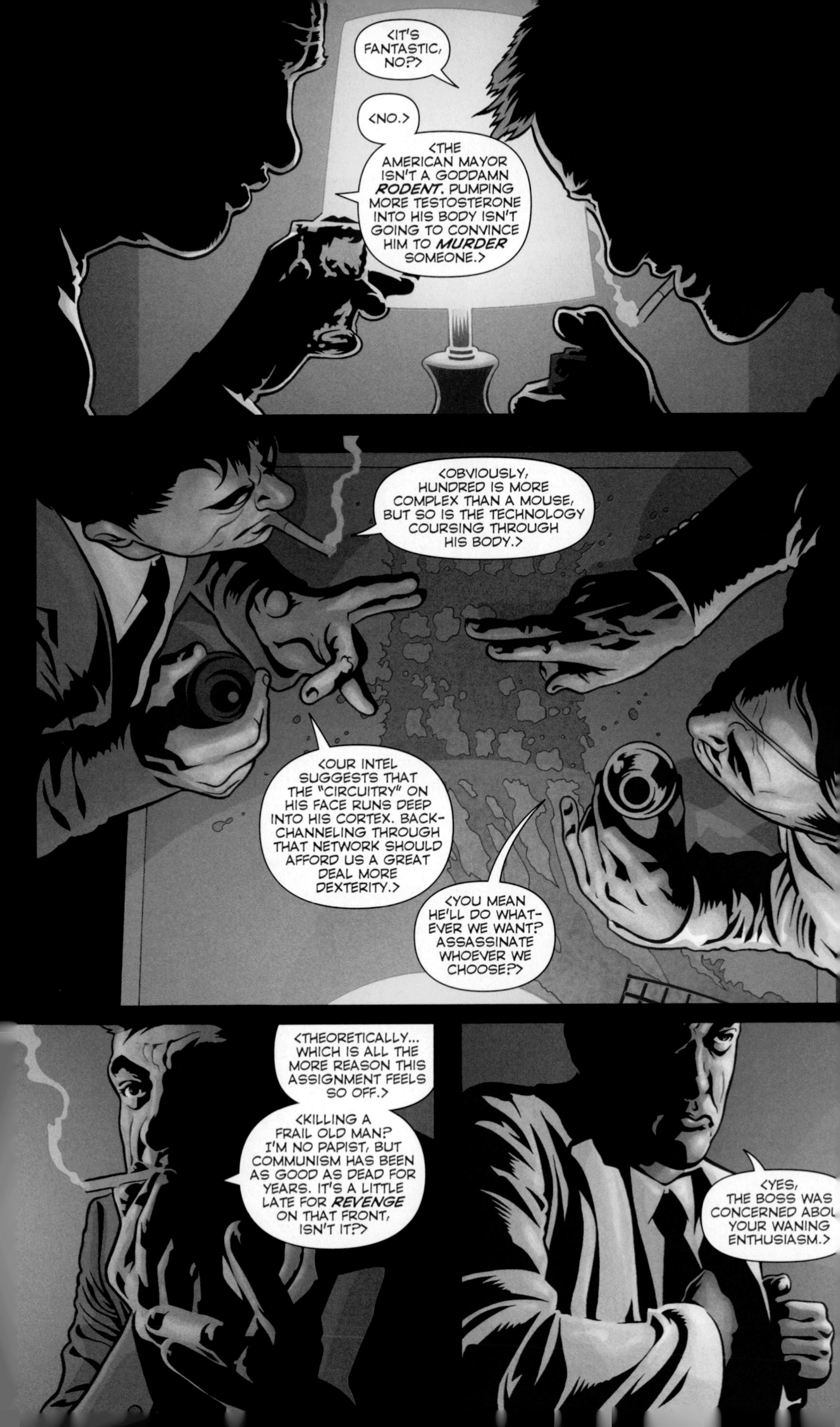
<IT'S FANTASTIC, NO?>
<NO.>
<THE AMERICAN MAYOR ISN'T A GODDAMN *RODENT*. PUMPING MORE TESTOSTERONE INTO HIS BODY ISN'T GOING TO CONVINCE HIM TO *MURDER* SOMEONE.>
<OBVIOUSLY, HUNDRED IS MORE COMPLEX THAN A MOUSE, BUT SO IS THE TECHNOLOGY COURSING THROUGH HIS BODY.>
<OUR INTEL SUGGESTS THAT THE "CIRCUITRY" ON HIS FACE RUNS DEEP INTO HIS CORTEX. BACK-CHANNELING THROUGH THAT NETWORK SHOULD AFFORD US A GREAT DEAL MORE DEXTERITY.>
<YOU MEAN HE'LL DO WHAT-EVER WE WANT? ASSASSINATE WHOEVER WE CHOOSE?>
<THEORETICALLY... WHICH IS ALL THE MORE REASON THIS ASSIGNMENT FEELS SO OFF.>
<KILLING A FRAIL OLD MAN? I'M NO PAPIST, BUT COMMUNISM HAS BEEN AS GOOD AS DEAD FOR YEARS. IT'S A LITTLE LATE FOR *REVENGE* ON THAT FRONT, ISN'T IT?>
<YES, THE BOSS WAS CONCERNED ABOU YOUR WANING ENTHUSIASM.>

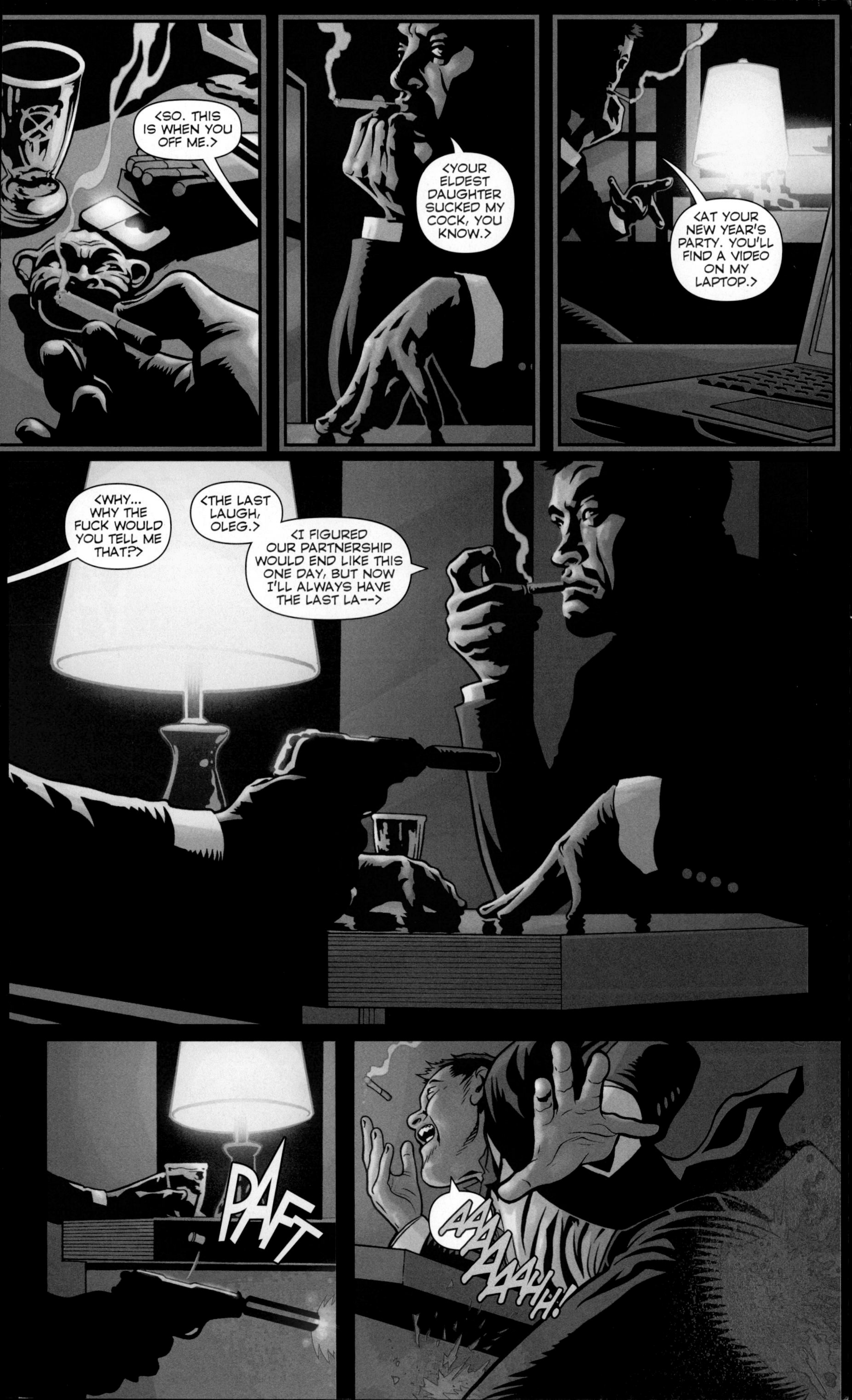
<SO. THIS IS WHEN YOU OFF ME.>
<YOUR ELDEST DAUGHTER SUCKED MY COCK, YOU KNOW.>
<AT YOUR NEW YEAR'S PARTY. YOU'LL FIND A VIDEO ON MY LAPTOP.>
<WHY... WHY THE FUCK WOULD YOU TELL ME THAT?>
<THE LAST LAUGH, OLEG.>
<I FIGURED OUR PARTNERSHIP WOULD END LIKE THIS ONE DAY, BUT NOW I'LL ALWAYS HAVE THE LAST LA-->
PAFT
AAAAAAAAAHH!

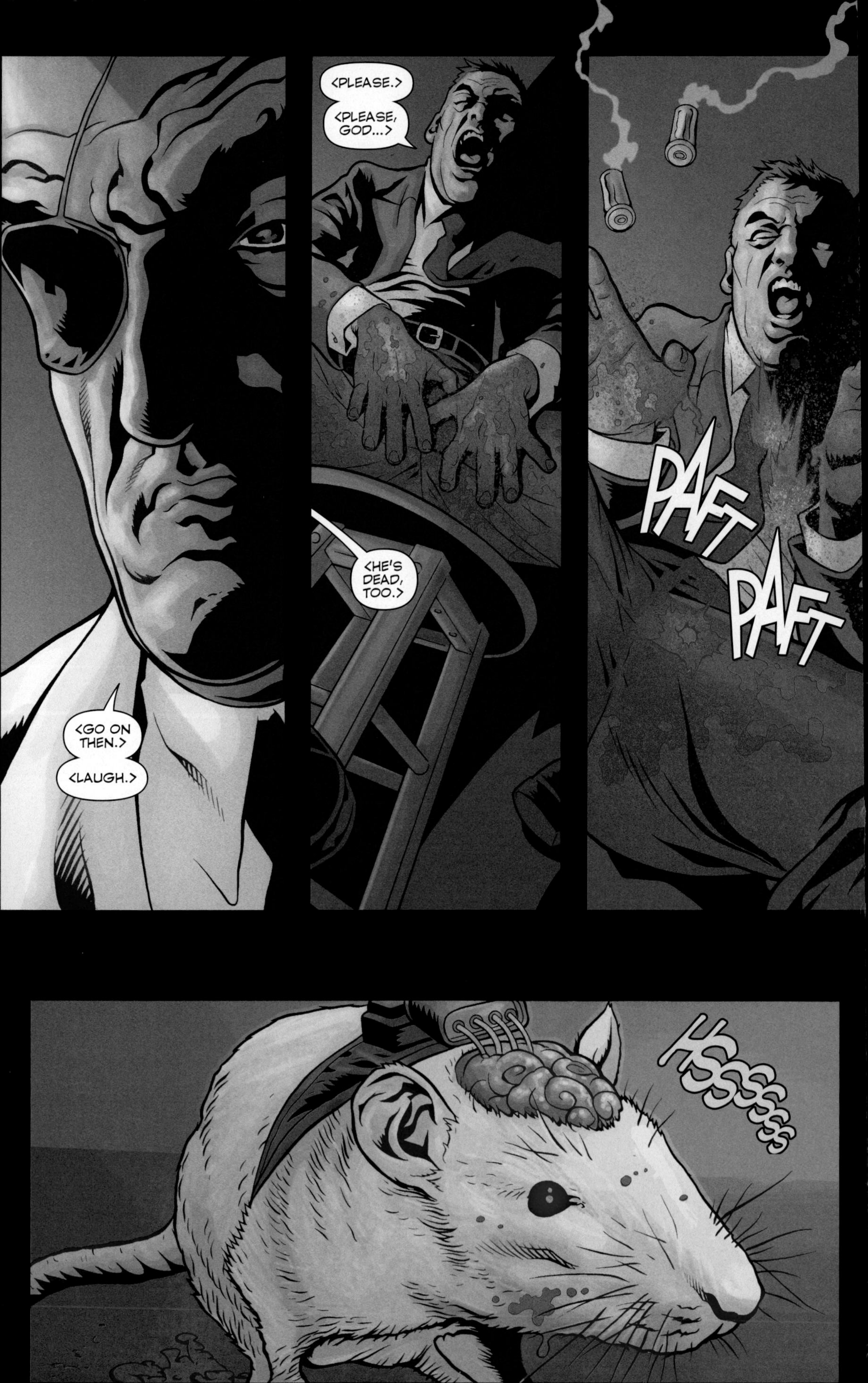
<GO ON THEN.>
<LAUGH.>
<PLEASE.>
<PLEASE, GOD...>
<HE'S DEAD, TOO.>
PAFT
PAFT
HSSSSSS

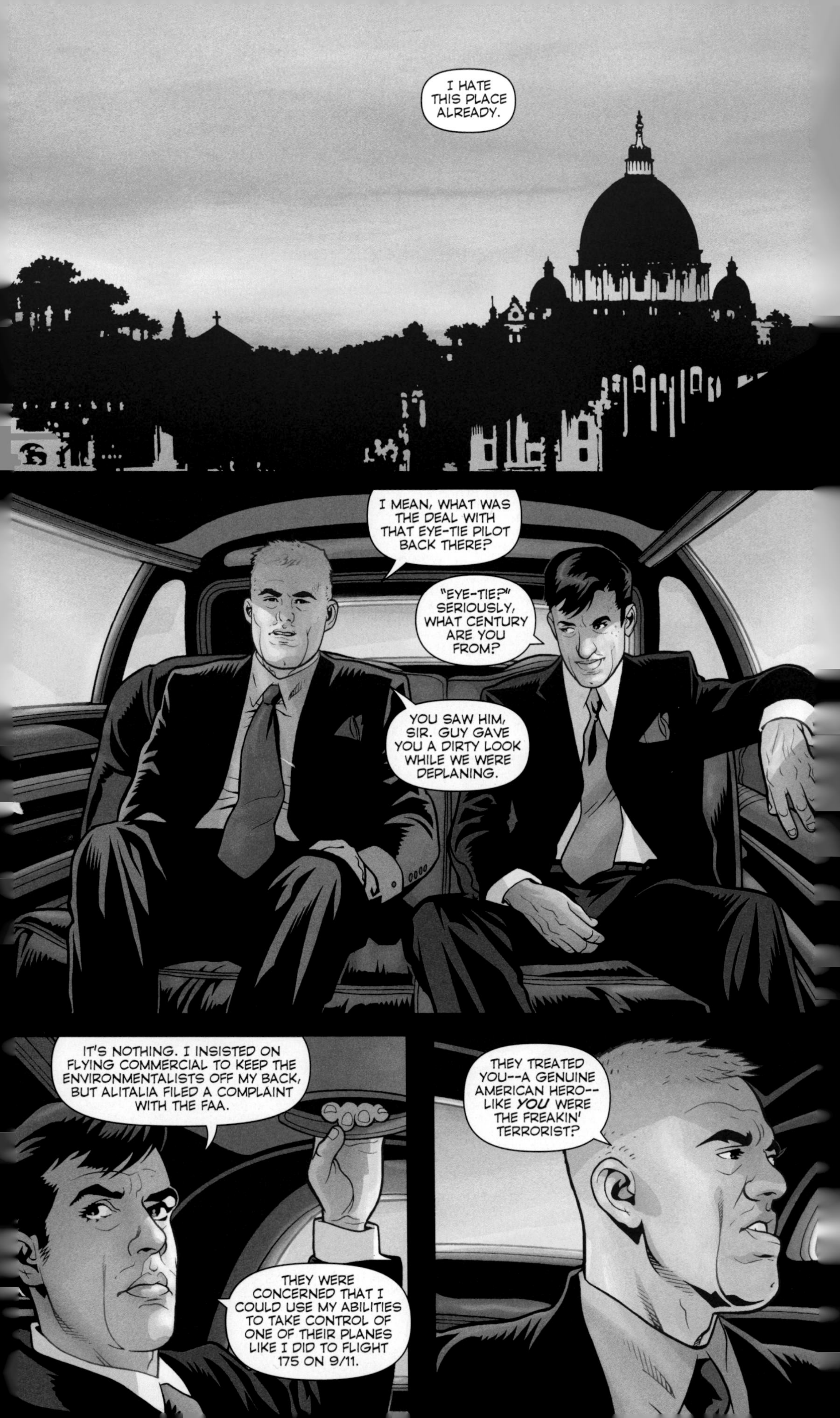
I HATE THIS PLACE ALREADY.
I MEAN, WHAT WAS THE DEAL WITH THAT EYE-TIE PILOT BACK THERE?
"EYE-TIE?" SERIOUSLY, WHAT CENTURY ARE YOU FROM?
YOU SAW HIM, SIR. GUY GAVE YOU A DIRTY LOOK WHILE WE WERE DEPLANING.
IT'S NOTHING. I INSISTED ON FLYING COMMERCIAL TO KEEP THE ENVIRONMENTALISTS OFF MY BACK, BUT ALITALIA FILED A COMPLAINT WITH THE FAA.
THEY WERE CONCERNED THAT I COULD USE MY ABILITIES TO TAKE CONTROL OF ONE OF THEIR PLANES LIKE I DID TO FLIGHT 175 ON 9/11.
THEY TREATED YOU--A GENUINE AMERICAN HERO--LIKE *YOU* WERE THE FREAKIN' TERRORIST?

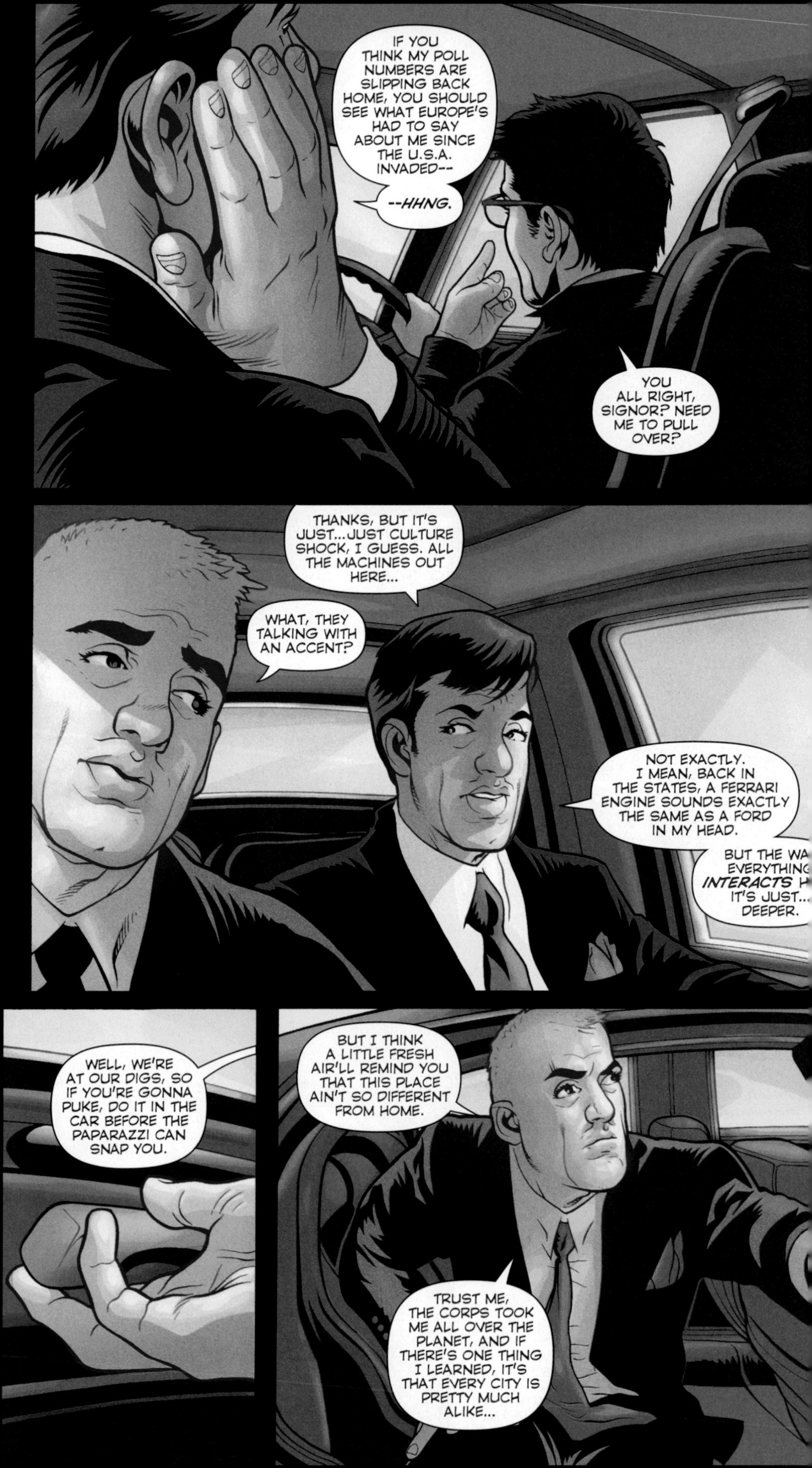
IF YOU THINK MY POLL NUMBERS ARE SLIPPING BACK HOME, YOU SHOULD SEE WHAT EUROPE'S HAD TO SAY ABOUT ME SINCE THE U.S.A. INVADED--
--HHNG.
YOU ALL RIGHT, SIGNOR? NEED ME TO PULL OVER?
THANKS, BUT IT'S JUST...JUST CULTURE SHOCK, I GUESS. ALL THE MACHINES OUT HERE...
WHAT, THEY TALKING WITH AN ACCENT?
NOT EXACTLY. I MEAN, BACK IN THE STATES, A FERRARI ENGINE SOUNDS EXACTLY THE SAME AS A FORD IN MY HEAD.
BUT THE WA EVERYTHING *INTERACTS* H IT'S JUST... DEEPER.
WELL, WE'RE AT OUR DIGS, SO IF YOU'RE GONNA PUKE, DO IT IN THE CAR BEFORE THE PAPARAZZI CAN SNAP YOU.
BUT I THINK A LITTLE FRESH AIR'LL REMIND YOU THAT THIS PLACE AIN'T SO DIFFERENT FROM HOME.
TRUST ME, THE CORPS TOOK ME ALL OVER THE PLANET, AND IF THERE'S ONE THING I LEARNED, IT'S THAT EVERY CITY IS PRETTY MUCH ALIKE...

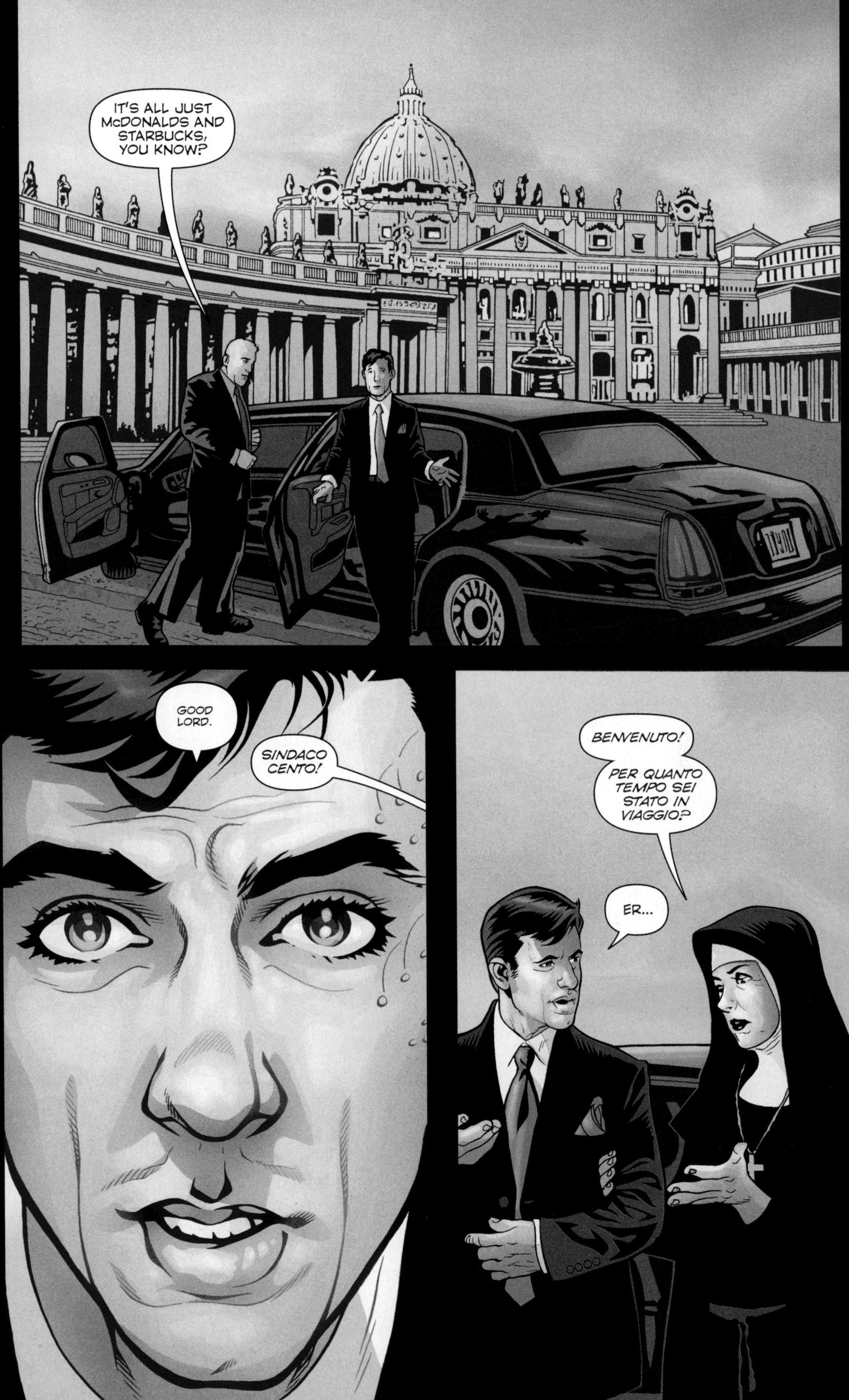
IT'S ALL JUST McDONALDS AND STARBUCKS, YOU KNOW?
GOOD LORD.
SINDACO CENTO!
BENVENUTO!
PER QUANTO TEMPO SEI STATO IN VIAGGIO?
ER...

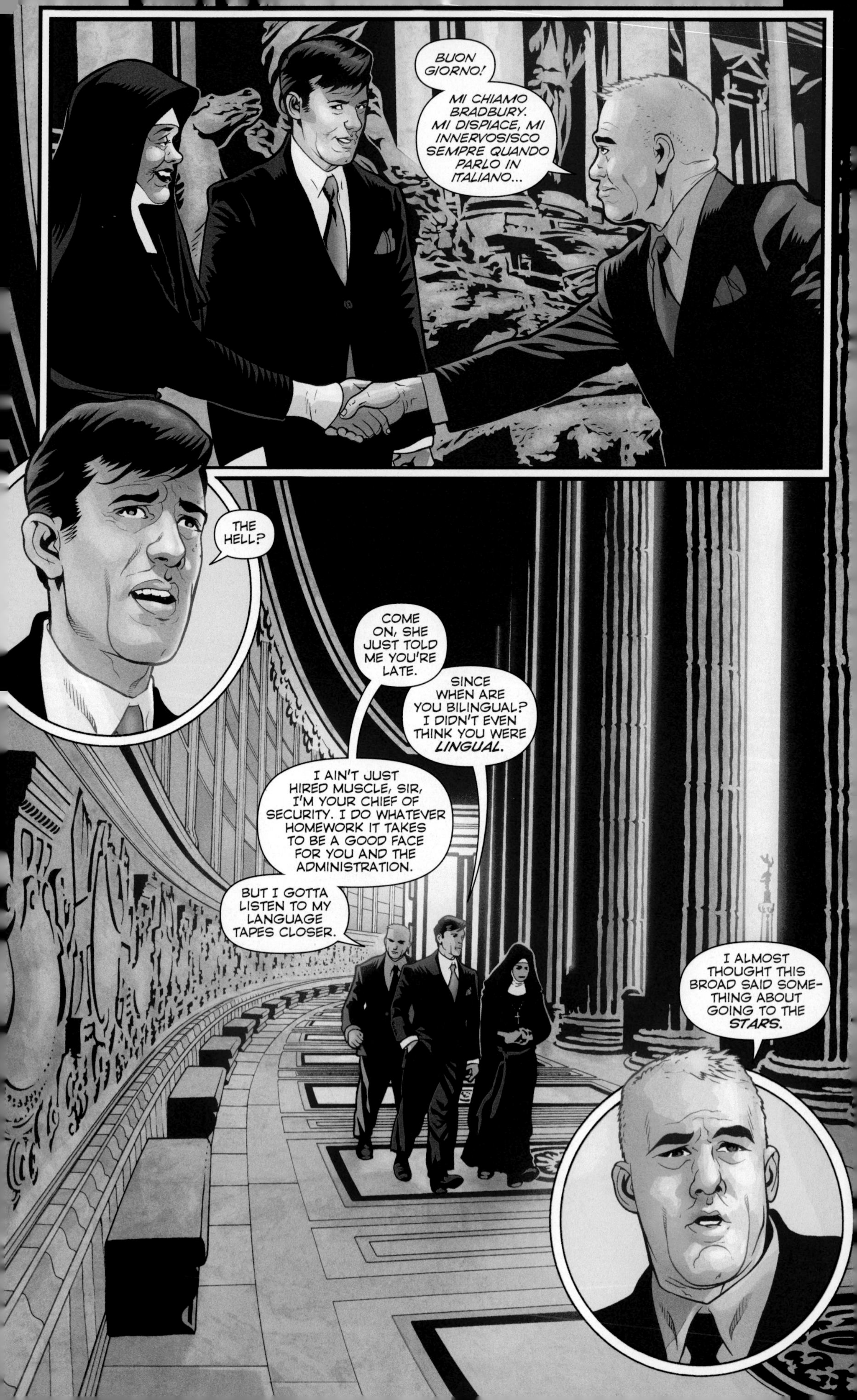
BUON GIORNO!
MI CHIAMO BRADBURY. MI DISPIACE, MI INNERVOSISCO SEMPRE QUANDO PARLO IN ITALIANO...
THE HELL?
COME ON, SHE JUST TOLD ME YOU'RE LATE.
SINCE WHEN ARE YOU BILINGUAL? I DIDN'T EVEN THINK YOU WERE LINGUAL.
I AIN'T JUST HIRED MUSCLE, SIR, I'M YOUR CHIEF OF SECURITY. I DO WHATEVER HOMEWORK IT TAKES TO BE A GOOD FACE FOR YOU AND THE ADMINISTRATION.
BUT I GOTTA LISTEN TO MY LANGUAGE TAPES CLOSER.
I ALMOST THOUGHT THIS BROAD SAID SOME-THING ABOUT GOING TO THE STARS.

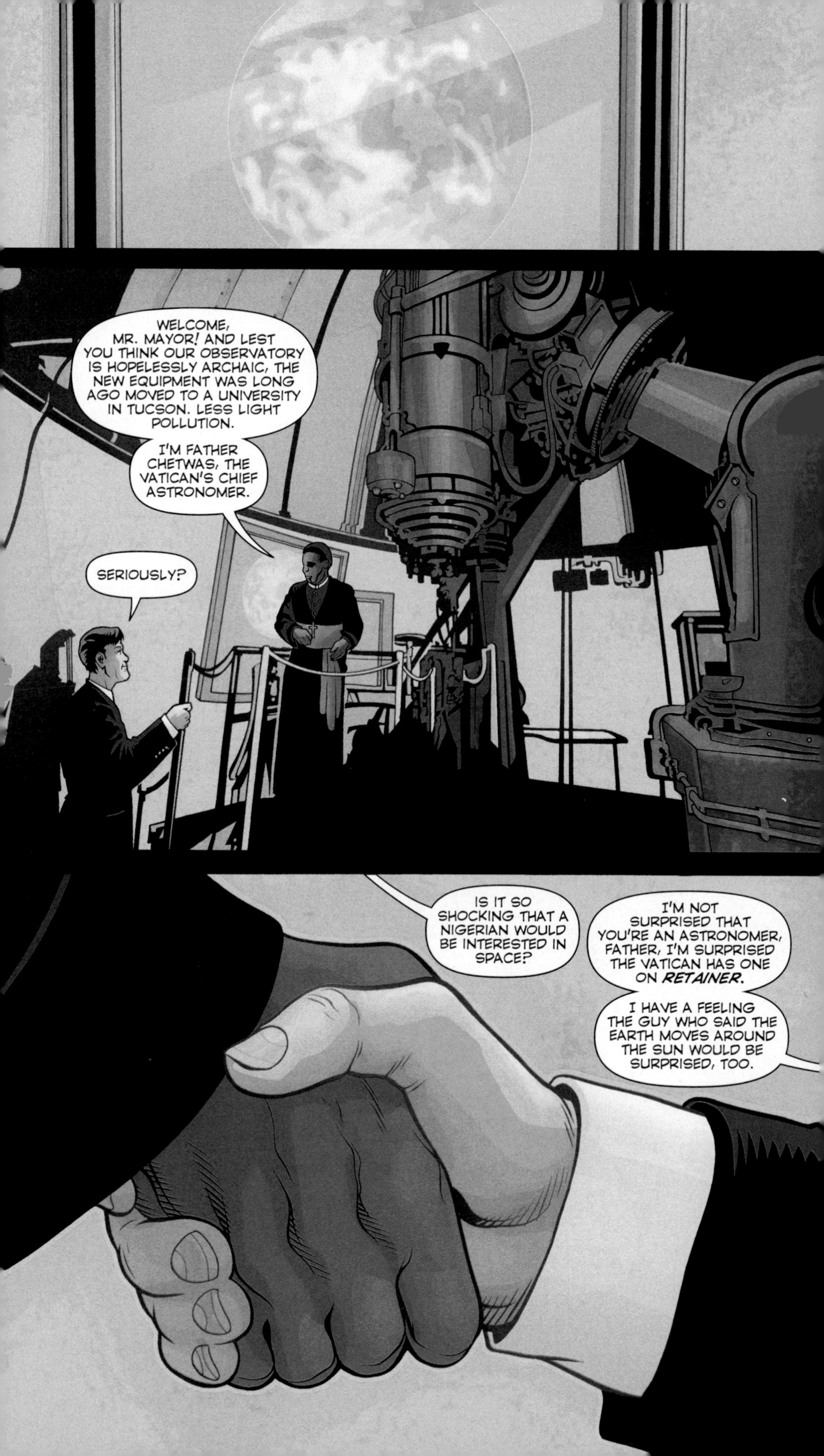
WELCOME, MR. MAYOR! AND LEST YOU THINK OUR OBSERVATORY IS HOPELESSLY ARCHAIC, THE NEW EQUIPMENT WAS LONG AGO MOVED TO A UNIVERSITY IN TUCSON. LESS LIGHT POLLUTION.
I'M FATHER CHETWAS, THE VATICAN'S CHIEF ASTRONOMER.
SERIOUSLY?
IS IT SO SHOCKING THAT A NIGERIAN WOULD BE INTERESTED IN SPACE?
I'M NOT SURPRISED THAT YOU'RE AN ASTRONOMER, FATHER, I'M SURPRISED THE VATICAN HAS ONE ON *RETAINER*.
I HAVE A FEELING THE GUY WHO SAID THE EARTH MOVES AROUND THE SUN WOULD BE SURPRISED, TOO.

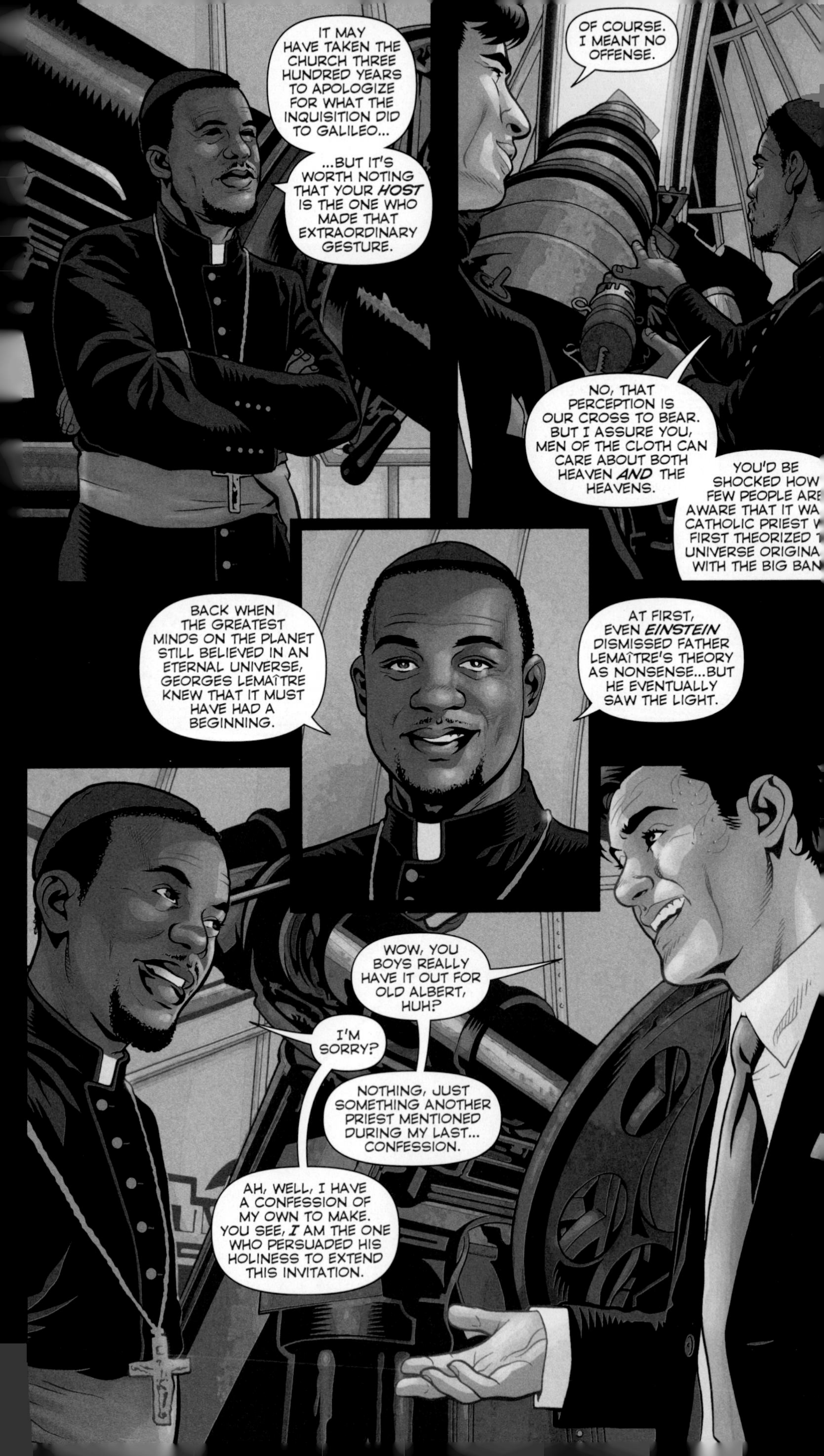
IT MAY HAVE TAKEN THE CHURCH THREE HUNDRED YEARS TO APOLOGIZE FOR WHAT THE INQUISITION DID TO GALILEO...
...BUT IT'S WORTH NOTING THAT YOUR *HOST* IS THE ONE WHO MADE THAT EXTRAORDINARY GESTURE.
OF COURSE. I MEANT NO OFFENSE.
NO, THAT PERCEPTION IS OUR CROSS TO BEAR. BUT I ASSURE YOU, MEN OF THE CLOTH CAN CARE ABOUT BOTH HEAVEN *AND* THE HEAVENS.
YOU'D BE SHOCKED HOW FEW PEOPLE ARE AWARE THAT IT WA CATHOLIC PRIEST W FIRST THEORIZED T UNIVERSE ORIGINA WITH THE BIG BAN
BACK WHEN THE GREATEST MINDS ON THE PLANET STILL BELIEVED IN AN ETERNAL UNIVERSE, GEORGES LEMAÎTRE KNEW THAT IT MUST HAVE HAD A BEGINNING.
AT FIRST, EVEN *EINSTEIN* DISMISSED FATHER LEMAÎTRE'S THEORY AS NONSENSE...BUT HE EVENTUALLY SAW THE LIGHT.
WOW, YOU BOYS REALLY HAVE IT OUT FOR OLD ALBERT, HUH?
I'M SORRY?
NOTHING, JUST SOMETHING ANOTHER PRIEST MENTIONED DURING MY LAST... CONFESSION.
AH, WELL, I HAVE A CONFESSION OF MY OWN TO MAKE. YOU SEE, *I* AM THE ONE WHO PERSUADED HIS HOLINESS TO EXTEND THIS INVITATION.

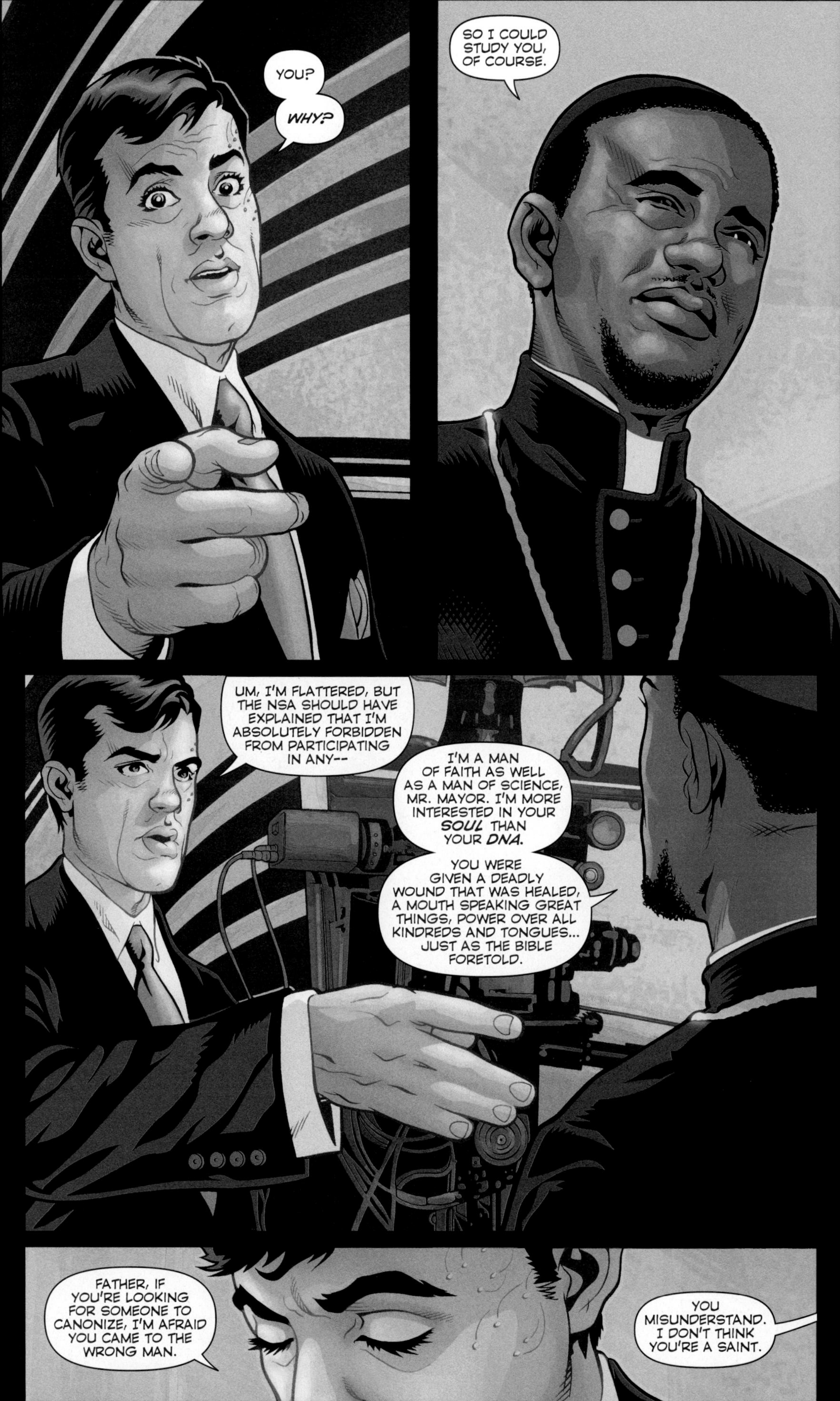

YOU?
WHY?
SO I COULD STUDY YOU, OF COURSE.
UM, I'M FLATTERED, BUT THE NSA SHOULD HAVE EXPLAINED THAT I'M ABSOLUTELY FORBIDDEN FROM PARTICIPATING IN ANY--
I'M A MAN OF FAITH AS WELL AS A MAN OF SCIENCE, MR. MAYOR. I'M MORE INTERESTED IN YOUR SOUL THAN YOUR DNA.
YOU WERE GIVEN A DEADLY WOUND THAT WAS HEALED, A MOUTH SPEAKING GREAT THINGS, POWER OVER ALL KINDREDS AND TONGUES... JUST AS THE BIBLE FORETOLD.
FATHER, IF YOU'RE LOOKING FOR SOMEONE TO CANONIZE, I'M AFRAID YOU CAME TO THE WRONG MAN.
YOU MISUNDERSTAND. I DON'T THINK YOU'RE A SAINT.

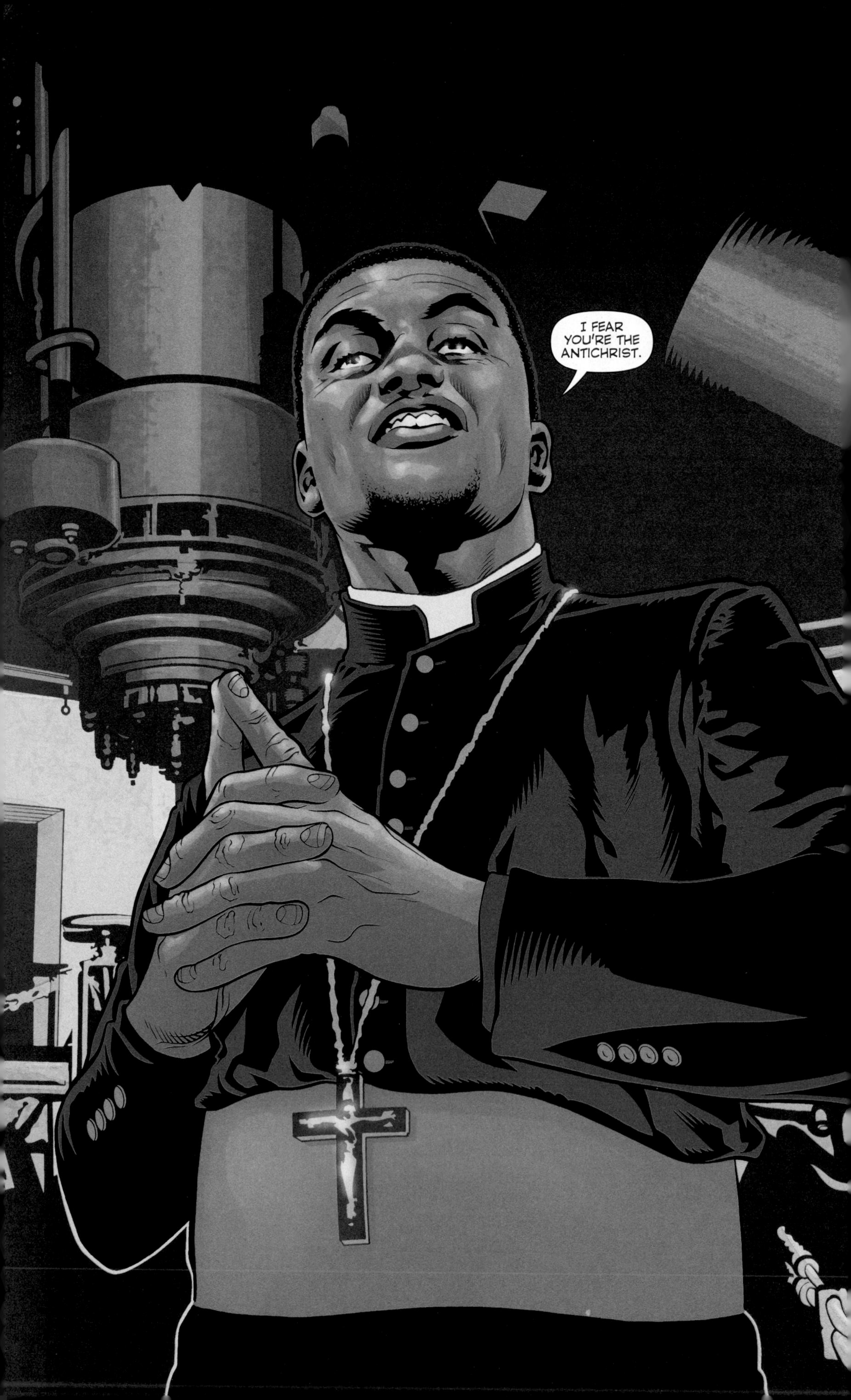
I FEAR YOU'RE THE ANTICHRIST.

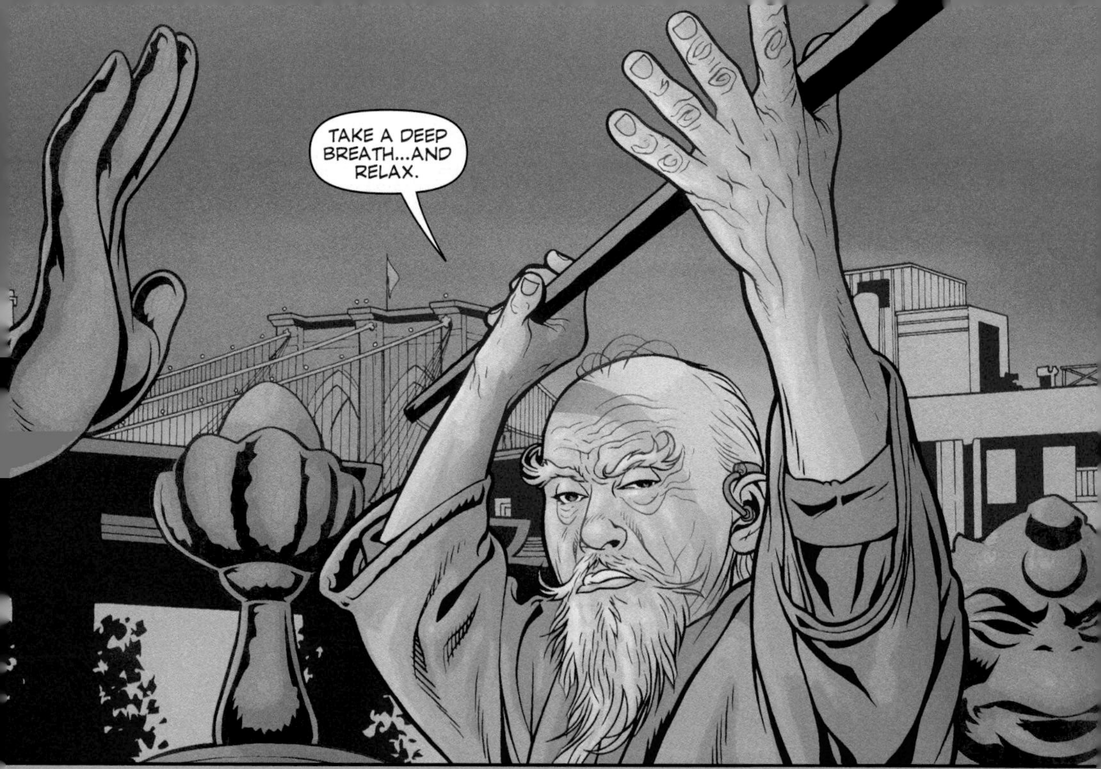
TAKE A DEEP BREATH...AND RELAX.

TUESDAY, MAY 29, 2001

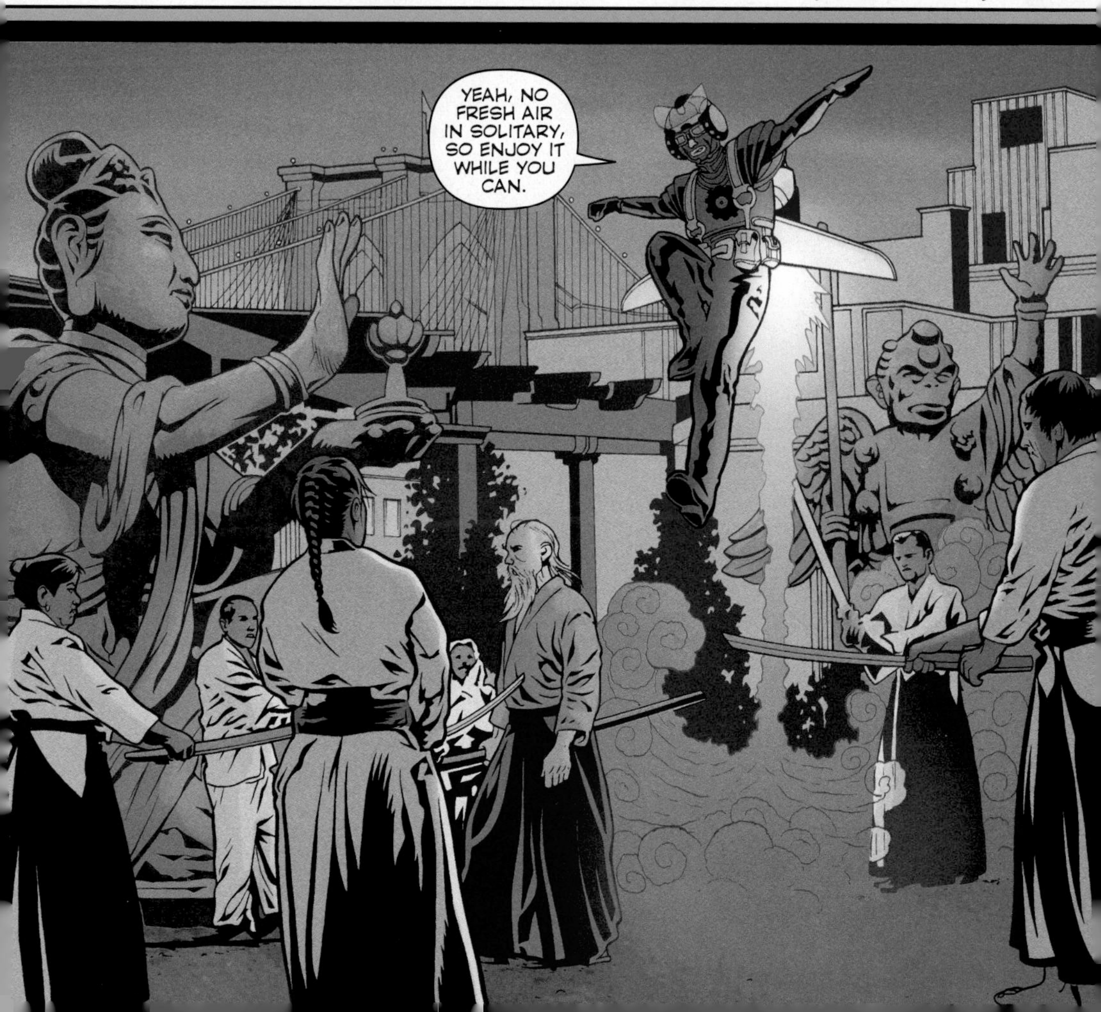
YEAH, NO FRESH AIR IN SOLITARY, SO ENJOY IT WHILE YOU CAN.

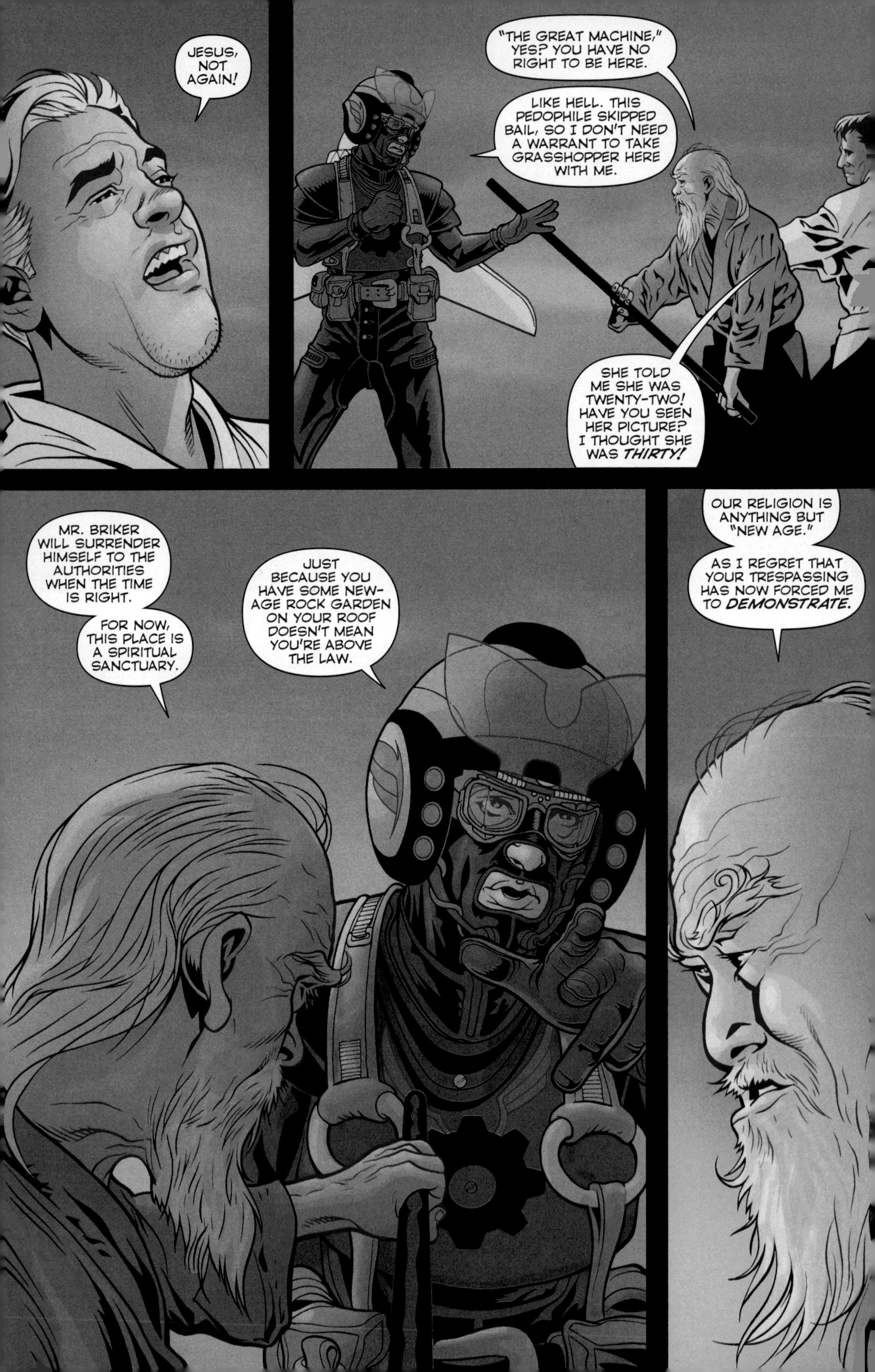
JESUS, NOT AGAIN!
"THE GREAT MACHINE," YES? YOU HAVE NO RIGHT TO BE HERE.
LIKE HELL. THIS PEDOPHILE SKIPPED BAIL, SO I DON'T NEED A WARRANT TO TAKE GRASSHOPPER HERE WITH ME.
SHE TOLD ME SHE WAS TWENTY-TWO! HAVE YOU SEEN HER PICTURE? I THOUGHT SHE WAS *THIRTY!*
MR. BRIKER WILL SURRENDER HIMSELF TO THE AUTHORITIES WHEN THE TIME IS RIGHT.
FOR NOW, THIS PLACE IS A SPIRITUAL SANCTUARY.
JUST BECAUSE YOU HAVE SOME NEW-AGE ROCK GARDEN ON YOUR ROOF DOESN'T MEAN YOU'RE ABOVE THE LAW.
OUR RELIGION IS ANYTHING BUT "NEW AGE."
AS I REGRET THAT YOUR TRESPASSING HAS NOW FORCED ME TO *DEMONSTRATE.*

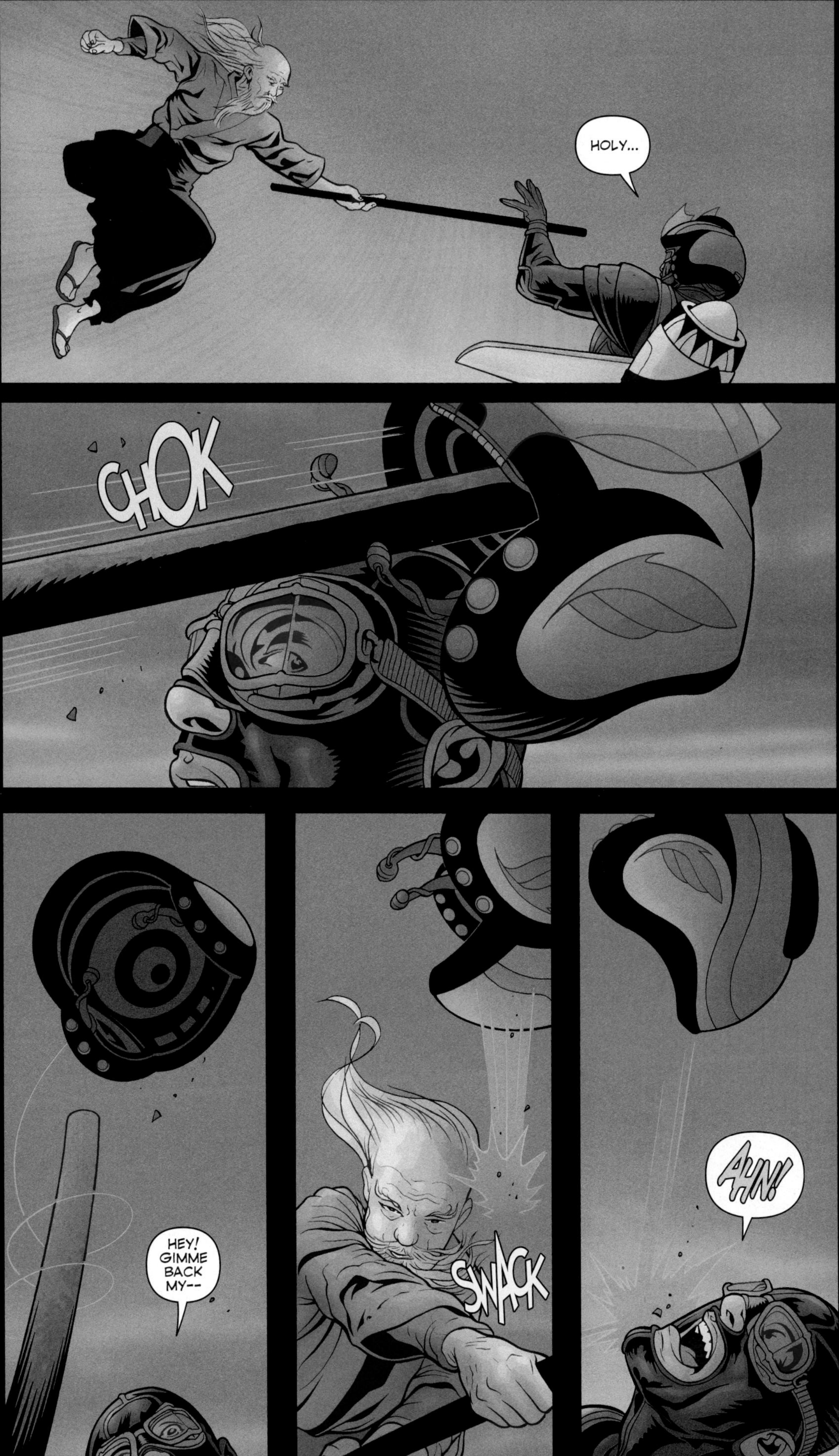
HOLY...
CHOK
HEY! GIMME BACK MY--
SWACK
AHN!

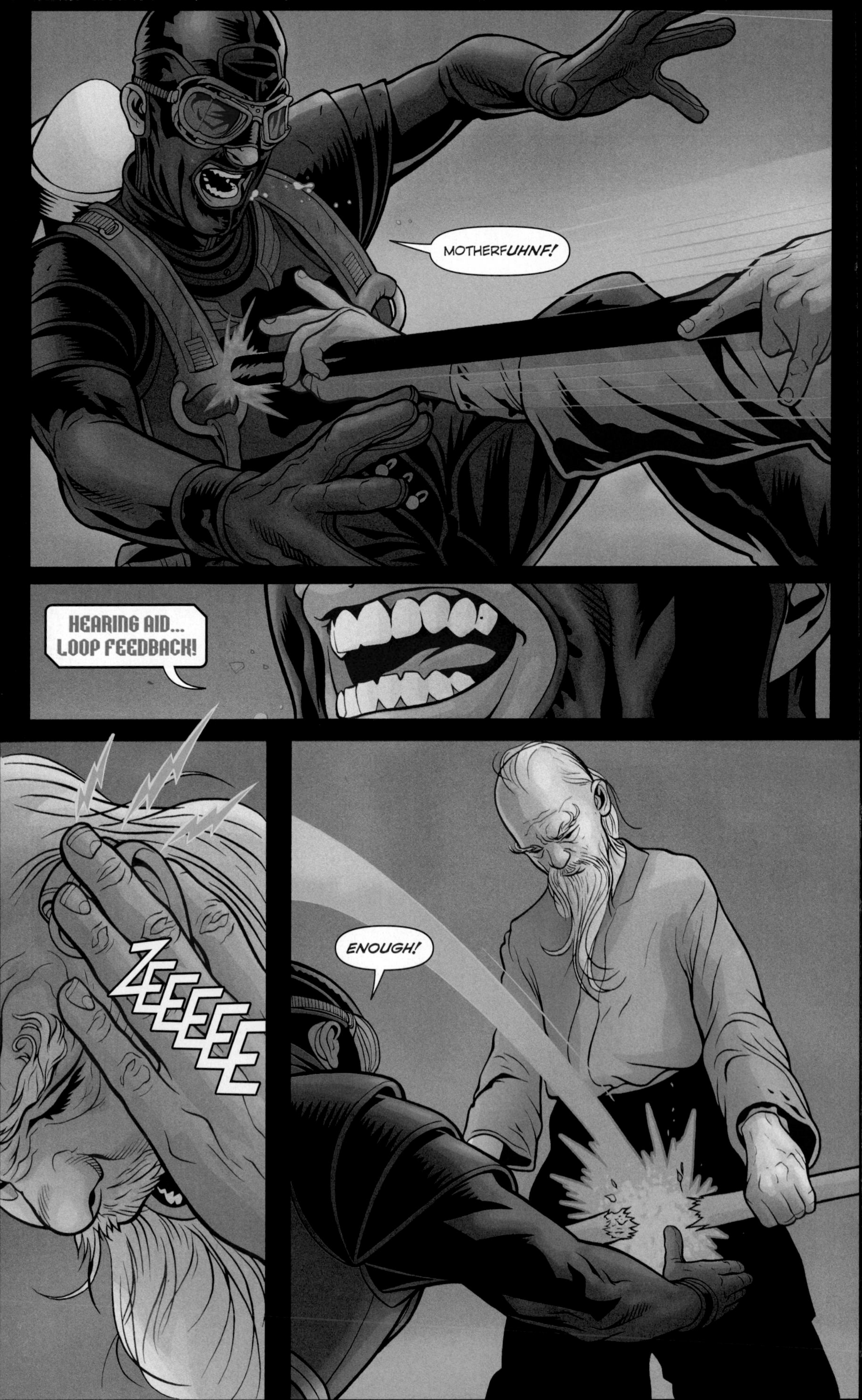
MOTHERFUHNF!
HEARING AID... LOOP FEEDBACK!
ZEEEEEE
ENOUGH!

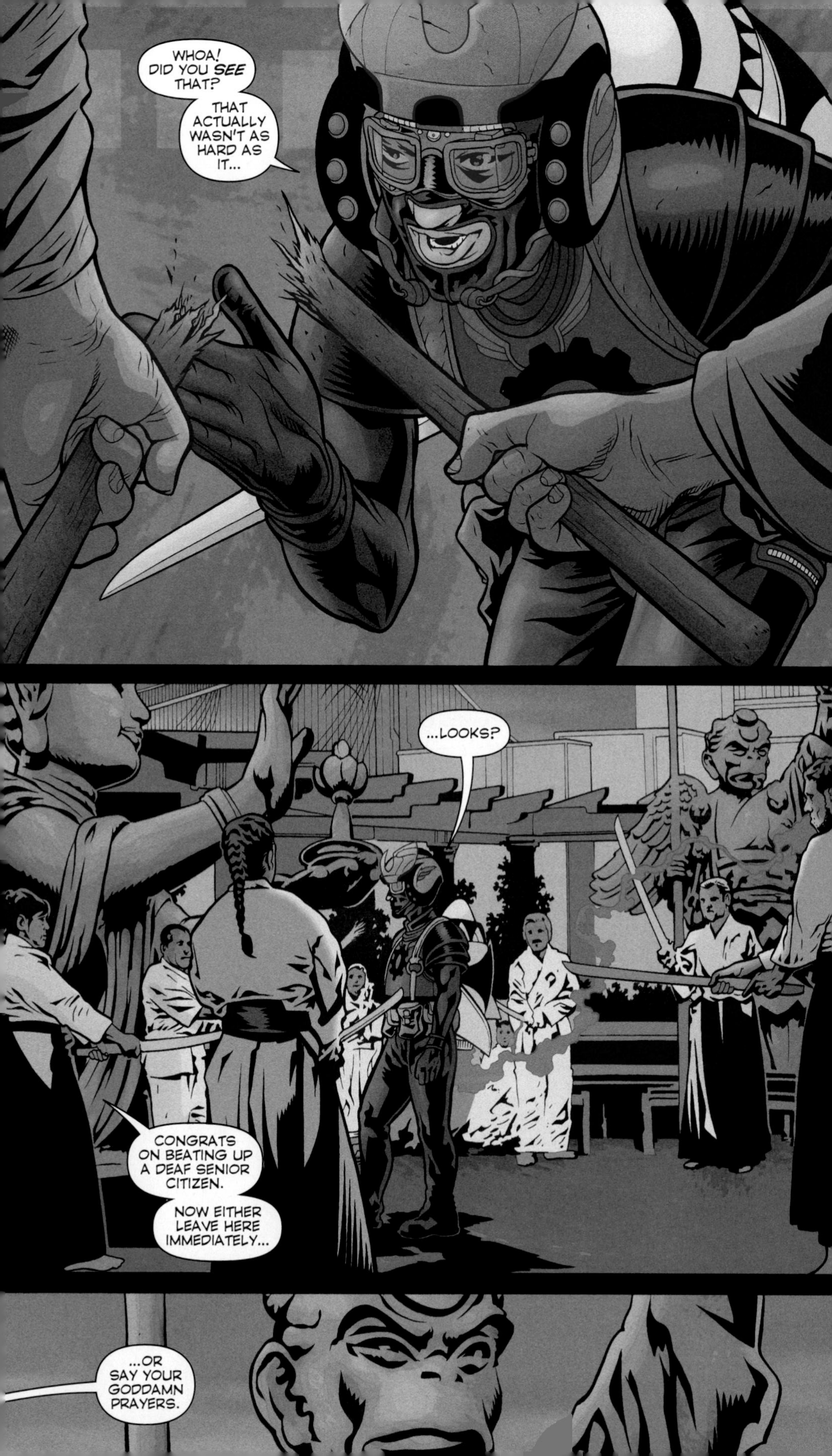
WHOA! DID YOU SEE THAT?
THAT ACTUALLY WASN'T AS HARD AS IT...
...LOOKS?
CONGRATS ON BEATING UP A DEAF SENIOR CITIZEN.
NOW EITHER LEAVE HERE IMMEDIATELY...
...OR SAY YOUR GODDAMN PRAYERS.

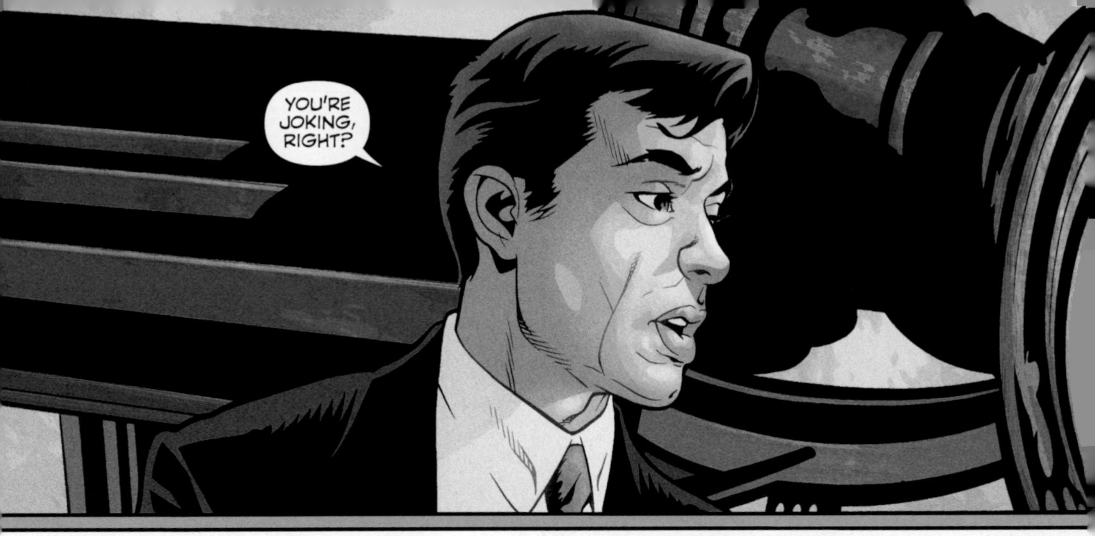
YOU'RE JOKING, RIGHT?

SUNDAY, DECEMBER 14, 2003

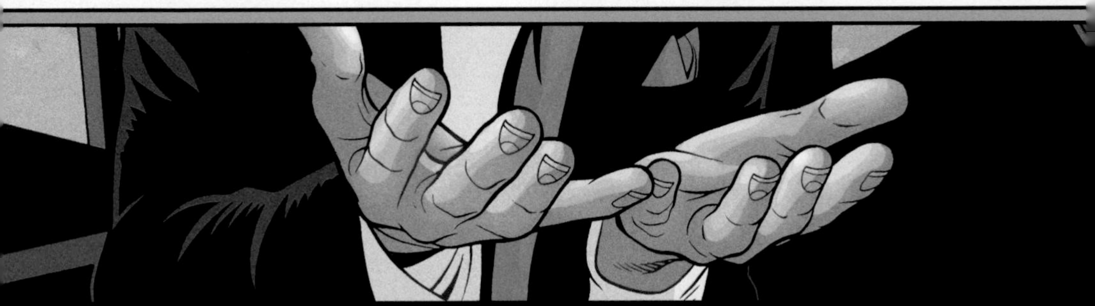

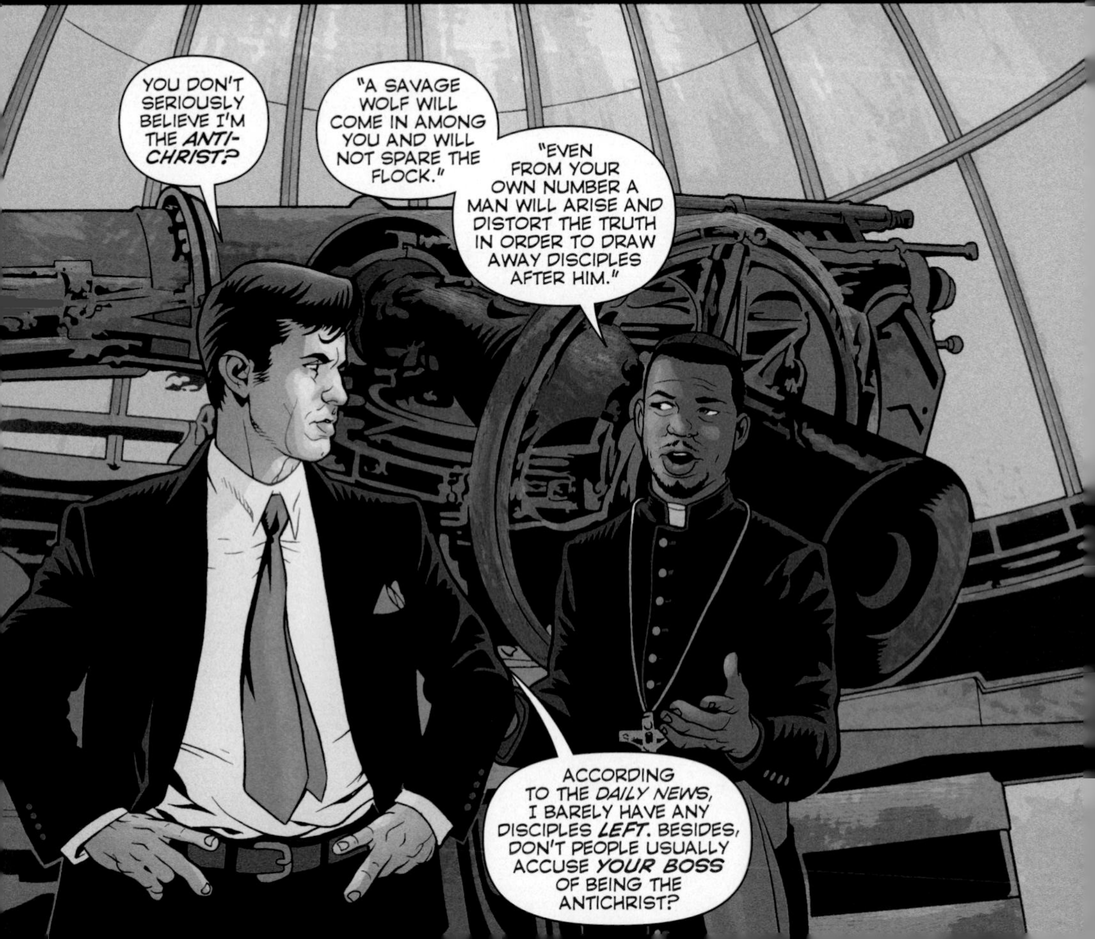
YOU DON'T SERIOUSLY BELIEVE I'M THE *ANTI-CHRIST?*
"A SAVAGE WOLF WILL COME IN AMONG YOU AND WILL NOT SPARE THE FLOCK."
"EVEN FROM YOUR OWN NUMBER A MAN WILL ARISE AND DISTORT THE TRUTH IN ORDER TO DRAW AWAY DISCIPLES AFTER HIM."
ACCORDING TO THE *DAILY NEWS*, I BARELY HAVE ANY DISCIPLES ***LEFT***. BESIDES, DON'T PEOPLE USUALLY ACCUSE ***YOUR BOSS*** OF BEING THE ANTICHRIST?

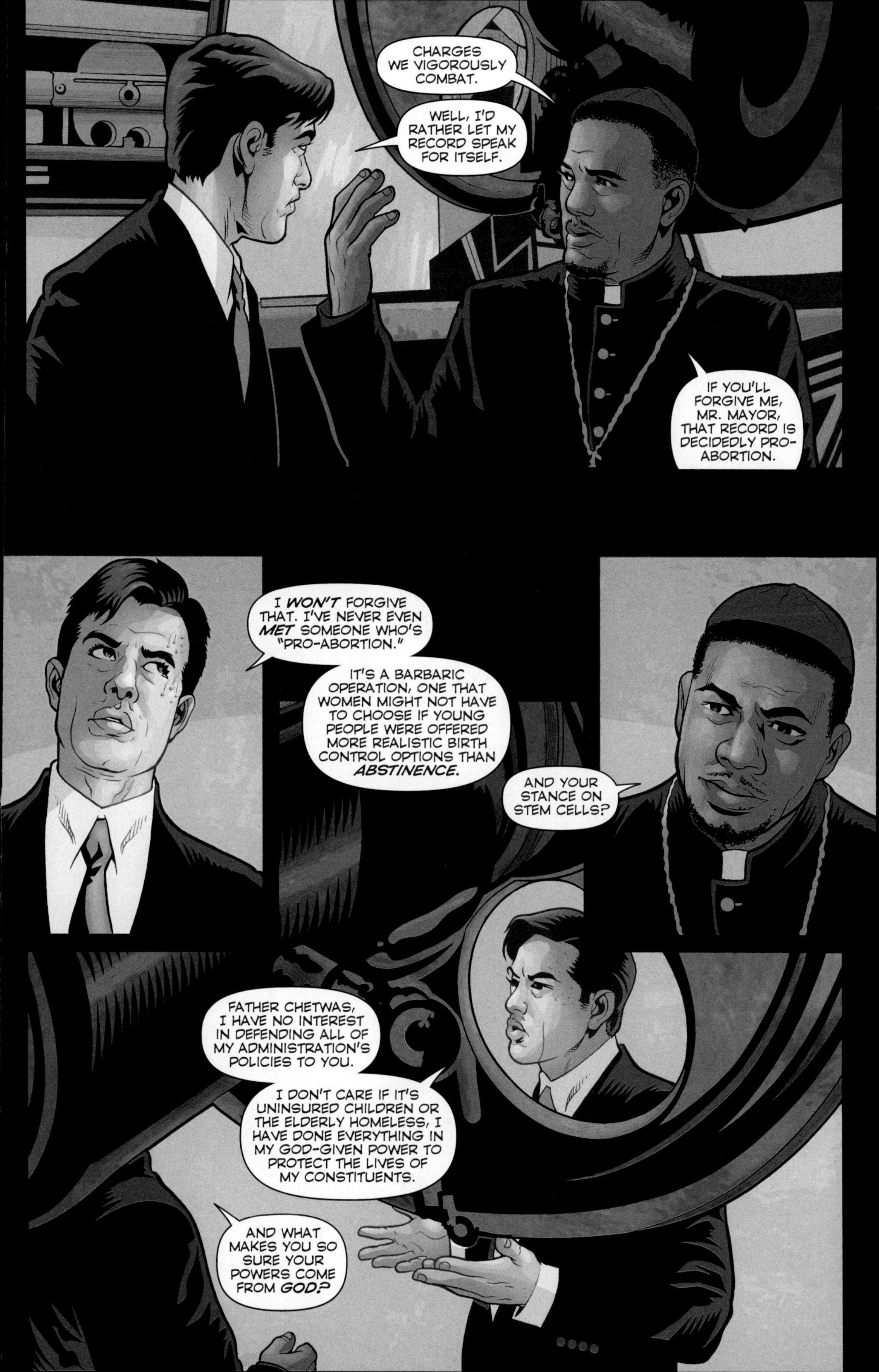
CHARGES WE VIGOROUSLY COMBAT.
WELL, I'D RATHER LET MY RECORD SPEAK FOR ITSELF.
IF YOU'LL FORGIVE ME, MR. MAYOR, THAT RECORD IS DECIDEDLY PRO-ABORTION.
I *WON'T* FORGIVE THAT. I'VE NEVER EVEN *MET* SOMEONE WHO'S "PRO-ABORTION."
IT'S A BARBARIC OPERATION, ONE THAT WOMEN MIGHT NOT HAVE TO CHOOSE IF YOUNG PEOPLE WERE OFFERED MORE REALISTIC BIRTH CONTROL OPTIONS THAN *ABSTINENCE*.
AND YOUR STANCE ON STEM CELLS?
FATHER CHETWAS, I HAVE NO INTEREST IN DEFENDING ALL OF MY ADMINISTRATION'S POLICIES TO YOU.
I DON'T CARE IF IT'S UNINSURED CHILDREN OR THE ELDERLY HOMELESS, I HAVE DONE EVERYTHING IN MY GOD-GIVEN POWER TO PROTECT THE LIVES OF MY CONSTITUENTS.
AND WHAT MAKES YOU SO SURE YOUR POWERS COME FROM *GOD?*

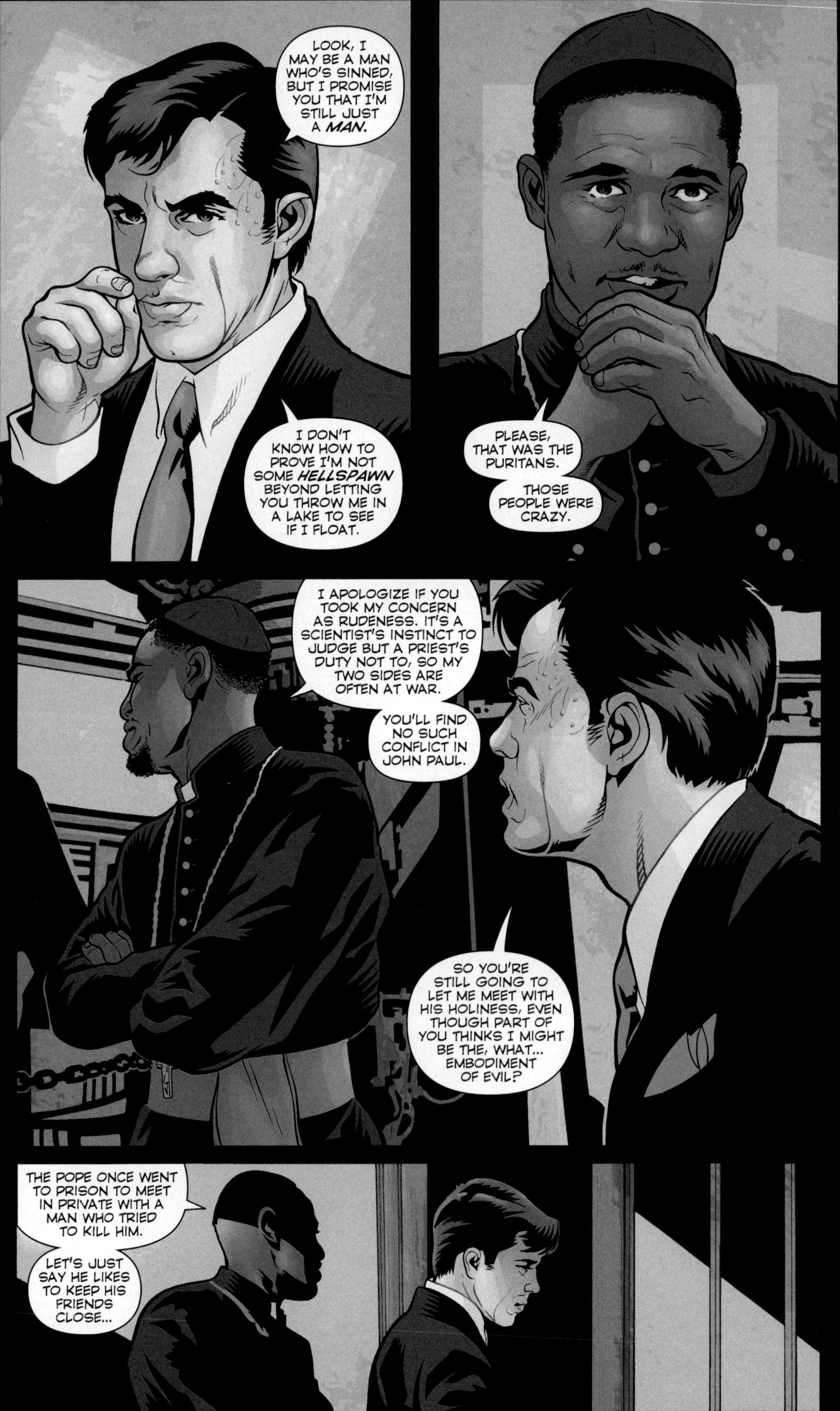

LOOK, I MAY BE A MAN WHO'S SINNED, BUT I PROMISE YOU THAT I'M STILL JUST A *MAN*.
I DON'T KNOW HOW TO PROVE I'M NOT SOME *HELLSPAWN* BEYOND LETTING YOU THROW ME IN A LAKE TO SEE IF I FLOAT.
PLEASE, THAT WAS THE PURITANS.
THOSE PEOPLE WERE CRAZY.
I APOLOGIZE IF YOU TOOK MY CONCERN AS RUDENESS. IT'S A SCIENTIST'S INSTINCT TO JUDGE BUT A PRIEST'S DUTY NOT TO, SO MY TWO SIDES ARE OFTEN AT WAR.
YOU'LL FIND NO SUCH CONFLICT IN JOHN PAUL.
SO YOU'RE STILL GOING TO LET ME MEET WITH HIS HOLINESS, EVEN THOUGH PART OF YOU THINKS I MIGHT BE THE, WHAT... EMBODIMENT OF EVIL?
THE POPE ONCE WENT TO PRISON TO MEET IN PRIVATE WITH A MAN WHO TRIED TO KILL HIM.
LET'S JUST SAY HE LIKES TO KEEP HIS FRIENDS CLOSE...

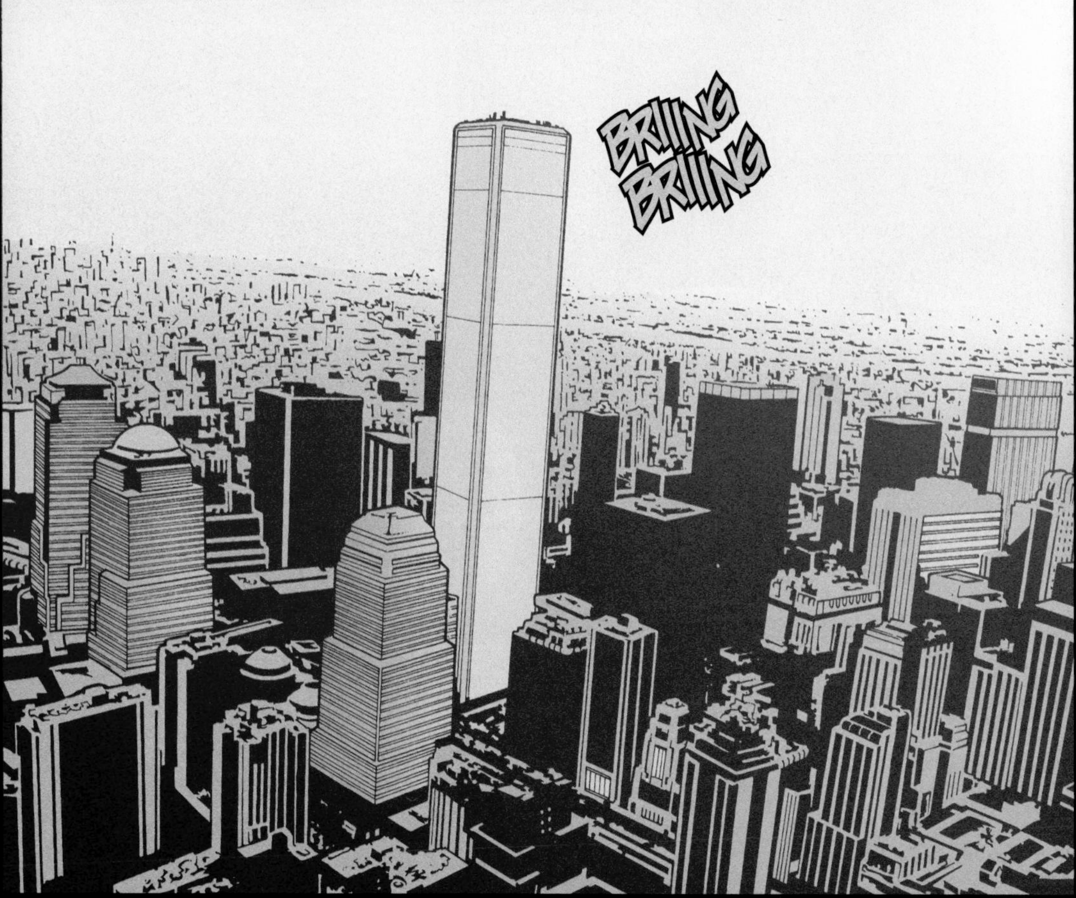
BRIIING
BRIIING

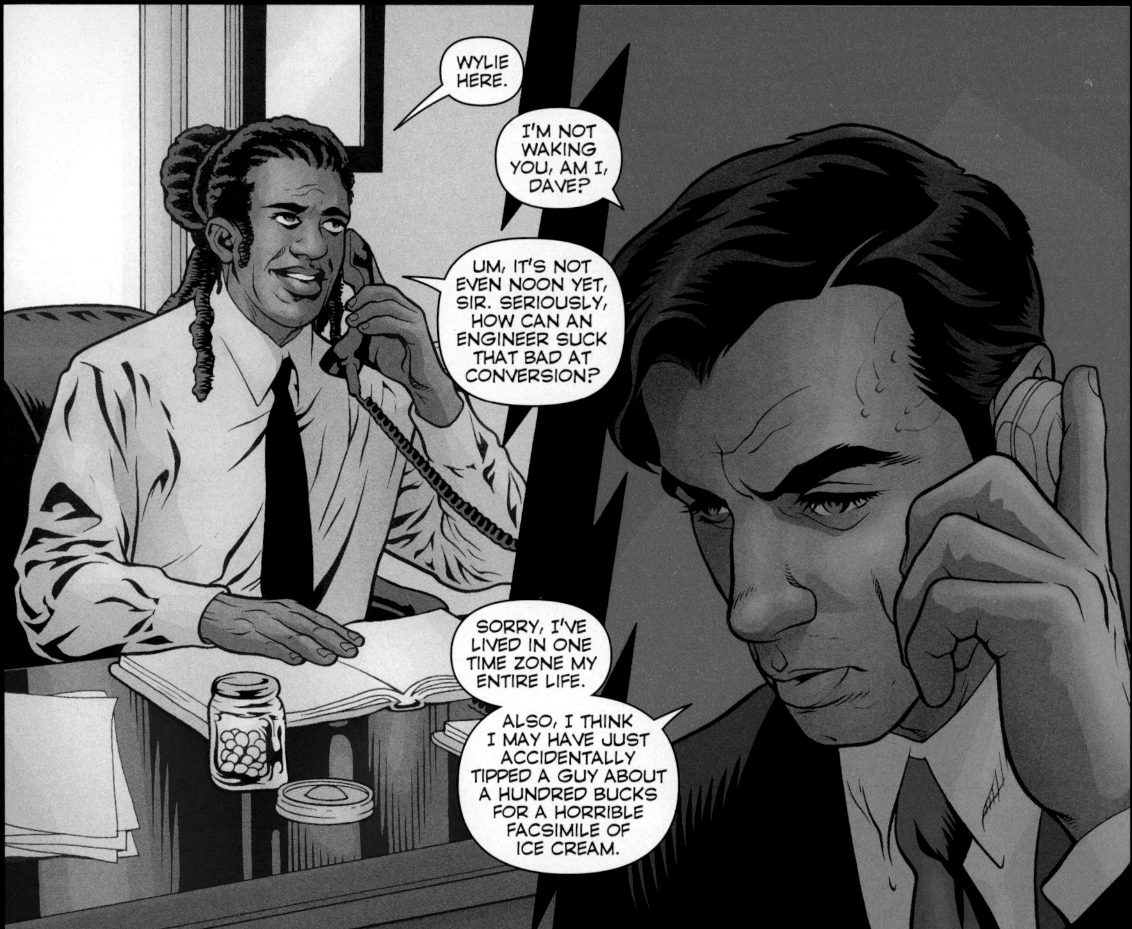
WYLIE HERE.
I'M NOT WAKING YOU, AM I, DAVE?
UM, IT'S NOT EVEN NOON YET, SIR. SERIOUSLY, HOW CAN AN ENGINEER SUCK THAT BAD AT CONVERSION?
SORRY, I'VE LIVED IN ONE TIME ZONE MY ENTIRE LIFE.
ALSO, I THINK I MAY HAVE JUST ACCIDENTALLY TIPPED A GUY ABOUT A HUNDRED BUCKS FOR A HORRIBLE FACSIMILE OF ICE CREAM.

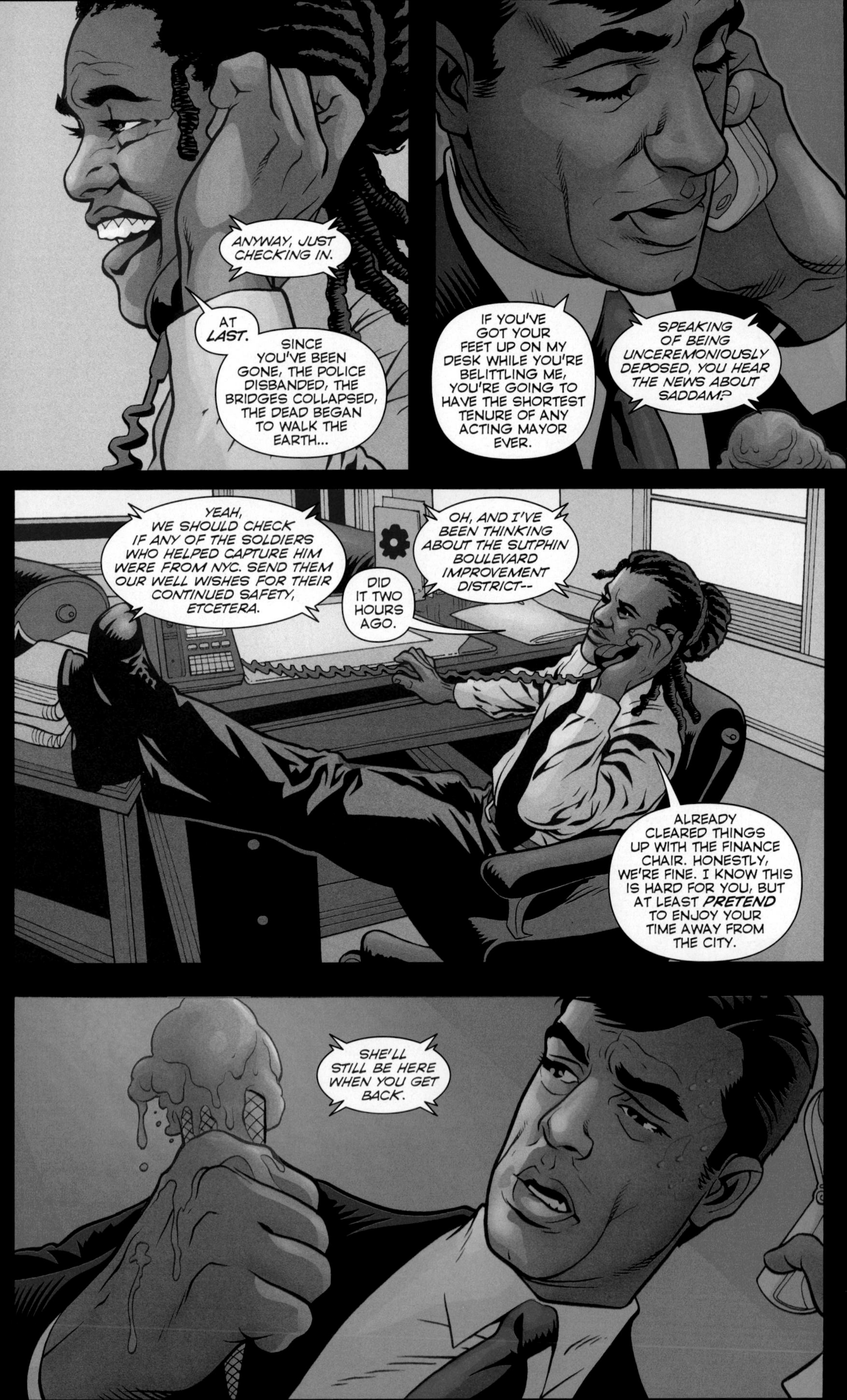
ANYWAY, JUST CHECKING IN.
AT LAST. SINCE YOU'VE BEEN GONE, THE POLICE DISBANDED, THE BRIDGES COLLAPSED, THE DEAD BEGAN TO WALK THE EARTH...
IF YOU'VE GOT YOUR FEET UP ON MY DESK WHILE YOU'RE BELITTLING ME, YOU'RE GOING TO HAVE THE SHORTEST TENURE OF ANY ACTING MAYOR EVER.
SPEAKING OF BEING UNCEREMONIOUSLY DEPOSED, YOU HEAR THE NEWS ABOUT SADDAM?
YEAH, WE SHOULD CHECK IF ANY OF THE SOLDIERS WHO HELPED CAPTURE HIM WERE FROM NYC. SEND THEM OUR WELL WISHES FOR THEIR CONTINUED SAFETY, ETCETERA.
DID IT TWO HOURS AGO.
OH, AND I'VE BEEN THINKING ABOUT THE SUTPHIN BOULEVARD IMPROVEMENT DISTRICT--
ALREADY CLEARED THINGS UP WITH THE FINANCE CHAIR. HONESTLY, WE'RE FINE. I KNOW THIS IS HARD FOR YOU, BUT AT LEAST PRETEND TO ENJOY YOUR TIME AWAY FROM THE CITY.
SHE'LL STILL BE HERE WHEN YOU GET BACK.

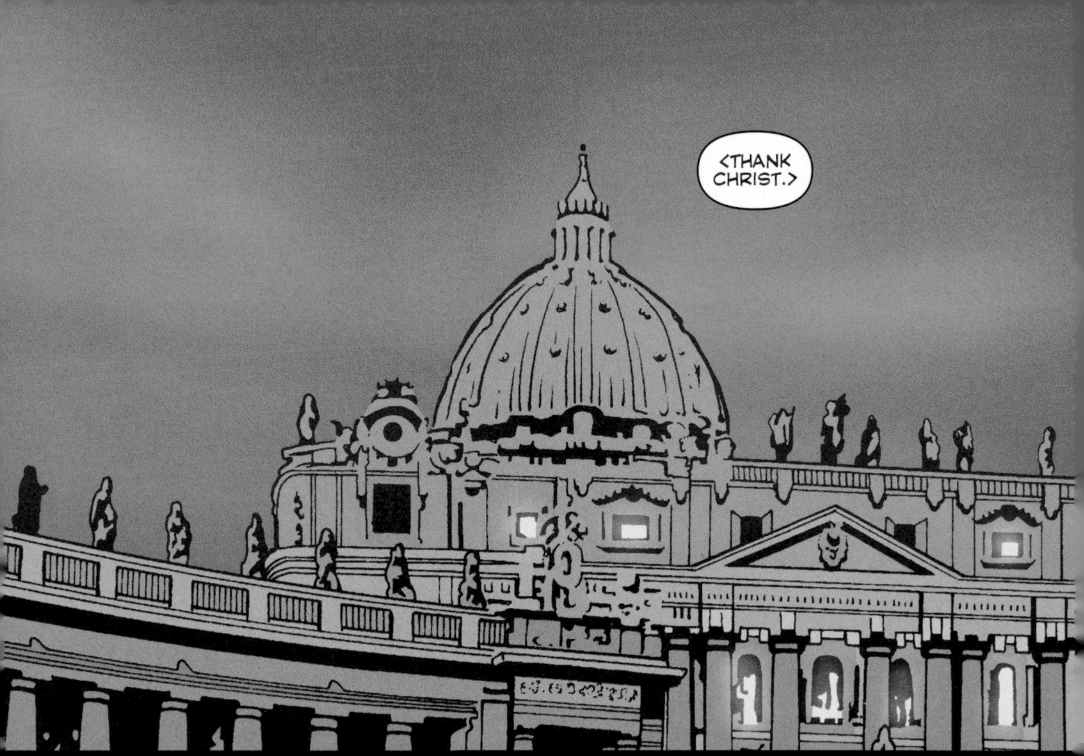
<THANK CHRIST.>

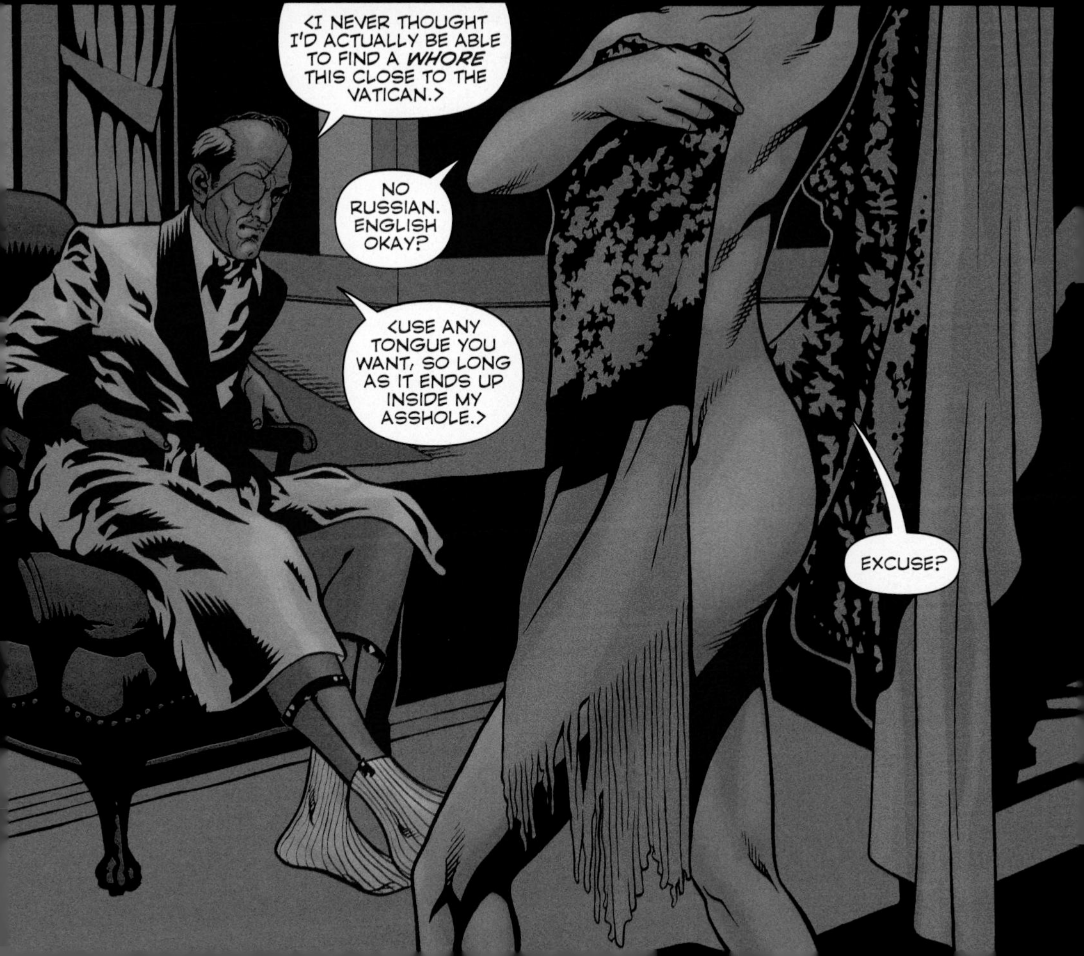
<I NEVER THOUGHT I'D ACTUALLY BE ABLE TO FIND A *WHORE* THIS CLOSE TO THE VATICAN.>
NO RUSSIAN. ENGLISH OKAY?
<USE ANY TONGUE YOU WANT, SO LONG AS IT ENDS UP INSIDE MY ASSHOLE.>
EXCUSE?

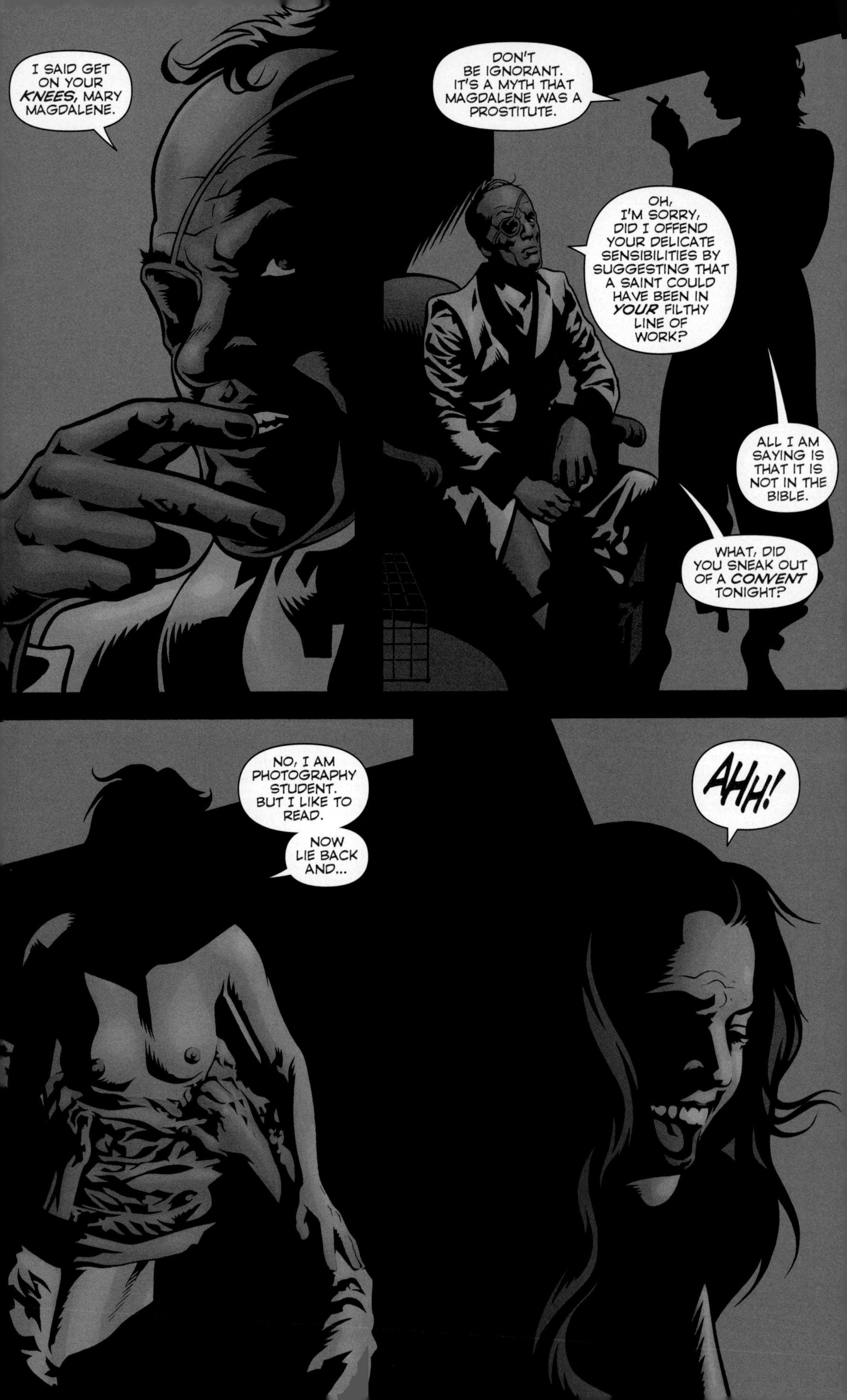
I SAID GET ON YOUR KNEES, MARY MAGDALENE.
DON'T BE IGNORANT. IT'S A MYTH THAT MAGDALENE WAS A PROSTITUTE.
OH, I'M SORRY, DID I OFFEND YOUR DELICATE SENSIBILITIES BY SUGGESTING THAT A SAINT COULD HAVE BEEN IN YOUR FILTHY LINE OF WORK?
ALL I AM SAYING IS THAT IT IS NOT IN THE BIBLE.
WHAT, DID YOU SNEAK OUT OF A CONVENT TONIGHT?
NO, I AM PHOTOGRAPHY STUDENT. BUT I LIKE TO READ.
NOW LIE BACK AND...
AHH!

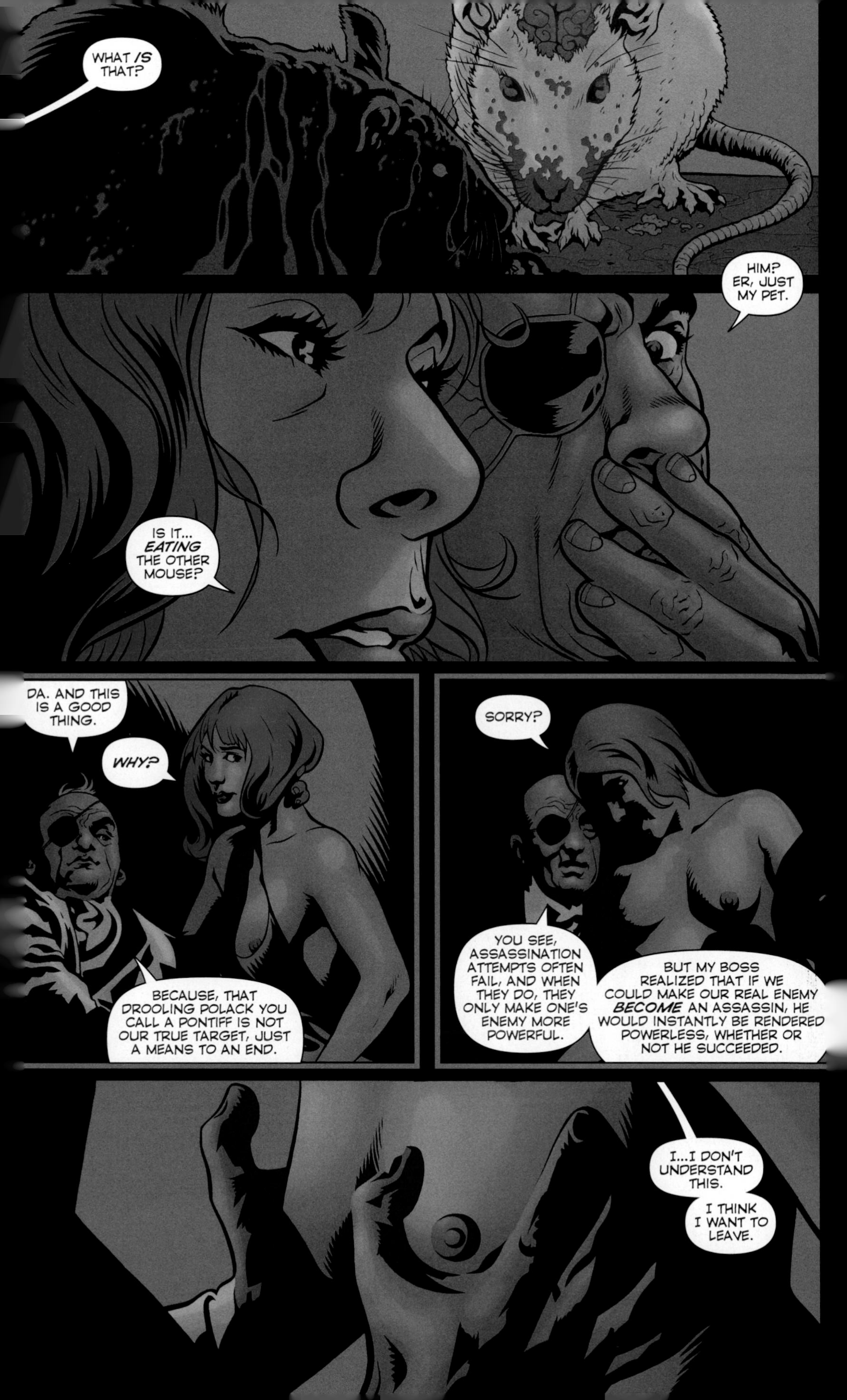
WHAT IS THAT?
HIM? ER, JUST MY PET.
IS IT... EATING THE OTHER MOUSE?
DA. AND THIS IS A GOOD THING.
WHY?
BECAUSE, THAT DROOLING POLACK YOU CALL A PONTIFF IS NOT OUR TRUE TARGET, JUST A MEANS TO AN END.
SORRY?
YOU SEE, ASSASSINATION ATTEMPTS OFTEN FAIL, AND WHEN THEY DO, THEY ONLY MAKE ONE'S ENEMY MORE POWERFUL.
BUT MY BOSS REALIZED THAT IF WE COULD MAKE OUR REAL ENEMY BECOME AN ASSASSIN, HE WOULD INSTANTLY BE RENDERED POWERLESS, WHETHER OR NOT HE SUCCEEDED.
I...I DON'T UNDERSTAND THIS.
I THINK I WANT TO LEAVE.

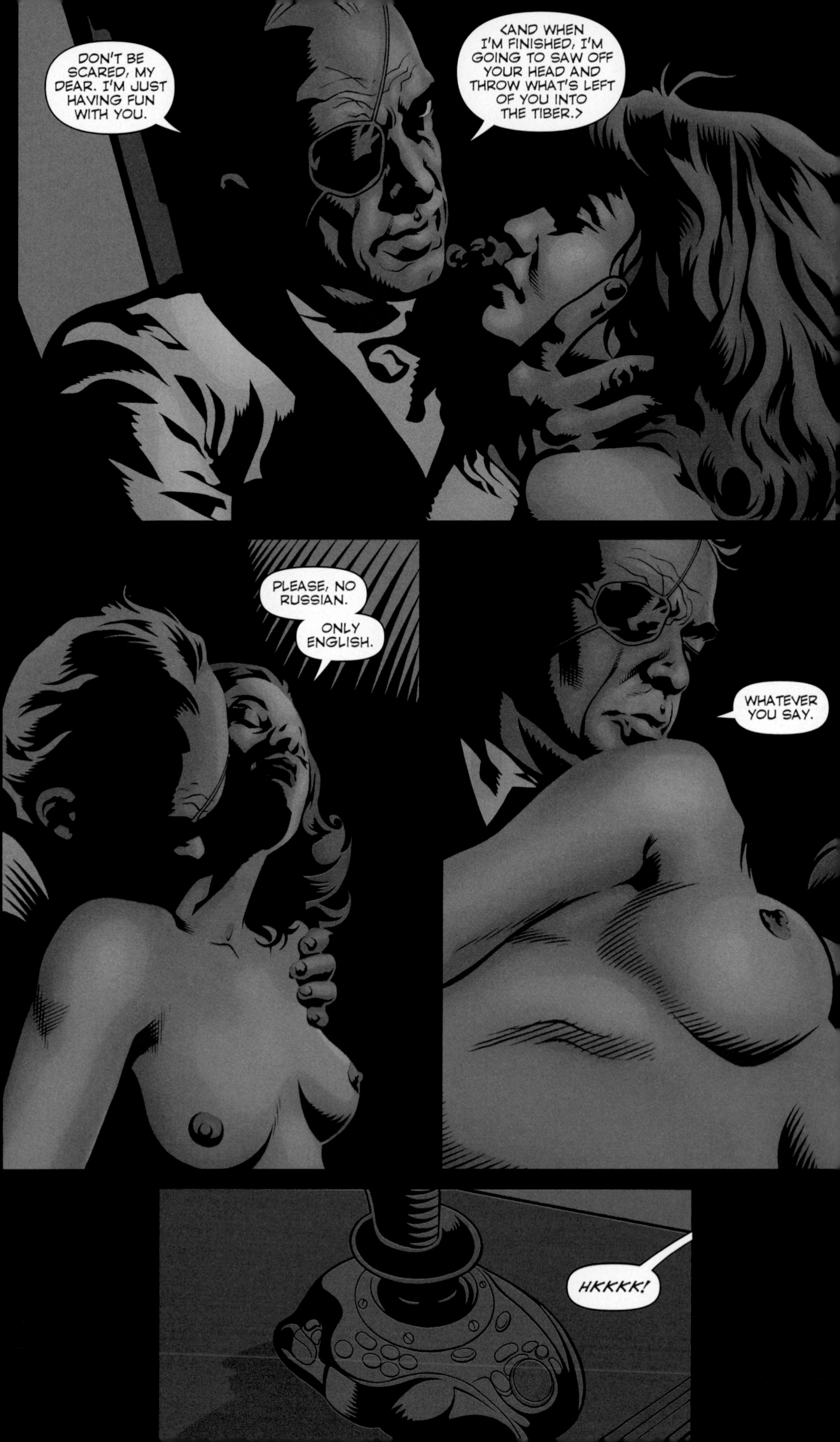
DON'T BE SCARED, MY DEAR. I'M JUST HAVING FUN WITH YOU.
<AND WHEN I'M FINISHED, I'M GOING TO SAW OFF YOUR HEAD AND THROW WHAT'S LEFT OF YOU INTO THE TIBER.>
PLEASE, NO RUSSIAN.
ONLY ENGLISH.
WHATEVER YOU SAY.
HKKKK!

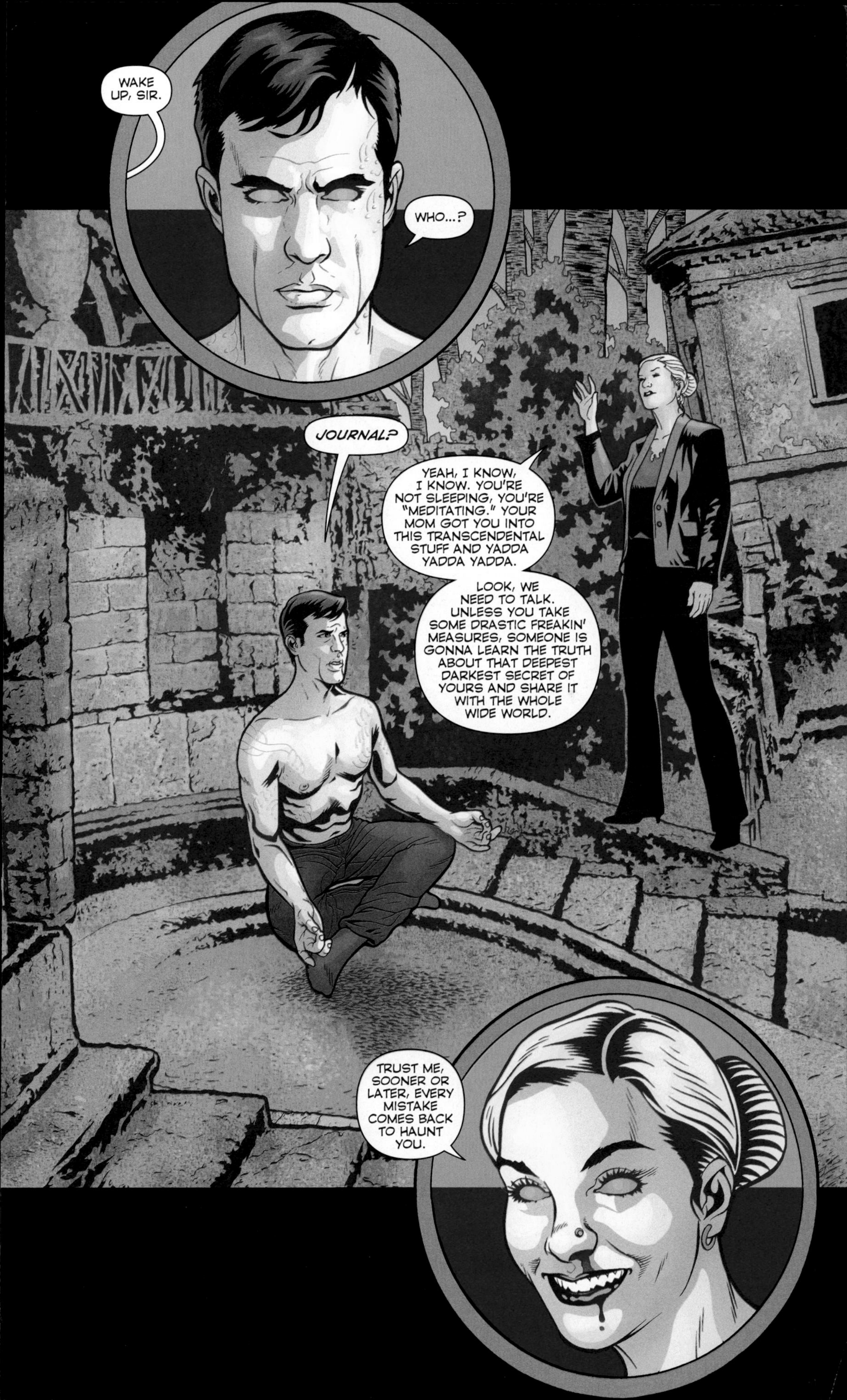
WAKE UP, SIR.
WHO...?
JOURNAL?
YEAH, I KNOW, I KNOW. YOU'RE NOT SLEEPING, YOU'RE "MEDITATING." YOUR MOM GOT YOU INTO THIS TRANSCENDENTAL STUFF AND YADDA YADDA YADDA.
LOOK, WE NEED TO TALK. UNLESS YOU TAKE SOME DRASTIC FREAKIN' MEASURES, SOMEONE IS GONNA LEARN THE TRUTH ABOUT THAT DEEPEST DARKEST SECRET OF YOURS AND SHARE IT WITH THE WHOLE WIDE WORLD.
TRUST ME, SOONER OR LATER, EVERY MISTAKE COMES BACK TO HAUNT YOU.

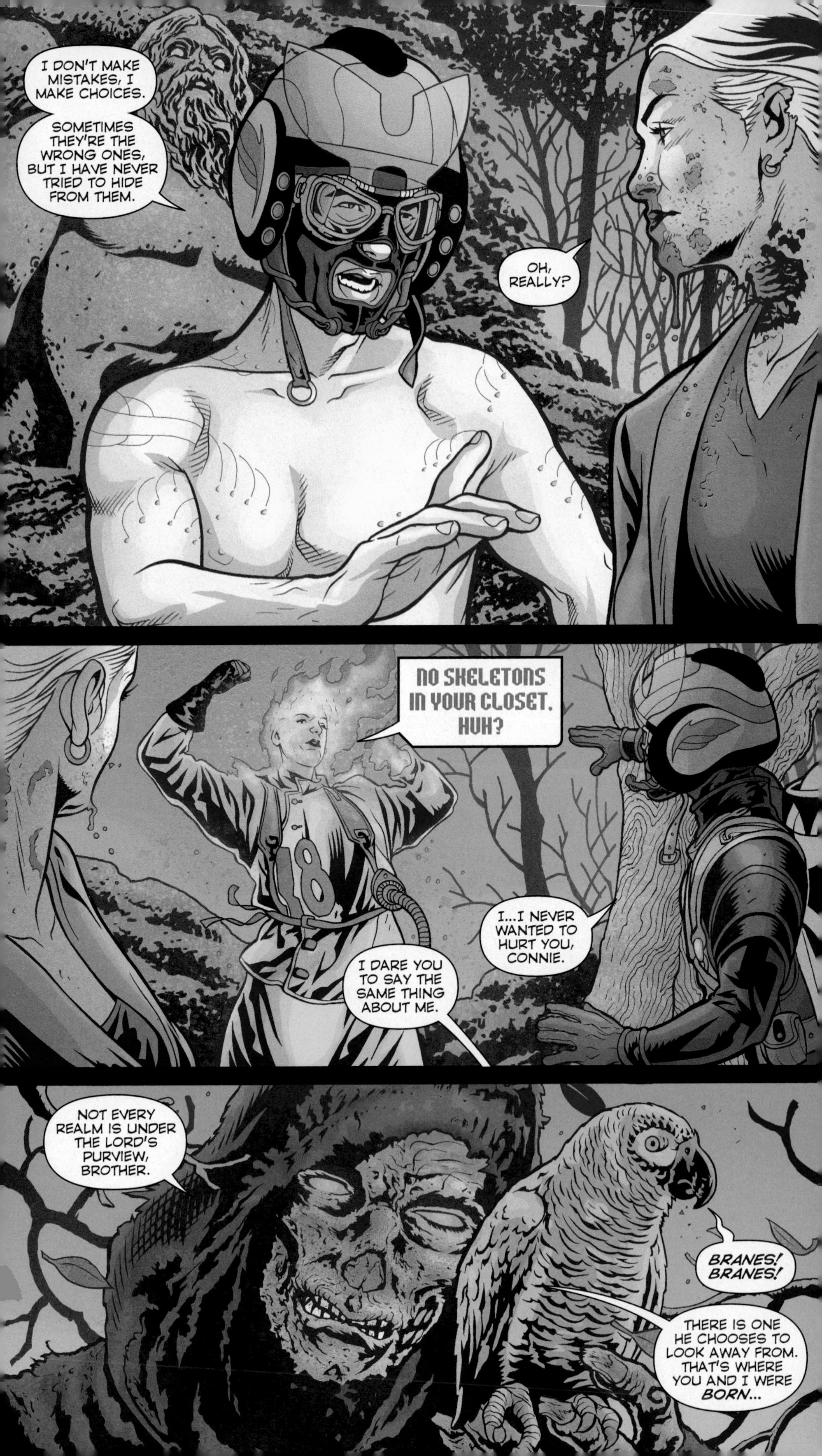
I DON'T MAKE MISTAKES, I MAKE CHOICES.
SOMETIMES THEY'RE THE WRONG ONES, BUT I HAVE NEVER TRIED TO HIDE FROM THEM.
OH, REALLY?
NO SKELETONS IN YOUR CLOSET. HUH?
I DARE YOU TO SAY THE SAME THING ABOUT ME.
I...I NEVER WANTED TO HURT YOU, CONNIE.
NOT EVERY REALM IS UNDER THE LORD'S PURVIEW, BROTHER.
BRANES! BRANES!
THERE IS ONE HE CHOOSES TO LOOK AWAY FROM. THAT'S WHERE YOU AND I WERE *BORN*...

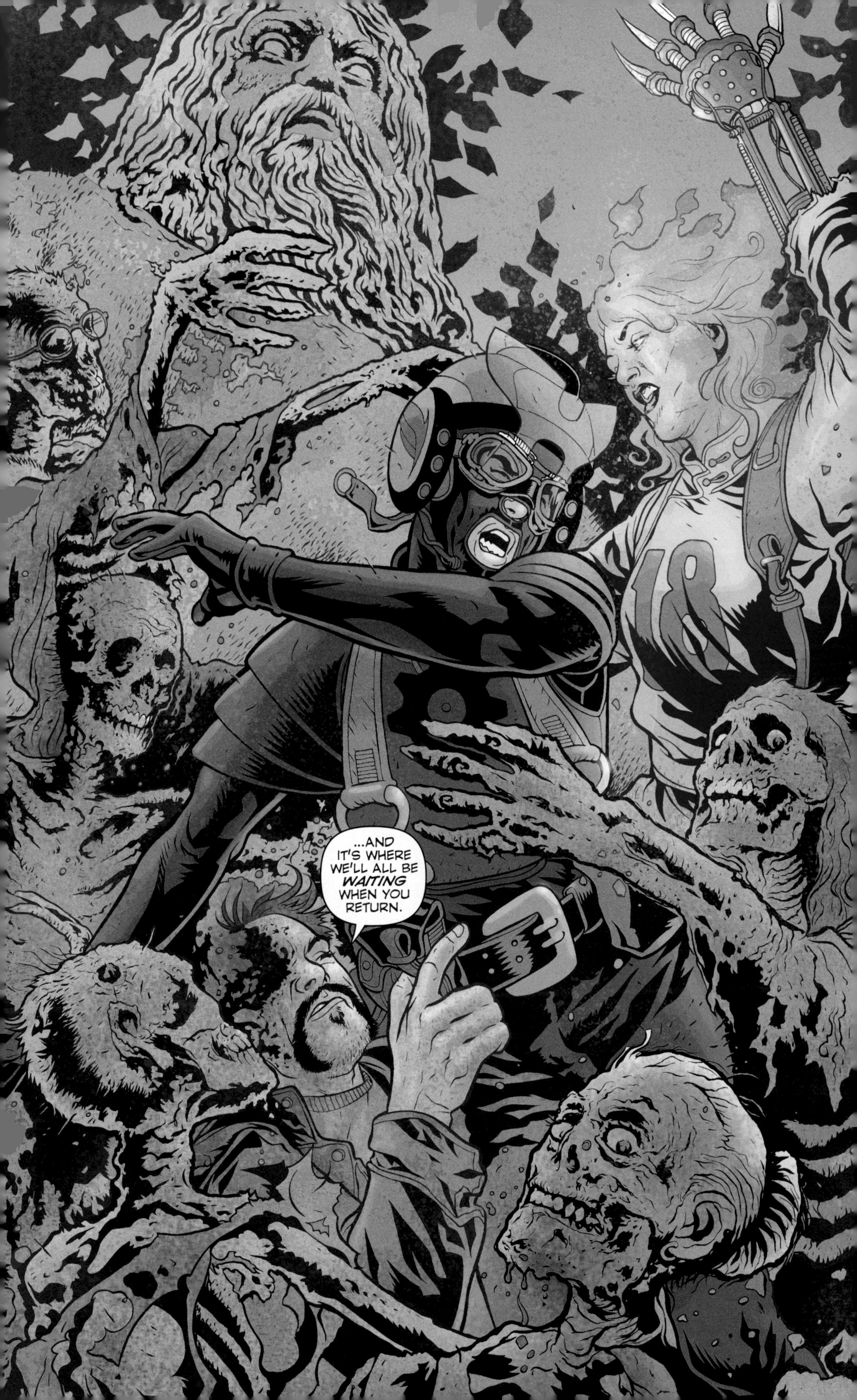
...AND IT'S WHERE WE'LL ALL BE *WAITING* WHEN YOU RETURN.

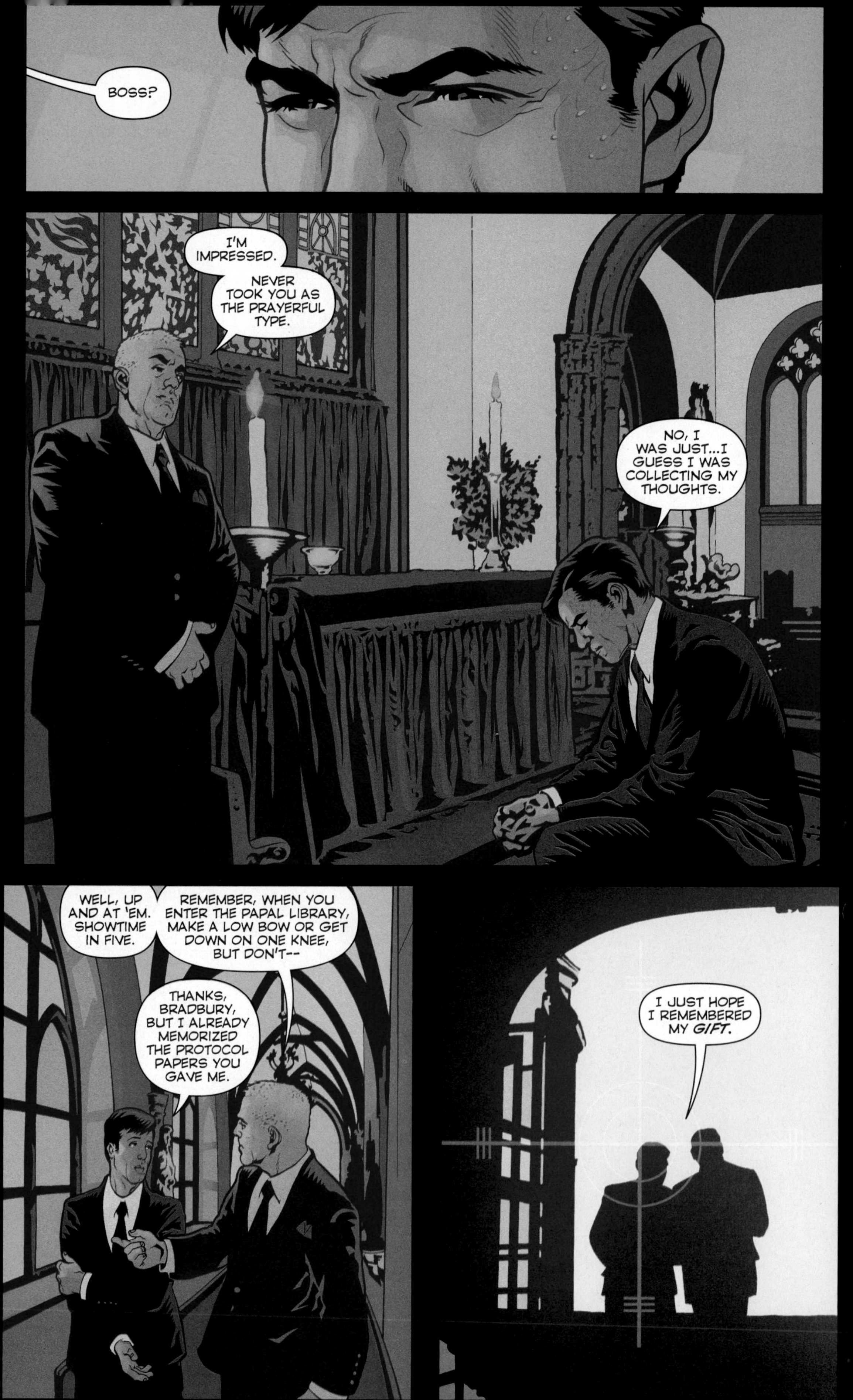
BOSS?
I'M IMPRESSED.
NEVER TOOK YOU AS THE PRAYERFUL TYPE.
NO, I WAS JUST...I GUESS I WAS COLLECTING MY THOUGHTS.
WELL, UP AND AT 'EM. SHOWTIME IN FIVE.
REMEMBER, WHEN YOU ENTER THE PAPAL LIBRARY, MAKE A LOW BOW OR GET DOWN ON ONE KNEE, BUT DON'T--
THANKS, BRADBURY, BUT I ALREADY MEMORIZED THE PROTOCOL PAPERS YOU GAVE ME.
I JUST HOPE I REMEMBERED MY *GIFT*.

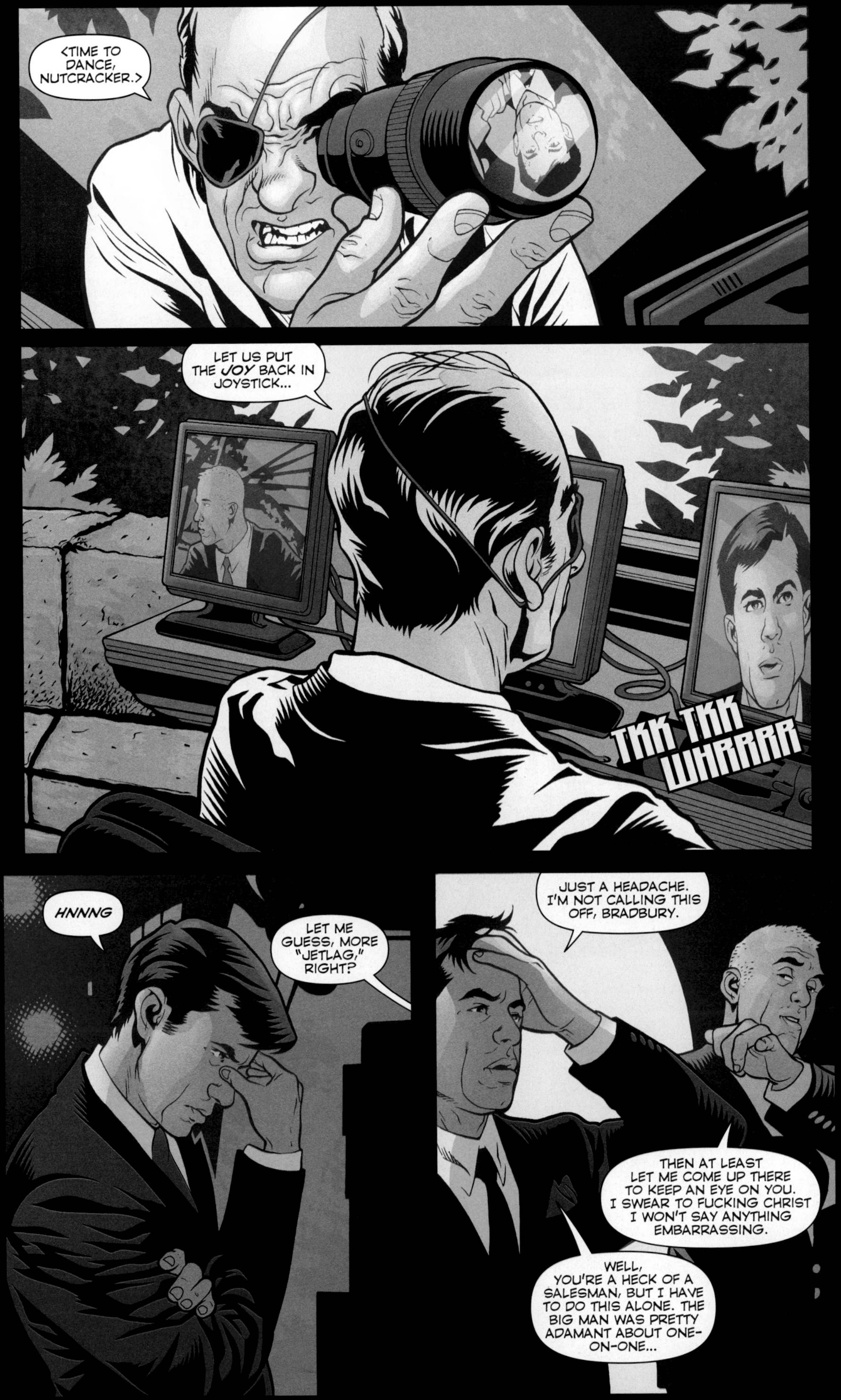

<TIME TO DANCE, NUTCRACKER.>
LET US PUT THE JOY BACK IN JOYSTICK...
TKK TKK WHRRRR
HNNNG
LET ME GUESS, MORE "JETLAG," RIGHT?
JUST A HEADACHE. I'M NOT CALLING THIS OFF, BRADBURY.
THEN AT LEAST LET ME COME UP THERE TO KEEP AN EYE ON YOU. I SWEAR TO FUCKING CHRIST I WON'T SAY ANYTHING EMBARRASSING.
WELL, YOU'RE A HECK OF A SALESMAN, BUT I HAVE TO DO THIS ALONE. THE BIG MAN WAS PRETTY ADAMANT ABOUT ONE-ON-ONE...

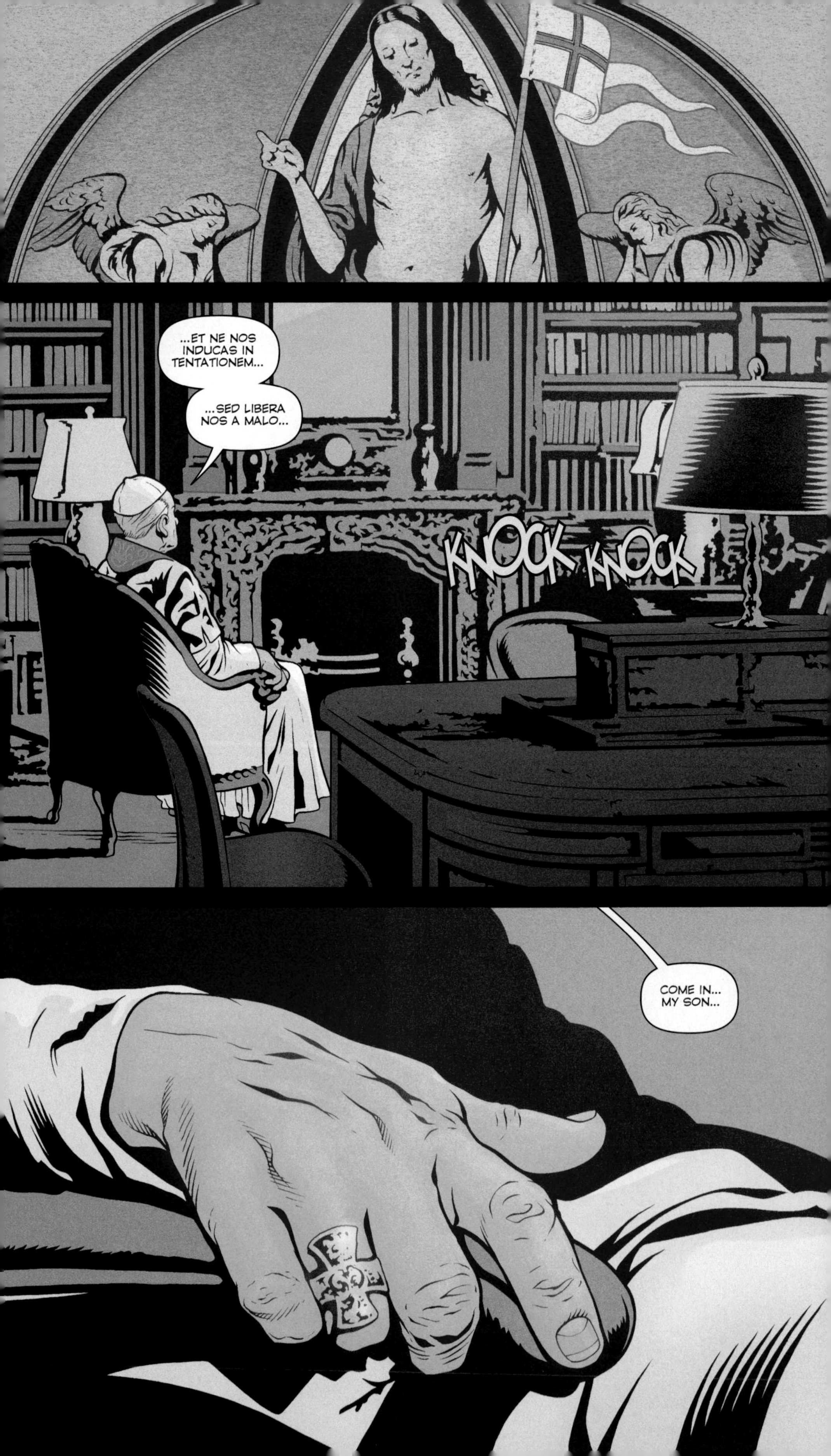
...ET NE NOS INDUCAS IN TENTATIONEM...
...SED LIBERA NOS A MALO...
KNOCK KNOCK
COME IN... MY SON...

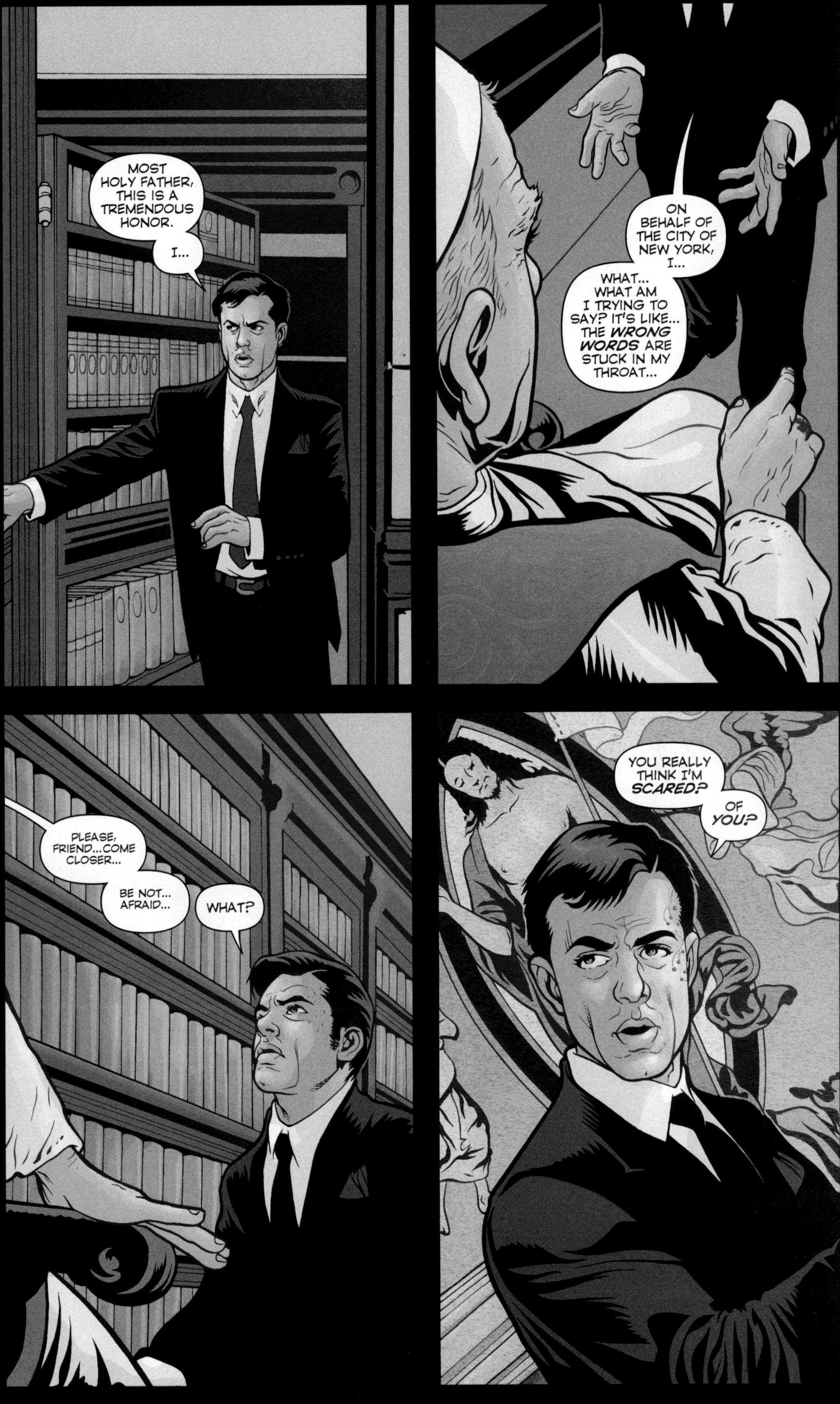
MOST HOLY FATHER, THIS IS A TREMENDOUS HONOR.
I...
ON BEHALF OF THE CITY OF NEW YORK, I...
WHAT... WHAT AM I TRYING TO SAY? IT'S LIKE... THE *WRONG WORDS* ARE STUCK IN MY THROAT...
PLEASE, FRIEND...COME CLOSER...
BE NOT... AFRAID...
WHAT?
YOU REALLY THINK I'M *SCARED?*
OF *YOU?*

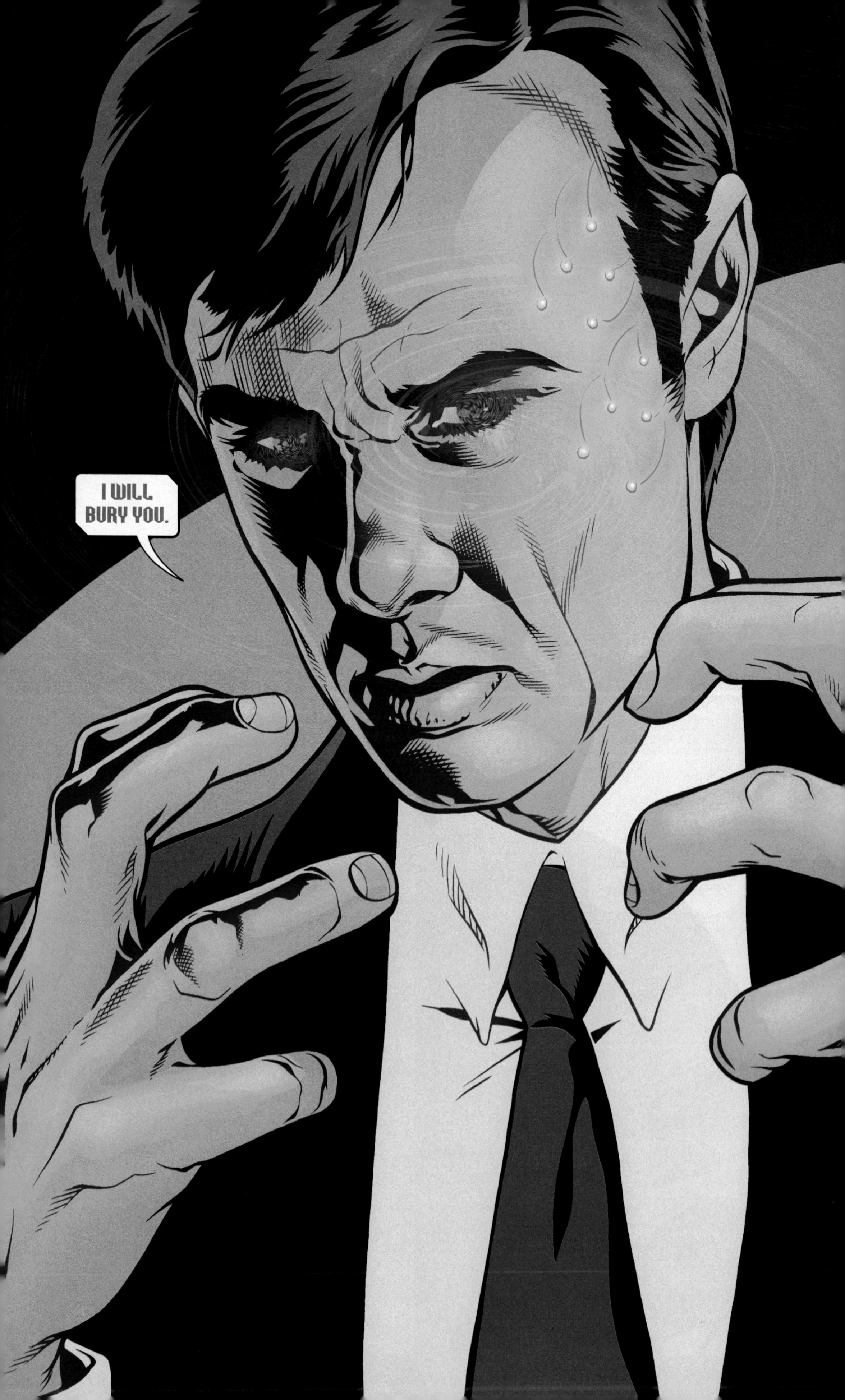
I WILL BURY YOU.

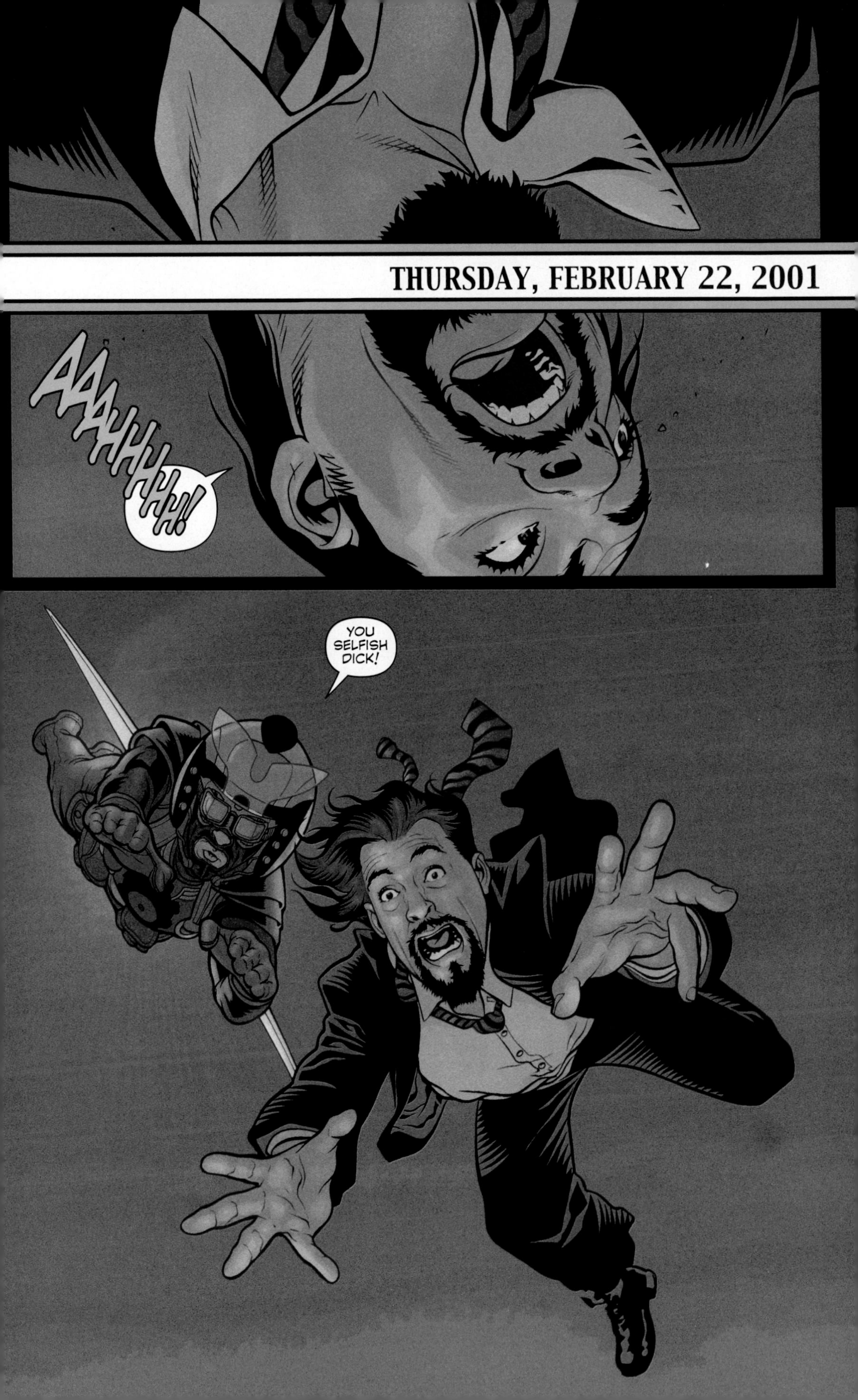
THURSDAY, FEBRUARY 22, 2001
AAAHHHHH!
YOU SELFISH DICK!

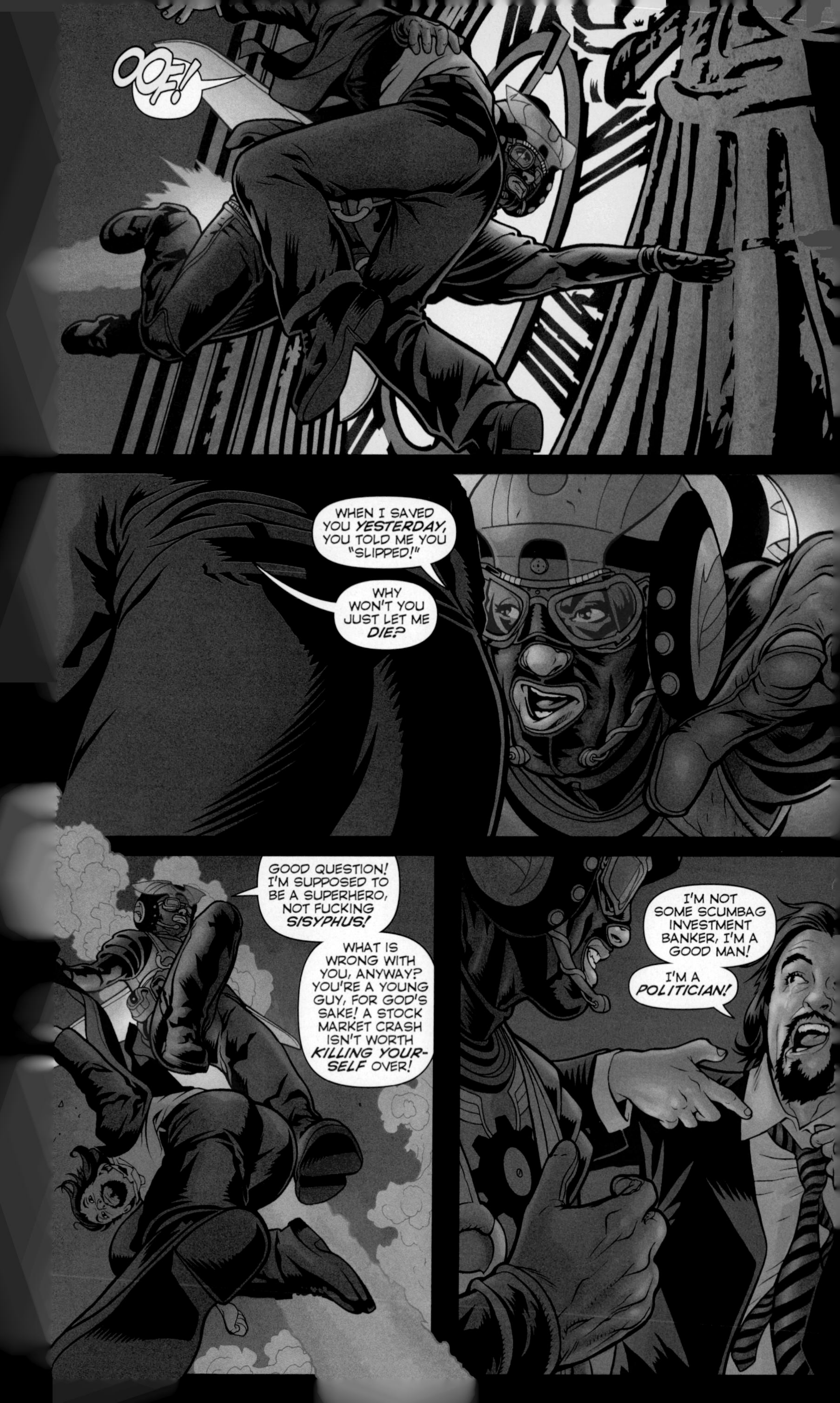
OOF!
WHEN I SAVED YOU YESTERDAY, YOU TOLD ME YOU "SLIPPED!"
WHY WON'T YOU JUST LET ME DIE?
GOOD QUESTION! I'M SUPPOSED TO BE A SUPERHERO, NOT FUCKING SISYPHUS!
WHAT IS WRONG WITH YOU, ANYWAY? YOU'RE A YOUNG GUY, FOR GOD'S SAKE! A STOCK MARKET CRASH ISN'T WORTH KILLING YOURSELF OVER!
I'M NOT SOME SCUMBAG INVESTMENT BANKER, I'M A GOOD MAN!
I'M A POLITICIAN!

I *WOULD* BE, ANYWAY, IF THAT ASSHOLE HADN'T DRAGGED RELIGION INTO THE DEBATE.

AM I SUPPOSED TO UNDERSTAND WHAT ANY OF THAT MEANS?

I SHOULD HAVE BEEN THE NEXT COUNCILMAN FOR THE 15TH DISTRICT.

I WAS GONNA WALK AWAY WITH THE SPECIAL ELECTION, BUT THEN THAT SON OF A BITCH HAD TO GO AND ASK ME IF I BELIEVED IN GOD. LIKE IT'S EVEN RELEVANT!

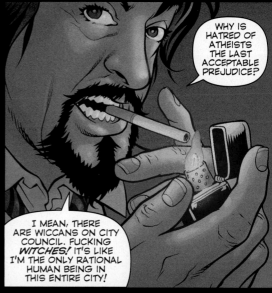

WHY IS HATRED OF ATHEISTS THE LAST ACCEPTABLE PREJUDICE?

I MEAN, THERE ARE WICCANS ON CITY COUNCIL. FUCKING *WITCHES!* IT'S LIKE I'M THE ONLY RATIONAL HUMAN BEING IN THIS ENTIRE CITY!

YOU'RE THROWING YOUR LIFE AWAY OVER *POLITICS?*

WHAT THE HELL IS RATIONAL ABOUT THAT?

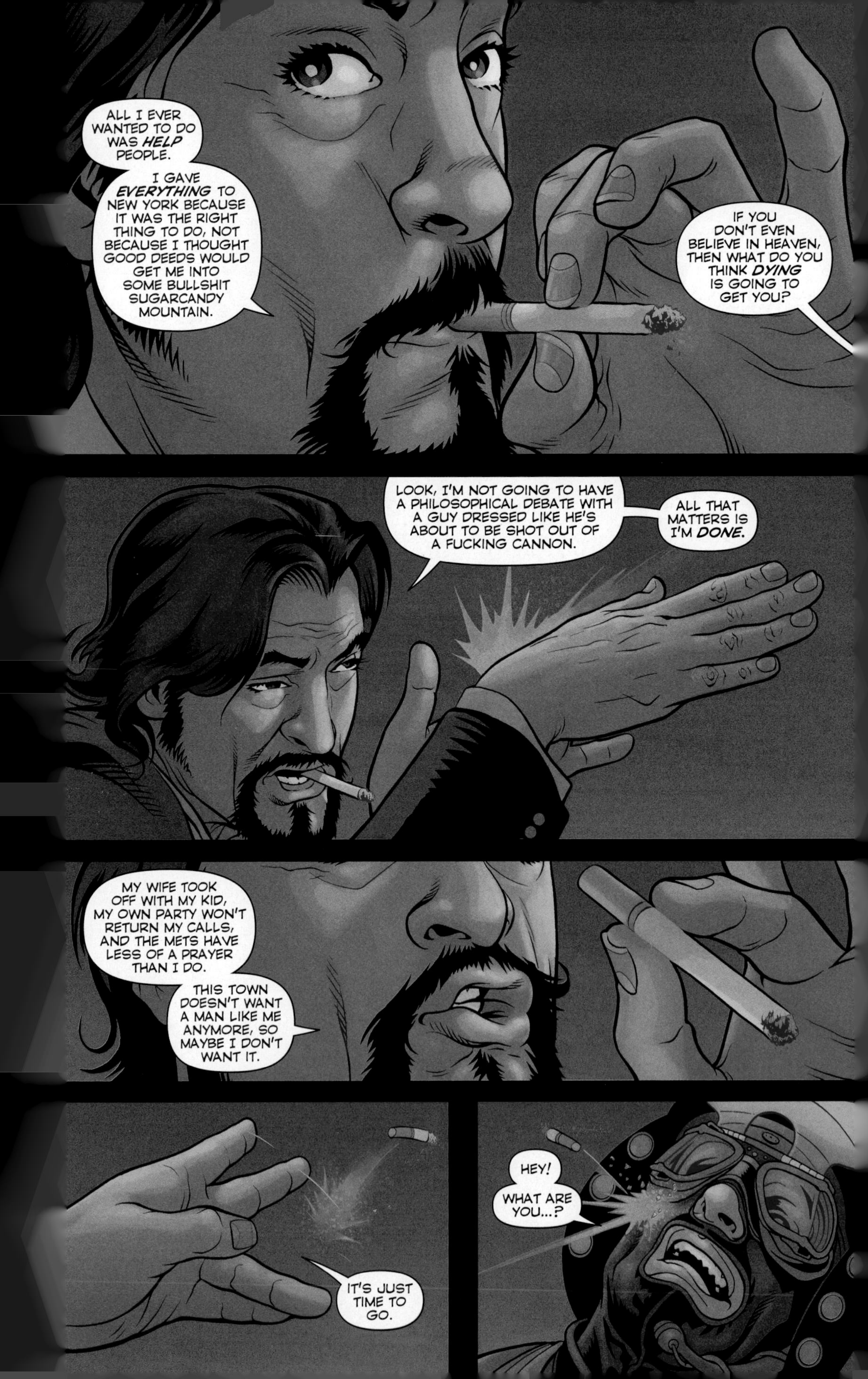
ALL I EVER WANTED TO DO WAS HELP PEOPLE.
I GAVE EVERYTHING TO NEW YORK BECAUSE IT WAS THE RIGHT THING TO DO, NOT BECAUSE I THOUGHT GOOD DEEDS WOULD GET ME INTO SOME BULLSHIT SUGARCANDY MOUNTAIN.
IF YOU DON'T EVEN BELIEVE IN HEAVEN, THEN WHAT DO YOU THINK DYING IS GOING TO GET YOU?
LOOK, I'M NOT GOING TO HAVE A PHILOSOPHICAL DEBATE WITH A GUY DRESSED LIKE HE'S ABOUT TO BE SHOT OUT OF A FUCKING CANNON.
ALL THAT MATTERS IS I'M DONE.
MY WIFE TOOK OFF WITH MY KID, MY OWN PARTY WON'T RETURN MY CALLS, AND THE METS HAVE LESS OF A PRAYER THAN I DO.
THIS TOWN DOESN'T WANT A MAN LIKE ME ANYMORE, SO MAYBE I DON'T WANT IT.
IT'S JUST TIME TO GO.
HEY!
WHAT ARE YOU...?

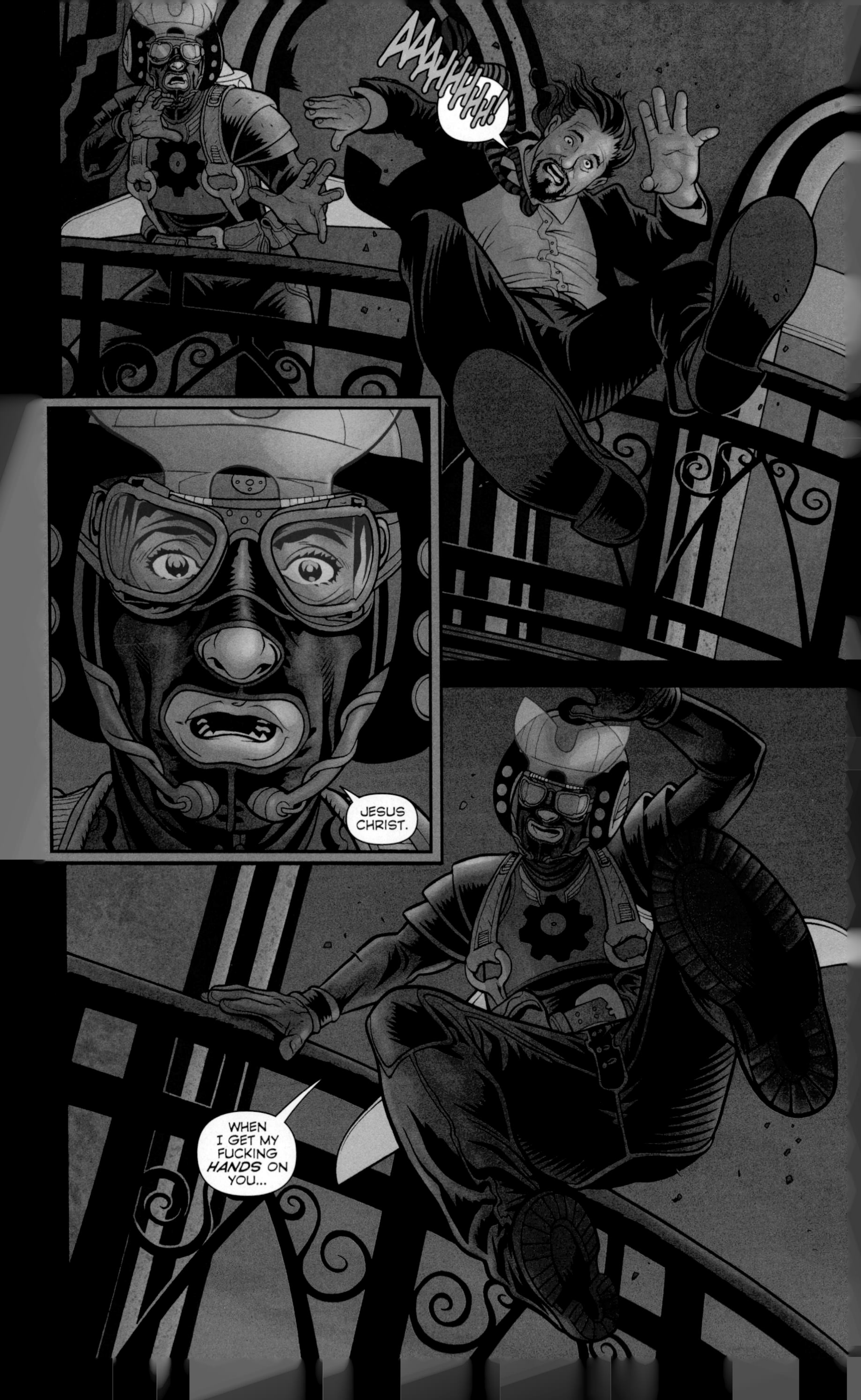
AAAHHHHH!
JESUS CHRIST.
WHEN I GET MY FUCKING HANDS ON YOU...

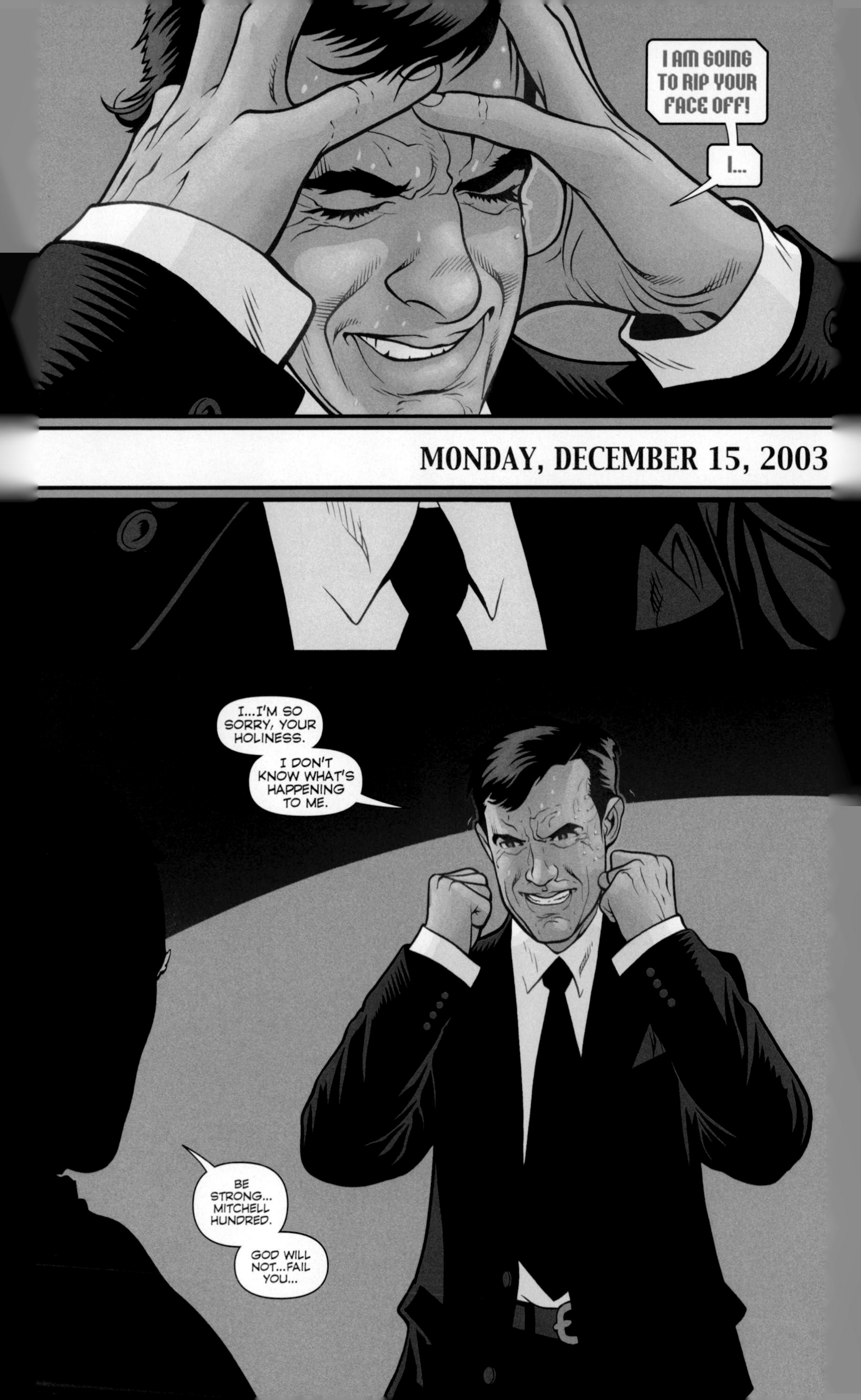
I AM GOING TO RIP YOUR FACE OFF!
I...
MONDAY, DECEMBER 15, 2003
I...I'M SO SORRY, YOUR HOLINESS.
I DON'T KNOW WHAT'S HAPPENING TO ME.
BE STRONG... MITCHELL HUNDRED.
GOD WILL NOT...FAIL YOU...

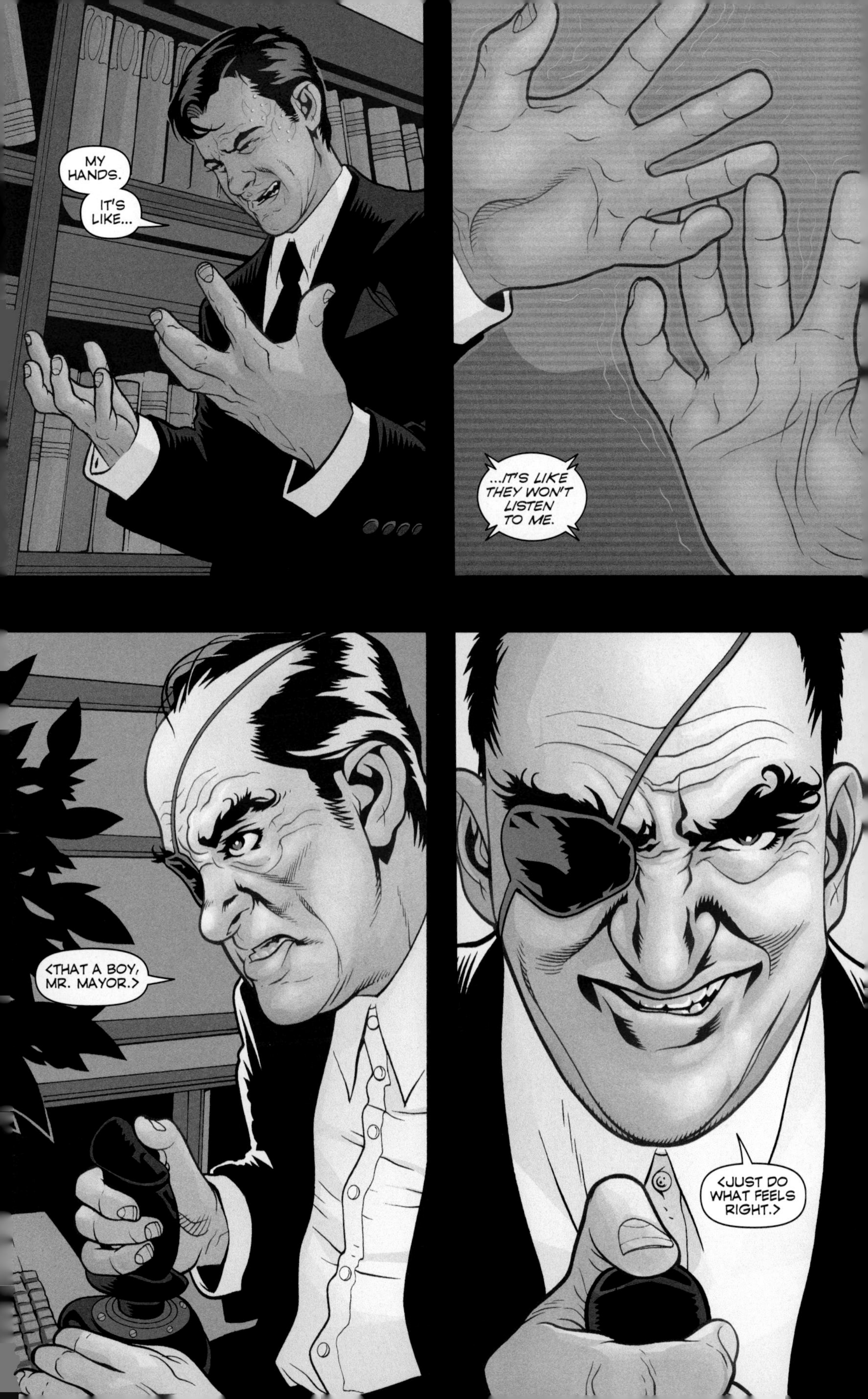
MY HANDS.
IT'S LIKE...
...IT'S LIKE THEY WON'T LISTEN TO ME.
<THAT A BOY, MR. MAYOR.>
<JUST DO WHAT FEELS RIGHT.>

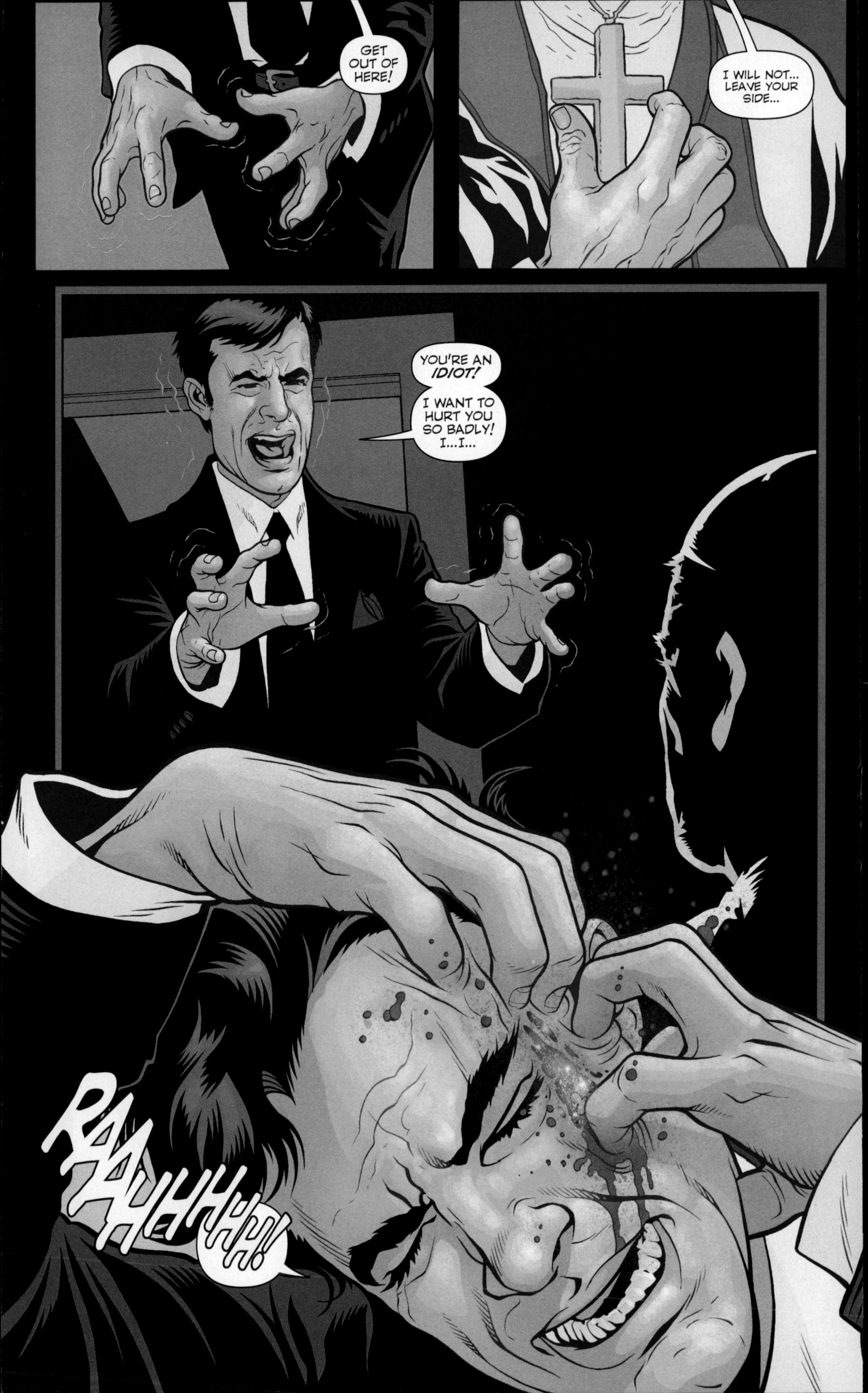
GET OUT OF HERE!
I WILL NOT... LEAVE YOUR SIDE...
YOU'RE AN IDIOT!
I WANT TO HURT YOU SO BADLY! I...I...
RAAHHHHH!

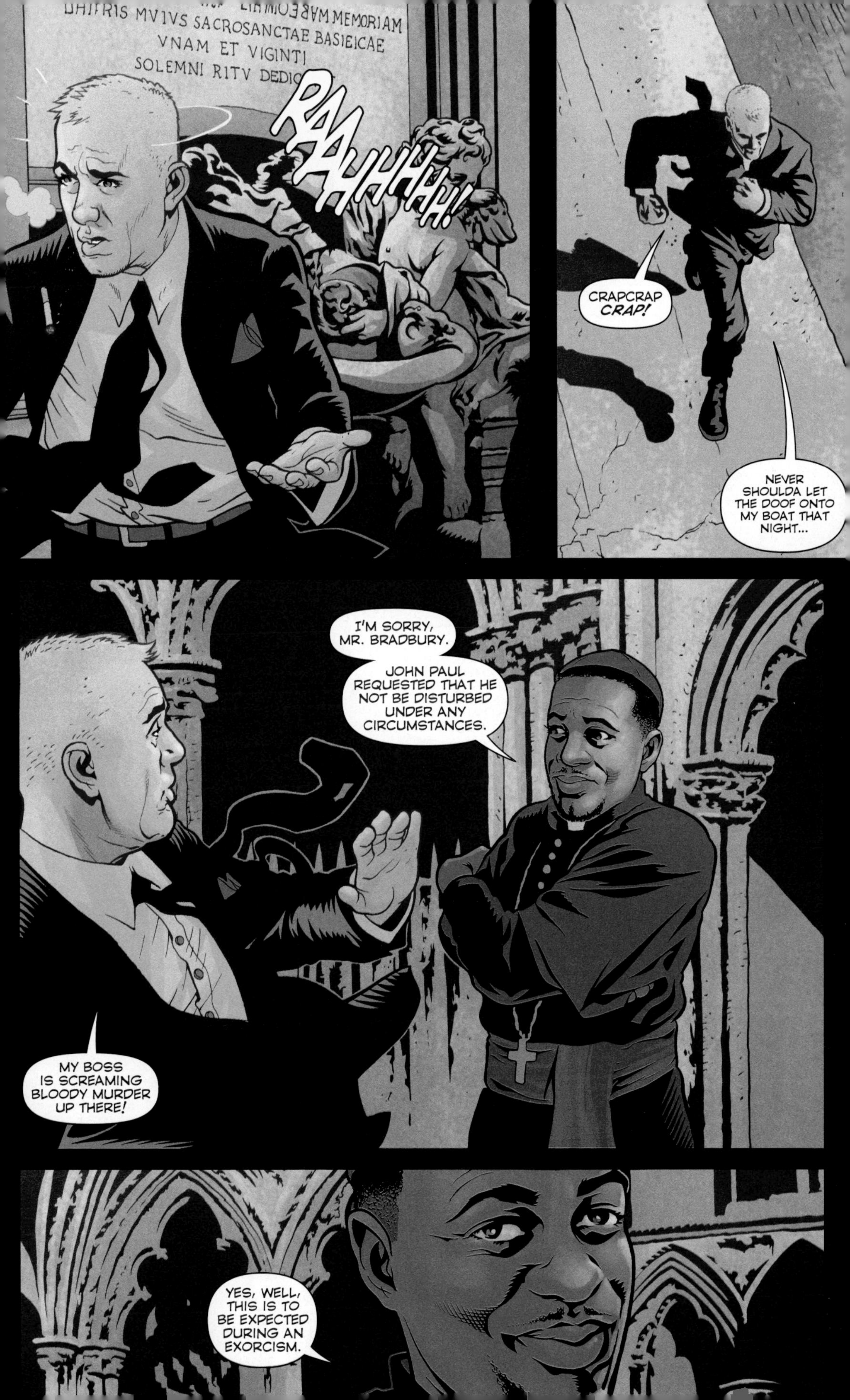

UHIFRIS MVIVS SACROSANCTAE BASIEICAE
VNAM ET VIGINTI
SOLEMNI RITV DEDIC
RAAAHHHHH!
CRAPCRAP CRAP!
NEVER SHOULDA LET THE DOOF ONTO MY BOAT THAT NIGHT...
MY BOSS IS SCREAMING BLOODY MURDER UP THERE!
I'M SORRY, MR. BRADBURY.
JOHN PAUL REQUESTED THAT HE NOT BE DISTURBED UNDER ANY CIRCUMSTANCES.
YES, WELL, THIS IS TO BE EXPECTED DURING AN EXORCISM.

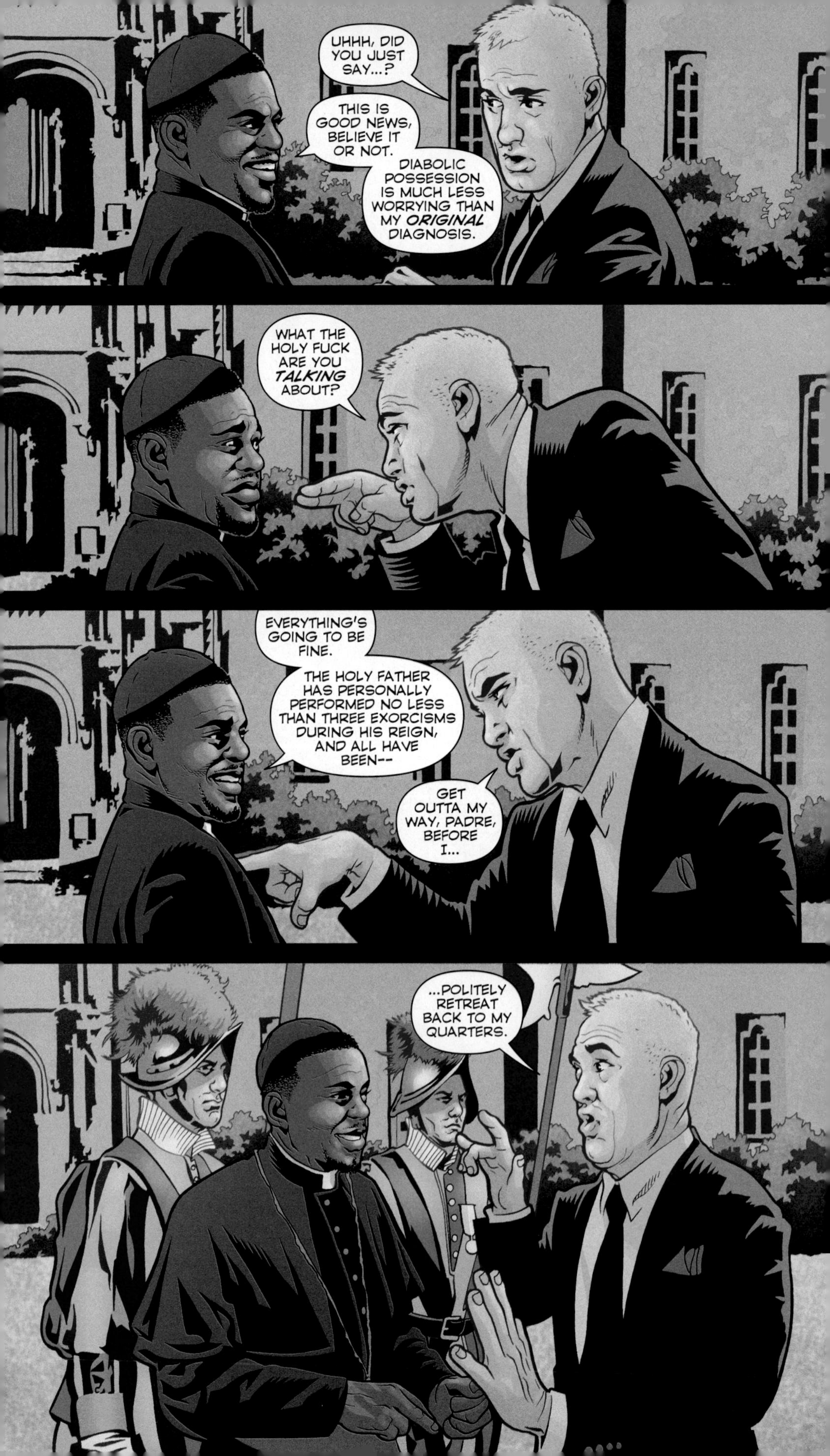
UHHH, DID YOU JUST SAY...?
THIS IS GOOD NEWS, BELIEVE IT OR NOT.
DIABOLIC POSSESSION IS MUCH LESS WORRYING THAN MY *ORIGINAL* DIAGNOSIS.
WHAT THE HOLY FUCK ARE YOU *TALKING* ABOUT?
EVERYTHING'S GOING TO BE FINE.
THE HOLY FATHER HAS PERSONALLY PERFORMED NO LESS THAN THREE EXORCISMS DURING HIS REIGN, AND ALL HAVE BEEN--
GET OUTTA MY WAY, PADRE, BEFORE I...
...POLITELY RETREAT BACK TO MY QUARTERS.

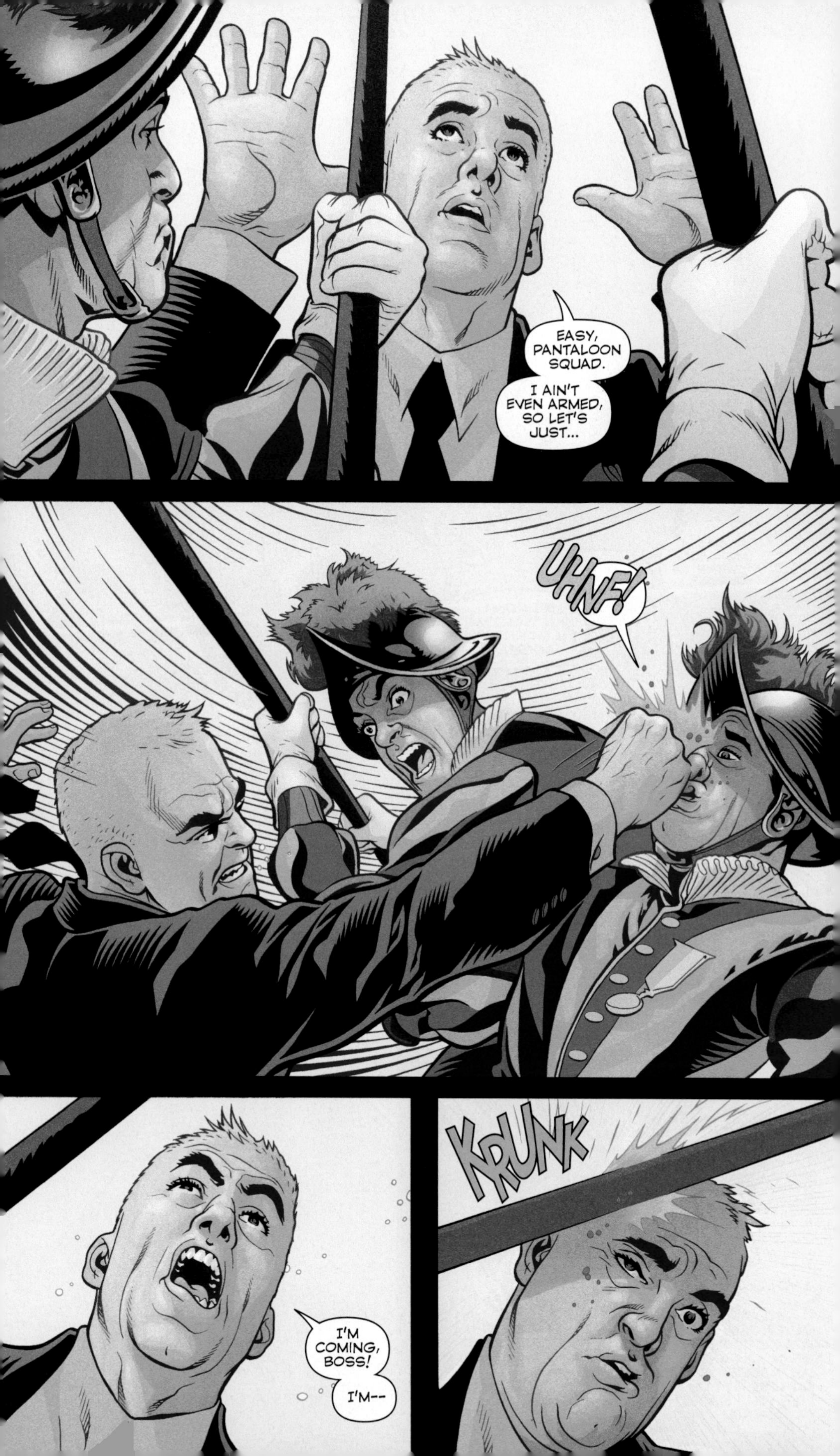
EASY, PANTALOON SQUAD.
I AIN'T EVEN ARMED, SO LET'S JUST...
UHNF!
I'M COMING, BOSS!
I'M--
KRUNK

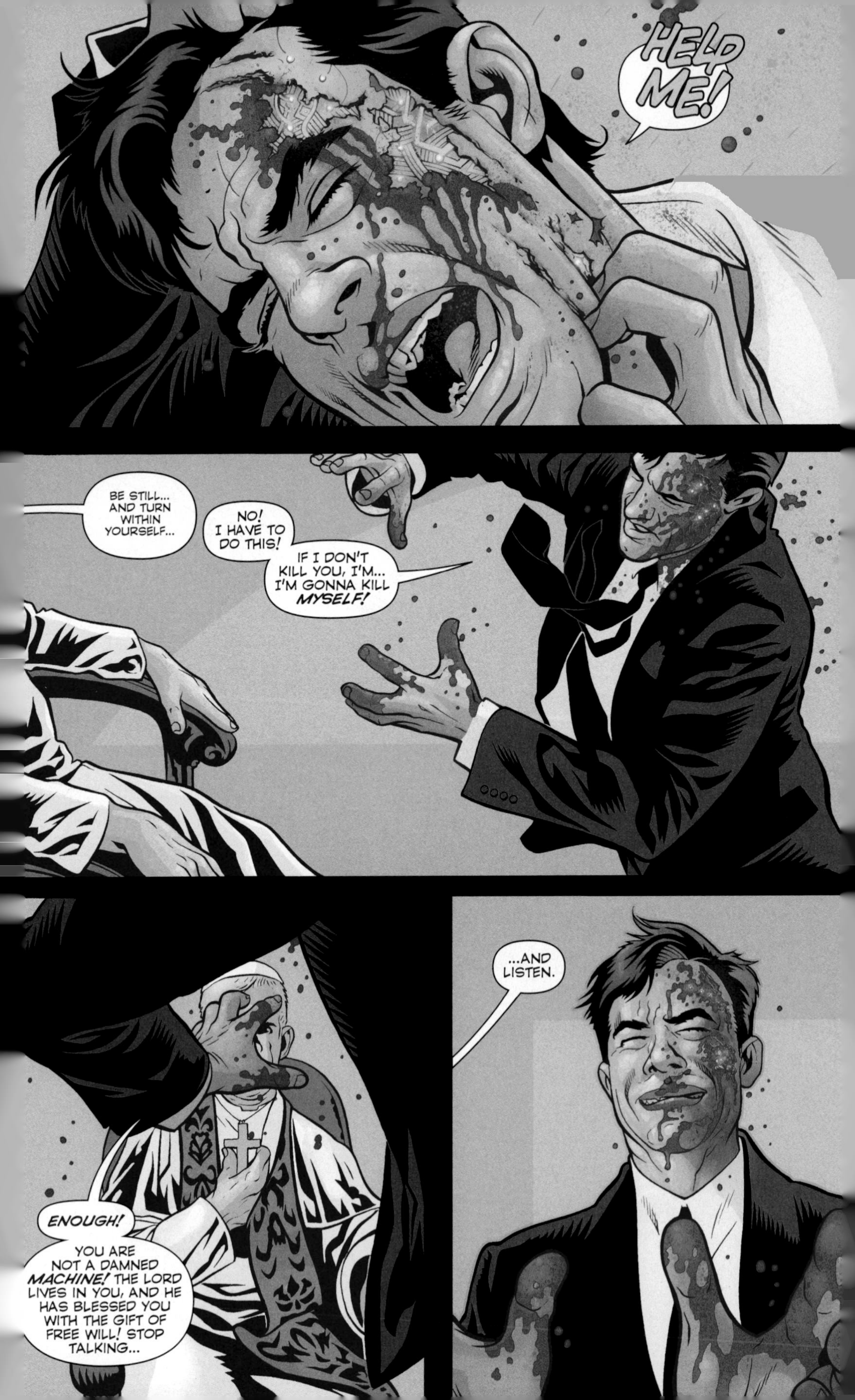

HELP ME!
BE STILL... AND TURN WITHIN YOURSELF...
NO! I HAVE TO DO THIS!
IF I DON'T KILL YOU, I'M... I'M GONNA KILL *MYSELF!*
ENOUGH!
YOU ARE NOT A DAMNED *MACHINE!* THE LORD LIVES IN YOU, AND HE HAS BLESSED YOU WITH THE GIFT OF FREE WILL! STOP TALKING...
...AND LISTEN.

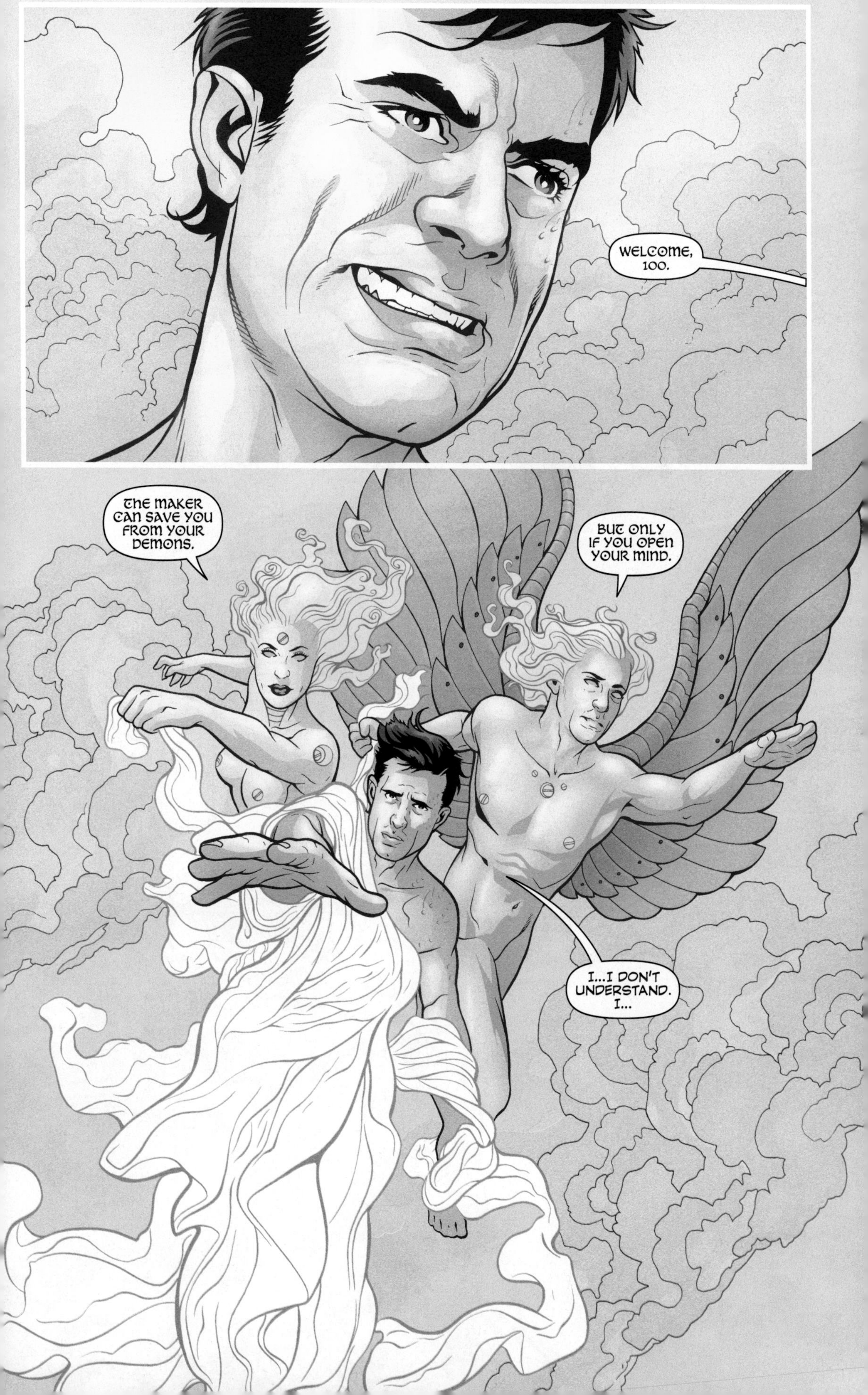
WELCOME, 100.
THE MAKER CAN SAVE YOU FROM YOUR DEMONS.
BUT ONLY IF YOU OPEN YOUR MIND.
I...I DON'T UNDERSTAND. I...

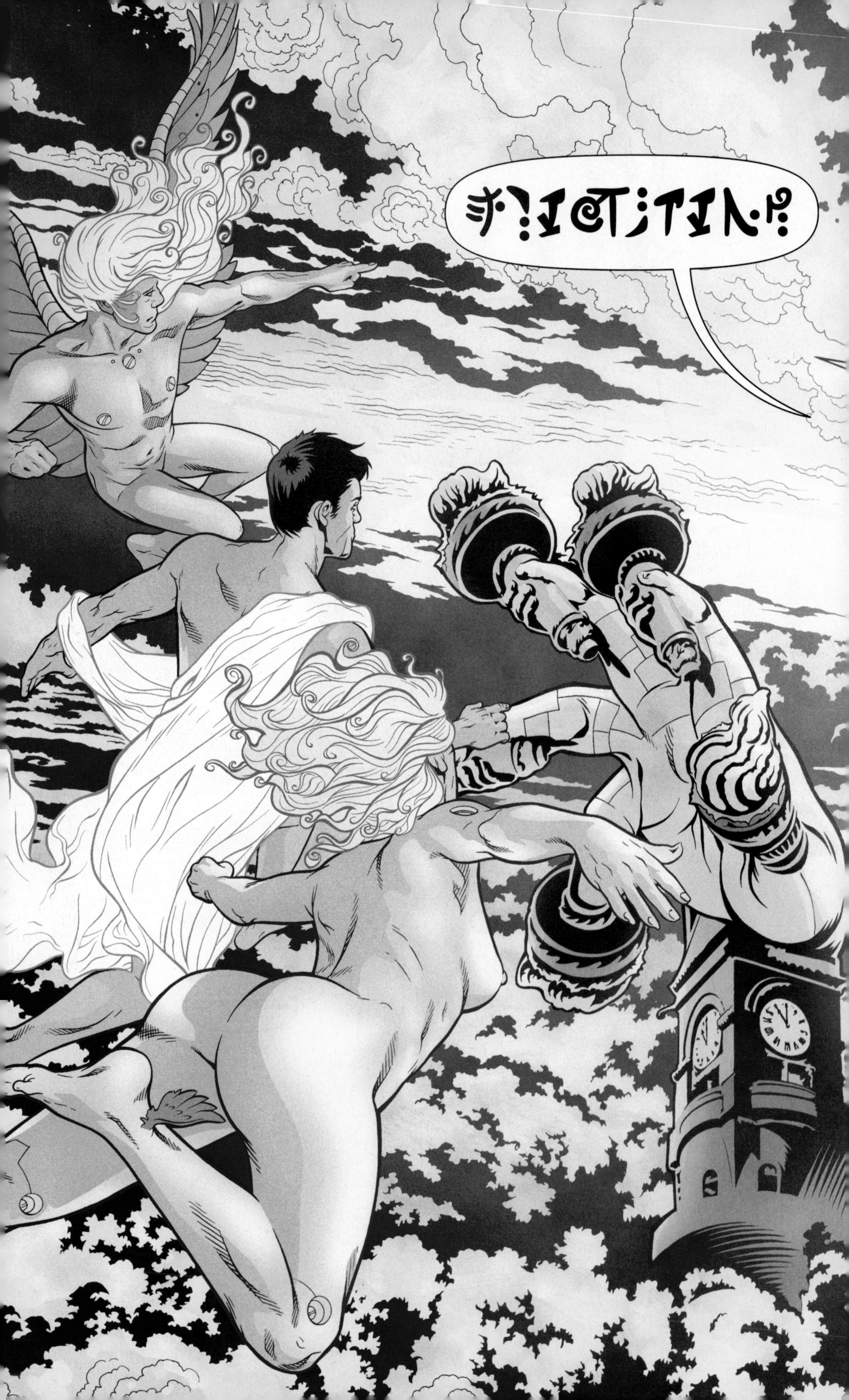

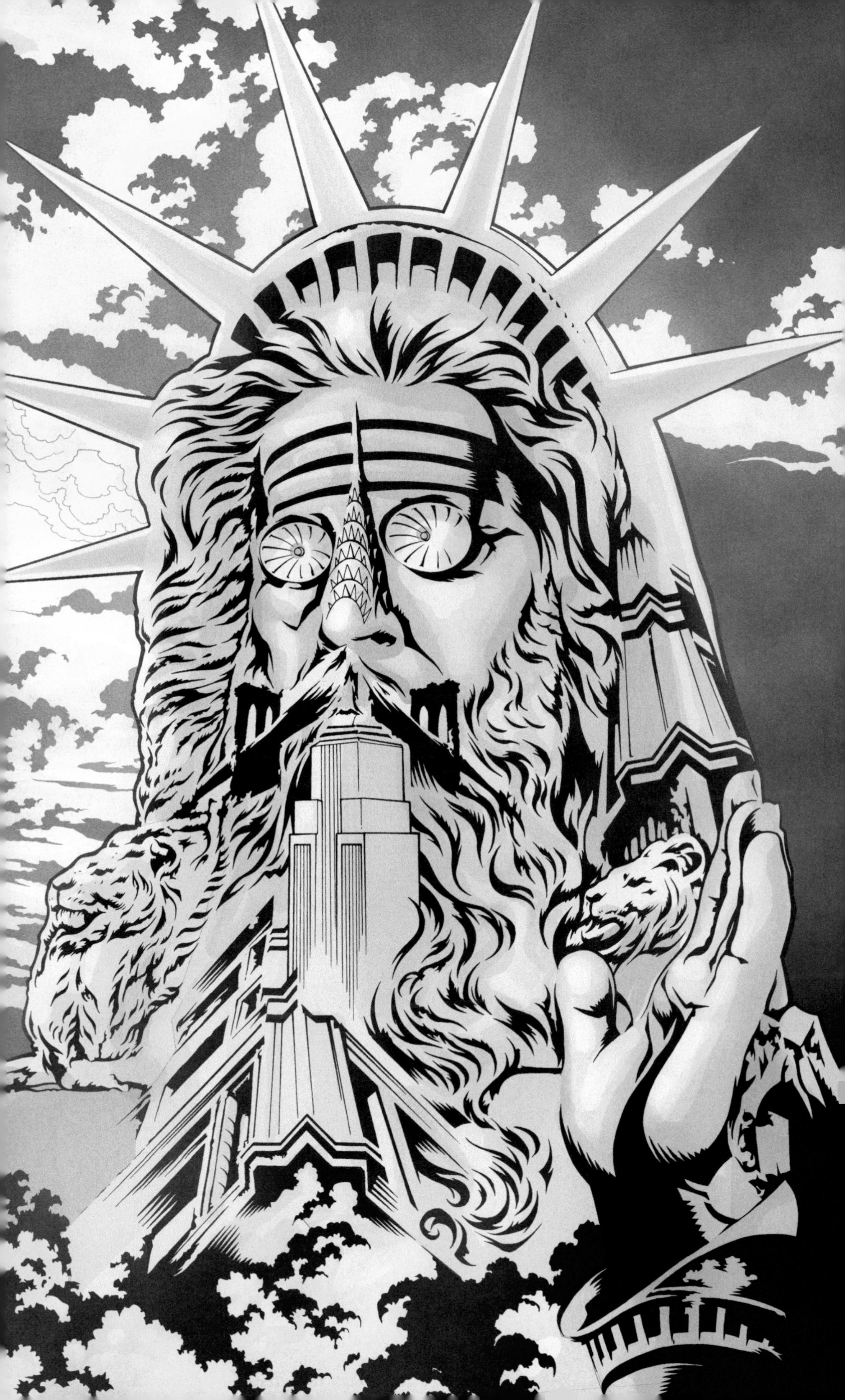

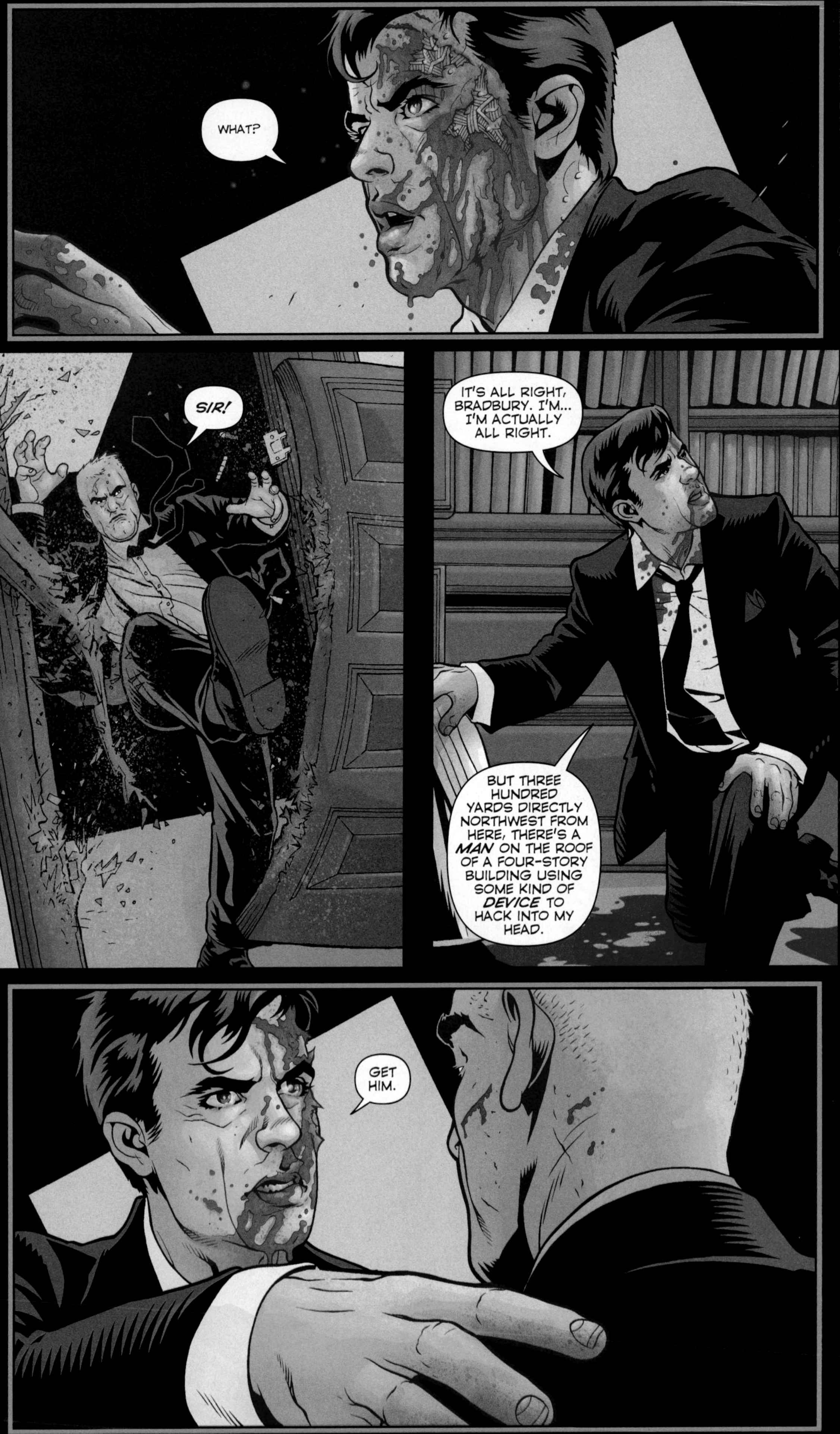
WHAT?
SIR!
IT'S ALL RIGHT, BRADBURY. I'M... I'M ACTUALLY ALL RIGHT.
BUT THREE HUNDRED YARDS DIRECTLY NORTHWEST FROM HERE, THERE'S A MAN ON THE ROOF OF A FOUR-STORY BUILDING USING SOME KIND OF DEVICE TO HACK INTO MY HEAD.
GET HIM.

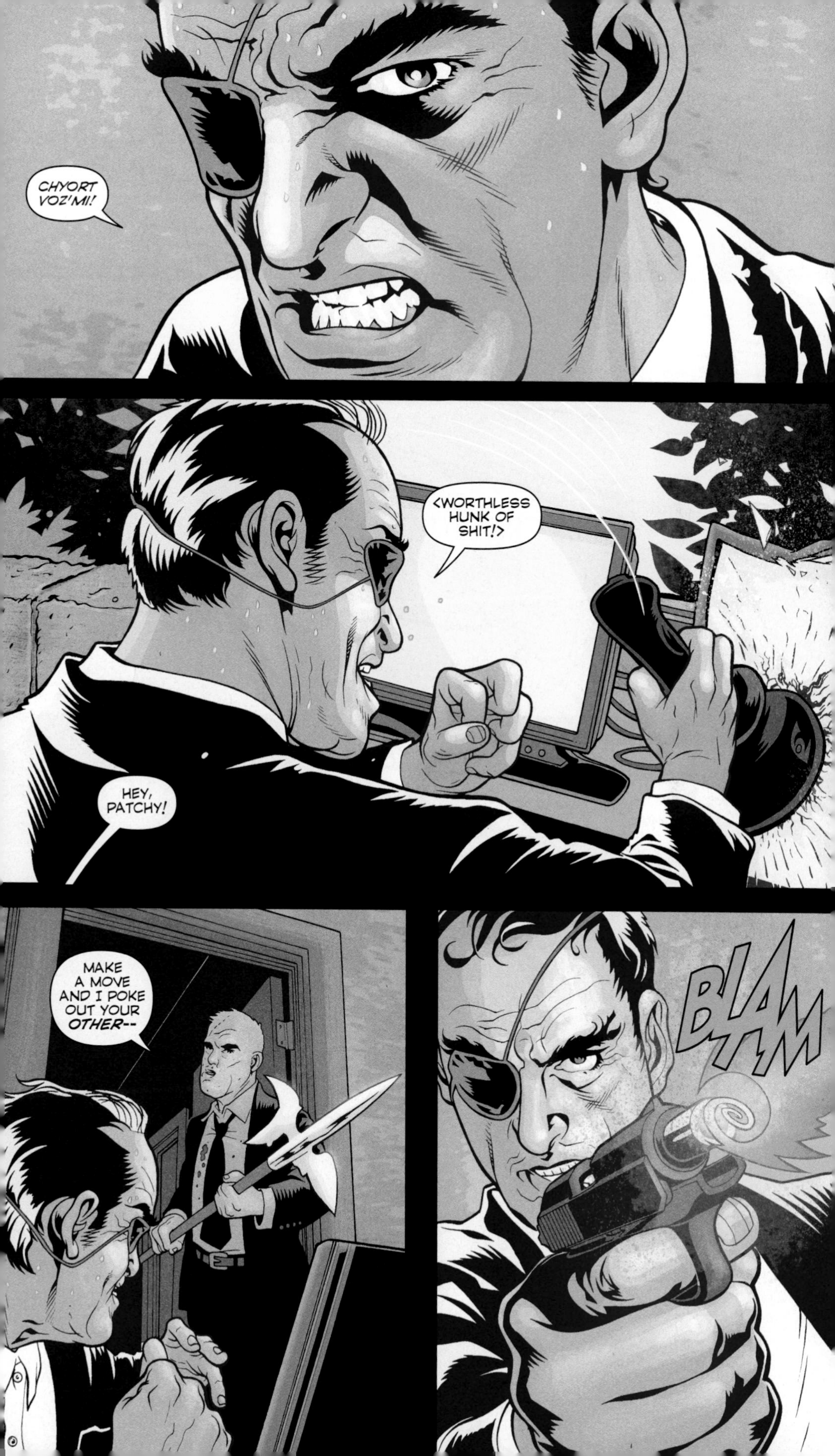
CHYORT VOZ'MI!
<WORTHLESS HUNK OF SHIT!>
HEY, PATCHY!
MAKE A MOVE AND I POKE OUT YOUR *OTHER*--
BLAM

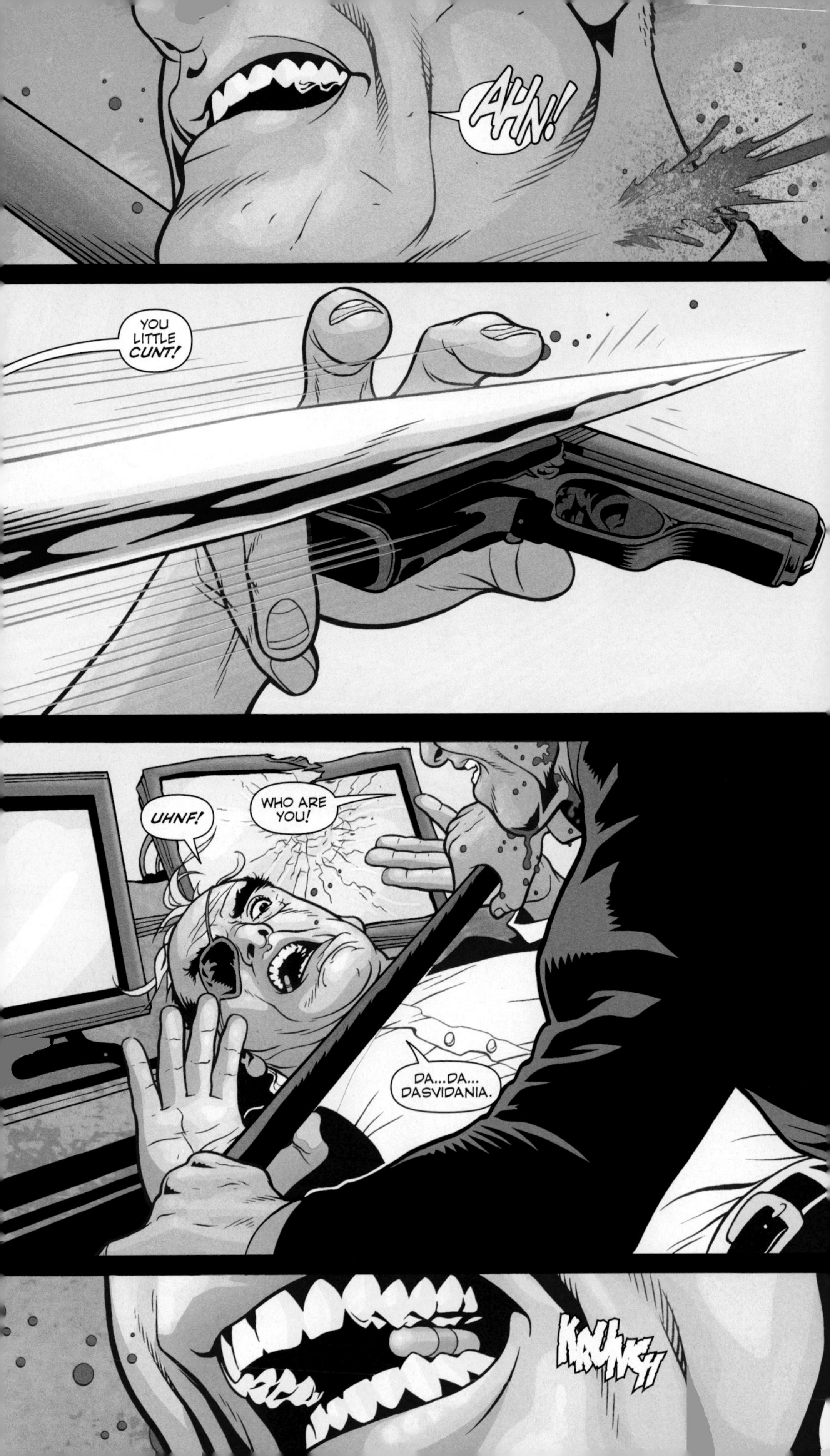
AHN!
YOU LITTLE CUNT!
UHNF!
WHO ARE YOU!
DA...DA... DASVIDANIA.
KRUNCH

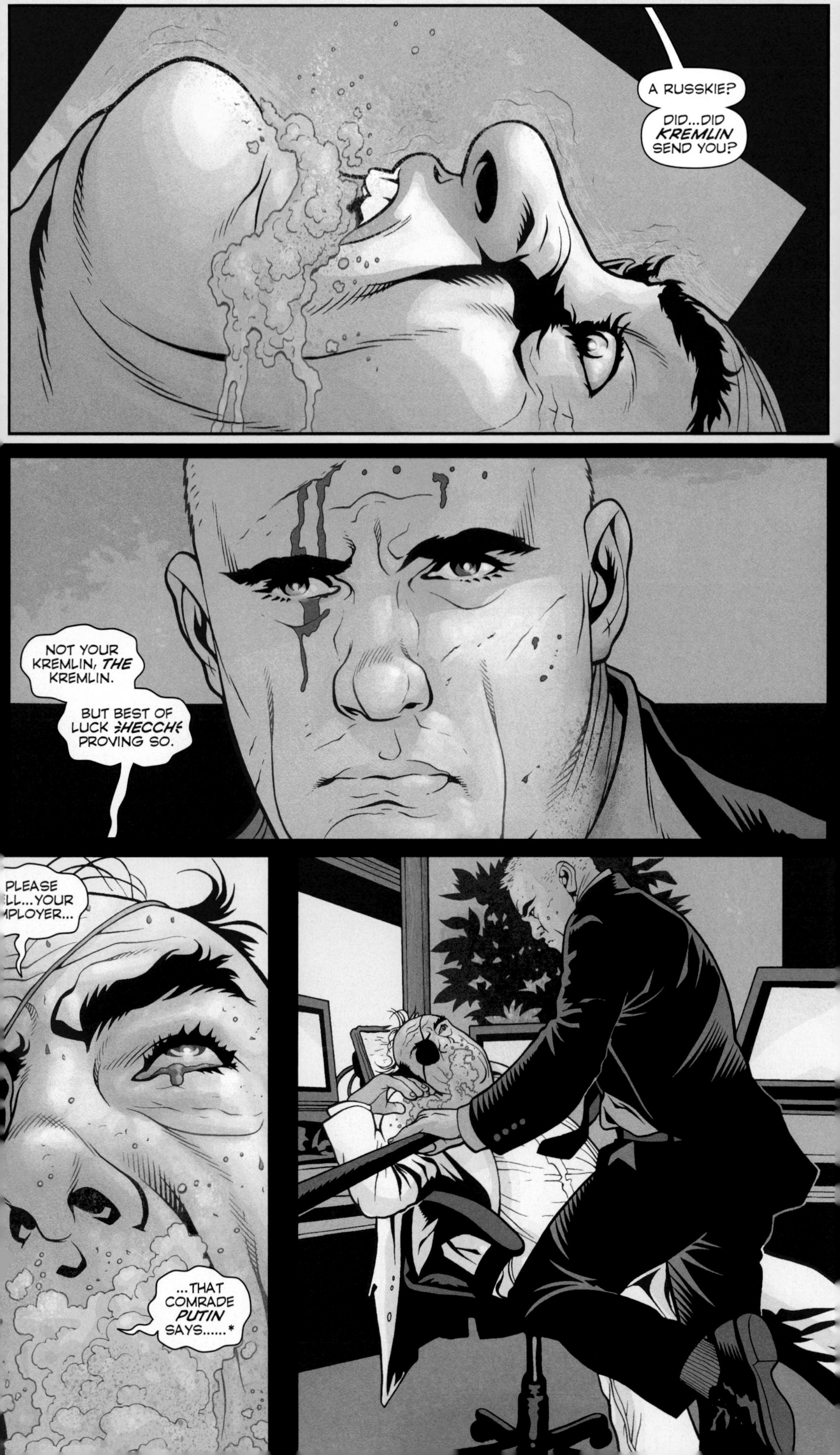

A RUSSKIE?
DID...DID *KREMLIN* SEND YOU?
NOT YOUR KREMLIN, *THE* KREMLIN.
BUT BEST OF LUCK *HECCH* PROVING SO.
PLEASE ELL...YOUR MPLOYER...
...THAT COMRADE *PUTIN* SAYS......*

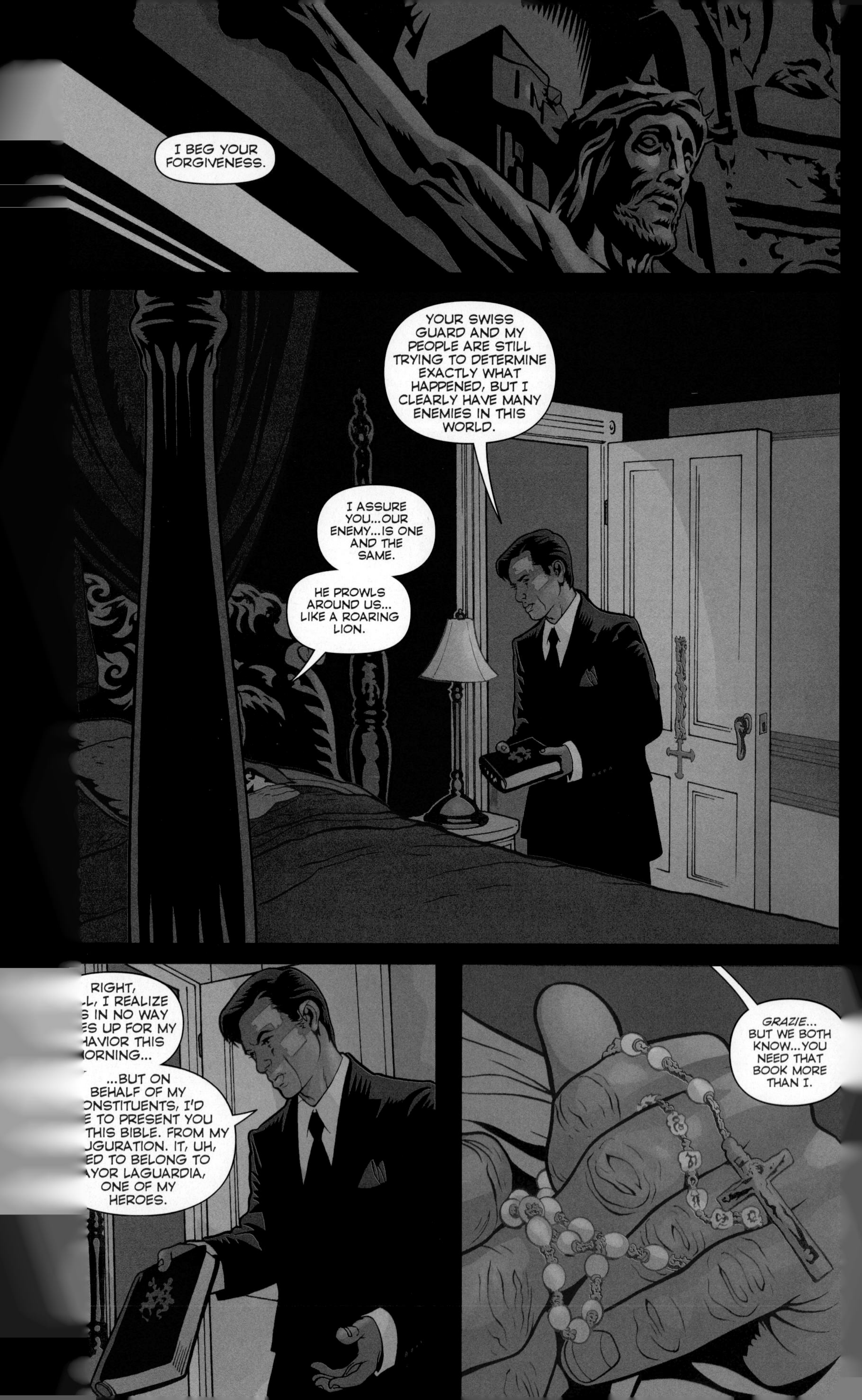
I BEG YOUR FORGIVENESS.
YOUR SWISS GUARD AND MY PEOPLE ARE STILL TRYING TO DETERMINE EXACTLY WHAT HAPPENED, BUT I CLEARLY HAVE MANY ENEMIES IN THIS WORLD.
I ASSURE YOU...OUR ENEMY...IS ONE AND THE SAME.
HE PROWLS AROUND US... LIKE A ROARING LION.
RIGHT, L, I REALIZE S IN NO WAY ES UP FOR MY HAVIOR THIS ORNING...
...BUT ON BEHALF OF MY ONSTITUENTS, I'D E TO PRESENT YOU THIS BIBLE. FROM MY UGURATION. IT, UH, ED TO BELONG TO AYOR LAGUARDIA, ONE OF MY HEROES.
GRAZIE... BUT WE BOTH KNOW...YOU NEED THAT BOOK MORE THAN I.

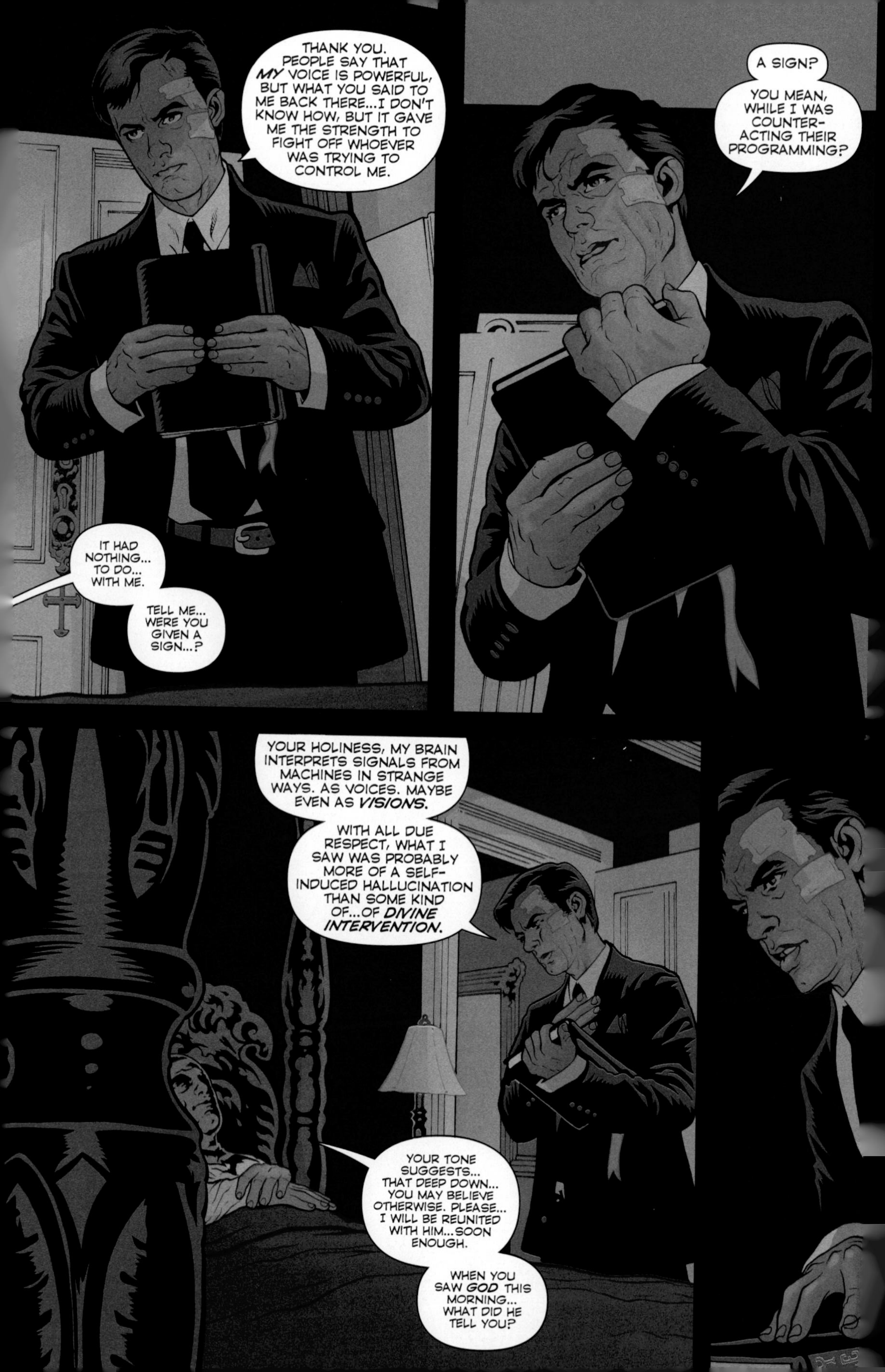
THANK YOU. PEOPLE SAY THAT *MY* VOICE IS POWERFUL, BUT WHAT YOU SAID TO ME BACK THERE...I DON'T KNOW HOW, BUT IT GAVE ME THE STRENGTH TO FIGHT OFF WHOEVER WAS TRYING TO CONTROL ME.
IT HAD NOTHING... TO DO... WITH ME.
TELL ME... WERE YOU GIVEN A SIGN...?
A SIGN?
YOU MEAN, WHILE I WAS COUNTER-ACTING THEIR PROGRAMMING?
YOUR HOLINESS, MY BRAIN INTERPRETS SIGNALS FROM MACHINES IN STRANGE WAYS. AS VOICES. MAYBE EVEN AS ***VISIONS***.
WITH ALL DUE RESPECT, WHAT I SAW WAS PROBABLY MORE OF A SELF-INDUCED HALLUCINATION THAN SOME KIND OF...OF ***DIVINE INTERVENTION***.
YOUR TONE SUGGESTS... THAT DEEP DOWN... YOU MAY BELIEVE OTHERWISE. PLEASE... I WILL BE REUNITED WITH HIM...SOON ENOUGH.
WHEN YOU SAW ***GOD*** THIS MORNING... WHAT DID HE TELL YOU?

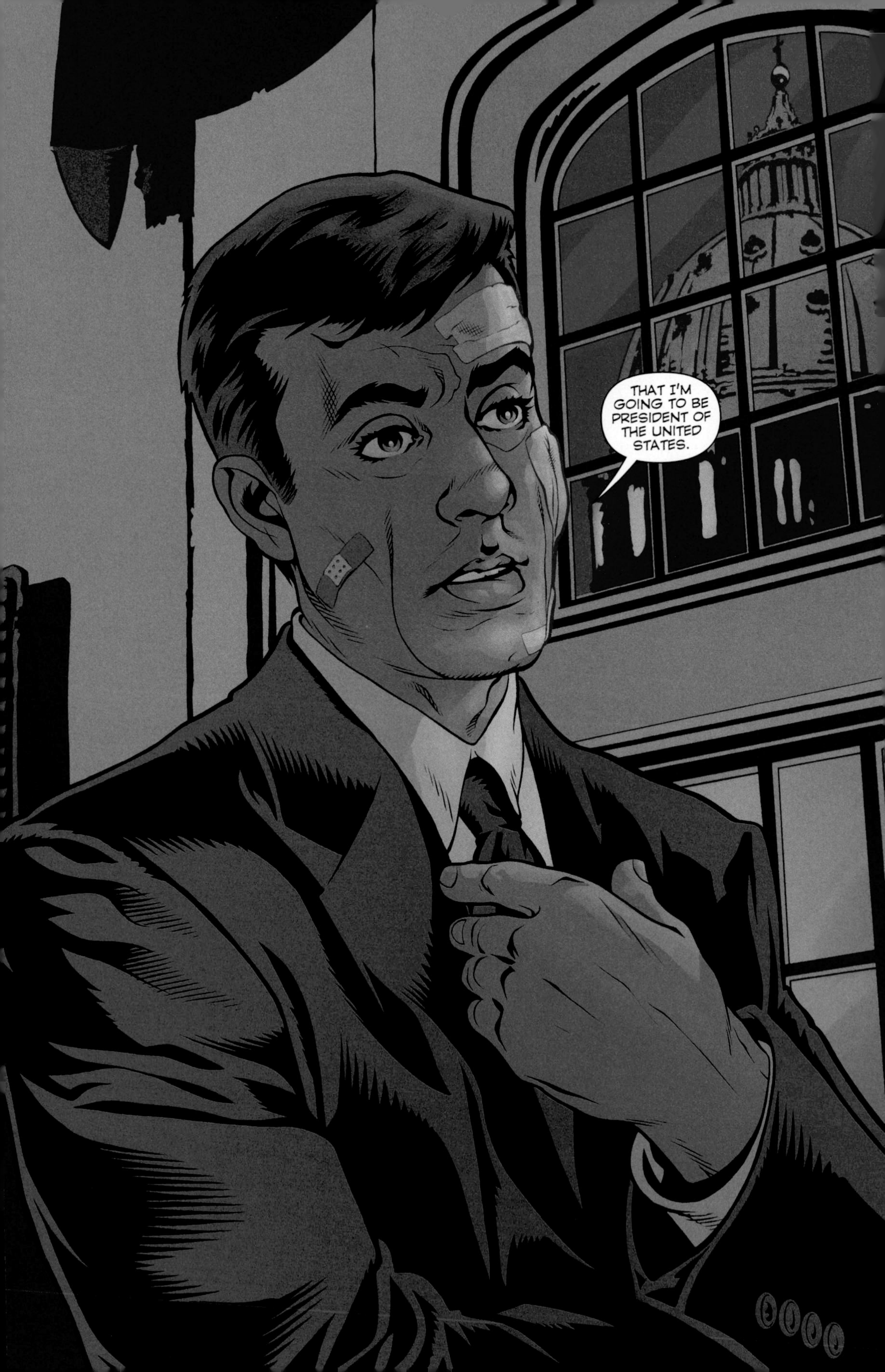
THAT I'M GOING TO BE PRESIDENT OF THE UNITED STATES.

CHAPTER 2 WORLD'S FINEST

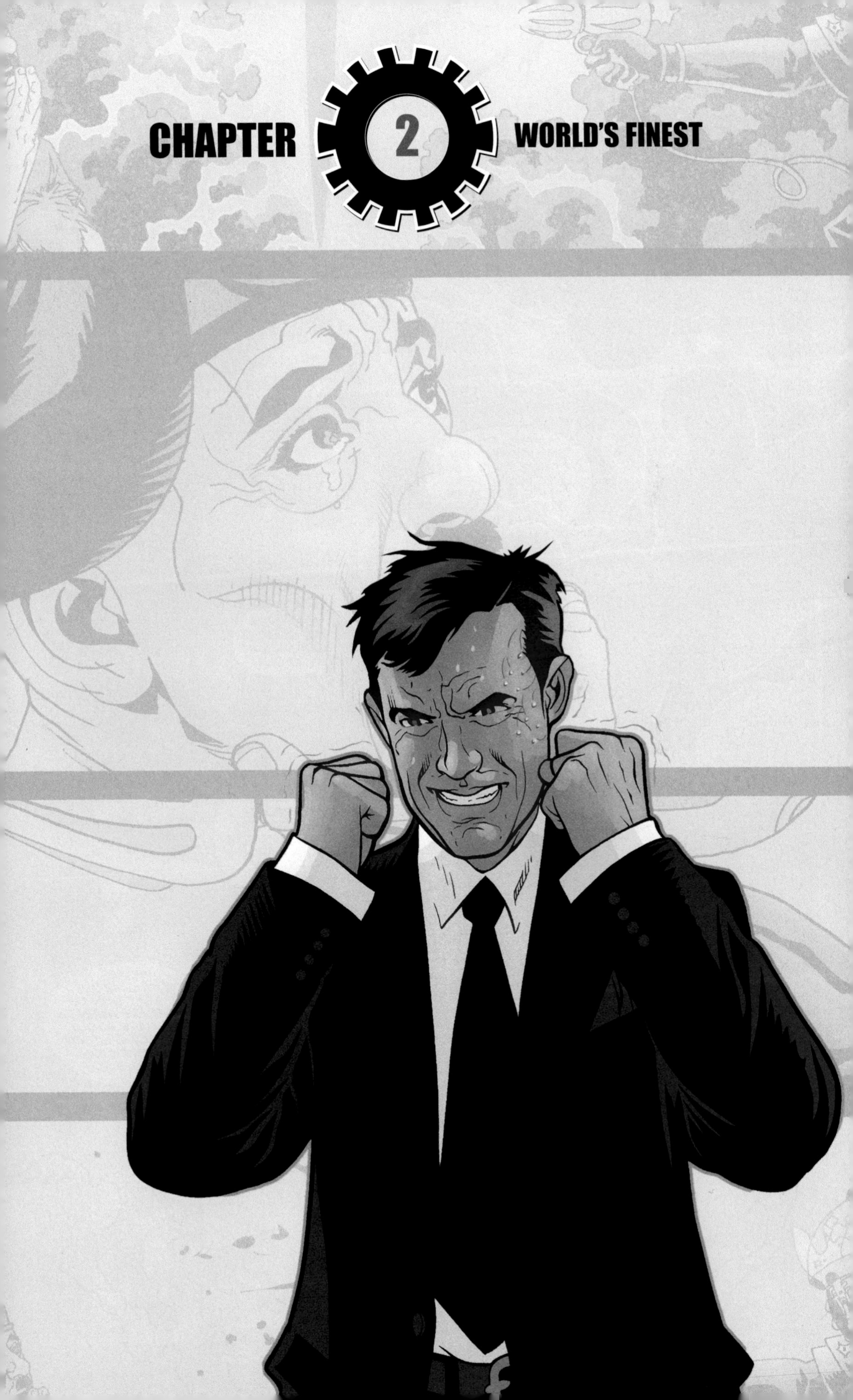

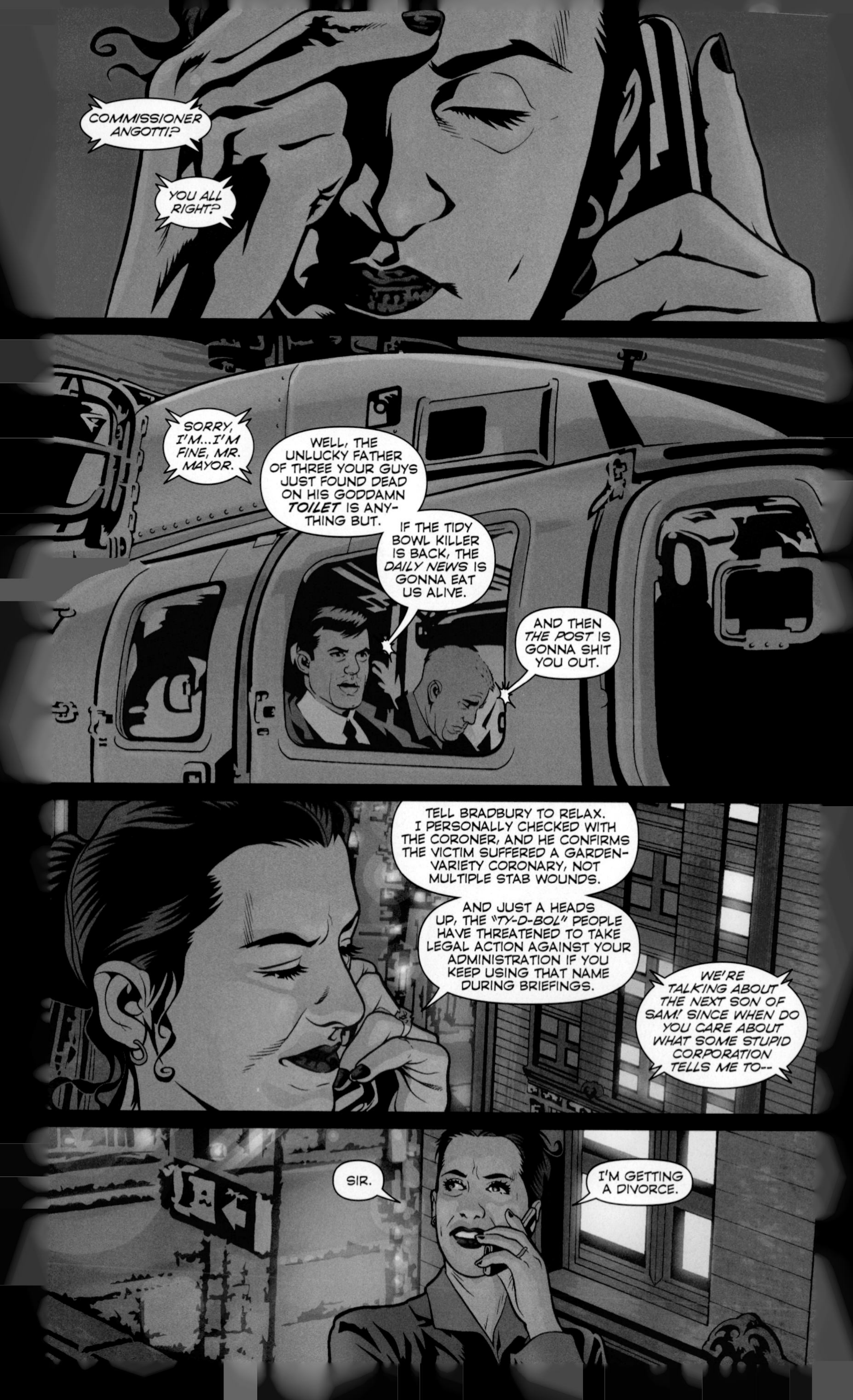
COMMISSIONER ANGOTTI?
YOU ALL RIGHT?
SORRY, I'M...I'M FINE, MR. MAYOR.
WELL, THE UNLUCKY FATHER OF THREE YOUR GUYS JUST FOUND DEAD ON HIS GODDAMN *TOILET* IS ANYTHING BUT.
IF THE TIDY BOWL KILLER IS BACK, THE *DAILY NEWS* IS GONNA EAT US ALIVE.
AND THEN *THE POST* IS GONNA SHIT YOU OUT.
TELL BRADBURY TO RELAX. I PERSONALLY CHECKED WITH THE CORONER, AND HE CONFIRMS THE VICTIM SUFFERED A GARDEN-VARIETY CORONARY, NOT MULTIPLE STAB WOUNDS.
AND JUST A HEADS UP, THE *"TY-D-BOL"* PEOPLE HAVE THREATENED TO TAKE LEGAL ACTION AGAINST YOUR ADMINISTRATION IF YOU KEEP USING THAT NAME DURING BRIEFINGS.
WE'RE TALKING ABOUT THE NEXT SON OF SAM! SINCE WHEN DO YOU CARE ABOUT WHAT SOME STUPID CORPORATION TELLS ME TO--
SIR.
I'M GETTING A DIVORCE.

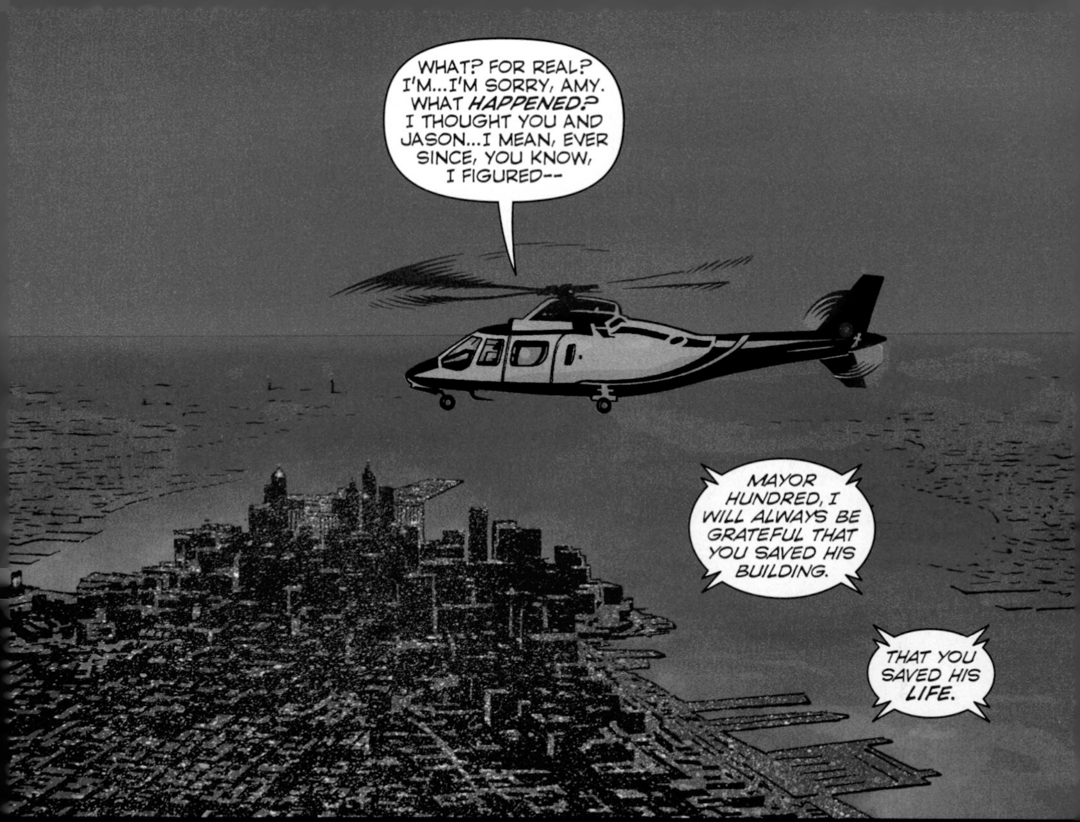
WHAT? FOR REAL? I'M...I'M SORRY, AMY. WHAT HAPPENED? I THOUGHT YOU AND JASON...I MEAN, EVER SINCE, YOU KNOW, I FIGURED--
MAYOR HUNDRED, I WILL ALWAYS BE GRATEFUL THAT YOU SAVED HIS BUILDING.
THAT YOU SAVED HIS LIFE.

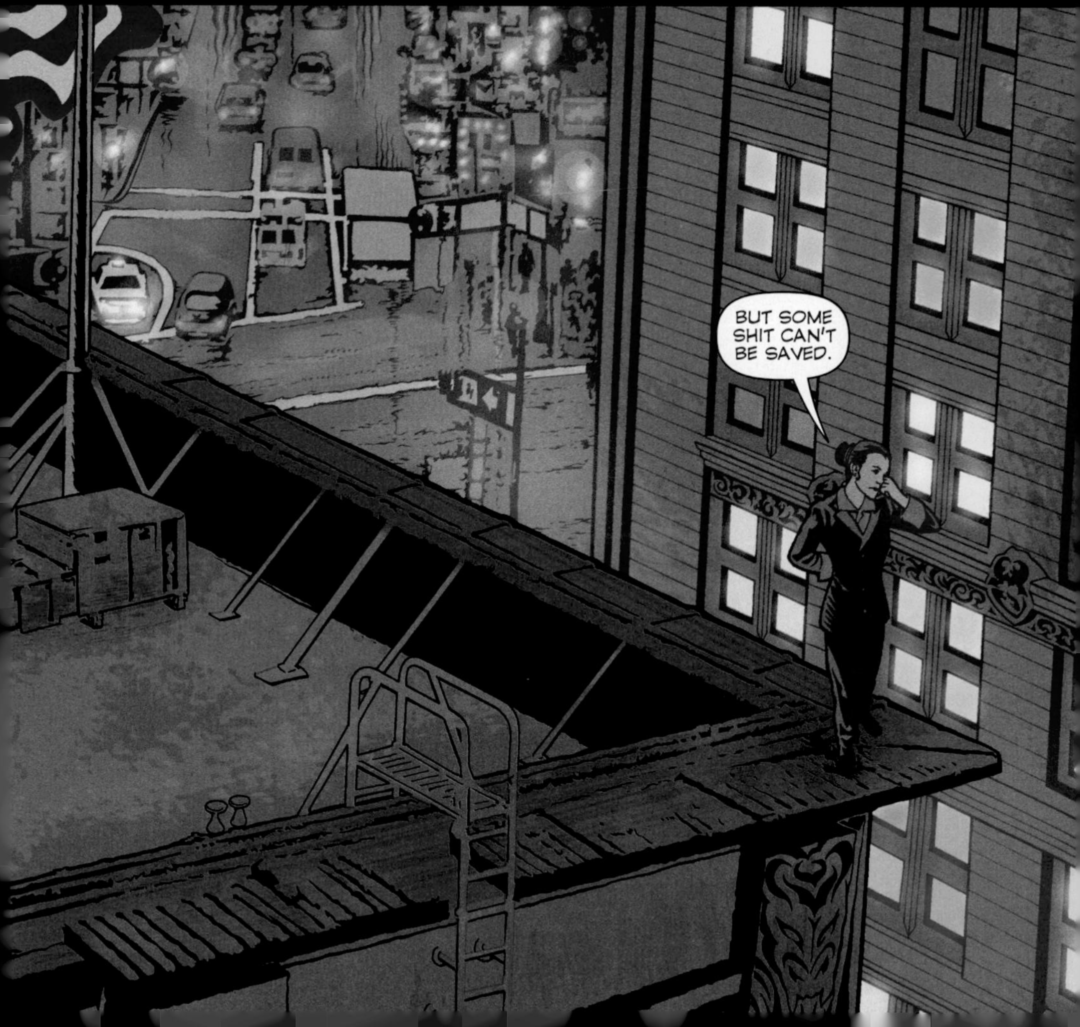
BUT SOME SHIT CAN'T BE SAVED.

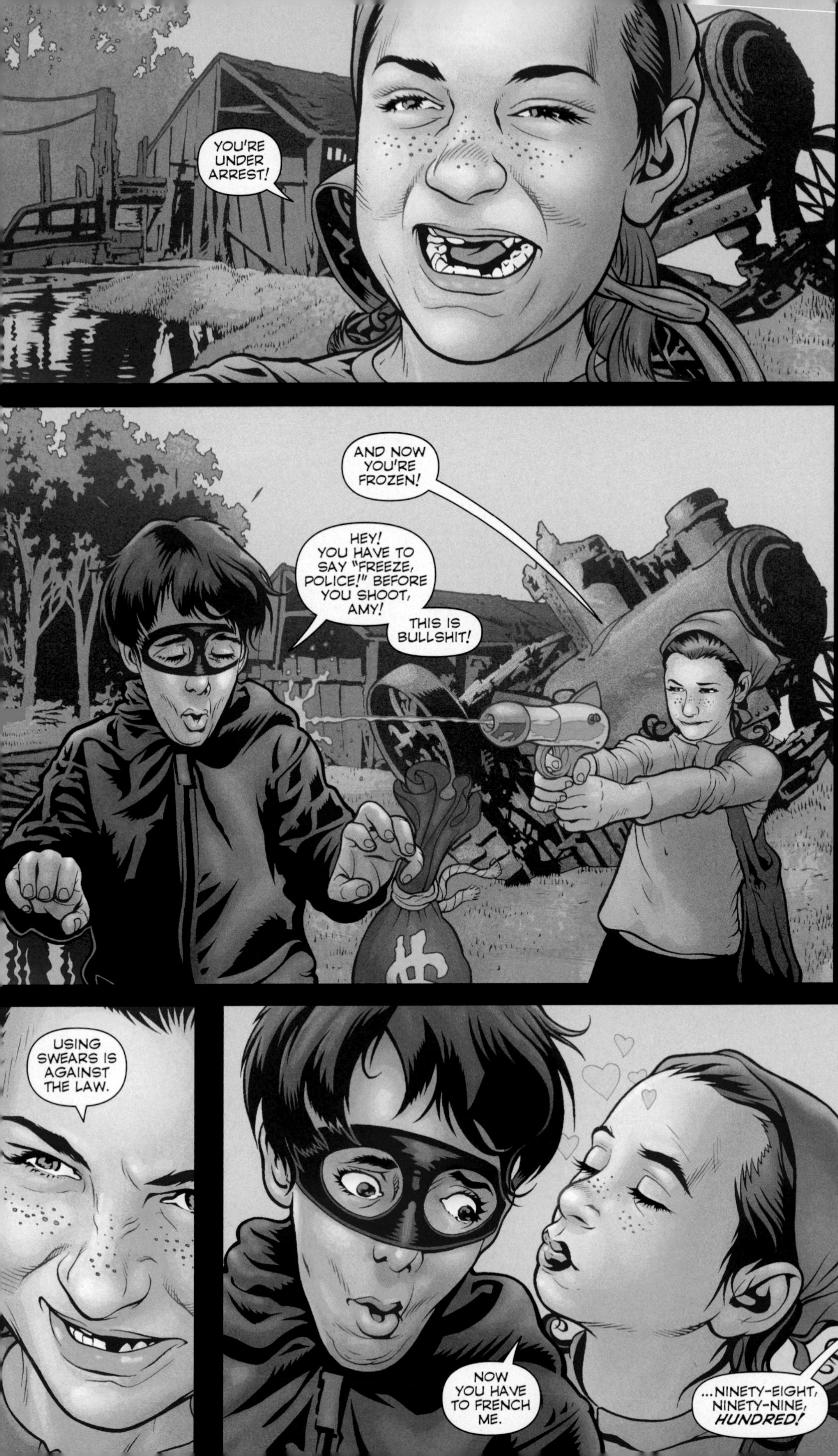
YOU'RE UNDER ARREST!
AND NOW YOU'RE FROZEN!
HEY! YOU HAVE TO SAY "FREEZE, POLICE!" BEFORE YOU SHOOT, AMY!
THIS IS BULLSHIT!
USING SWEARS IS AGAINST THE LAW.
NOW YOU HAVE TO FRENCH ME.
...NINETY-EIGHT, NINETY-NINE, *HUNDRED!*

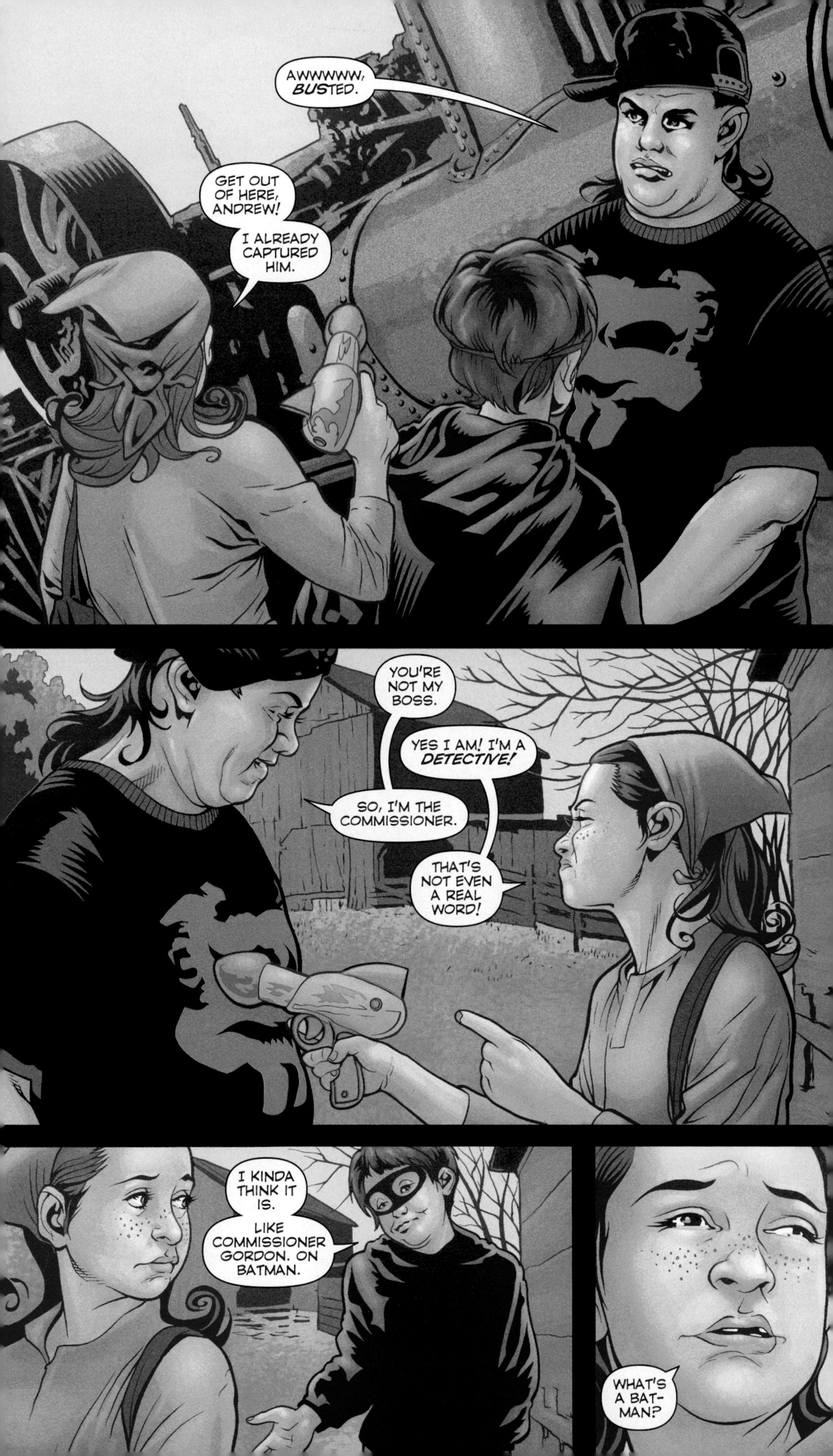
AWWWWW, *BUS*TED.
GET OUT OF HERE, ANDREW!
I ALREADY CAPTURED HIM.
YOU'RE NOT MY BOSS.
YES I AM! I'M A *DETECTIVE!*
SO, I'M THE COMMISSIONER.
THAT'S NOT EVEN A REAL WORD!
I KINDA THINK IT IS.
LIKE COMMISSIONER GORDON. ON BATMAN.
WHAT'S A BAT-MAN?

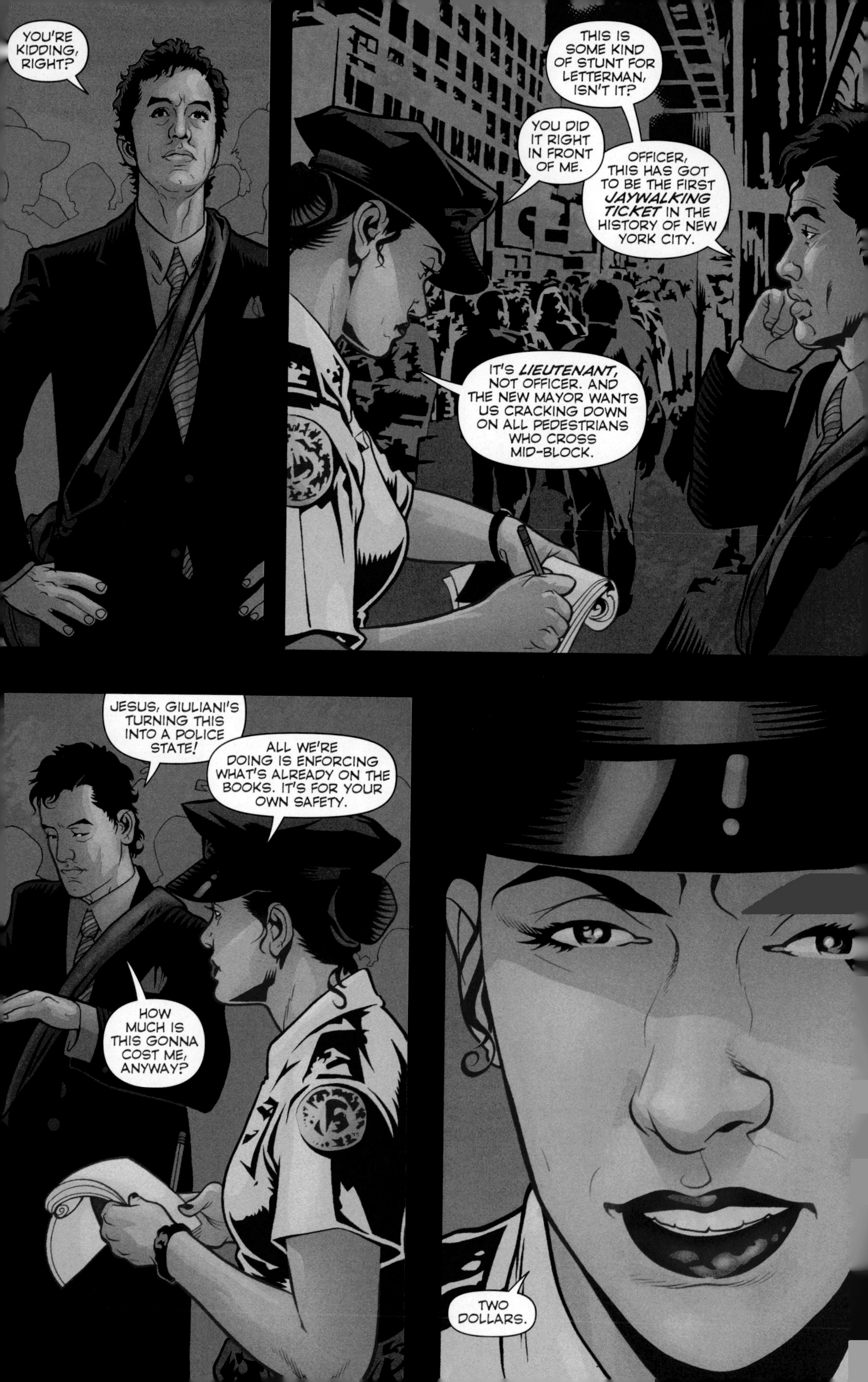
YOU'RE KIDDING, RIGHT?
THIS IS SOME KIND OF STUNT FOR LETTERMAN, ISN'T IT?
YOU DID IT RIGHT IN FRONT OF ME.
OFFICER, THIS HAS GOT TO BE THE FIRST JAYWALKING TICKET IN THE HISTORY OF NEW YORK CITY.
IT'S LIEUTENANT, NOT OFFICER. AND THE NEW MAYOR WANTS US CRACKING DOWN ON ALL PEDESTRIANS WHO CROSS MID-BLOCK.
JESUS, GIULIANI'S TURNING THIS INTO A POLICE STATE!
ALL WE'RE DOING IS ENFORCING WHAT'S ALREADY ON THE BOOKS. IT'S FOR YOUR OWN SAFETY.
HOW MUCH IS THIS GONNA COST ME, ANYWAY?
TWO DOLLARS.

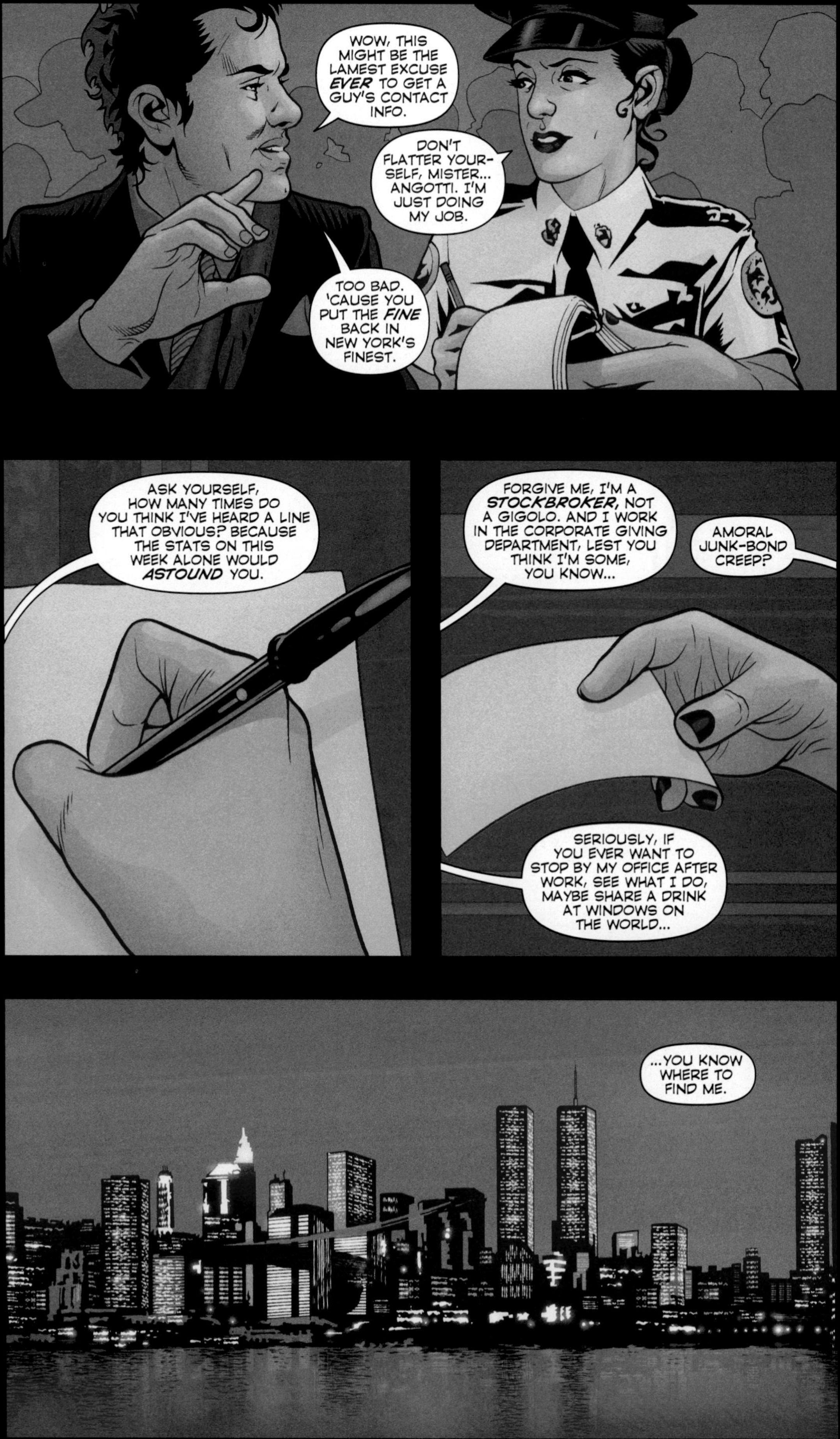
WOW, THIS MIGHT BE THE LAMEST EXCUSE EVER TO GET A GUY'S CONTACT INFO.
DON'T FLATTER YOURSELF, MISTER... ANGOTTI. I'M JUST DOING MY JOB.
TOO BAD. 'CAUSE YOU PUT THE FINE BACK IN NEW YORK'S FINEST.
ASK YOURSELF, HOW MANY TIMES DO YOU THINK I'VE HEARD A LINE THAT OBVIOUS? BECAUSE THE STATS ON THIS WEEK ALONE WOULD ASTOUND YOU.
FORGIVE ME, I'M A STOCKBROKER, NOT A GIGOLO. AND I WORK IN THE CORPORATE GIVING DEPARTMENT, LEST YOU THINK I'M SOME, YOU KNOW...
AMORAL JUNK-BOND CREEP?
SERIOUSLY, IF YOU EVER WANT TO STOP BY MY OFFICE AFTER WORK, SEE WHAT I DO, MAYBE SHARE A DRINK AT WINDOWS ON THE WORLD...
...YOU KNOW WHERE TO FIND ME.

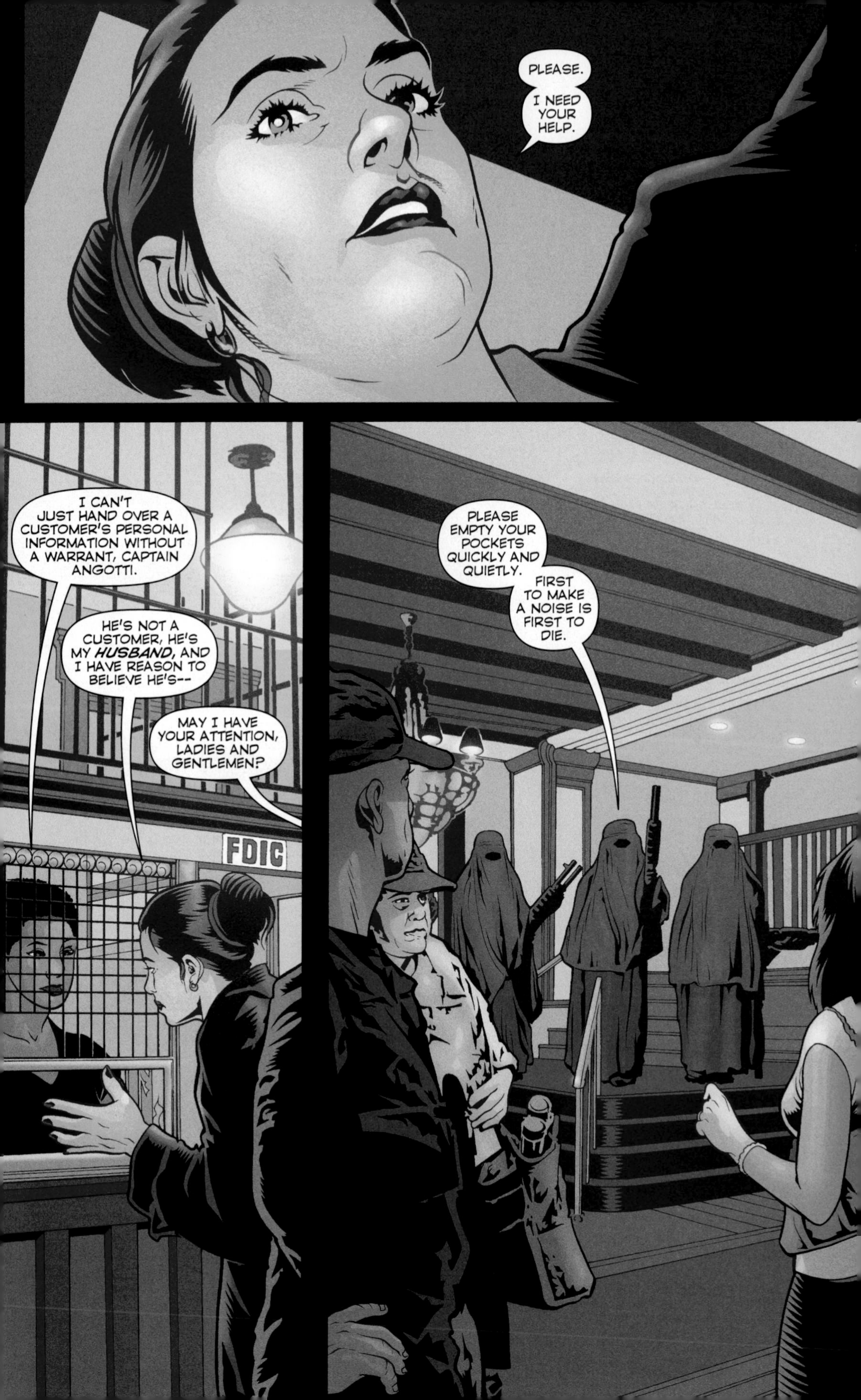
PLEASE.
I NEED YOUR HELP.
I CAN'T JUST HAND OVER A CUSTOMER'S PERSONAL INFORMATION WITHOUT A WARRANT, CAPTAIN ANGOTTI.
HE'S NOT A CUSTOMER, HE'S MY *HUSBAND,* AND I HAVE REASON TO BELIEVE HE'S--
MAY I HAVE YOUR ATTENTION, LADIES AND GENTLEMEN?
FDIC
PLEASE EMPTY YOUR POCKETS QUICKLY AND QUIETLY.
FIRST TO MAKE A NOISE IS FIRST TO DIE.

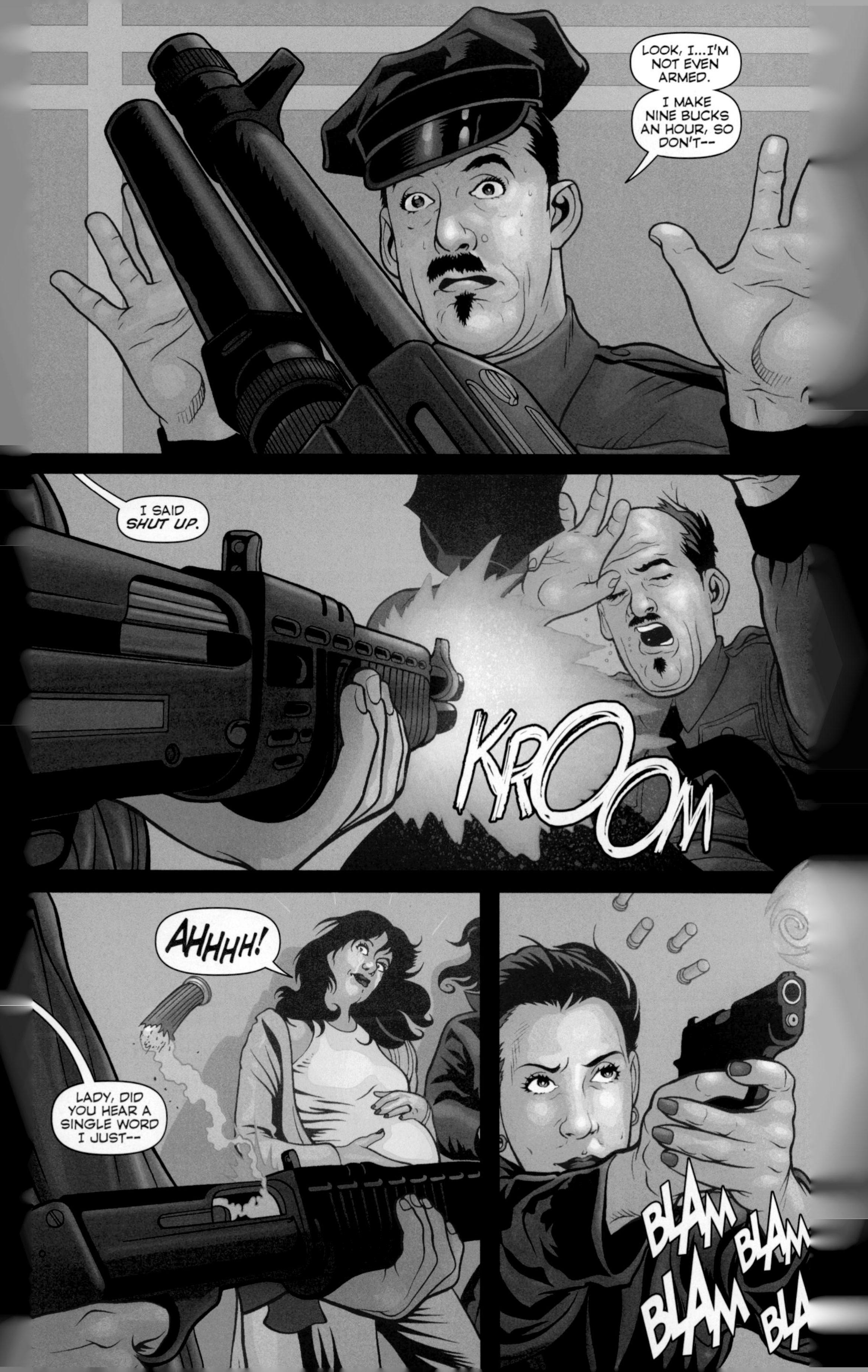
LOOK, I...I'M NOT EVEN ARMED.
I MAKE NINE BUCKS AN HOUR, SO DON'T--
I SAID SHUT UP.
KROOOM
AHHHH!
LADY, DID YOU HEAR A SINGLE WORD I JUST--
BLAM BLAM
BLAM BLA

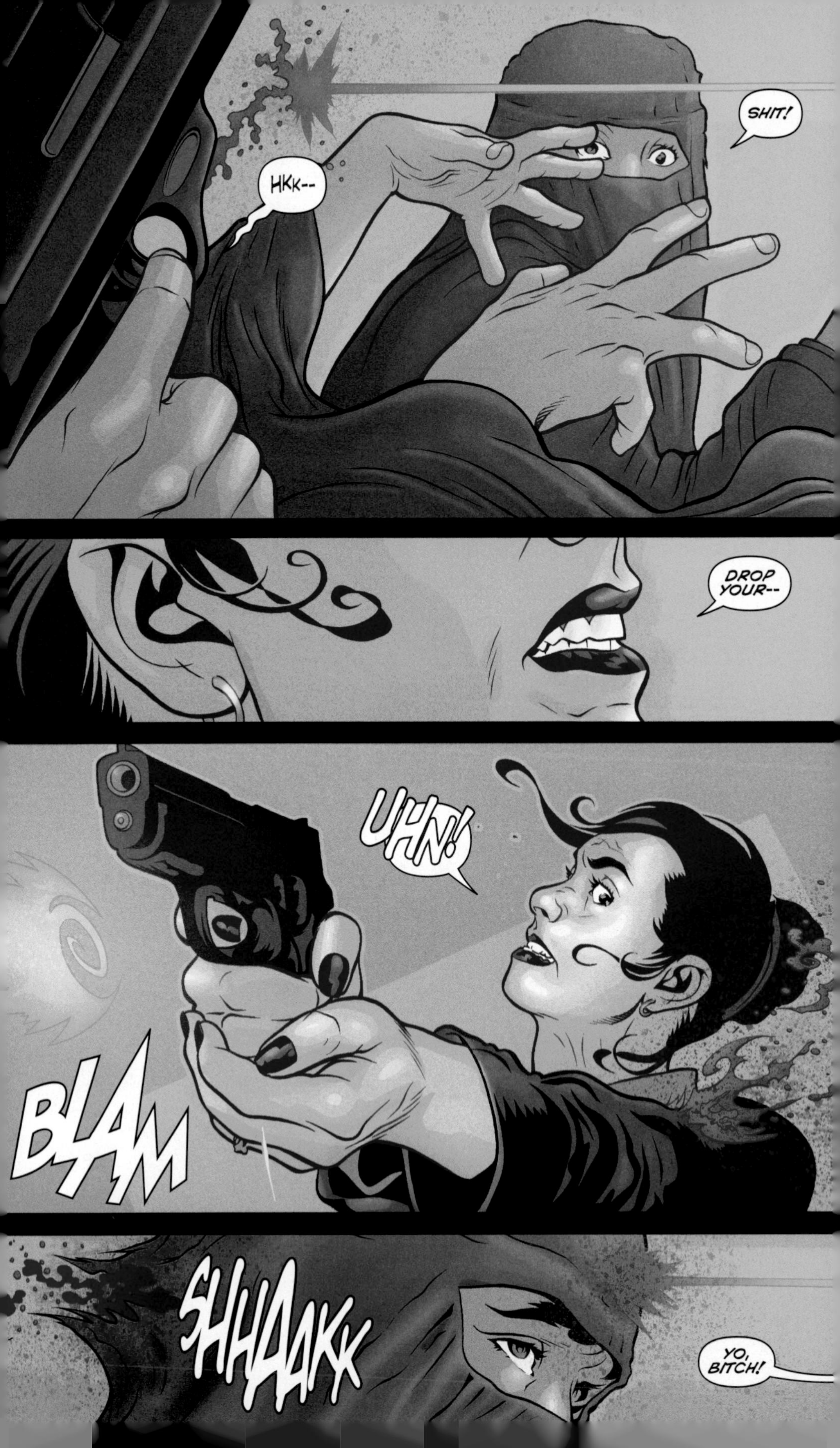
SHIT!
HKK--
DROP YOUR--
UHN!
BLAM
SHHAAKK
YO, BITCH!

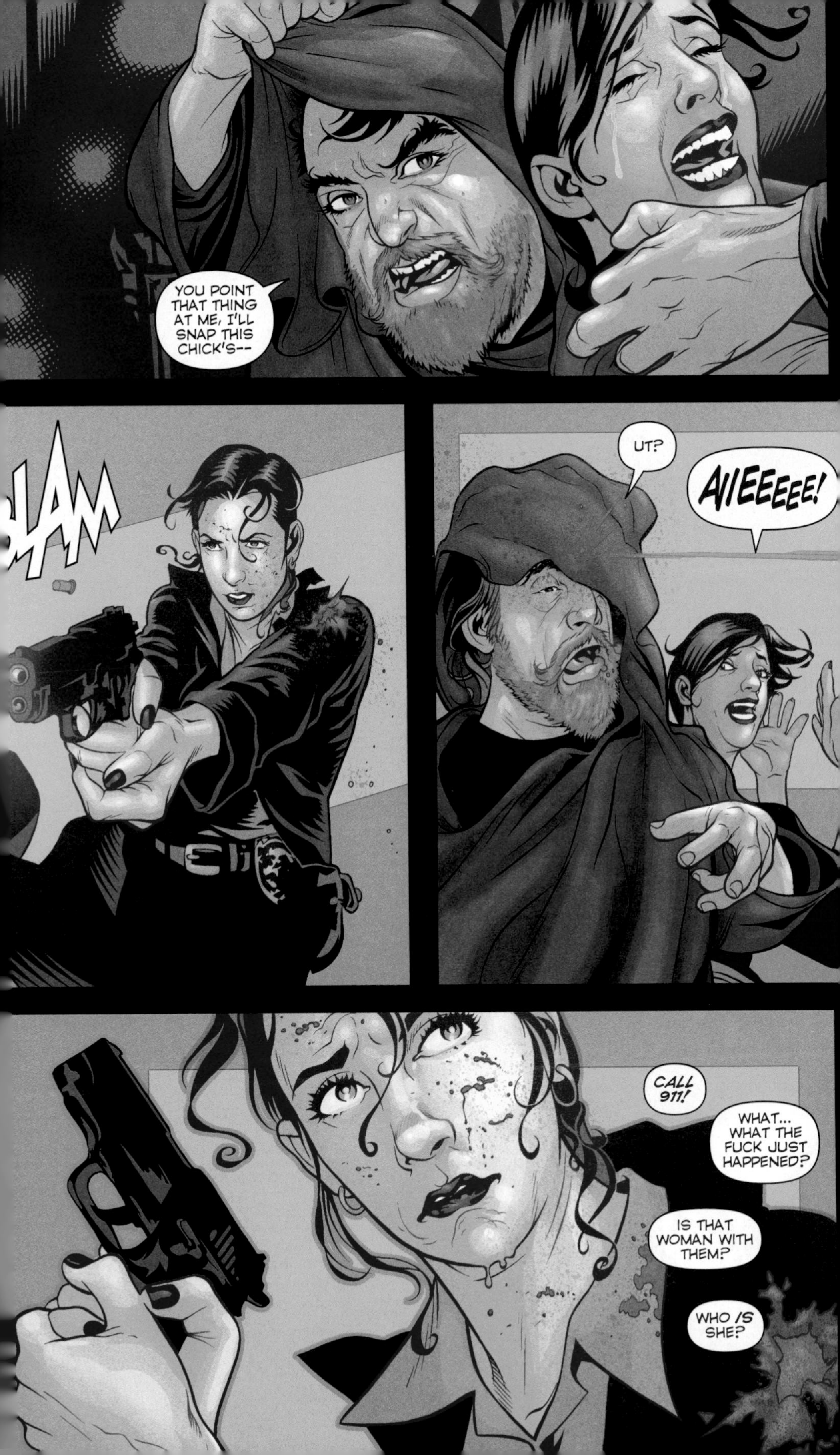
YOU POINT THAT THING AT ME, I'LL SNAP THIS CHICK'S--
BLAM
UT?
AIIEEEEEE!
CALL 911!
WHAT... WHAT THE FUCK JUST HAPPENED?
IS THAT WOMAN WITH THEM?
WHO IS SHE?

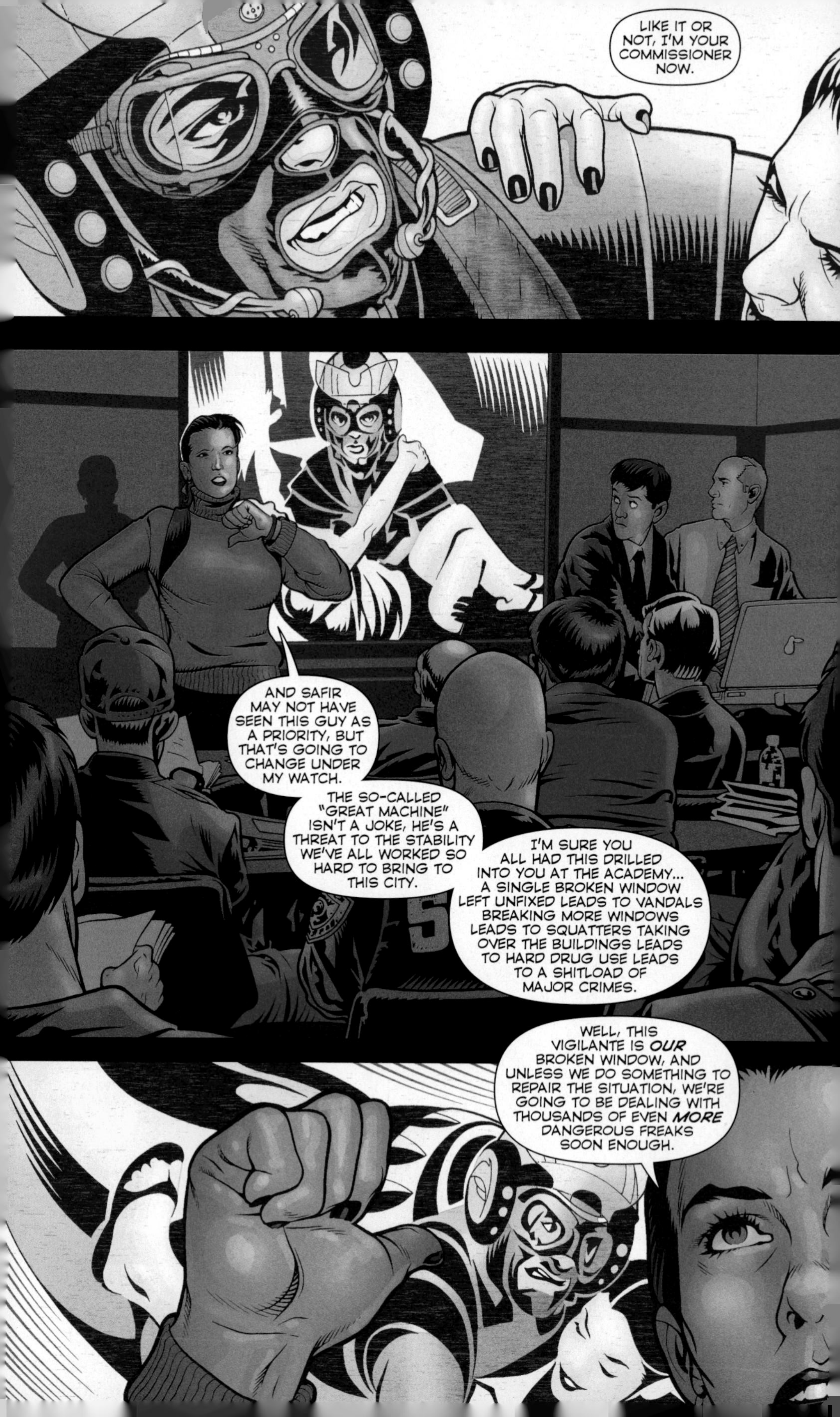
LIKE IT OR NOT, I'M YOUR COMMISSIONER NOW.
AND SAFIR MAY NOT HAVE SEEN THIS GUY AS A PRIORITY, BUT THAT'S GOING TO CHANGE UNDER MY WATCH.
THE SO-CALLED "GREAT MACHINE" ISN'T A JOKE, HE'S A THREAT TO THE STABILITY WE'VE ALL WORKED SO HARD TO BRING TO THIS CITY.
I'M SURE YOU ALL HAD THIS DRILLED INTO YOU AT THE ACADEMY... A SINGLE BROKEN WINDOW LEFT UNFIXED LEADS TO VANDALS BREAKING MORE WINDOWS LEADS TO SQUATTERS TAKING OVER THE BUILDINGS LEADS TO HARD DRUG USE LEADS TO A SHITLOAD OF MAJOR CRIMES.
WELL, THIS VIGILANTE IS *OUR* BROKEN WINDOW, AND UNLESS WE DO SOMETHING TO REPAIR THE SITUATION, WE'RE GOING TO BE DEALING WITH THOUSANDS OF EVEN *MORE* DANGEROUS FREAKS SOON ENOUGH.

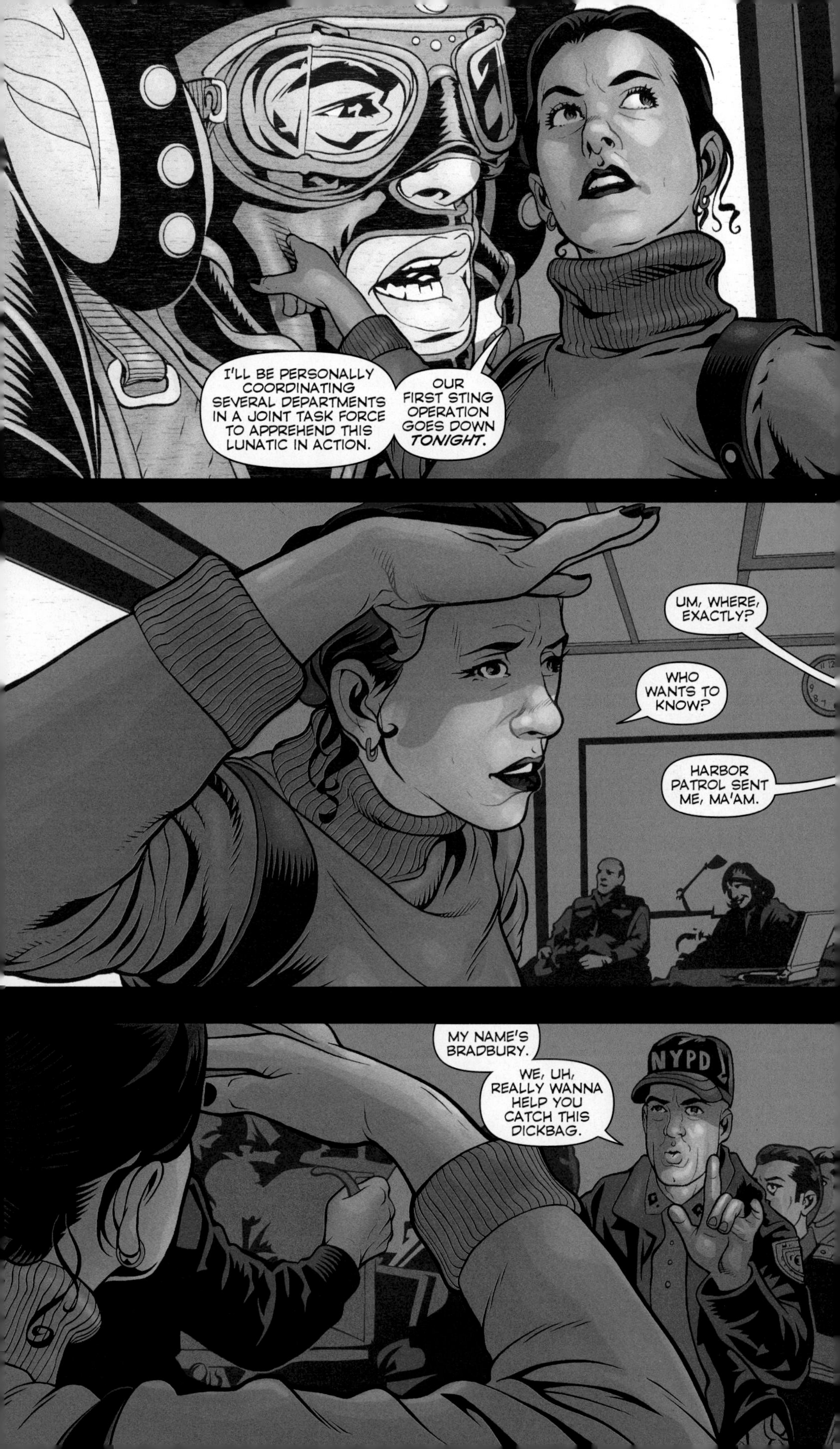
I'LL BE PERSONALLY COORDINATING SEVERAL DEPARTMENTS IN A JOINT TASK FORCE TO APPREHEND THIS LUNATIC IN ACTION.
OUR FIRST STING OPERATION GOES DOWN *TONIGHT*.
UM, WHERE, EXACTLY?
WHO WANTS TO KNOW?
HARBOR PATROL SENT ME, MA'AM.
MY NAME'S BRADBURY.
WE, UH, REALLY WANNA HELP YOU CATCH THIS DICKBAG.
NYPD

ASSHOLE.

AMY? GOD, COME TO BED ALREADY.

IN A BIT, JASON. SCANNER SAYS PUBLIC ENEMY NUMBER ONE WAS SPOTTED IN OUR NEIGHBORHOOD.

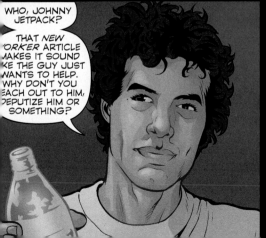

WHO, JOHNNY JETPACK?

THAT *NEW YORKER* ARTICLE MAKES IT SOUND LIKE THE GUY JUST WANTS TO HELP. WHY DON'T YOU REACH OUT TO HIM, DEPUTIZE HIM OR SOMETHING?

WHAT THE FUCK DID YOU SAY?

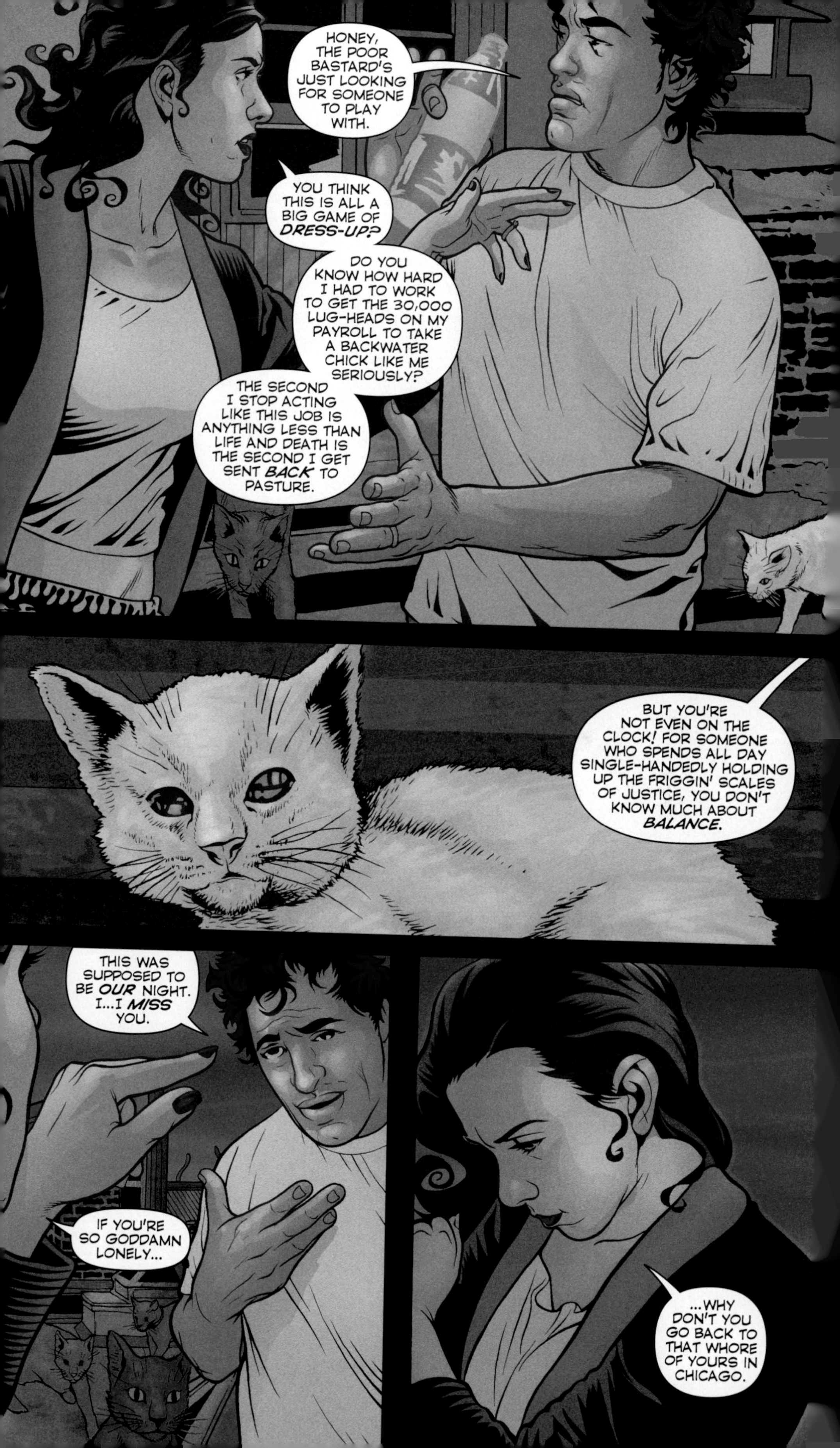
HONEY, THE POOR BASTARD'S JUST LOOKING FOR SOMEONE TO PLAY WITH.
YOU THINK THIS IS ALL A BIG GAME OF DRESS-UP?
DO YOU KNOW HOW HARD I HAD TO WORK TO GET THE 30,000 LUG-HEADS ON MY PAYROLL TO TAKE A BACKWATER CHICK LIKE ME SERIOUSLY?
THE SECOND I STOP ACTING LIKE THIS JOB IS ANYTHING LESS THAN LIFE AND DEATH IS THE SECOND I GET SENT BACK TO PASTURE.
BUT YOU'RE NOT EVEN ON THE CLOCK! FOR SOMEONE WHO SPENDS ALL DAY SINGLE-HANDEDLY HOLDING UP THE FRIGGIN' SCALES OF JUSTICE, YOU DON'T KNOW MUCH ABOUT BALANCE.
THIS WAS SUPPOSED TO BE OUR NIGHT. I...I MISS YOU.
IF YOU'RE SO GODDAMN LONELY...
...WHY DON'T YOU GO BACK TO THAT WHORE OF YOURS IN CHICAGO.

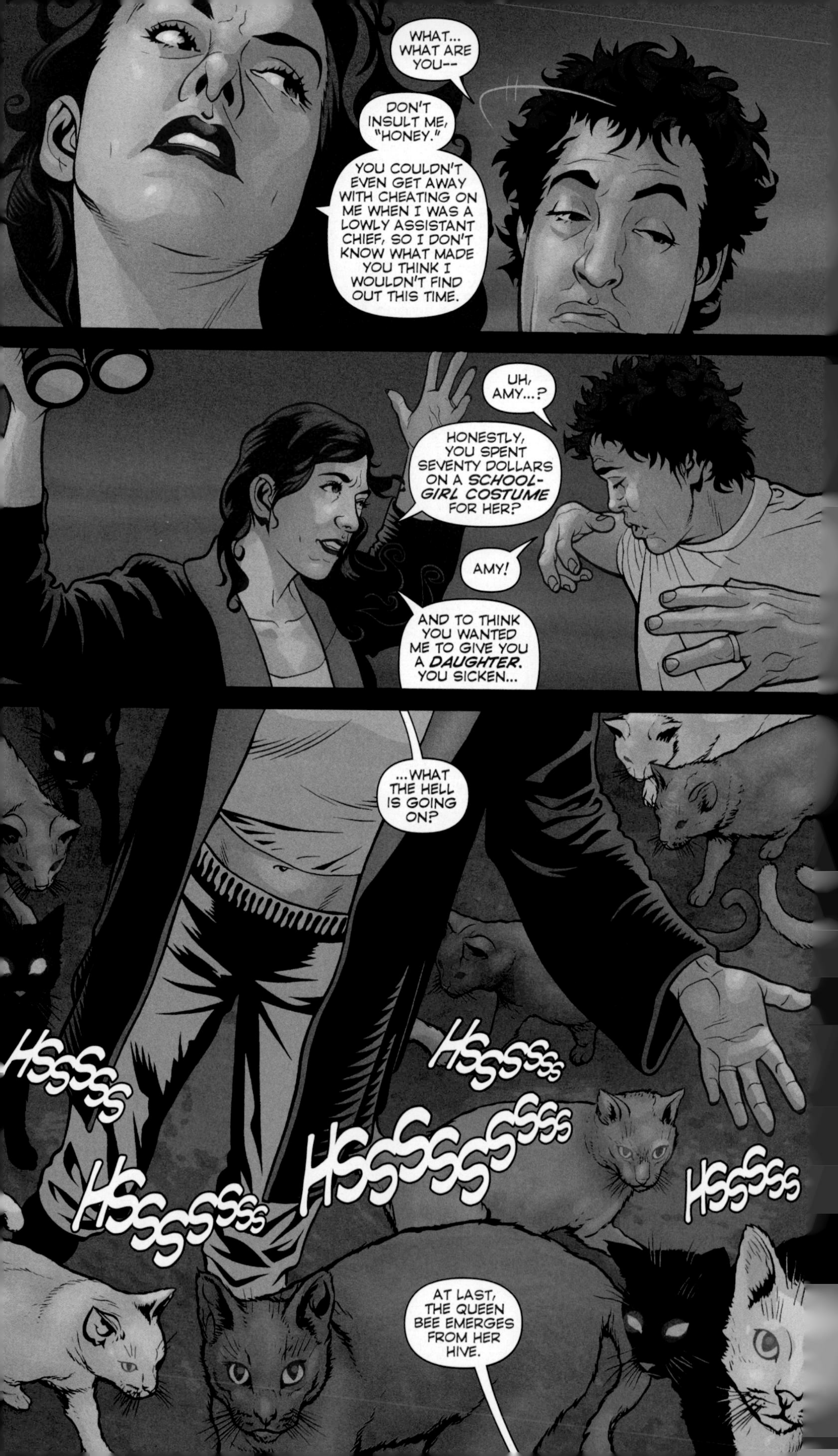
WHAT... WHAT ARE YOU--
DON'T INSULT ME, "HONEY."
YOU COULDN'T EVEN GET AWAY WITH CHEATING ON ME WHEN I WAS A LOWLY ASSISTANT CHIEF, SO I DON'T KNOW WHAT MADE YOU THINK I WOULDN'T FIND OUT THIS TIME.
UH, AMY...?
HONESTLY, YOU SPENT SEVENTY DOLLARS ON A *SCHOOL-GIRL COSTUME* FOR HER?
AMY!
AND TO THINK YOU WANTED ME TO GIVE YOU A *DAUGHTER*. YOU SICKEN...
...WHAT THE HELL IS GOING ON?
HSSSSS
HSSSSSS
HSSSSSSSS
HSSSSSSSSSSS
HSSSSS
AT LAST, THE QUEEN BEE EMERGES FROM HER HIVE.

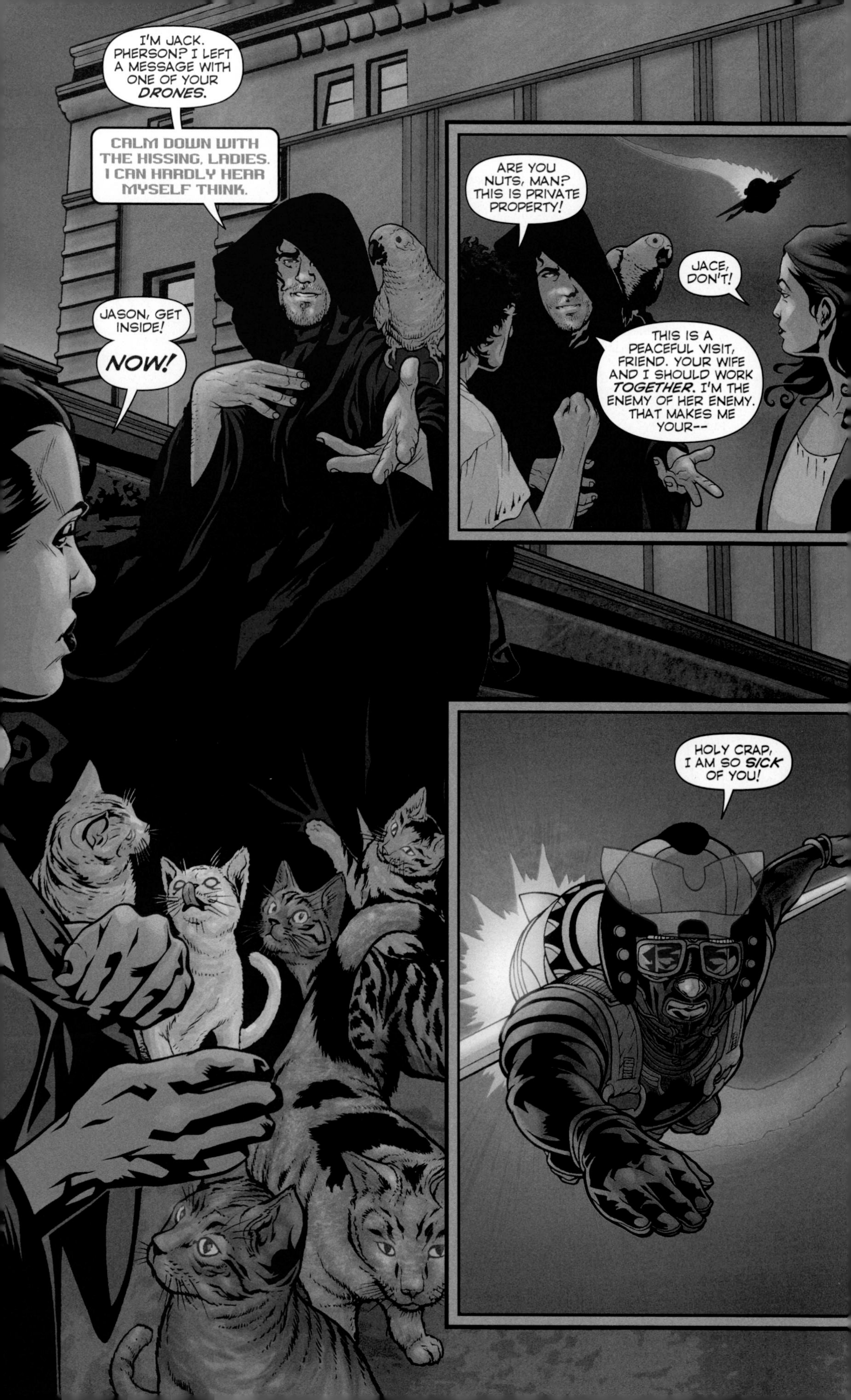
I'M JACK. PHERSON? I LEFT A MESSAGE WITH ONE OF YOUR *DRONES*.
CALM DOWN WITH THE HISSING, LADIES. I CAN HARDLY HEAR MYSELF THINK.
JASON, GET INSIDE!
NOW!
ARE YOU NUTS, MAN? THIS IS PRIVATE PROPERTY!
JACE, DON'T!
THIS IS A PEACEFUL VISIT, FRIEND. YOUR WIFE AND I SHOULD WORK *TOGETHER*. I'M THE ENEMY OF HER ENEMY. THAT MAKES ME YOUR--
HOLY CRAP, I AM SO *SICK* OF YOU!

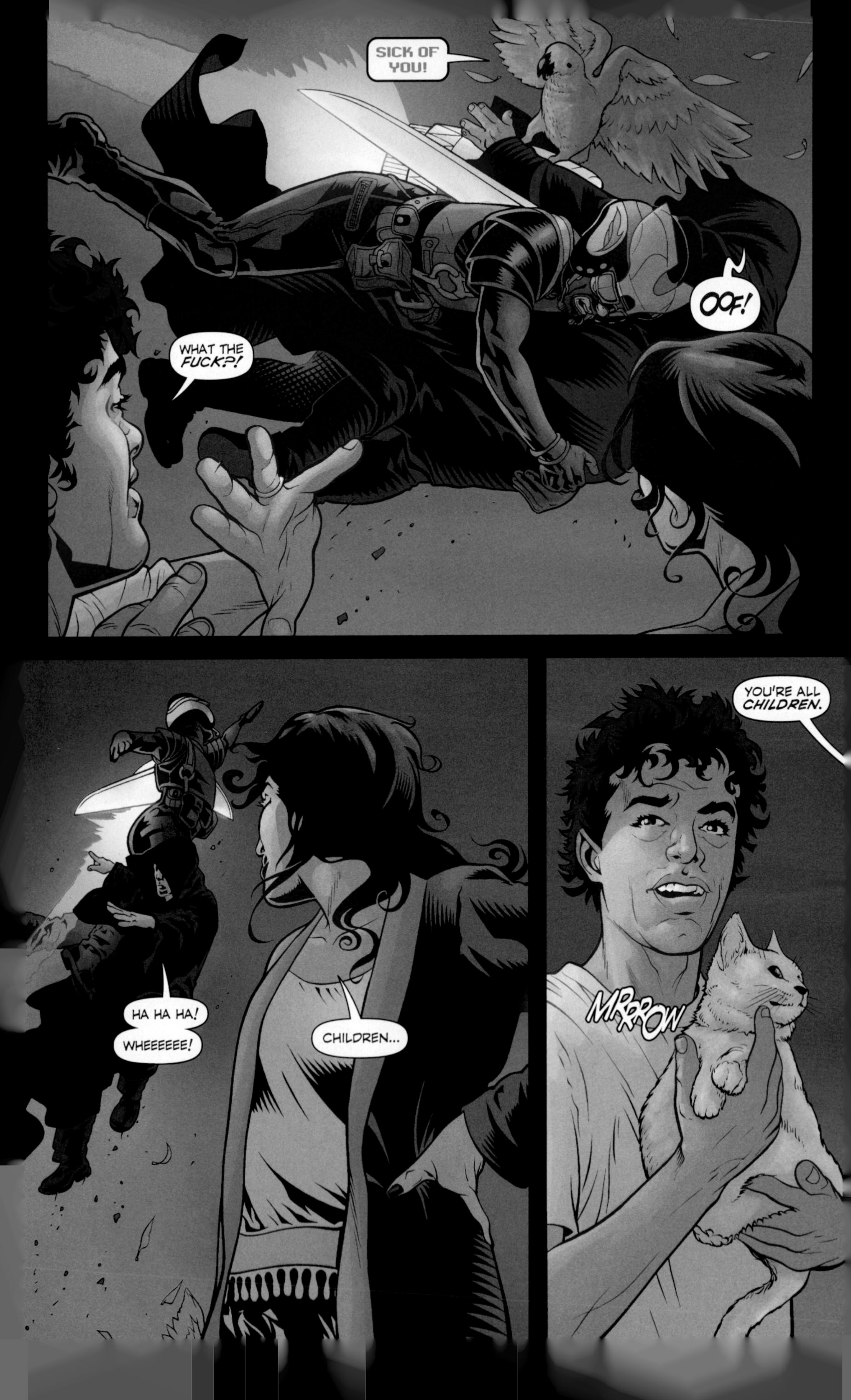
SICK OF YOU!
OOF!
WHAT THE FUCK?!
HA HA HA!
WHEEEEEE!
CHILDREN...
YOU'RE ALL CHILDREN.
MRRROW

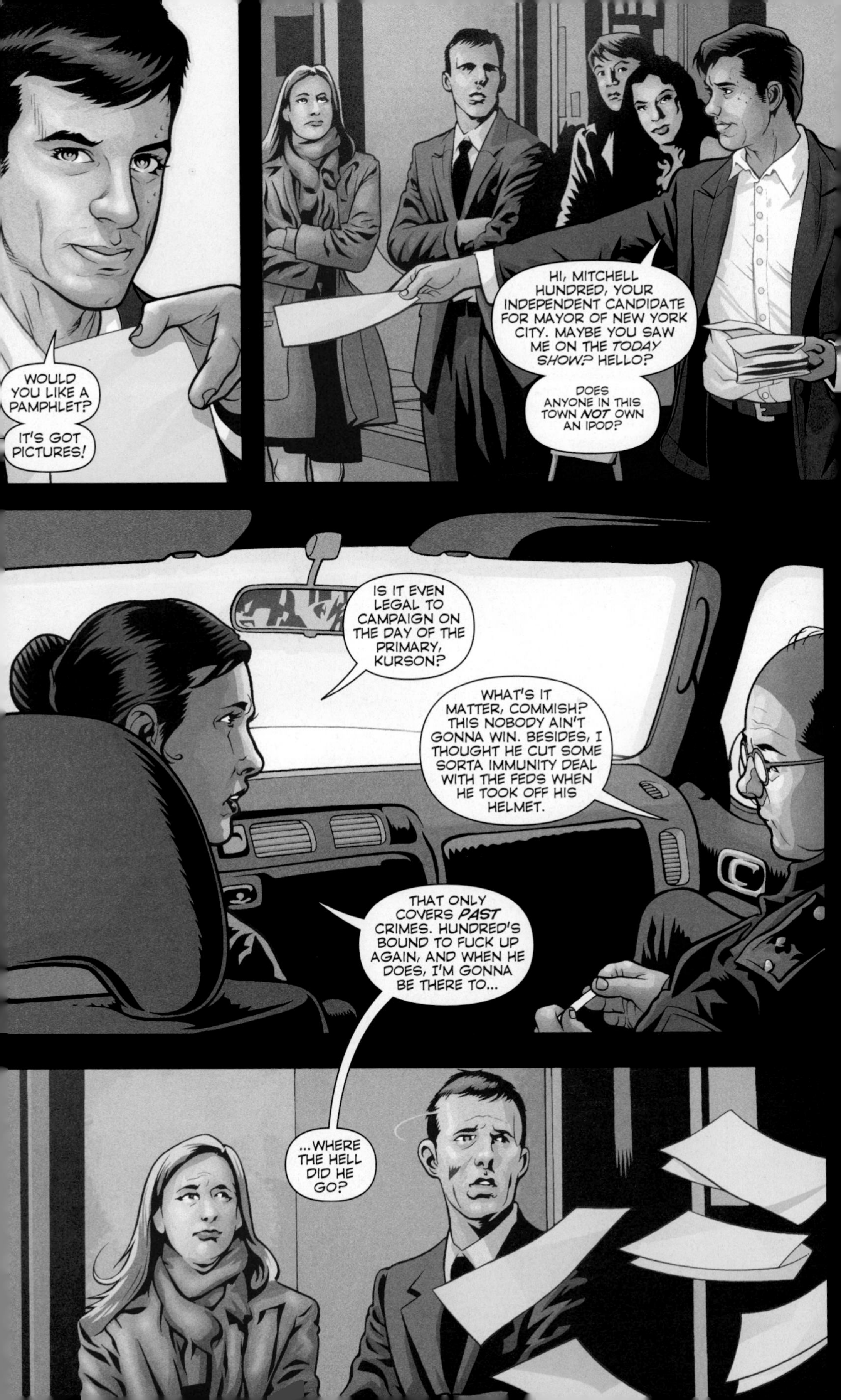
WOULD YOU LIKE A PAMPHLET?
IT'S GOT PICTURES!
HI, MITCHELL HUNDRED, YOUR INDEPENDENT CANDIDATE FOR MAYOR OF NEW YORK CITY. MAYBE YOU SAW ME ON THE *TODAY SHOW?* HELLO?
DOES ANYONE IN THIS TOWN *NOT* OWN AN IPOD?
IS IT EVEN LEGAL TO CAMPAIGN ON THE DAY OF THE PRIMARY, KURSON?
WHAT'S IT MATTER, COMMISH? THIS NOBODY AIN'T GONNA WIN. BESIDES, I THOUGHT HE CUT SOME SORTA IMMUNITY DEAL WITH THE FEDS WHEN HE TOOK OFF HIS HELMET.
THAT ONLY COVERS *PAST* CRIMES. HUNDRED'S BOUND TO FUCK UP AGAIN, AND WHEN HE DOES, I'M GONNA BE THERE TO...
...WHERE THE HELL DID HE GO?

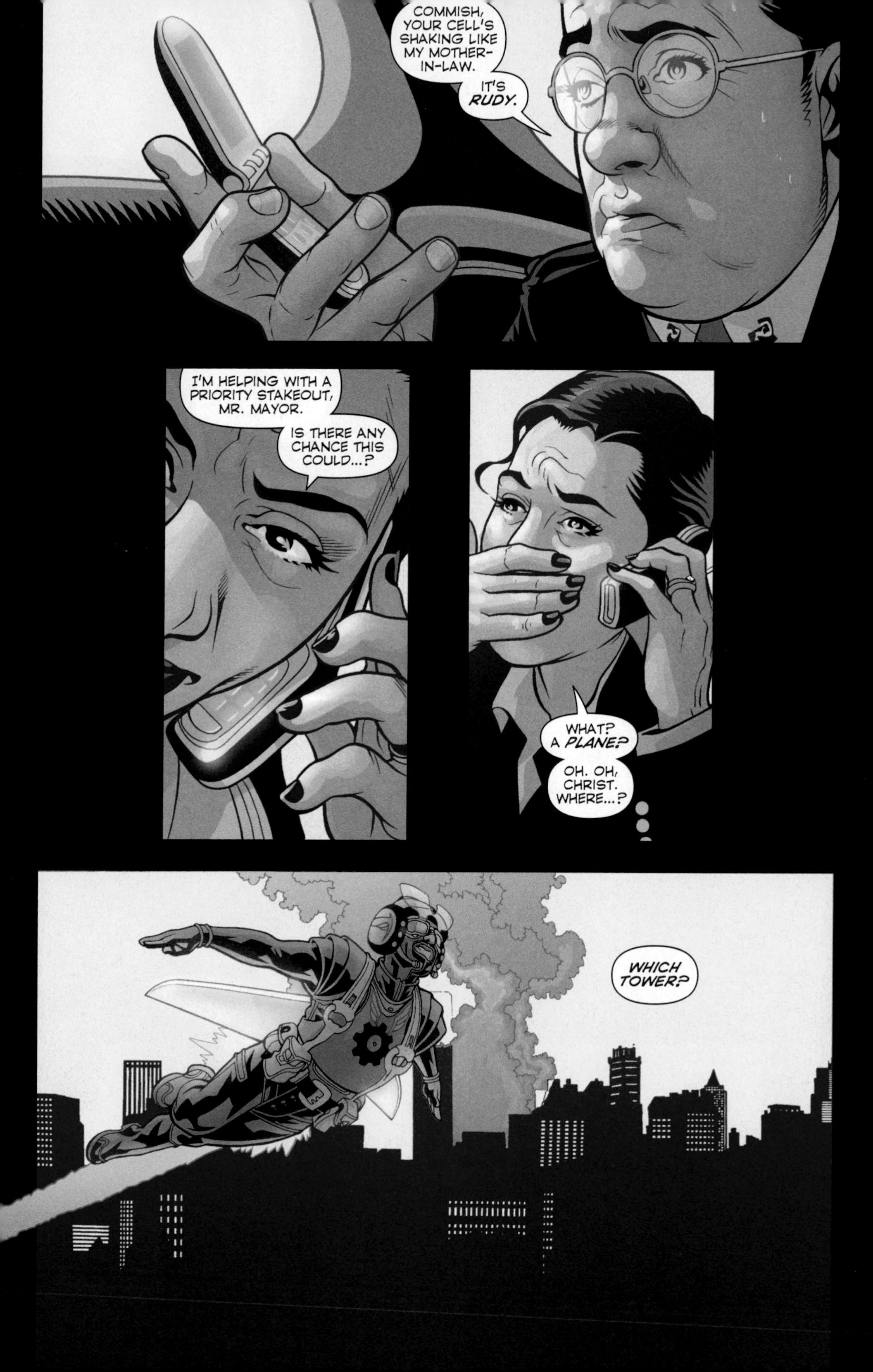
COMMISH, YOUR CELL'S SHAKING LIKE MY MOTHER-IN-LAW.
IT'S *RUDY.*
I'M HELPING WITH A PRIORITY STAKEOUT, MR. MAYOR.
IS THERE ANY CHANCE THIS COULD...?
WHAT? A *PLANE?*
OH. OH, CHRIST. WHERE...?
WHICH TOWER?

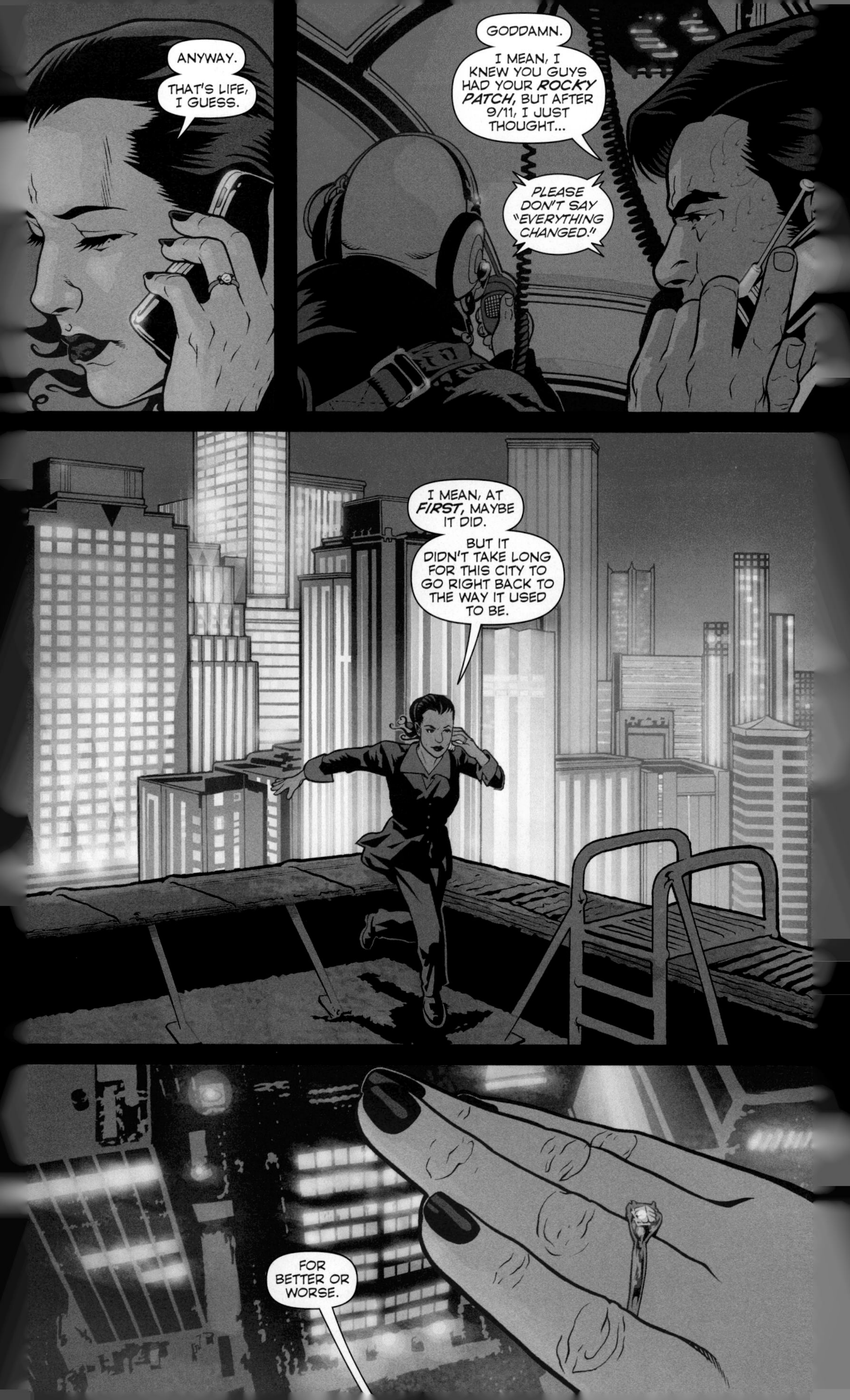
ANYWAY.
THAT'S LIFE, I GUESS.
GODDAMN.
I MEAN, I KNEW YOU GUYS HAD YOUR ROCKY PATCH, BUT AFTER 9/11, I JUST THOUGHT...
PLEASE DON'T SAY "EVERYTHING CHANGED."
I MEAN, AT FIRST, MAYBE IT DID.
BUT IT DIDN'T TAKE LONG FOR THIS CITY TO GO RIGHT BACK TO THE WAY IT USED TO BE.
FOR BETTER OR WORSE.

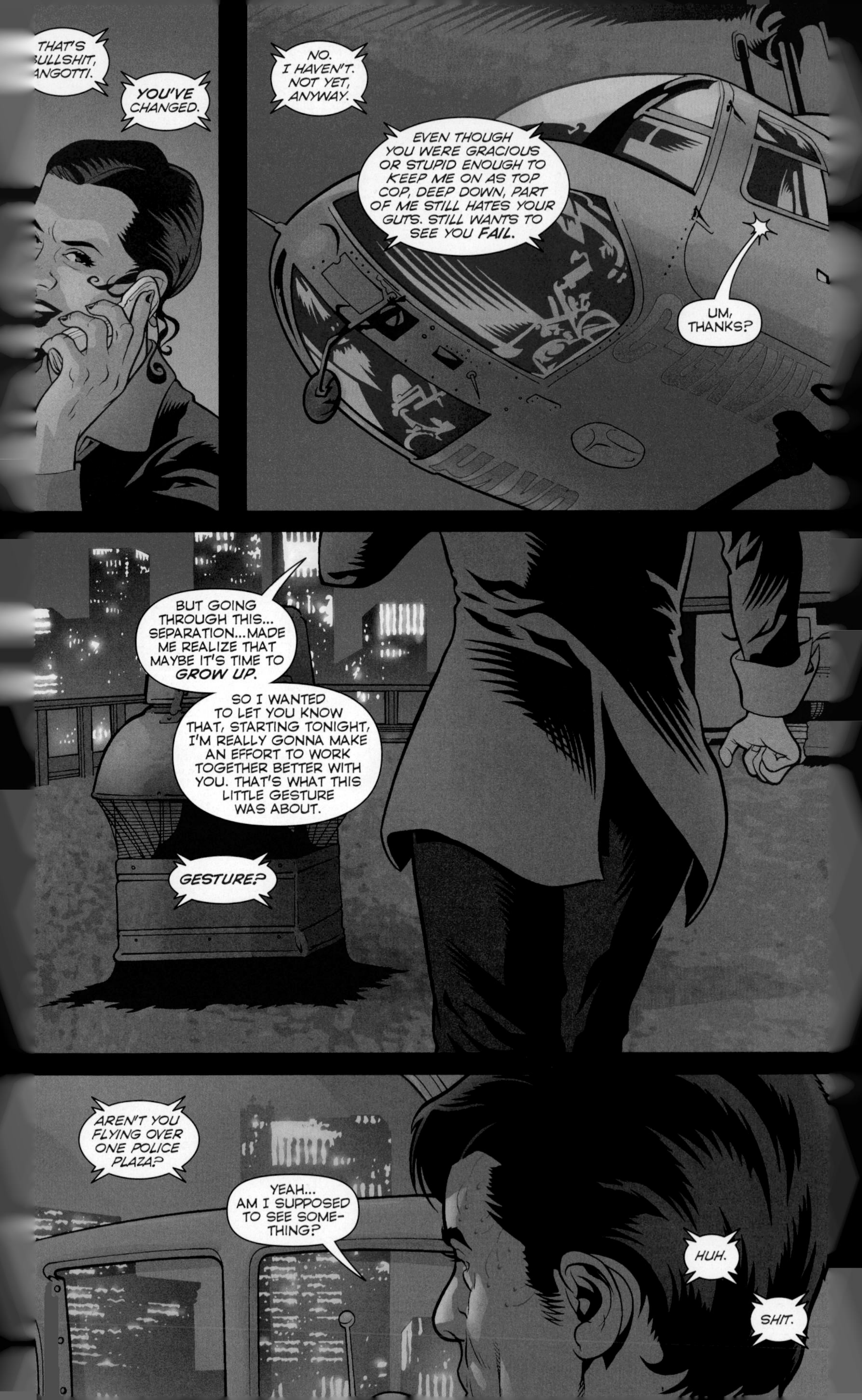
THAT'S BULLSHIT, ANGOTTI.
YOU'VE CHANGED.
NO. I HAVEN'T. NOT YET, ANYWAY.
EVEN THOUGH YOU WERE GRACIOUS OR STUPID ENOUGH TO KEEP ME ON AS TOP COP, DEEP DOWN, PART OF ME STILL HATES YOUR GUTS. STILL WANTS TO SEE YOU FAIL.
UM, THANKS?
BUT GOING THROUGH THIS... SEPARATION...MADE ME REALIZE THAT MAYBE IT'S TIME TO GROW UP.
SO I WANTED TO LET YOU KNOW THAT, STARTING TONIGHT, I'M REALLY GONNA MAKE AN EFFORT TO WORK TOGETHER BETTER WITH YOU. THAT'S WHAT THIS LITTLE GESTURE WAS ABOUT.
GESTURE?
AREN'T YOU FLYING OVER ONE POLICE PLAZA?
YEAH... AM I SUPPOSED TO SEE SOME-THING?
HUH.
SHIT.

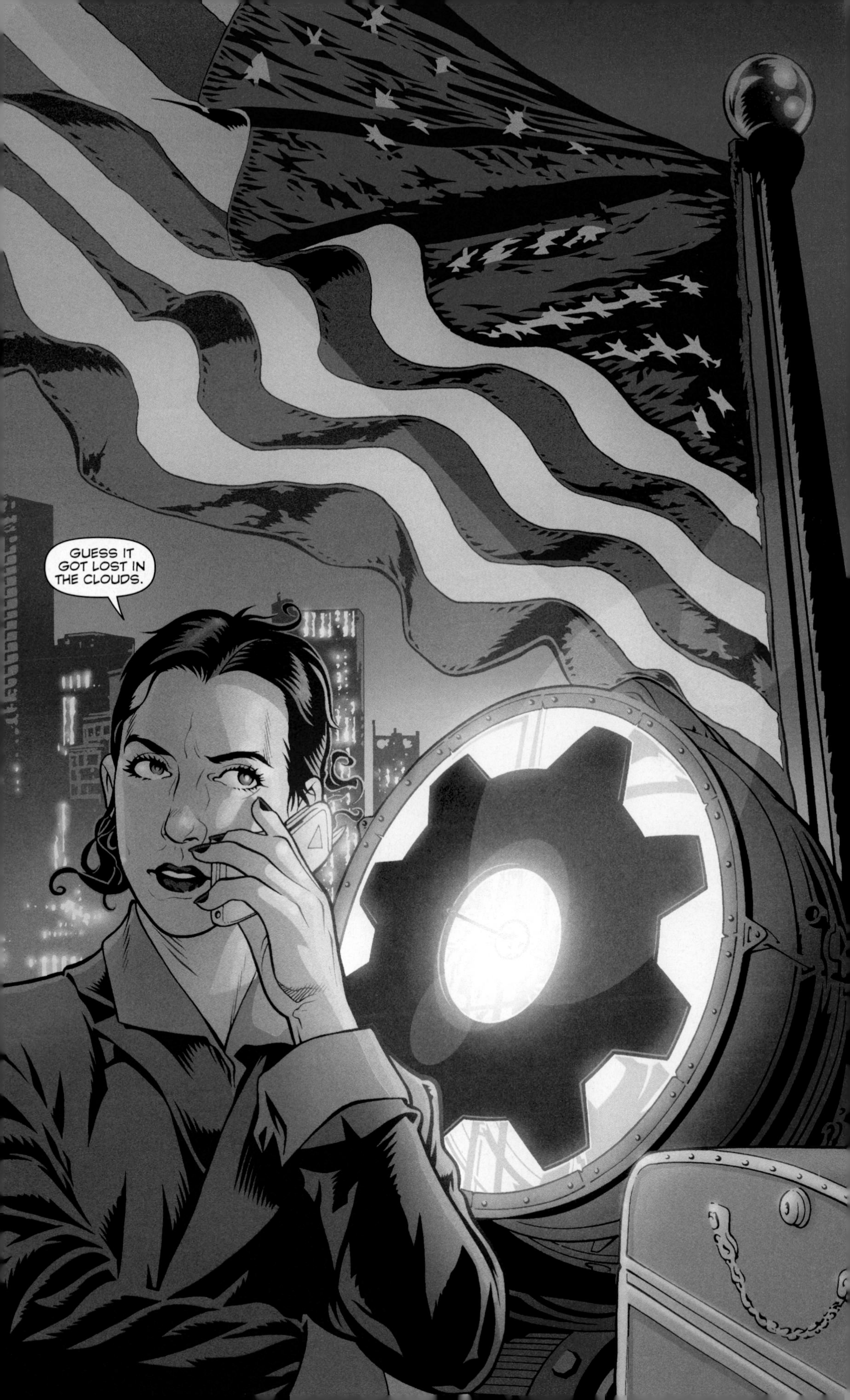
GUESS IT GOT LOST IN THE CLOUDS.

CHAPTER 3 THE RACE

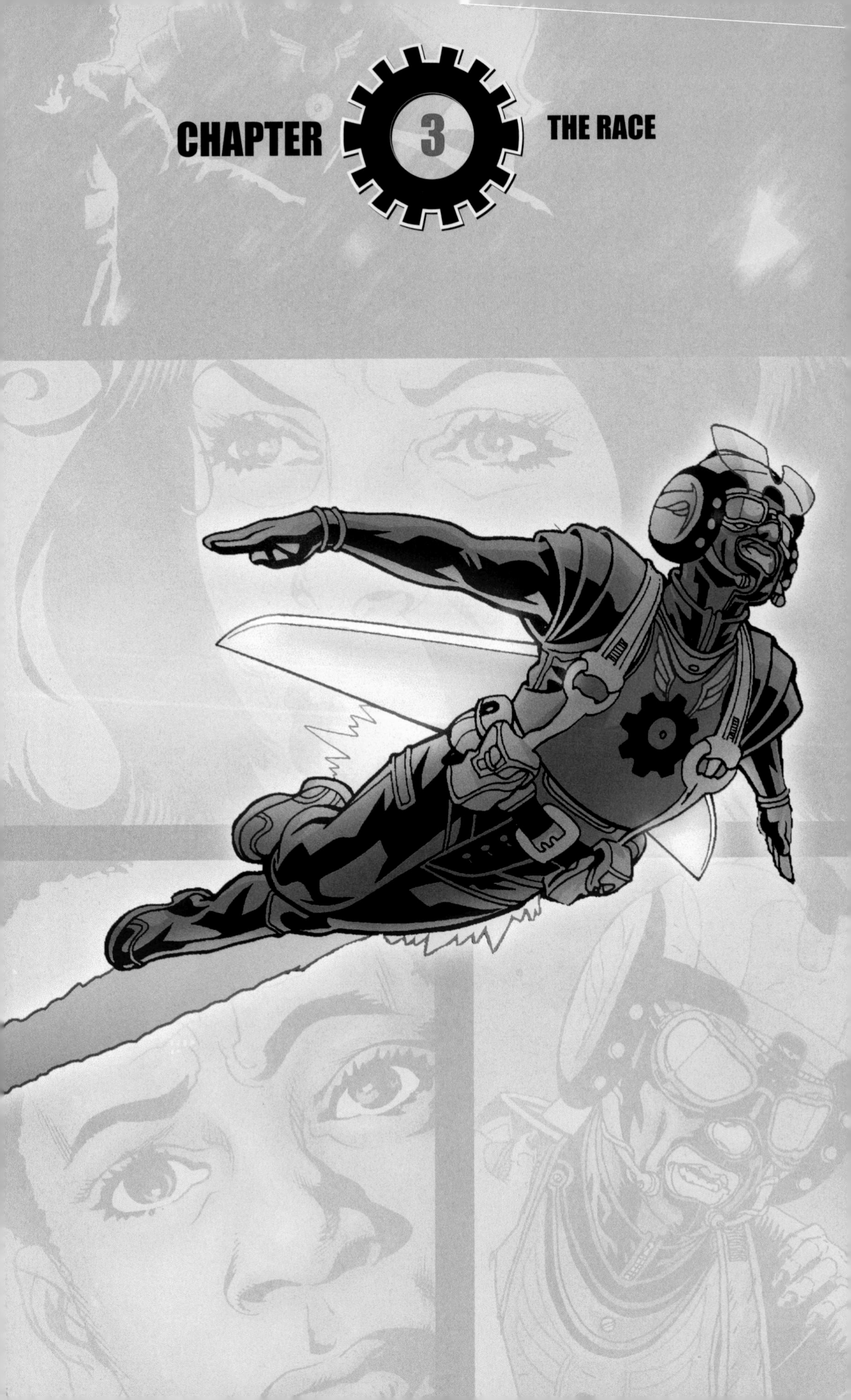

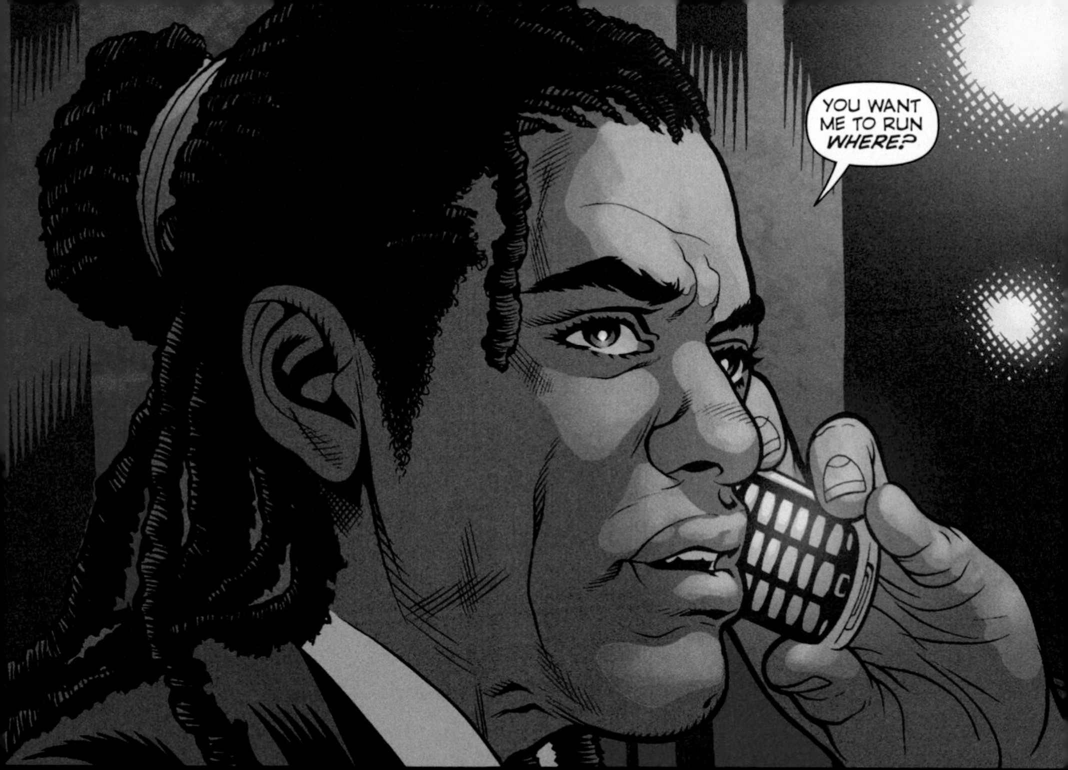
YOU WANT ME TO RUN *WHERE?*

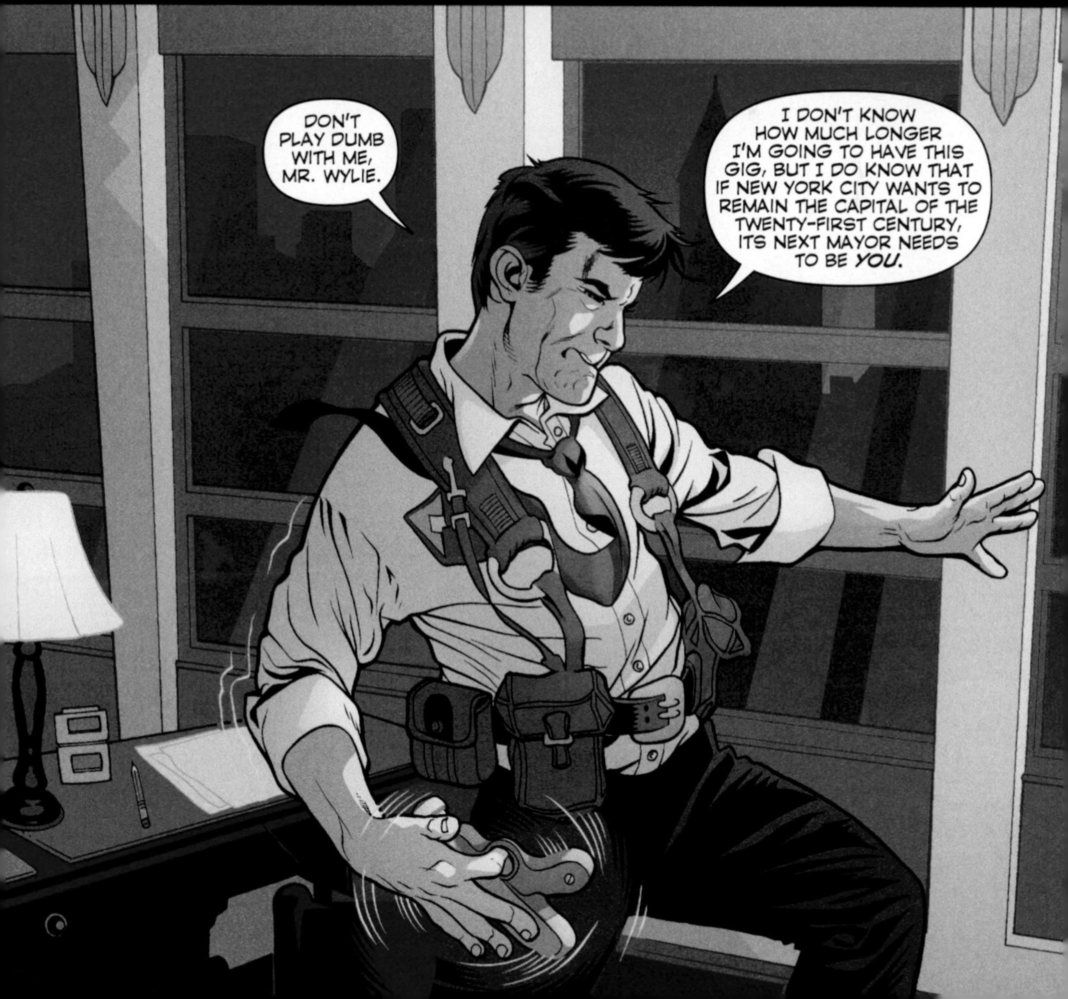
DON'T PLAY DUMB WITH ME, MR. WYLIE.
I DON'T KNOW HOW MUCH LONGER I'M GOING TO HAVE THIS GIG, BUT I DO KNOW THAT IF NEW YORK CITY WANTS TO REMAIN THE CAPITAL OF THE TWENTY-FIRST CENTURY, ITS NEXT MAYOR NEEDS TO BE *YOU*.

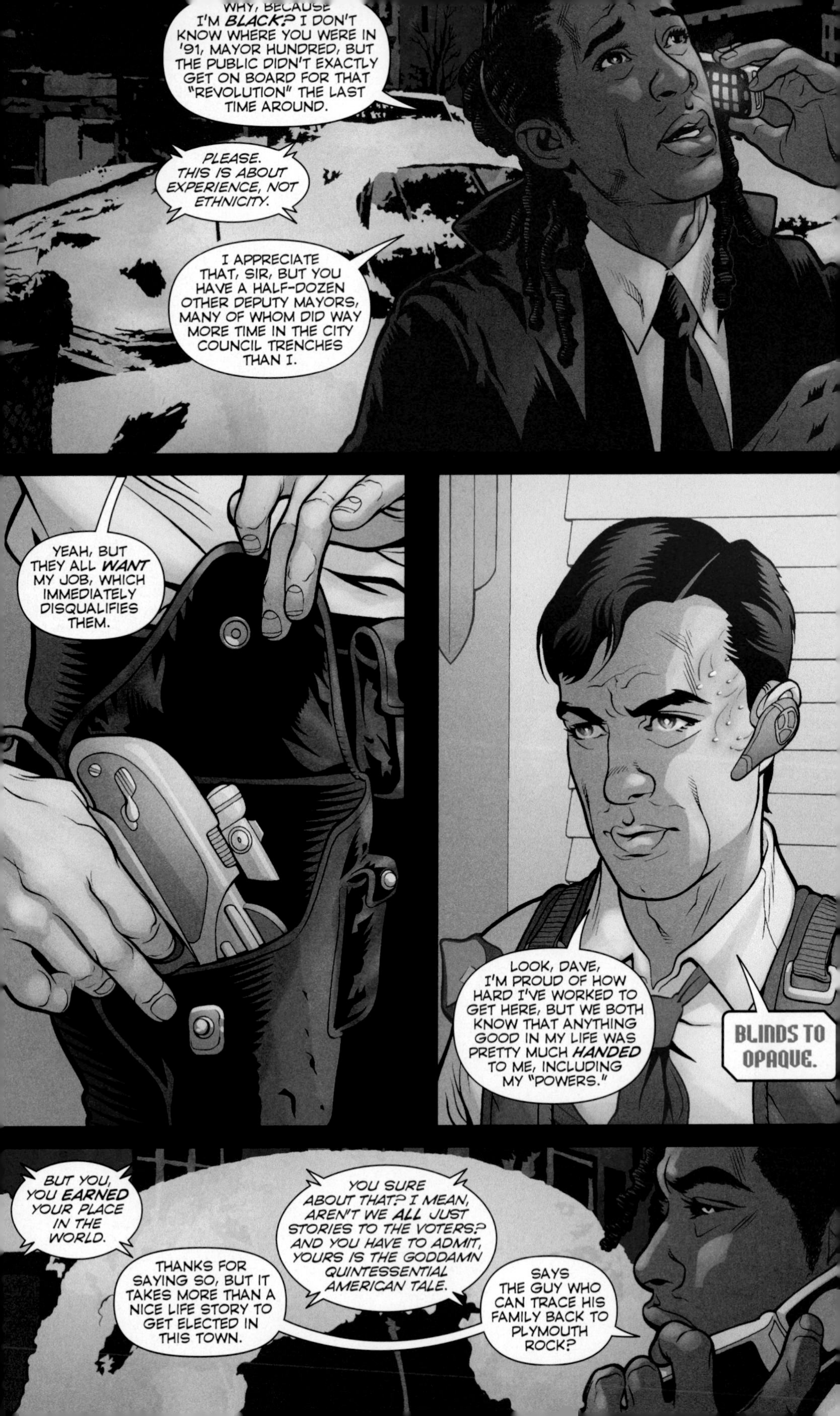
WHY, BECAUSE I'M *BLACK?* I DON'T KNOW WHERE YOU WERE IN '91, MAYOR HUNDRED, BUT THE PUBLIC DIDN'T EXACTLY GET ON BOARD FOR THAT "REVOLUTION" THE LAST TIME AROUND.
PLEASE. THIS IS ABOUT EXPERIENCE, NOT ETHNICITY.
I APPRECIATE THAT, SIR, BUT YOU HAVE A HALF-DOZEN OTHER DEPUTY MAYORS, MANY OF WHOM DID WAY MORE TIME IN THE CITY COUNCIL TRENCHES THAN I.
YEAH, BUT THEY ALL *WANT* MY JOB, WHICH IMMEDIATELY DISQUALIFIES THEM.
LOOK, DAVE, I'M PROUD OF HOW HARD I'VE WORKED TO GET HERE, BUT WE BOTH KNOW THAT ANYTHING GOOD IN MY LIFE WAS PRETTY MUCH *HANDED* TO ME, INCLUDING MY "POWERS."
BLINDS TO OPAQUE.
BUT YOU, YOU *EARNED* YOUR PLACE IN THE WORLD.
THANKS FOR SAYING SO, BUT IT TAKES MORE THAN A NICE LIFE STORY TO GET ELECTED IN THIS TOWN.
YOU SURE ABOUT THAT? I MEAN, AREN'T WE *ALL* JUST STORIES TO THE VOTERS? AND YOU HAVE TO ADMIT, YOURS IS THE GODDAMN QUINTESSENTIAL AMERICAN TALE.
SAYS THE GUY WHO CAN TRACE HIS FAMILY BACK TO PLYMOUTH ROCK?

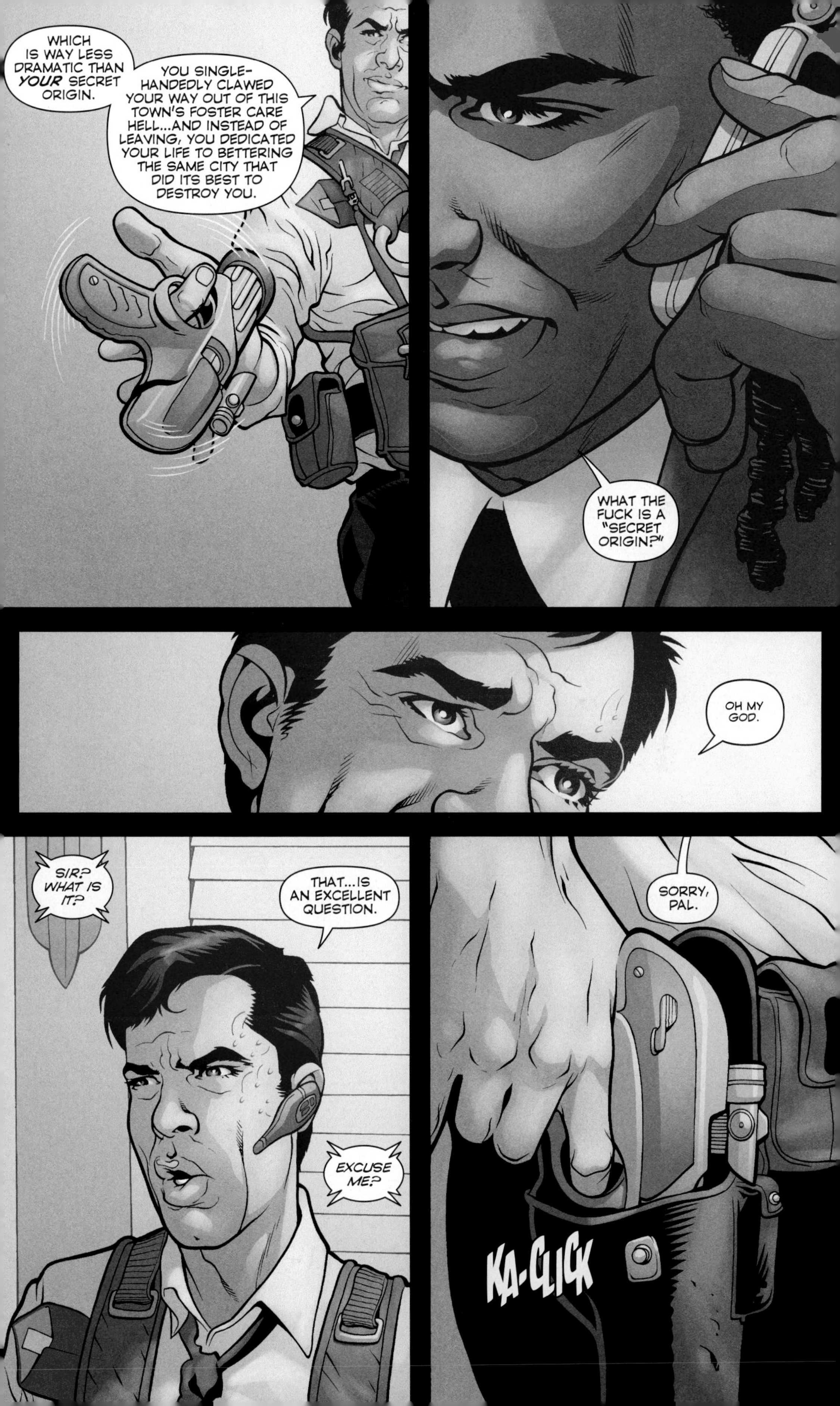
WHICH IS WAY LESS DRAMATIC THAN *YOUR* SECRET ORIGIN.
YOU SINGLE-HANDEDLY CLAWED YOUR WAY OUT OF THIS TOWN'S FOSTER CARE HELL...AND INSTEAD OF LEAVING, YOU DEDICATED YOUR LIFE TO BETTERING THE SAME CITY THAT DID ITS BEST TO DESTROY YOU.
WHAT THE FUCK IS A "SECRET ORIGIN?"
OH MY GOD.
SIR? WHAT IS IT?
THAT...IS AN EXCELLENT QUESTION.
EXCUSE ME?
SORRY, PAL.
KA-CLICK

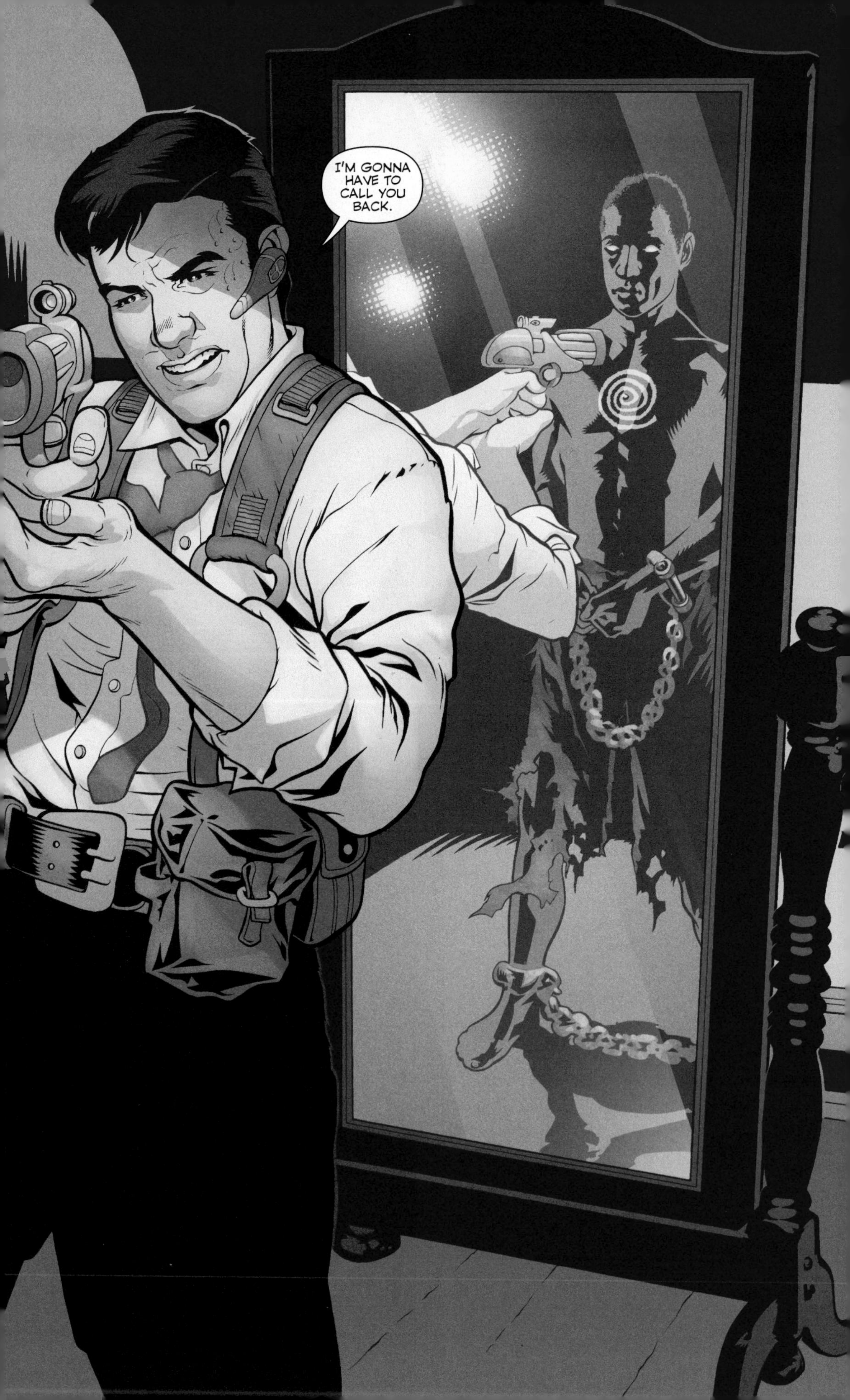
I'M GONNA HAVE TO CALL YOU BACK.

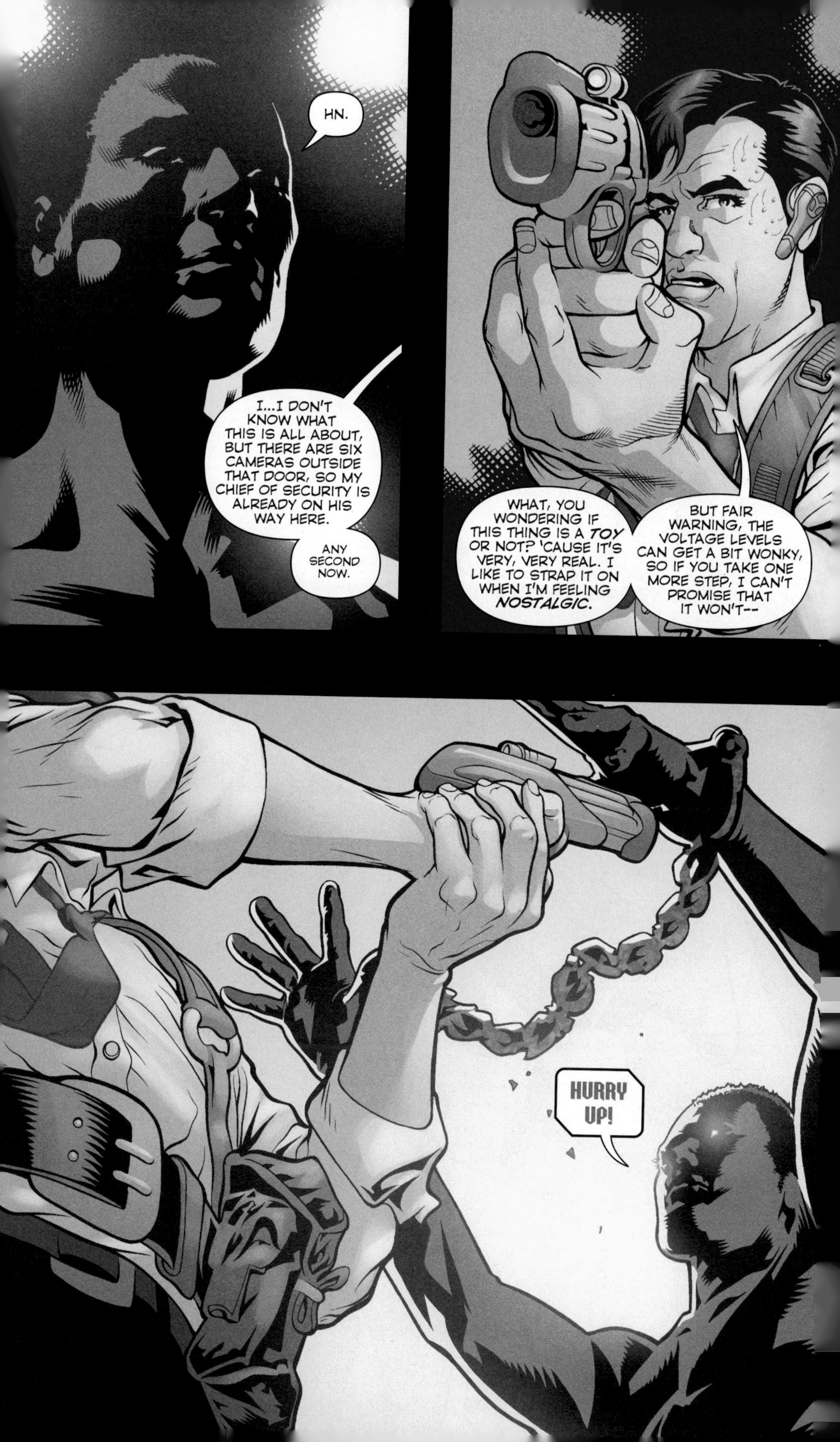
HN.
I...I DON'T KNOW WHAT THIS IS ALL ABOUT, BUT THERE ARE SIX CAMERAS OUTSIDE THAT DOOR, SO MY CHIEF OF SECURITY IS ALREADY ON HIS WAY HERE.
ANY SECOND NOW.
WHAT, YOU WONDERING IF THIS THING IS A TOY OR NOT? 'CAUSE IT'S VERY, VERY REAL. I LIKE TO STRAP IT ON WHEN I'M FEELING NOSTALGIC.
BUT FAIR WARNING, THE VOLTAGE LEVELS CAN GET A BIT WONKY, SO IF YOU TAKE ONE MORE STEP, I CAN'T PROMISE THAT IT WON'T--
HURRY UP!

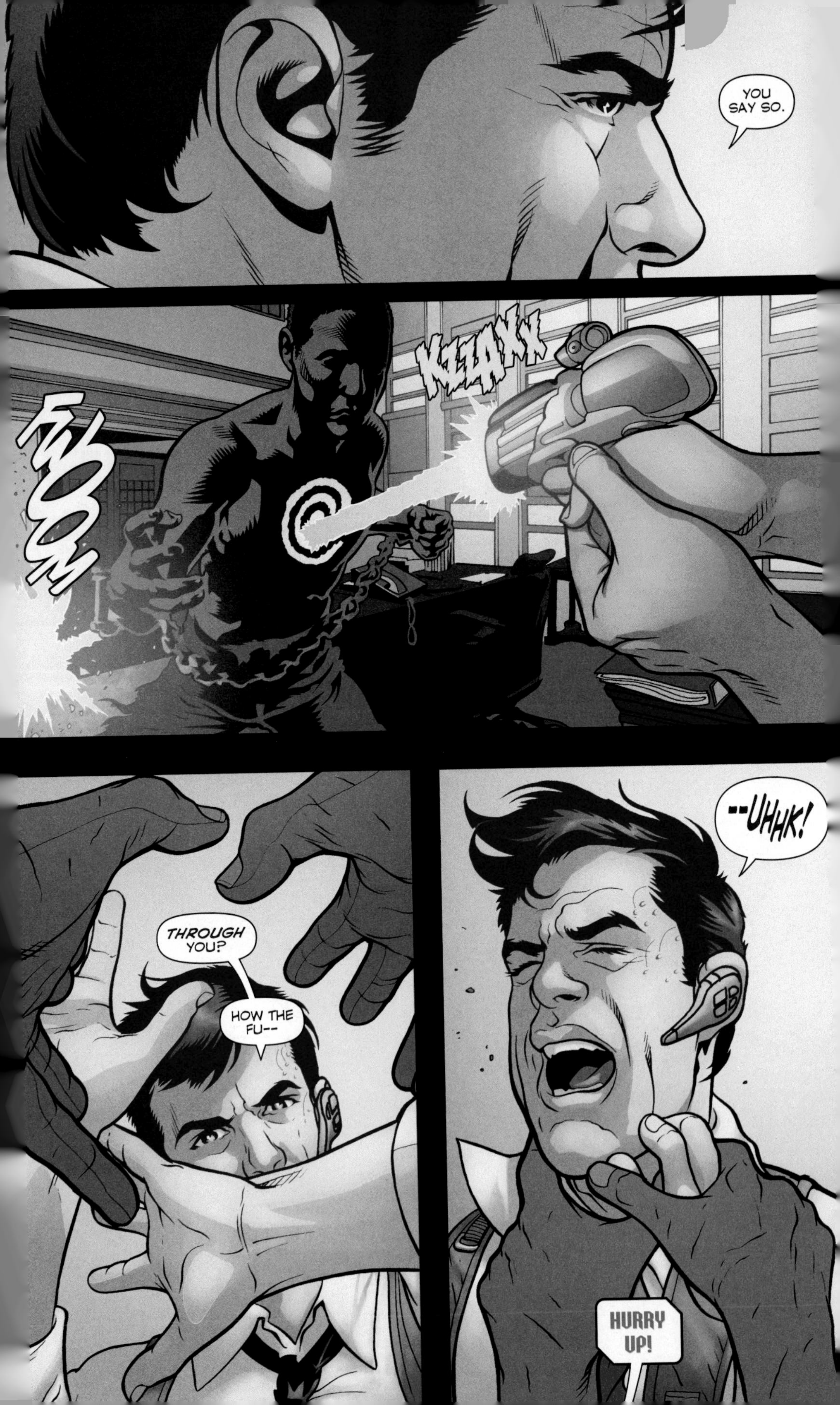
YOU SAY SO.
KZZAXX
FWOOM
THROUGH YOU?
HOW THE FU--
--UHHK!
HURRY UP!

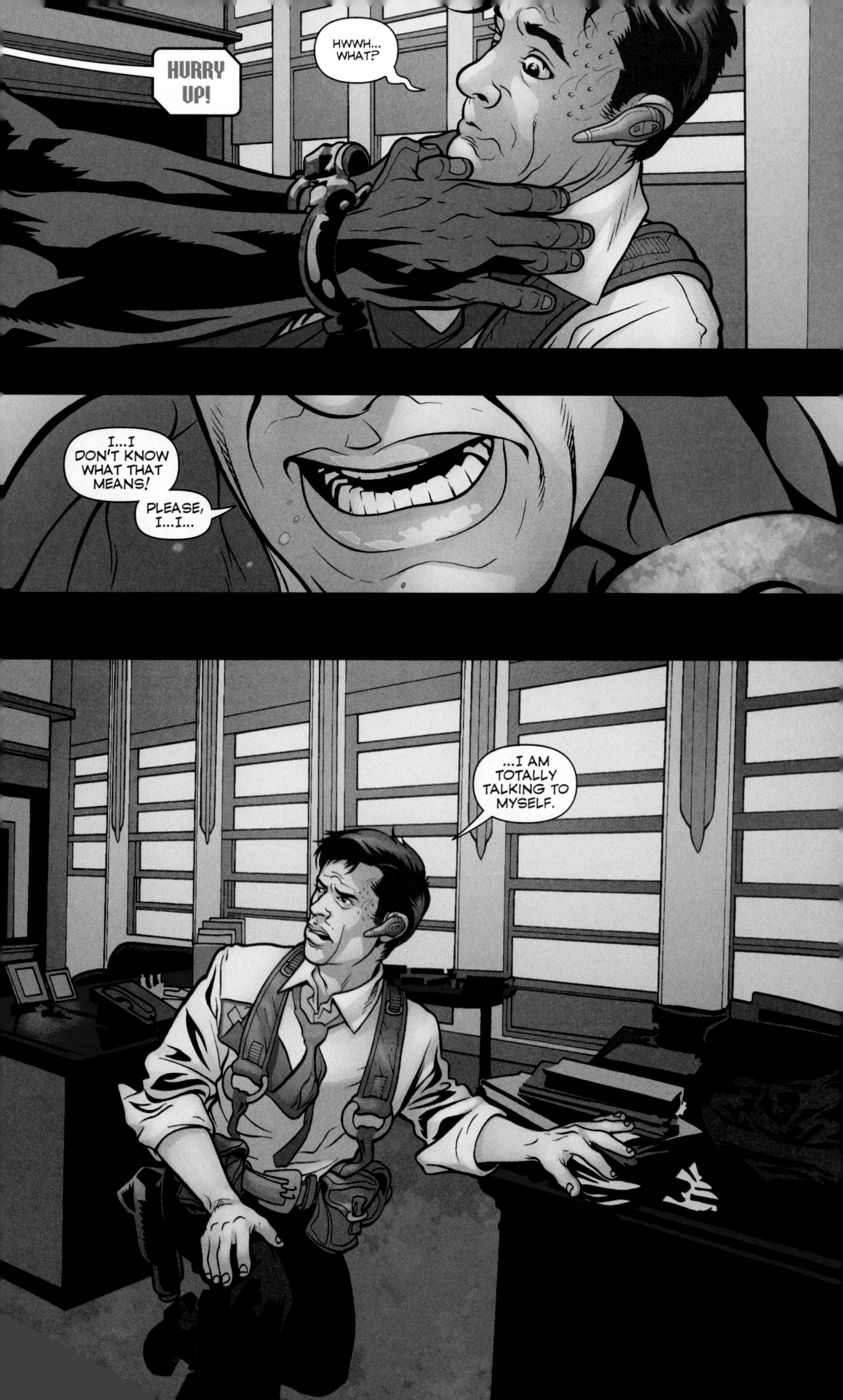
HURRY UP!
HWWH... WHAT?
I...I DON'T KNOW WHAT THAT MEANS!
PLEASE, I...I...
...I AM TOTALLY TALKING TO MYSELF.

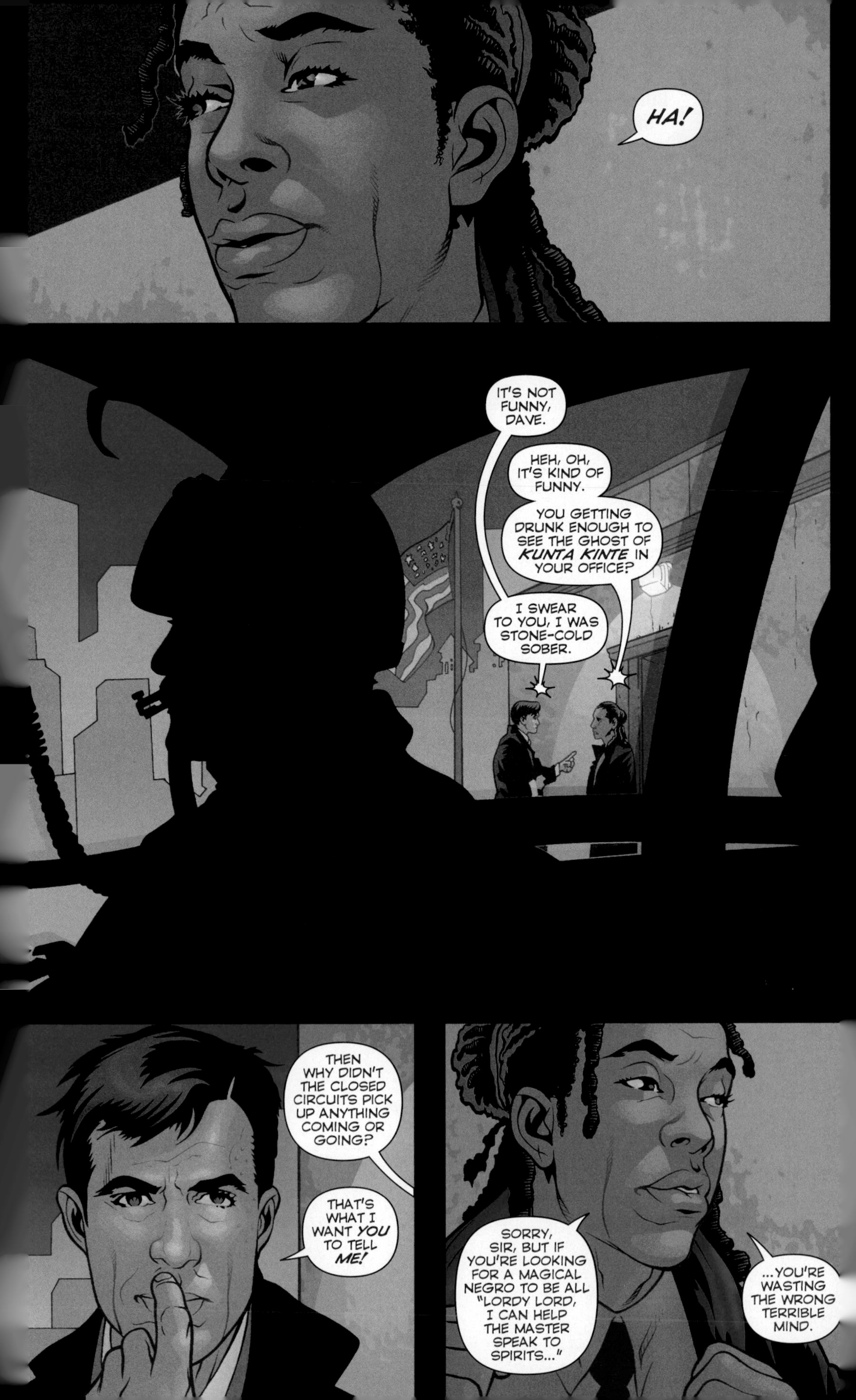
HA!
IT'S NOT FUNNY, DAVE.
HEH, OH, IT'S KIND OF FUNNY.
YOU GETTING DRUNK ENOUGH TO SEE THE GHOST OF *KUNTA KINTE* IN YOUR OFFICE?
I SWEAR TO YOU, I WAS STONE-COLD SOBER.
THEN WHY DIDN'T THE CLOSED CIRCUITS PICK UP ANYTHING COMING OR GOING?
THAT'S WHAT I WANT *YOU* TO TELL *ME!*
SORRY, SIR, BUT IF YOU'RE LOOKING FOR A MAGICAL NEGRO TO BE ALL "LORDY LORD, I CAN HELP THE MASTER SPEAK TO SPIRITS..."
...YOU'RE WASTING THE WRONG TERRIBLE MIND.

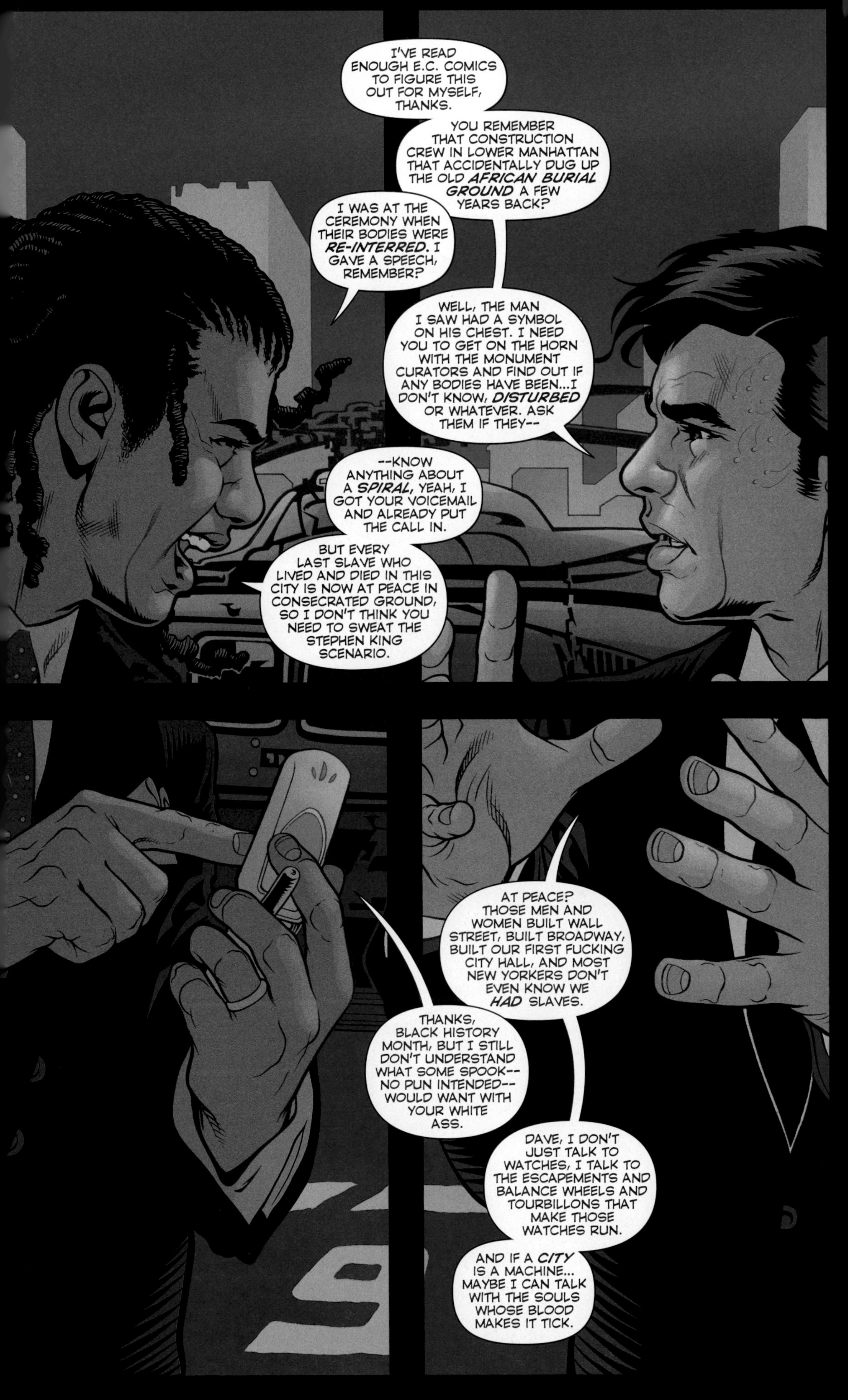
I'VE READ ENOUGH E.C. COMICS TO FIGURE THIS OUT FOR MYSELF, THANKS.
YOU REMEMBER THAT CONSTRUCTION CREW IN LOWER MANHATTAN THAT ACCIDENTALLY DUG UP THE OLD *AFRICAN BURIAL GROUND* A FEW YEARS BACK?
I WAS AT THE CEREMONY WHEN THEIR BODIES WERE *RE-INTERRED*. I GAVE A SPEECH, REMEMBER?
WELL, THE MAN I SAW HAD A SYMBOL ON HIS CHEST. I NEED YOU TO GET ON THE HORN WITH THE MONUMENT CURATORS AND FIND OUT IF ANY BODIES HAVE BEEN...I DON'T KNOW, *DISTURBED* OR WHATEVER. ASK THEM IF THEY--
--KNOW ANYTHING ABOUT A *SPIRAL*, YEAH, I GOT YOUR VOICEMAIL AND ALREADY PUT THE CALL IN.
BUT EVERY LAST SLAVE WHO LIVED AND DIED IN THIS CITY IS NOW AT PEACE IN CONSECRATED GROUND, SO I DON'T THINK YOU NEED TO SWEAT THE STEPHEN KING SCENARIO.
AT PEACE? THOSE MEN AND WOMEN BUILT WALL STREET, BUILT BROADWAY, BUILT OUR FIRST FUCKING CITY HALL, AND MOST NEW YORKERS DON'T EVEN KNOW WE *HAD* SLAVES.
THANKS, BLACK HISTORY MONTH, BUT I STILL DON'T UNDERSTAND WHAT SOME SPOOK-- NO PUN INTENDED-- WOULD WANT WITH YOUR WHITE ASS.
DAVE, I DON'T JUST TALK TO WATCHES, I TALK TO THE ESCAPEMENTS AND BALANCE WHEELS AND TOURBILLONS THAT MAKE THOSE WATCHES RUN.
AND IF A *CITY* IS A MACHINE... MAYBE I CAN TALK WITH THE SOULS WHOSE BLOOD MAKES IT TICK.

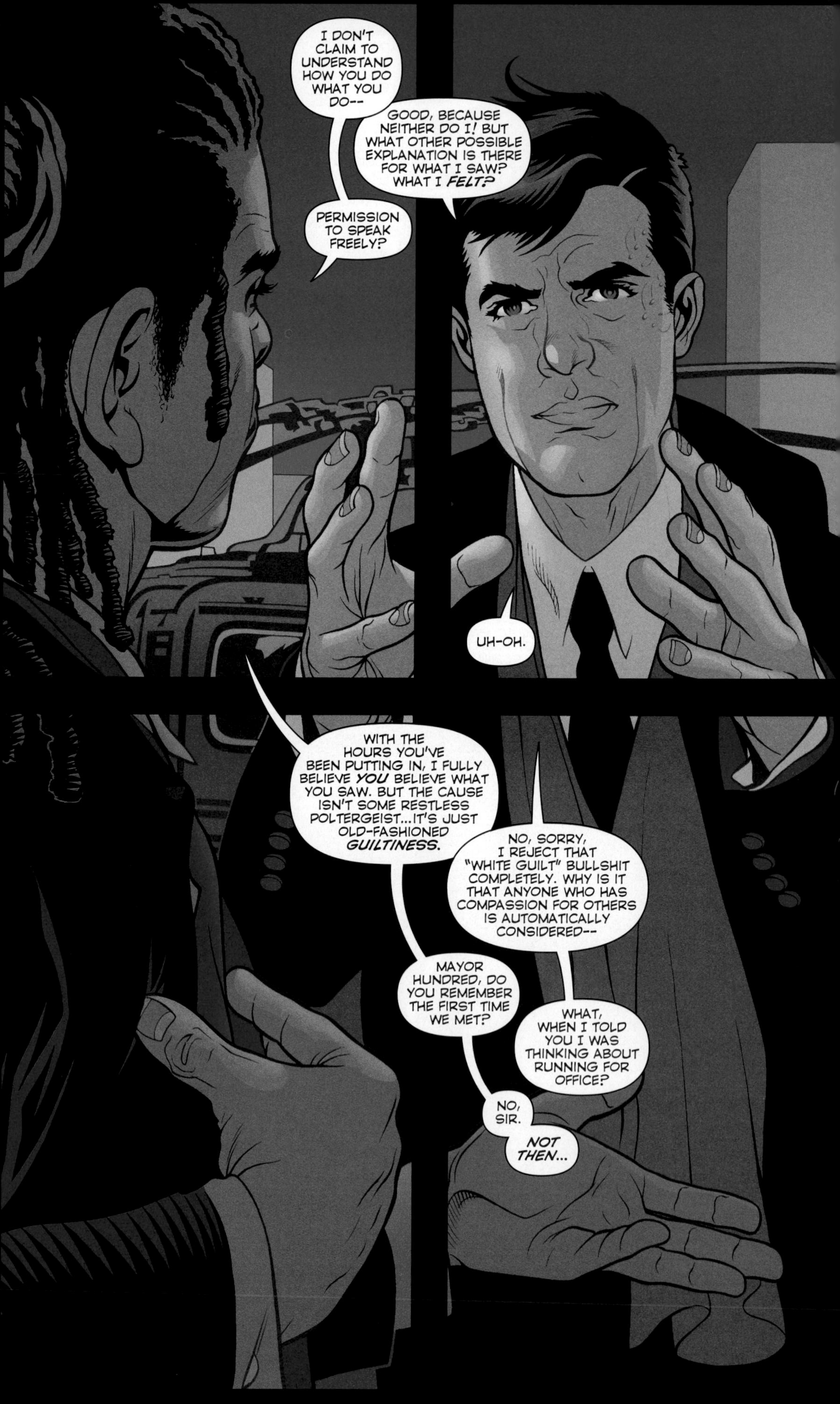

I DON'T CLAIM TO UNDERSTAND HOW YOU DO WHAT YOU DO--
GOOD, BECAUSE NEITHER DO I! BUT WHAT OTHER POSSIBLE EXPLANATION IS THERE FOR WHAT I SAW? WHAT I *FELT?*
PERMISSION TO SPEAK FREELY?
UH-OH.
WITH THE HOURS YOU'VE BEEN PUTTING IN, I FULLY BELIEVE ***YOU*** BELIEVE WHAT YOU SAW. BUT THE CAUSE ISN'T SOME RESTLESS POLTERGEIST...IT'S JUST OLD-FASHIONED ***GUILTINESS.***
NO, SORRY, I REJECT THAT "WHITE GUILT" BULLSHIT COMPLETELY. WHY IS IT THAT ANYONE WHO HAS COMPASSION FOR OTHERS IS AUTOMATICALLY CONSIDERED--
MAYOR HUNDRED, DO YOU REMEMBER THE FIRST TIME WE MET?
WHAT, WHEN I TOLD YOU I WAS THINKING ABOUT RUNNING FOR OFFICE?
NO, SIR.
NOT THEN...

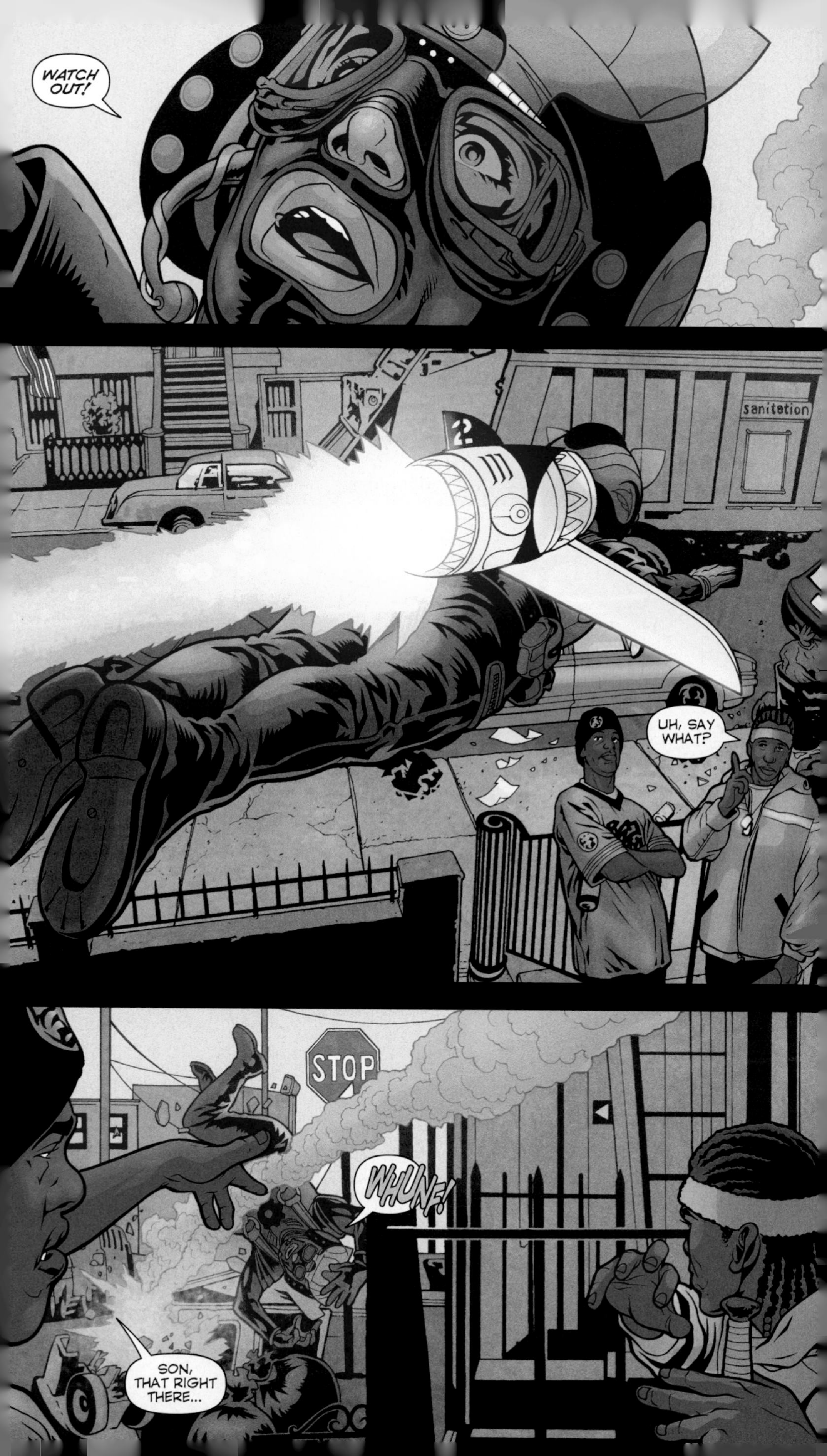
WATCH OUT!
UH, SAY WHAT?
sanitation
2
STOP
WHUNF!
SON, THAT RIGHT THERE...

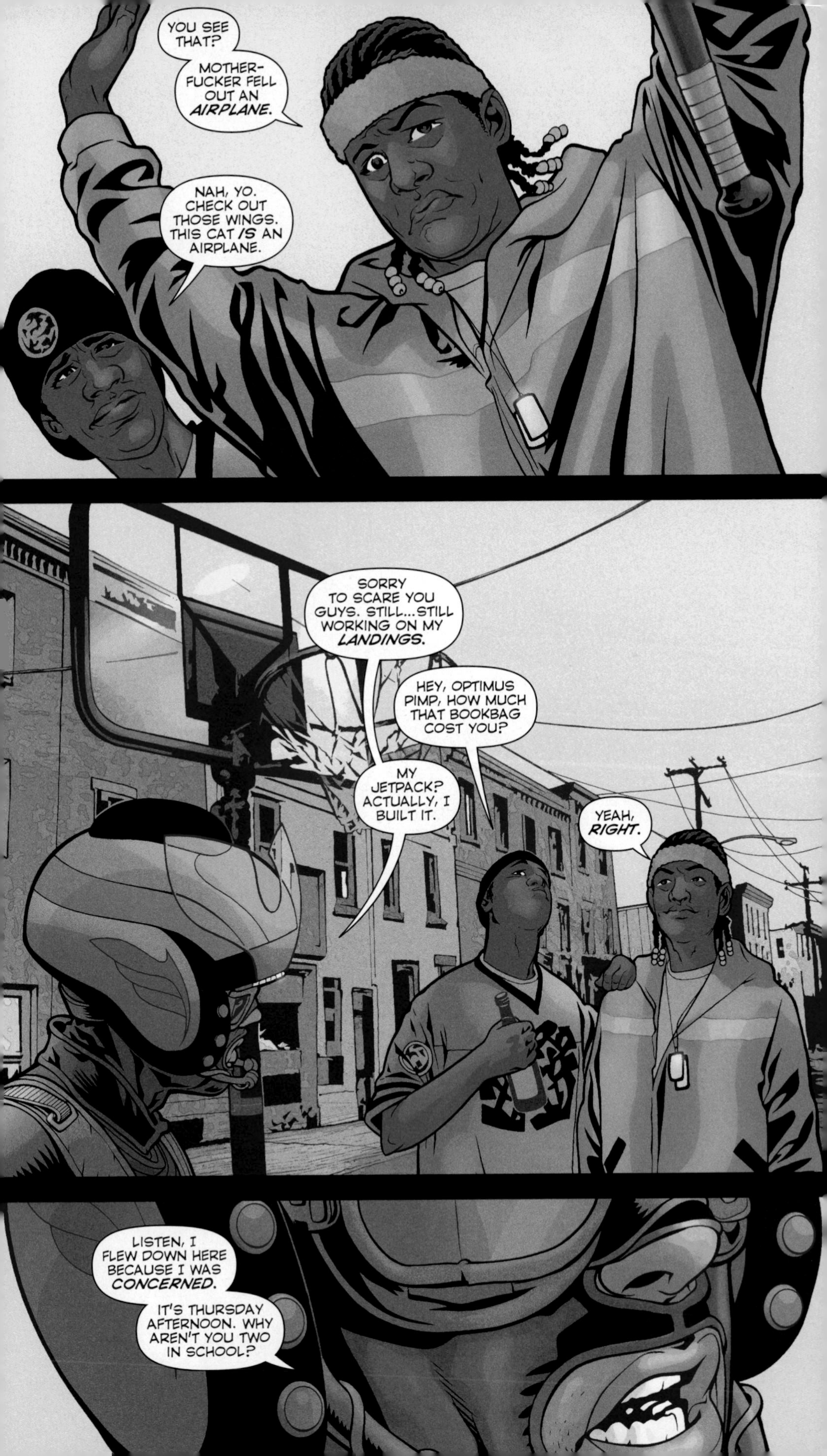
YOU SEE THAT?
MOTHER-FUCKER FELL OUT AN *AIRPLANE*.
NAH, YO. CHECK OUT THOSE WINGS. THIS CAT *IS* AN AIRPLANE.
SORRY TO SCARE YOU GUYS. STILL...STILL WORKING ON MY *LANDINGS*.
HEY, OPTIMUS PIMP, HOW MUCH THAT BOOKBAG COST YOU?
MY JETPACK? ACTUALLY, I BUILT IT.
YEAH, *RIGHT*.
LISTEN, I FLEW DOWN HERE BECAUSE I WAS *CONCERNED*.
IT'S THURSDAY AFTERNOON. WHY AREN'T YOU TWO IN SCHOOL?

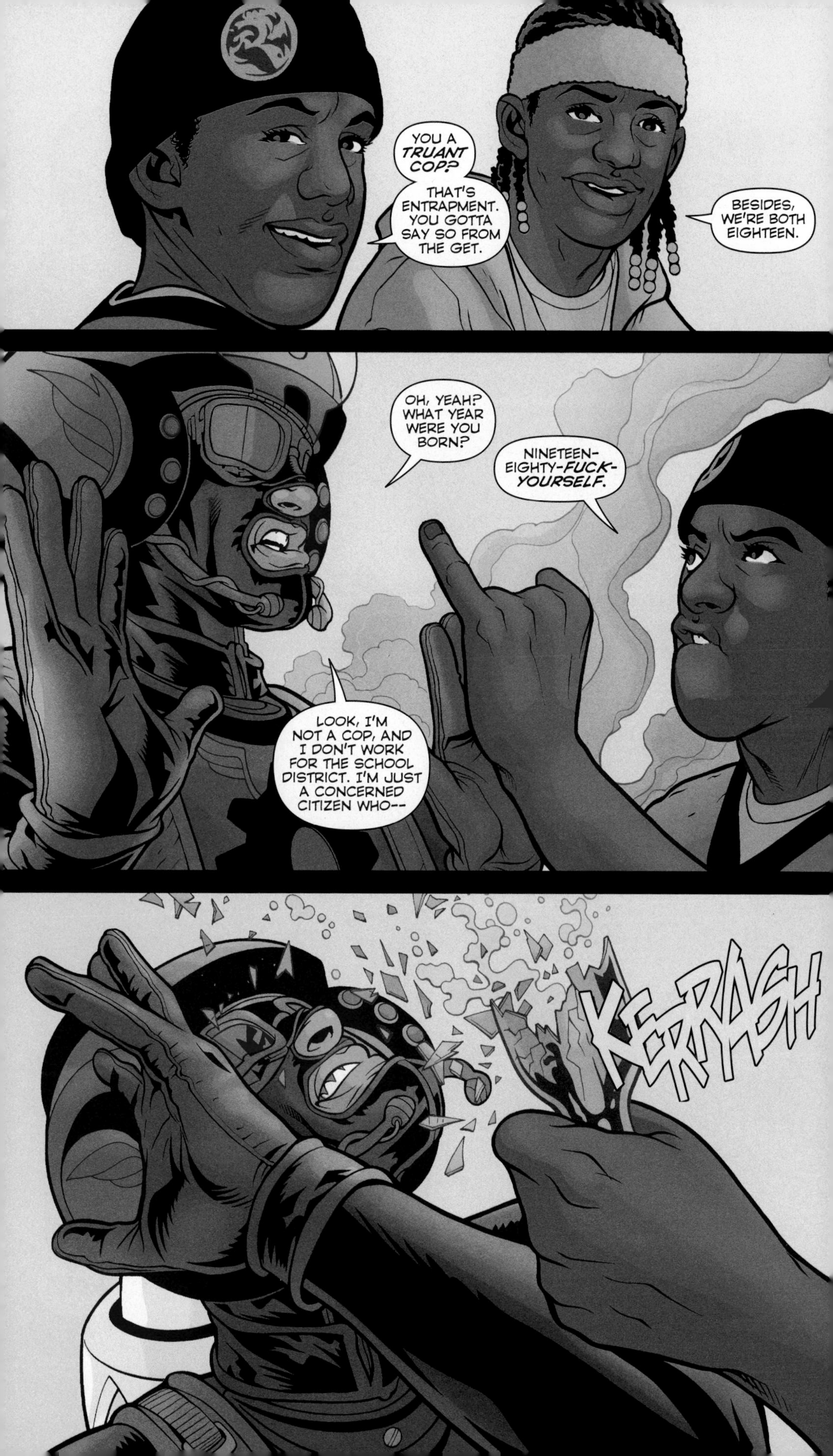
YOU A *TRUANT COP?*
THAT'S ENTRAPMENT. YOU GOTTA SAY SO FROM THE GET.
BESIDES, WE'RE BOTH EIGHTEEN.
OH, YEAH? WHAT YEAR WERE YOU BORN?
NINETEEN-EIGHTY-*FUCK-YOURSELF.*
LOOK, I'M NOT A COP, AND I DON'T WORK FOR THE SCHOOL DISTRICT. I'M JUST A CONCERNED CITIZEN WHO--
KRASH

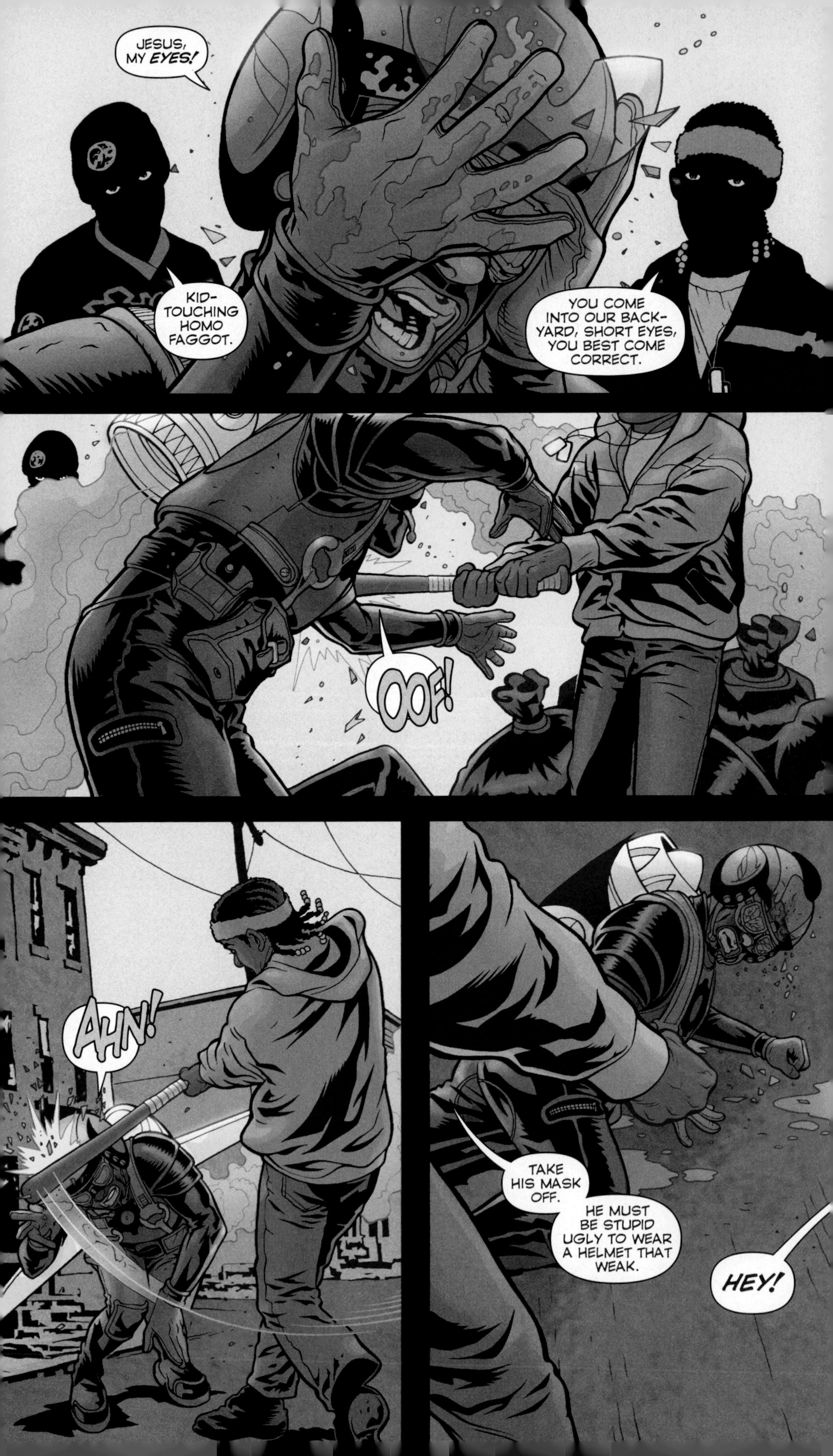
JESUS, MY *EYES!*
KID-TOUCHING HOMO FAGGOT.
YOU COME INTO OUR BACK-YARD, SHORT EYES, YOU BEST COME CORRECT.
OOF!
AHN!
TAKE HIS MASK OFF.
HE MUST BE STUPID UGLY TO WEAR A HELMET THAT WEAK.
HEY!

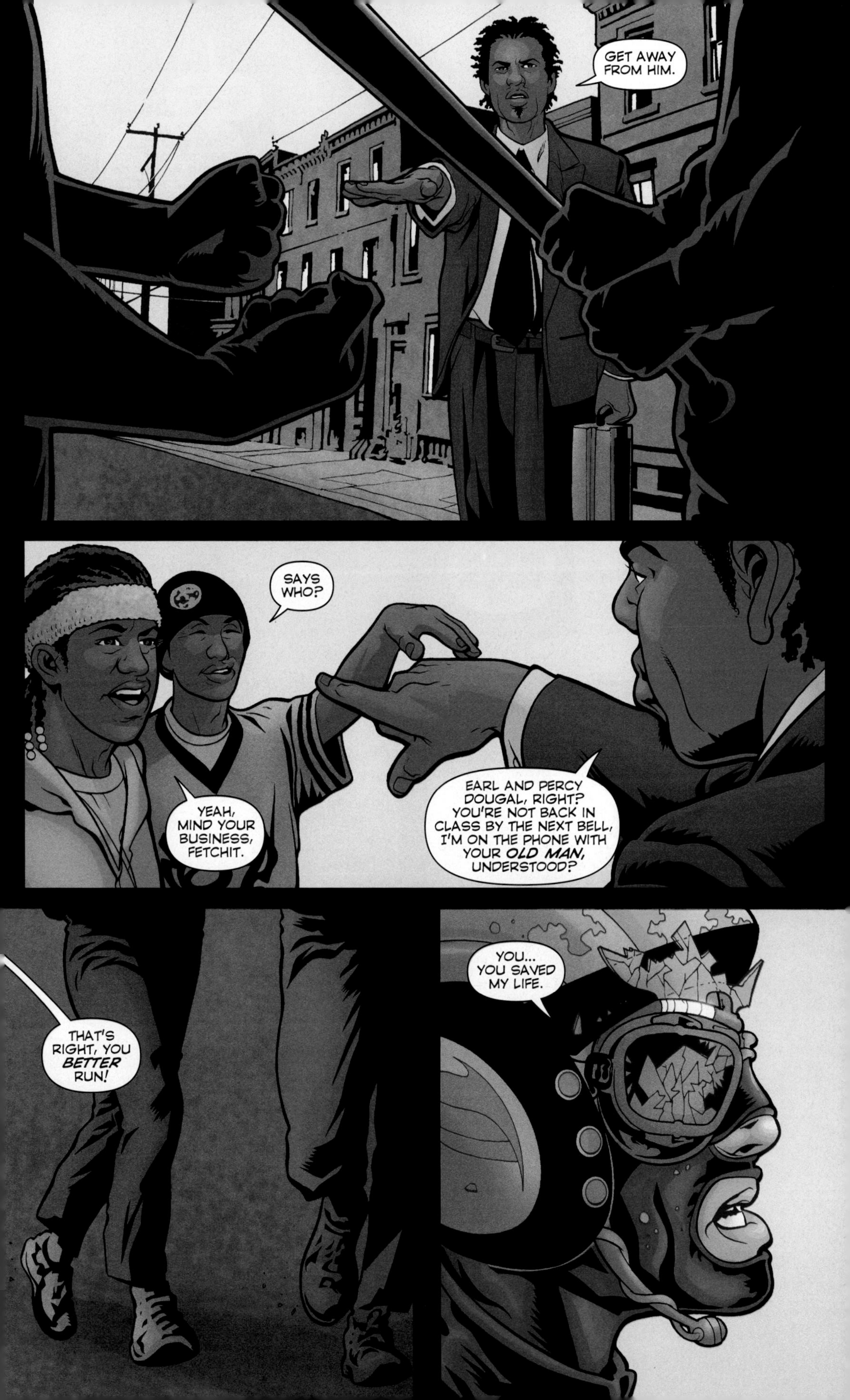
GET AWAY FROM HIM.
SAYS WHO?
YEAH, MIND YOUR BUSINESS, FETCHIT.
EARL AND PERCY DOUGAL, RIGHT? YOU'RE NOT BACK IN CLASS BY THE NEXT BELL, I'M ON THE PHONE WITH YOUR *OLD MAN,* UNDERSTOOD?
THAT'S RIGHT, YOU *BETTER* RUN!
YOU... YOU SAVED MY LIFE.

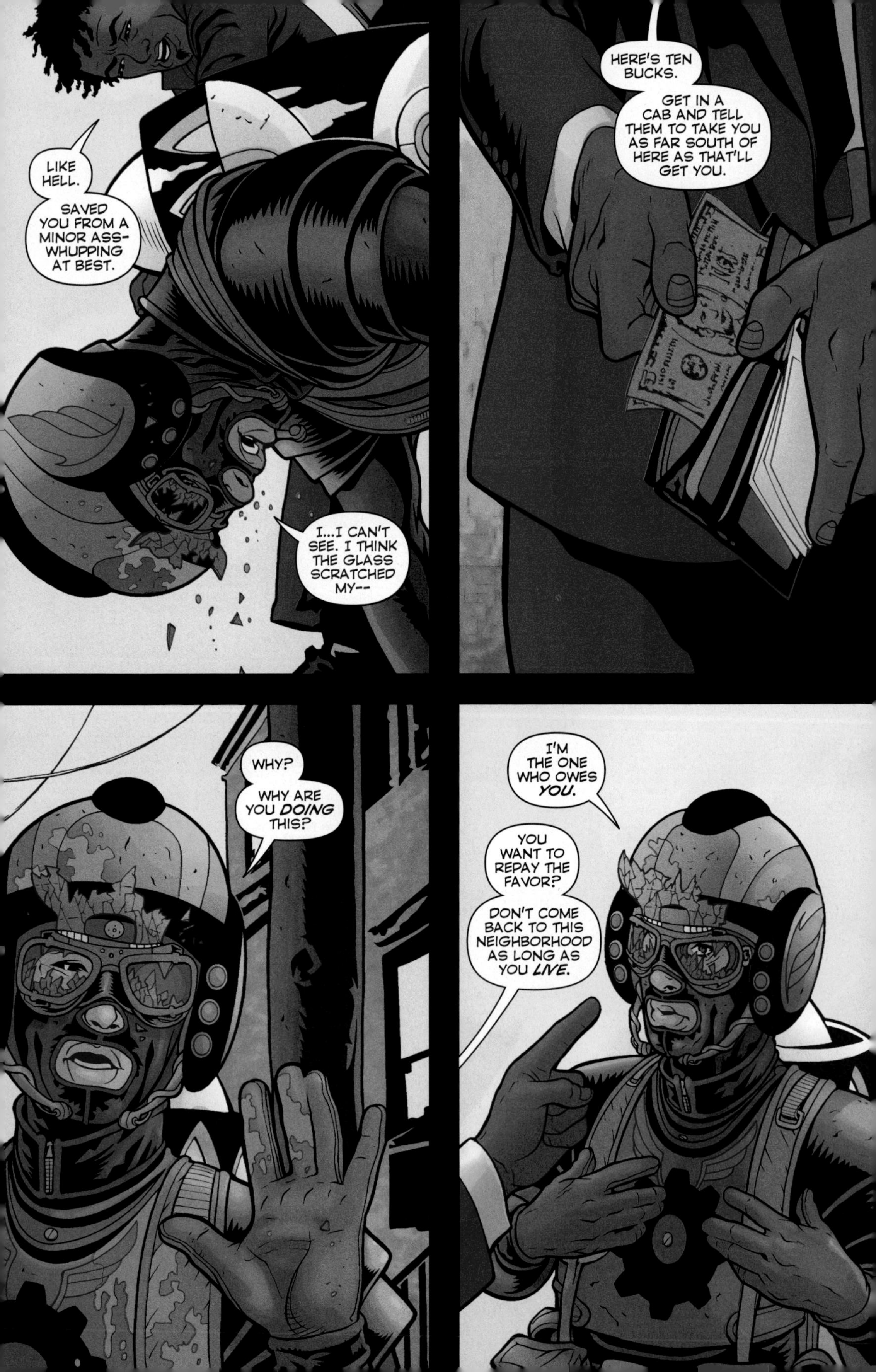
LIKE HELL.
SAVED YOU FROM A MINOR ASS-WHUPPING AT BEST.
I...I CAN'T SEE. I THINK THE GLASS SCRATCHED MY--
HERE'S TEN BUCKS.
GET IN A CAB AND TELL THEM TO TAKE YOU AS FAR SOUTH OF HERE AS THAT'LL GET YOU.
WHY?
WHY ARE YOU *DOING* THIS?
I'M THE ONE WHO OWES *YOU*.
YOU WANT TO REPAY THE FAVOR?
DON'T COME BACK TO THIS NEIGHBORHOOD AS LONG AS YOU *LIVE*.

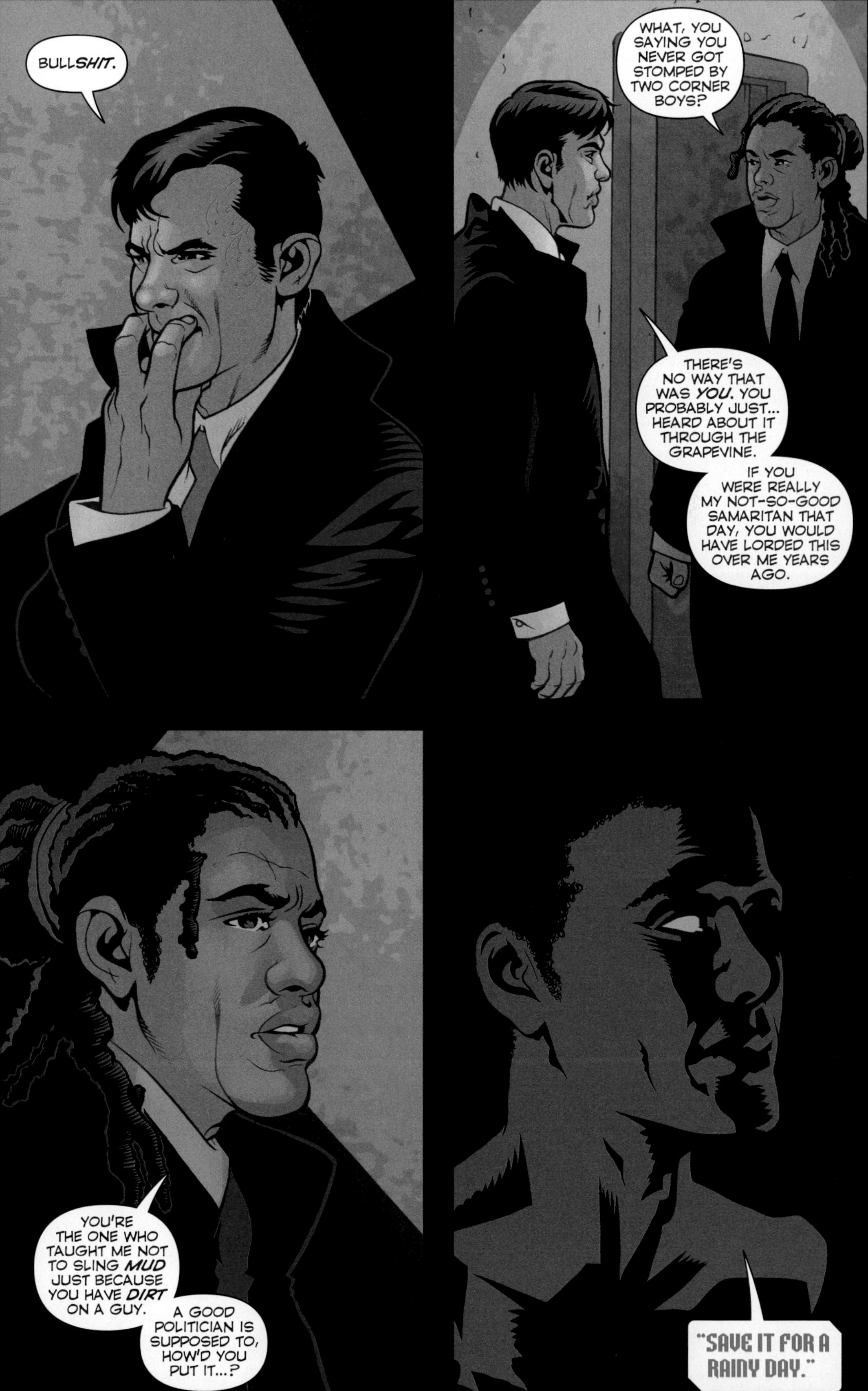
BULLSHIT.
WHAT, YOU SAYING YOU NEVER GOT STOMPED BY TWO CORNER BOYS?
THERE'S NO WAY THAT WAS YOU. YOU PROBABLY JUST... HEARD ABOUT IT THROUGH THE GRAPEVINE.
IF YOU WERE REALLY MY NOT-SO-GOOD SAMARITAN THAT DAY, YOU WOULD HAVE LORDED THIS OVER ME YEARS AGO.
YOU'RE THE ONE WHO TAUGHT ME NOT TO SLING MUD JUST BECAUSE YOU HAVE DIRT ON A GUY.
A GOOD POLITICIAN IS SUPPOSED TO, HOW'D YOU PUT IT...?
"SAVE IT FOR A RAINY DAY."

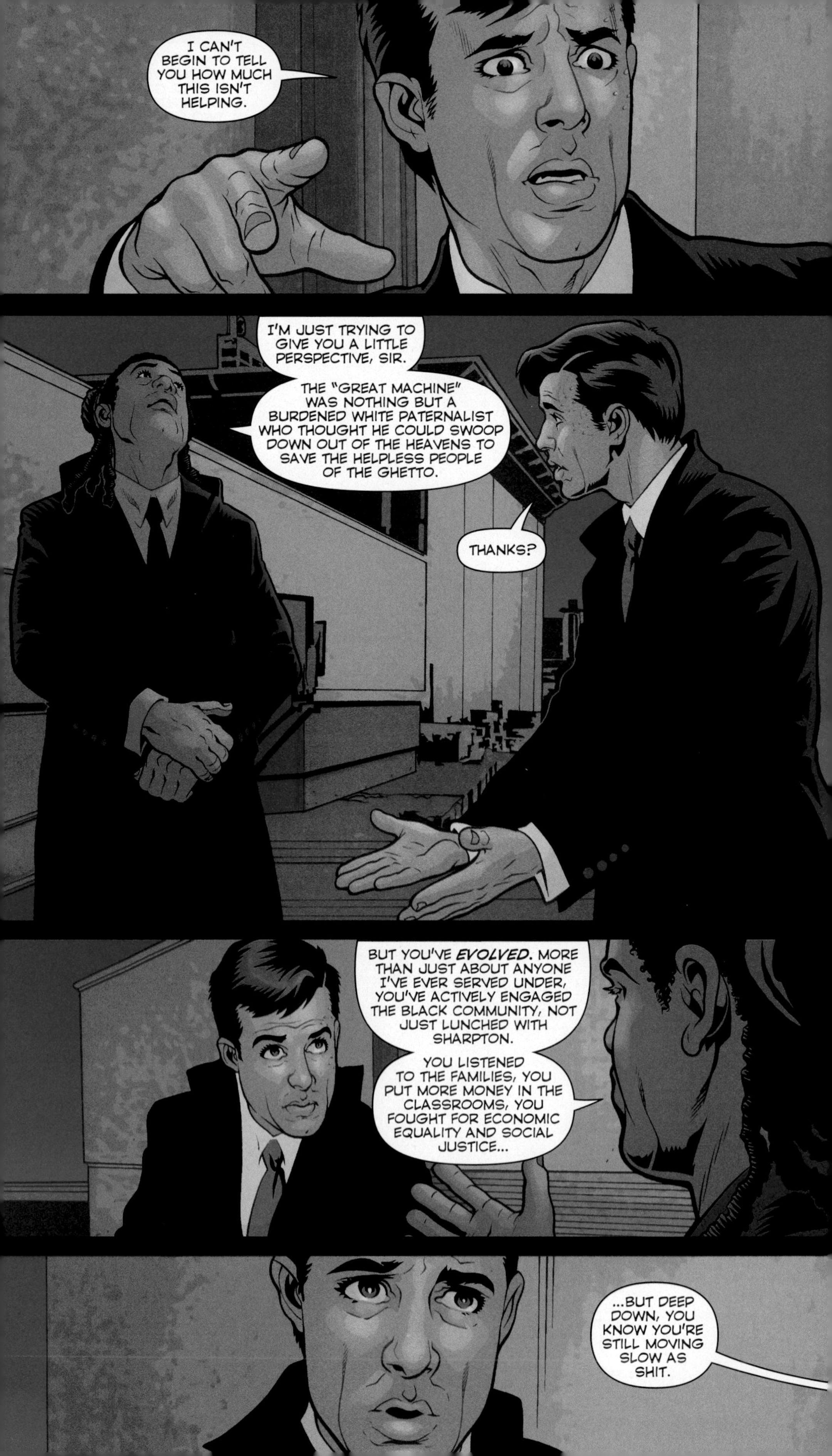
I CAN'T BEGIN TO TELL YOU HOW MUCH THIS ISN'T HELPING.
I'M JUST TRYING TO GIVE YOU A LITTLE PERSPECTIVE, SIR.
THE "GREAT MACHINE" WAS NOTHING BUT A BURDENED WHITE PATERNALIST WHO THOUGHT HE COULD SWOOP DOWN OUT OF THE HEAVENS TO SAVE THE HELPLESS PEOPLE OF THE GHETTO.
THANKS?
BUT YOU'VE *EVOLVED.* MORE THAN JUST ABOUT ANYONE I'VE EVER SERVED UNDER, YOU'VE ACTIVELY ENGAGED THE BLACK COMMUNITY, NOT JUST LUNCHED WITH SHARPTON.
YOU LISTENED TO THE FAMILIES, YOU PUT MORE MONEY IN THE CLASSROOMS, YOU FOUGHT FOR ECONOMIC EQUALITY AND SOCIAL JUSTICE...
...BUT DEEP DOWN, YOU KNOW YOU'RE STILL MOVING SLOW AS SHIT.

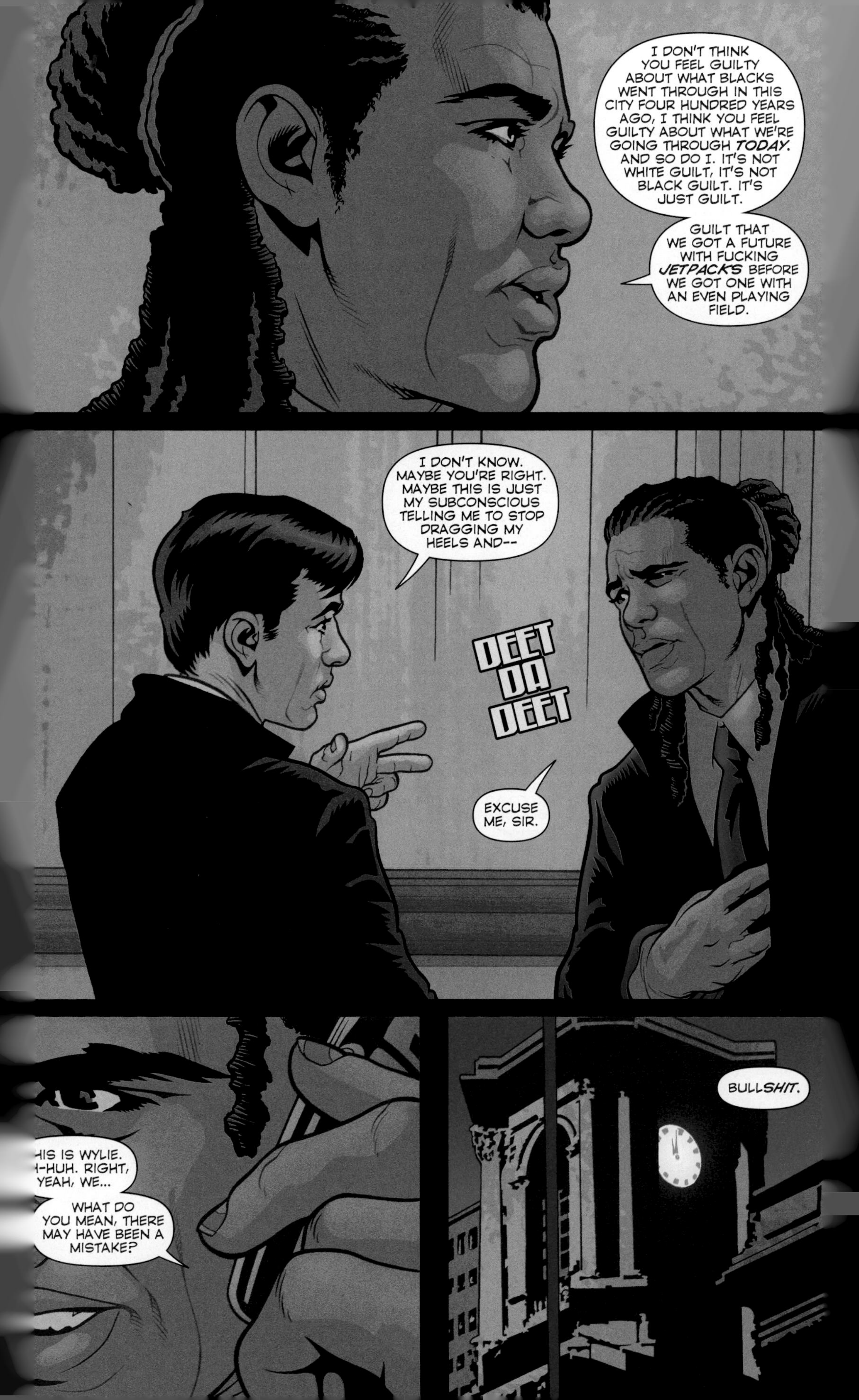
I DON'T THINK YOU FEEL GUILTY ABOUT WHAT BLACKS WENT THROUGH IN THIS CITY FOUR HUNDRED YEARS AGO, I THINK YOU FEEL GUILTY ABOUT WHAT WE'RE GOING THROUGH TODAY. AND SO DO I. IT'S NOT WHITE GUILT, IT'S NOT BLACK GUILT. IT'S JUST GUILT.
GUILT THAT WE GOT A FUTURE WITH FUCKING JETPACKS BEFORE WE GOT ONE WITH AN EVEN PLAYING FIELD.
I DON'T KNOW. MAYBE YOU'RE RIGHT. MAYBE THIS IS JUST MY SUBCONSCIOUS TELLING ME TO STOP DRAGGING MY HEELS AND--
DEET DA DEET
EXCUSE ME, SIR.
HIS IS WYLIE. H-HUH. RIGHT, YEAH, WE...
WHAT DO YOU MEAN, THERE MAY HAVE BEEN A MISTAKE?
BULLSHIT.

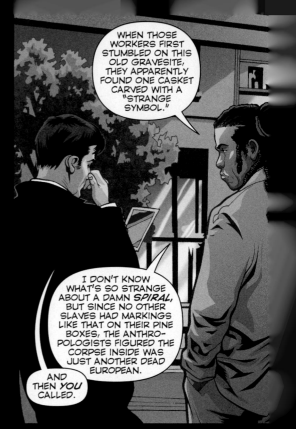

WHEN THOSE WORKERS FIRST STUMBLED ON THIS OLD GRAVESITE, THEY APPARENTLY FOUND ONE CASKET CARVED WITH A "STRANGE SYMBOL."

I DON'T KNOW WHAT'S SO STRANGE ABOUT A DAMN *SPIRAL*, BUT SINCE NO OTHER SLAVES HAD MARKINGS LIKE THAT ON THEIR PINE BOXES, THE ANTHROPOLOGISTS FIGURED THE CORPSE INSIDE WAS JUST ANOTHER DEAD EUROPEAN.

AND THEN *YOU* CALLED.

GOD, I HATE WHEN YOU'RE RIGHT.

THE BRAIN TRUST AT HOWARD U. REEXAMINED THOSE REMAINS AND NOTICED THAT THE SKULL'S UPPER INCISORS HAD BEEN *FILED*, A MUTILATION SPECIFIC TO AFRICAN SLAVES.

SIR, IF YOU HADN'T TOLD ANYONE WHAT YOU SAW, THIS MAN NEVER WOULD HAVE BEEN GIVEN A PROPER RESTING SPOT...NEXT TO HIS BROTHERS AND SISTERS WHERE HE BELONGS.

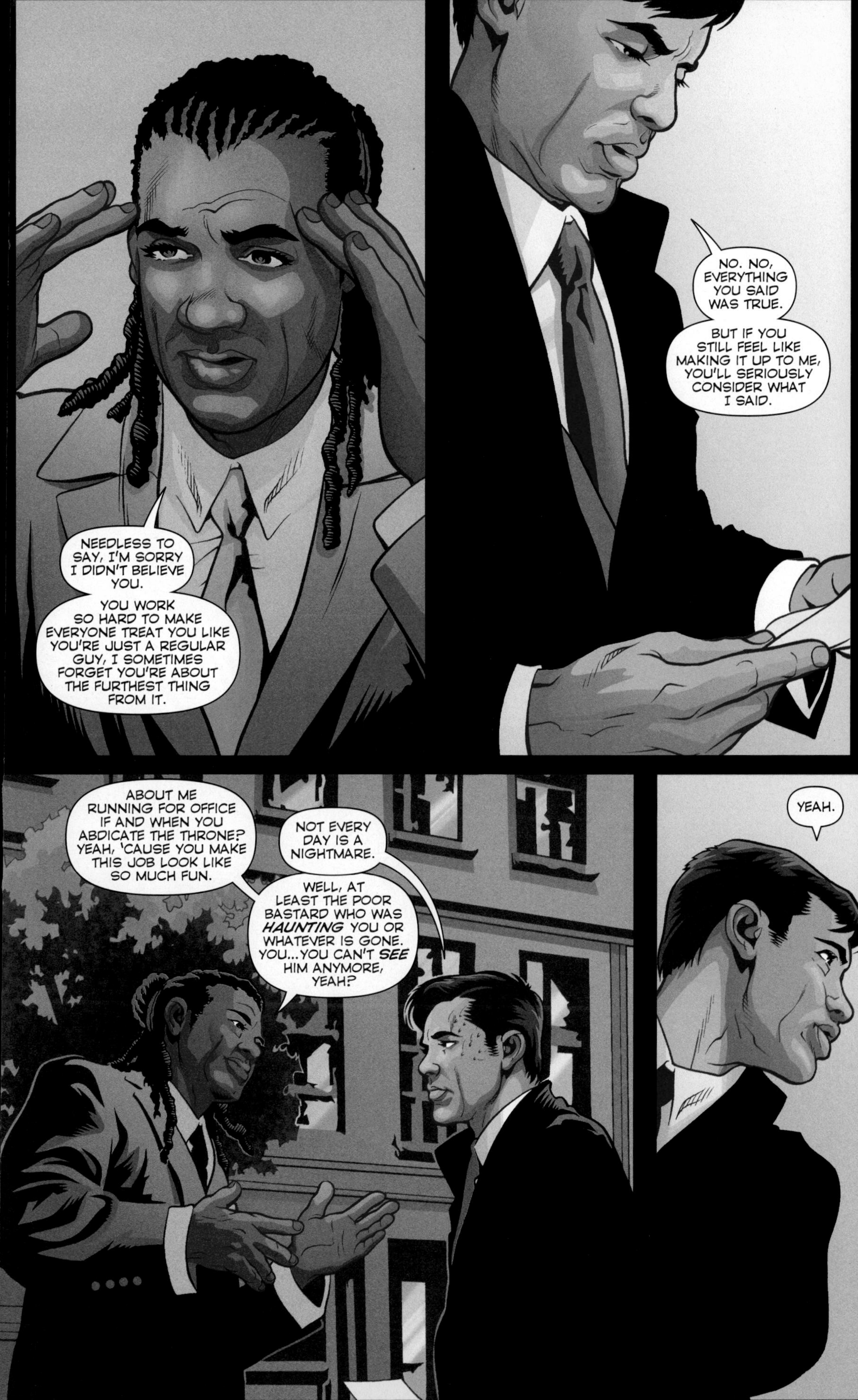
NEEDLESS TO SAY, I'M SORRY I DIDN'T BELIEVE YOU.
YOU WORK SO HARD TO MAKE EVERYONE TREAT YOU LIKE YOU'RE JUST A REGULAR GUY, I SOMETIMES FORGET YOU'RE ABOUT THE FURTHEST THING FROM IT.
NO. NO, EVERYTHING YOU SAID WAS TRUE.
BUT IF YOU STILL FEEL LIKE MAKING IT UP TO ME, YOU'LL SERIOUSLY CONSIDER WHAT I SAID.
ABOUT ME RUNNING FOR OFFICE IF AND WHEN YOU ABDICATE THE THRONE? YEAH, 'CAUSE YOU MAKE THIS JOB LOOK LIKE SO MUCH FUN.
NOT EVERY DAY IS A NIGHTMARE.
WELL, AT LEAST THE POOR BASTARD WHO WAS *HAUNTING* YOU OR WHATEVER IS GONE. YOU...YOU CAN'T *SEE* HIM ANYMORE, YEAH?
YEAH.

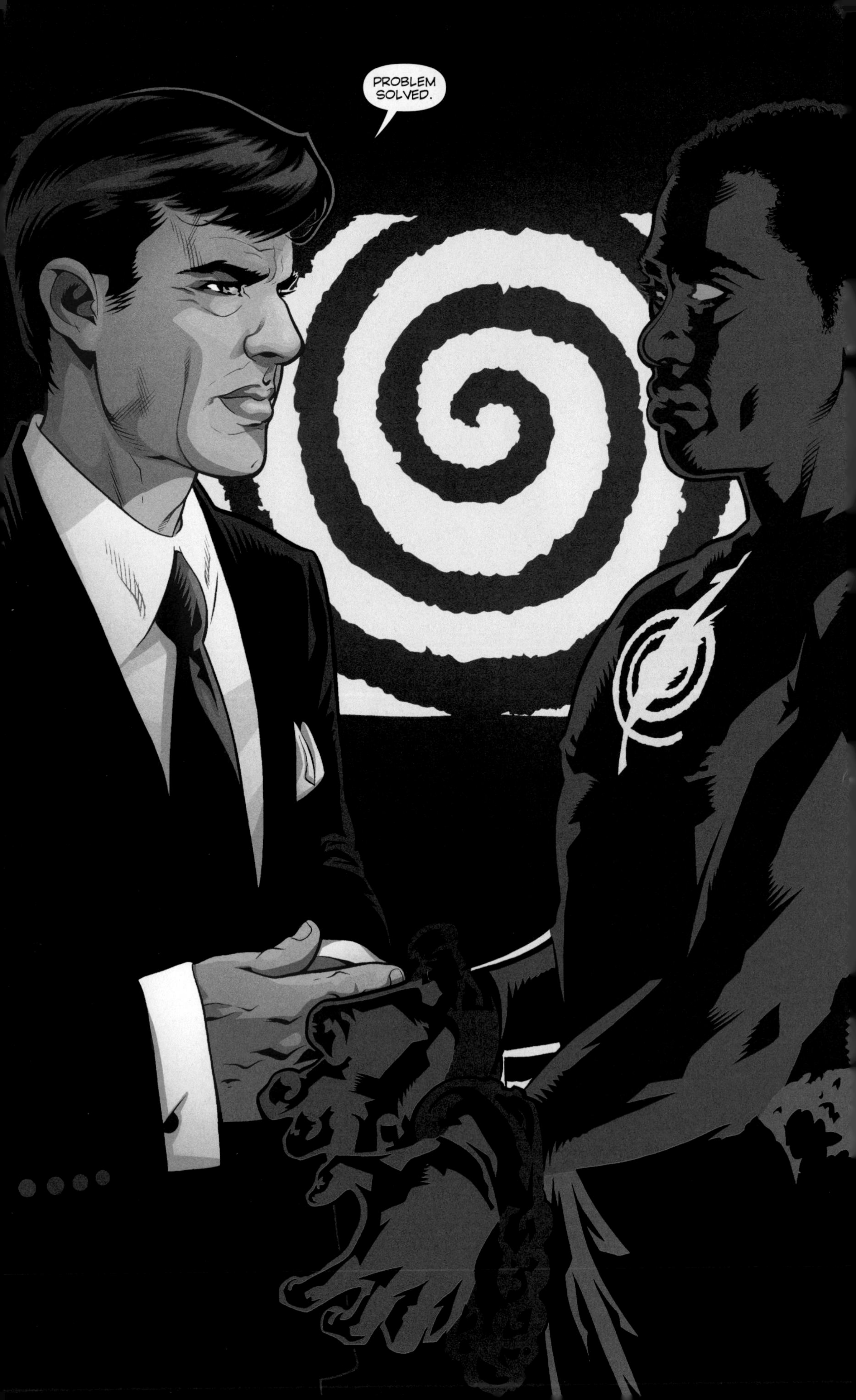
PROBLEM SOLVED.

CHAPTER 4 DIRTY TRICKS

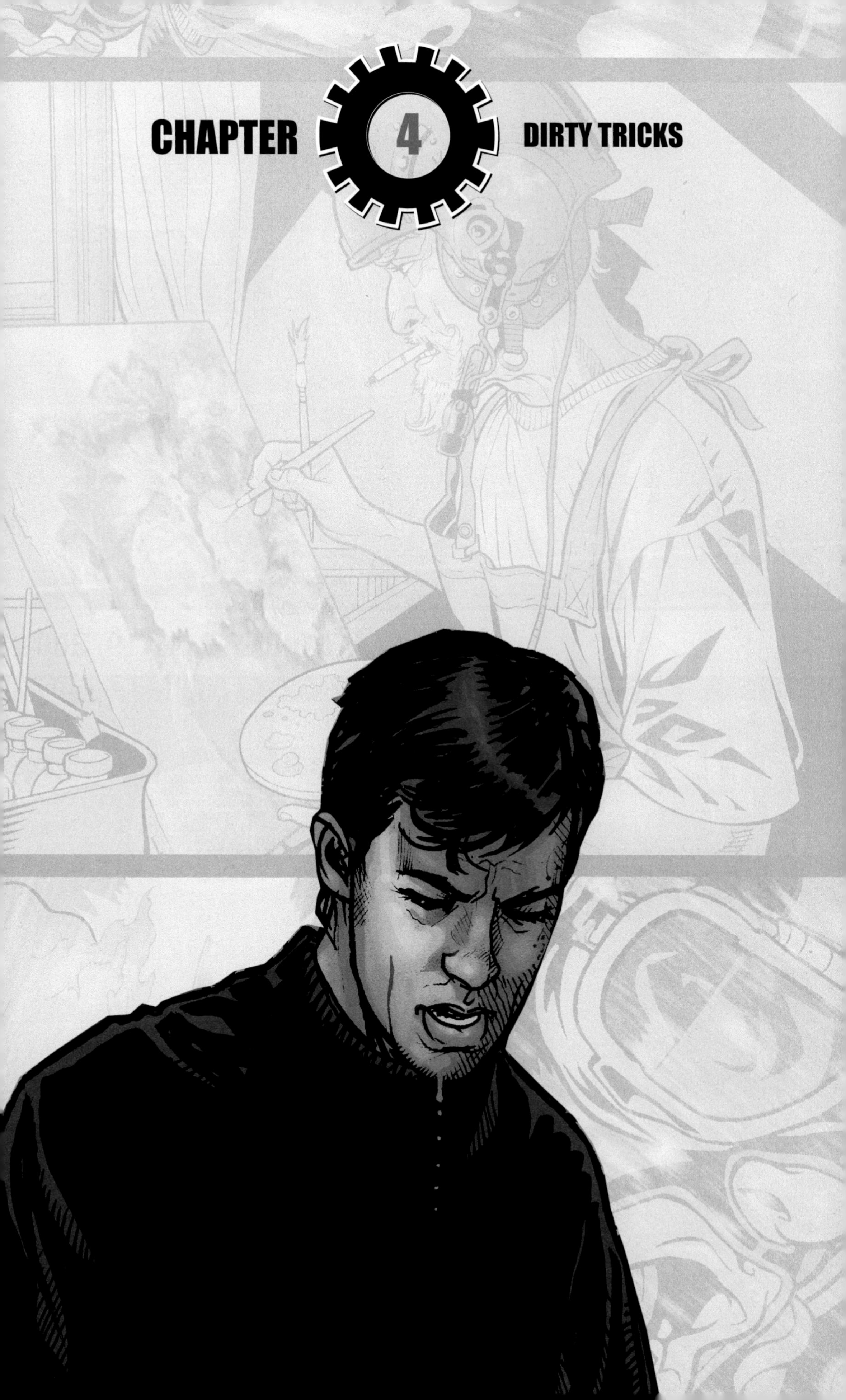

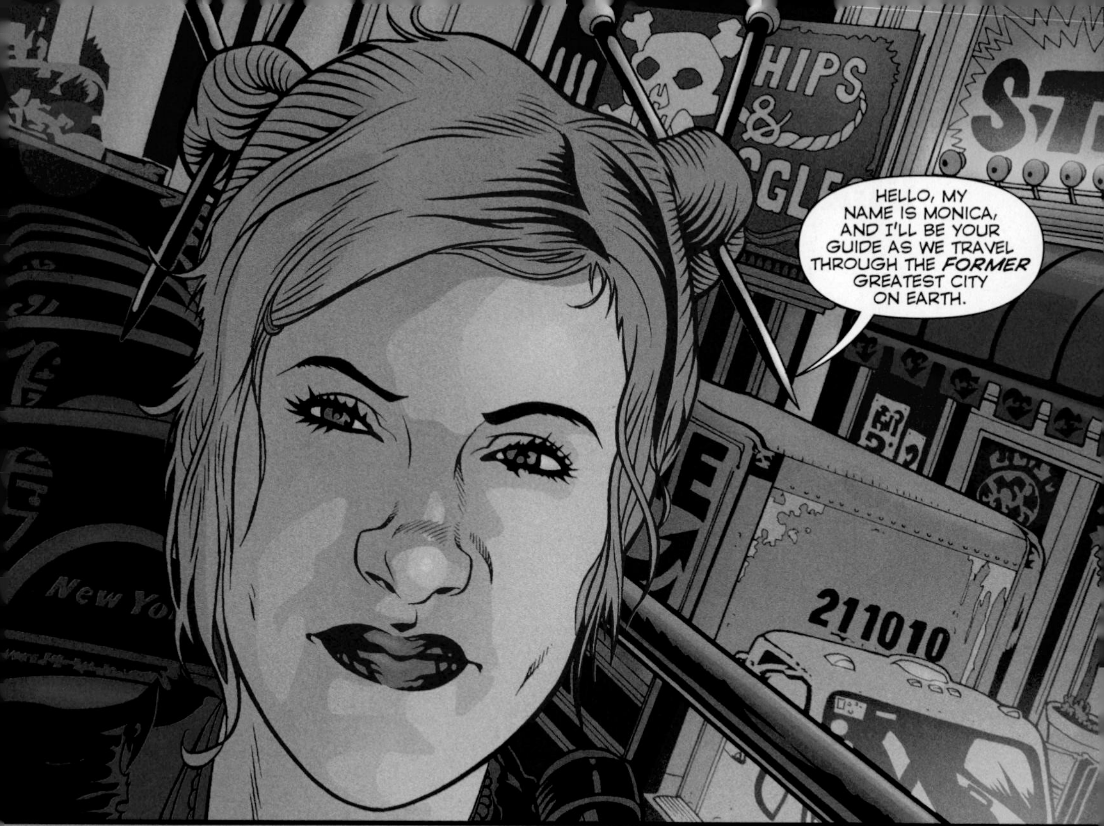
HELLO, MY NAME IS MONICA, AND I'LL BE YOUR GUIDE AS WE TRAVEL THROUGH THE *FORMER* GREATEST CITY ON EARTH.
211010

SATURDAY, MAY 19, 2001

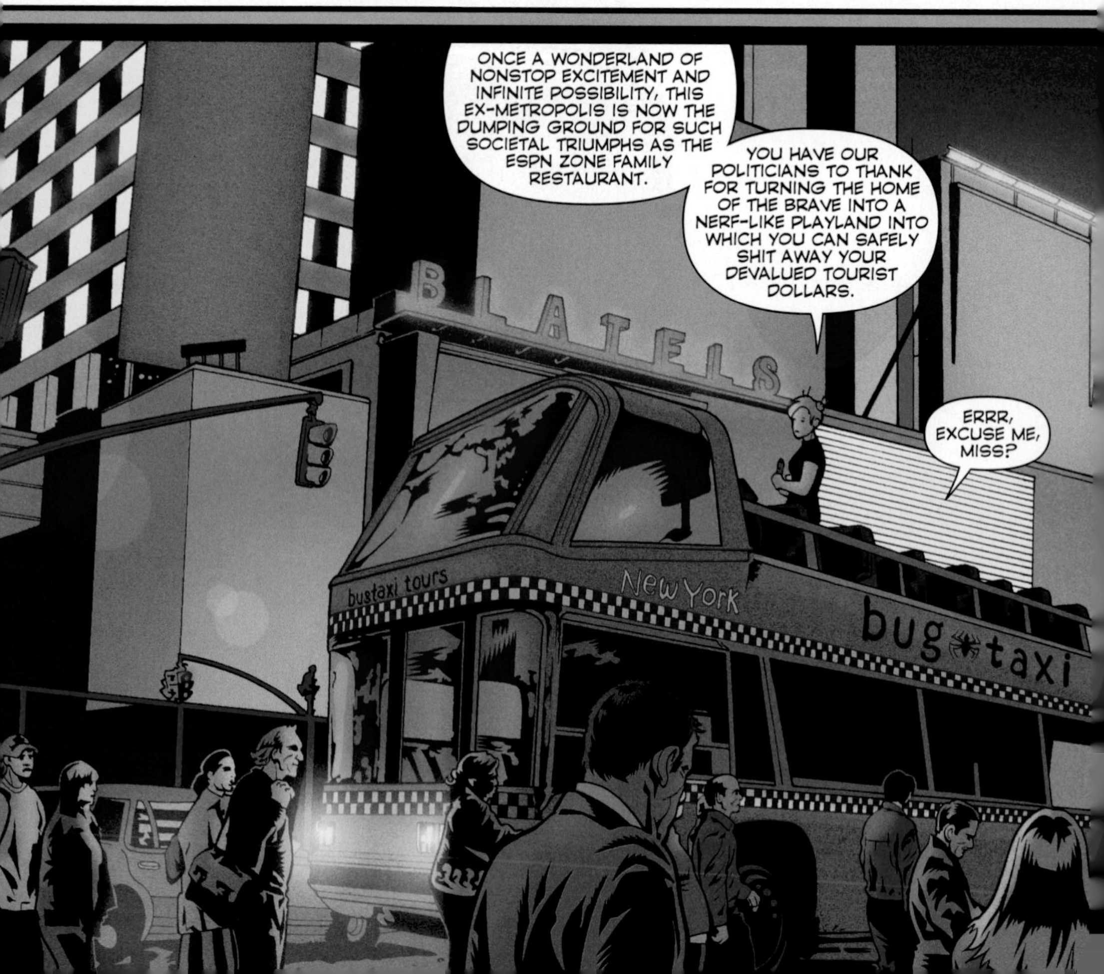
ONCE A WONDERLAND OF NONSTOP EXCITEMENT AND INFINITE POSSIBILITY, THIS EX-METROPOLIS IS NOW THE DUMPING GROUND FOR SUCH SOCIETAL TRIUMPHS AS THE ESPN ZONE FAMILY RESTAURANT.
YOU HAVE OUR POLITICIANS TO THANK FOR TURNING THE HOME OF THE BRAVE INTO A NERF-LIKE PLAYLAND INTO WHICH YOU CAN SAFELY SHIT AWAY YOUR DEVALUED TOURIST DOLLARS.
ERRR, EXCUSE ME, MISS?
bustaxi tours
New York
bug taxi

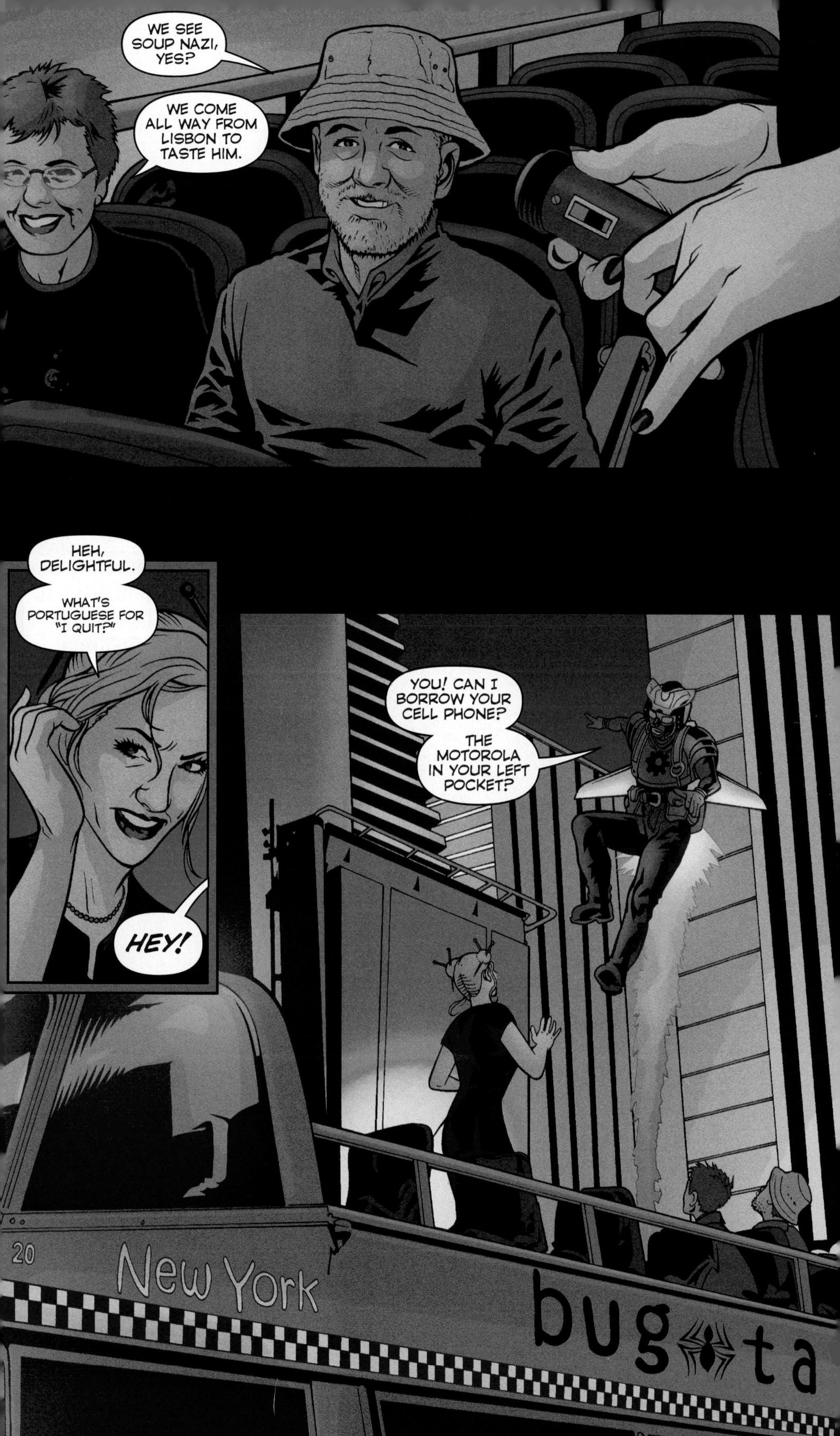
WE SEE SOUP NAZI, YES?
WE COME ALL WAY FROM LISBON TO TASTE HIM.
HEH, DELIGHTFUL.
WHAT'S PORTUGUESE FOR "I QUIT?"
HEY!
YOU! CAN I BORROW YOUR CELL PHONE?
THE MOTOROLA IN YOUR LEFT POCKET?
20
New York
bug ta

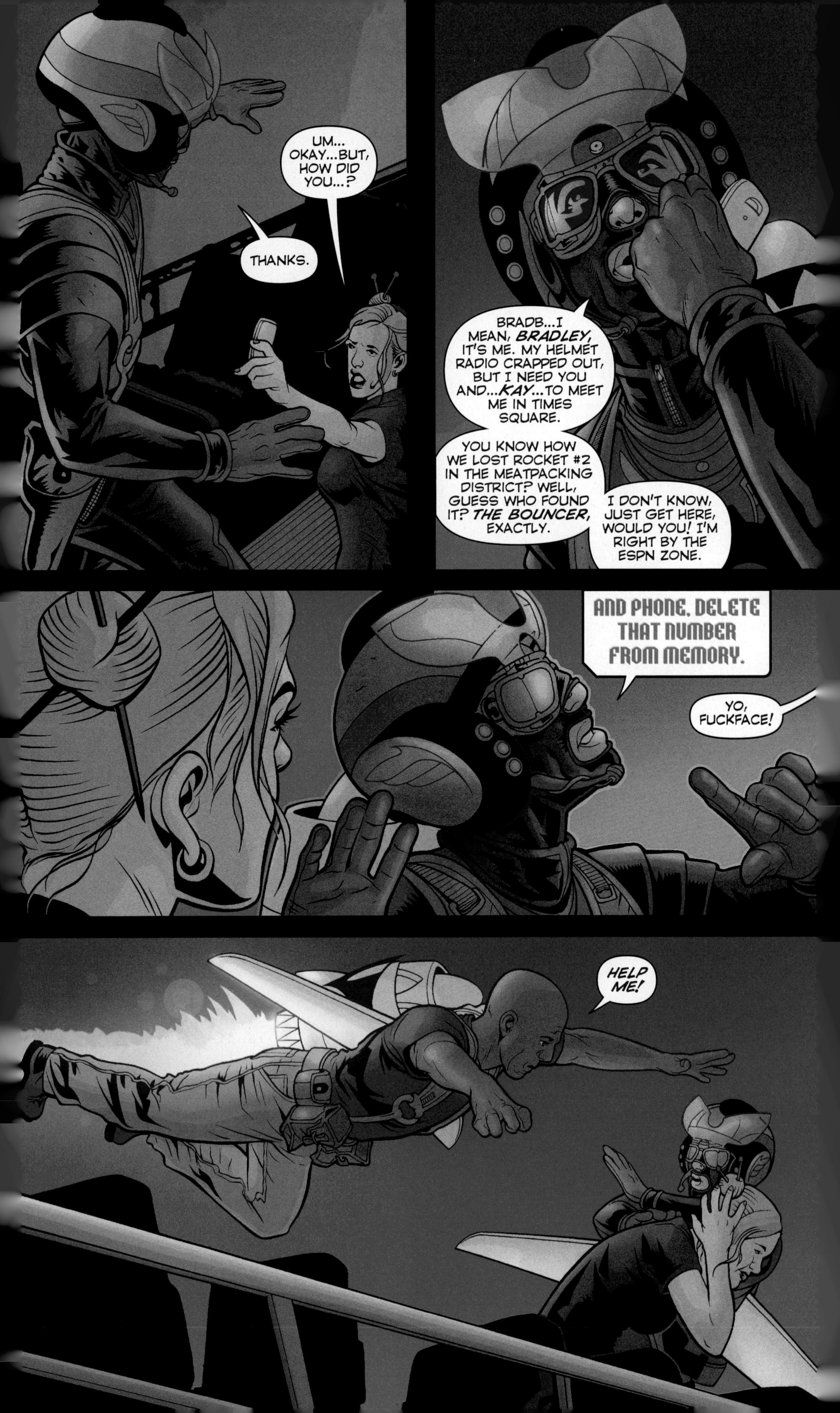
UM... OKAY...BUT, HOW DID YOU...?
THANKS.
BRADB...I MEAN, BRADLEY, IT'S ME. MY HELMET RADIO CRAPPED OUT, BUT I NEED YOU AND...KAY...TO MEET ME IN TIMES SQUARE.
YOU KNOW HOW WE LOST ROCKET #2 IN THE MEATPACKING DISTRICT? WELL, GUESS WHO FOUND IT? THE BOUNCER, EXACTLY.
I DON'T KNOW, JUST GET HERE, WOULD YOU! I'M RIGHT BY THE ESPN ZONE.
AND PHONE, DELETE THAT NUMBER FROM MEMORY.
YO, FUCKFACE!
HELP ME!

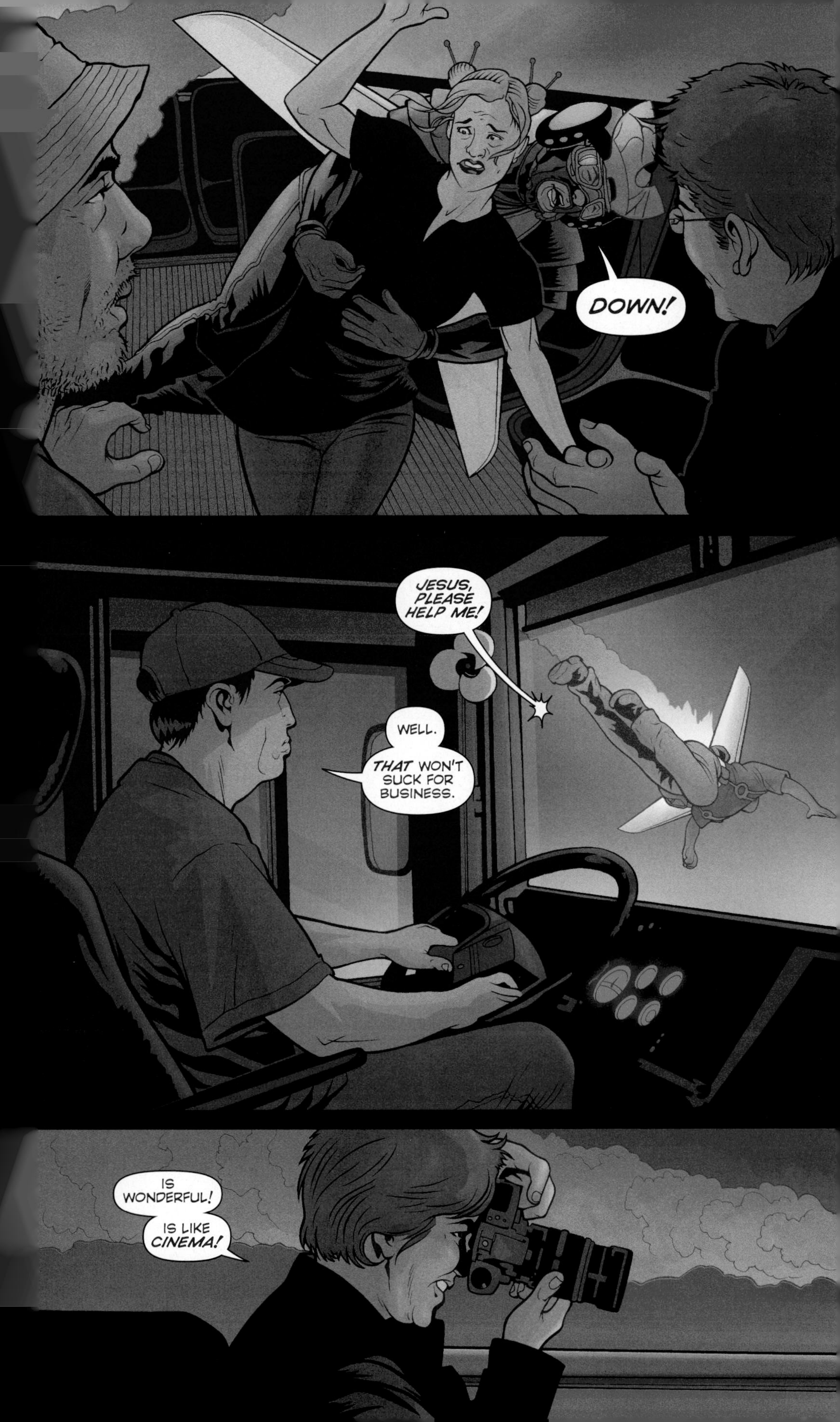
DOWN!
JESUS, PLEASE HELP ME!
WELL.
THAT WON'T SUCK FOR BUSINESS.
IS WONDERFUL!
IS LIKE CINEMA!

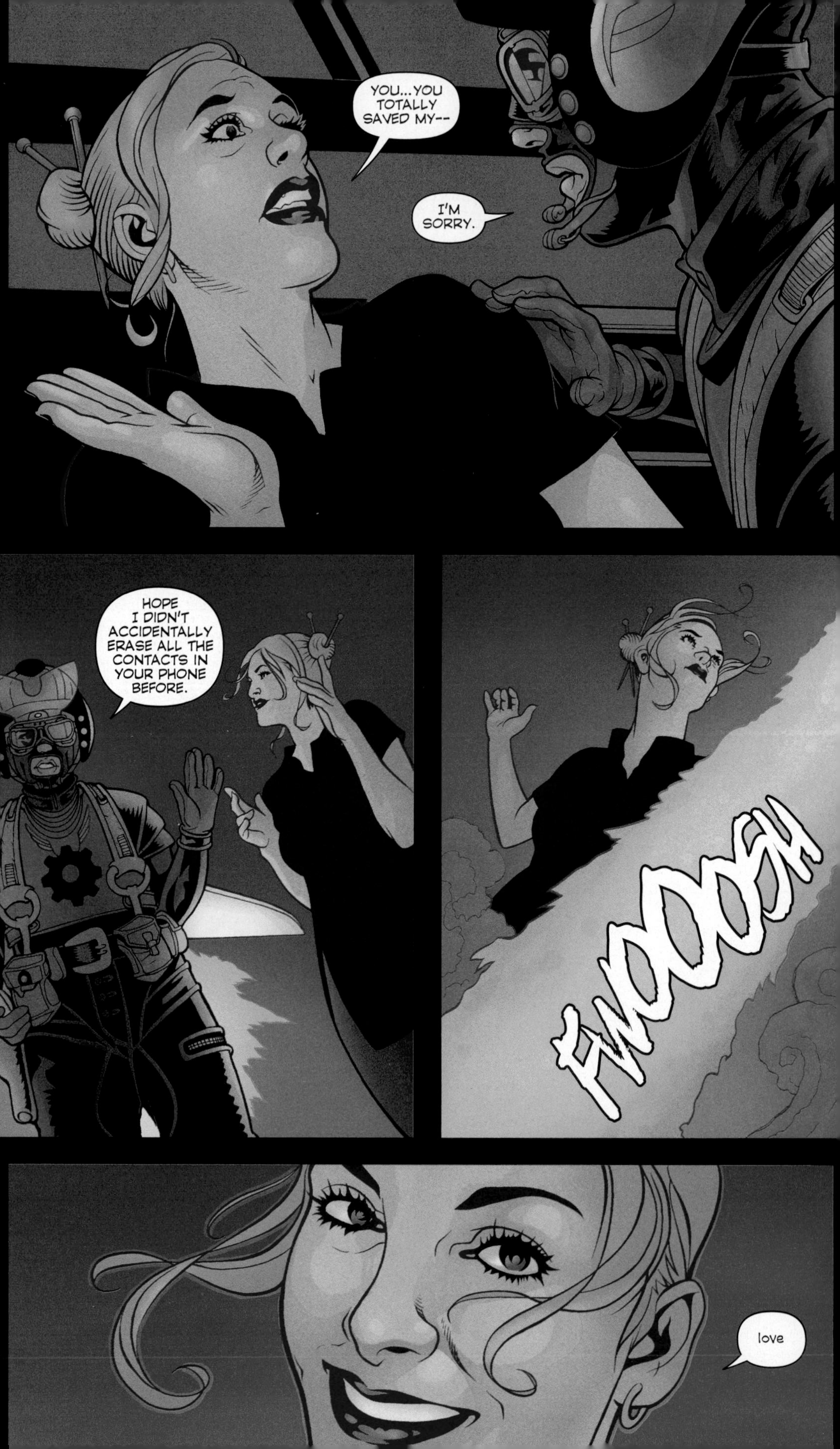
YOU...YOU TOTALLY SAVED MY--
I'M SORRY.
HOPE I DIDN'T ACCIDENTALLY ERASE ALL THE CONTACTS IN YOUR PHONE BEFORE.
FWOOOSH
love

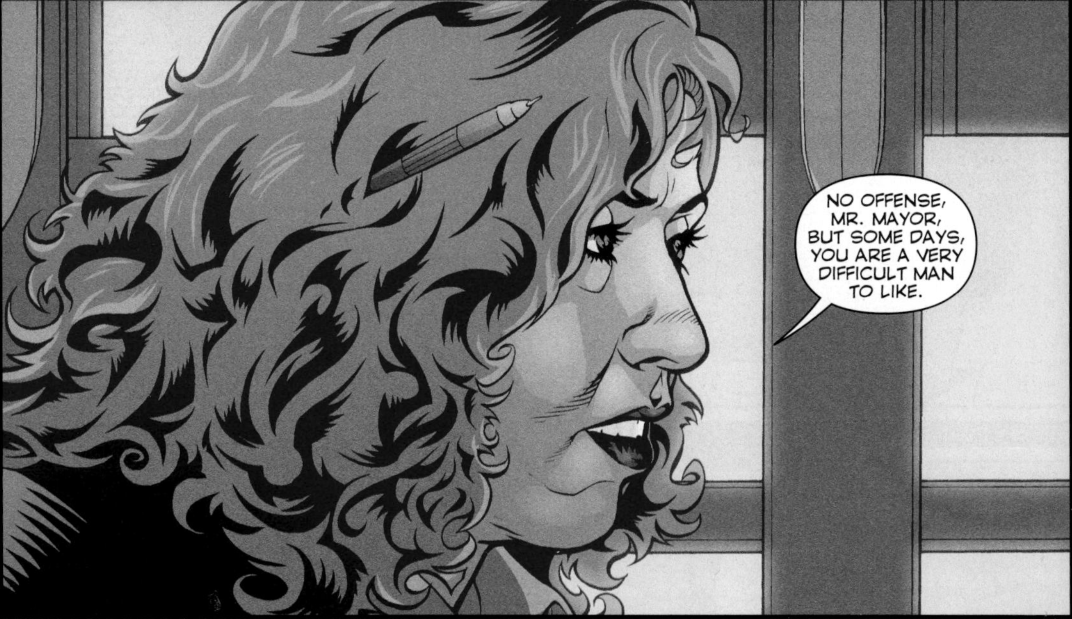
NO OFFENSE, MR. MAYOR, BUT SOME DAYS, YOU ARE A VERY DIFFICULT MAN TO LIKE.

THURSDAY, JULY 29, 2004

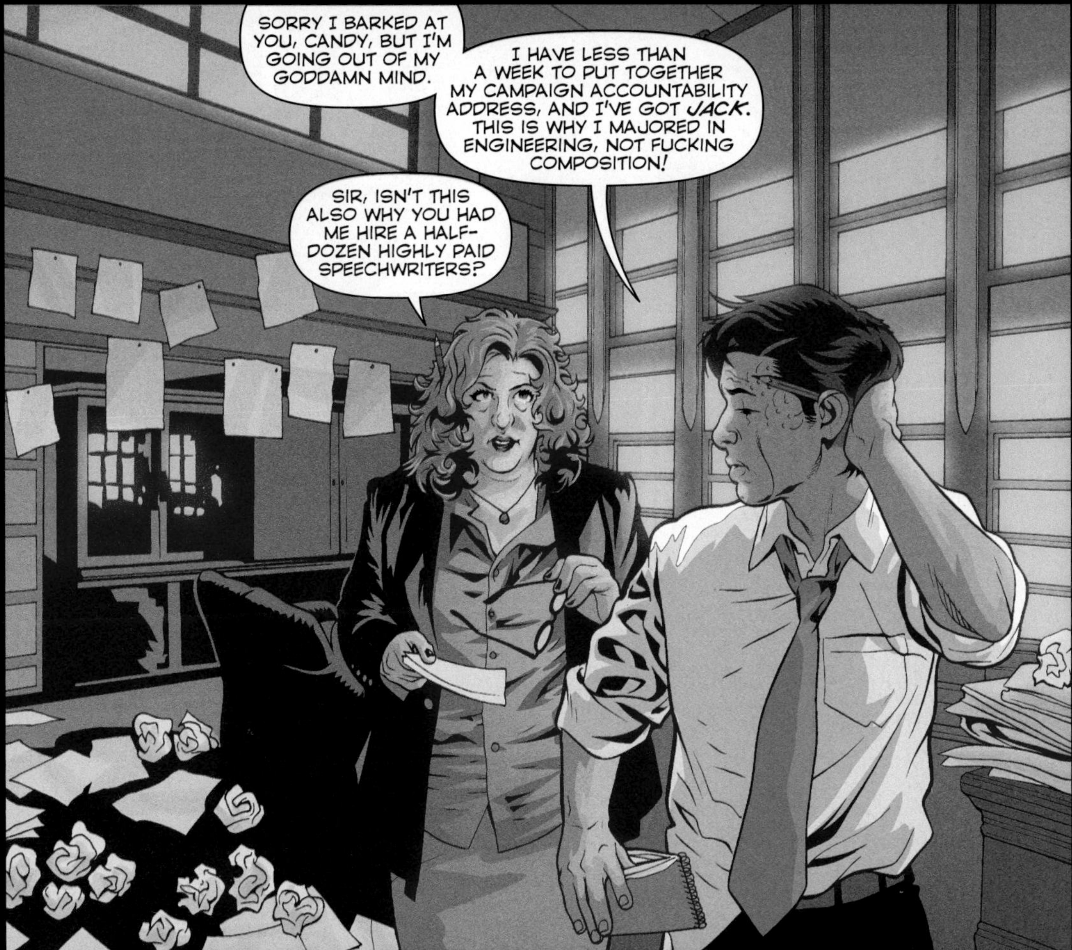
SORRY I BARKED AT YOU, CANDY, BUT I'M GOING OUT OF MY GODDAMN MIND.
I HAVE LESS THAN A WEEK TO PUT TOGETHER MY CAMPAIGN ACCOUNTABILITY ADDRESS, AND I'VE GOT *JACK*. THIS IS WHY I MAJORED IN ENGINEERING, NOT FUCKING COMPOSITION!
SIR, ISN'T THIS ALSO WHY YOU HAD ME HIRE A HALF-DOZEN HIGHLY PAID SPEECHWRITERS?

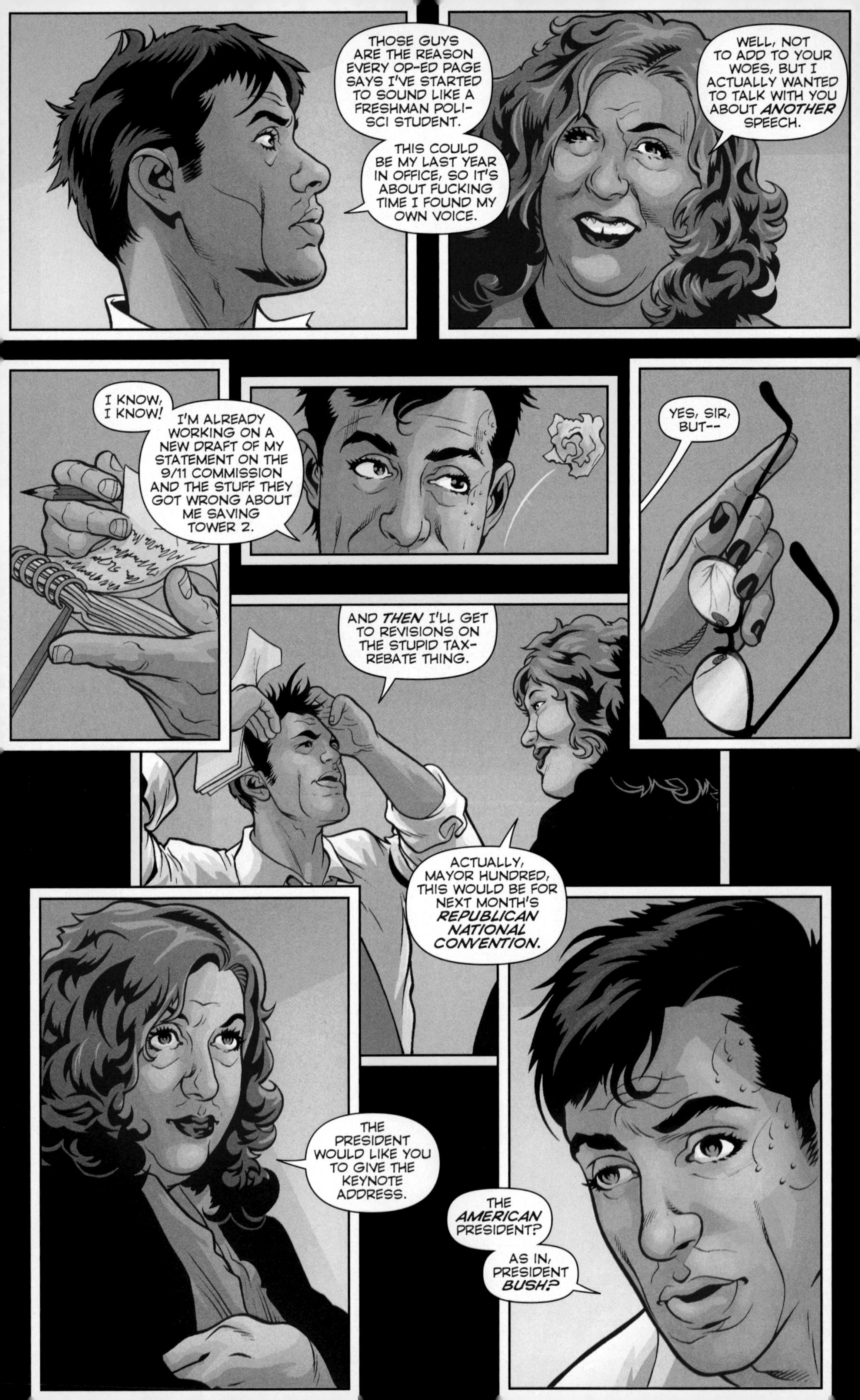
THOSE GUYS ARE THE REASON EVERY OP-ED PAGE SAYS I'VE STARTED TO SOUND LIKE A FRESHMAN POLI-SCI STUDENT.
THIS COULD BE MY LAST YEAR IN OFFICE, SO IT'S ABOUT FUCKING TIME I FOUND MY OWN VOICE.
WELL, NOT TO ADD TO YOUR WOES, BUT I ACTUALLY WANTED TO TALK WITH YOU ABOUT ANOTHER SPEECH.
I KNOW, I KNOW!
I'M ALREADY WORKING ON A NEW DRAFT OF MY STATEMENT ON THE 9/11 COMMISSION AND THE STUFF THEY GOT WRONG ABOUT ME SAVING TOWER 2.
YES, SIR, BUT--
AND THEN I'LL GET TO REVISIONS ON THE STUPID TAX-REBATE THING.
ACTUALLY, MAYOR HUNDRED, THIS WOULD BE FOR NEXT MONTH'S REPUBLICAN NATIONAL CONVENTION.
THE PRESIDENT WOULD LIKE YOU TO GIVE THE KEYNOTE ADDRESS.
THE AMERICAN PRESIDENT?
AS IN, PRESIDENT BUSH?

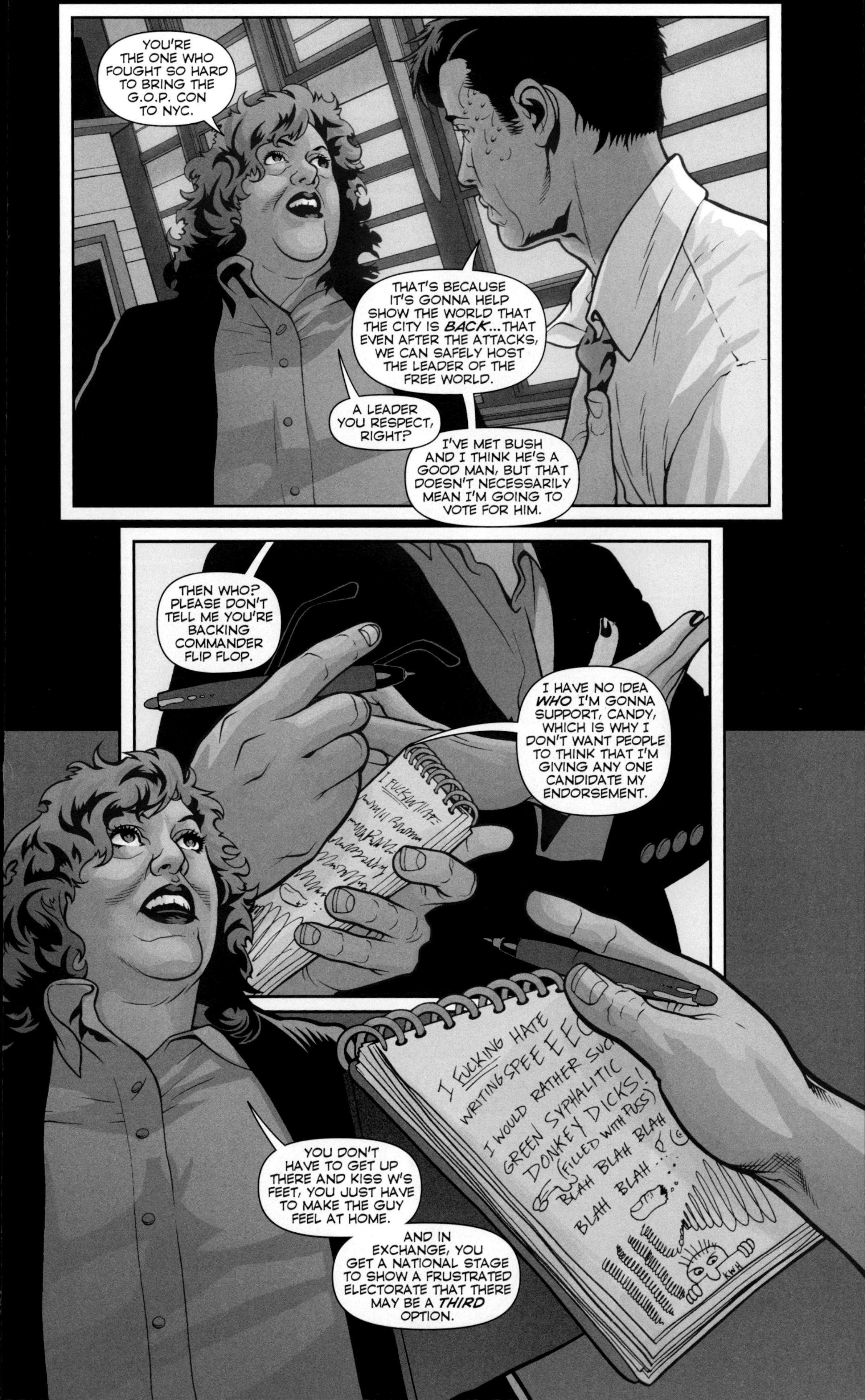
YOU'RE THE ONE WHO FOUGHT SO HARD TO BRING THE G.O.P. CON TO NYC.
THAT'S BECAUSE IT'S GONNA HELP SHOW THE WORLD THAT THE CITY IS *BACK*... THAT EVEN AFTER THE ATTACKS, WE CAN SAFELY HOST THE LEADER OF THE FREE WORLD.
A LEADER YOU RESPECT, RIGHT?
I'VE MET BUSH AND I THINK HE'S A GOOD MAN, BUT THAT DOESN'T NECESSARILY MEAN I'M GOING TO VOTE FOR HIM.
THEN WHO? PLEASE DON'T TELL ME YOU'RE BACKING COMMANDER FLIP FLOP.
I HAVE NO IDEA ***WHO*** I'M GONNA SUPPORT, CANDY, WHICH IS WHY I DON'T WANT PEOPLE TO THINK THAT I'M GIVING ANY ONE CANDIDATE MY ENDORSEMENT.
I FUCKING HATE
GREEN SYPHALITIC
DONKEY DICKS!
(FILLED WITH PUSS)
BLAH BLAH BLAH
BLAH BLAH...
BLAH
YOU DON'T HAVE TO GET UP THERE AND KISS W'S FEET, YOU JUST HAVE TO MAKE THE GUY FEEL AT HOME.
AND IN EXCHANGE, YOU GET A NATIONAL STAGE TO SHOW A FRUSTRATED ELECTORATE THAT THERE MAY BE A *THIRD* OPTION.

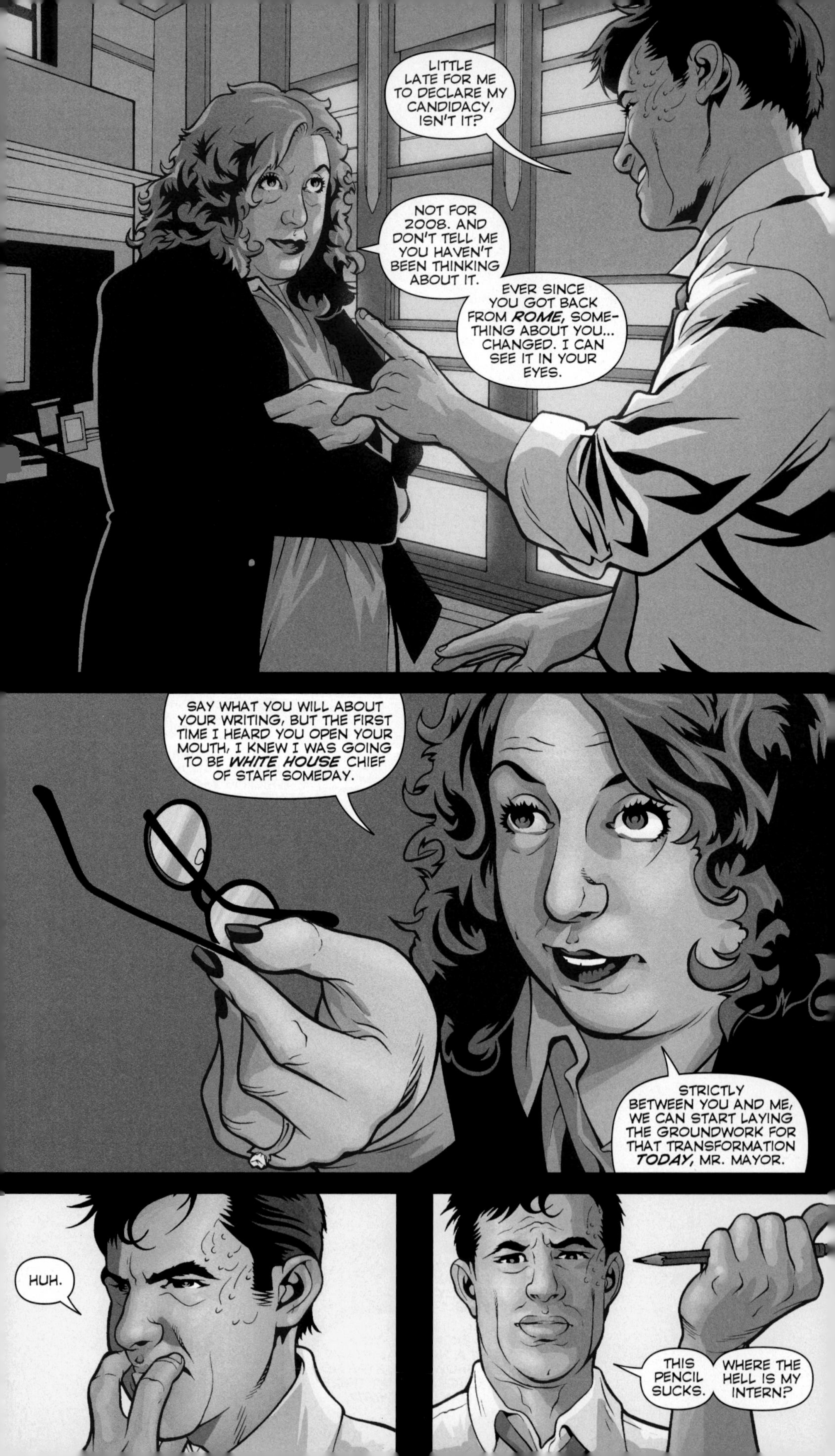
LITTLE LATE FOR ME TO DECLARE MY CANDIDACY, ISN'T IT?
NOT FOR 2008. AND DON'T TELL ME YOU HAVEN'T BEEN THINKING ABOUT IT.
EVER SINCE YOU GOT BACK FROM ROME, SOMETHING ABOUT YOU... CHANGED. I CAN SEE IT IN YOUR EYES.
SAY WHAT YOU WILL ABOUT YOUR WRITING, BUT THE FIRST TIME I HEARD YOU OPEN YOUR MOUTH, I KNEW I WAS GOING TO BE WHITE HOUSE CHIEF OF STAFF SOMEDAY.
STRICTLY BETWEEN YOU AND ME, WE CAN START LAYING THE GROUNDWORK FOR THAT TRANSFORMATION TODAY, MR. MAYOR.
HUH.
THIS PENCIL SUCKS.
WHERE THE HELL IS MY INTERN?

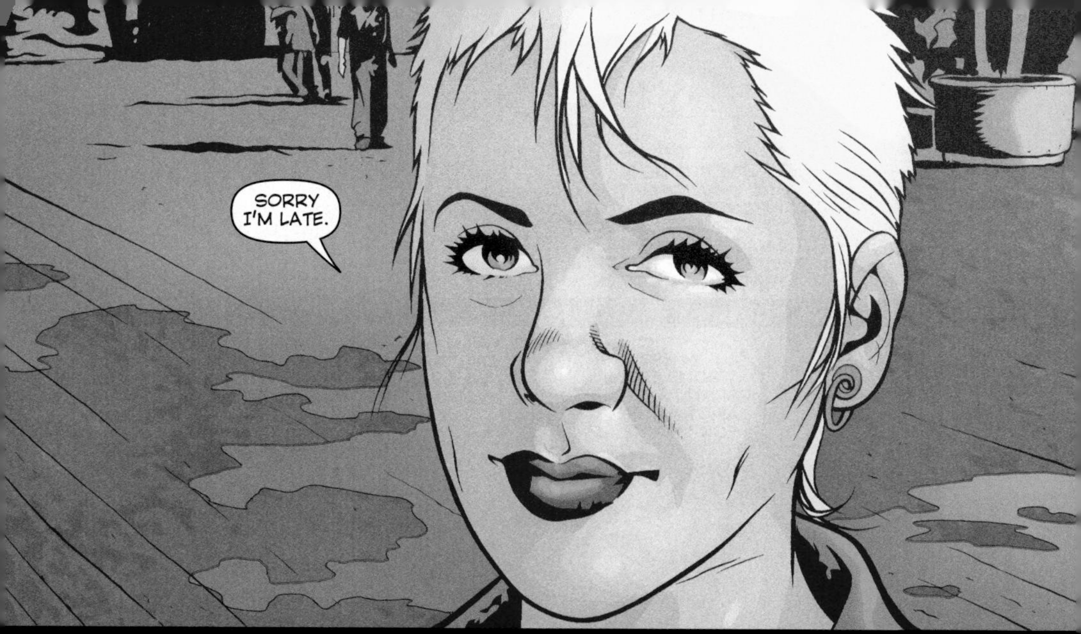
SORRY I'M LATE.

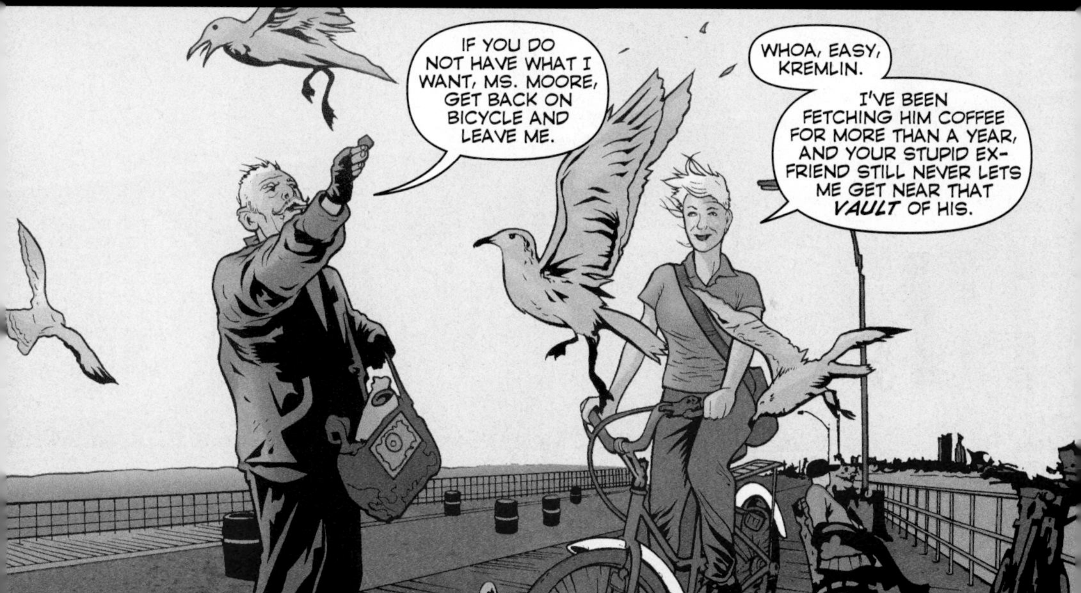
IF YOU DO NOT HAVE WHAT I WANT, MS. MOORE, GET BACK ON BICYCLE AND LEAVE ME.
WHOA, EASY, KREMLIN.
I'VE BEEN FETCHING HIM COFFEE FOR MORE THAN A YEAR, AND YOUR STUPID EX-FRIEND STILL NEVER LETS ME GET NEAR THAT *VAULT* OF HIS.

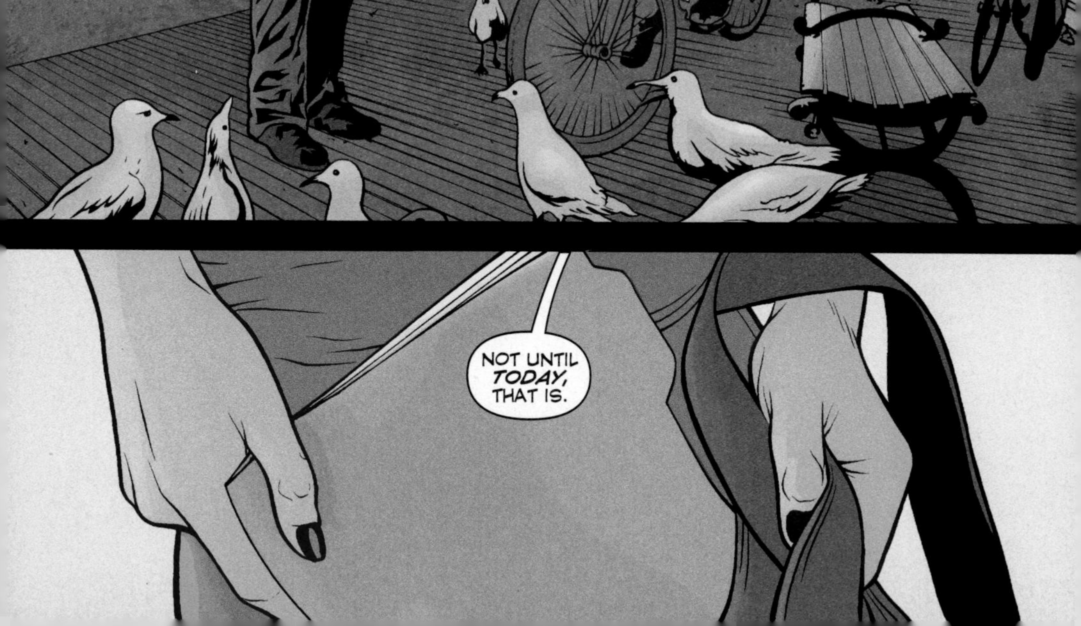
NOT UNTIL *TODAY,* THAT IS.

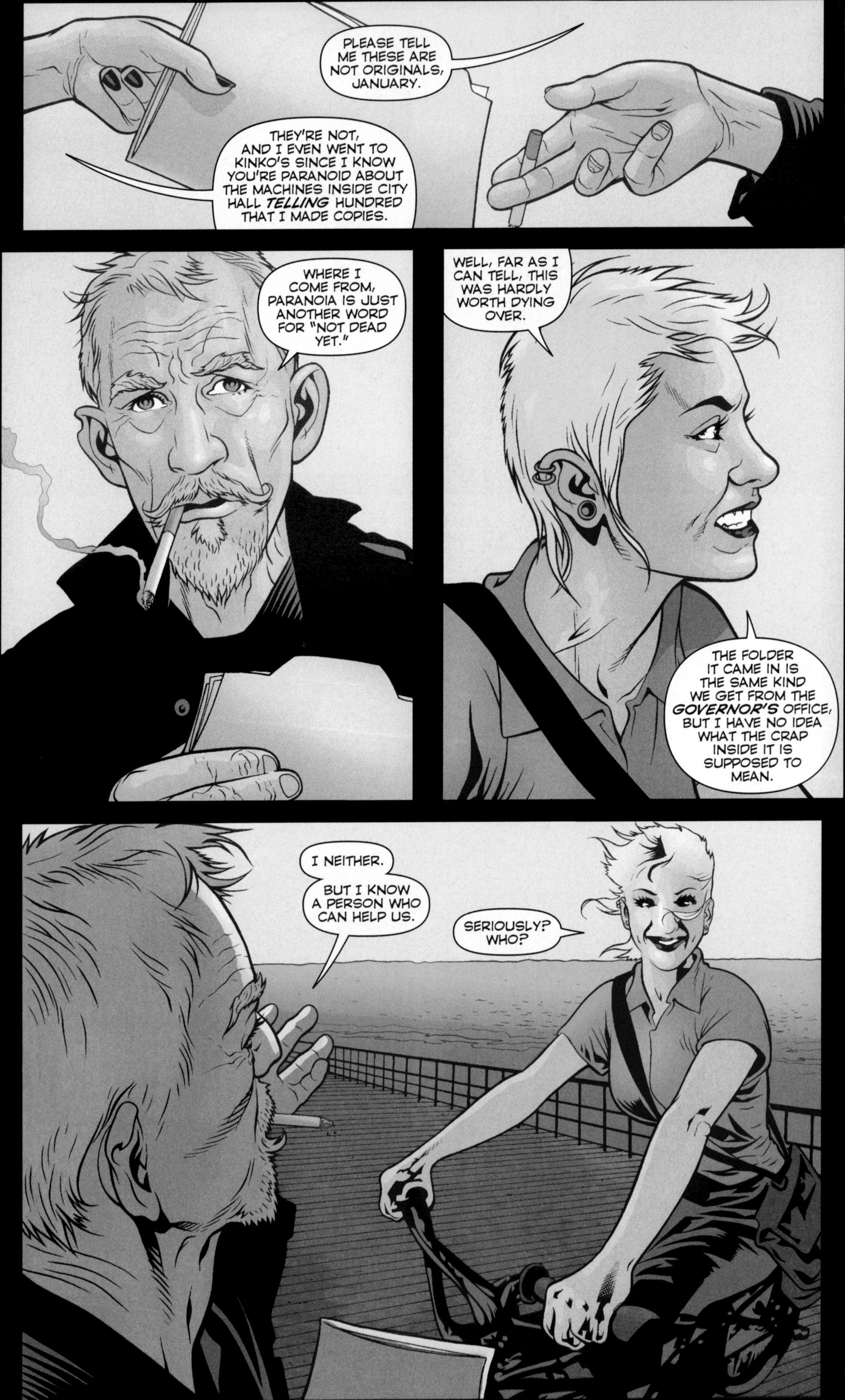
PLEASE TELL ME THESE ARE NOT ORIGINALS, JANUARY.
THEY'RE NOT, AND I EVEN WENT TO KINKO'S SINCE I KNOW YOU'RE PARANOID ABOUT THE MACHINES INSIDE CITY HALL TELLING HUNDRED THAT I MADE COPIES.
WHERE I COME FROM, PARANOIA IS JUST ANOTHER WORD FOR "NOT DEAD YET."
WELL, FAR AS I CAN TELL, THIS WAS HARDLY WORTH DYING OVER.
THE FOLDER IT CAME IN IS THE SAME KIND WE GET FROM THE GOVERNOR'S OFFICE, BUT I HAVE NO IDEA WHAT THE CRAP INSIDE IT IS SUPPOSED TO MEAN.
I NEITHER.
BUT I KNOW A PERSON WHO CAN HELP US.
SERIOUSLY? WHO?

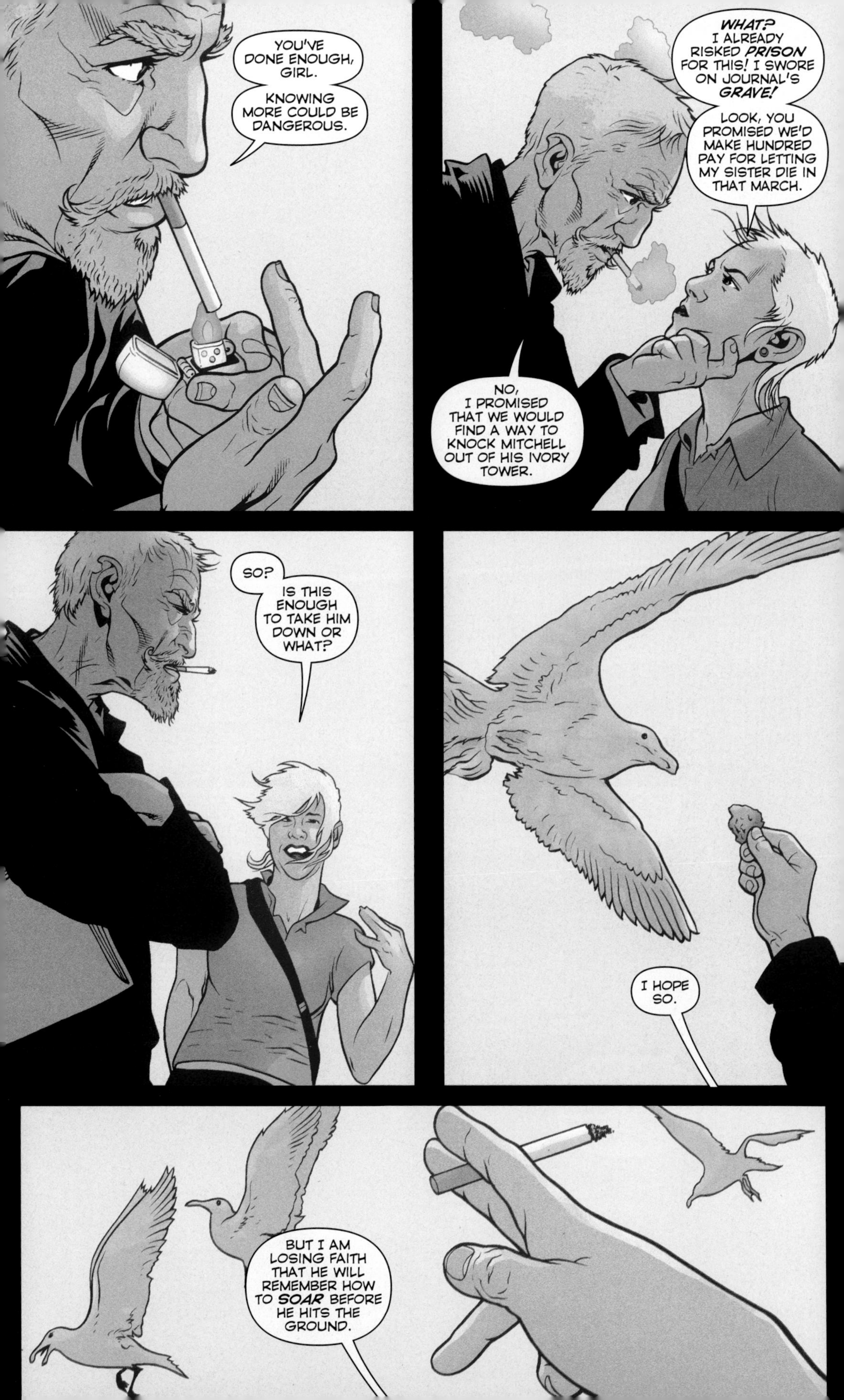

YOU'VE DONE ENOUGH, GIRL.
KNOWING MORE COULD BE DANGEROUS.
WHAT? I ALREADY RISKED PRISON FOR THIS! I SWORE ON JOURNAL'S GRAVE!
LOOK, YOU PROMISED WE'D MAKE HUNDRED PAY FOR LETTING MY SISTER DIE IN THAT MARCH.
NO, I PROMISED THAT WE WOULD FIND A WAY TO KNOCK MITCHELL OUT OF HIS IVORY TOWER.
SO?
IS THIS ENOUGH TO TAKE HIM DOWN OR WHAT?
I HOPE SO.
BUT I AM LOSING FAITH THAT HE WILL REMEMBER HOW TO SOAR BEFORE HE HITS THE GROUND.

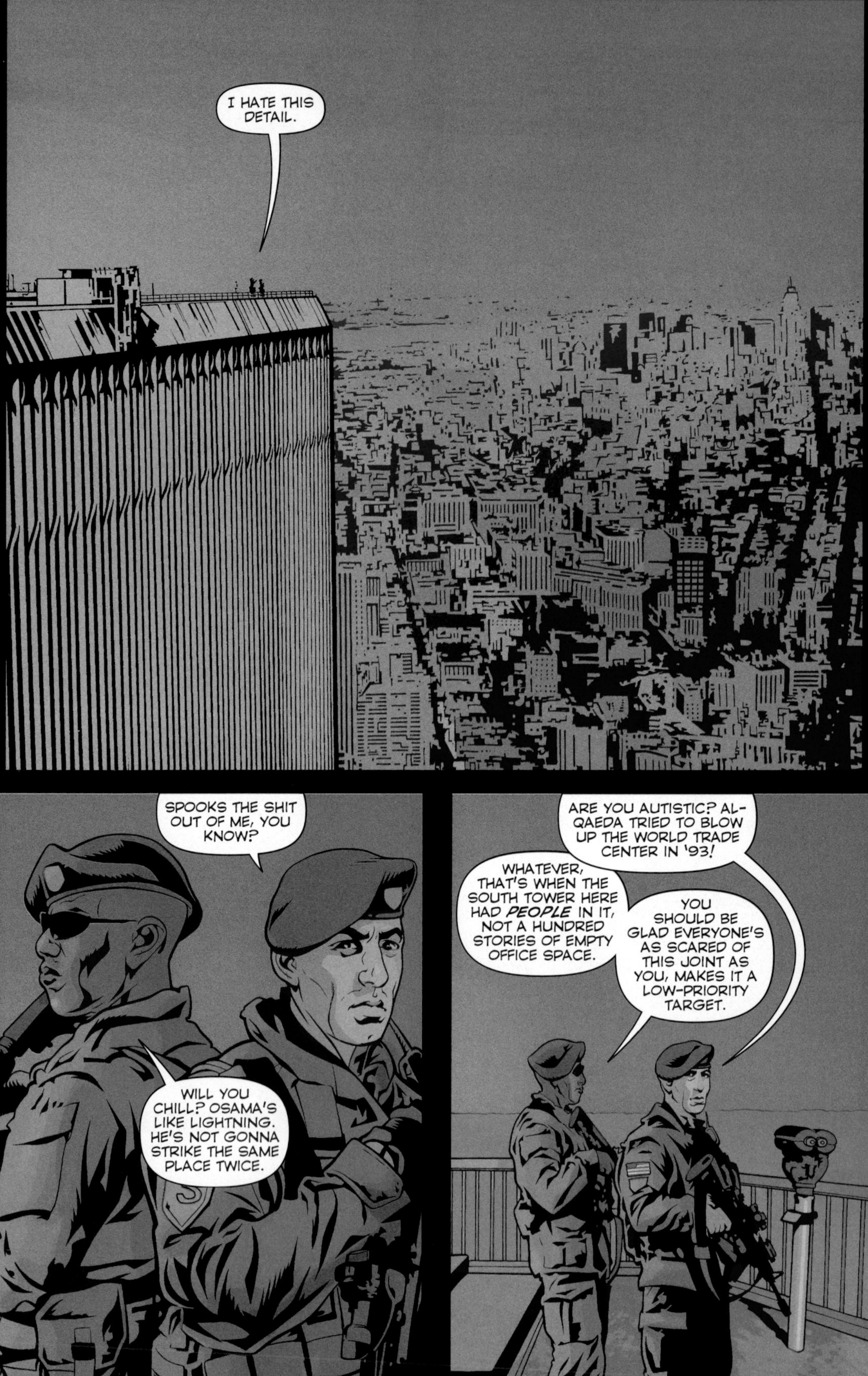
I HATE THIS DETAIL.
SPOOKS THE SHIT OUT OF ME, YOU KNOW?
WILL YOU CHILL? OSAMA'S LIKE LIGHTNING. HE'S NOT GONNA STRIKE THE SAME PLACE TWICE.
ARE YOU AUTISTIC? AL-QAEDA TRIED TO BLOW UP THE WORLD TRADE CENTER IN '93!
WHATEVER, THAT'S WHEN THE SOUTH TOWER HERE HAD *PEOPLE* IN IT, NOT A HUNDRED STORIES OF EMPTY OFFICE SPACE.
YOU SHOULD BE GLAD EVERYONE'S AS SCARED OF THIS JOINT AS YOU, MAKES IT A LOW-PRIORITY TARGET.

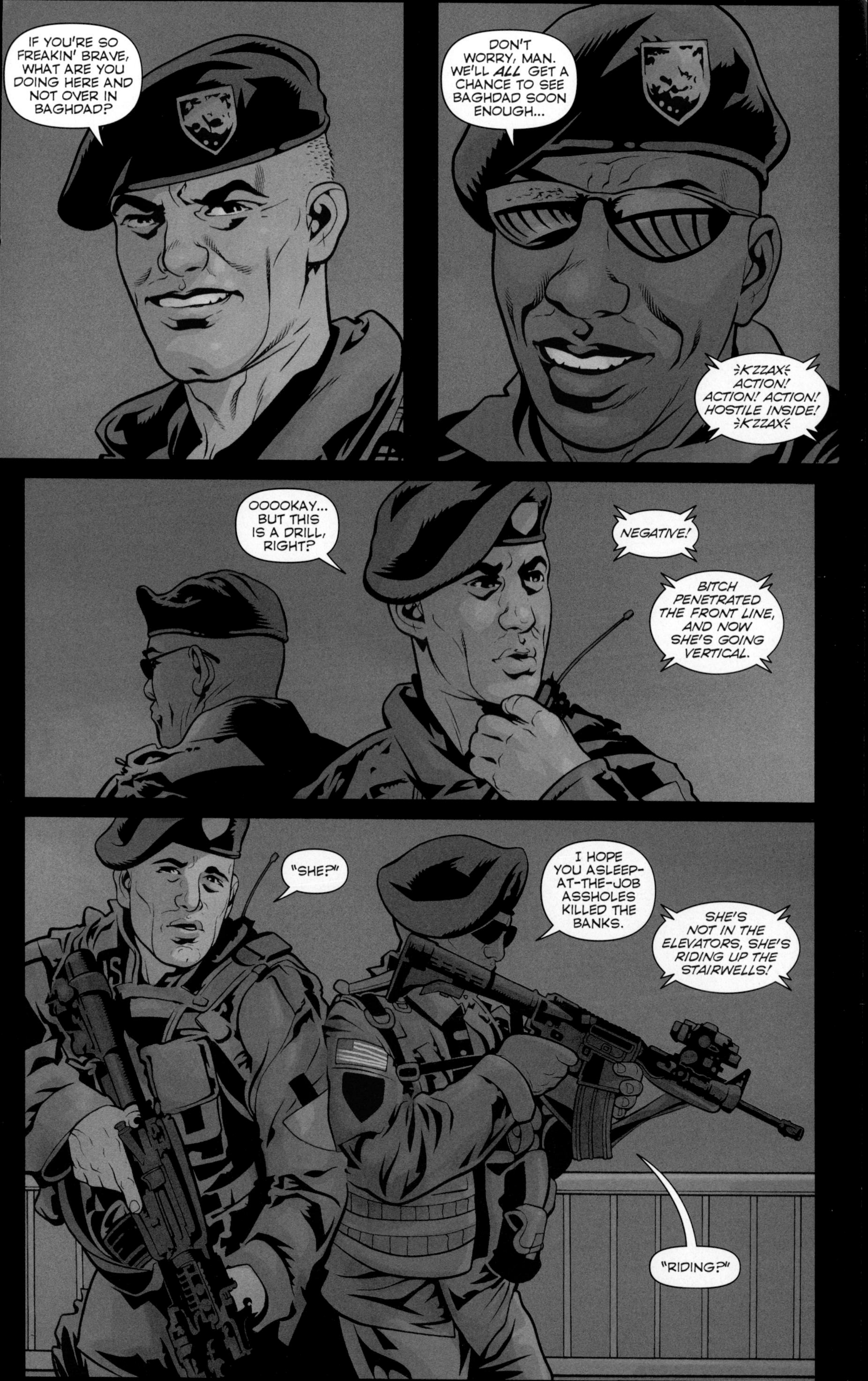
IF YOU'RE SO FREAKIN' BRAVE, WHAT ARE YOU DOING HERE AND NOT OVER IN BAGHDAD?
DON'T WORRY, MAN. WE'LL ALL GET A CHANCE TO SEE BAGHDAD SOON ENOUGH...
KZZAX ACTION! ACTION! ACTION! HOSTILE INSIDE! KZZAX
OOOOKAY... BUT THIS IS A DRILL, RIGHT?
NEGATIVE!
BITCH PENETRATED THE FRONT LINE, AND NOW SHE'S GOING VERTICAL.
"SHE?"
I HOPE YOU ASLEEP-AT-THE-JOB ASSHOLES KILLED THE BANKS.
SHE'S NOT IN THE ELEVATORS, SHE'S RIDING UP THE STAIRWELLS!
"RIDING?"

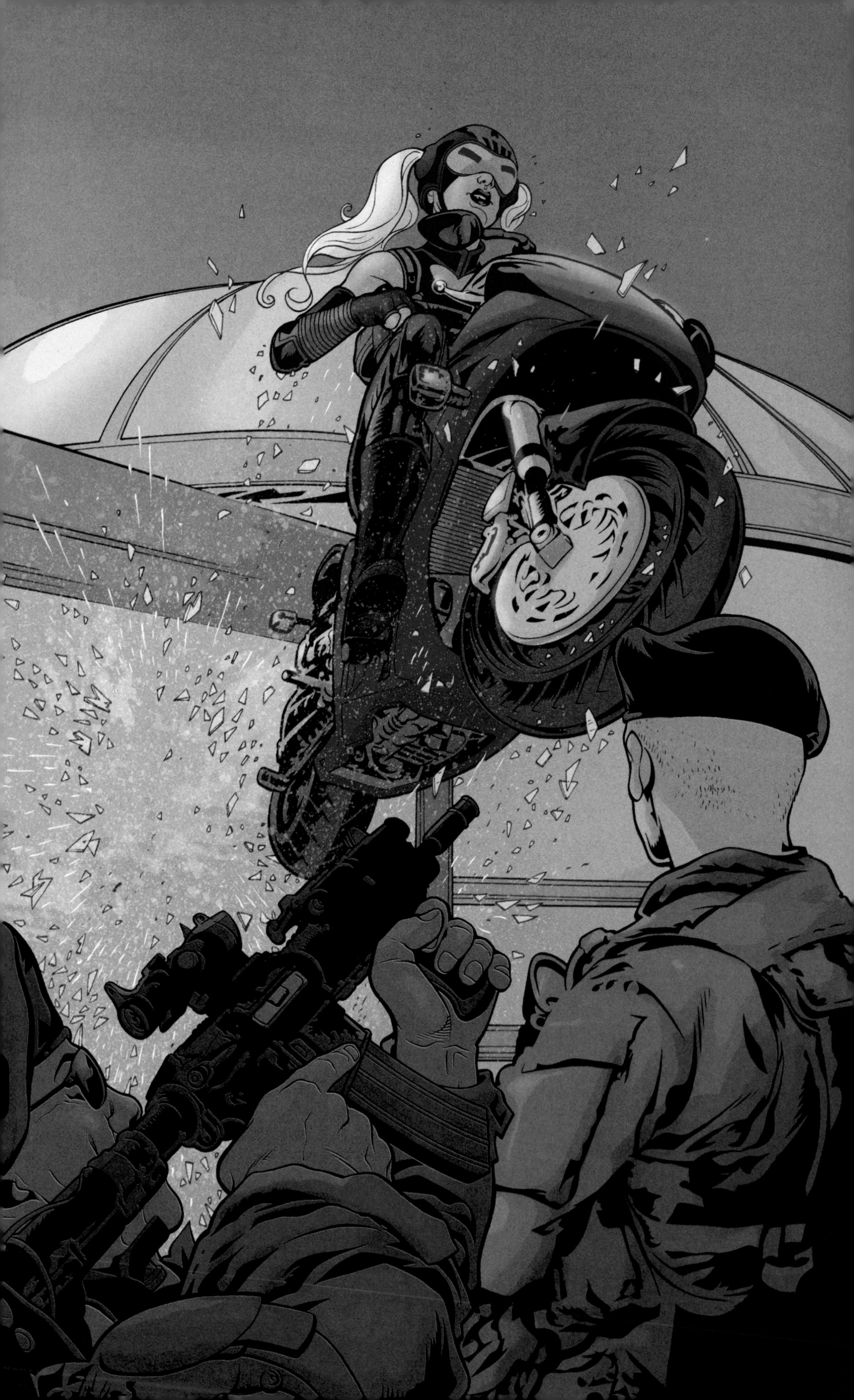

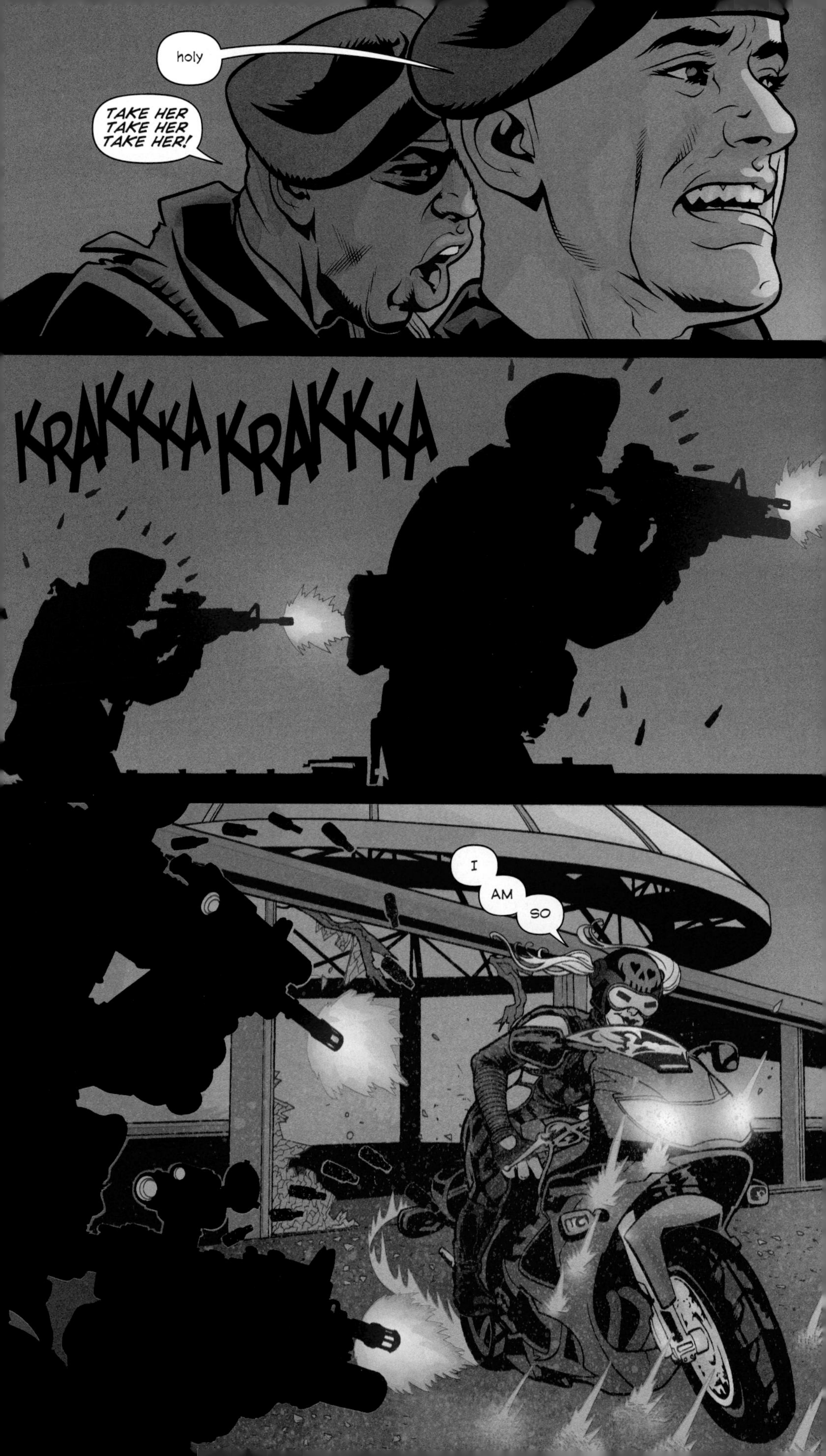
holy
TAKE HER TAKE HER TAKE HER!
KRAKKKA KRAKKKA
I AM SO

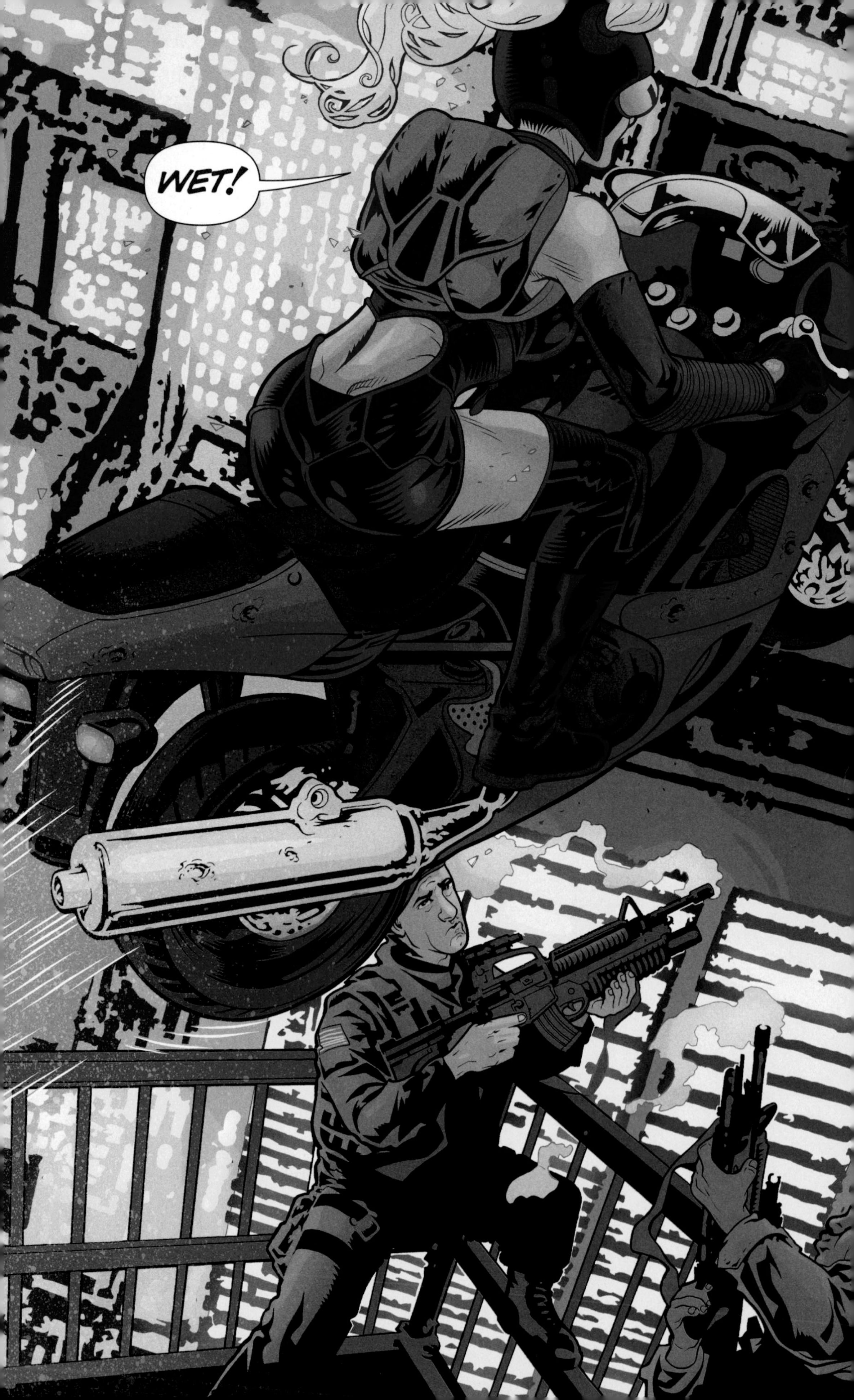
WET!

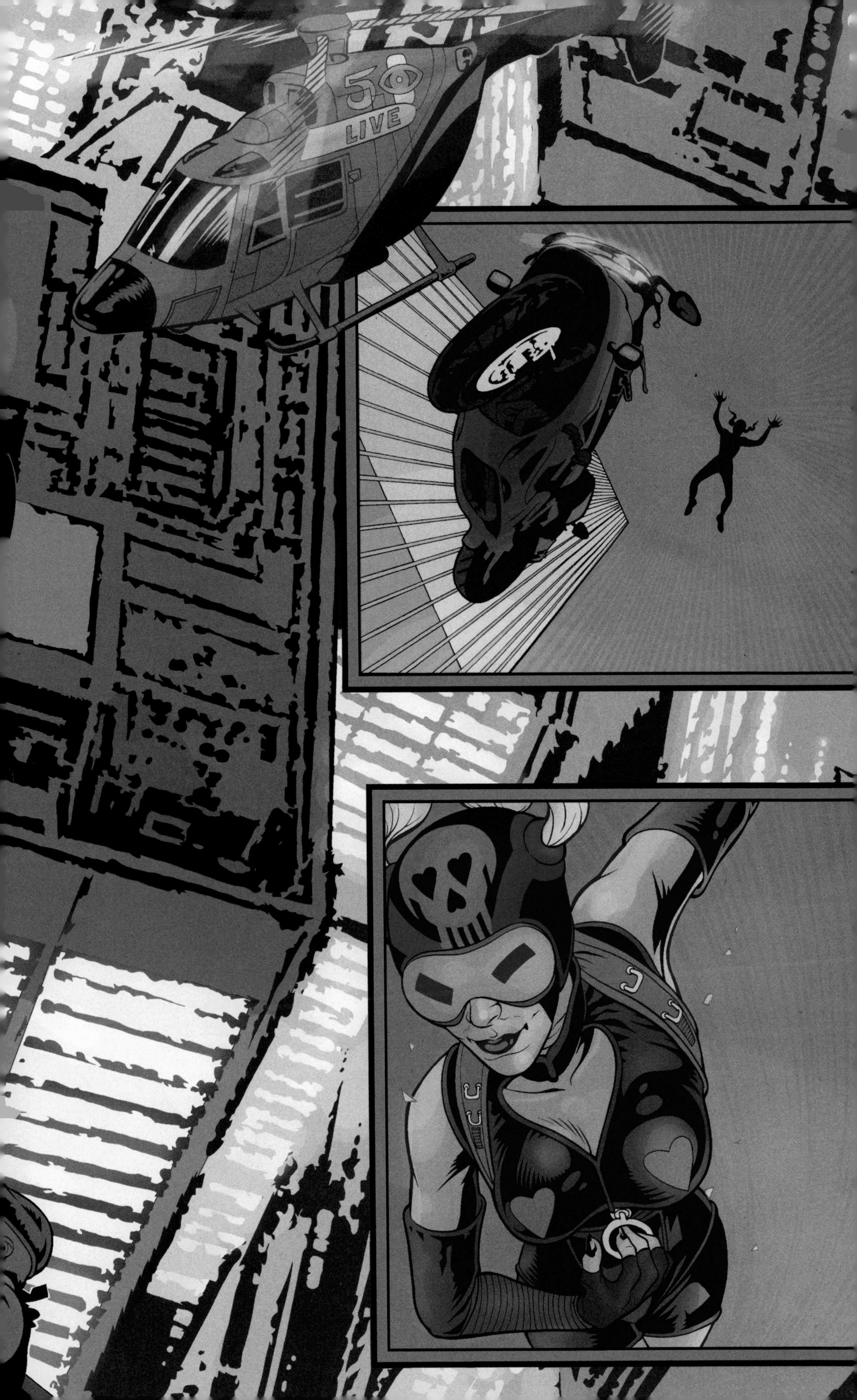
LIVE

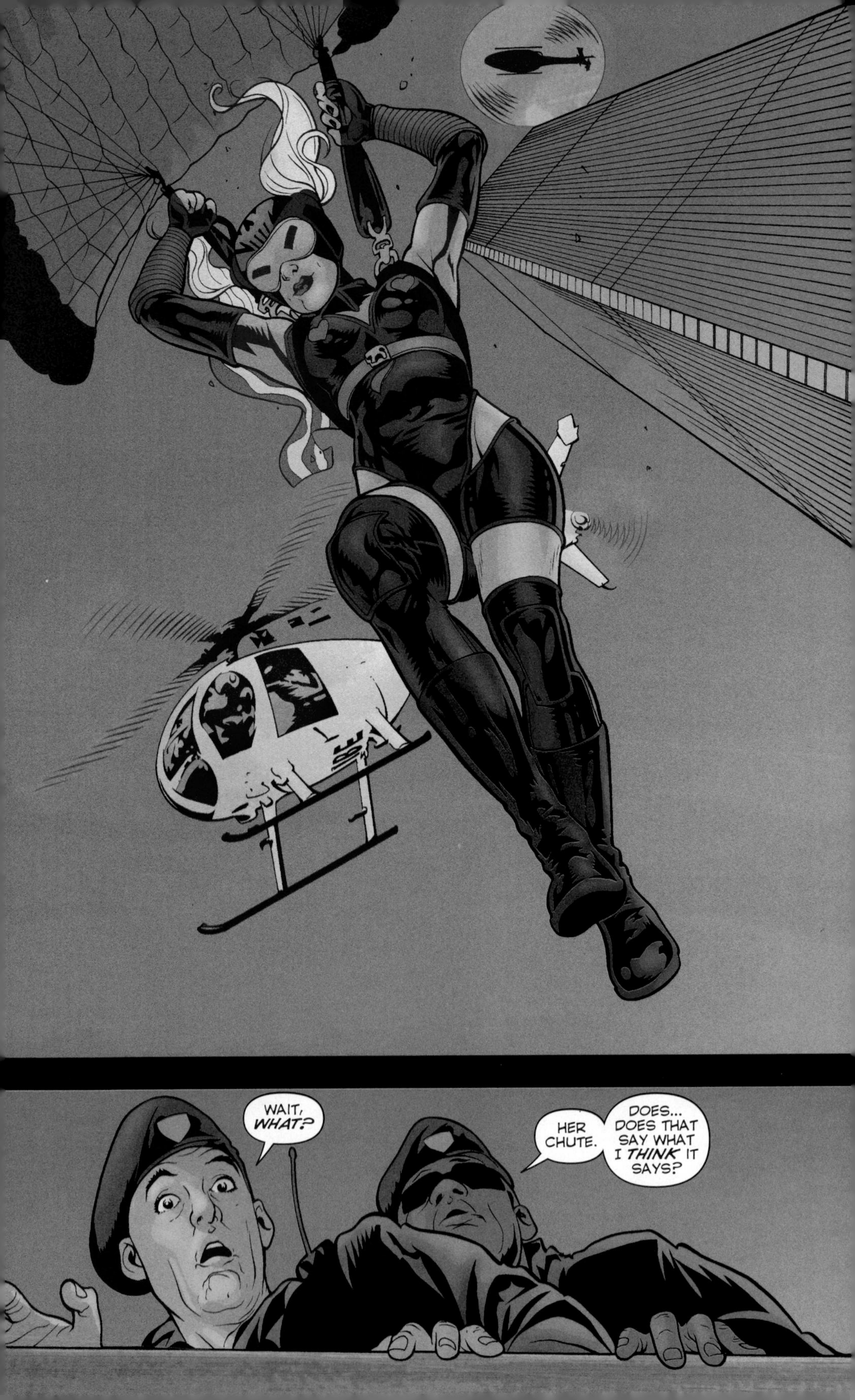
WAIT, *WHAT?*
HER CHUTE.
DOES... DOES THAT SAY WHAT I *THINK* IT SAYS?

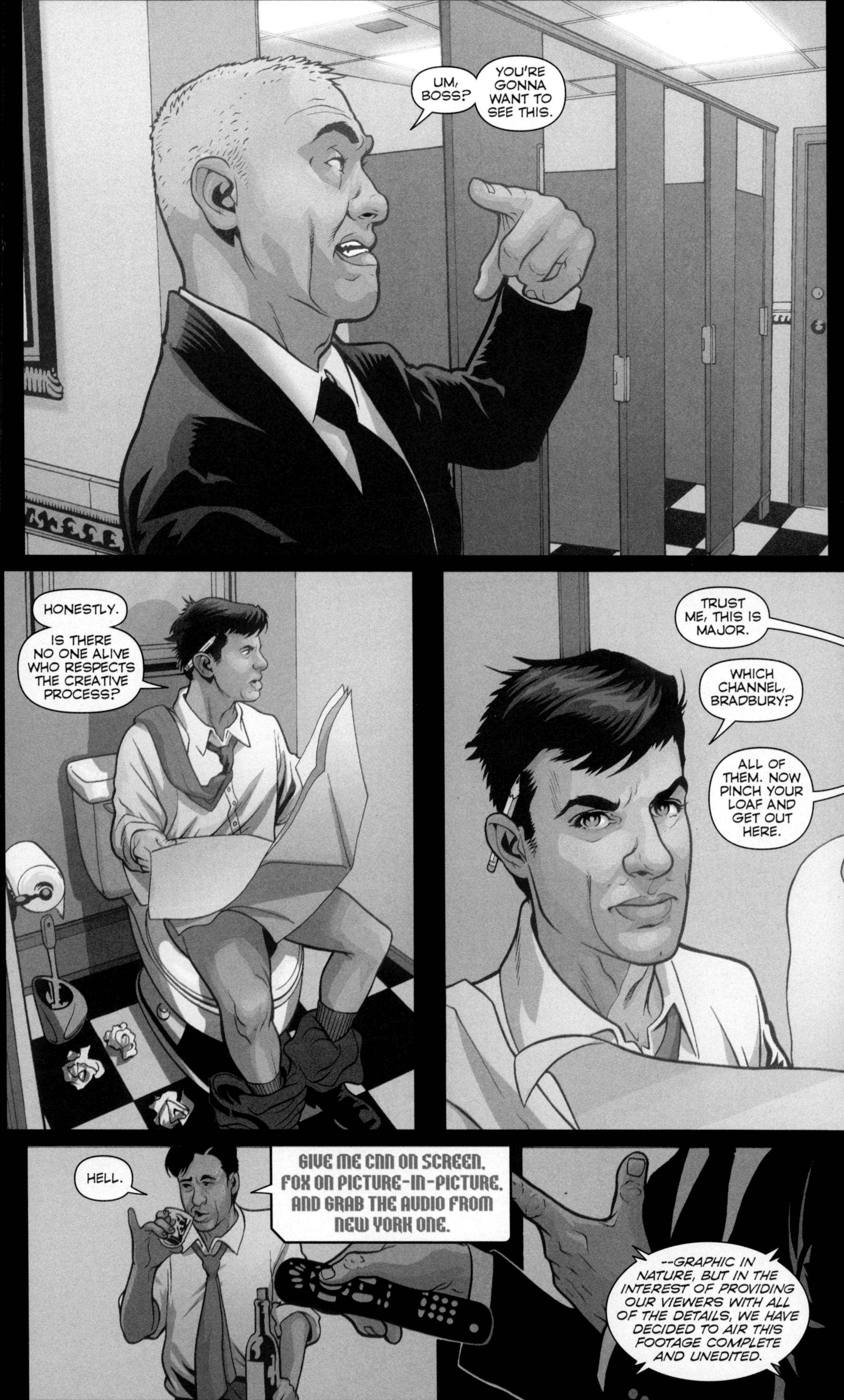

UM, BOSS?
YOU'RE GONNA WANT TO SEE THIS.
HONESTLY.
IS THERE NO ONE ALIVE WHO RESPECTS THE CREATIVE PROCESS?
TRUST ME, THIS IS MAJOR.
WHICH CHANNEL, BRADBURY?
ALL OF THEM. NOW PINCH YOUR LOAF AND GET OUT HERE.
HELL.
GIVE ME CNN ON SCREEN, FOX ON PICTURE-IN-PICTURE, AND GRAB THE AUDIO FROM NEW YORK ONE.
--GRAPHIC IN NATURE, BUT IN THE INTEREST OF PROVIDING OUR VIEWERS WITH ALL OF THE DETAILS, WE HAVE DECIDED TO AIR THIS FOOTAGE COMPLETE AND UNEDITED.

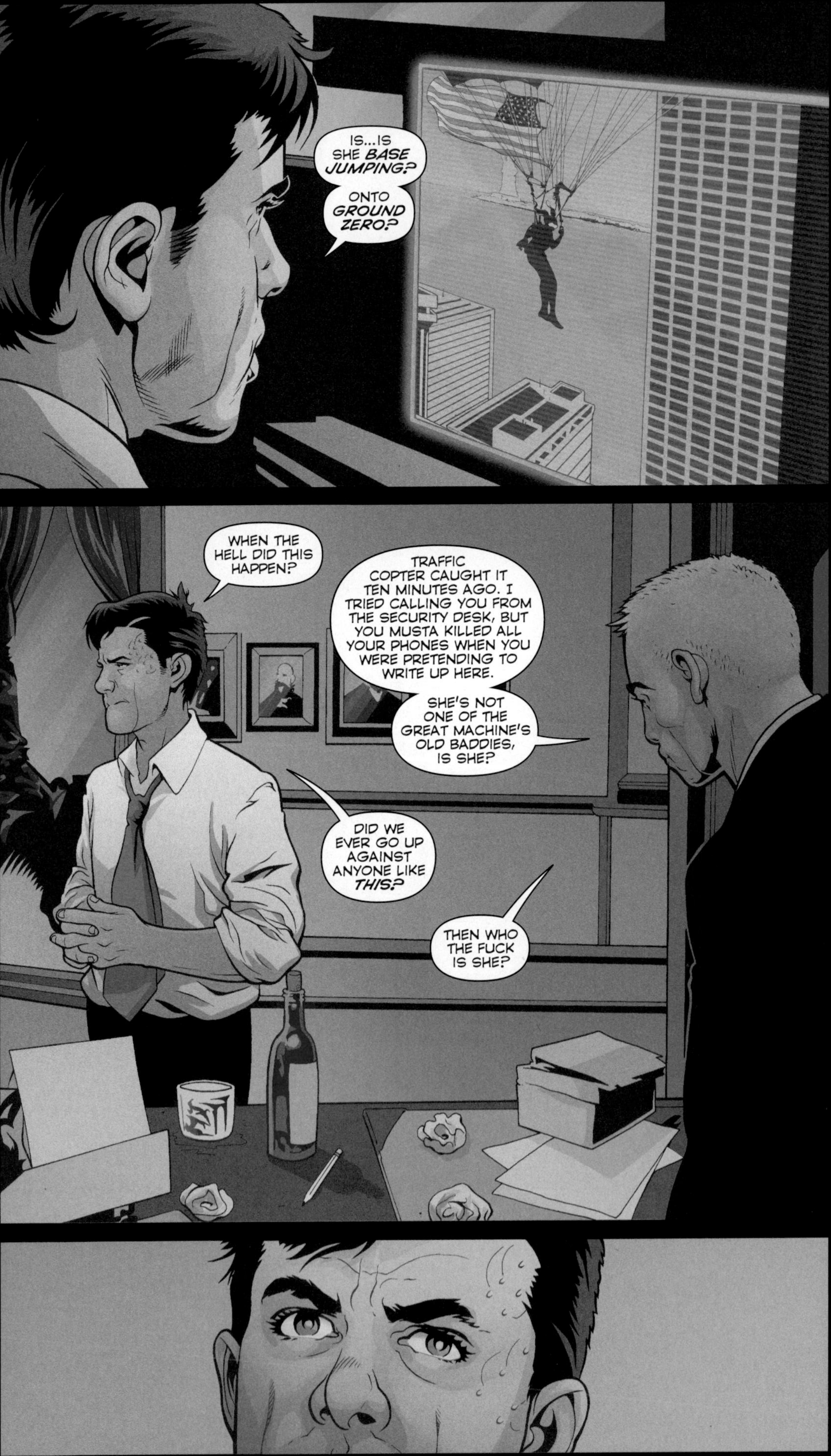
IS...IS SHE *BASE JUMPING?*
ONTO *GROUND ZERO?*
WHEN THE HELL DID THIS HAPPEN?
TRAFFIC COPTER CAUGHT IT TEN MINUTES AGO. I TRIED CALLING YOU FROM THE SECURITY DESK, BUT YOU MUSTA KILLED ALL YOUR PHONES WHEN YOU WERE PRETENDING TO WRITE UP HERE.
SHE'S NOT ONE OF THE GREAT MACHINE'S OLD BADDIES, IS SHE?
DID WE EVER GO UP AGAINST ANYONE LIKE *THIS?*
THEN WHO THE FUCK IS SHE?

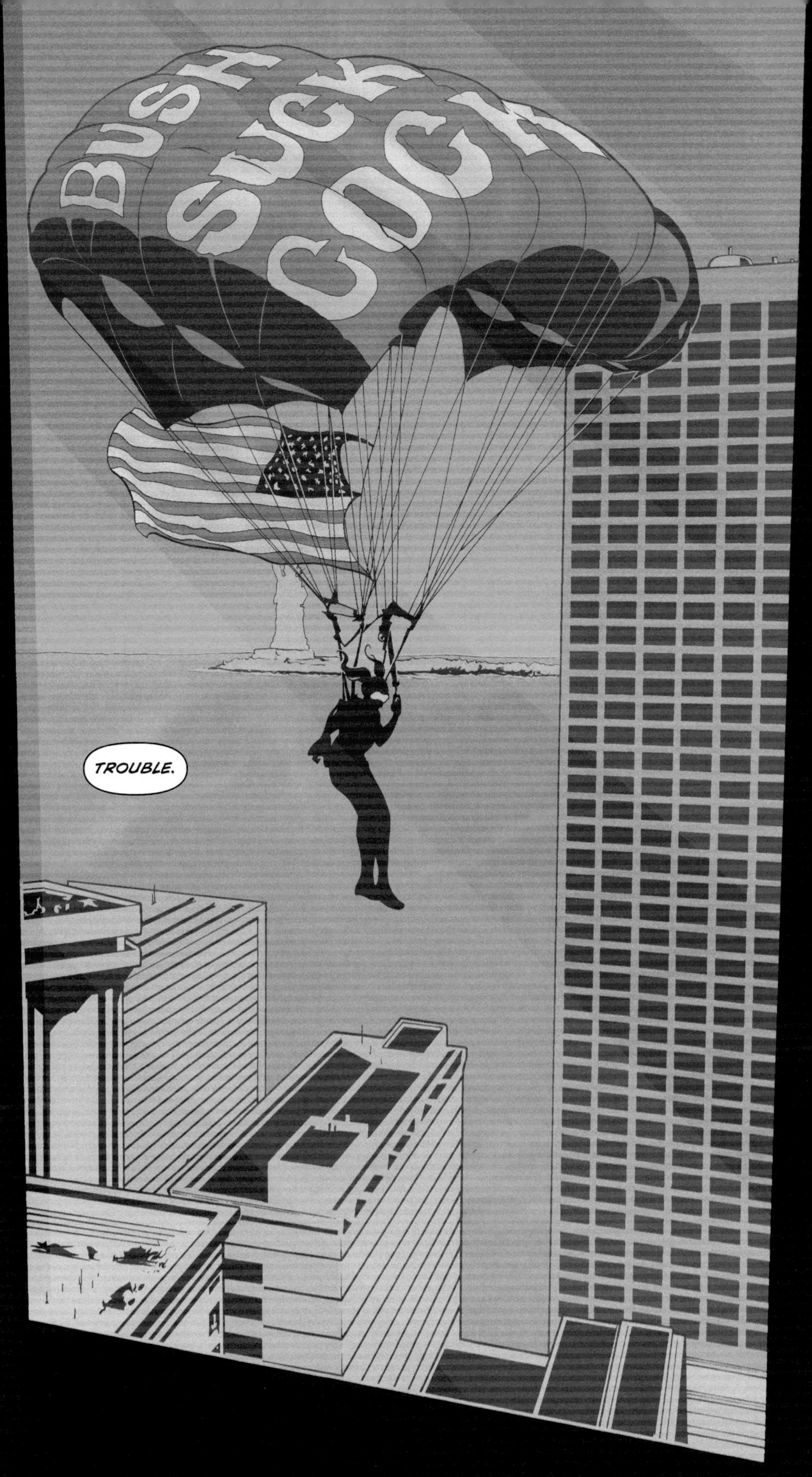
BUSH SUCK COCK
TROUBLE.

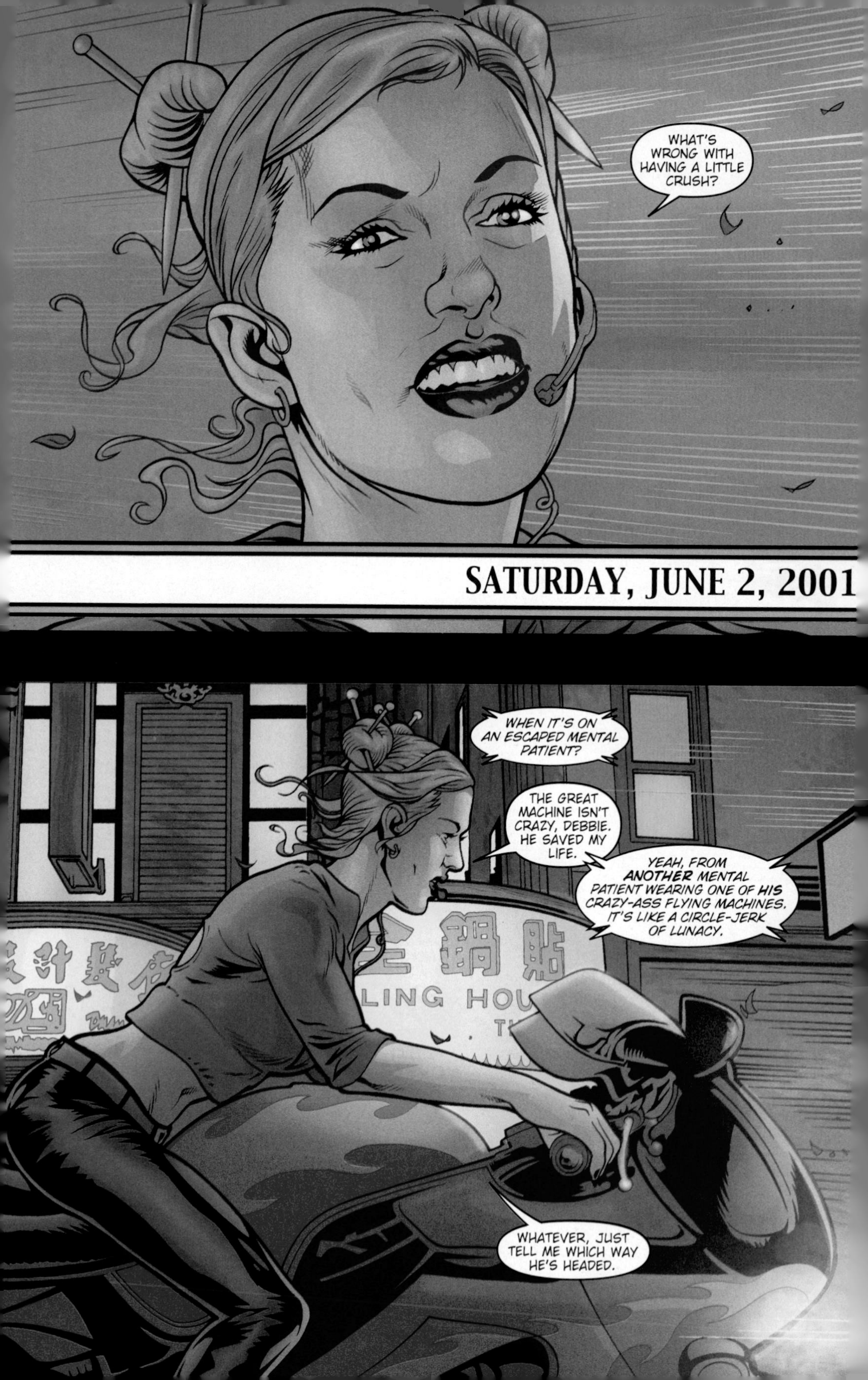
WHAT'S WRONG WITH HAVING A LITTLE CRUSH?
SATURDAY, JUNE 2, 2001
WHEN IT'S ON AN ESCAPED MENTAL PATIENT?
THE GREAT MACHINE ISN'T CRAZY, DEBBIE. HE SAVED MY LIFE.
YEAH, FROM ANOTHER MENTAL PATIENT WEARING ONE OF HIS CRAZY-ASS FLYING MACHINES. IT'S LIKE A CIRCLE-JERK OF LUNACY.
WHATEVER, JUST TELL ME WHICH WAY HE'S HEADED.

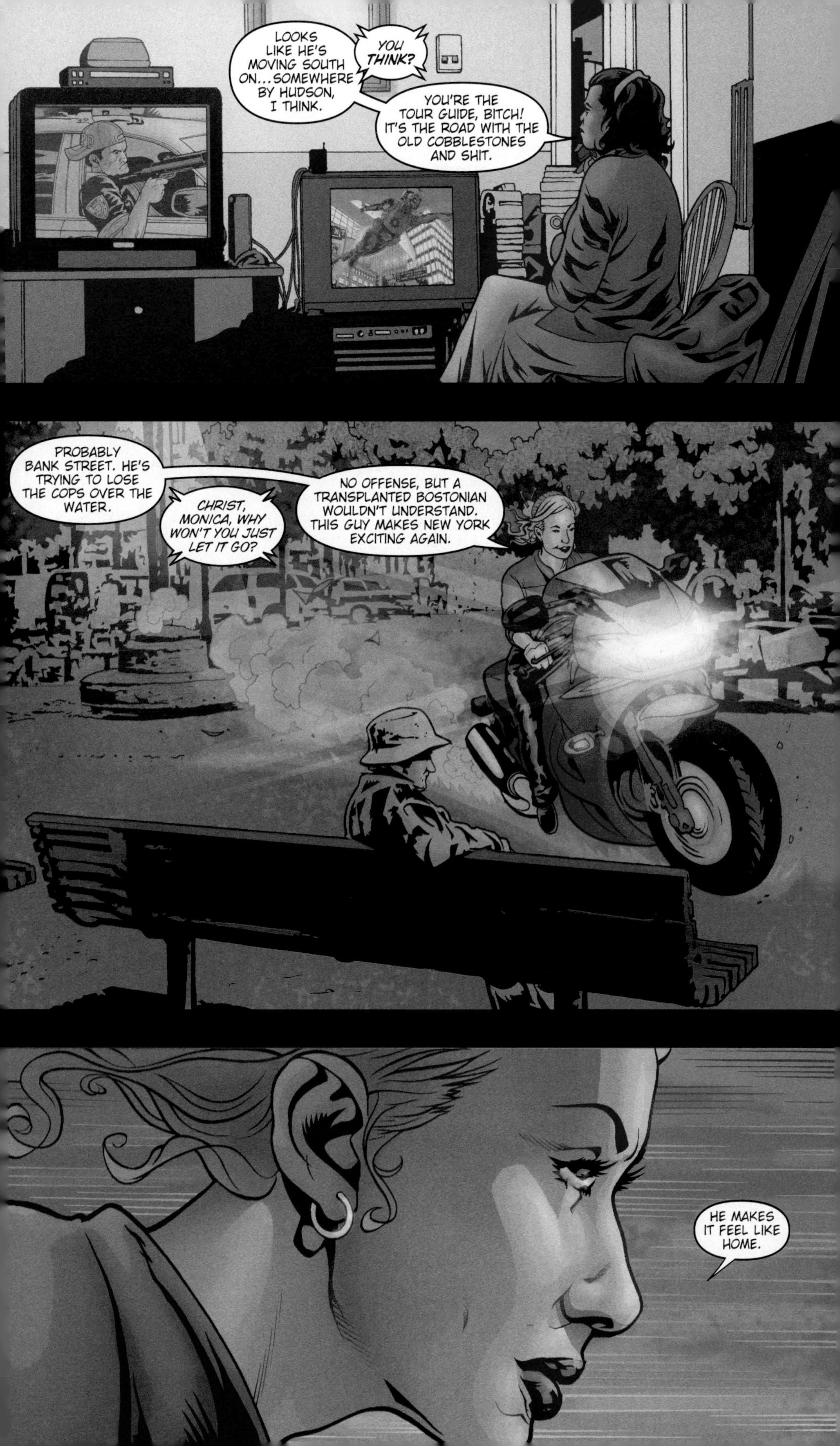
LOOKS LIKE HE'S MOVING SOUTH ON... SOMEWHERE BY HUDSON, I THINK.
YOU THINK?
YOU'RE THE TOUR GUIDE, BITCH! IT'S THE ROAD WITH THE OLD COBBLESTONES AND SHIT.
PROBABLY BANK STREET. HE'S TRYING TO LOSE THE COPS OVER THE WATER.
CHRIST, MONICA, WHY WON'T YOU JUST LET IT GO?
NO OFFENSE, BUT A TRANSPLANTED BOSTONIAN WOULDN'T UNDERSTAND. THIS GUY MAKES NEW YORK EXCITING AGAIN.
HE MAKES IT FEEL LIKE HOME.

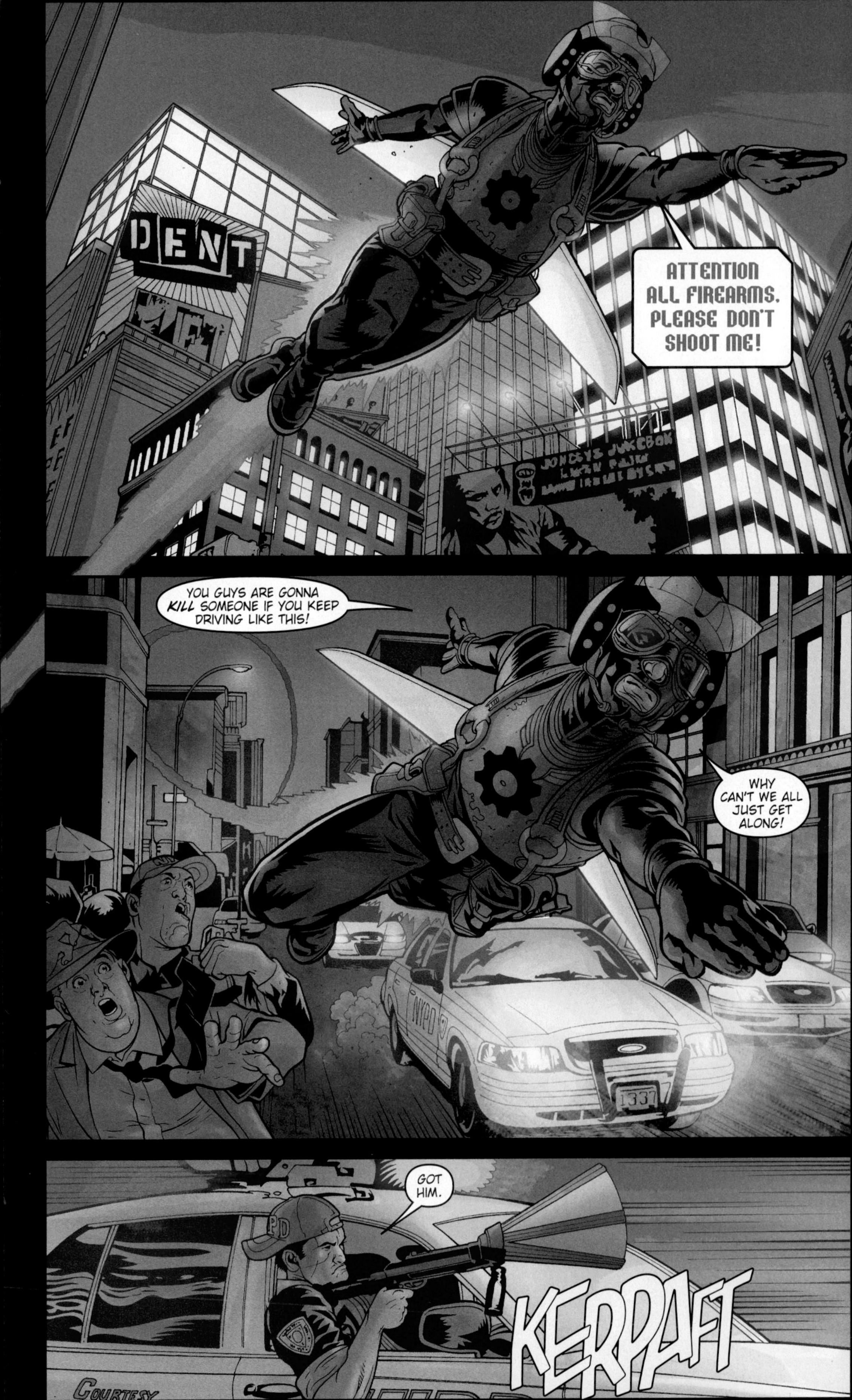
DENT
ATTENTION ALL FIREARMS. PLEASE DON'T SHOOT ME!
YOU GUYS ARE GONNA KILL SOMEONE IF YOU KEEP DRIVING LIKE THIS!
WHY CAN'T WE ALL JUST GET ALONG!
NYPD
1337
GOT HIM.
KERPAFT
COURTESY

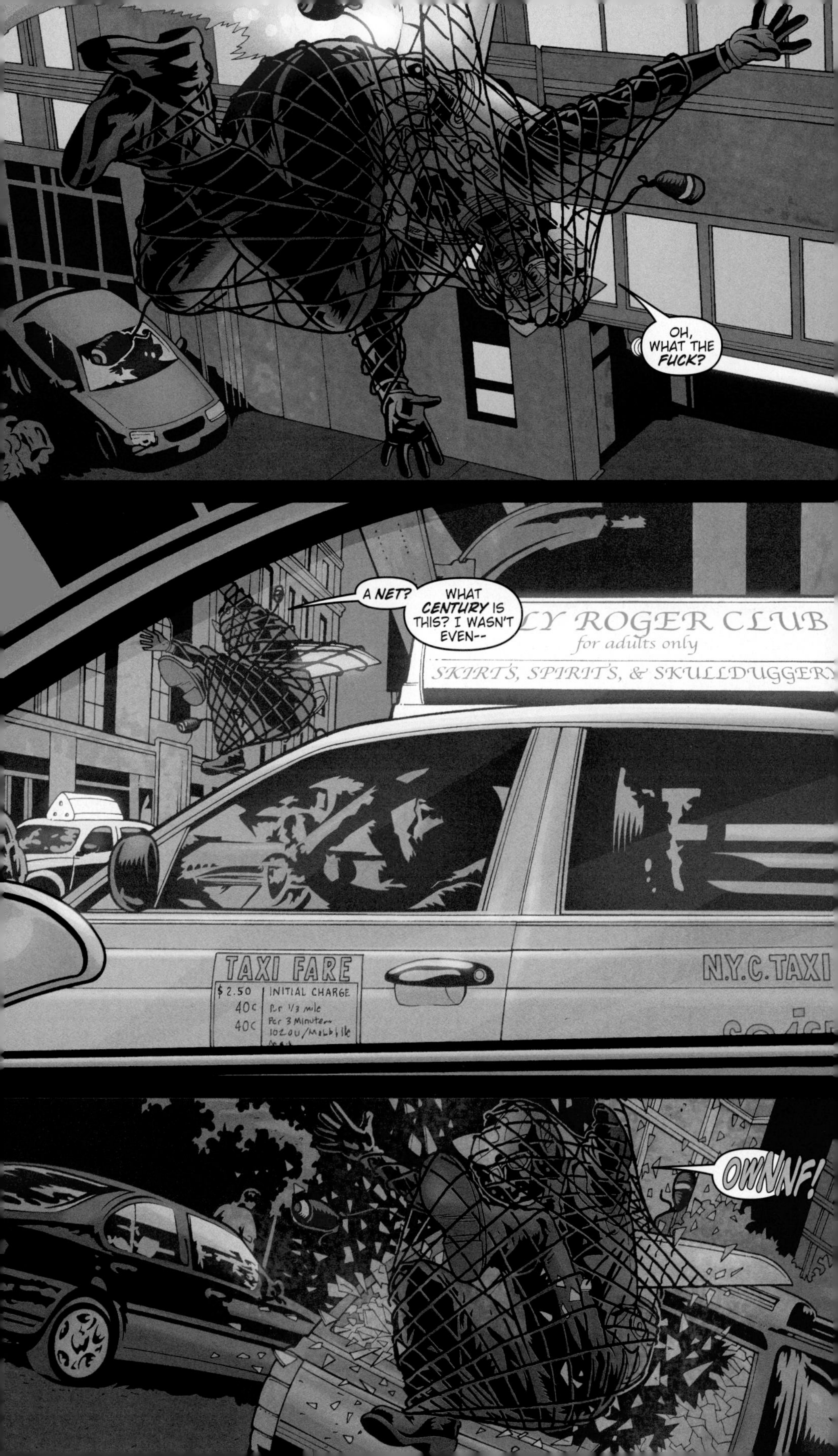
OH, WHAT THE FUCK?
A NET?
WHAT CENTURY IS THIS? I WASN'T EVEN--
LY ROGER CLUB
for adults only
TAXI FARE
$2.50 INITIAL CHARGE
40¢ Per 1/3 mile
40¢ Per 3 Minutes
N.Y.C. TAXI
OWNNF!

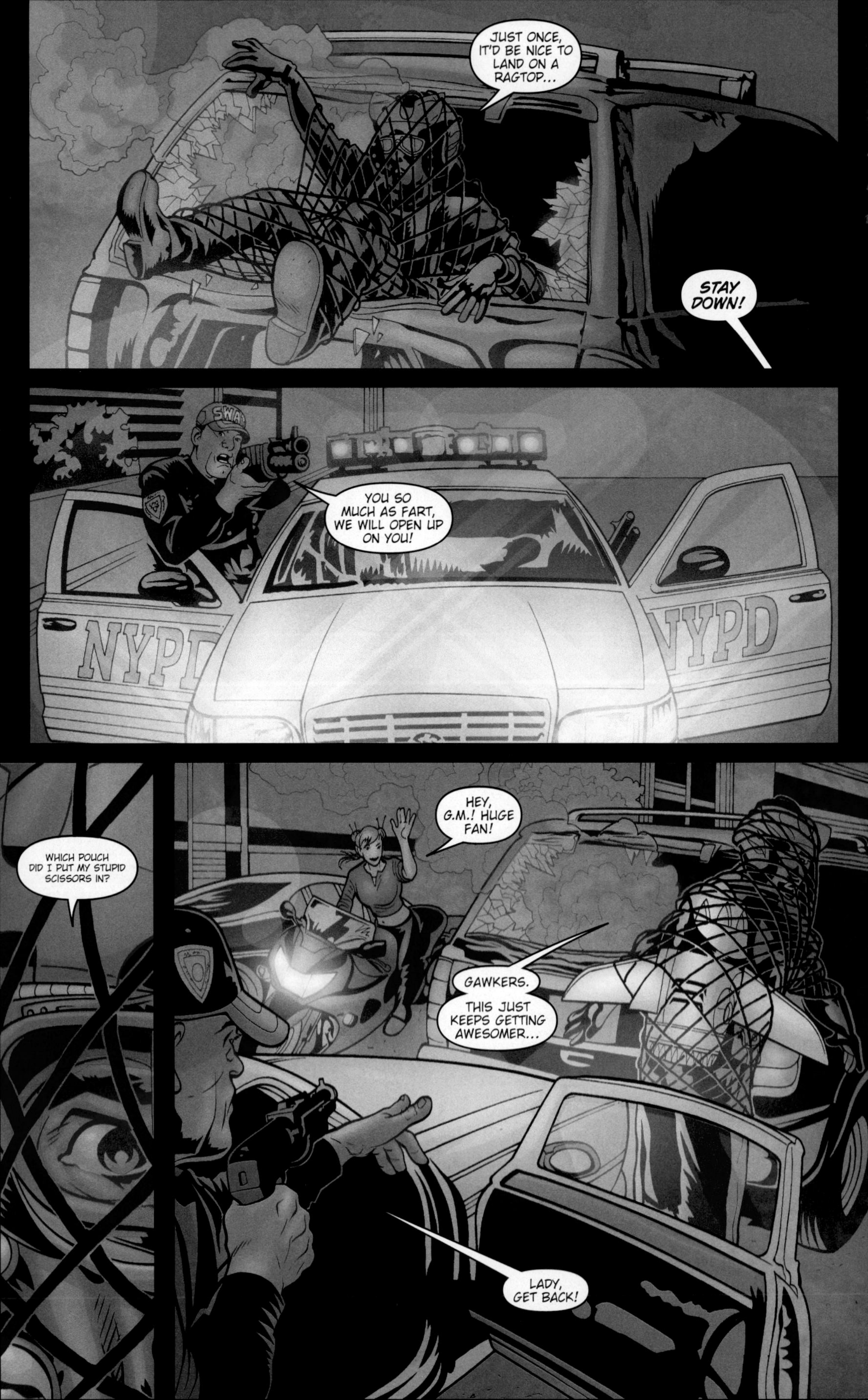
JUST ONCE, IT'D BE NICE TO LAND ON A RAGTOP...
STAY DOWN!
YOU SO MUCH AS FART, WE WILL OPEN UP ON YOU!
NYPD
NYPD
WHICH POUCH DID I PUT MY STUPID SCISSORS IN?
HEY, G.M.! HUGE FAN!
GAWKERS.
THIS JUST KEEPS GETTING AWESOMER...
LADY, GET BACK!

YOU GET BACK! HE ISN'T HURTING *ANYONE!*

LOOK, SISTER, DON'T MAKE ME CUFF YOU FOR INTERFERIN' WITH--

FOR THE LAST TIME, I'M NOT A VILLAIN, I'M A MOTHERFUCKING *GOOD GUY!*

YOU'RE WELCOME...

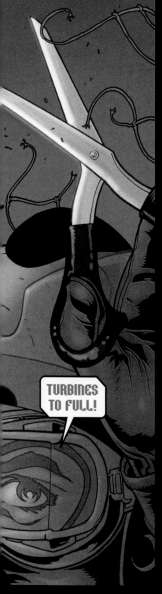

TURBINES TO FULL!

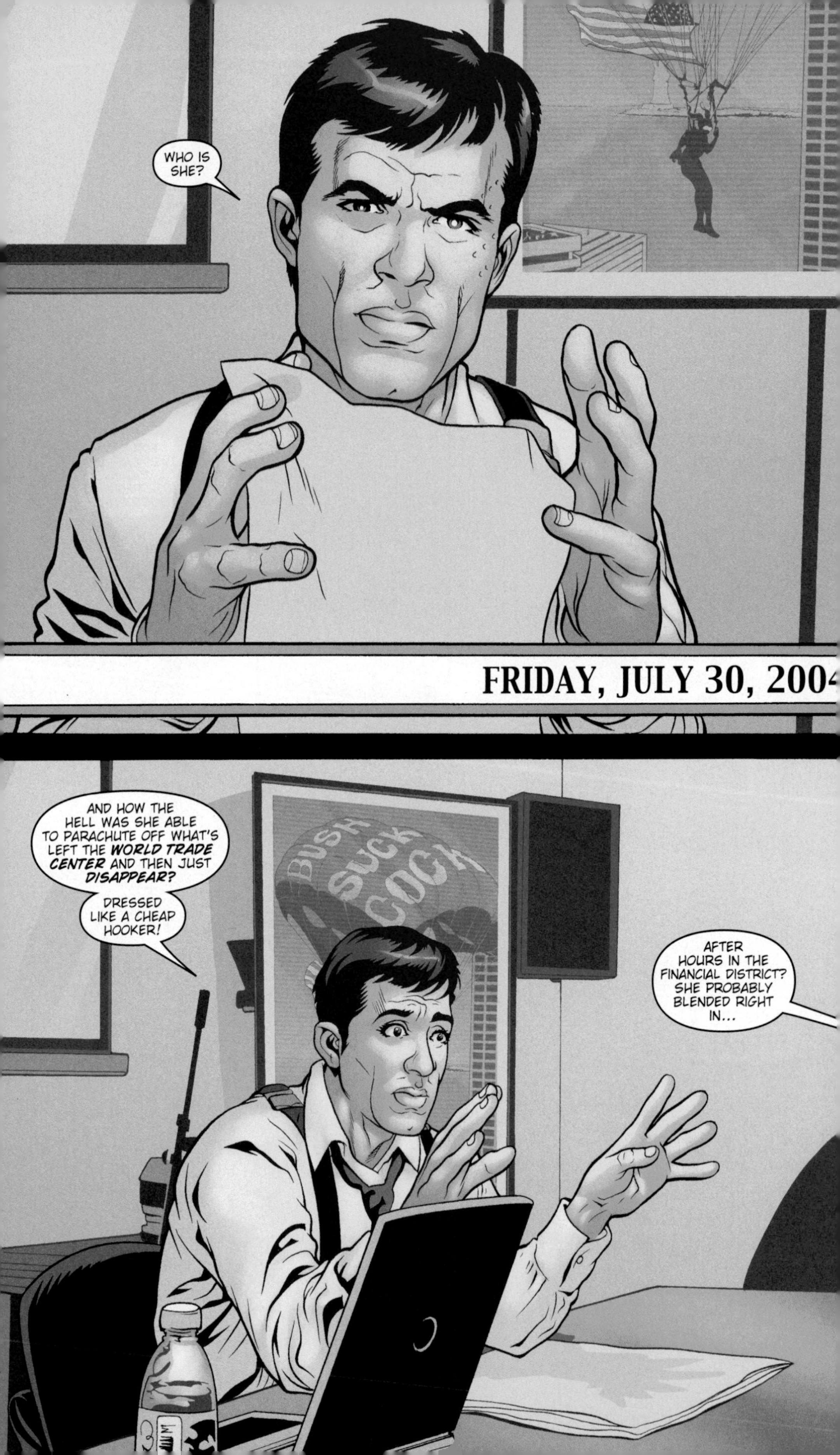
WHO IS SHE?
FRIDAY, JULY 30, 2004
AND HOW THE HELL WAS SHE ABLE TO PARACHUTE OFF WHAT'S LEFT THE ***WORLD TRADE CENTER*** AND THEN JUST ***DISAPPEAR?***
DRESSED LIKE A CHEAP HOOKER!
BUSH SUCK COCK
AFTER HOURS IN THE FINANCIAL DISTRICT? SHE PROBABLY BLENDED RIGHT IN...

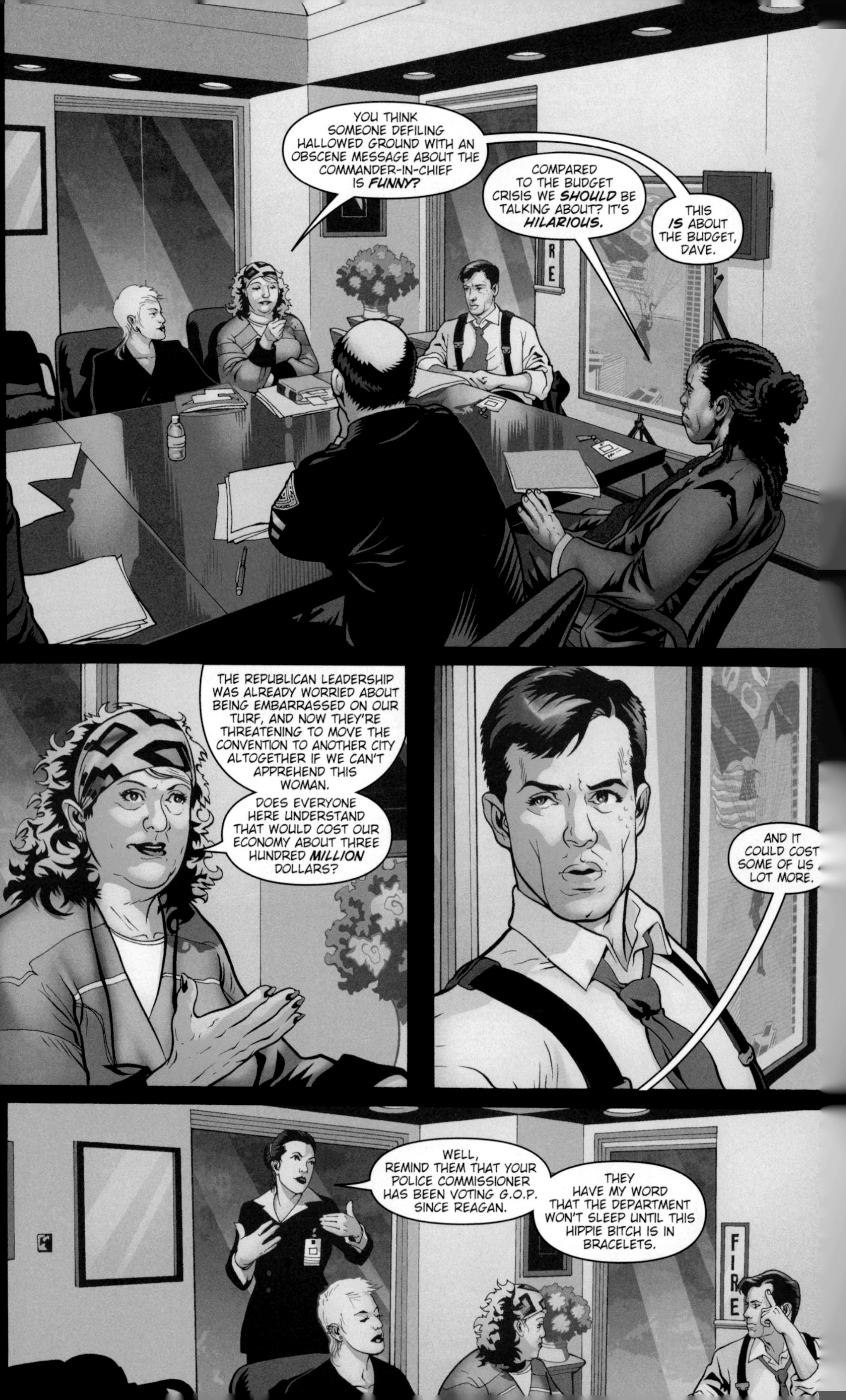
YOU THINK SOMEONE DEFILING HALLOWED GROUND WITH AN OBSCENE MESSAGE ABOUT THE COMMANDER-IN-CHIEF IS *FUNNY?*
COMPARED TO THE BUDGET CRISIS WE *SHOULD* BE TALKING ABOUT? IT'S *HILARIOUS.*
THIS *IS* ABOUT THE BUDGET, DAVE.
FIRE
THE REPUBLICAN LEADERSHIP WAS ALREADY WORRIED ABOUT BEING EMBARRASSED ON OUR TURF, AND NOW THEY'RE THREATENING TO MOVE THE CONVENTION TO ANOTHER CITY ALTOGETHER IF WE CAN'T APPREHEND THIS WOMAN.
DOES EVERYONE HERE UNDERSTAND THAT WOULD COST OUR ECONOMY ABOUT THREE HUNDRED *MILLION* DOLLARS?
AND IT COULD COST SOME OF US LOT MORE.
WELL, REMIND THEM THAT YOUR POLICE COMMISSIONER HAS BEEN VOTING G.O.P. SINCE REAGAN.
THEY HAVE MY WORD THAT THE DEPARTMENT WON'T SLEEP UNTIL THIS HIPPIE BITCH IS IN BRACELETS.
FIRE

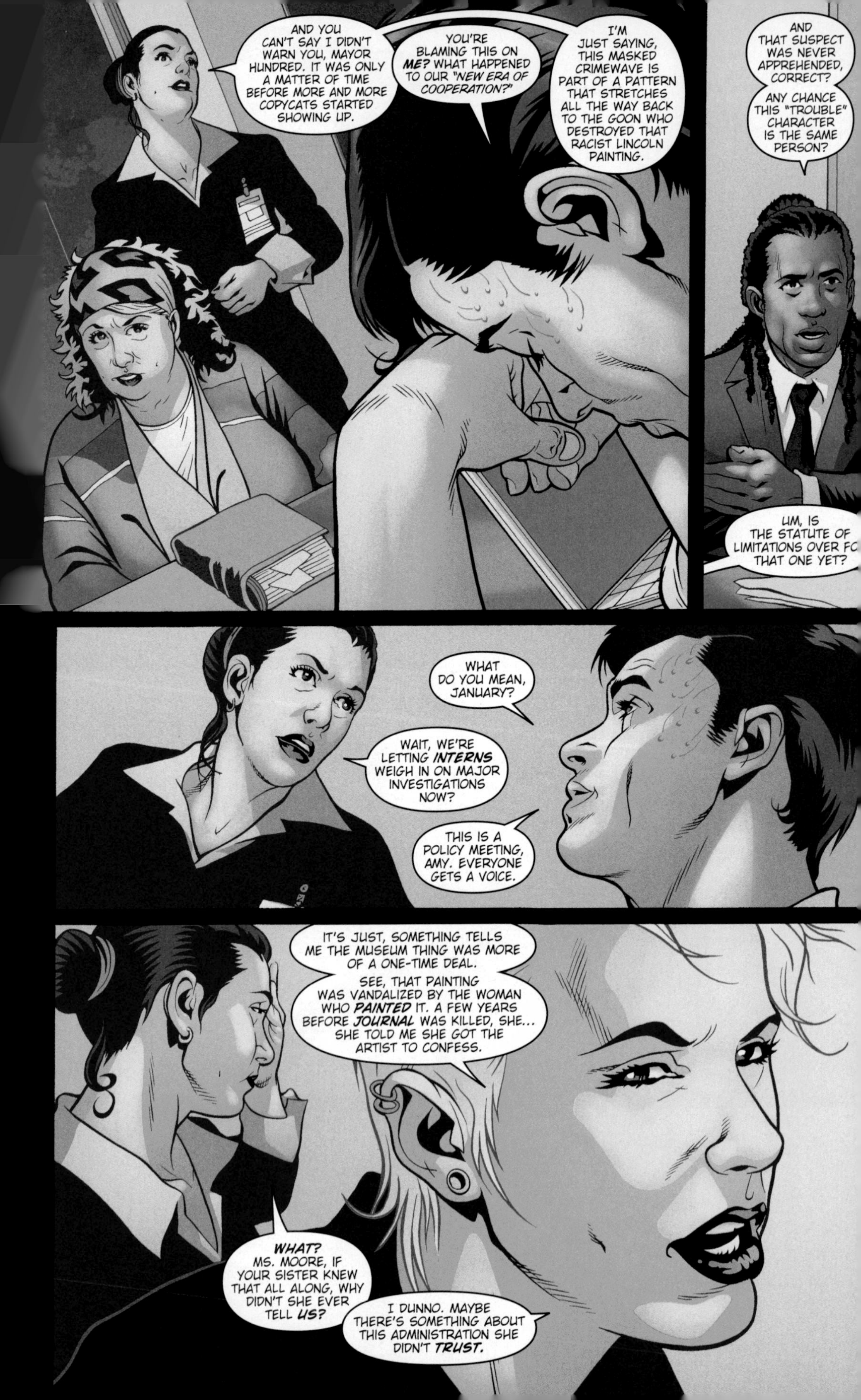
AND YOU CAN'T SAY I DIDN'T WARN YOU, MAYOR HUNDRED. IT WAS ONLY A MATTER OF TIME BEFORE MORE AND MORE COPYCATS STARTED SHOWING UP.
YOU'RE BLAMING THIS ON ME? WHAT HAPPENED TO OUR "NEW ERA OF COOPERATION?"
I'M JUST SAYING, THIS MASKED CRIMEWAVE IS PART OF A PATTERN THAT STRETCHES ALL THE WAY BACK TO THE GOON WHO DESTROYED THAT RACIST LINCOLN PAINTING.
AND THAT SUSPECT WAS NEVER APPREHENDED, CORRECT?
ANY CHANCE THIS "TROUBLE" CHARACTER IS THE SAME PERSON?
UM, IS THE STATUTE OF LIMITATIONS OVER FO THAT ONE YET?
WHAT DO YOU MEAN, JANUARY?
WAIT, WE'RE LETTING INTERNS WEIGH IN ON MAJOR INVESTIGATIONS NOW?
THIS IS A POLICY MEETING, AMY. EVERYONE GETS A VOICE.
IT'S JUST, SOMETHING TELLS ME THE MUSEUM THING WAS MORE OF A ONE-TIME DEAL.
SEE, THAT PAINTING WAS VANDALIZED BY THE WOMAN WHO PAINTED IT. A FEW YEARS BEFORE JOURNAL WAS KILLED, SHE... SHE TOLD ME SHE GOT THE ARTIST TO CONFESS.
WHAT? MS. MOORE, IF YOUR SISTER KNEW THAT ALL ALONG, WHY DIDN'T SHE EVER TELL US?
I DUNNO. MAYBE THERE'S SOMETHING ABOUT THIS ADMINISTRATION SHE DIDN'T TRUST.

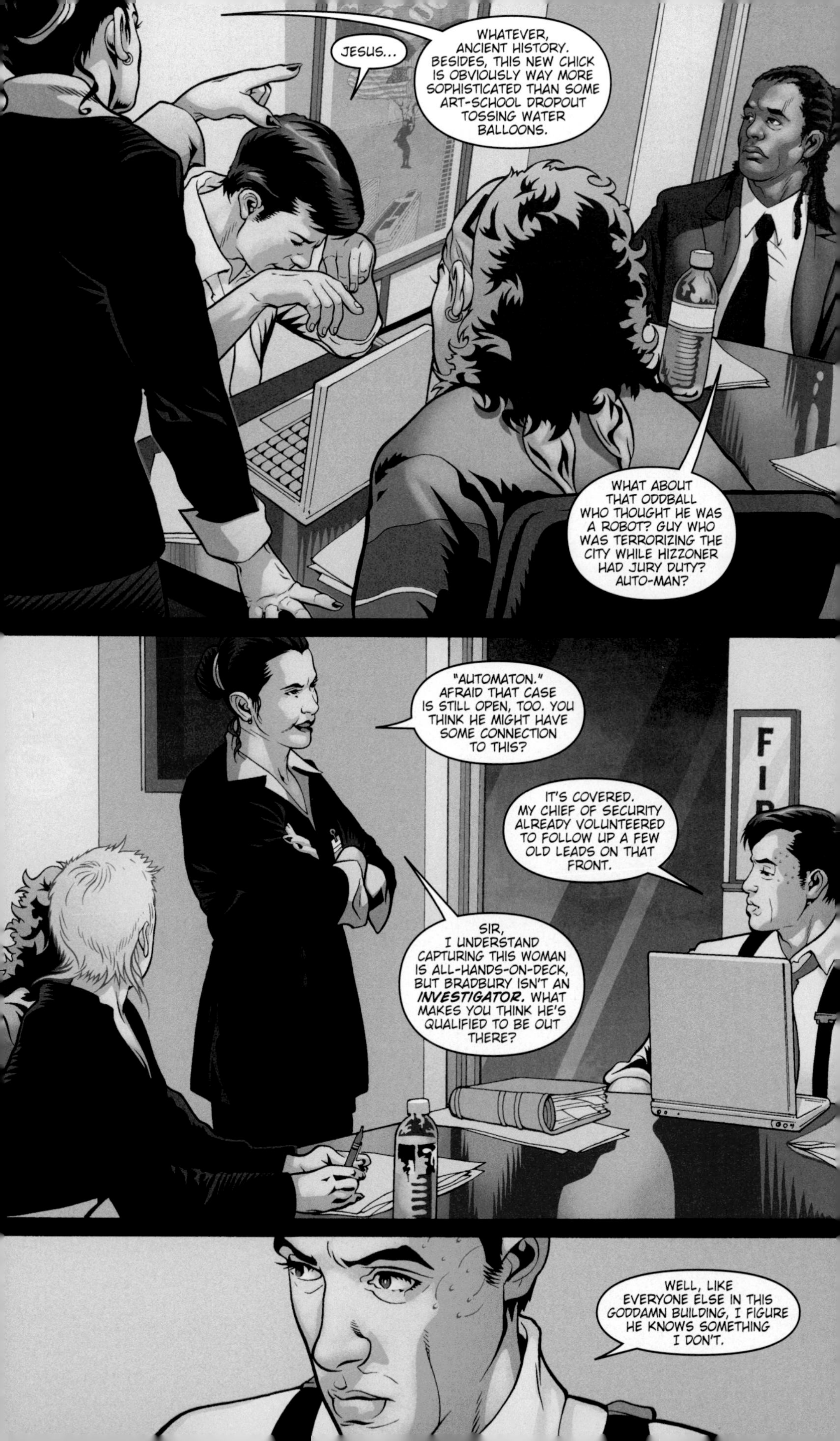
JESUS...
WHATEVER, ANCIENT HISTORY. BESIDES, THIS NEW CHICK IS OBVIOUSLY WAY MORE SOPHISTICATED THAN SOME ART-SCHOOL DROPOUT TOSSING WATER BALLOONS.
WHAT ABOUT THAT ODDBALL WHO THOUGHT HE WAS A ROBOT? GUY WHO WAS TERRORIZING THE CITY WHILE HIZZONER HAD JURY DUTY? AUTO-MAN?
"AUTOMATON." AFRAID THAT CASE IS STILL OPEN, TOO. YOU THINK HE MIGHT HAVE SOME CONNECTION TO THIS?
IT'S COVERED. MY CHIEF OF SECURITY ALREADY VOLUNTEERED TO FOLLOW UP A FEW OLD LEADS ON THAT FRONT.
SIR, I UNDERSTAND CAPTURING THIS WOMAN IS ALL-HANDS-ON-DECK, BUT BRADBURY ISN'T AN ***INVESTIGATOR.*** WHAT MAKES YOU THINK HE'S QUALIFIED TO BE OUT THERE?
WELL, LIKE EVERYONE ELSE IN THIS GODDAMN BUILDING, I FIGURE HE KNOWS SOMETHING I DON'T.

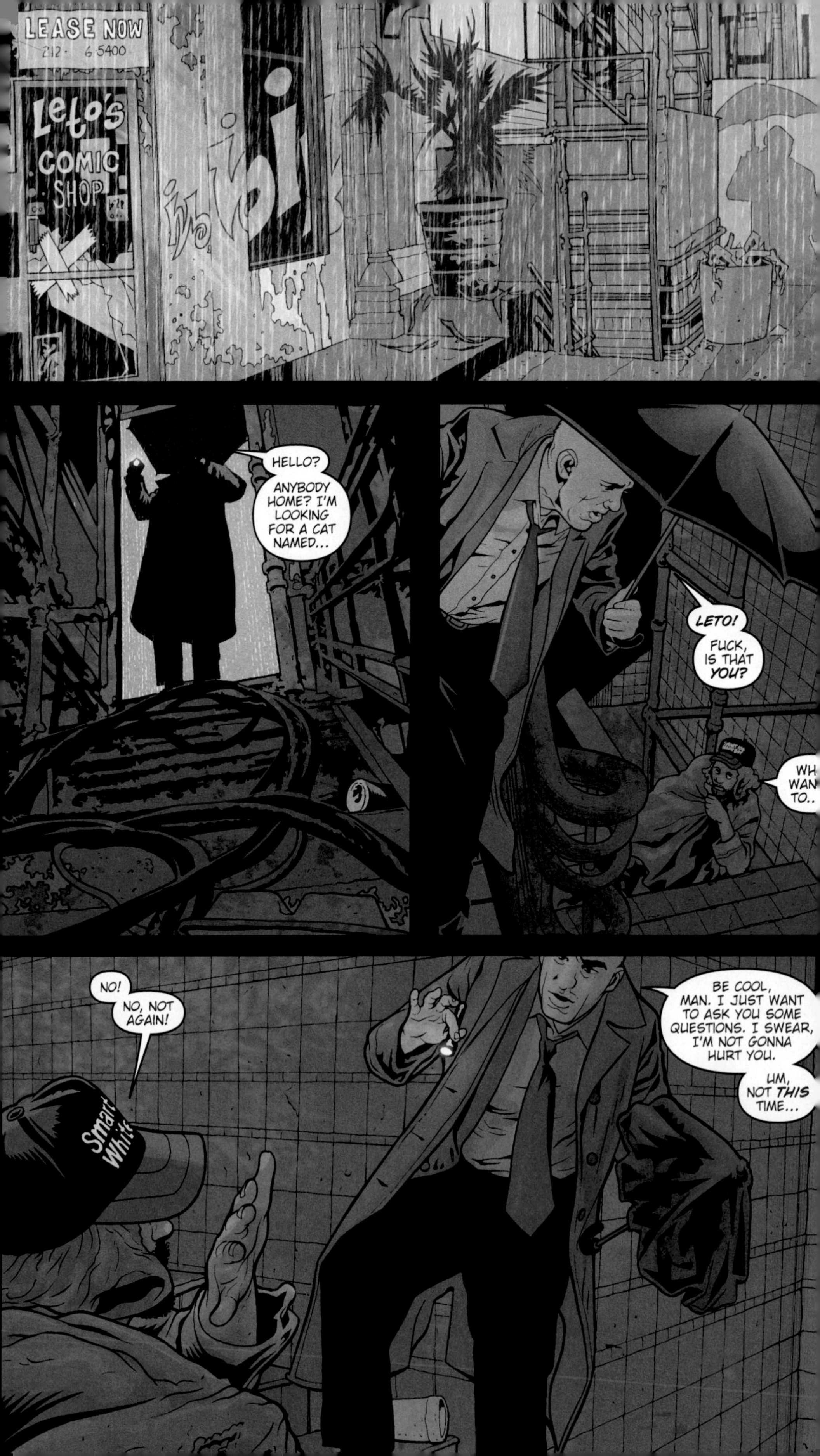
LEASE NOW
212- 6 5400
Leto's
COMIC
SHOP
HELLO?
ANYBODY HOME? I'M LOOKING FOR A CAT NAMED...
LETO!
FUCK, IS THAT YOU?
NO!
NO, NOT AGAIN!
BE COOL, MAN. I JUST WANT TO ASK YOU SOME QUESTIONS. I SWEAR, I'M NOT GONNA HURT YOU.
UM, NOT THIS TIME...

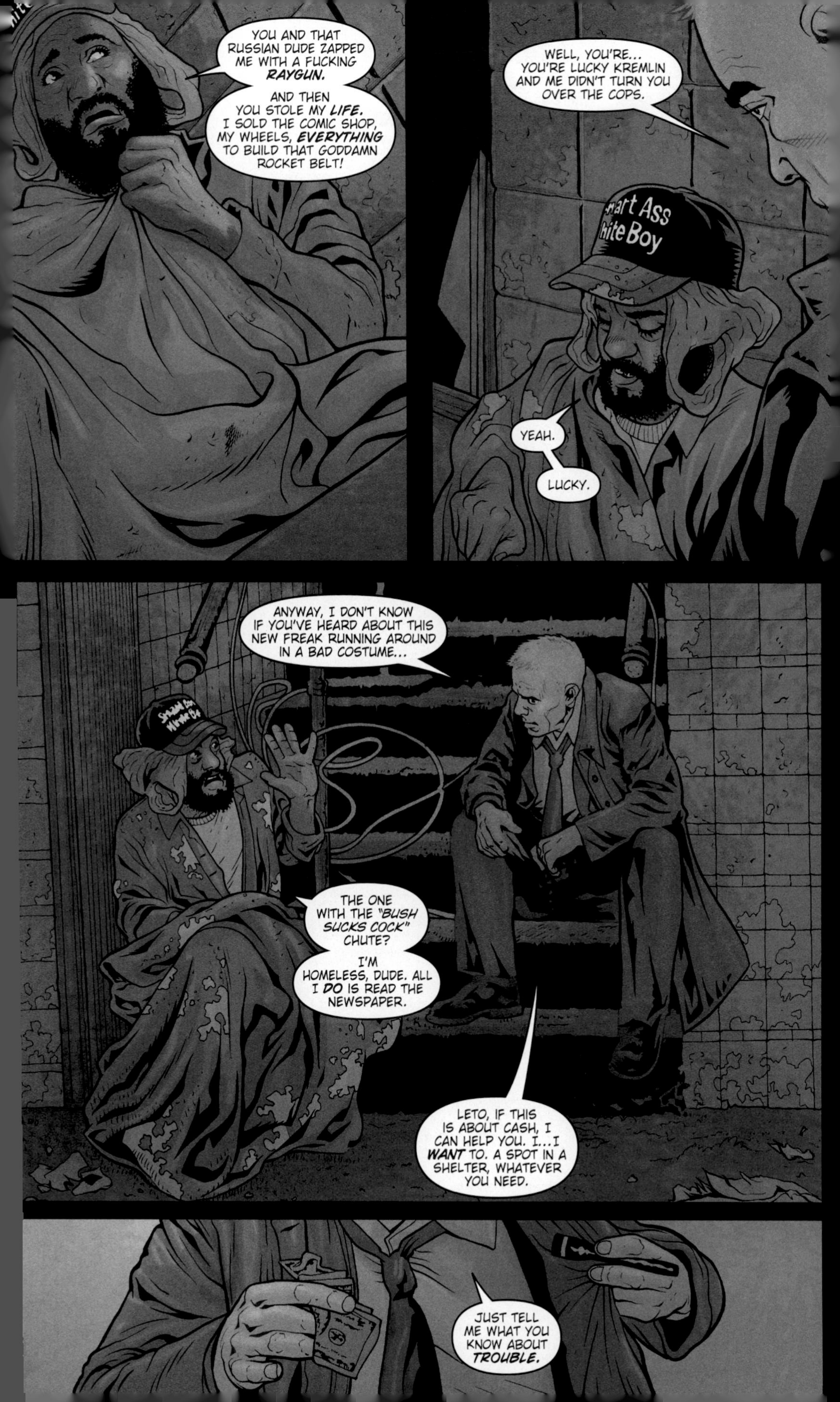
YOU AND THAT RUSSIAN DUDE ZAPPED ME WITH A FUCKING RAYGUN.
AND THEN YOU STOLE MY LIFE. I SOLD THE COMIC SHOP, MY WHEELS, EVERYTHING TO BUILD THAT GODDAMN ROCKET BELT!
WELL, YOU'RE... YOU'RE LUCKY KREMLIN AND ME DIDN'T TURN YOU OVER THE COPS.
Smart Ass White Boy
YEAH.
LUCKY.
ANYWAY, I DON'T KNOW IF YOU'VE HEARD ABOUT THIS NEW FREAK RUNNING AROUND IN A BAD COSTUME...
THE ONE WITH THE "BUSH SUCKS COCK" CHUTE?
I'M HOMELESS, DUDE. ALL I DO IS READ THE NEWSPAPER.
LETO, IF THIS IS ABOUT CASH, I CAN HELP YOU. I...I WANT TO. A SPOT IN A SHELTER, WHATEVER YOU NEED.
JUST TELL ME WHAT YOU KNOW ABOUT TROUBLE.

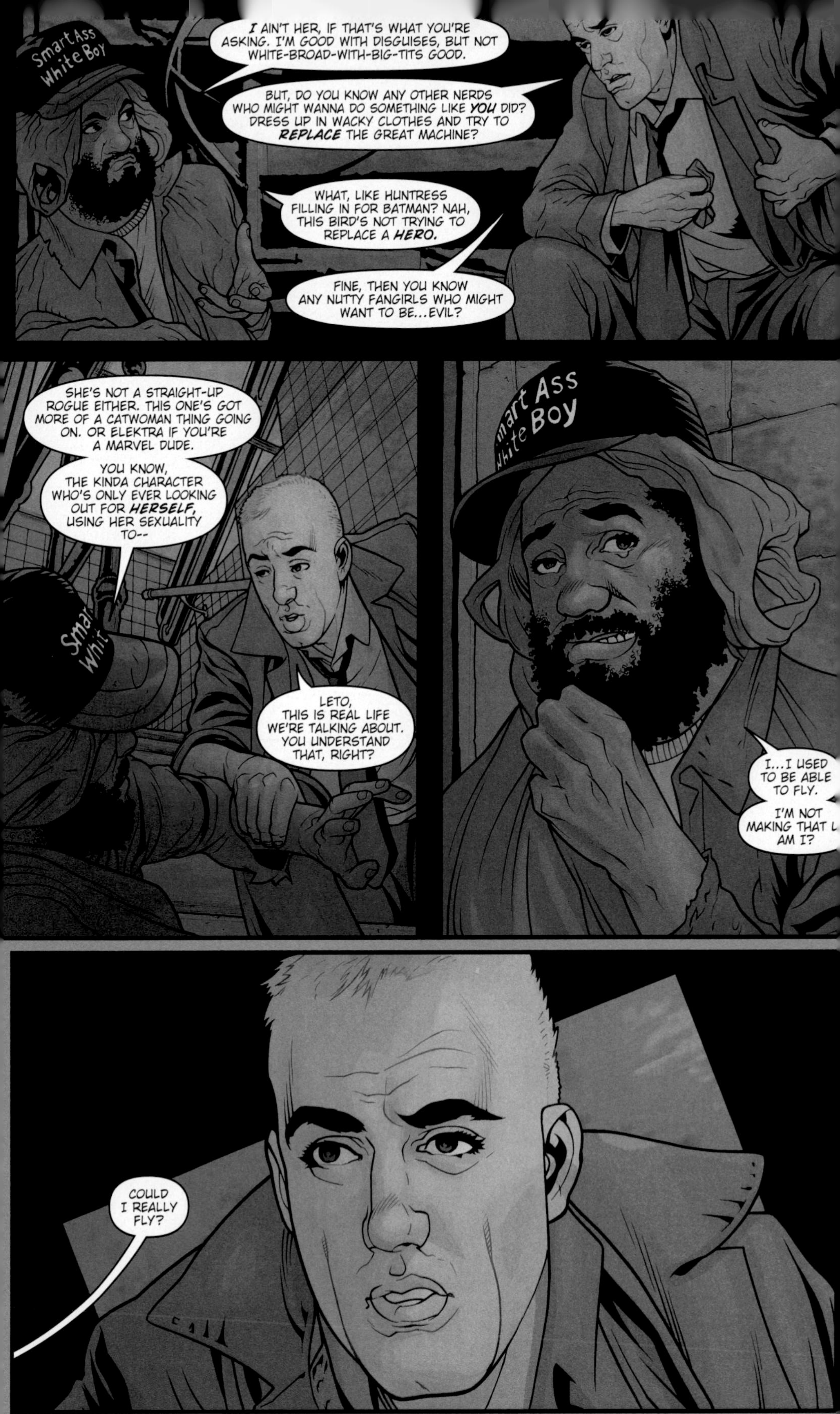
Smart Ass White Boy
I AIN'T HER, IF THAT'S WHAT YOU'RE ASKING. I'M GOOD WITH DISGUISES, BUT NOT WHITE-BROAD-WITH-BIG-TITS GOOD.
BUT, DO YOU KNOW ANY OTHER NERDS WHO MIGHT WANNA DO SOMETHING LIKE YOU DID? DRESS UP IN WACKY CLOTHES AND TRY TO REPLACE THE GREAT MACHINE?
WHAT, LIKE HUNTRESS FILLING IN FOR BATMAN? NAH, THIS BIRD'S NOT TRYING TO REPLACE A HERO.
FINE, THEN YOU KNOW ANY NUTTY FANGIRLS WHO MIGHT WANT TO BE...EVIL?
SHE'S NOT A STRAIGHT-UP ROGUE EITHER. THIS ONE'S GOT MORE OF A CATWOMAN THING GOING ON. OR ELEKTRA IF YOU'RE A MARVEL DUDE.
YOU KNOW, THE KINDA CHARACTER WHO'S ONLY EVER LOOKING OUT FOR HERSELF, USING HER SEXUALITY TO--
LETO, THIS IS REAL LIFE WE'RE TALKING ABOUT. YOU UNDERSTAND THAT, RIGHT?
Smart Ass White Boy
I...I USED TO BE ABLE TO FLY.
I'M NOT MAKING THAT
AM I?
COULD I REALLY FLY?

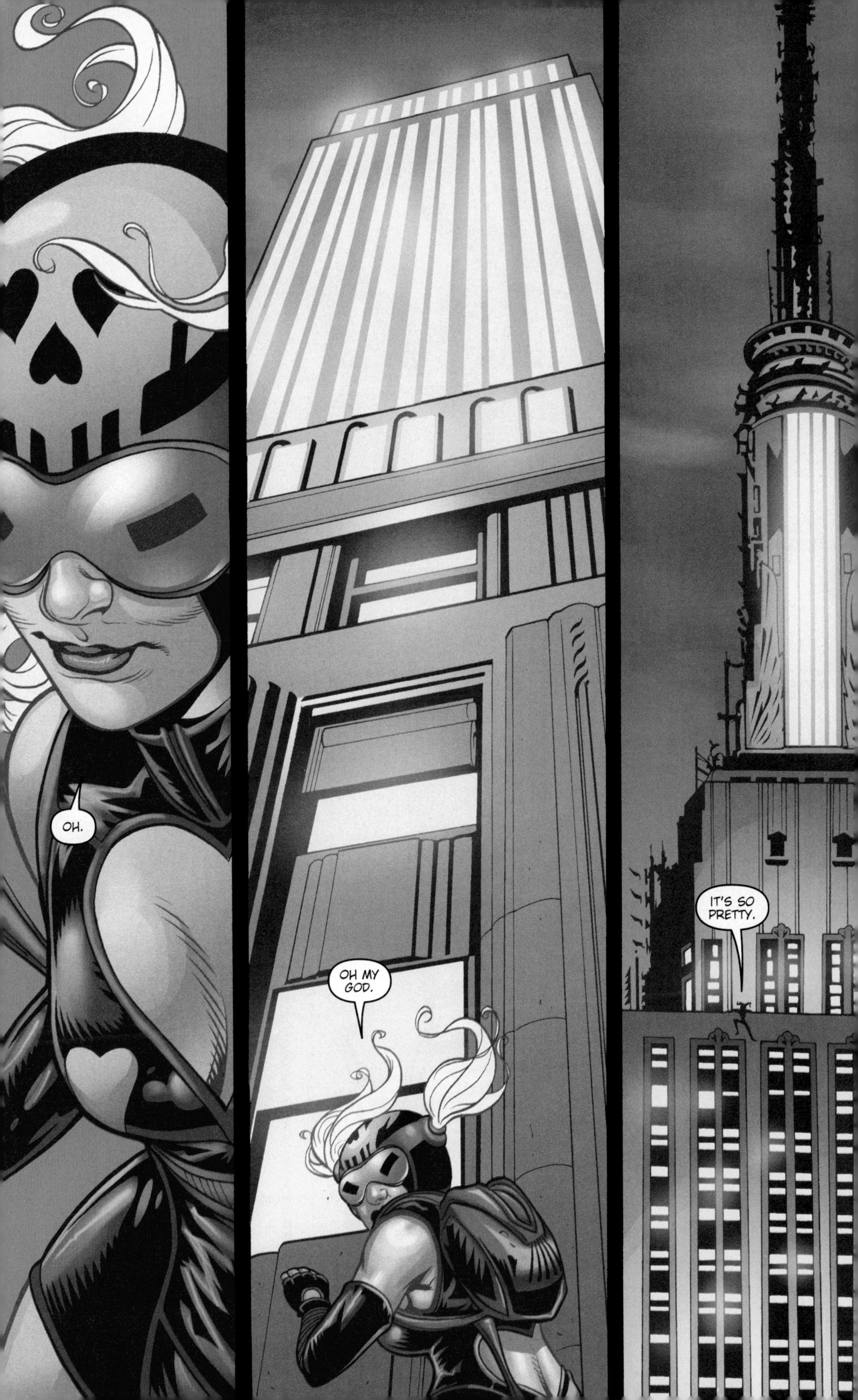
OH.
OH MY GOD.
IT'S SO PRETTY.

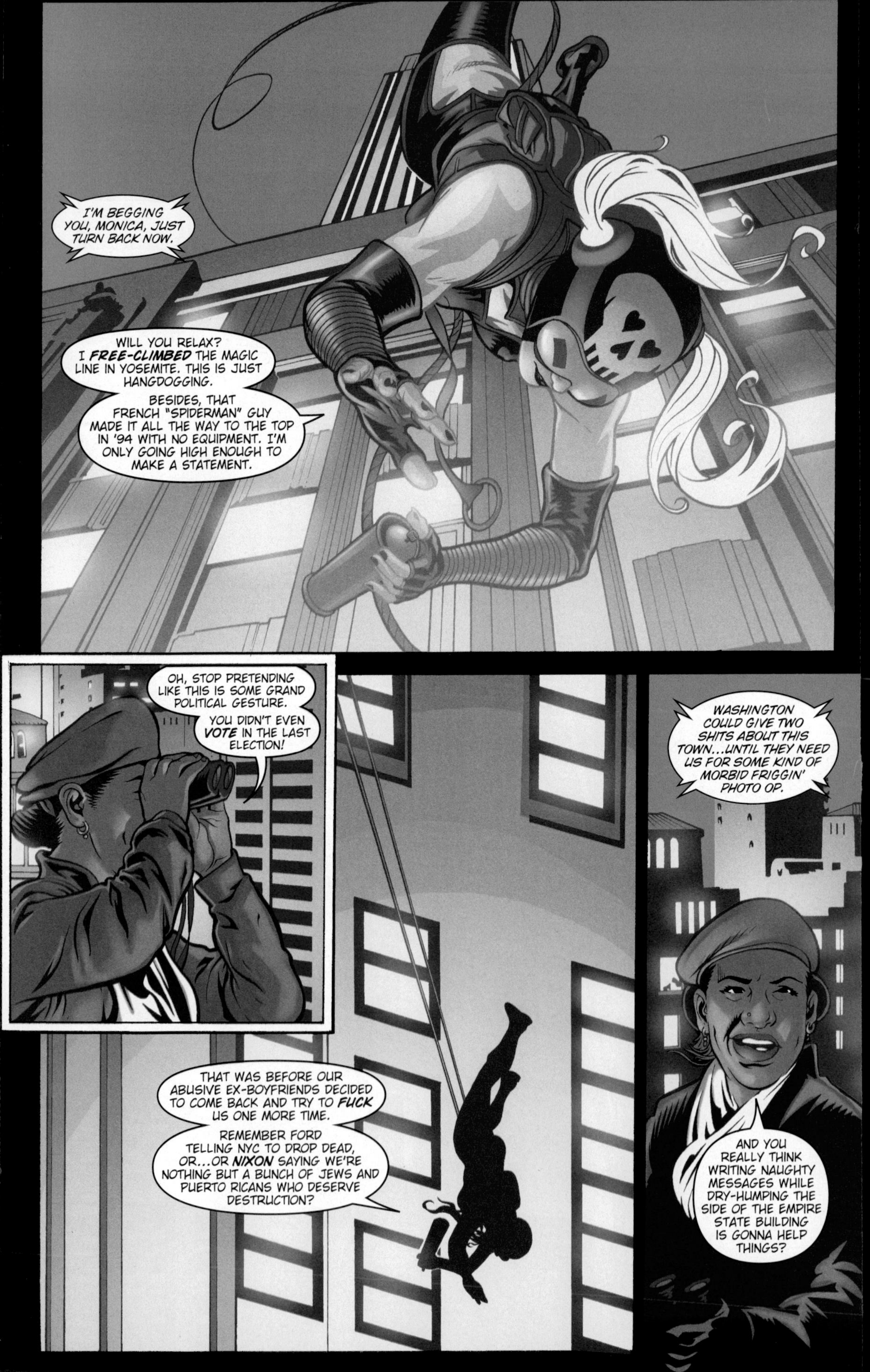
I'M BEGGING YOU, MONICA, JUST TURN BACK NOW.
WILL YOU RELAX? I FREE-CLIMBED THE MAGIC LINE IN YOSEMITE. THIS IS JUST HANGDOGGING.
BESIDES, THAT FRENCH "SPIDERMAN" GUY MADE IT ALL THE WAY TO THE TOP IN '94 WITH NO EQUIPMENT. I'M ONLY GOING HIGH ENOUGH TO MAKE A STATEMENT.
OH, STOP PRETENDING LIKE THIS IS SOME GRAND POLITICAL GESTURE.
YOU DIDN'T EVEN VOTE IN THE LAST ELECTION!
THAT WAS BEFORE OUR ABUSIVE EX-BOYFRIENDS DECIDED TO COME BACK AND TRY TO FUCK US ONE MORE TIME.
REMEMBER FORD TELLING NYC TO DROP DEAD, OR...OR NIXON SAYING WE'RE NOTHING BUT A BUNCH OF JEWS AND PUERTO RICANS WHO DESERVE DESTRUCTION?
WASHINGTON COULD GIVE TWO SHITS ABOUT THIS TOWN...UNTIL THEY NEED US FOR SOME KIND OF MORBID FRIGGIN' PHOTO OP.
AND YOU REALLY THINK WRITING NAUGHTY MESSAGES WHILE DRY-HUMPING THE SIDE OF THE EMPIRE STATE BUILDING IS GONNA HELP THINGS?

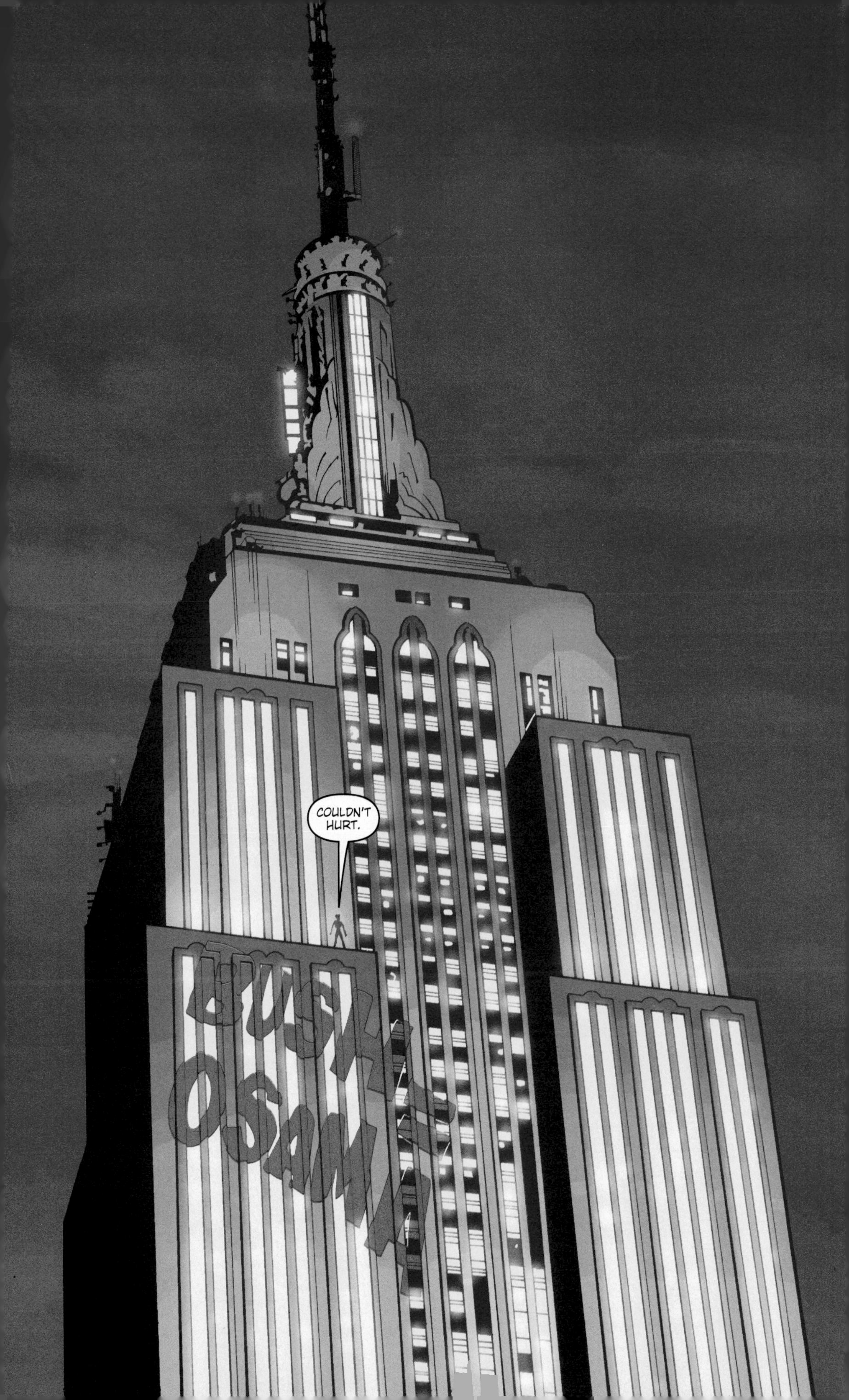
COULDN'T HURT.

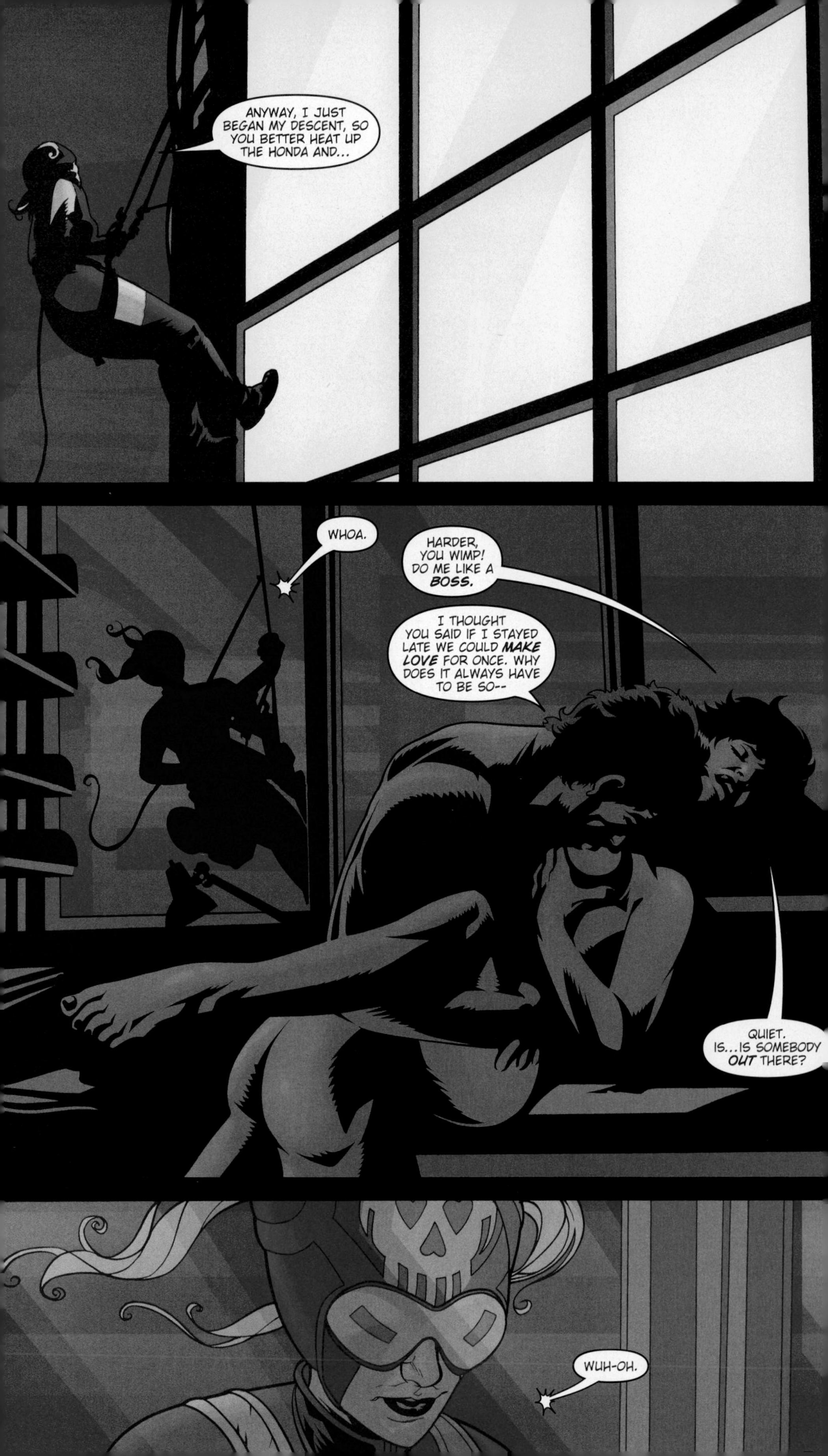
ANYWAY, I JUST BEGAN MY DESCENT, SO YOU BETTER HEAT UP THE HONDA AND...
WHOA.
HARDER, YOU WIMP! DO ME LIKE A ***BOSS.***
I THOUGHT YOU SAID IF I STAYED LATE WE COULD ***MAKE LOVE*** FOR ONCE. WHY DOES IT ALWAYS HAVE TO BE SO--
QUIET. IS...IS SOMEBODY ***OUT*** THERE?
WUH-OH.

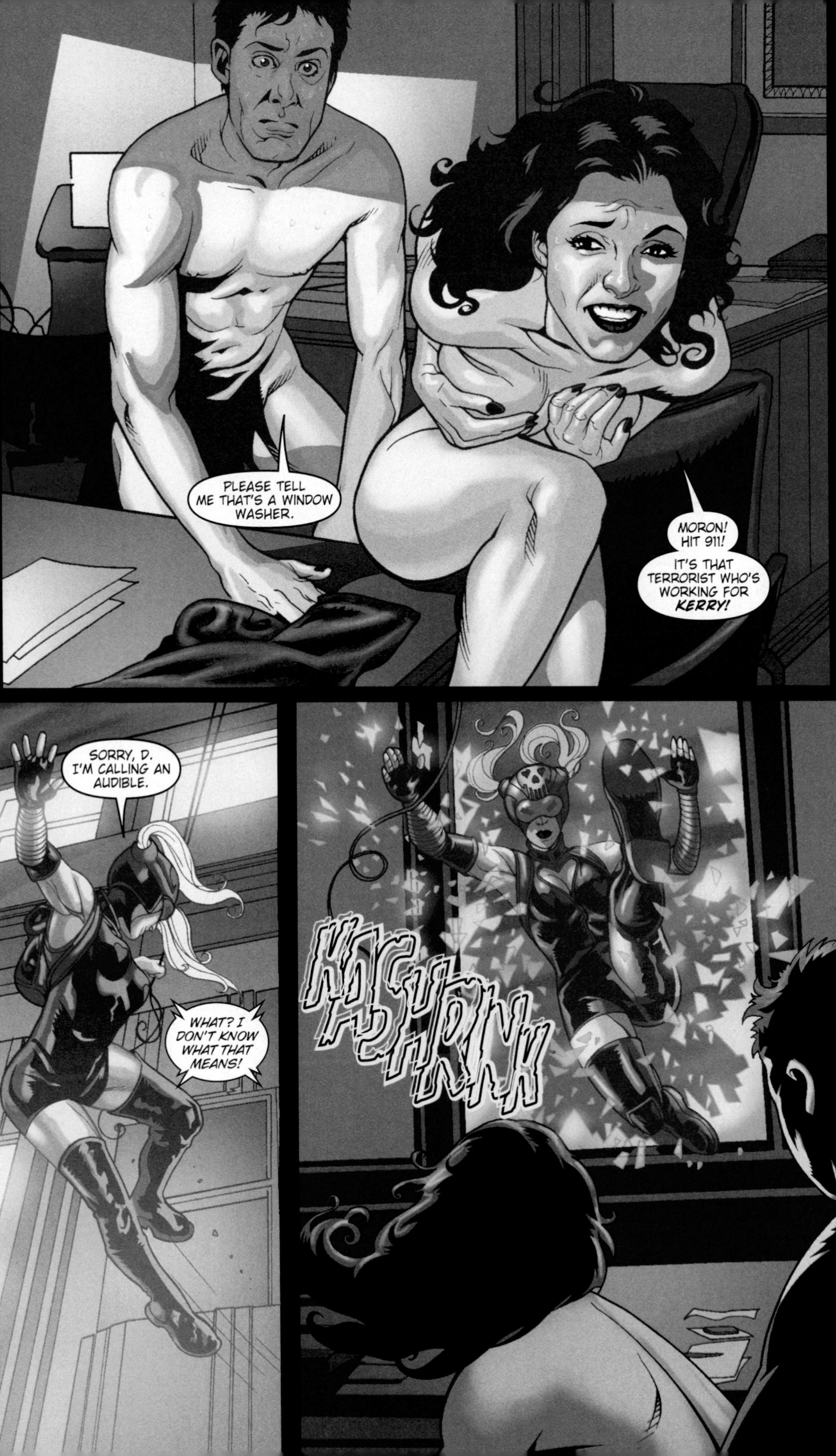
PLEASE TELL ME THAT'S A WINDOW WASHER.
MORON! HIT 911!
IT'S THAT TERRORIST WHO'S WORKING FOR KERRY!
SORRY, D. I'M CALLING AN AUDIBLE.
WHAT? I DON'T KNOW WHAT THAT MEANS!

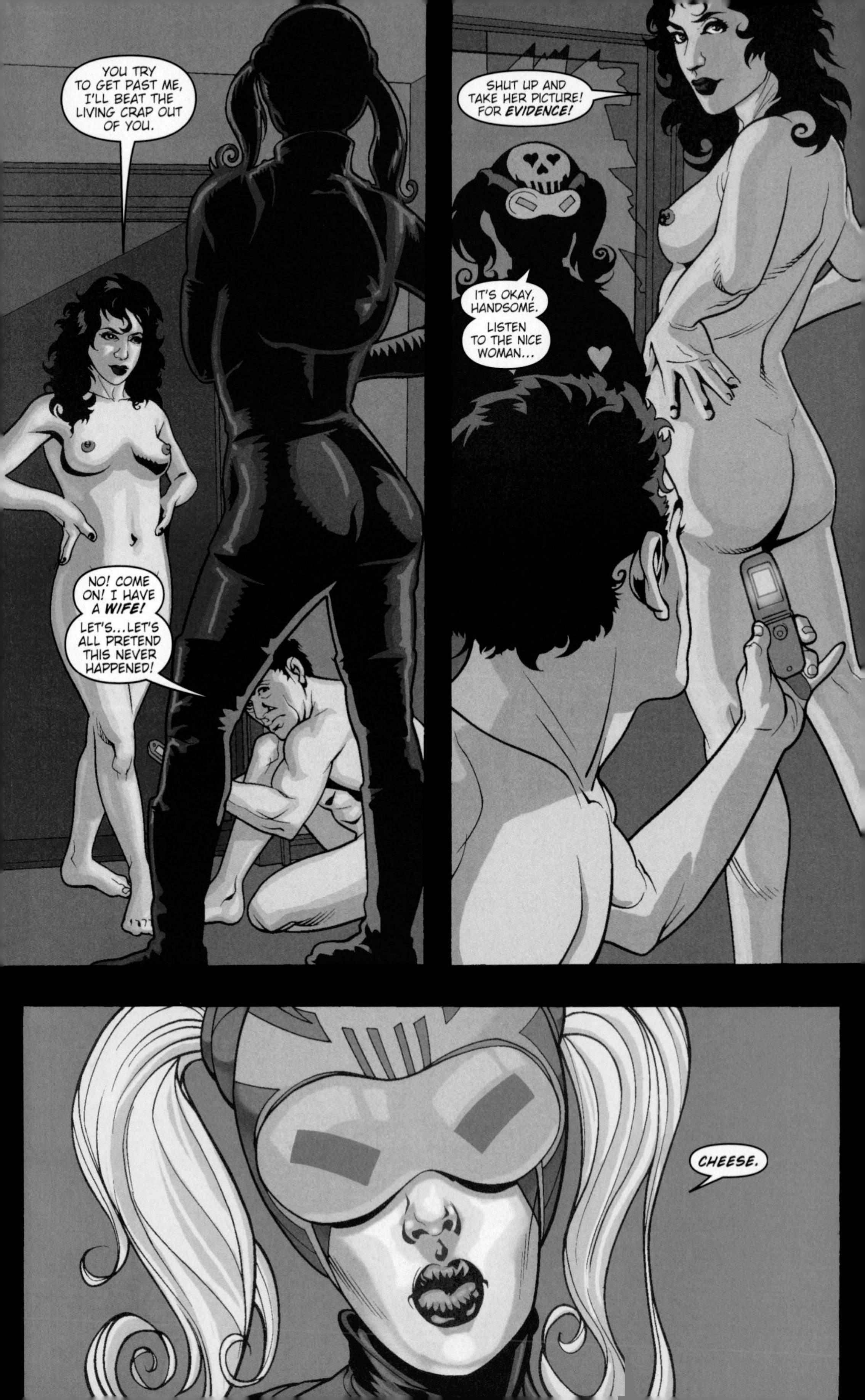
YOU TRY TO GET PAST ME, I'LL BEAT THE LIVING CRAP OUT OF YOU.
NO! COME ON! I HAVE A WIFE!
LET'S...LET'S ALL PRETEND THIS NEVER HAPPENED!
SHUT UP AND TAKE HER PICTURE! FOR EVIDENCE!
IT'S OKAY, HANDSOME.
LISTEN TO THE NICE WOMAN...
CHEESE.

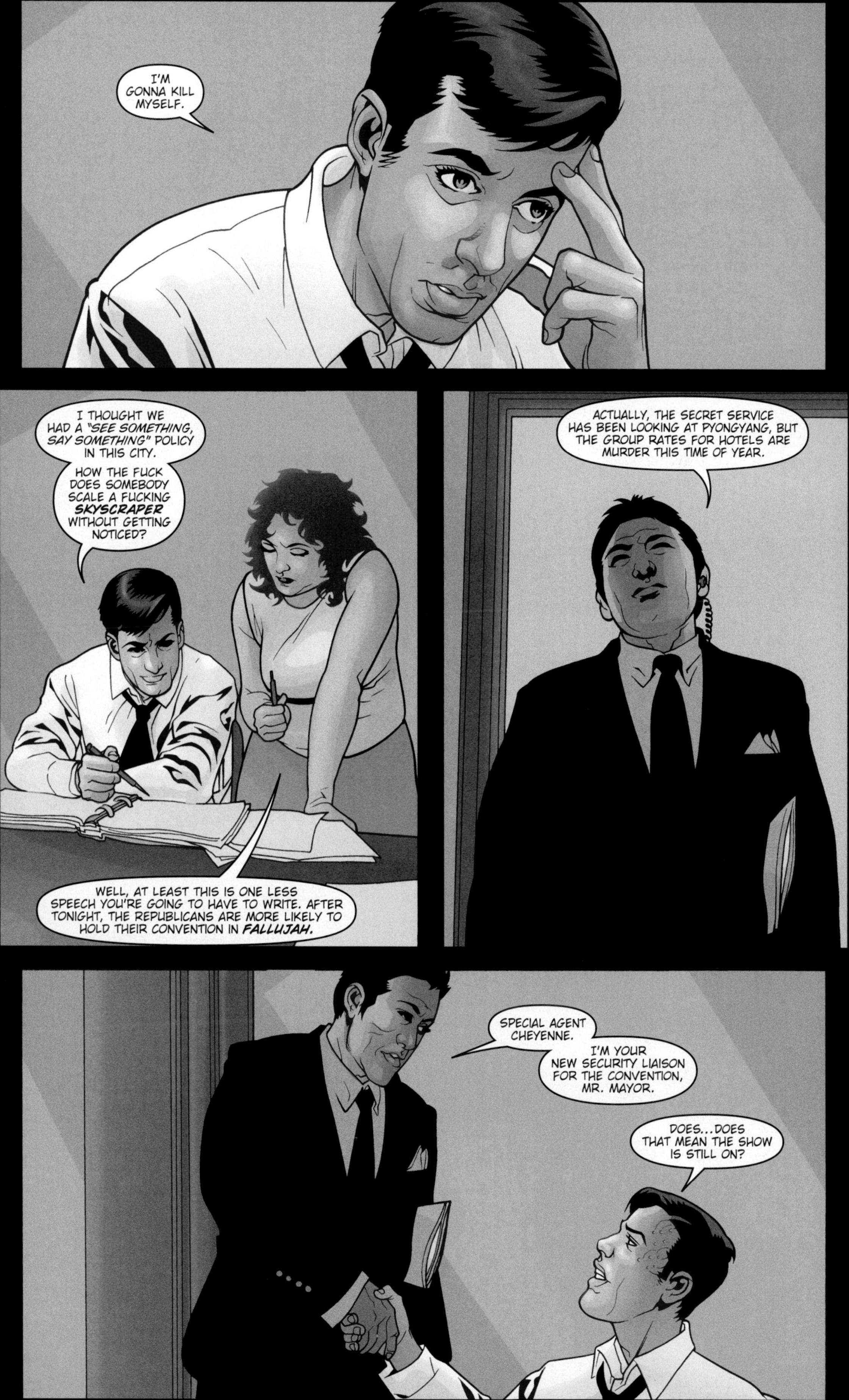
I'M GONNA KILL MYSELF.
I THOUGHT WE HAD A "SEE SOMETHING, SAY SOMETHING" POLICY IN THIS CITY.
HOW THE FUCK DOES SOMEBODY SCALE A FUCKING SKYSCRAPER WITHOUT GETTING NOTICED?
WELL, AT LEAST THIS IS ONE LESS SPEECH YOU'RE GOING TO HAVE TO WRITE. AFTER TONIGHT, THE REPUBLICANS ARE MORE LIKELY TO HOLD THEIR CONVENTION IN FALLUJAH.
ACTUALLY, THE SECRET SERVICE HAS BEEN LOOKING AT PYONGYANG, BUT THE GROUP RATES FOR HOTELS ARE MURDER THIS TIME OF YEAR.
SPECIAL AGENT CHEYENNE.
I'M YOUR NEW SECURITY LIAISON FOR THE CONVENTION, MR. MAYOR.
DOES...DOES THAT MEAN THE SHOW IS STILL ON?

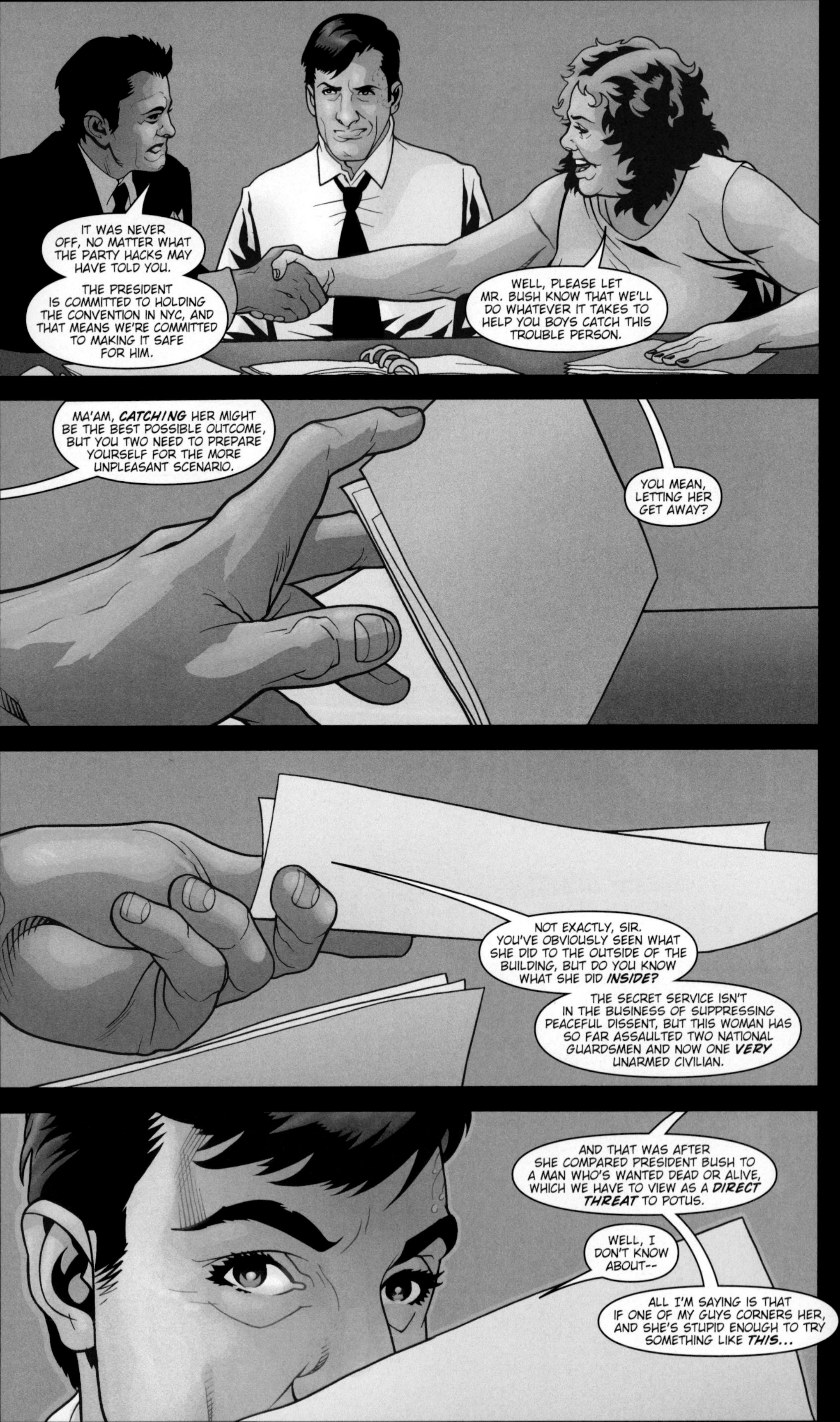
IT WAS NEVER OFF, NO MATTER WHAT THE PARTY HACKS MAY HAVE TOLD YOU.
THE PRESIDENT IS COMMITTED TO HOLDING THE CONVENTION IN NYC, AND THAT MEANS WE'RE COMMITTED TO MAKING IT SAFE FOR HIM.
WELL, PLEASE LET MR. BUSH KNOW THAT WE'LL DO WHATEVER IT TAKES TO HELP YOU BOYS CATCH THIS TROUBLE PERSON.
MA'AM, CATCHING HER MIGHT BE THE BEST POSSIBLE OUTCOME, BUT YOU TWO NEED TO PREPARE YOURSELF FOR THE MORE UNPLEASANT SCENARIO.
YOU MEAN, LETTING HER GET AWAY?
NOT EXACTLY, SIR. YOU'VE OBVIOUSLY SEEN WHAT SHE DID TO THE OUTSIDE OF THE BUILDING, BUT DO YOU KNOW WHAT SHE DID INSIDE?
THE SECRET SERVICE ISN'T IN THE BUSINESS OF SUPPRESSING PEACEFUL DISSENT, BUT THIS WOMAN HAS SO FAR ASSAULTED TWO NATIONAL GUARDSMEN AND NOW ONE VERY UNARMED CIVILIAN.
AND THAT WAS AFTER SHE COMPARED PRESIDENT BUSH TO A MAN WHO'S WANTED DEAD OR ALIVE, WHICH WE HAVE TO VIEW AS A DIRECT THREAT TO POTUS.
WELL, I DON'T KNOW ABOUT--
ALL I'M SAYING IS THAT IF ONE OF MY GUYS CORNERS HER, AND SHE'S STUPID ENOUGH TO TRY SOMETHING LIKE THIS...

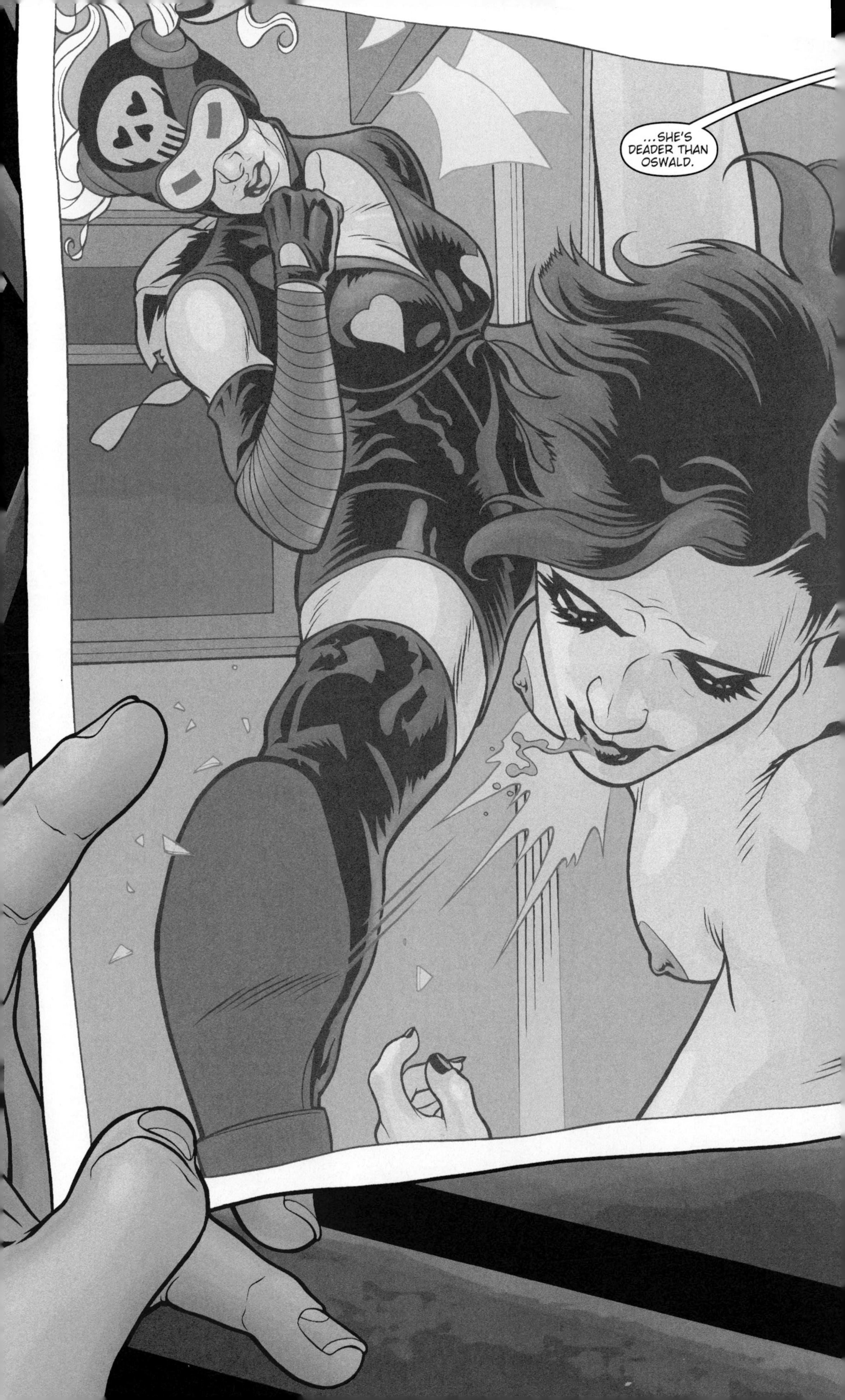
...SHE'S DEADER THAN OSWALD.

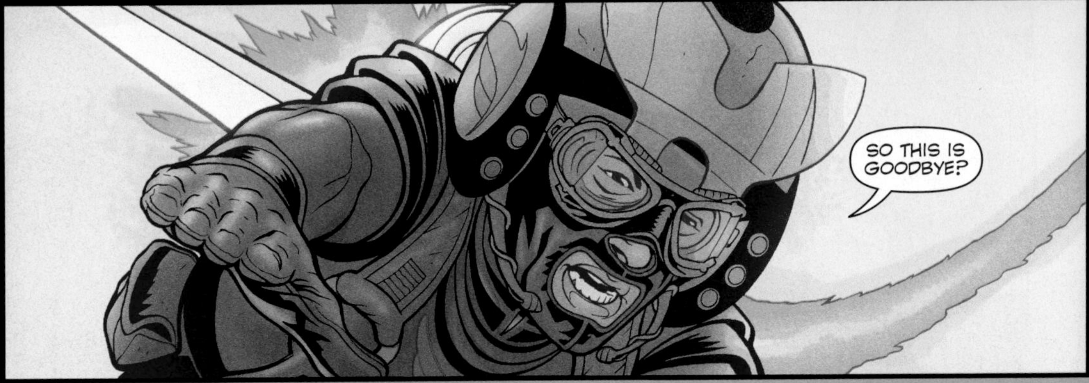
SO THIS IS GOODBYE?

WEDNESDAY, JULY 4, 2001

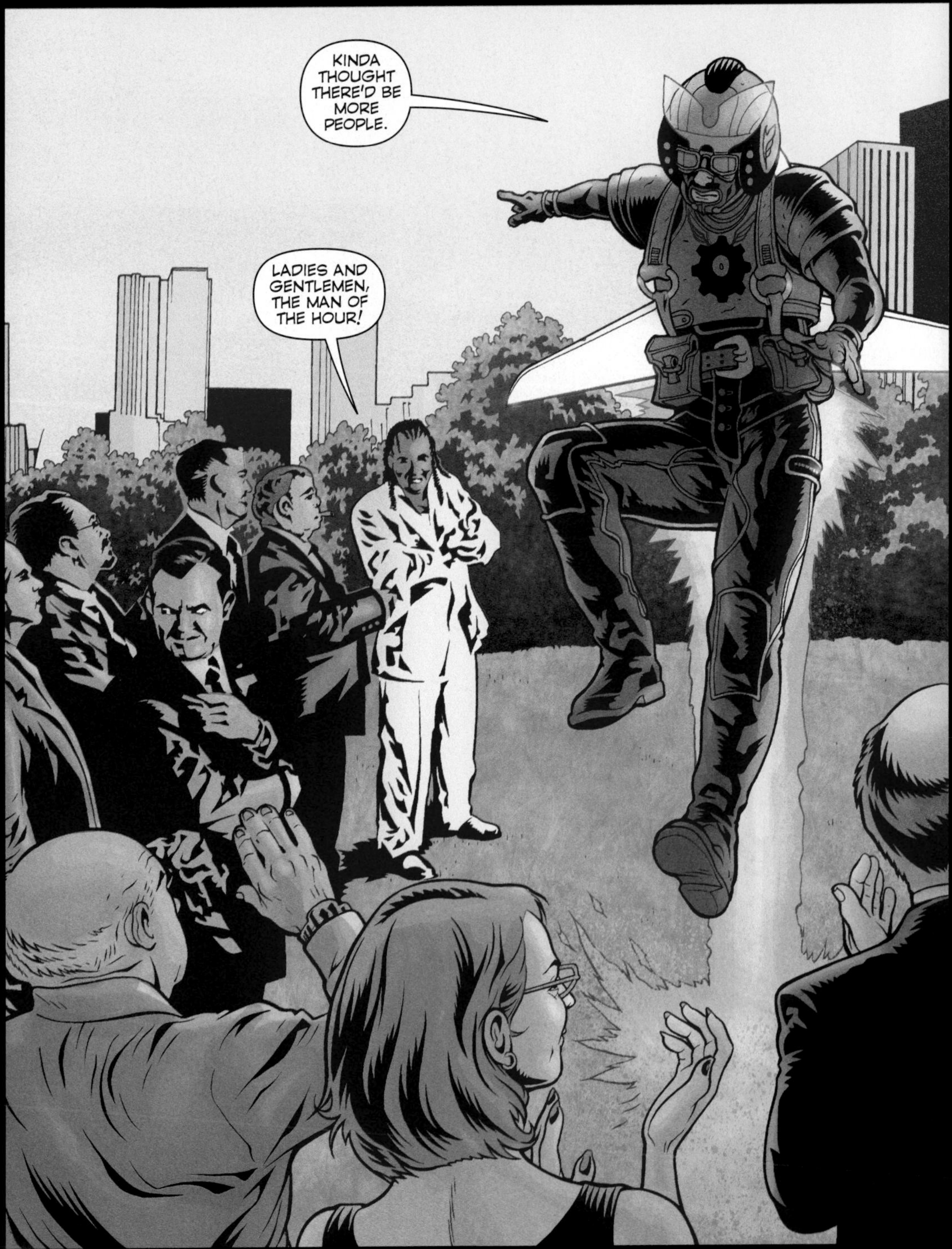
KINDA THOUGHT THERE'D BE MORE PEOPLE.
LADIES AND GENTLEMEN, THE MAN OF THE HOUR!

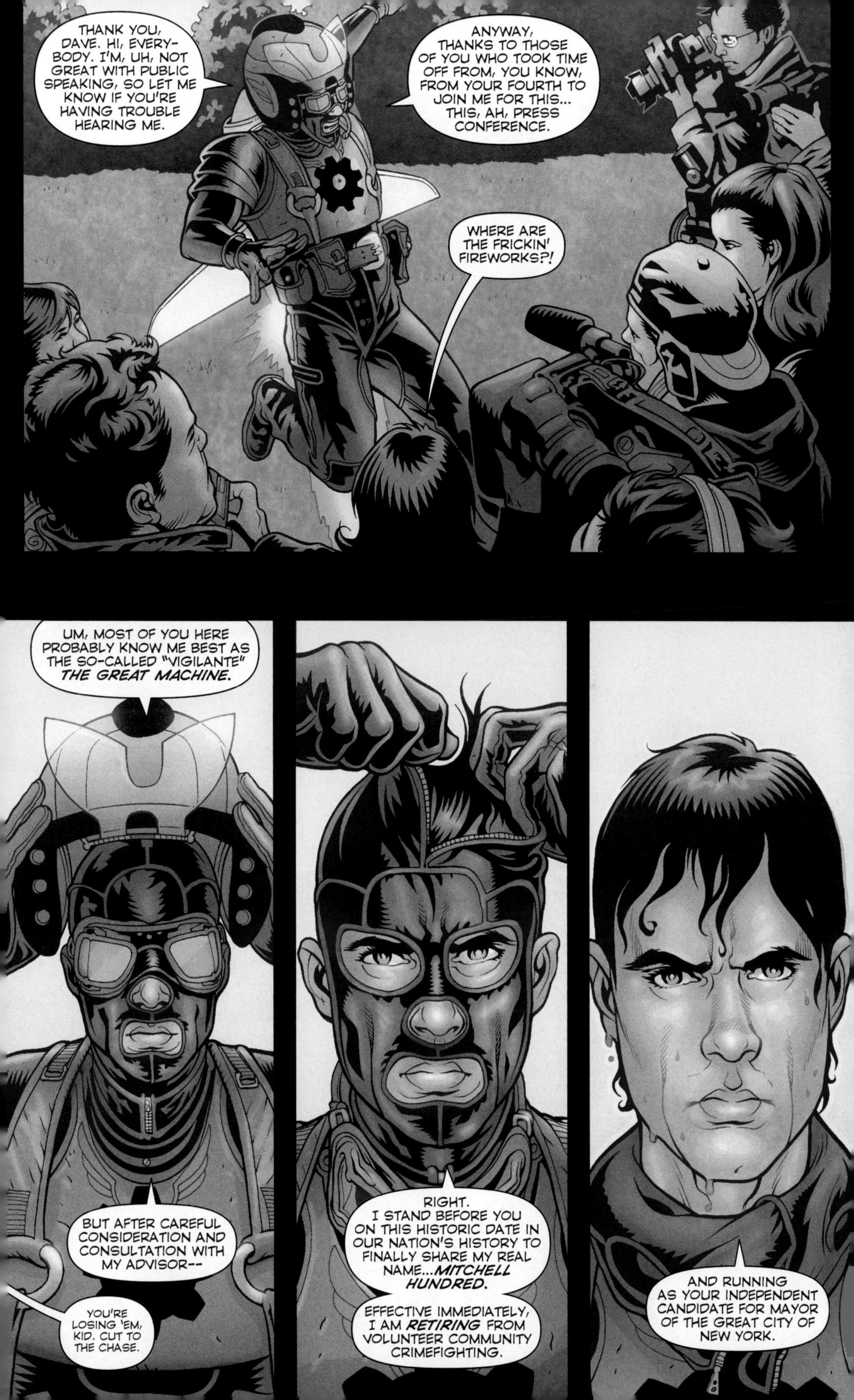
THANK YOU, DAVE. HI, EVERYBODY. I'M, UH, NOT GREAT WITH PUBLIC SPEAKING, SO LET ME KNOW IF YOU'RE HAVING TROUBLE HEARING ME.
ANYWAY, THANKS TO THOSE OF YOU WHO TOOK TIME OFF FROM, YOU KNOW, FROM YOUR FOURTH TO JOIN ME FOR THIS... THIS, AH, PRESS CONFERENCE.
WHERE ARE THE FRICKIN' FIREWORKS?!
UM, MOST OF YOU HERE PROBABLY KNOW ME BEST AS THE SO-CALLED "VIGILANTE" *THE GREAT MACHINE*.
BUT AFTER CAREFUL CONSIDERATION AND CONSULTATION WITH MY ADVISOR--
YOU'RE LOSING 'EM, KID. CUT TO THE CHASE.
RIGHT. I STAND BEFORE YOU ON THIS HISTORIC DATE IN OUR NATION'S HISTORY TO FINALLY SHARE MY REAL NAME...*MITCHELL HUNDRED*.
EFFECTIVE IMMEDIATELY, I AM *RETIRING* FROM VOLUNTEER COMMUNITY CRIMEFIGHTING.
AND RUNNING AS YOUR INDEPENDENT CANDIDATE FOR MAYOR OF THE GREAT CITY OF NEW YORK.

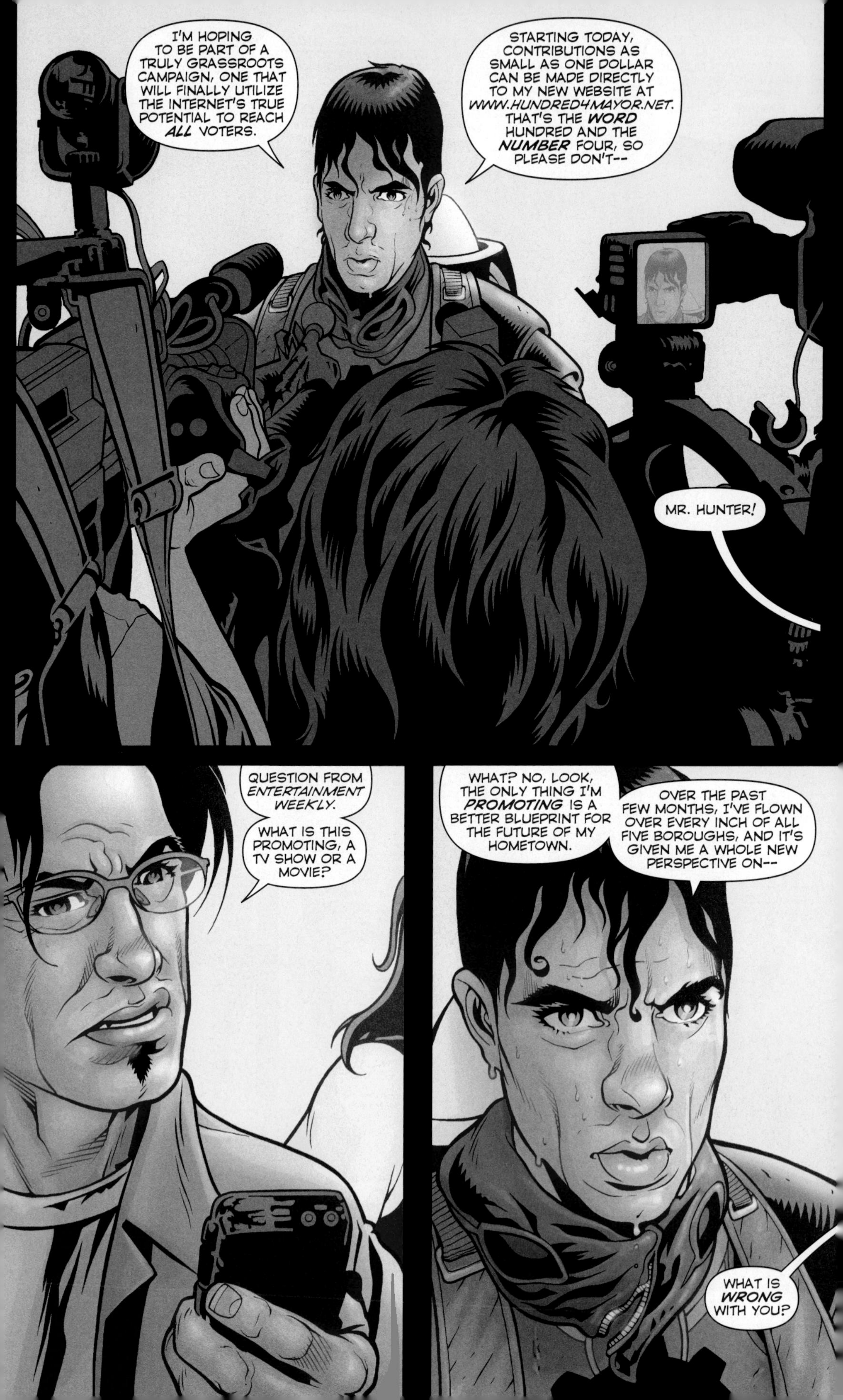

I'M HOPING TO BE PART OF A TRULY GRASSROOTS CAMPAIGN, ONE THAT WILL FINALLY UTILIZE THE INTERNET'S TRUE POTENTIAL TO REACH *ALL* VOTERS.
STARTING TODAY, CONTRIBUTIONS AS SMALL AS ONE DOLLAR CAN BE MADE DIRECTLY TO MY NEW WEBSITE AT *WWW.HUNDRED4MAYOR.NET.* THAT'S THE ***WORD*** HUNDRED AND THE ***NUMBER*** FOUR, SO PLEASE DON'T--
MR. HUNTER!
QUESTION FROM *ENTERTAINMENT WEEKLY.*
WHAT IS THIS PROMOTING, A TV SHOW OR A MOVIE?
WHAT? NO, LOOK, THE ONLY THING I'M ***PROMOTING*** IS A BETTER BLUEPRINT FOR THE FUTURE OF MY HOMETOWN.
OVER THE PAST FEW MONTHS, I'VE FLOWN OVER EVERY INCH OF ALL FIVE BOROUGHS, AND IT'S GIVEN ME A WHOLE NEW PERSPECTIVE ON--
WHAT IS ***WRONG*** WITH YOU?

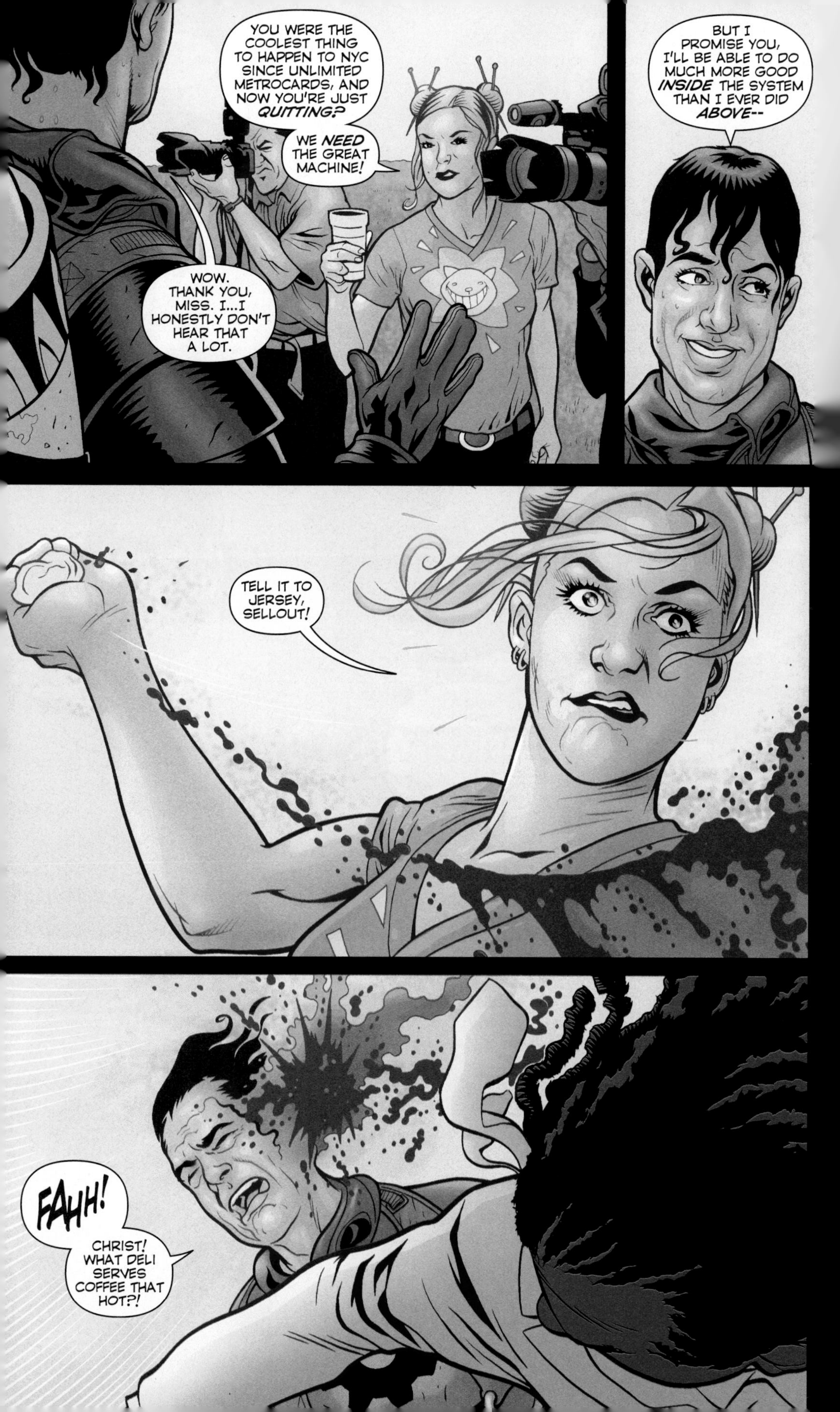
YOU WERE THE COOLEST THING TO HAPPEN TO NYC SINCE UNLIMITED METROCARDS, AND NOW YOU'RE JUST *QUITTING?*
WE *NEED* THE GREAT MACHINE!
WOW. THANK YOU, MISS. I...I HONESTLY DON'T HEAR THAT A LOT.
BUT I PROMISE YOU, I'LL BE ABLE TO DO MUCH MORE GOOD *INSIDE* THE SYSTEM THAN I EVER DID *ABOVE*--
TELL IT TO JERSEY, SELLOUT!
FAHH!
CHRIST! WHAT DELI SERVES COFFEE THAT HOT?!

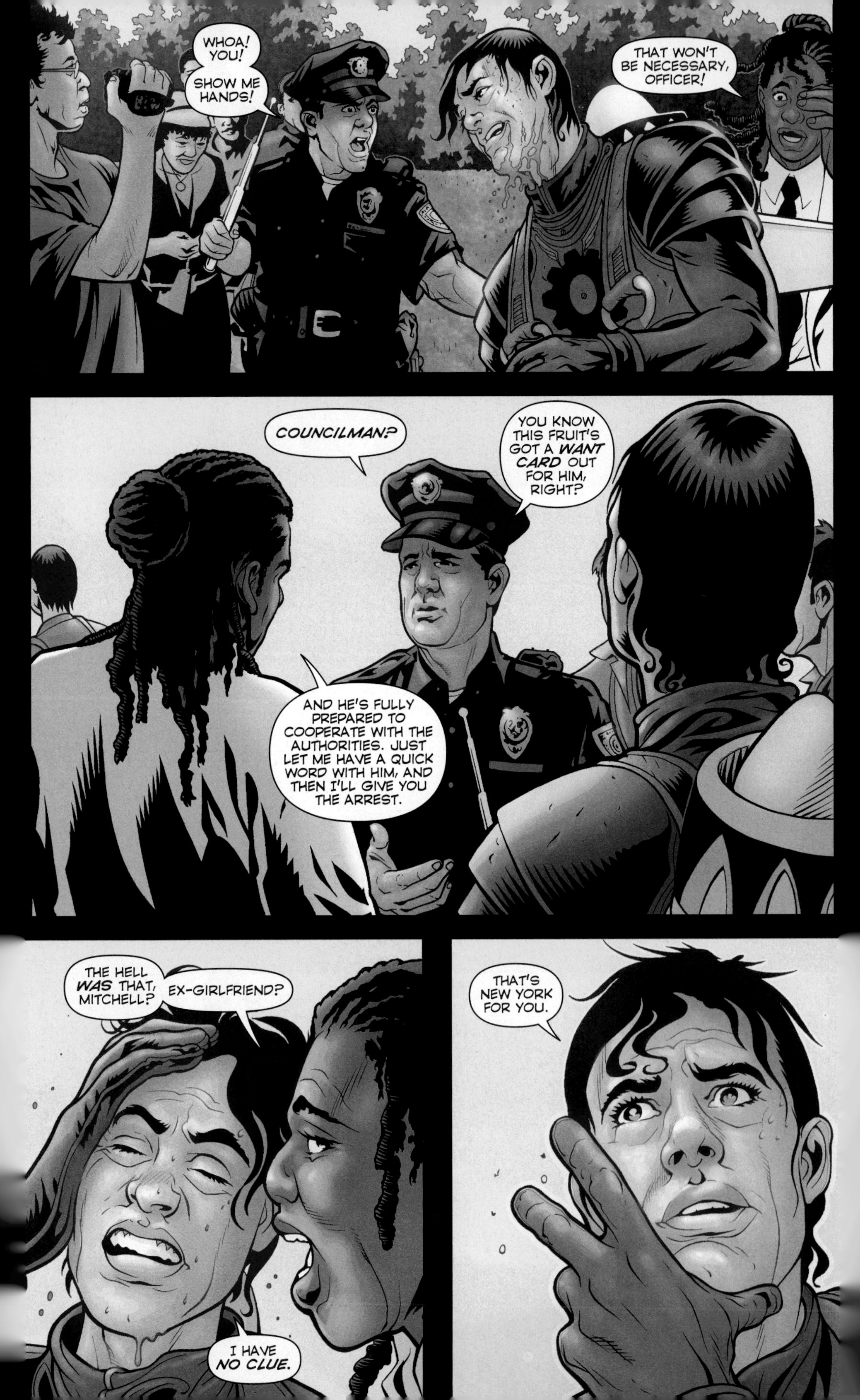
WHOA! YOU!
SHOW ME HANDS!
THAT WON'T BE NECESSARY, OFFICER!
COUNCILMAN?
YOU KNOW THIS FRUIT'S GOT A WANT CARD OUT FOR HIM, RIGHT?
AND HE'S FULLY PREPARED TO COOPERATE WITH THE AUTHORITIES. JUST LET ME HAVE A QUICK WORD WITH HIM, AND THEN I'LL GIVE YOU THE ARREST.
THE HELL WAS THAT, MITCHELL?
EX-GIRLFRIEND?
I HAVE NO CLUE.
THAT'S NEW YORK FOR YOU.

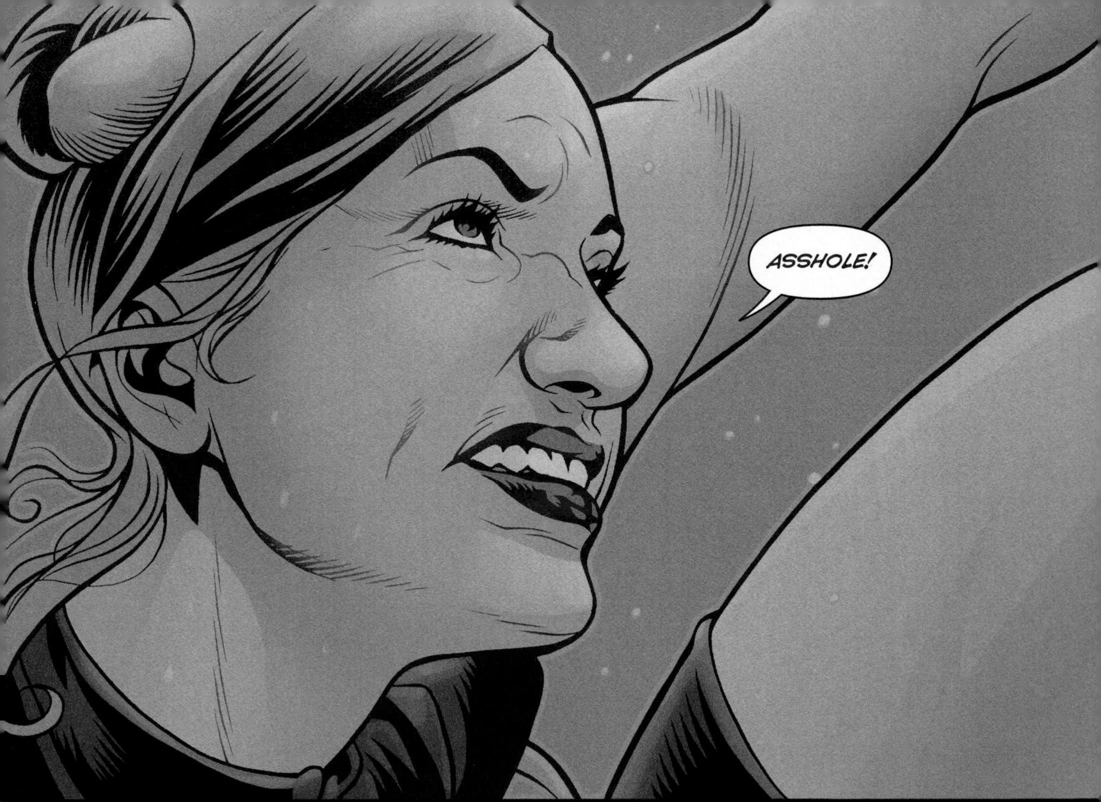
ASSHOLE!

FRIDAY, AUGUST 27, 2004

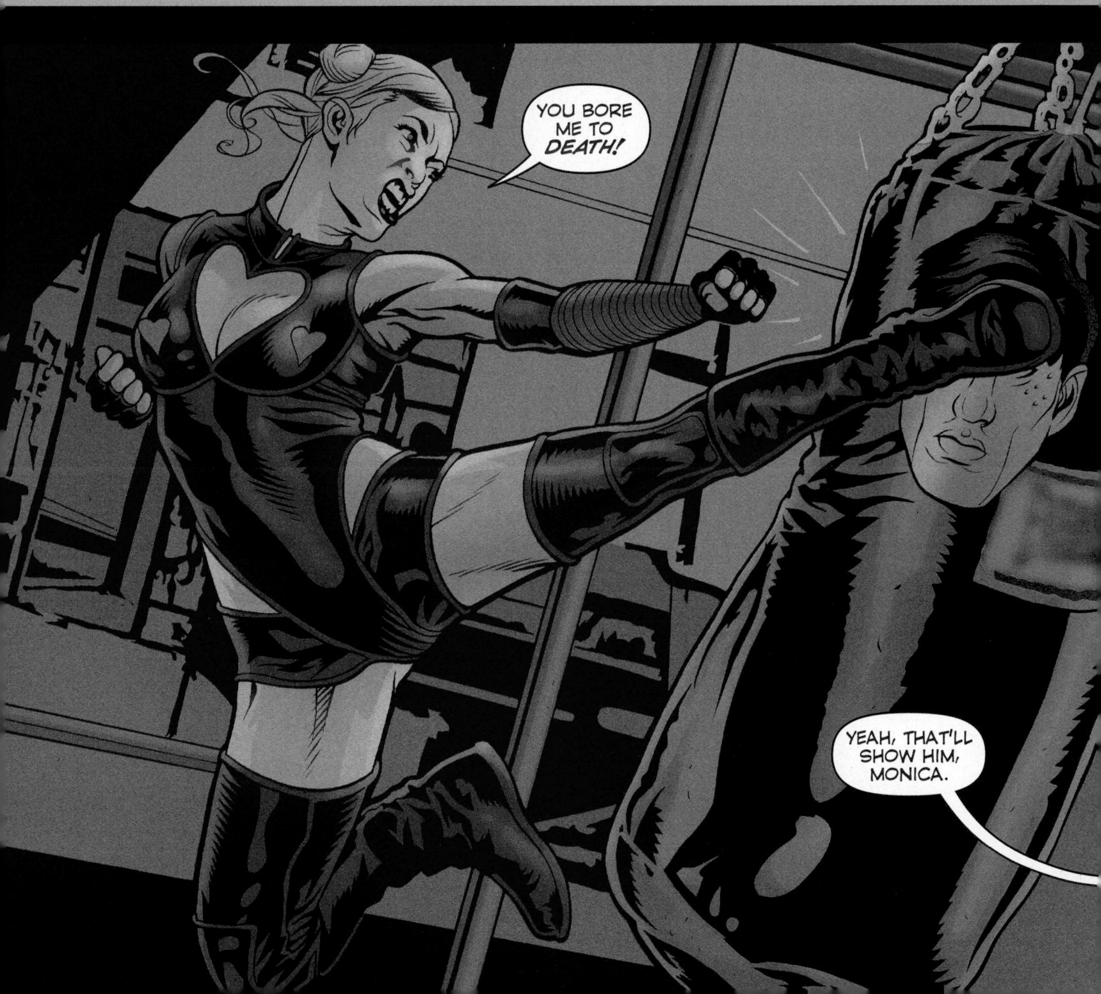
YOU BORE ME TO DEATH!
YEAH, THAT'LL SHOW HIM, MONICA.

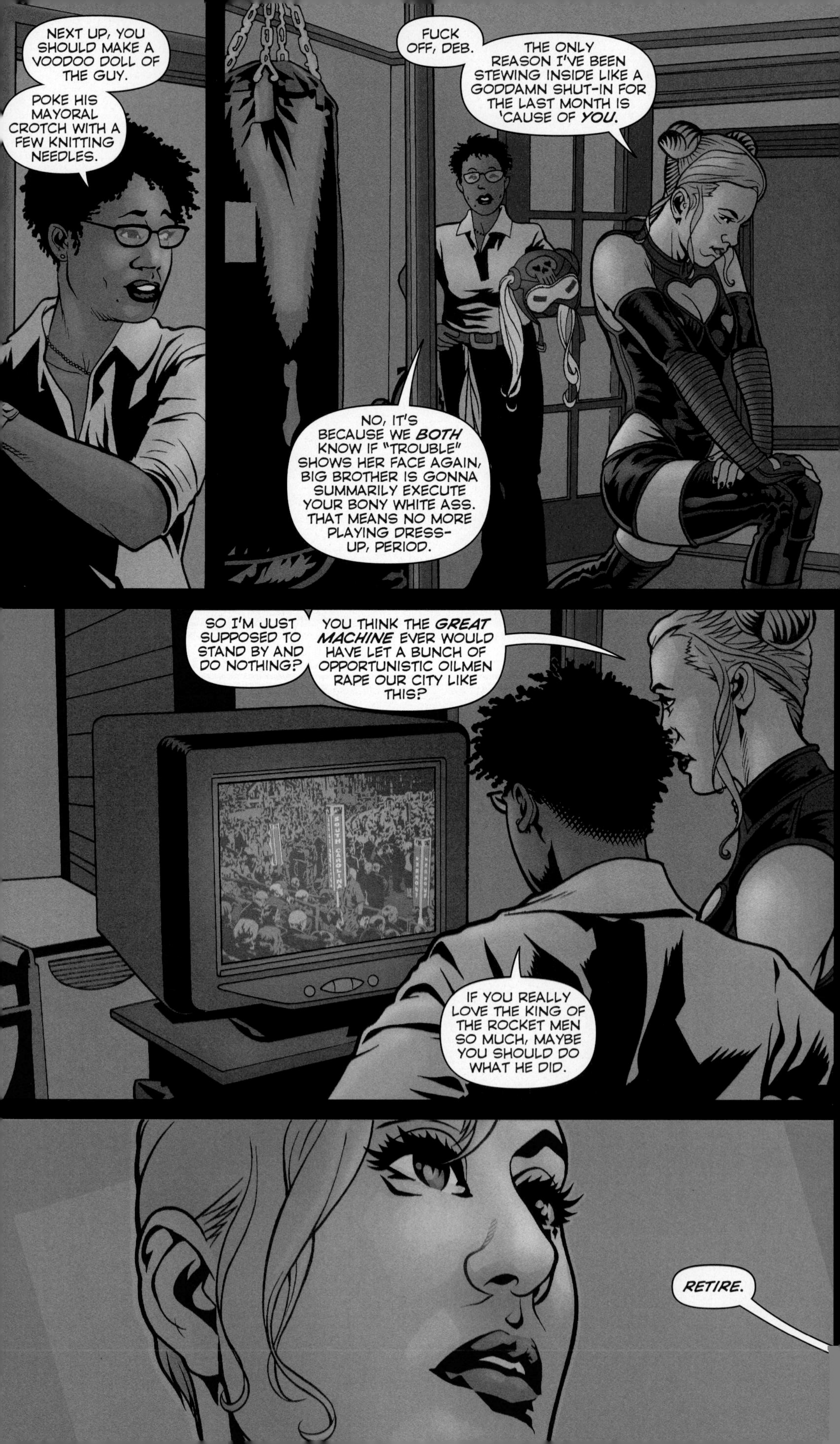
NEXT UP, YOU SHOULD MAKE A VOODOO DOLL OF THE GUY.
POKE HIS MAYORAL CROTCH WITH A FEW KNITTING NEEDLES.
FUCK OFF, DEB.
THE ONLY REASON I'VE BEEN STEWING INSIDE LIKE A GODDAMN SHUT-IN FOR THE LAST MONTH IS 'CAUSE OF *YOU.*
NO, IT'S BECAUSE WE *BOTH* KNOW IF "TROUBLE" SHOWS HER FACE AGAIN, BIG BROTHER IS GONNA SUMMARILY EXECUTE YOUR BONY WHITE ASS. THAT MEANS NO MORE PLAYING DRESS-UP, PERIOD.
SO I'M JUST SUPPOSED TO STAND BY AND DO NOTHING?
YOU THINK THE *GREAT MACHINE* EVER WOULD HAVE LET A BUNCH OF OPPORTUNISTIC OILMEN RAPE OUR CITY LIKE THIS?
IF YOU REALLY LOVE THE KING OF THE ROCKET MEN SO MUCH, MAYBE YOU SHOULD DO WHAT HE DID.
RETIRE.

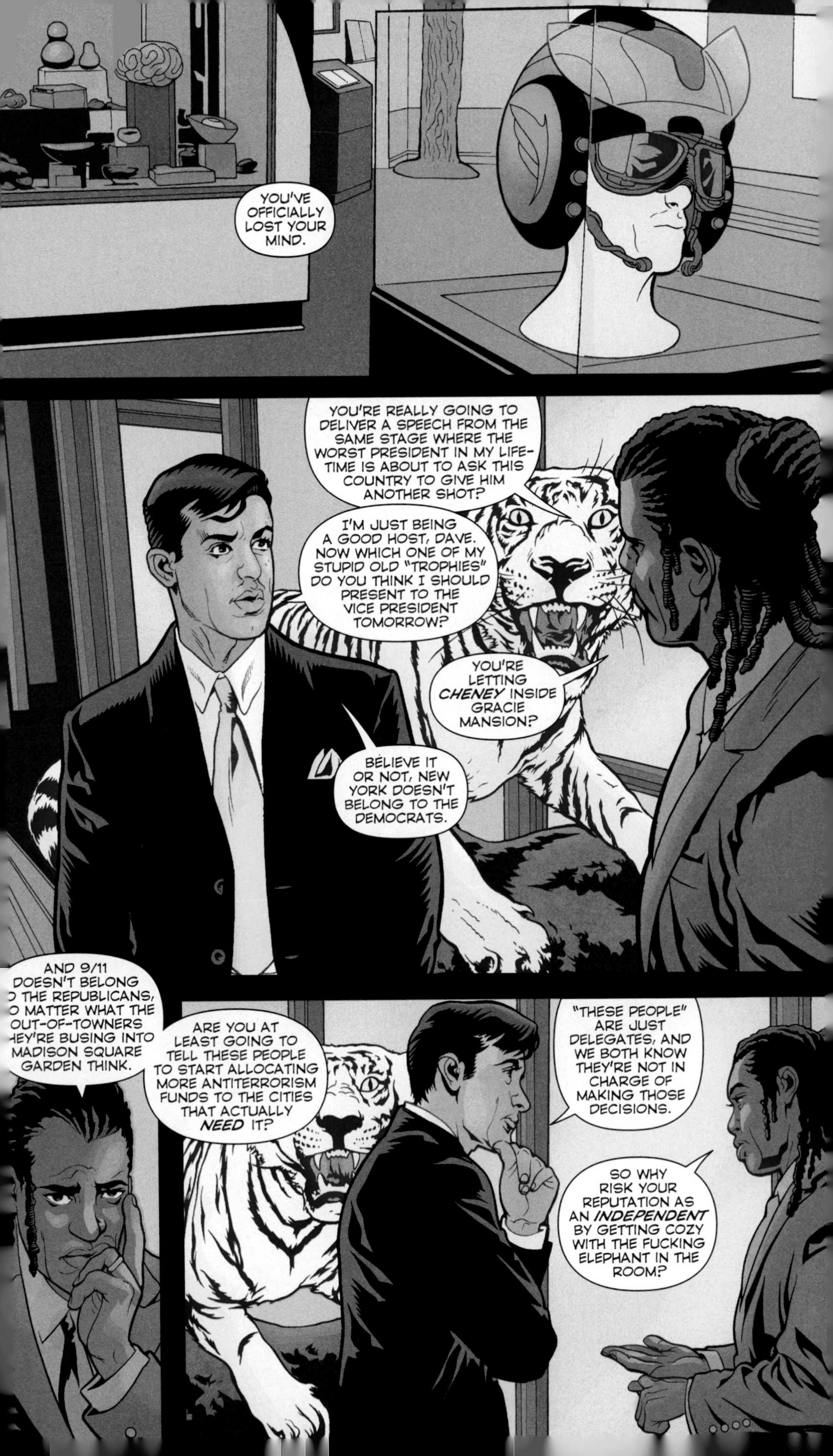

YOU'VE OFFICIALLY LOST YOUR MIND.
YOU'RE REALLY GOING TO DELIVER A SPEECH FROM THE SAME STAGE WHERE THE WORST PRESIDENT IN MY LIFE-TIME IS ABOUT TO ASK THIS COUNTRY TO GIVE HIM ANOTHER SHOT?
I'M JUST BEING A GOOD HOST, DAVE. NOW WHICH ONE OF MY STUPID OLD "TROPHIES" DO YOU THINK I SHOULD PRESENT TO THE VICE PRESIDENT TOMORROW?
YOU'RE LETTING CHENEY INSIDE GRACIE MANSION?
BELIEVE IT OR NOT, NEW YORK DOESN'T BELONG TO THE DEMOCRATS.
AND 9/11 DOESN'T BELONG O THE REPUBLICANS, O MATTER WHAT THE OUT-OF-TOWNERS HEY'RE BUSING INTO MADISON SQUARE GARDEN THINK.
ARE YOU AT LEAST GOING TO TELL THESE PEOPLE TO START ALLOCATING MORE ANTITERRORISM FUNDS TO THE CITIES THAT ACTUALLY NEED IT?
"THESE PEOPLE" ARE JUST DELEGATES, AND WE BOTH KNOW THEY'RE NOT IN CHARGE OF MAKING THOSE DECISIONS.
SO WHY RISK YOUR REPUTATION AS AN INDEPENDENT BY GETTING COZY WITH THE FUCKING ELEPHANT IN THE ROOM?

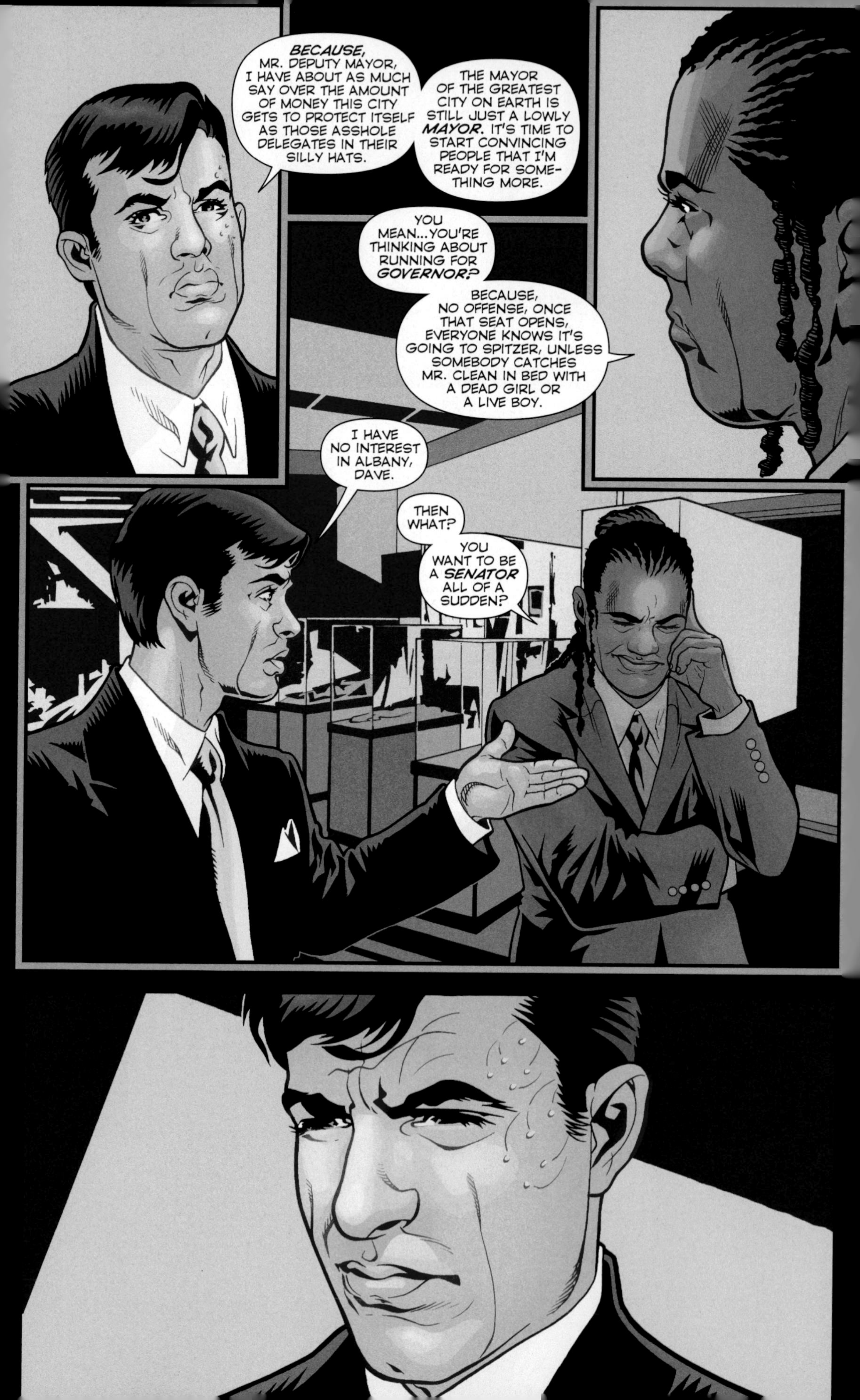
BECAUSE, MR. DEPUTY MAYOR, I HAVE ABOUT AS MUCH SAY OVER THE AMOUNT OF MONEY THIS CITY GETS TO PROTECT ITSELF AS THOSE ASSHOLE DELEGATES IN THEIR SILLY HATS.
THE MAYOR OF THE GREATEST CITY ON EARTH IS STILL JUST A LOWLY MAYOR. IT'S TIME TO START CONVINCING PEOPLE THAT I'M READY FOR SOME-THING MORE.
YOU MEAN...YOU'RE THINKING ABOUT RUNNING FOR GOVERNOR?
BECAUSE, NO OFFENSE, ONCE THAT SEAT OPENS, EVERYONE KNOWS IT'S GOING TO SPITZER, UNLESS SOMEBODY CATCHES MR. CLEAN IN BED WITH A DEAD GIRL OR A LIVE BOY.
I HAVE NO INTEREST IN ALBANY, DAVE.
THEN WHAT?
YOU WANT TO BE A SENATOR ALL OF A SUDDEN?

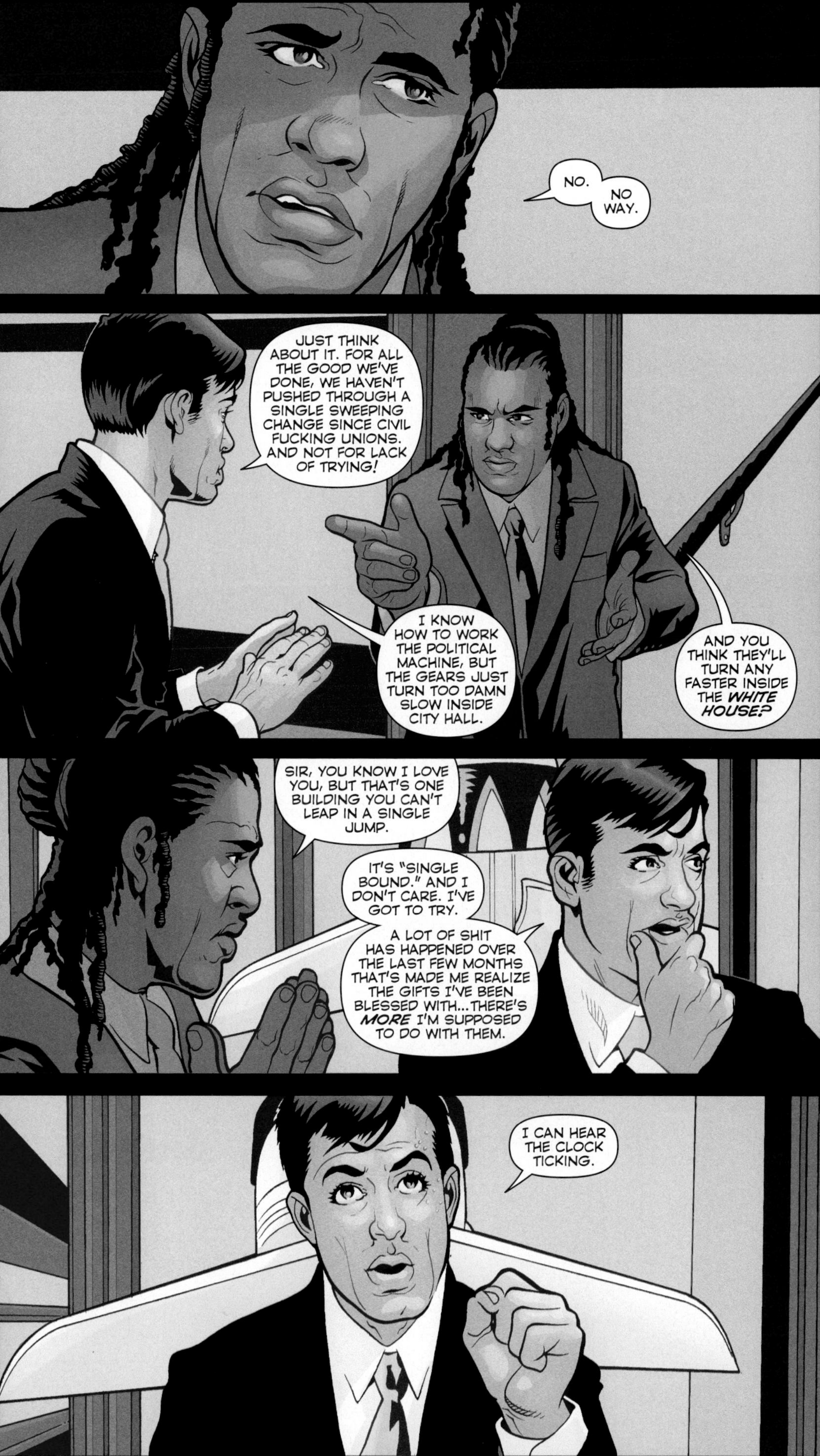
NO.
NO WAY.
JUST THINK ABOUT IT. FOR ALL THE GOOD WE'VE DONE, WE HAVEN'T PUSHED THROUGH A SINGLE SWEEPING CHANGE SINCE CIVIL FUCKING UNIONS. AND NOT FOR LACK OF TRYING!
I KNOW HOW TO WORK THE POLITICAL MACHINE, BUT THE GEARS JUST TURN TOO DAMN SLOW INSIDE CITY HALL.
AND YOU THINK THEY'LL TURN ANY FASTER INSIDE THE *WHITE HOUSE?*
SIR, YOU KNOW I LOVE YOU, BUT THAT'S ONE BUILDING YOU CAN'T LEAP IN A SINGLE JUMP.
IT'S "SINGLE BOUND." AND I DON'T CARE. I'VE GOT TO TRY.
A LOT OF SHIT HAS HAPPENED OVER THE LAST FEW MONTHS THAT'S MADE ME REALIZE THE GIFTS I'VE BEEN BLESSED WITH...THERE'S *MORE* I'M SUPPOSED TO DO WITH THEM.
I CAN HEAR THE CLOCK TICKING.

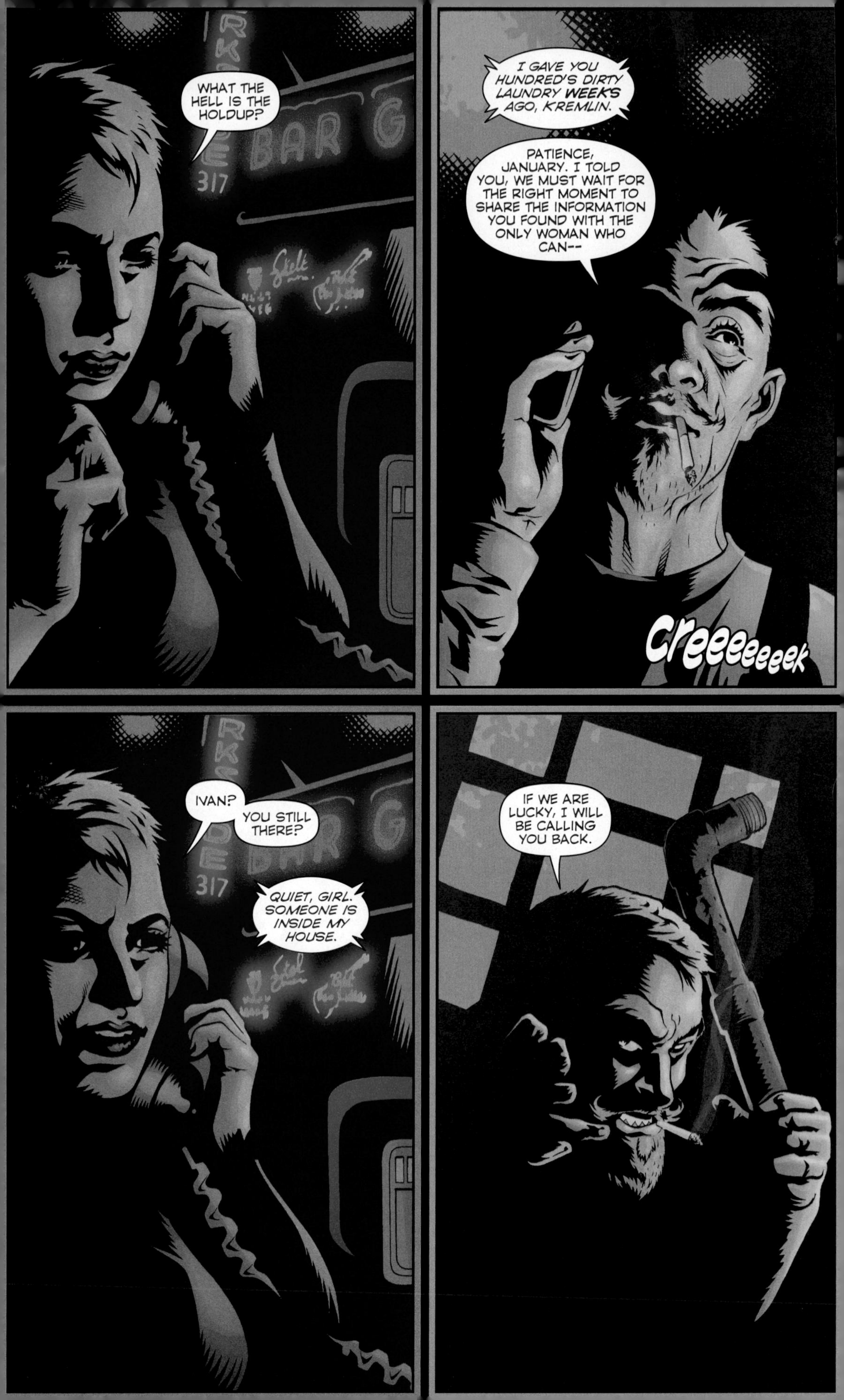
WHAT THE HELL IS THE HOLDUP?
I GAVE YOU HUNDRED'S DIRTY LAUNDRY WEEKS AGO, KREMLIN.
PATIENCE, JANUARY. I TOLD YOU, WE MUST WAIT FOR THE RIGHT MOMENT TO SHARE THE INFORMATION YOU FOUND WITH THE ONLY WOMAN WHO CAN--
CREEEEEEEK
IVAN?
YOU STILL THERE?
QUIET, GIRL. SOMEONE IS INSIDE MY HOUSE.
IF WE ARE LUCKY, I WILL BE CALLING YOU BACK.

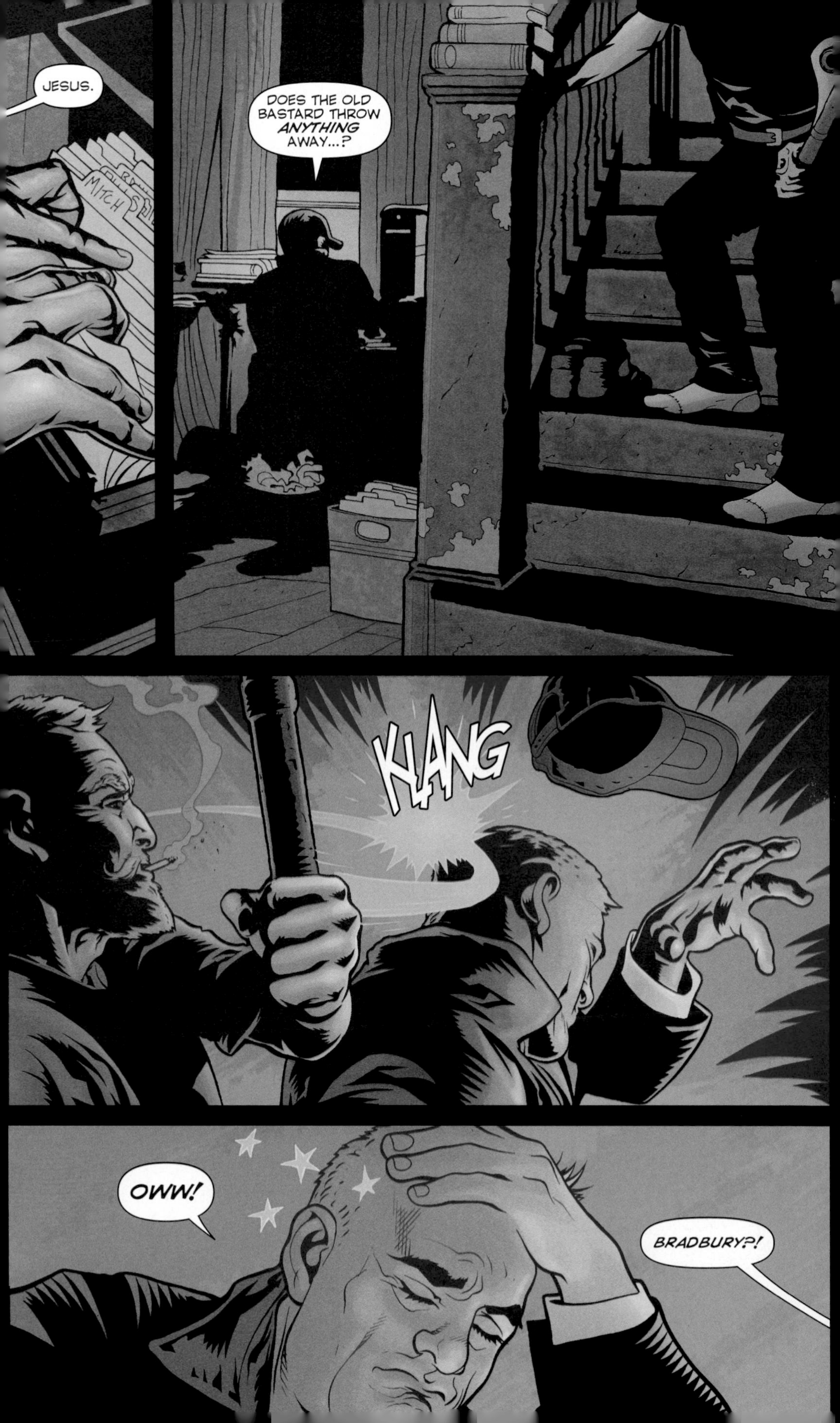
JESUS.
MITCH
DOES THE OLD BASTARD THROW *ANYTHING* AWAY...?
KLANG
OWW!
BRADBURY?!

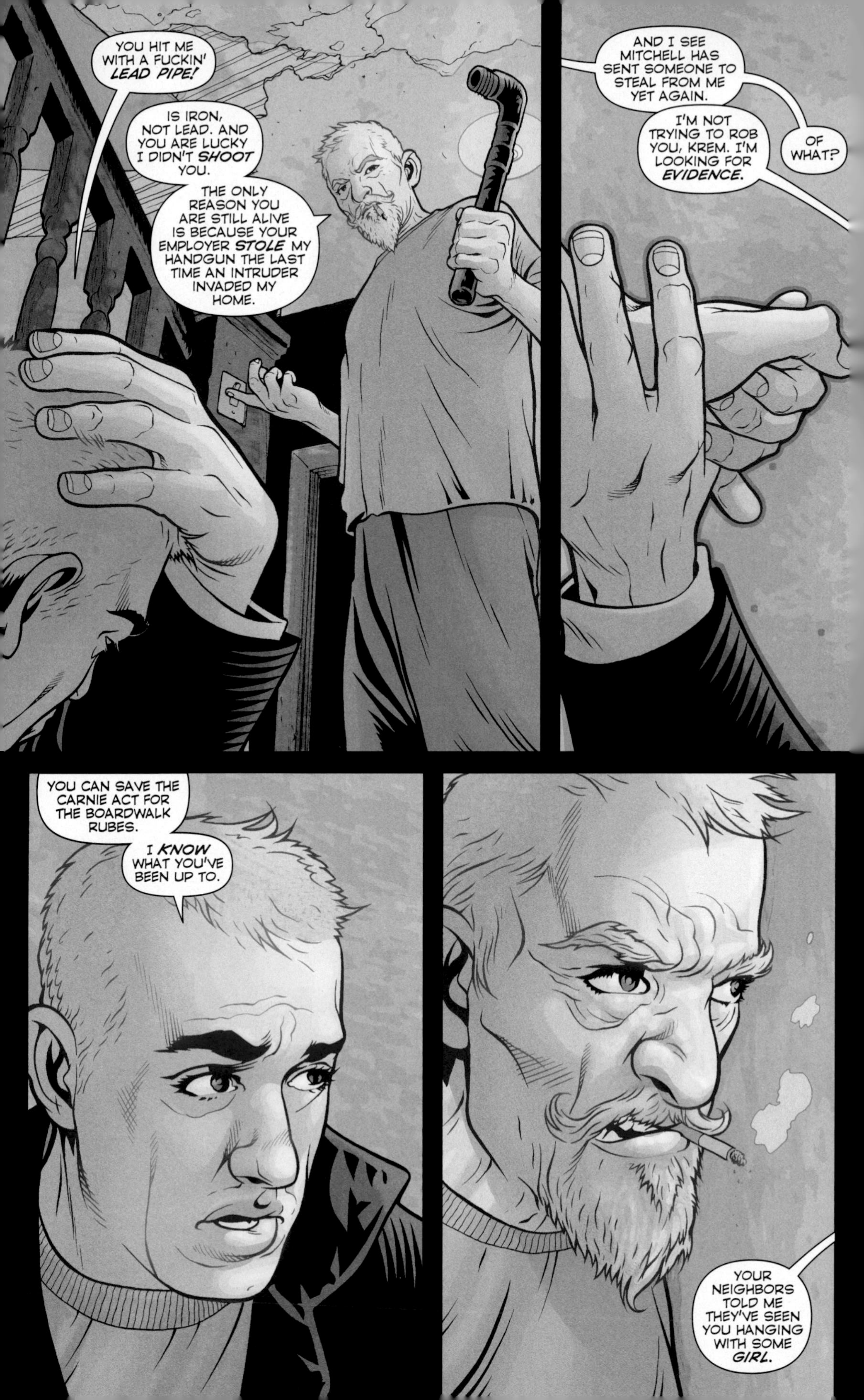
YOU HIT ME WITH A FUCKIN' LEAD PIPE!
IS IRON, NOT LEAD. AND YOU ARE LUCKY I DIDN'T SHOOT YOU.
THE ONLY REASON YOU ARE STILL ALIVE IS BECAUSE YOUR EMPLOYER STOLE MY HANDGUN THE LAST TIME AN INTRUDER INVADED MY HOME.
AND I SEE MITCHELL HAS SENT SOMEONE TO STEAL FROM ME YET AGAIN.
I'M NOT TRYING TO ROB YOU, KREM. I'M LOOKING FOR EVIDENCE.
OF WHAT?
YOU CAN SAVE THE CARNIE ACT FOR THE BOARDWALK RUBES.
I KNOW WHAT YOU'VE BEEN UP TO.
YOUR NEIGHBORS TOLD ME THEY'VE SEEN YOU HANGING WITH SOME GIRL.

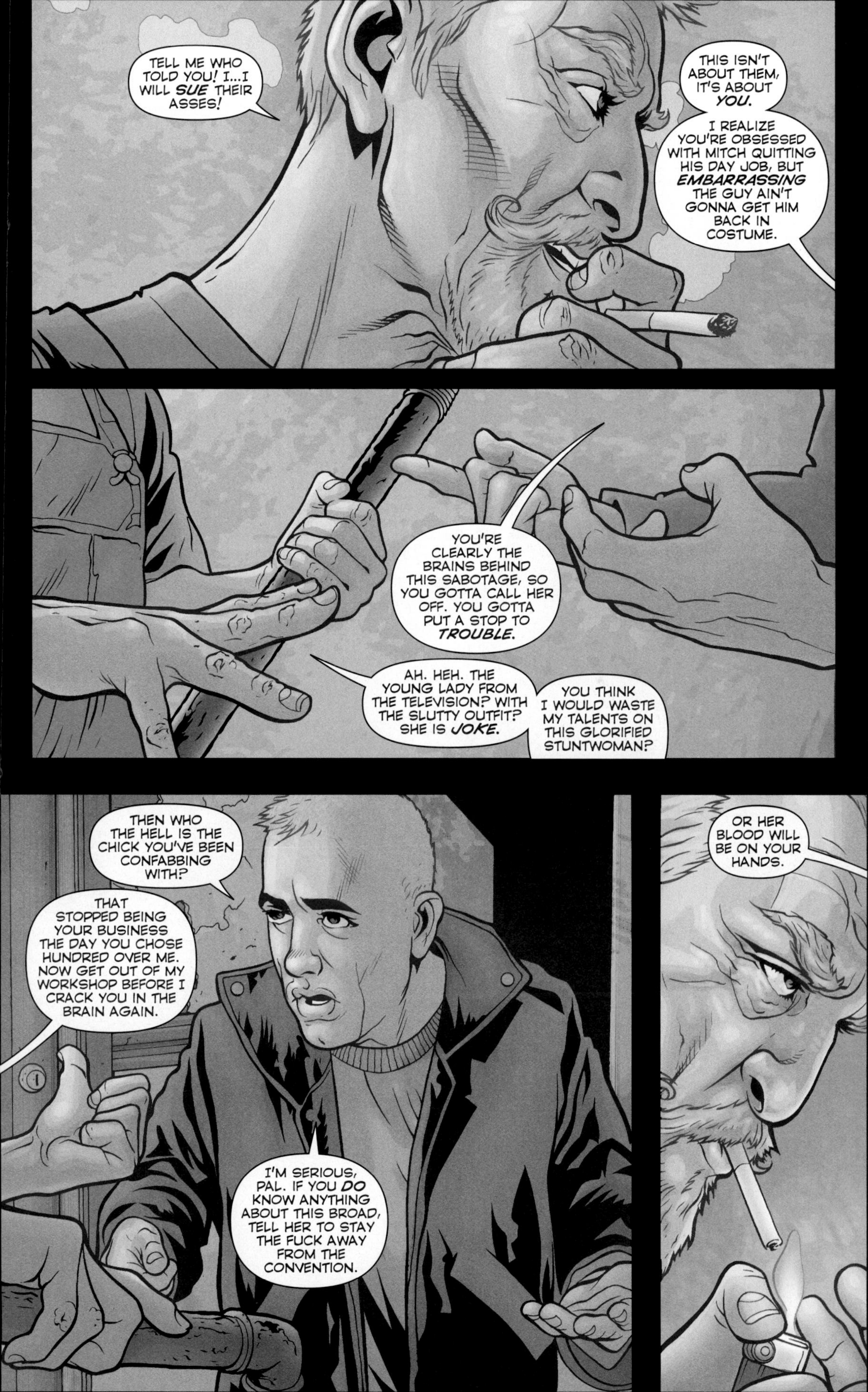
TELL ME WHO TOLD YOU! I...I WILL *SUE* THEIR ASSES!
THIS ISN'T ABOUT THEM, IT'S ABOUT *YOU.*
I REALIZE YOU'RE OBSESSED WITH MITCH QUITTING HIS DAY JOB, BUT *EMBARRASSING* THE GUY AIN'T GONNA GET HIM BACK IN COSTUME.
YOU'RE CLEARLY THE BRAINS BEHIND THIS SABOTAGE, SO YOU GOTTA CALL HER OFF. YOU GOTTA PUT A STOP TO *TROUBLE.*
AH. HEH. THE YOUNG LADY FROM THE TELEVISION? WITH THE SLUTTY OUTFIT? SHE IS *JOKE.*
YOU THINK I WOULD WASTE MY TALENTS ON THIS GLORIFIED STUNTWOMAN?
THEN WHO THE HELL IS THE CHICK YOU'VE BEEN CONFABBING WITH?
THAT STOPPED BEING YOUR BUSINESS THE DAY YOU CHOSE HUNDRED OVER ME. NOW GET OUT OF MY WORKSHOP BEFORE I CRACK YOU IN THE BRAIN AGAIN.
I'M SERIOUS, PAL. IF YOU *DO* KNOW ANYTHING ABOUT THIS BROAD, TELL HER TO STAY THE FUCK AWAY FROM THE CONVENTION.
OR HER BLOOD WILL BE ON YOUR HANDS.

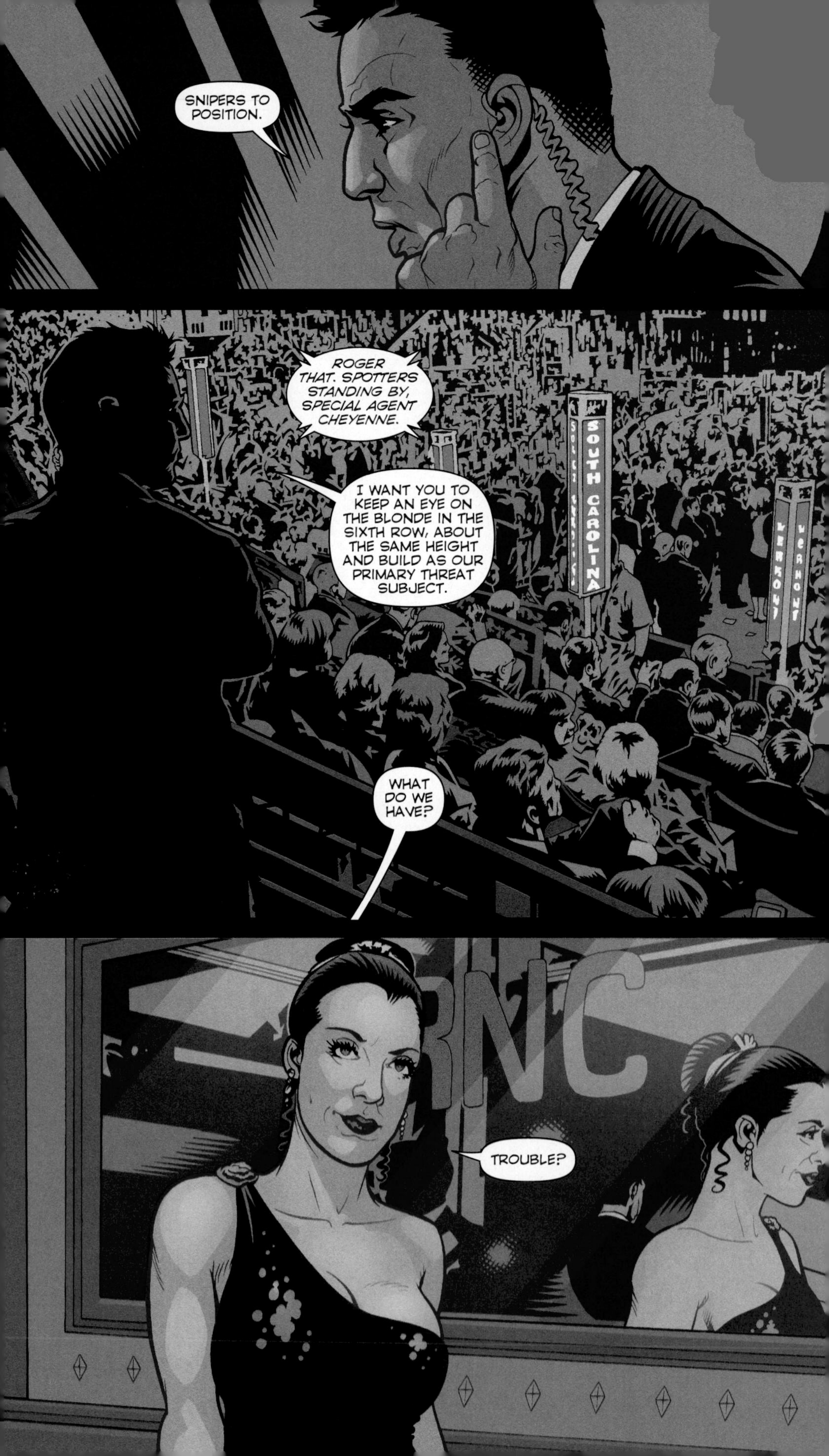

SNIPERS TO POSITION.
ROGER THAT. SPOTTERS STANDING BY, SPECIAL AGENT CHEYENNE.
I WANT YOU TO KEEP AN EYE ON THE BLONDE IN THE SIXTH ROW, ABOUT THE SAME HEIGHT AND BUILD AS OUR PRIMARY THREAT SUBJECT.
SOUTH CAROLINA
WHAT DO WE HAVE?
RNC
TROUBLE?

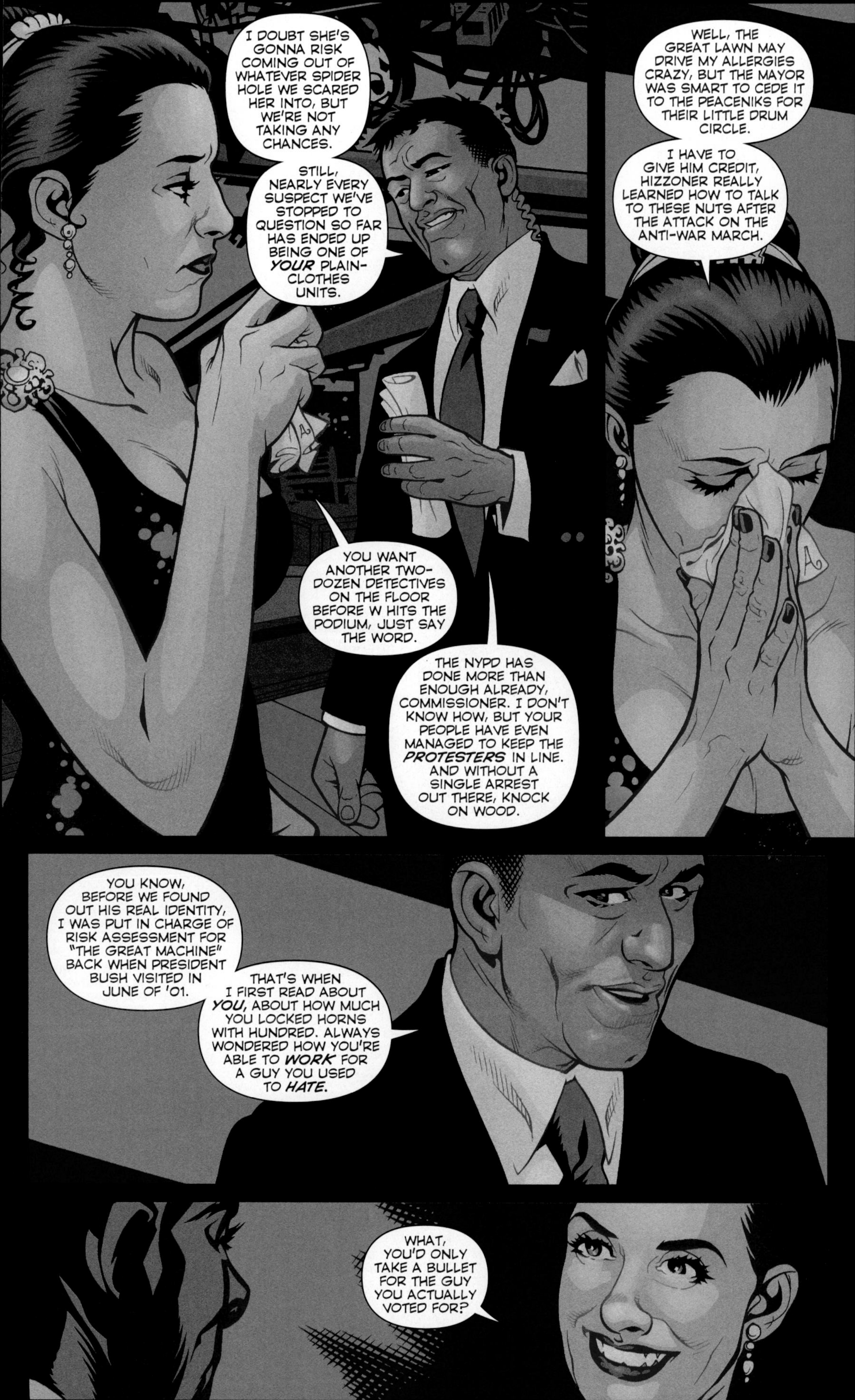
I DOUBT SHE'S GONNA RISK COMING OUT OF WHATEVER SPIDER HOLE WE SCARED HER INTO, BUT WE'RE NOT TAKING ANY CHANCES.
STILL, NEARLY EVERY SUSPECT WE'VE STOPPED TO QUESTION SO FAR HAS ENDED UP BEING ONE OF *YOUR* PLAIN-CLOTHES UNITS.
YOU WANT ANOTHER TWO-DOZEN DETECTIVES ON THE FLOOR BEFORE W HITS THE PODIUM, JUST SAY THE WORD.
THE NYPD HAS DONE MORE THAN ENOUGH ALREADY, COMMISSIONER. I DON'T KNOW HOW, BUT YOUR PEOPLE HAVE EVEN MANAGED TO KEEP THE *PROTESTERS* IN LINE. AND WITHOUT A SINGLE ARREST OUT THERE, KNOCK ON WOOD.
WELL, THE GREAT LAWN MAY DRIVE MY ALLERGIES CRAZY, BUT THE MAYOR WAS SMART TO CEDE IT TO THE PEACENIKS FOR THEIR LITTLE DRUM CIRCLE.
I HAVE TO GIVE HIM CREDIT, HIZZONER REALLY LEARNED HOW TO TALK TO THESE NUTS AFTER THE ATTACK ON THE ANTI-WAR MARCH.
YOU KNOW, BEFORE WE FOUND OUT HIS REAL IDENTITY, I WAS PUT IN CHARGE OF RISK ASSESSMENT FOR "THE GREAT MACHINE" BACK WHEN PRESIDENT BUSH VISITED IN JUNE OF '01.
THAT'S WHEN I FIRST READ ABOUT *YOU,* ABOUT HOW MUCH YOU LOCKED HORNS WITH HUNDRED. ALWAYS WONDERED HOW YOU'RE ABLE TO *WORK* FOR A GUY YOU USED TO *HATE.*
WHAT, YOU'D ONLY TAKE A BULLET FOR THE GUY YOU ACTUALLY VOTED FOR?

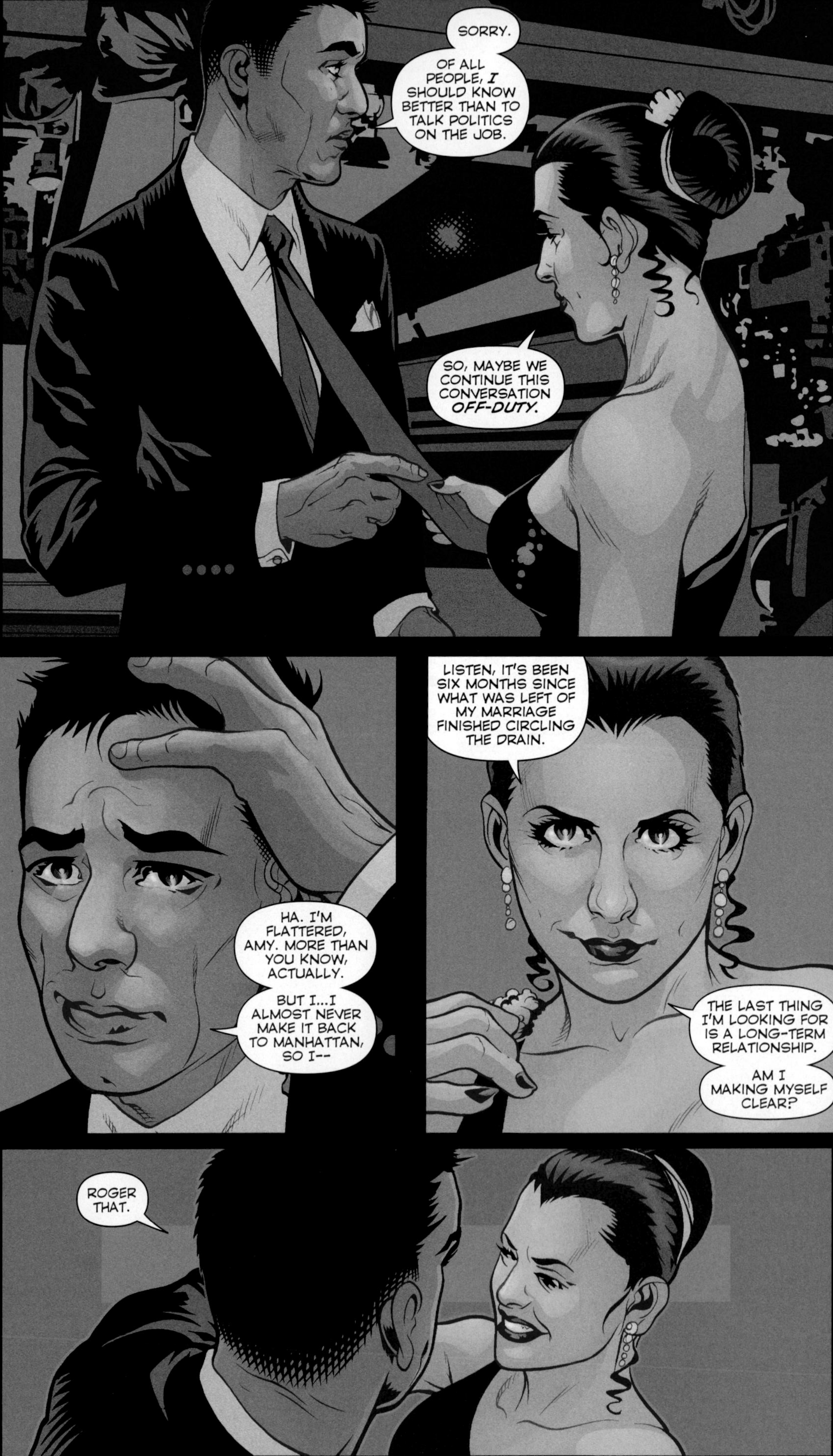

SORRY.
OF ALL PEOPLE, *I* SHOULD KNOW BETTER THAN TO TALK POLITICS ON THE JOB.
SO, MAYBE WE CONTINUE THIS CONVERSATION *OFF-DUTY*.
HA. I'M FLATTERED, AMY. MORE THAN YOU KNOW, ACTUALLY.
BUT I...I ALMOST NEVER MAKE IT BACK TO MANHATTAN, SO I--
LISTEN, IT'S BEEN SIX MONTHS SINCE WHAT WAS LEFT OF MY MARRIAGE FINISHED CIRCLING THE DRAIN.
THE LAST THING I'M LOOKING FOR IS A LONG-TERM RELATIONSHIP.
AM I MAKING MYSELF CLEAR?
ROGER THAT.

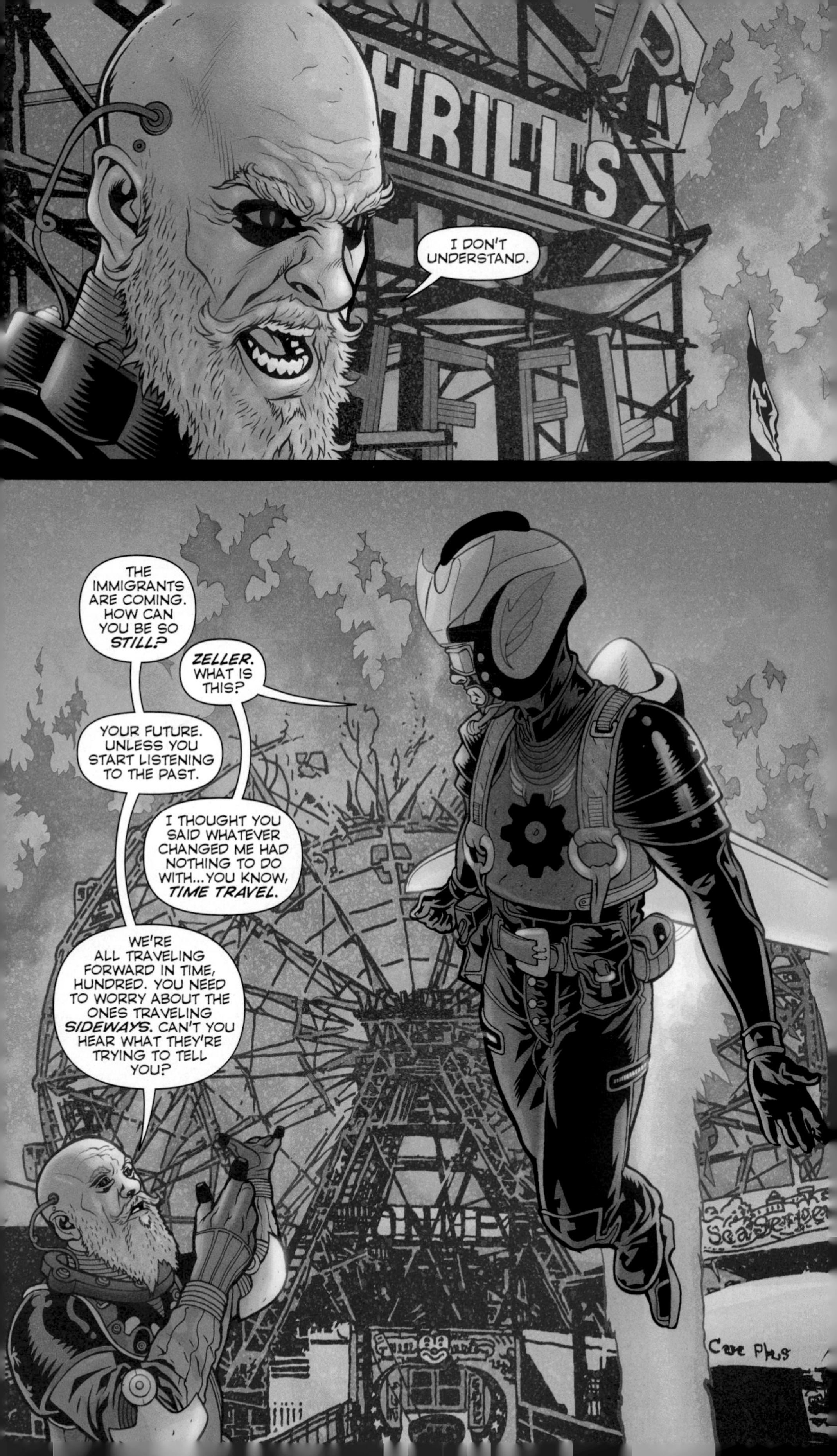
I DON'T UNDERSTAND.
THE IMMIGRANTS ARE COMING. HOW CAN YOU BE SO STILL?
ZELLER. WHAT IS THIS?
YOUR FUTURE. UNLESS YOU START LISTENING TO THE PAST.
I THOUGHT YOU SAID WHATEVER CHANGED ME HAD NOTHING TO DO WITH...YOU KNOW, TIME TRAVEL.
WE'RE ALL TRAVELING FORWARD IN TIME, HUNDRED. YOU NEED TO WORRY ABOUT THE ONES TRAVELING SIDEWAYS. CAN'T YOU HEAR WHAT THEY'RE TRYING TO TELL YOU?

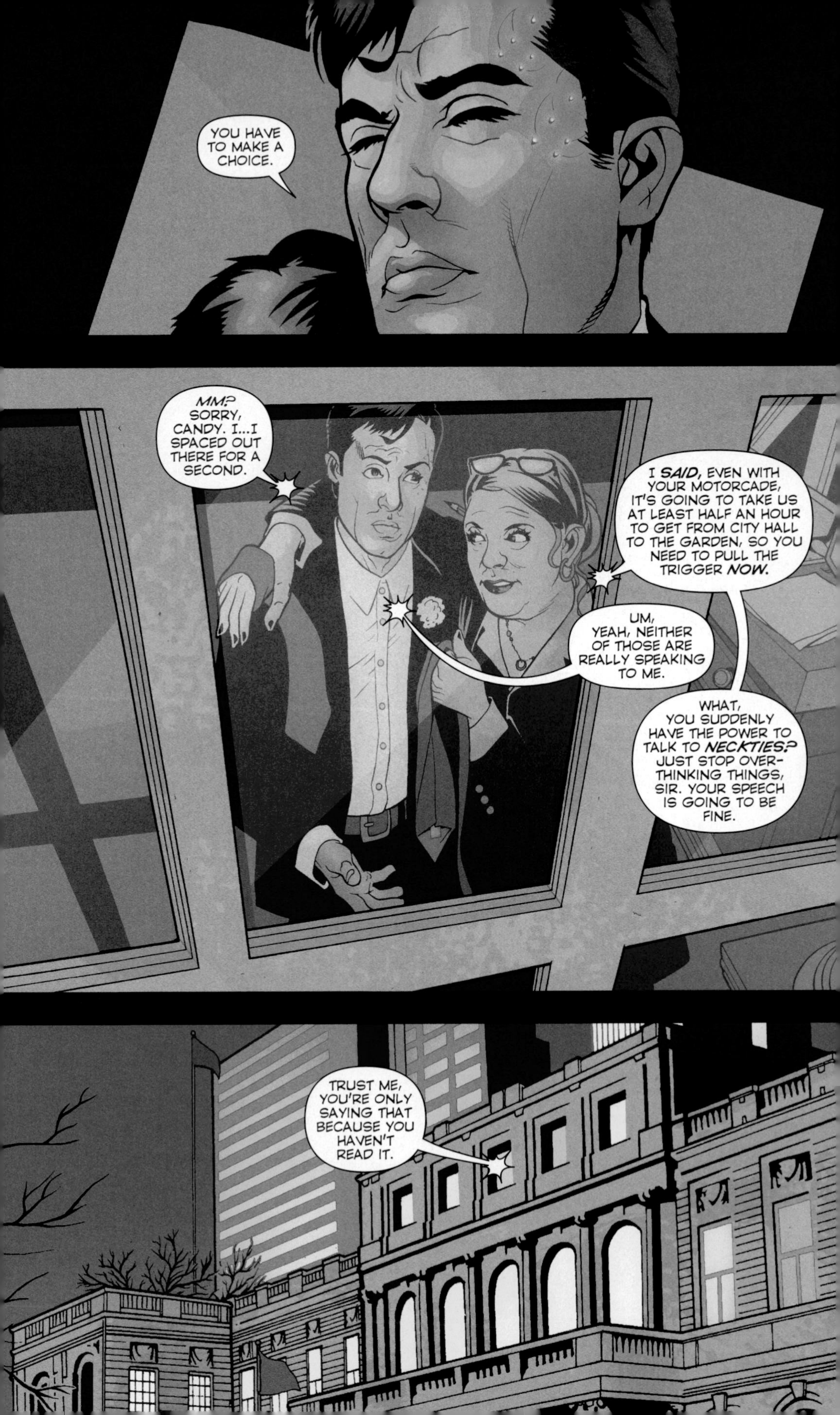
YOU HAVE TO MAKE A CHOICE.
MM? SORRY, CANDY. I...I SPACED OUT THERE FOR A SECOND.
I *SAID,* EVEN WITH YOUR MOTORCADE, IT'S GOING TO TAKE US AT LEAST HALF AN HOUR TO GET FROM CITY HALL TO THE GARDEN, SO YOU NEED TO PULL THE TRIGGER *NOW.*
UM, YEAH, NEITHER OF THOSE ARE REALLY SPEAKING TO ME.
WHAT, YOU SUDDENLY HAVE THE POWER TO TALK TO *NECKTIES?* JUST STOP OVER-THINKING THINGS, SIR. YOUR SPEECH IS GOING TO BE FINE.
TRUST ME, YOU'RE ONLY SAYING THAT BECAUSE YOU HAVEN'T READ IT.

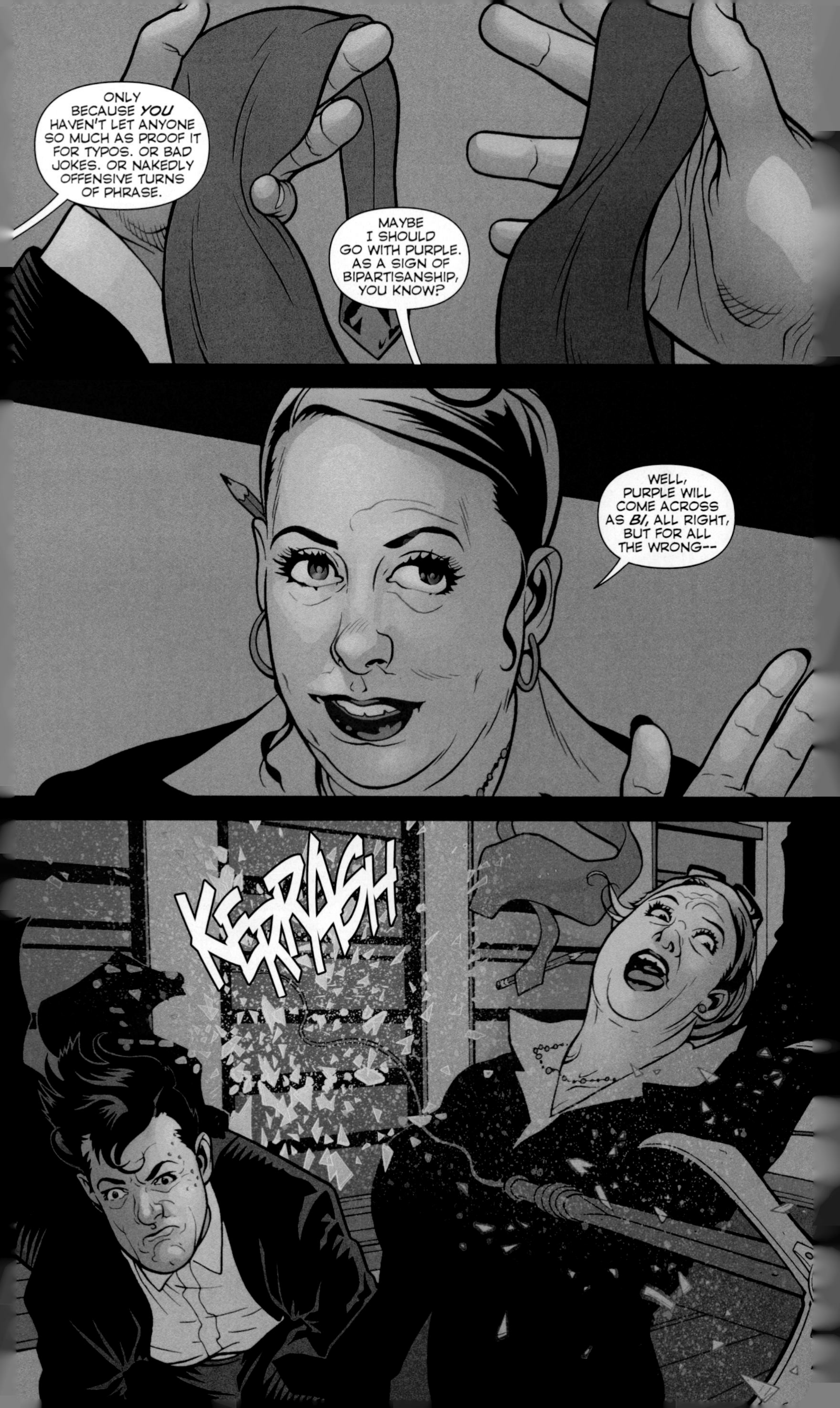
ONLY BECAUSE *YOU* HAVEN'T LET ANYONE SO MUCH AS PROOF IT FOR TYPOS. OR BAD JOKES. OR NAKEDLY OFFENSIVE TURNS OF PHRASE.
MAYBE I SHOULD GO WITH PURPLE. AS A SIGN OF BIPARTISANSHIP, YOU KNOW?
WELL, PURPLE WILL COME ACROSS AS *BI*, ALL RIGHT, BUT FOR ALL THE WRONG--
KERRASH

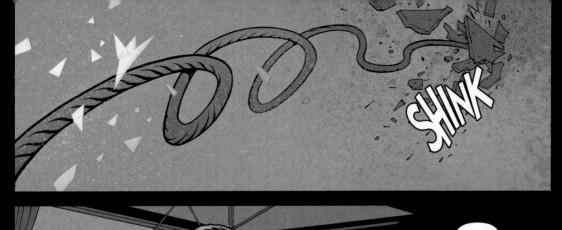

SHINK

DON'T TOUCH IT!

RELAX.

IF THIS THING WERE A BOMB, IT ALREADY WOULD HAVE TOLD ME SO.

deep boo deep beep!

answer me:)

UM, YEAH?

HOWDY, HANDSOME.

WHO IS THIS?

LOOK OUT YOUR WINDOW. BUT DO IT FAST...

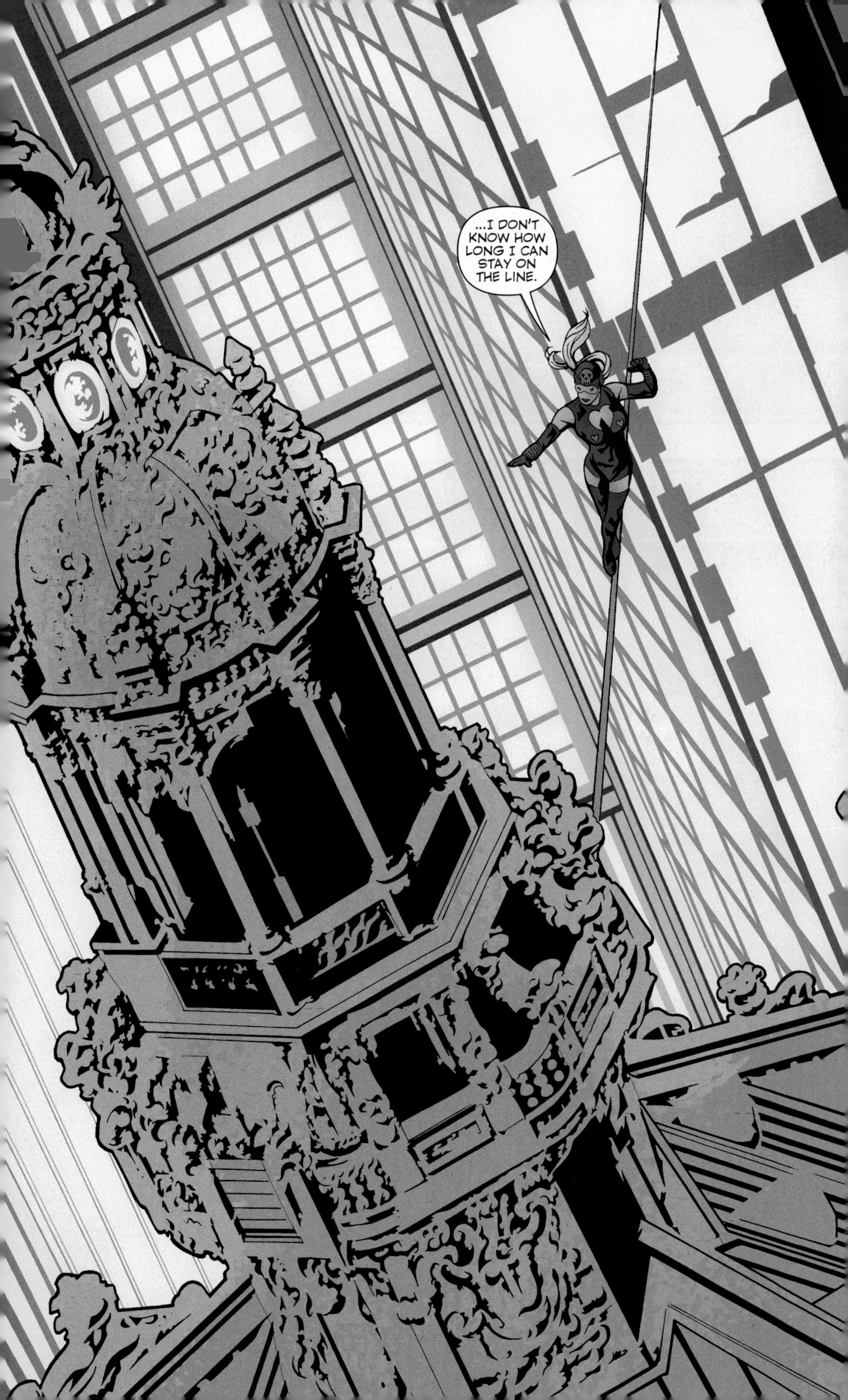
...I DON'T KNOW HOW LONG I CAN STAY ON THE LINE.

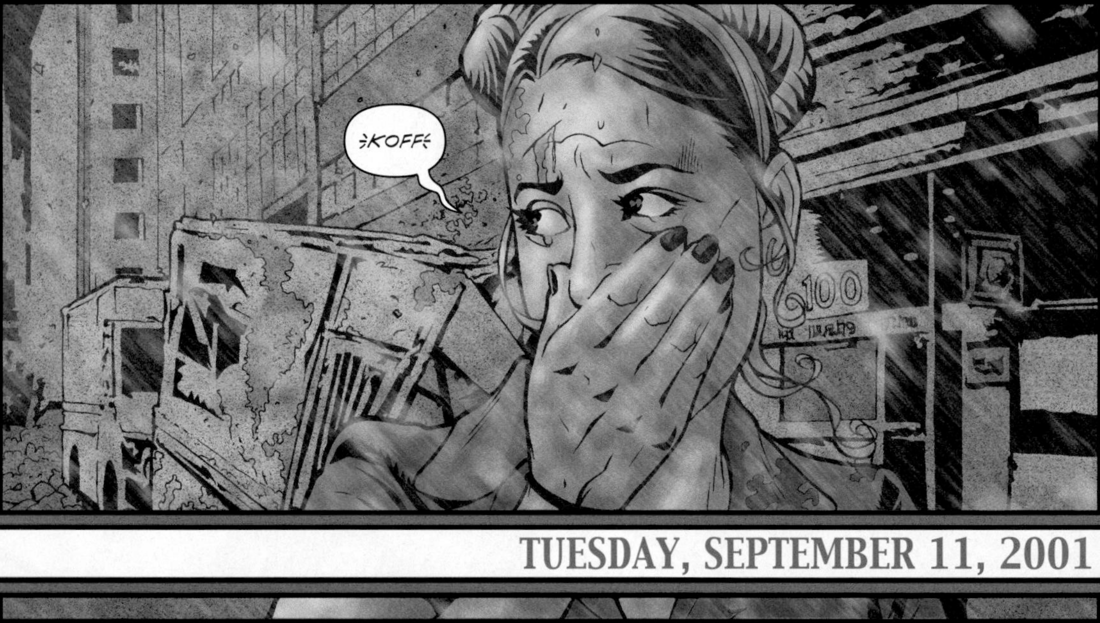
KOFF
TUESDAY, SEPTEMBER 11, 2001

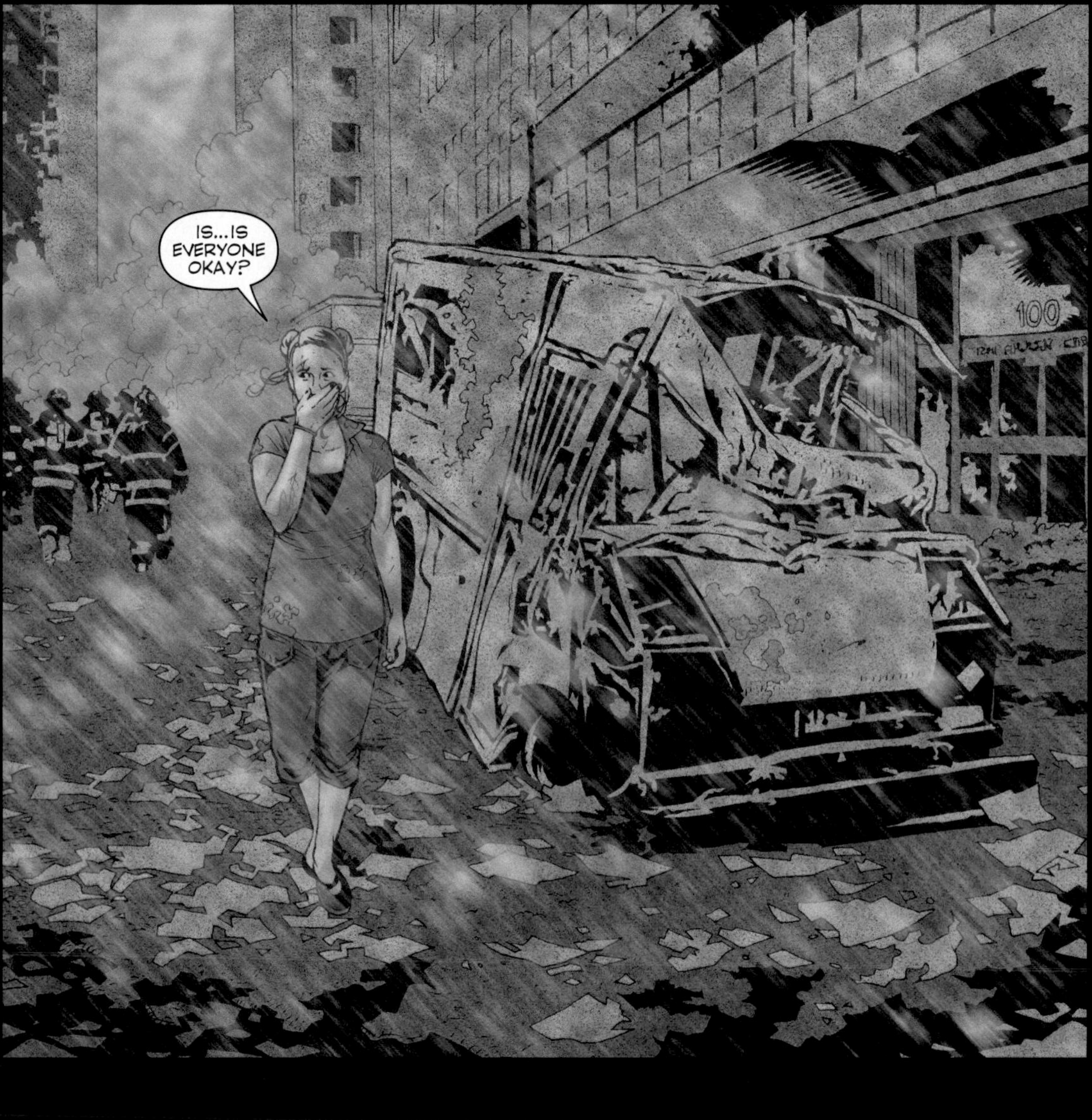
IS...IS EVERYONE OKAY?

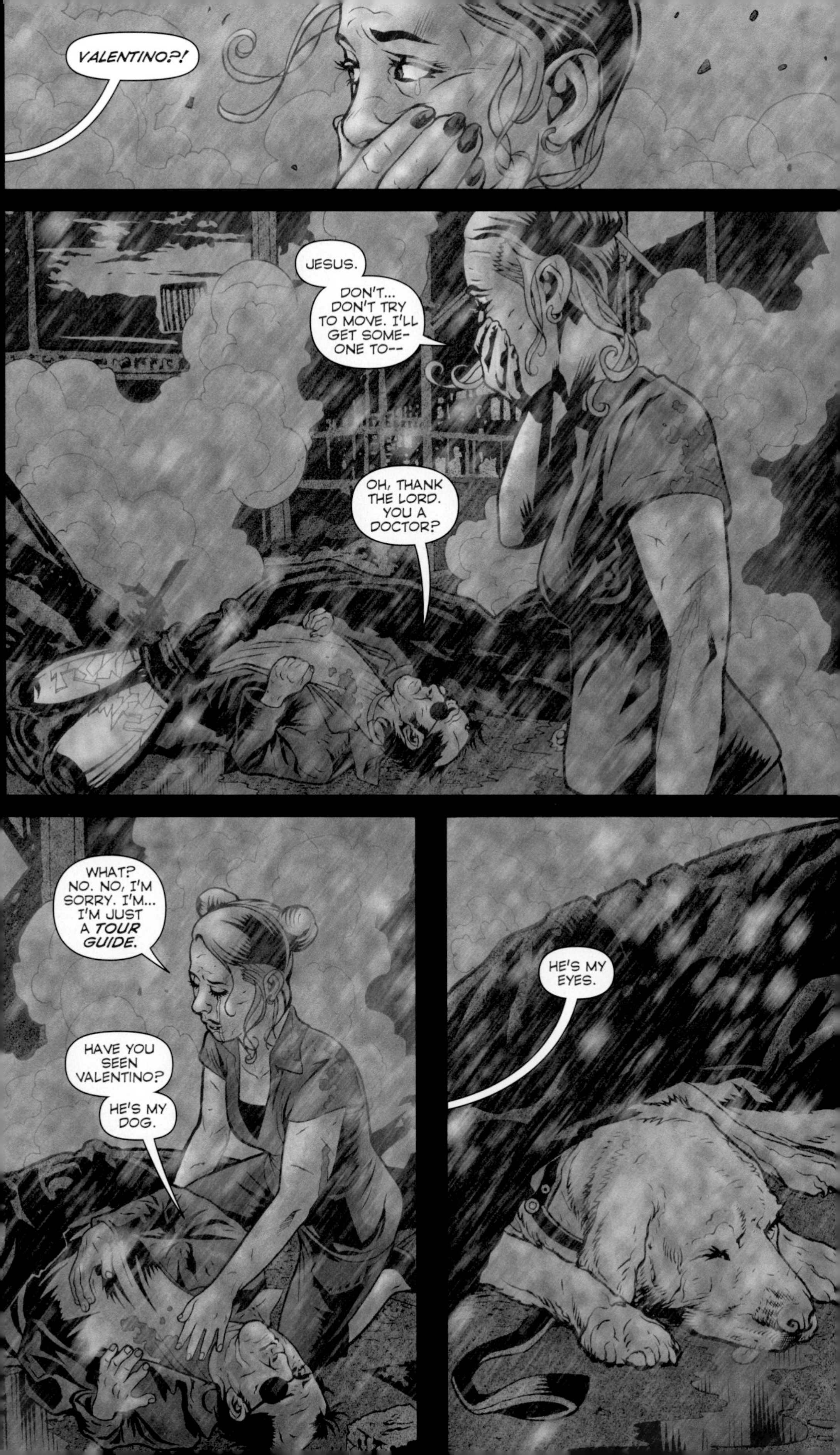

VALENTINO?!
JESUS.
DON'T... DON'T TRY TO MOVE. I'LL GET SOME-ONE TO--
OH, THANK THE LORD. YOU A DOCTOR?
WHAT? NO. NO, I'M SORRY. I'M... I'M JUST A TOUR GUIDE.
HAVE YOU SEEN VALENTINO?
HE'S MY DOG.
HE'S MY EYES.

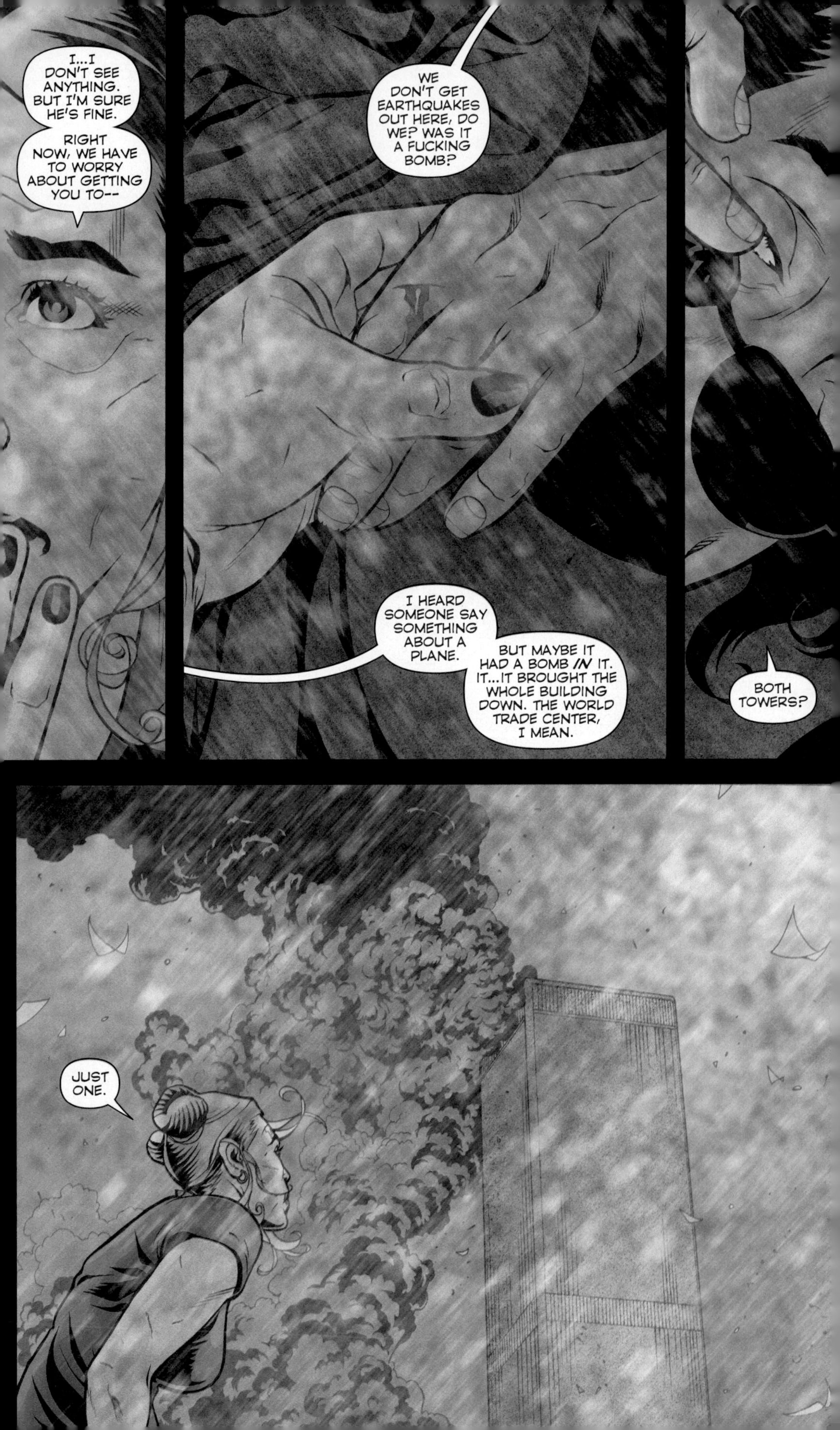
I...I DON'T SEE ANYTHING. BUT I'M SURE HE'S FINE.
RIGHT NOW, WE HAVE TO WORRY ABOUT GETTING YOU TO--
WE DON'T GET EARTHQUAKES OUT HERE, DO WE? WAS IT A FUCKING BOMB?
I HEARD SOMEONE SAY SOMETHING ABOUT A PLANE.
BUT MAYBE IT HAD A BOMB *IN* IT. IT...IT BROUGHT THE WHOLE BUILDING DOWN. THE WORLD TRADE CENTER, I MEAN.
BOTH TOWERS?
JUST ONE.

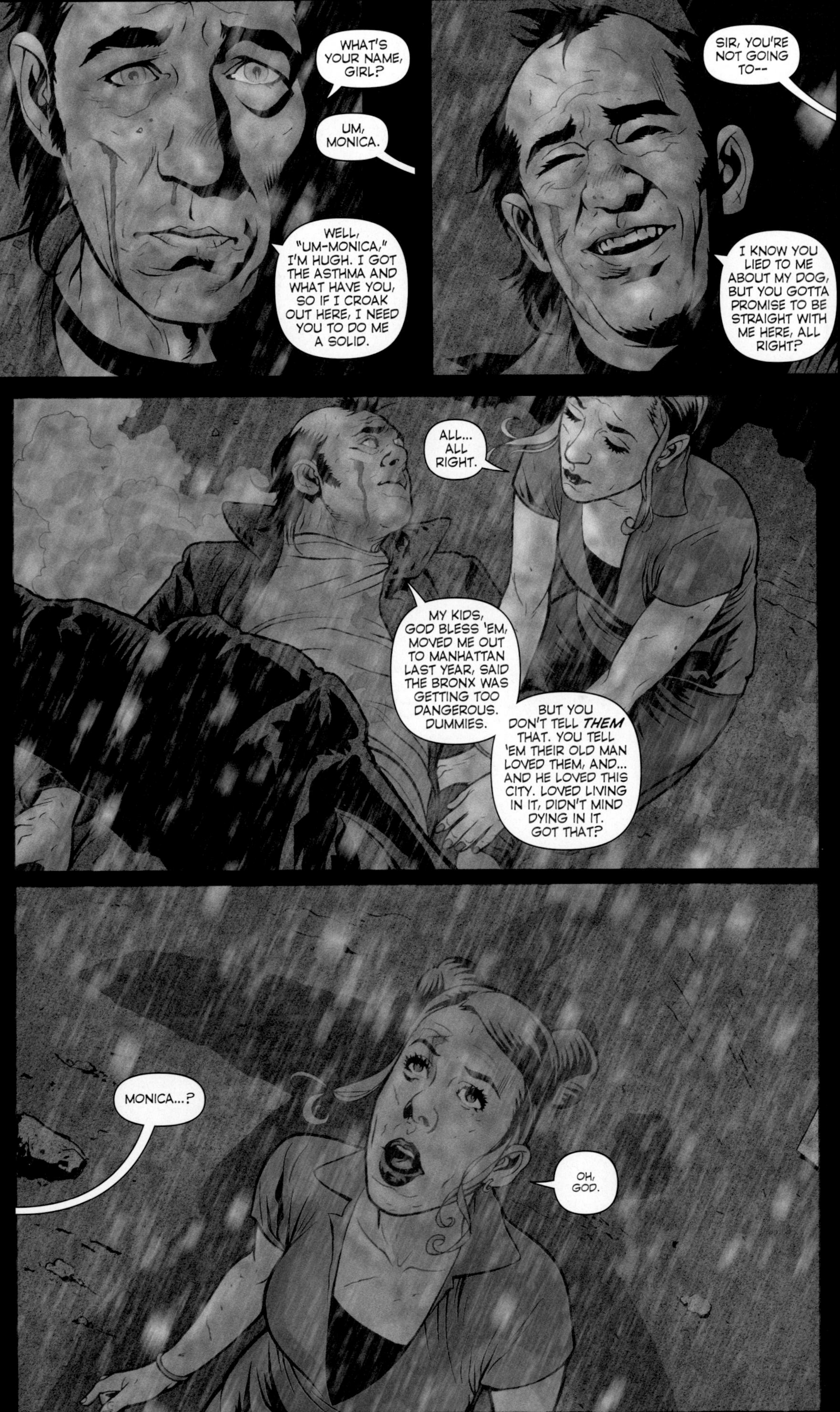
WHAT'S YOUR NAME, GIRL?
UM, MONICA.
WELL, "UM-MONICA," I'M HUGH. I GOT THE ASTHMA AND WHAT HAVE YOU, SO IF I CROAK OUT HERE, I NEED YOU TO DO ME A SOLID.
SIR, YOU'RE NOT GOING TO--
I KNOW YOU LIED TO ME ABOUT MY DOG, BUT YOU GOTTA PROMISE TO BE STRAIGHT WITH ME HERE, ALL RIGHT?
ALL... ALL RIGHT.
MY KIDS, GOD BLESS 'EM, MOVED ME OUT TO MANHATTAN LAST YEAR, SAID THE BRONX WAS GETTING TOO DANGEROUS. DUMMIES.
BUT YOU DON'T TELL *THEM* THAT. YOU TELL 'EM THEIR OLD MAN LOVED THEM, AND... AND HE LOVED THIS CITY. LOVED LIVING IN IT, DIDN'T MIND DYING IN IT. GOT THAT?
MONICA...?
OH, GOD.

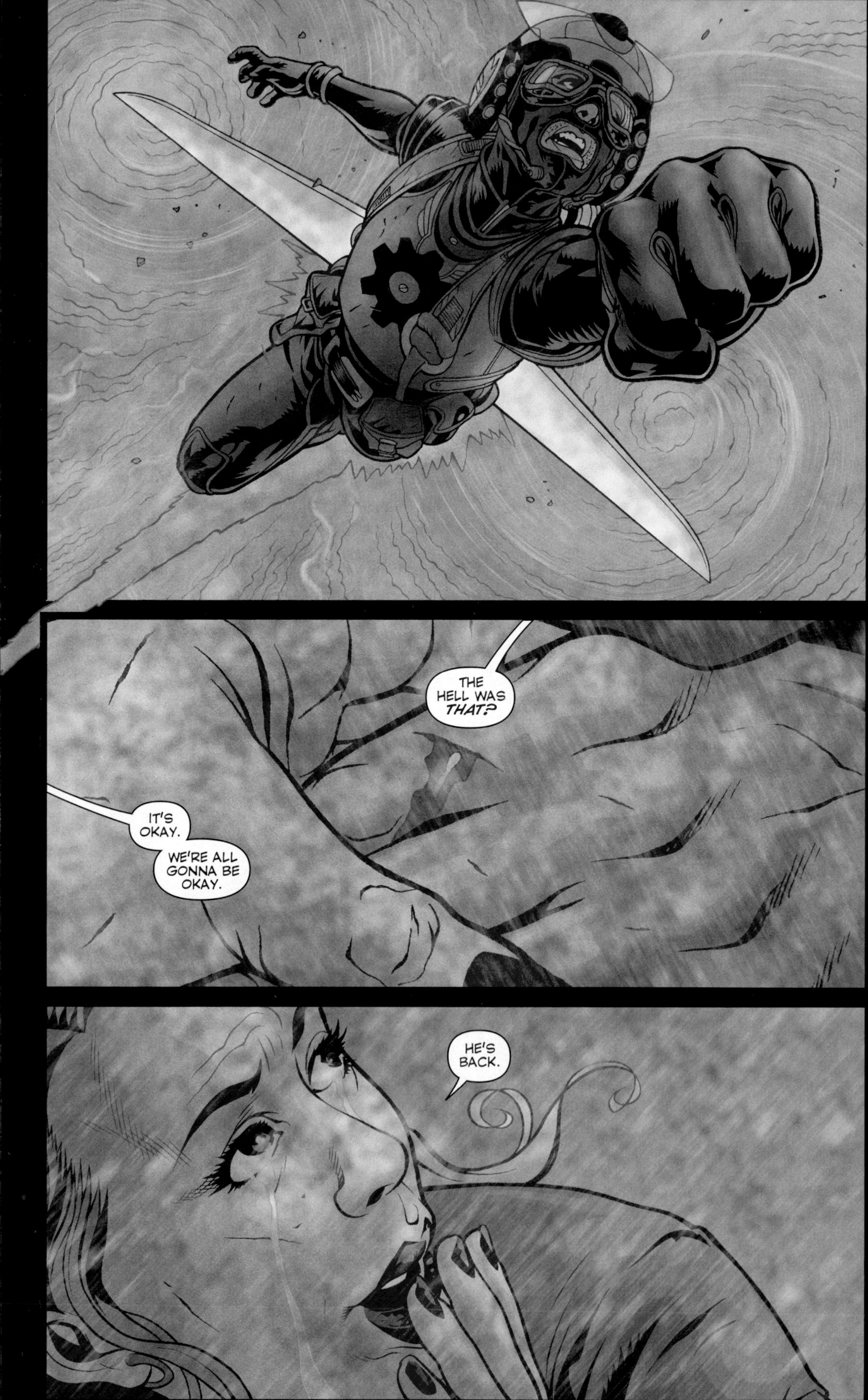
THE HELL WAS THAT?
IT'S OKAY.
WE'RE ALL GONNA BE OKAY.
HE'S BACK.

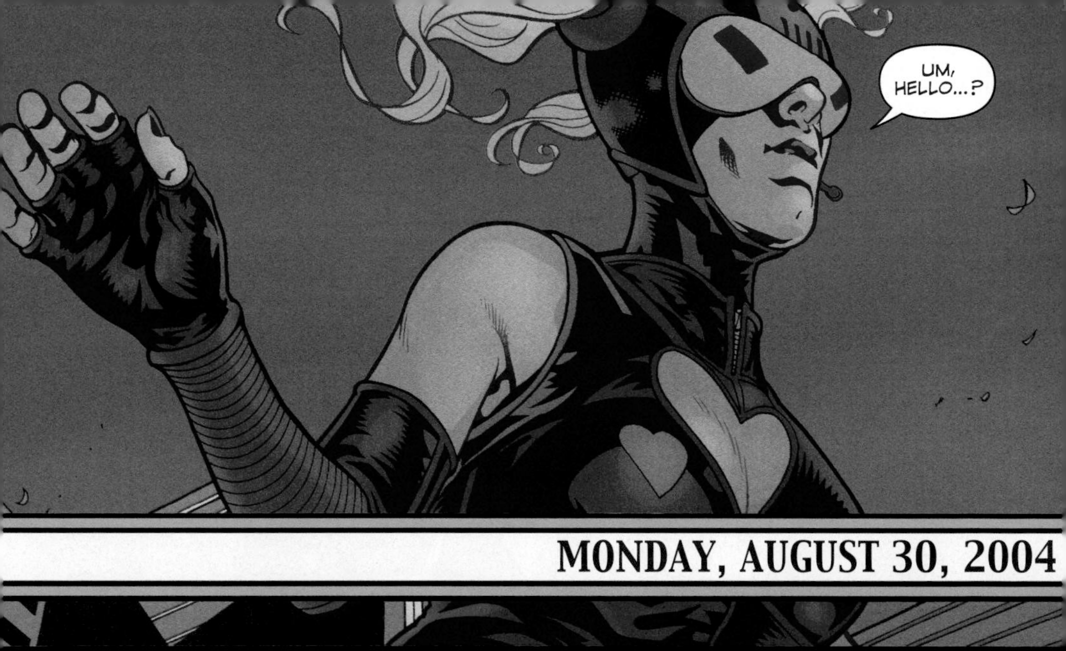
UM, HELLO...?
MONDAY, AUGUST 30, 2004

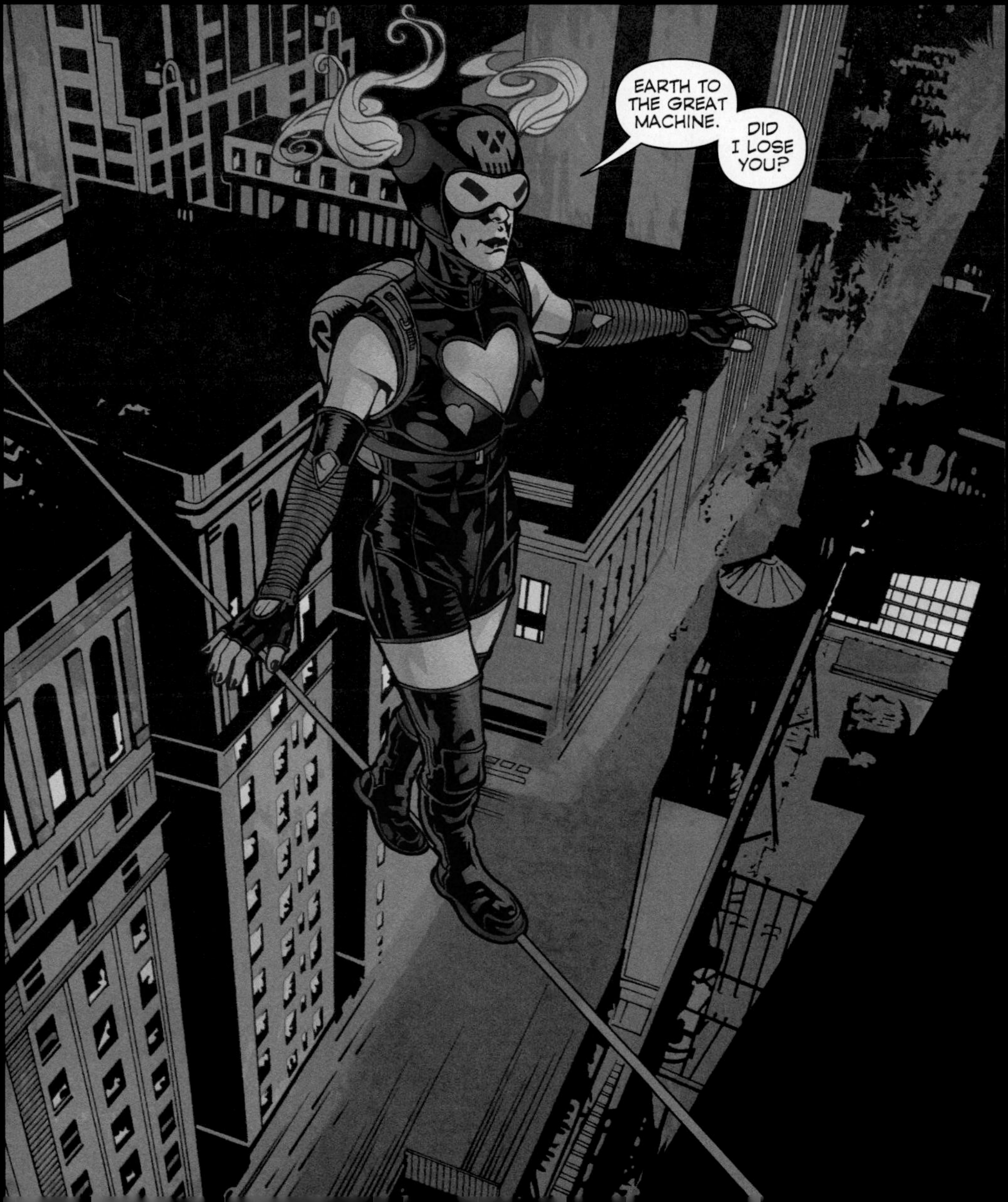
EARTH TO THE GREAT MACHINE.
DID I LOSE YOU?

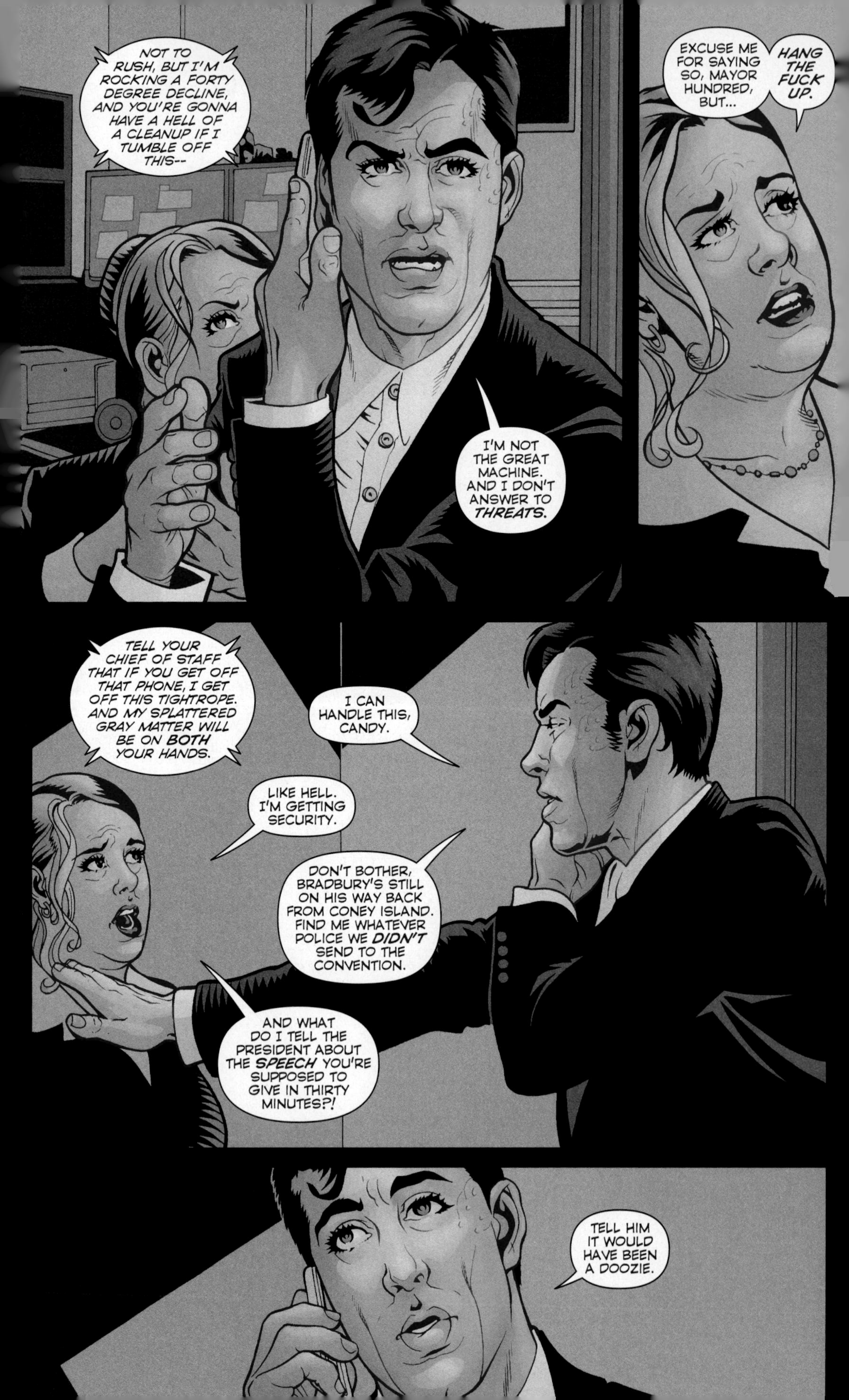
NOT TO RUSH, BUT I'M ROCKING A FORTY DEGREE DECLINE, AND YOU'RE GONNA HAVE A HELL OF A CLEANUP IF I TUMBLE OFF THIS--
I'M NOT THE GREAT MACHINE. AND I DON'T ANSWER TO THREATS.
EXCUSE ME FOR SAYING SO, MAYOR HUNDRED, BUT...
HANG THE FUCK UP.
TELL YOUR CHIEF OF STAFF THAT IF YOU GET OFF THAT PHONE, I GET OFF THIS TIGHTROPE. AND MY SPLATTERED GRAY MATTER WILL BE ON BOTH YOUR HANDS.
I CAN HANDLE THIS, CANDY.
LIKE HELL. I'M GETTING SECURITY.
DON'T BOTHER, BRADBURY'S STILL ON HIS WAY BACK FROM CONEY ISLAND. FIND ME WHATEVER POLICE WE DIDN'T SEND TO THE CONVENTION.
AND WHAT DO I TELL THE PRESIDENT ABOUT THE SPEECH YOU'RE SUPPOSED TO GIVE IN THIRTY MINUTES?!
TELL HIM IT WOULD HAVE BEEN A DOOZIE.

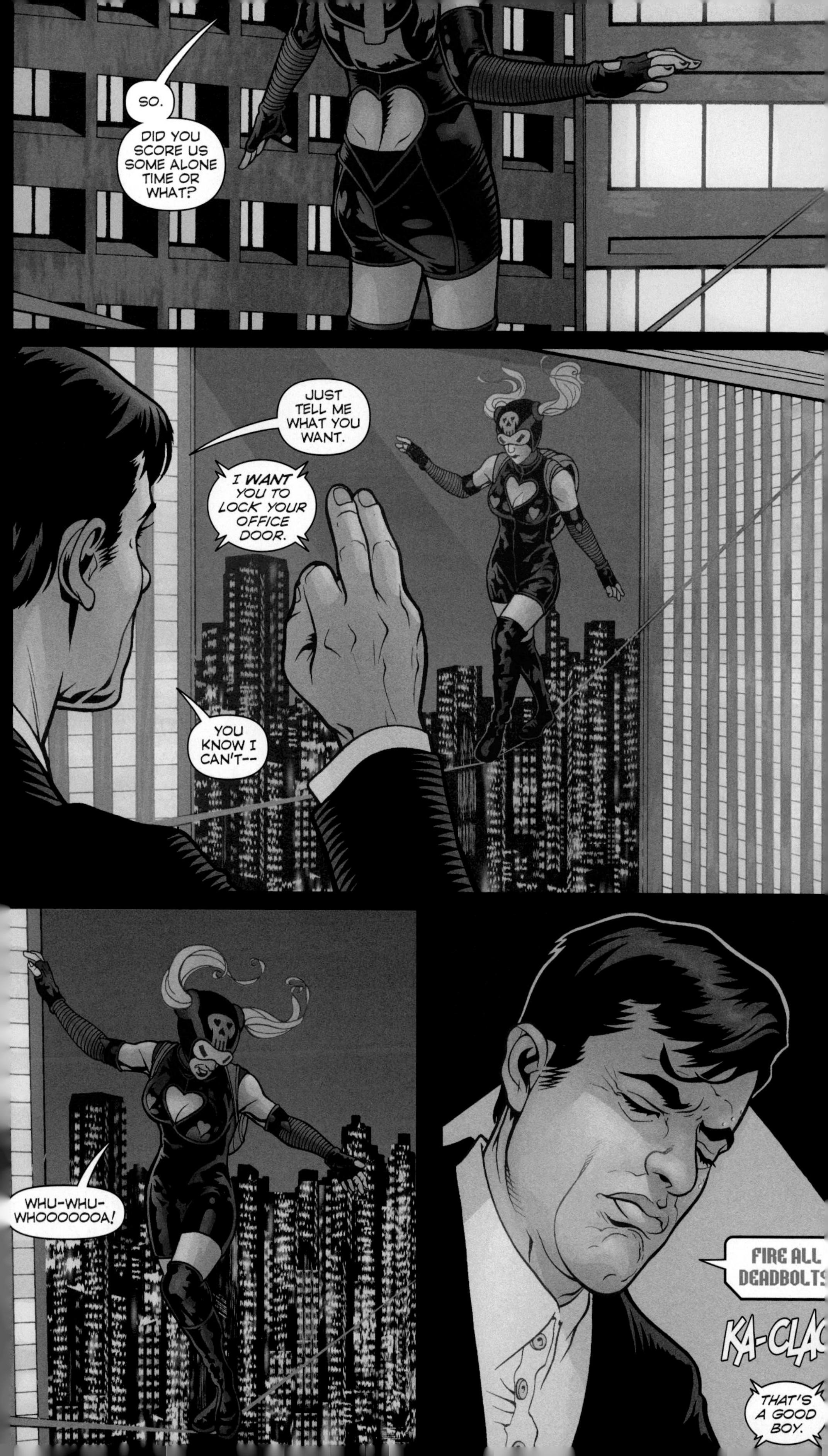
SO.
DID YOU SCORE US SOME ALONE TIME OR WHAT?
JUST TELL ME WHAT YOU WANT.
I WANT YOU TO LOCK YOUR OFFICE DOOR.
YOU KNOW I CAN'T--
WHU-WHU-WHOOOOOOA!
FIRE ALL DEADBOLTS
KA-CLAC
THAT'S A GOOD BOY.

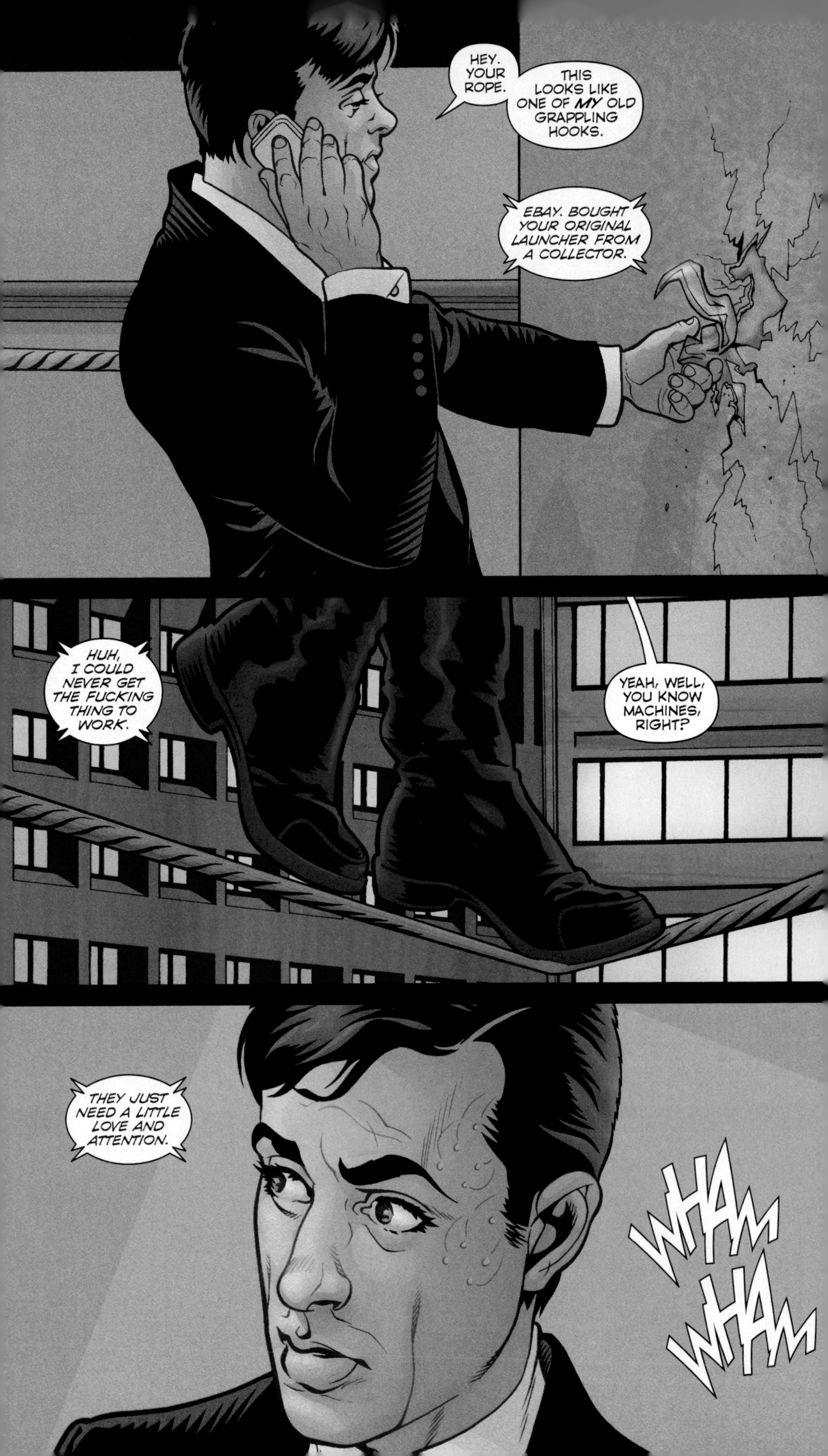
HEY. YOUR ROPE.
THIS LOOKS LIKE ONE OF *MY* OLD GRAPPLING HOOKS.
EBAY. BOUGHT YOUR ORIGINAL LAUNCHER FROM A COLLECTOR.
HUH, I COULD NEVER GET THE FUCKING THING TO WORK.
YEAH, WELL, YOU KNOW MACHINES, RIGHT?
THEY JUST NEED A LITTLE LOVE AND ATTENTION.
WHAM
WHAM

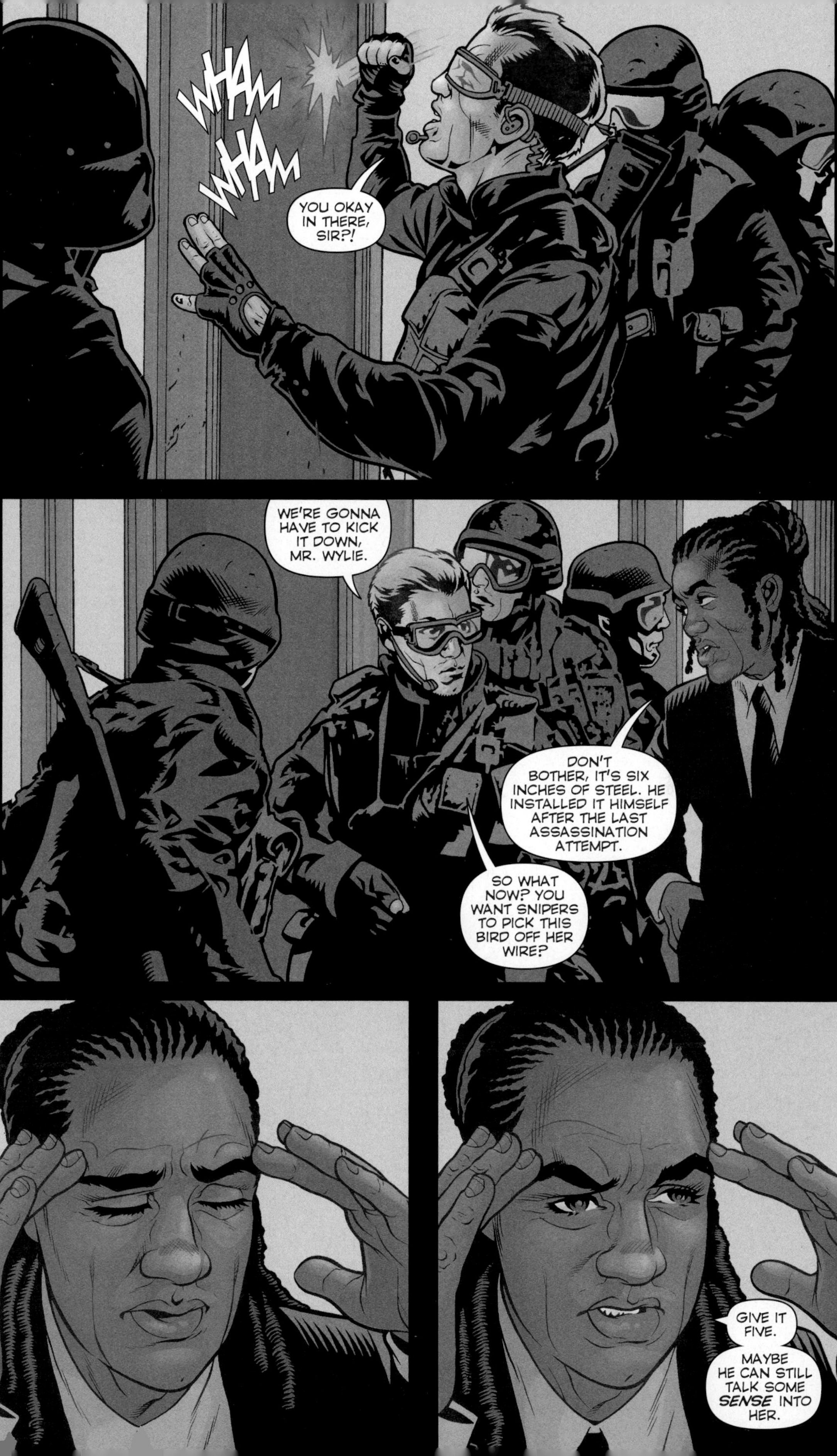
WHAM
WHAM
YOU OKAY IN THERE, SIR?!
WE'RE GONNA HAVE TO KICK IT DOWN, MR. WYLIE.
DON'T BOTHER, IT'S SIX INCHES OF STEEL. HE INSTALLED IT HIMSELF AFTER THE LAST ASSASSINATION ATTEMPT.
SO WHAT NOW? YOU WANT SNIPERS TO PICK THIS BIRD OFF HER WIRE?
GIVE IT FIVE.
MAYBE HE CAN STILL TALK SOME *SENSE* INTO HER.

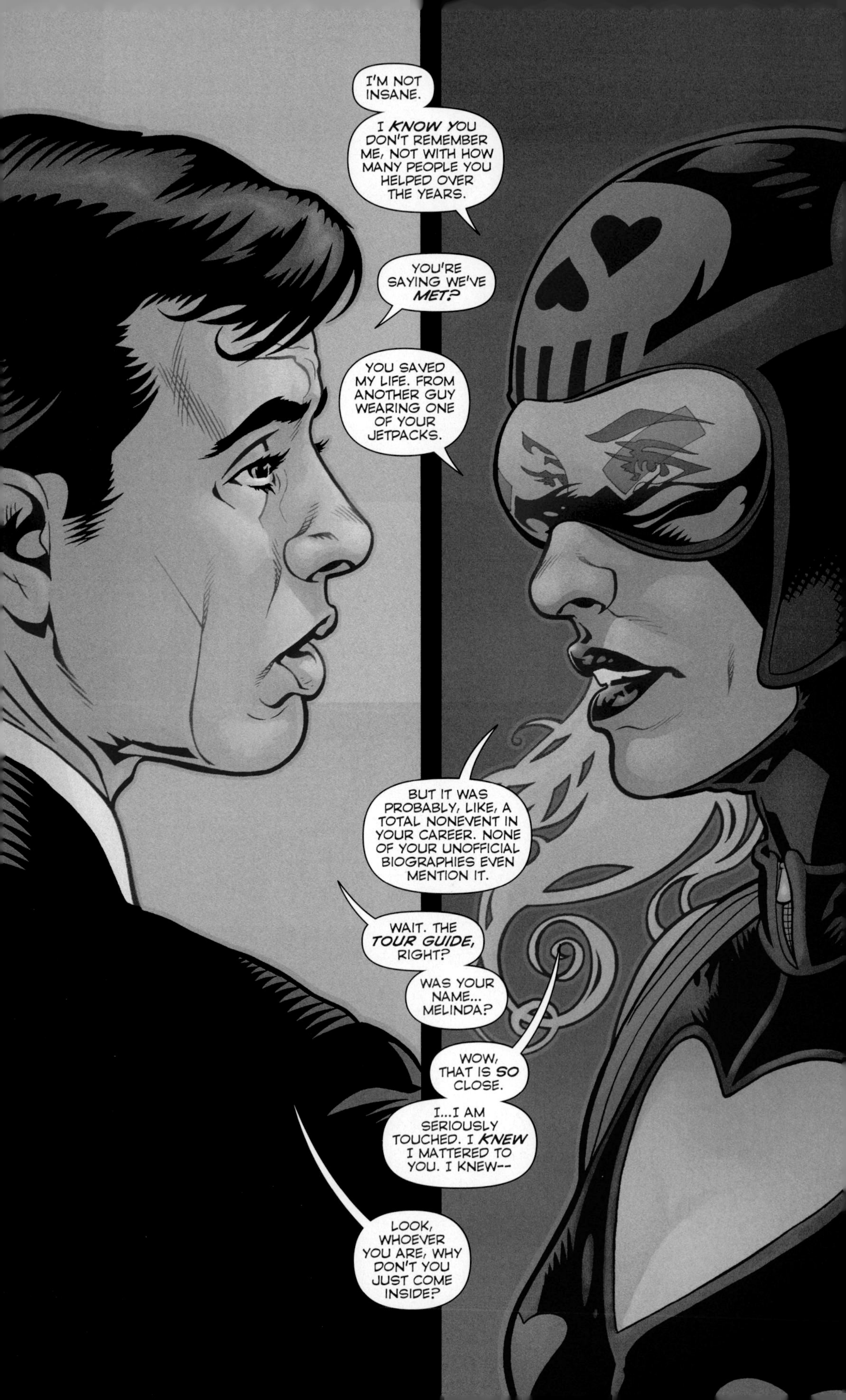
I'M NOT INSANE.
I KNOW YOU DON'T REMEMBER ME, NOT WITH HOW MANY PEOPLE YOU HELPED OVER THE YEARS.
YOU'RE SAYING WE'VE MET?
YOU SAVED MY LIFE. FROM ANOTHER GUY WEARING ONE OF YOUR JETPACKS.
BUT IT WAS PROBABLY, LIKE, A TOTAL NONEVENT IN YOUR CAREER. NONE OF YOUR UNOFFICIAL BIOGRAPHIES EVEN MENTION IT.
WAIT. THE TOUR GUIDE, RIGHT?
WAS YOUR NAME... MELINDA?
WOW, THAT IS SO CLOSE.
I...I AM SERIOUSLY TOUCHED. I KNEW I MATTERED TO YOU. I KNEW--
LOOK, WHOEVER YOU ARE, WHY DON'T YOU JUST COME INSIDE?

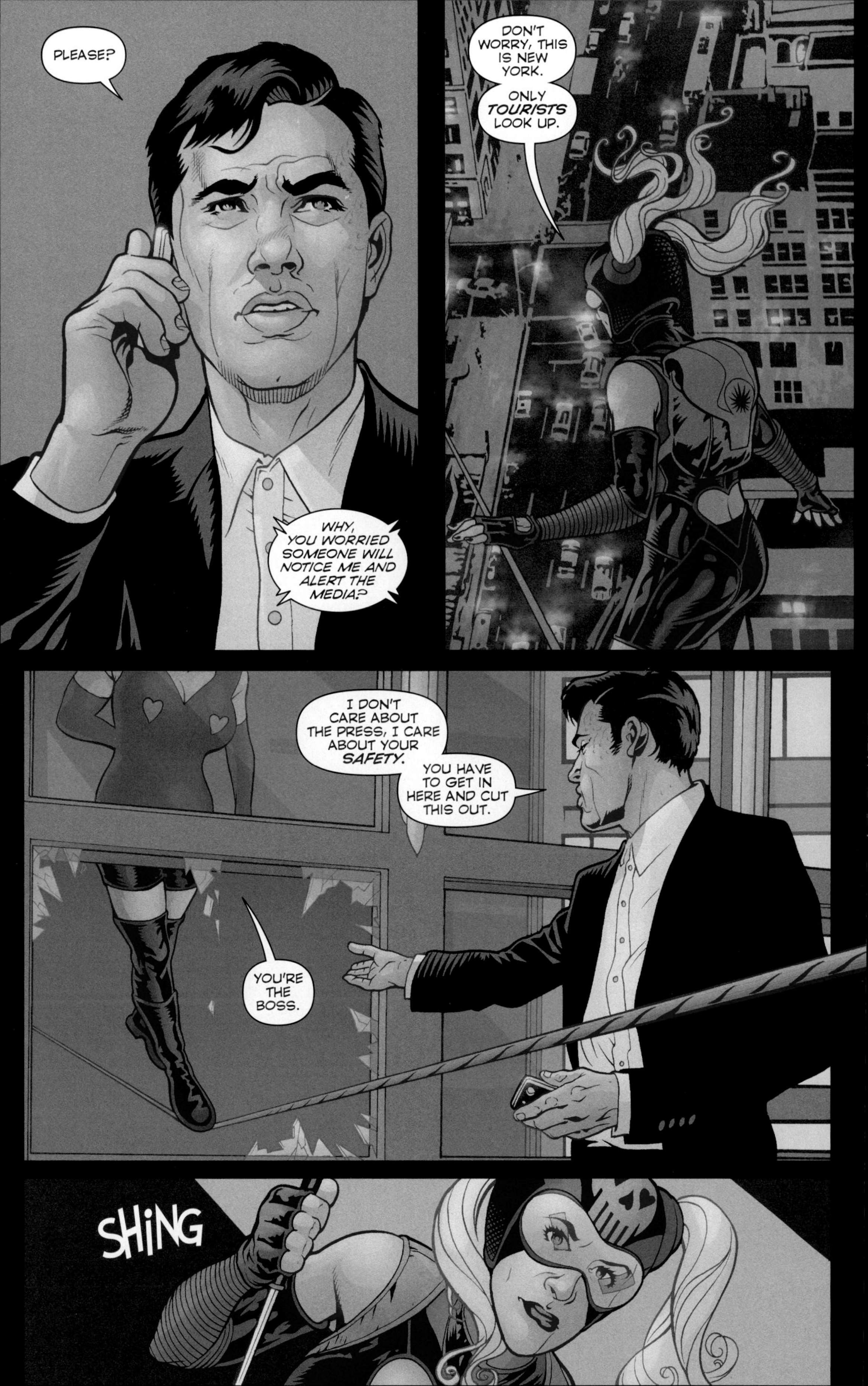
PLEASE?
DON'T WORRY, THIS IS NEW YORK.
ONLY *TOURISTS* LOOK UP.
WHY, YOU WORRIED SOMEONE WILL NOTICE ME AND ALERT THE MEDIA?
I DON'T CARE ABOUT THE PRESS, I CARE ABOUT YOUR *SAFETY*.
YOU HAVE TO GET IN HERE AND CUT THIS OUT.
YOU'RE THE BOSS.
SHING

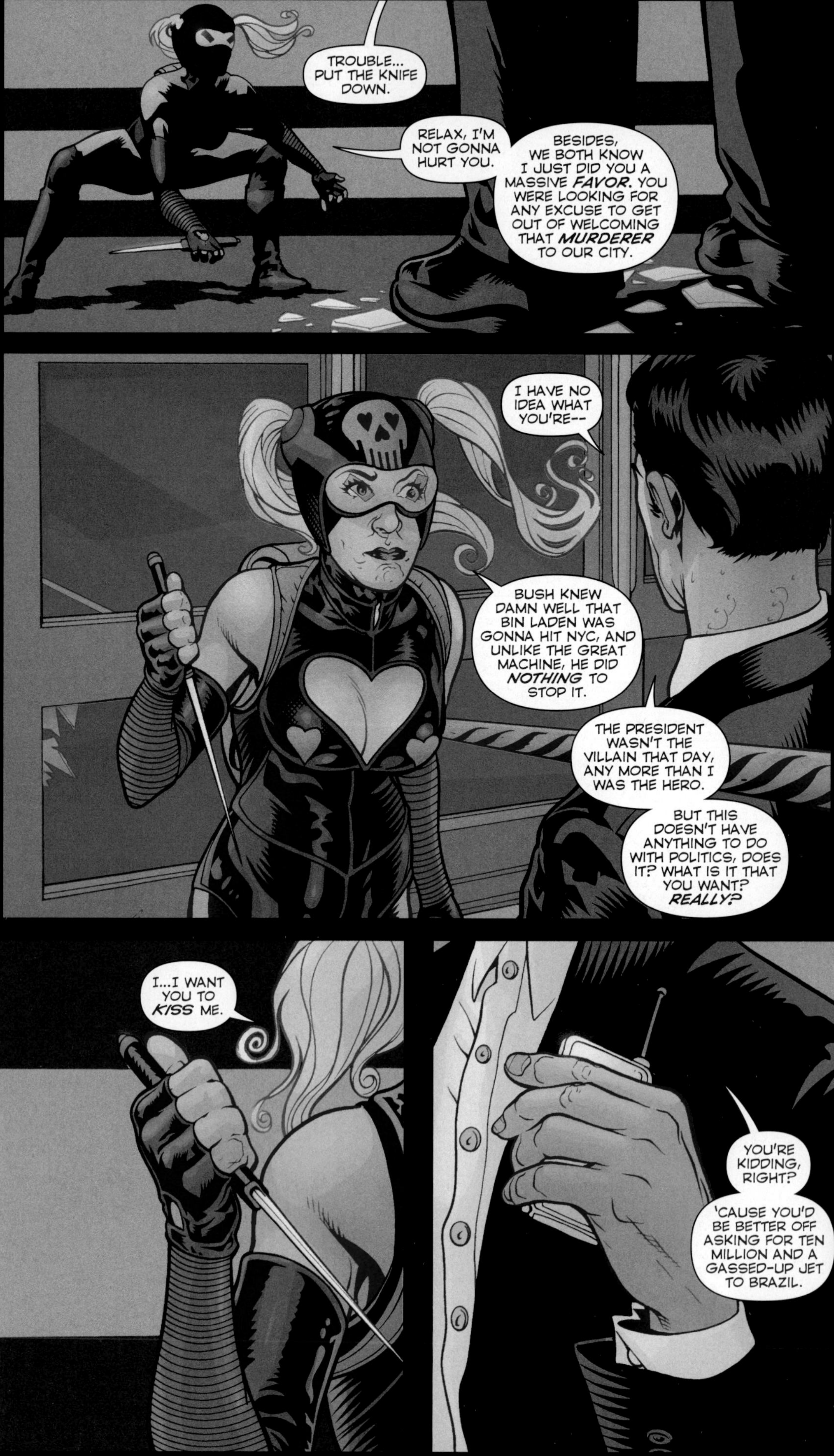
TROUBLE... PUT THE KNIFE DOWN.
RELAX, I'M NOT GONNA HURT YOU.
BESIDES, WE BOTH KNOW I JUST DID YOU A MASSIVE FAVOR. YOU WERE LOOKING FOR ANY EXCUSE TO GET OUT OF WELCOMING THAT MURDERER TO OUR CITY.
I HAVE NO IDEA WHAT YOU'RE--
BUSH KNEW DAMN WELL THAT BIN LADEN WAS GONNA HIT NYC, AND UNLIKE THE GREAT MACHINE, HE DID NOTHING TO STOP IT.
THE PRESIDENT WASN'T THE VILLAIN THAT DAY, ANY MORE THAN I WAS THE HERO.
BUT THIS DOESN'T HAVE ANYTHING TO DO WITH POLITICS, DOES IT? WHAT IS IT THAT YOU WANT? REALLY?
I...I WANT YOU TO KISS ME.
YOU'RE KIDDING, RIGHT?
'CAUSE YOU'D BE BETTER OFF ASKING FOR TEN MILLION AND A GASSED-UP JET TO BRAZIL.

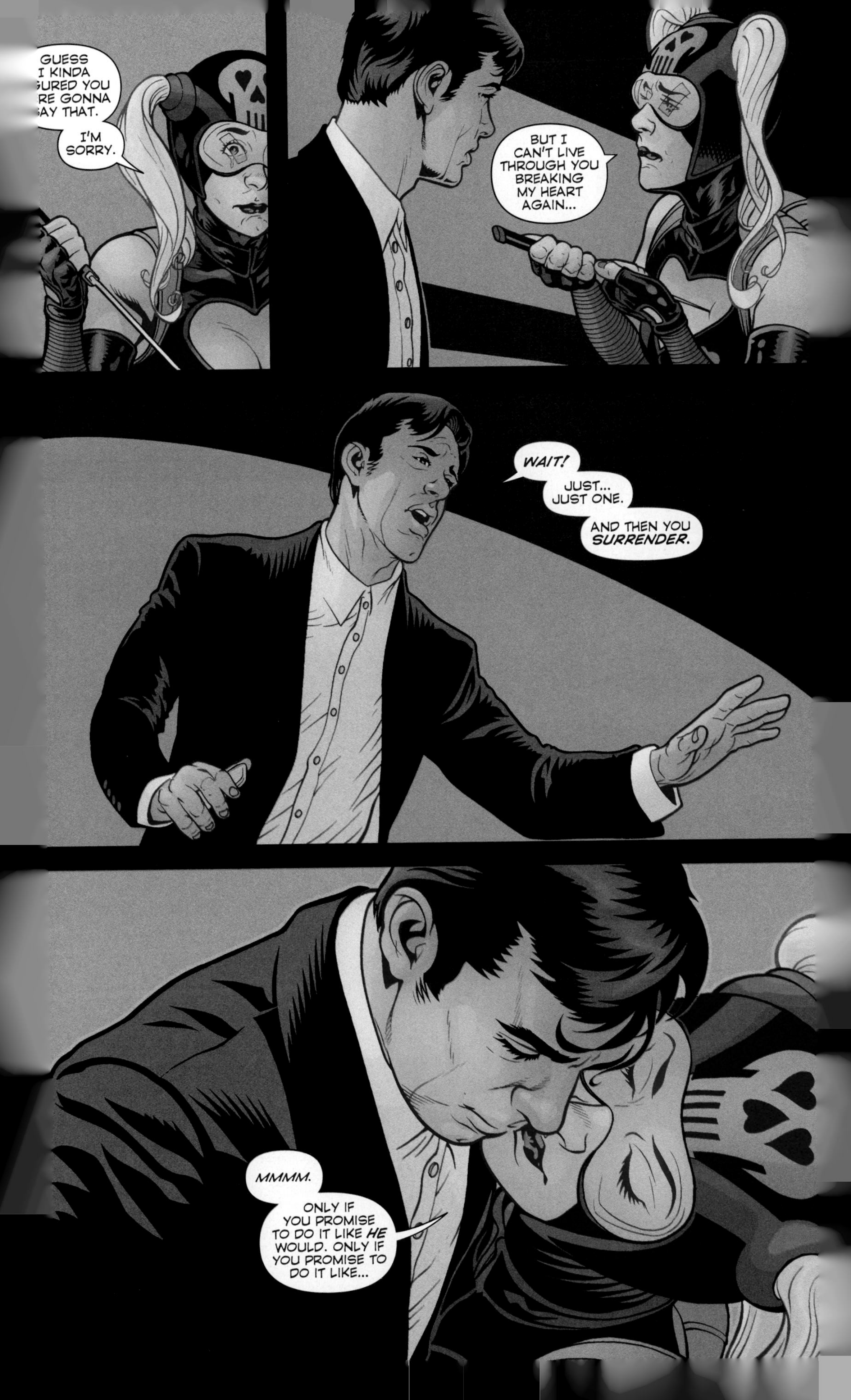
GUESS I KINDA ...GURED YOU ...RE GONNA ...AY THAT.
I'M SORRY.
BUT I CAN'T LIVE THROUGH YOU BREAKING MY HEART AGAIN...
WAIT!
JUST... JUST ONE.
AND THEN YOU SURRENDER.
MMMM.
ONLY IF YOU PROMISE TO DO IT LIKE HE WOULD. ONLY IF YOU PROMISE TO DO IT LIKE...

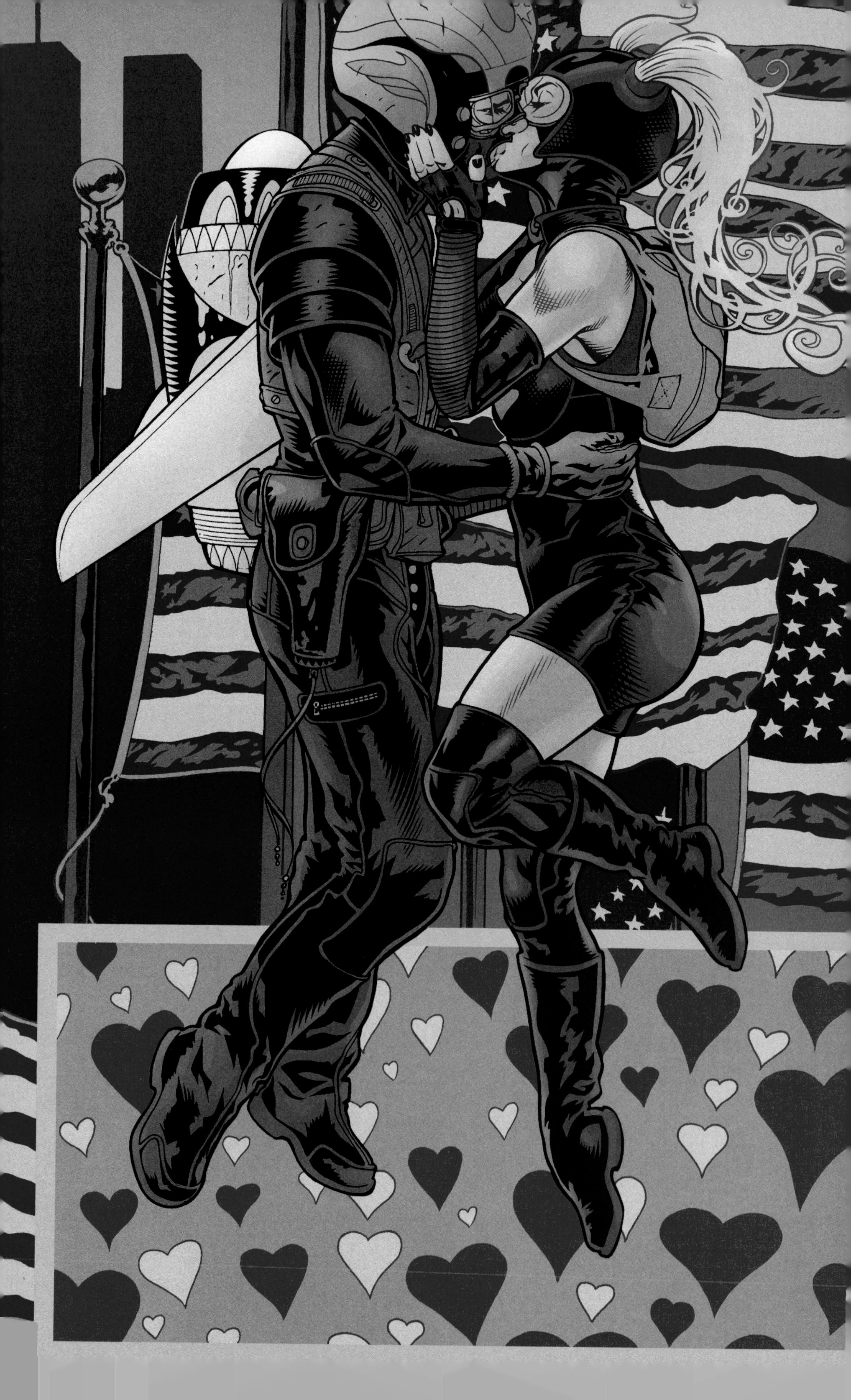

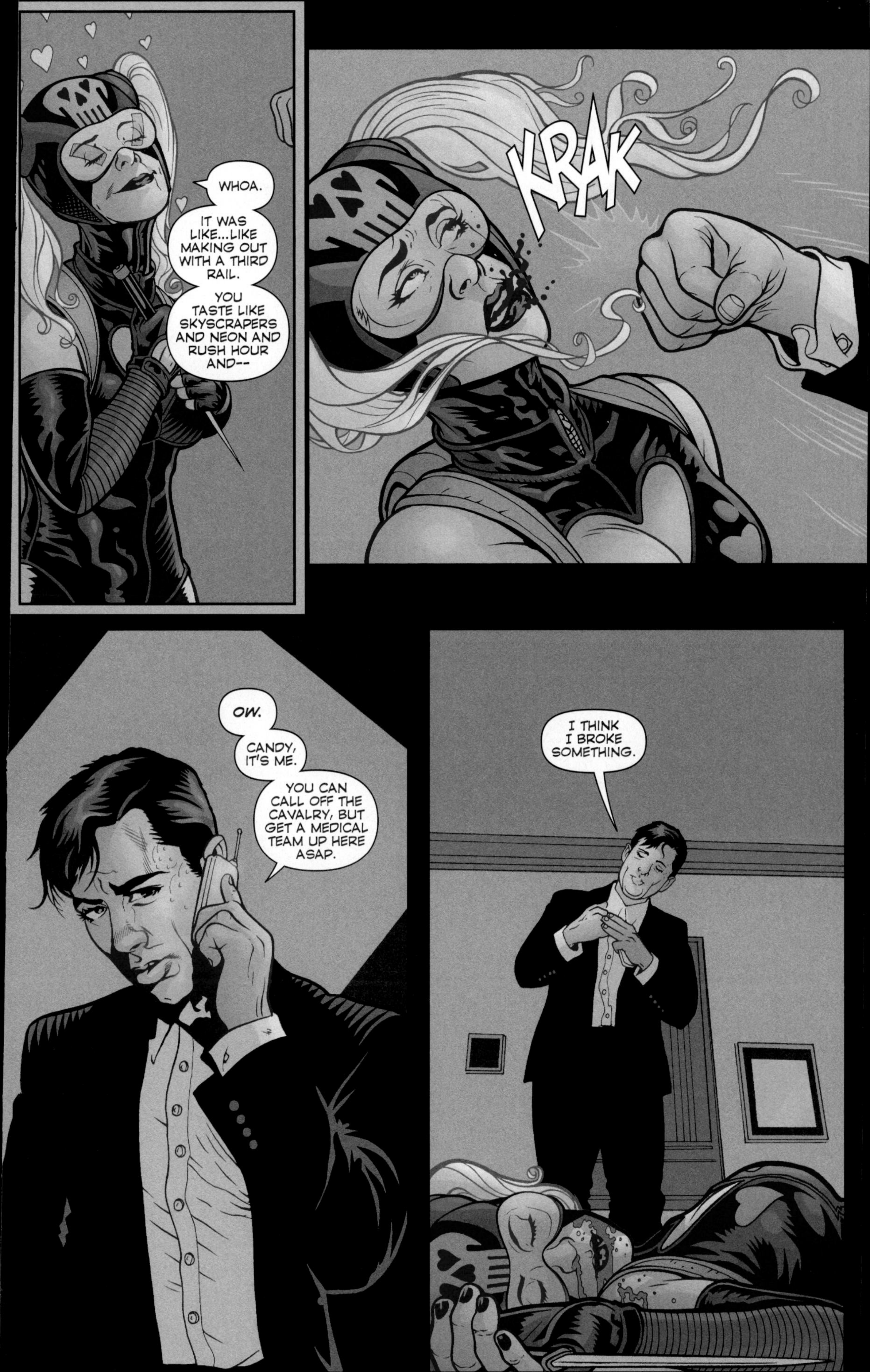
WHOA.
IT WAS LIKE...LIKE MAKING OUT WITH A THIRD RAIL.
YOU TASTE LIKE SKYSCRAPERS AND NEON AND RUSH HOUR AND--
KRAK
OW.
CANDY, IT'S ME.
YOU CAN CALL OFF THE CAVALRY, BUT GET A MEDICAL TEAM UP HERE ASAP.
I THINK I BROKE SOMETHING.

TROUBLE NO MORE!
Hizzoner helps nab G.O.P. nightmare
by SUZANNE PADILLA

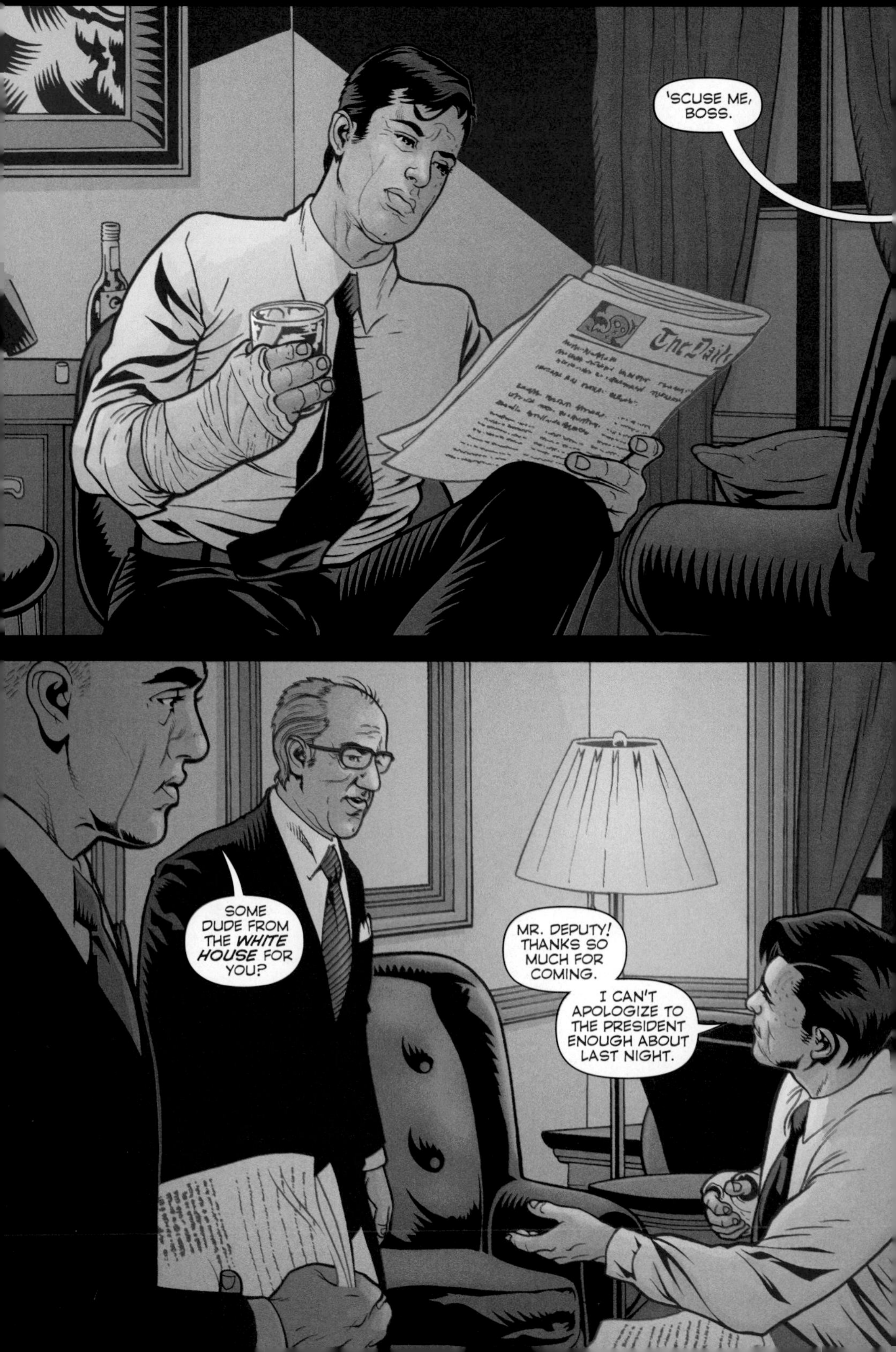
'SCUSE ME, BOSS.
SOME DUDE FROM THE *WHITE HOUSE* FOR YOU?
MR. DEPUTY! THANKS SO MUCH FOR COMING.
I CAN'T APOLOGIZE TO THE PRESIDENT ENOUGH ABOUT LAST NIGHT.

DON'T BE ABSURD. WHO KNOWS WHAT THAT GIRL MIGHT HAVE TRIED AT THE BIG SHOW IF SHE HADN'T HAD YOU TO GO AFTER.
FAR AS THIS ADMINISTRATION IS CONCERNED, YOU TOOK ONE FOR THE TEAM.
WELL, I'LL HAVE TO HAVE MR. BUSH SIGN MY CAST.
ACTUALLY, THE PRESIDENT WANTED ME TO ASK YOU HOW YOU MIGHT RESPOND TO THE OFFER OF AN AMBASSADORSHIP.
HA, THANK YOU, THAT'S VERY NICE, BUT MUCH AS I LOVE NORDIC WALKING, I'M NOT QUITE READY TO RELOCATE TO FINLAND.
ACTUALLY, YOU WOULDN'T EVEN HAVE TO LEAVE YOUR AREA CODE FOR THIS POST.
HOW WOULD YOU FEEL ABOUT REPRESENTING US TO THE WORLD AT THE UNITED NATIONS?
ARE...ARE YOU SERIOUS? I HAVE JUST ABOUT ZERO INTERNATIONAL EXPERIENCE.
YOU HAVE ALL THE EXPERIENCE YOU NEED TO SPEAK FOR AMERICA'S INTERESTS. WE THINK YOU'LL BE ESPECIALLY EFFECTIVE ON THE SECURITY COUNCIL.
PLUS, YOU'LL BE CONFIRMED IN A NEW YORK MINUTE. NO DEMOCRAT IS GOING TO VOTE AGAINST THE MAN WHO SAVED THE SECOND TOWER.

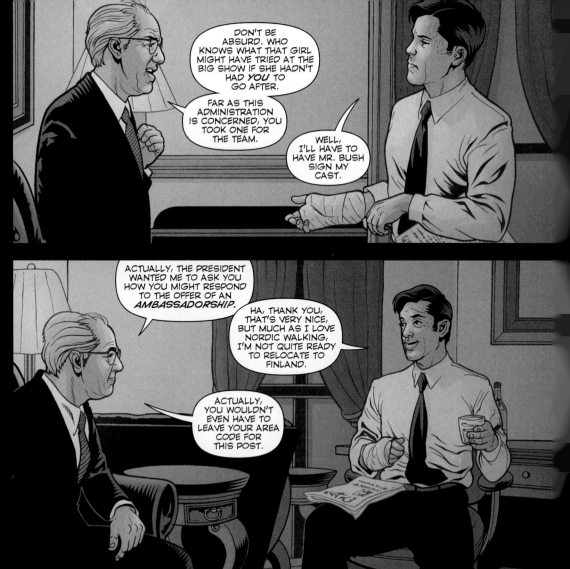

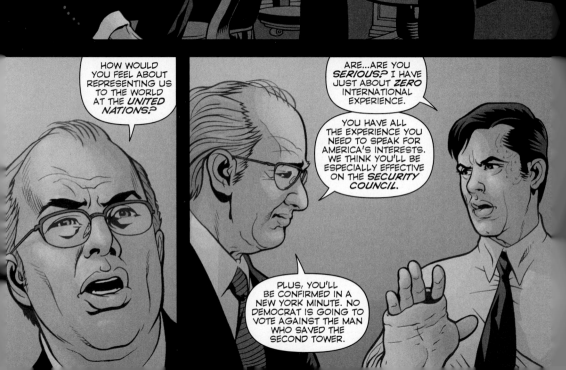

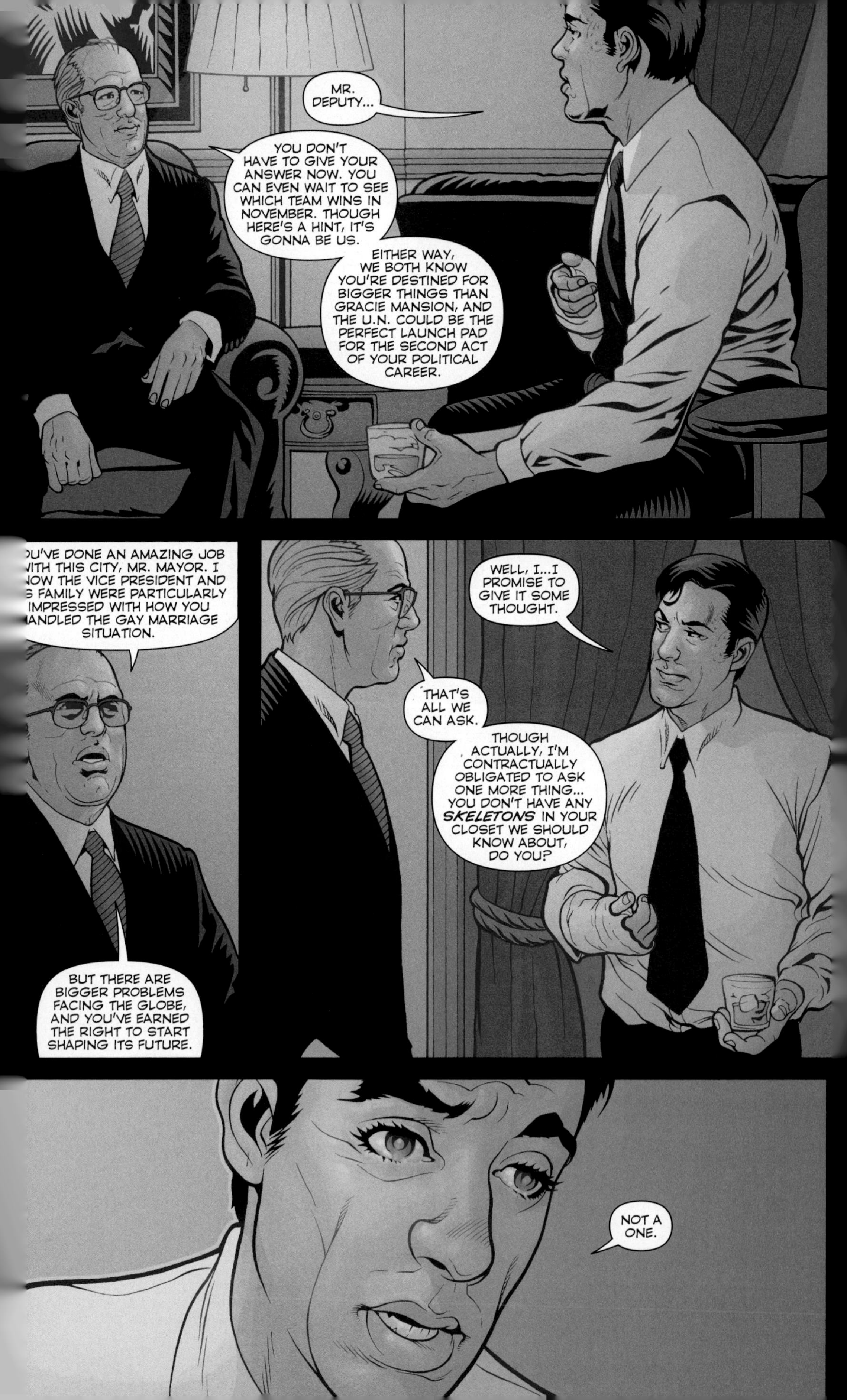
MR. DEPUTY...
YOU DON'T HAVE TO GIVE YOUR ANSWER NOW. YOU CAN EVEN WAIT TO SEE WHICH TEAM WINS IN NOVEMBER. THOUGH HERE'S A HINT, IT'S GONNA BE US.
EITHER WAY, WE BOTH KNOW YOU'RE DESTINED FOR BIGGER THINGS THAN GRACIE MANSION, AND THE U.N. COULD BE THE PERFECT LAUNCH PAD FOR THE SECOND ACT OF YOUR POLITICAL CAREER.
OU'VE DONE AN AMAZING JOB WITH THIS CITY, MR. MAYOR. I NOW THE VICE PRESIDENT AND S FAMILY WERE PARTICULARLY IMPRESSED WITH HOW YOU ANDLED THE GAY MARRIAGE SITUATION.
BUT THERE ARE BIGGER PROBLEMS FACING THE GLOBE, AND YOU'VE EARNED THE RIGHT TO START SHAPING ITS FUTURE.
WELL, I...I PROMISE TO GIVE IT SOME THOUGHT.
THAT'S ALL WE CAN ASK.
THOUGH ACTUALLY, I'M CONTRACTUALLY OBLIGATED TO ASK ONE MORE THING... YOU DON'T HAVE ANY *SKELETONS* IN YOUR CLOSET WE SHOULD KNOW ABOUT, DO YOU?
NOT A ONE.

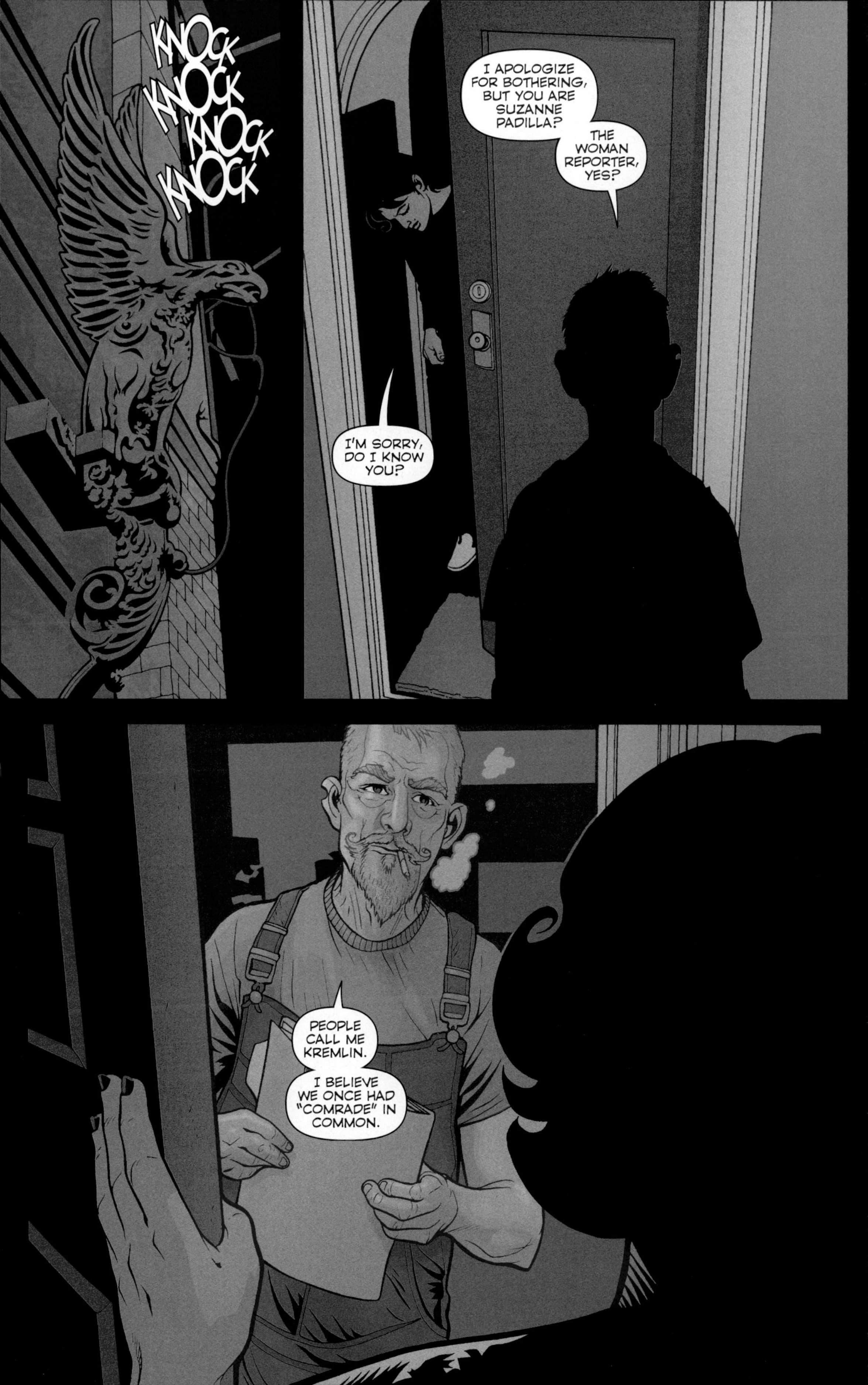
KNOCK KNOCK KNOCK KNOCK
I APOLOGIZE FOR BOTHERING, BUT YOU ARE SUZANNE PADILLA?
THE WOMAN REPORTER, YES?
I'M SORRY, DO I KNOW YOU?
PEOPLE CALL ME KREMLIN.
I BELIEVE WE ONCE HAD "COMRADE" IN COMMON.

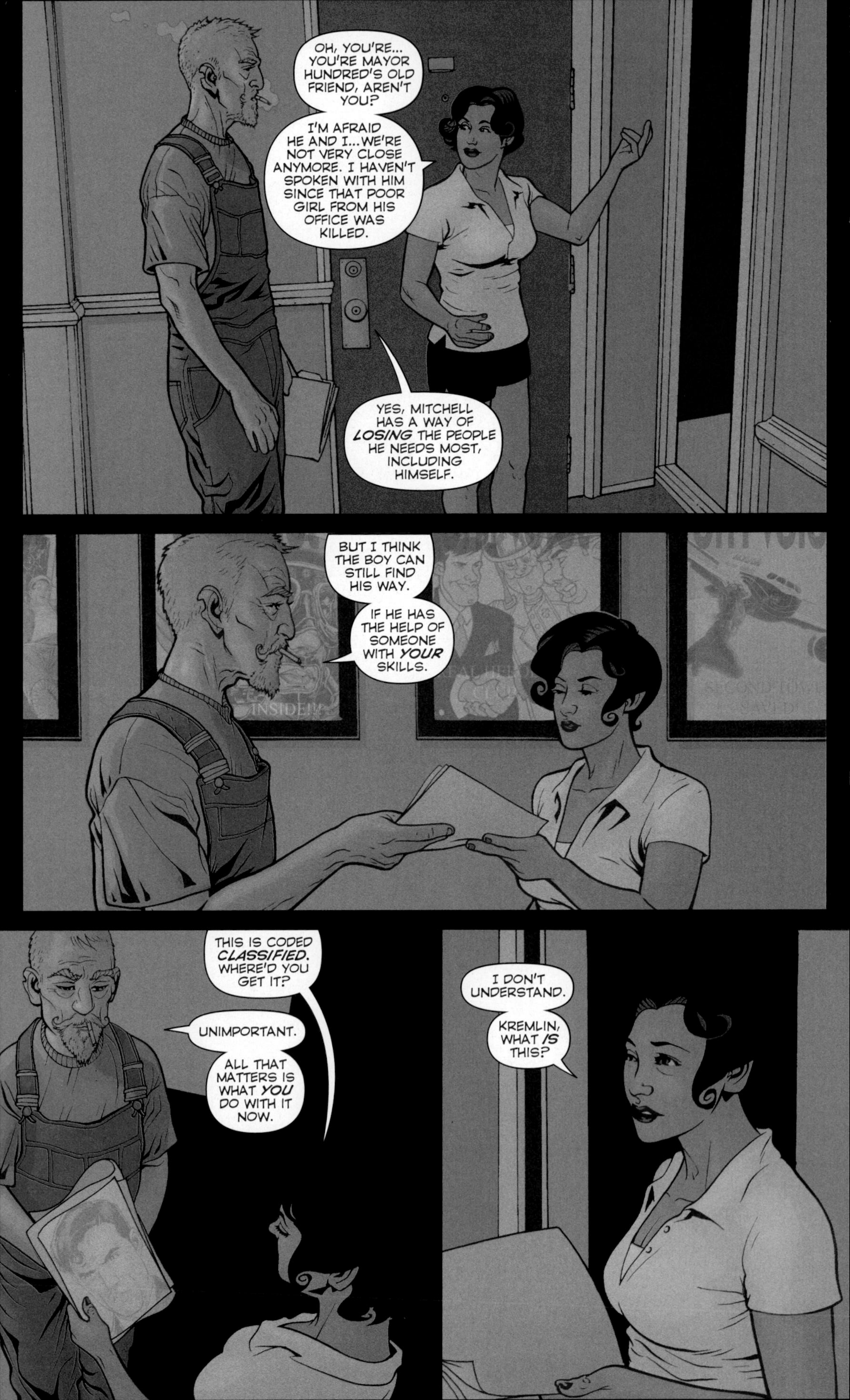
OH, YOU'RE... YOU'RE MAYOR HUNDRED'S OLD FRIEND, AREN'T YOU?
I'M AFRAID HE AND I...WE'RE NOT VERY CLOSE ANYMORE. I HAVEN'T SPOKEN WITH HIM SINCE THAT POOR GIRL FROM HIS OFFICE WAS KILLED.
YES, MITCHELL HAS A WAY OF *LOSING* THE PEOPLE HE NEEDS MOST, INCLUDING HIMSELF.
BUT I THINK THE BOY CAN STILL FIND HIS WAY.
IF HE HAS THE HELP OF SOMEONE WITH *YOUR* SKILLS.
THIS IS CODED *CLASSIFIED*. WHERE'D YOU GET IT?
UNIMPORTANT.
ALL THAT MATTERS IS WHAT *YOU* DO WITH IT NOW.
I DON'T UNDERSTAND.
KREMLIN, WHAT *IS* THIS?

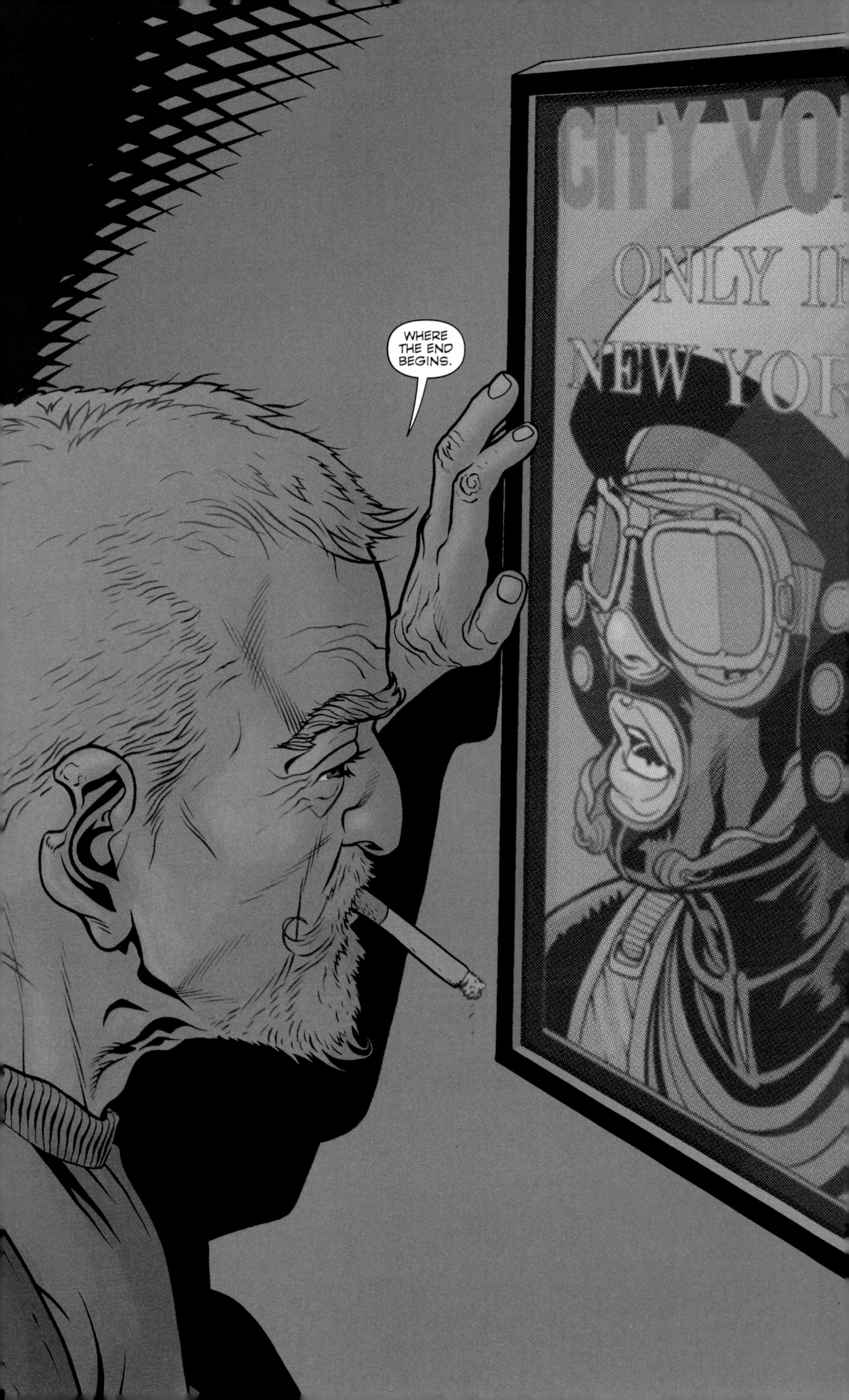
WHERE THE END BEGINS.

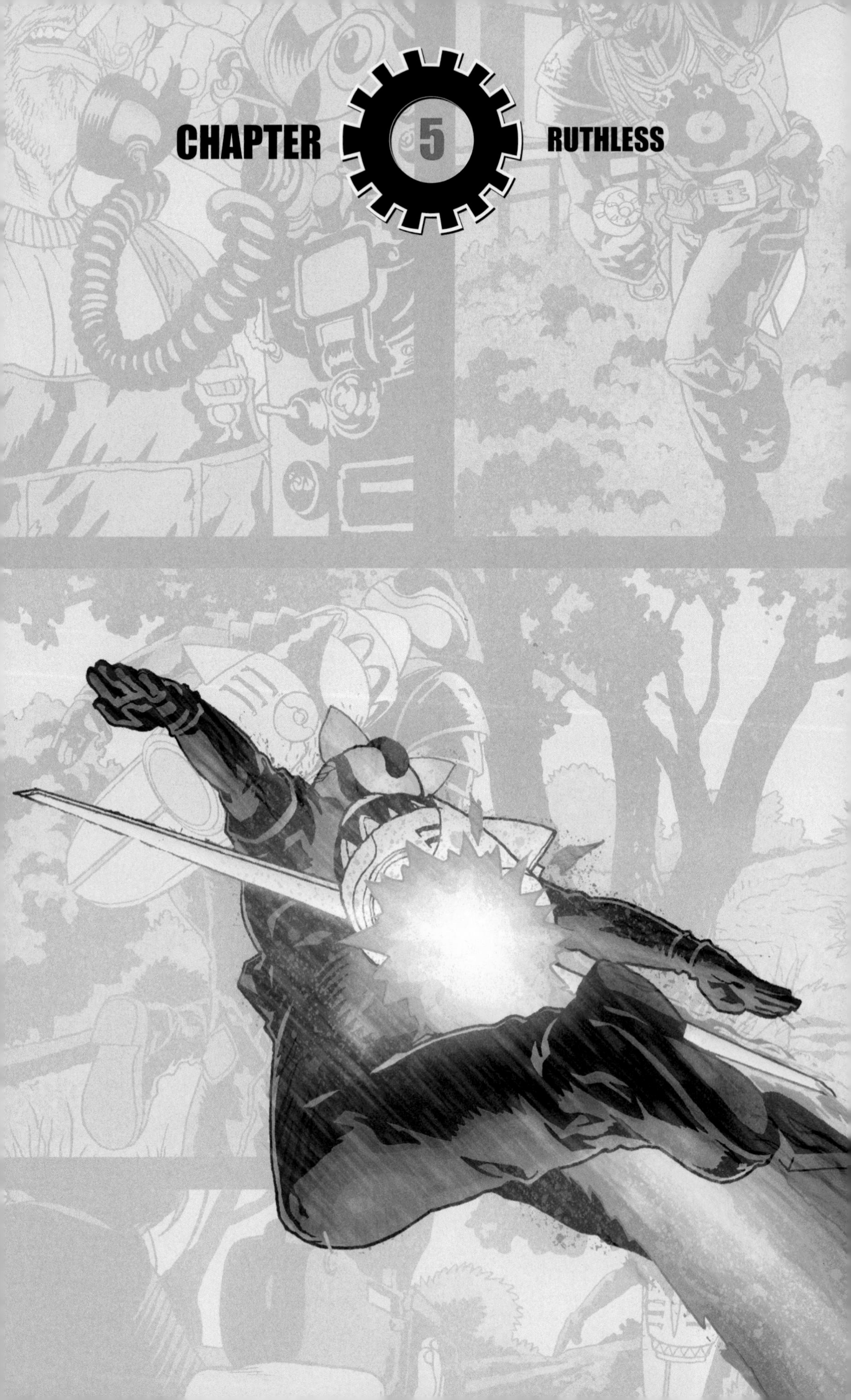
CHAPTER
5
RUTHLESS

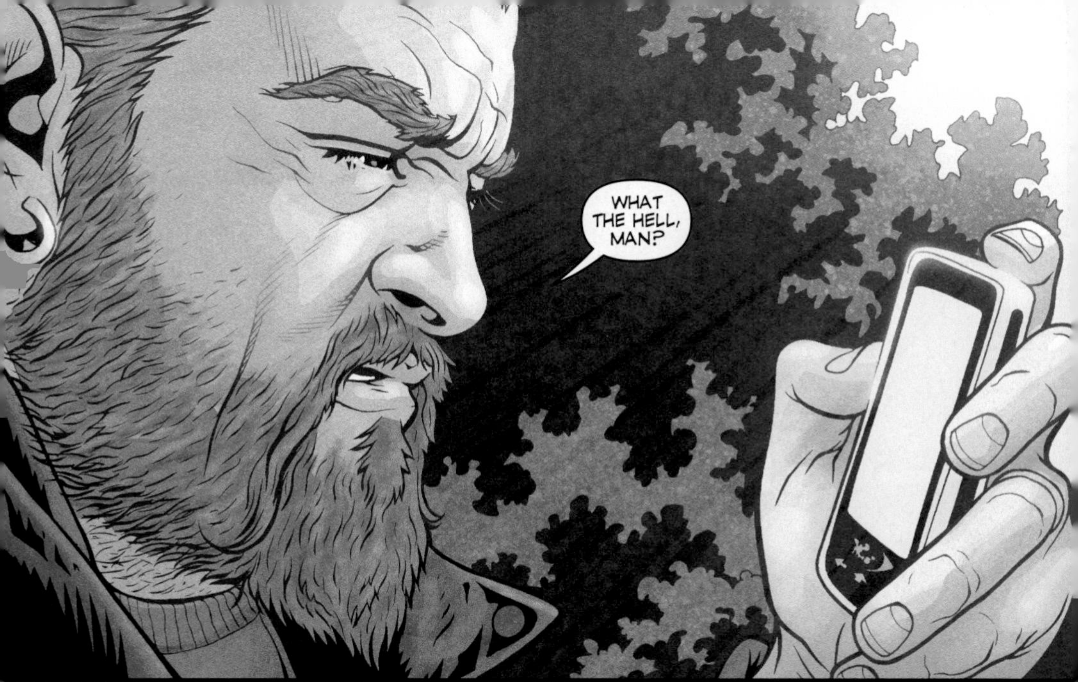
WHAT THE HELL, MAN?

WEDNESDAY, OCTOBER 6, 2004

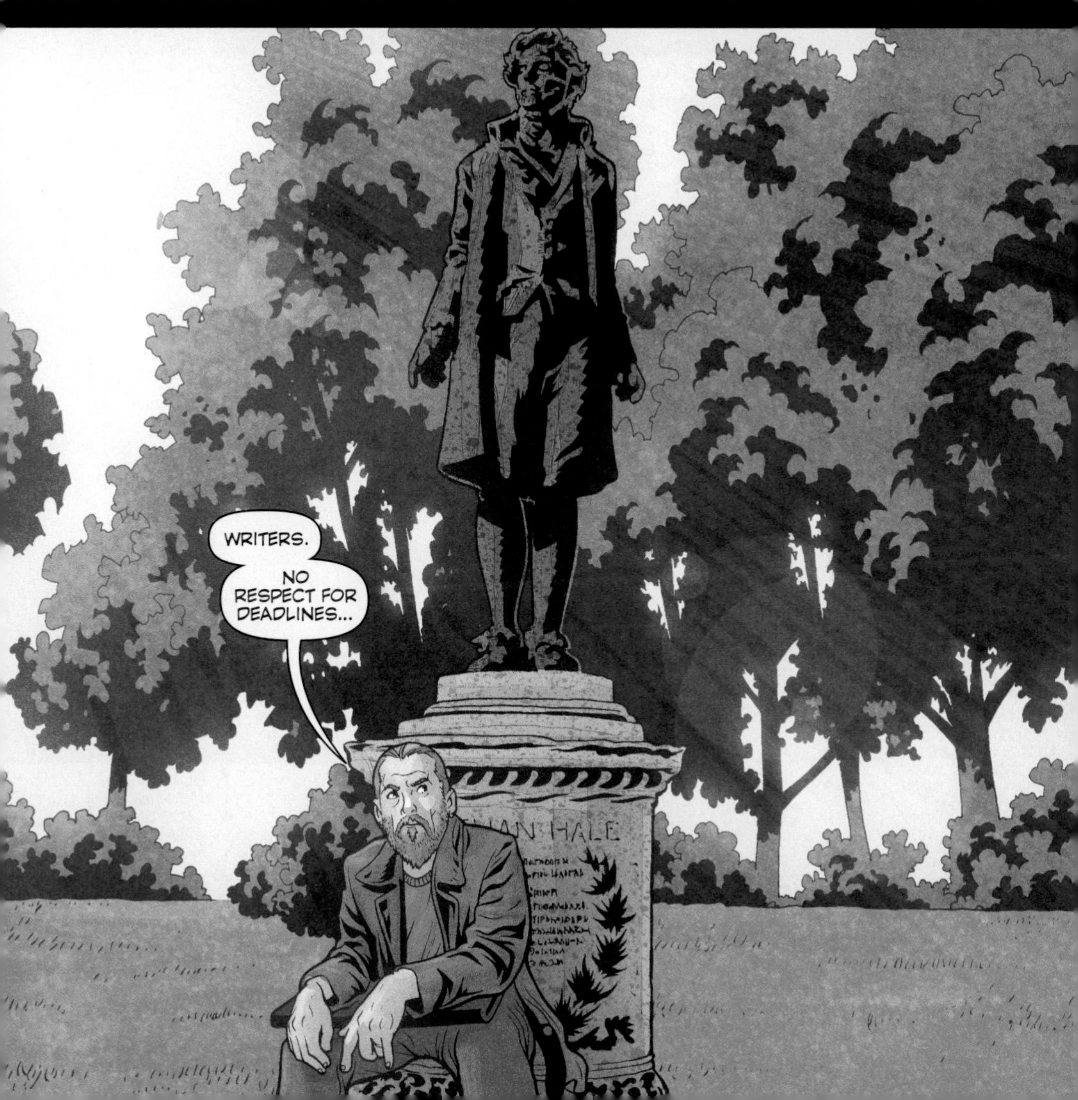
WRITERS.
NO RESPECT FOR DEADLINES...

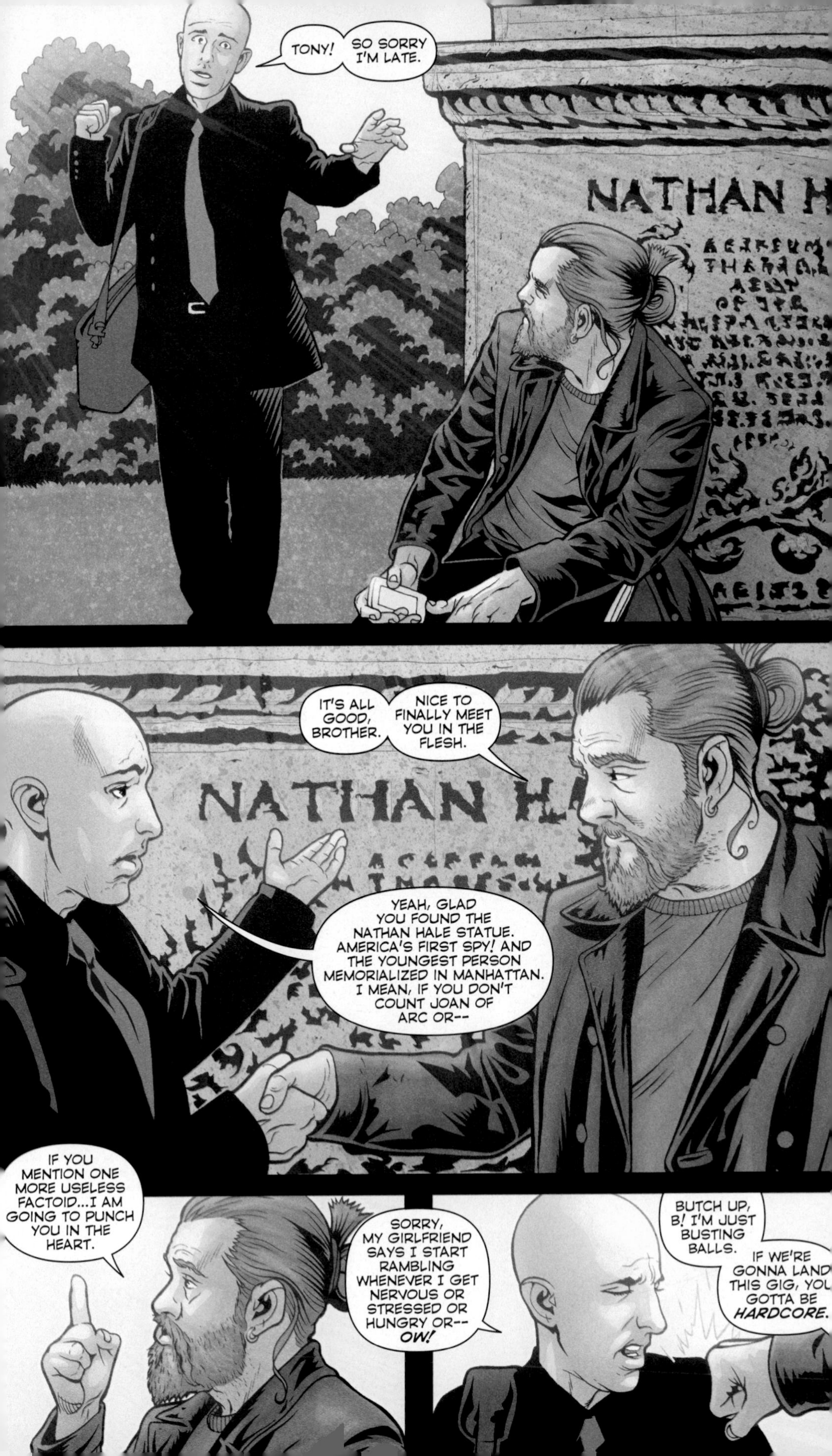
TONY!
SO SORRY I'M LATE.
IT'S ALL GOOD, BROTHER.
NICE TO FINALLY MEET YOU IN THE FLESH.
YEAH, GLAD YOU FOUND THE NATHAN HALE STATUE. AMERICA'S FIRST SPY! AND THE YOUNGEST PERSON MEMORIALIZED IN MANHATTAN. I MEAN, IF YOU DON'T COUNT JOAN OF ARC OR--
IF YOU MENTION ONE MORE USELESS FACTOID...I AM GOING TO PUNCH YOU IN THE HEART.
SORRY, MY GIRLFRIEND SAYS I START RAMBLING WHENEVER I GET NERVOUS OR STRESSED OR HUNGRY OR-- *OW!*
BUTCH UP, B! I'M JUST BUSTING BALLS.
IF WE'RE GONNA LAND THIS GIG, YOU GOTTA BE *HARDCORE*.

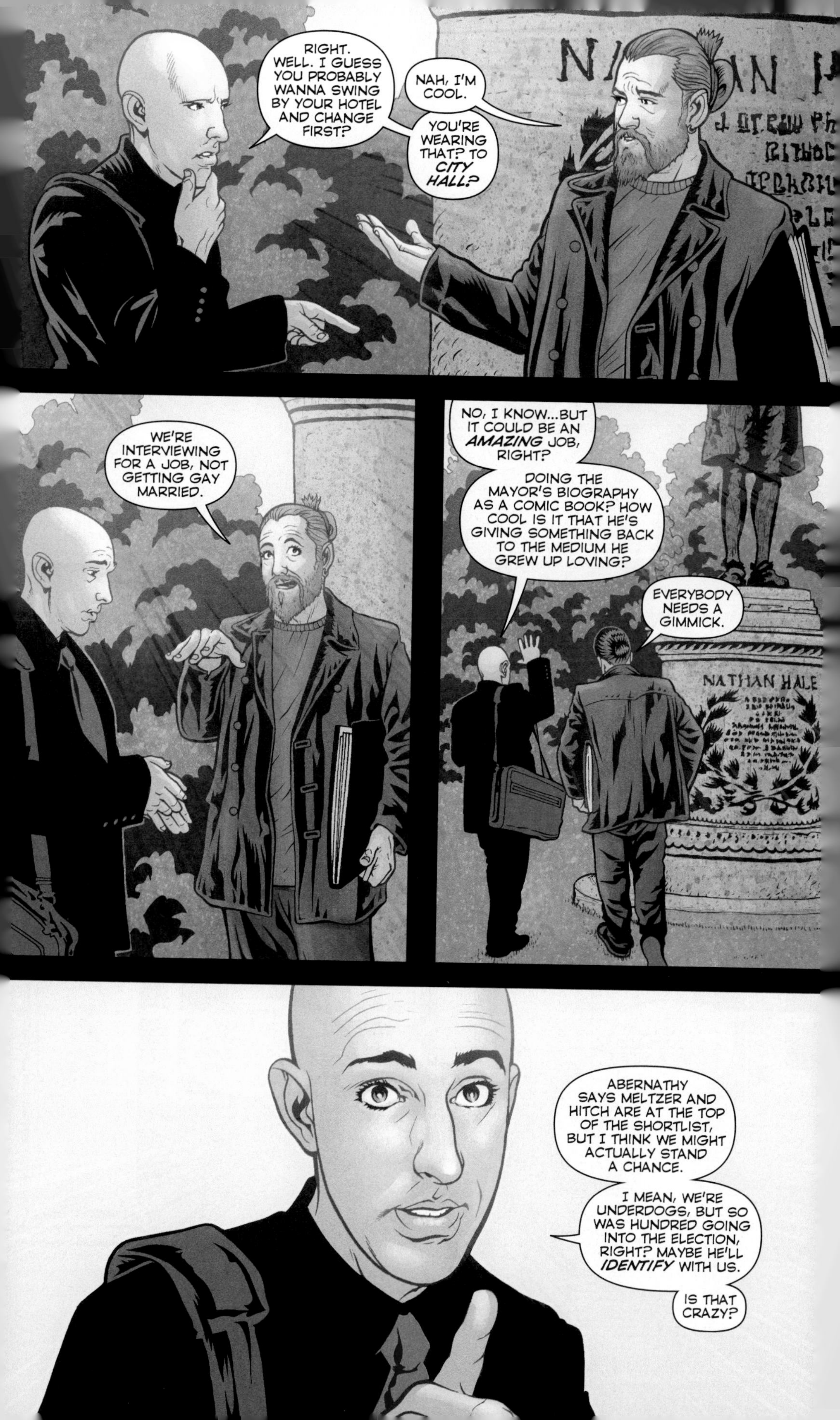
RIGHT. WELL. I GUESS YOU PROBABLY WANNA SWING BY YOUR HOTEL AND CHANGE FIRST?
NAH, I'M COOL.
YOU'RE WEARING THAT? TO CITY HALL?
WE'RE INTERVIEWING FOR A JOB, NOT GETTING GAY MARRIED.
NO, I KNOW...BUT IT COULD BE AN AMAZING JOB, RIGHT?
DOING THE MAYOR'S BIOGRAPHY AS A COMIC BOOK? HOW COOL IS IT THAT HE'S GIVING SOMETHING BACK TO THE MEDIUM HE GREW UP LOVING?
EVERYBODY NEEDS A GIMMICK.
NATHAN HALE
ABERNATHY SAYS MELTZER AND HITCH ARE AT THE TOP OF THE SHORTLIST, BUT I THINK WE MIGHT ACTUALLY STAND A CHANCE.
I MEAN, WE'RE UNDERDOGS, BUT SO WAS HUNDRED GOING INTO THE ELECTION, RIGHT? MAYBE HE'LL IDENTIFY WITH US.
IS THAT CRAZY?

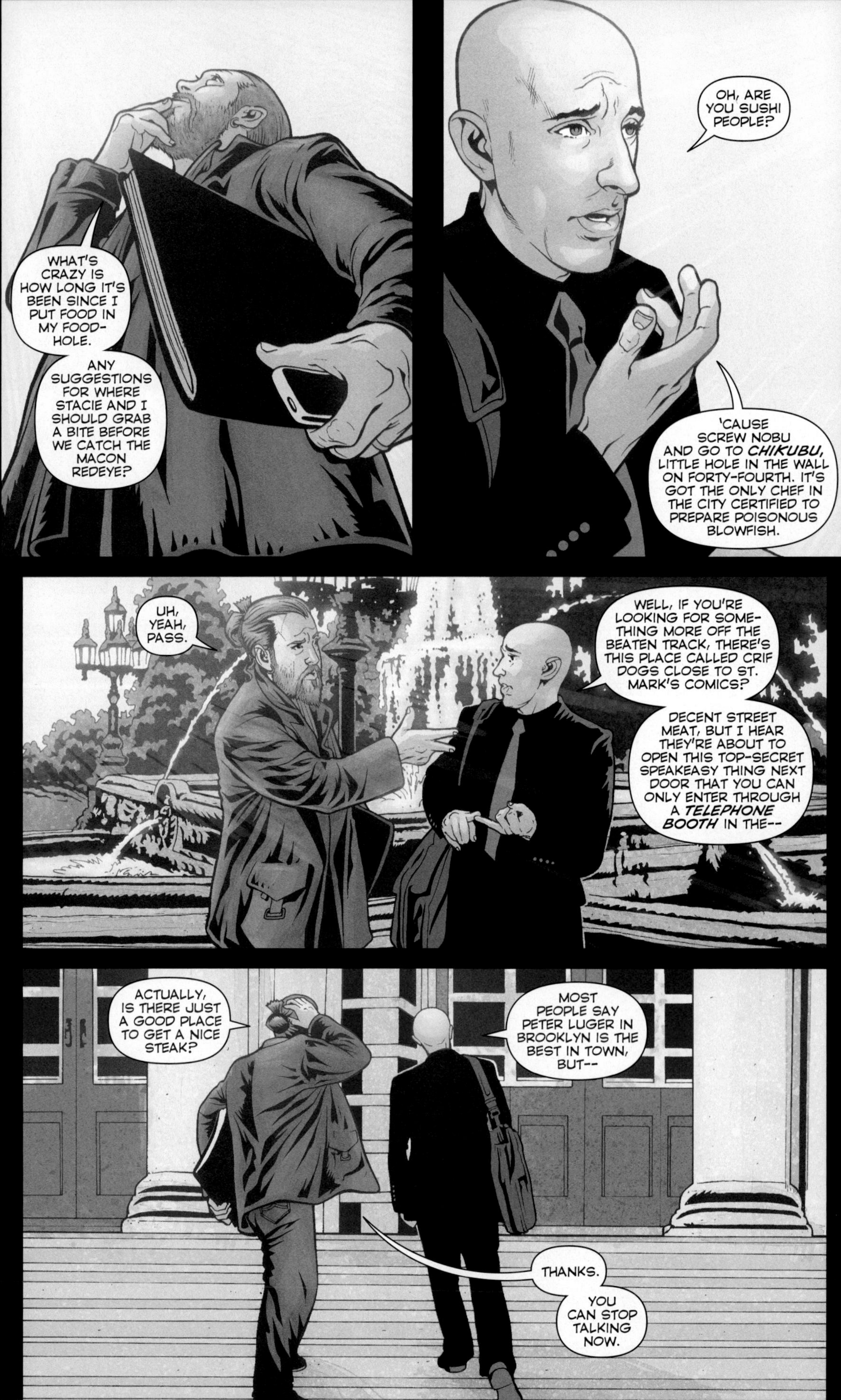
WHAT'S CRAZY IS HOW LONG IT'S BEEN SINCE I PUT FOOD IN MY FOOD-HOLE.
ANY SUGGESTIONS FOR WHERE STACIE AND I SHOULD GRAB A BITE BEFORE WE CATCH THE MACON REDEYE?
OH, ARE YOU SUSHI PEOPLE?
'CAUSE SCREW NOBU AND GO TO CHIKUBU, LITTLE HOLE IN THE WALL ON FORTY-FOURTH. IT'S GOT THE ONLY CHEF IN THE CITY CERTIFIED TO PREPARE POISONOUS BLOWFISH.
UH, YEAH, PASS.
WELL, IF YOU'RE LOOKING FOR SOME-THING MORE OFF THE BEATEN TRACK, THERE'S THIS PLACE CALLED CRIF DOGS CLOSE TO ST. MARK'S COMICS?
DECENT STREET MEAT, BUT I HEAR THEY'RE ABOUT TO OPEN THIS TOP-SECRET SPEAKEASY THING NEXT DOOR THAT YOU CAN ONLY ENTER THROUGH A TELEPHONE BOOTH IN THE--
ACTUALLY, IS THERE JUST A GOOD PLACE TO GET A NICE STEAK?
MOST PEOPLE SAY PETER LUGER IN BROOKLYN IS THE BEST IN TOWN, BUT--
THANKS.
YOU CAN STOP TALKING NOW.

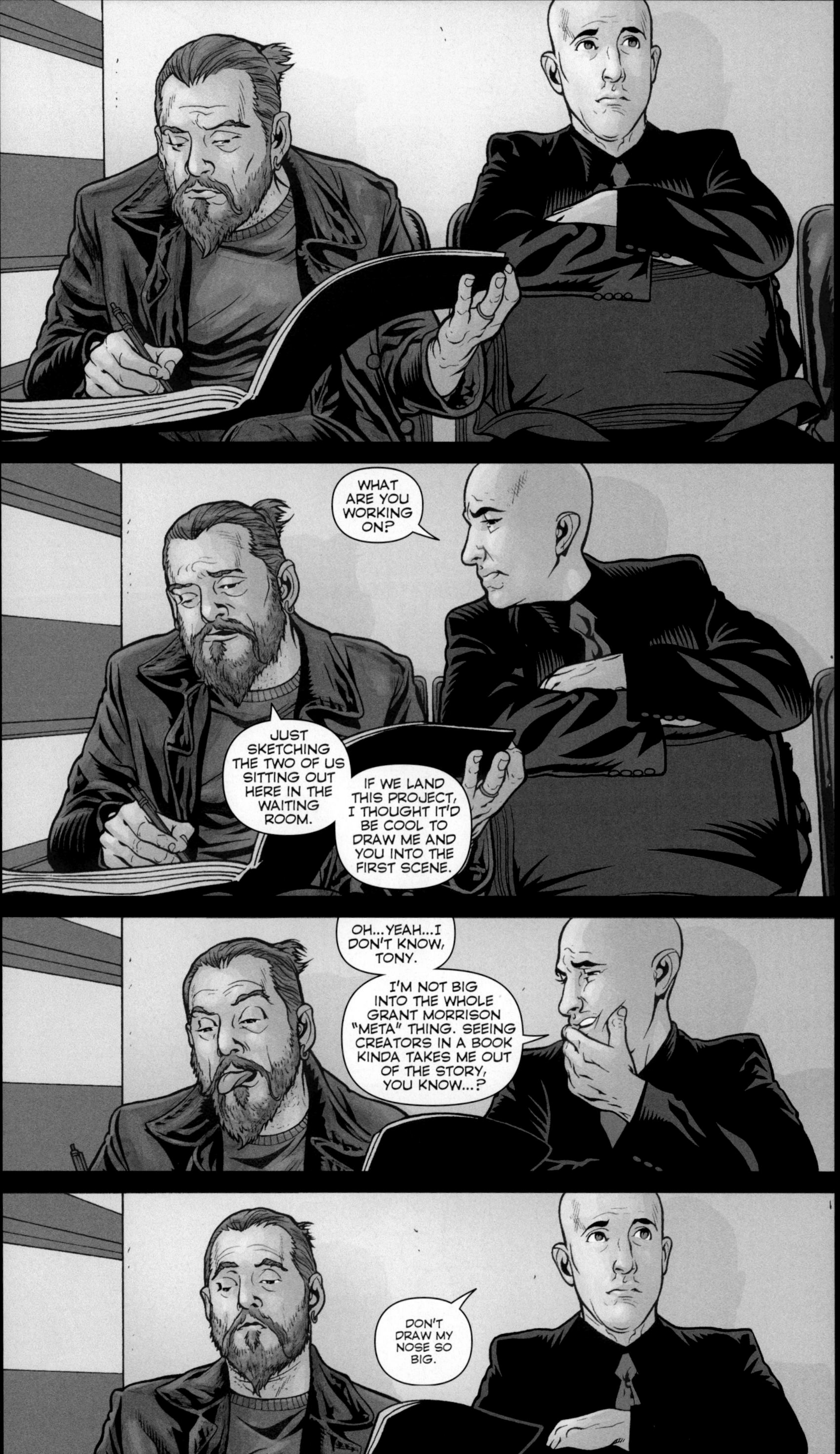
WHAT ARE YOU WORKING ON?
JUST SKETCHING THE TWO OF US SITTING OUT HERE IN THE WAITING ROOM.
IF WE LAND THIS PROJECT, I THOUGHT IT'D BE COOL TO DRAW ME AND YOU INTO THE FIRST SCENE.
OH...YEAH...I DON'T KNOW, TONY.
I'M NOT BIG INTO THE WHOLE GRANT MORRISON "META" THING. SEEING CREATORS IN A BOOK KINDA TAKES ME OUT OF THE STORY, YOU KNOW...?
DON'T DRAW MY NOSE SO BIG.

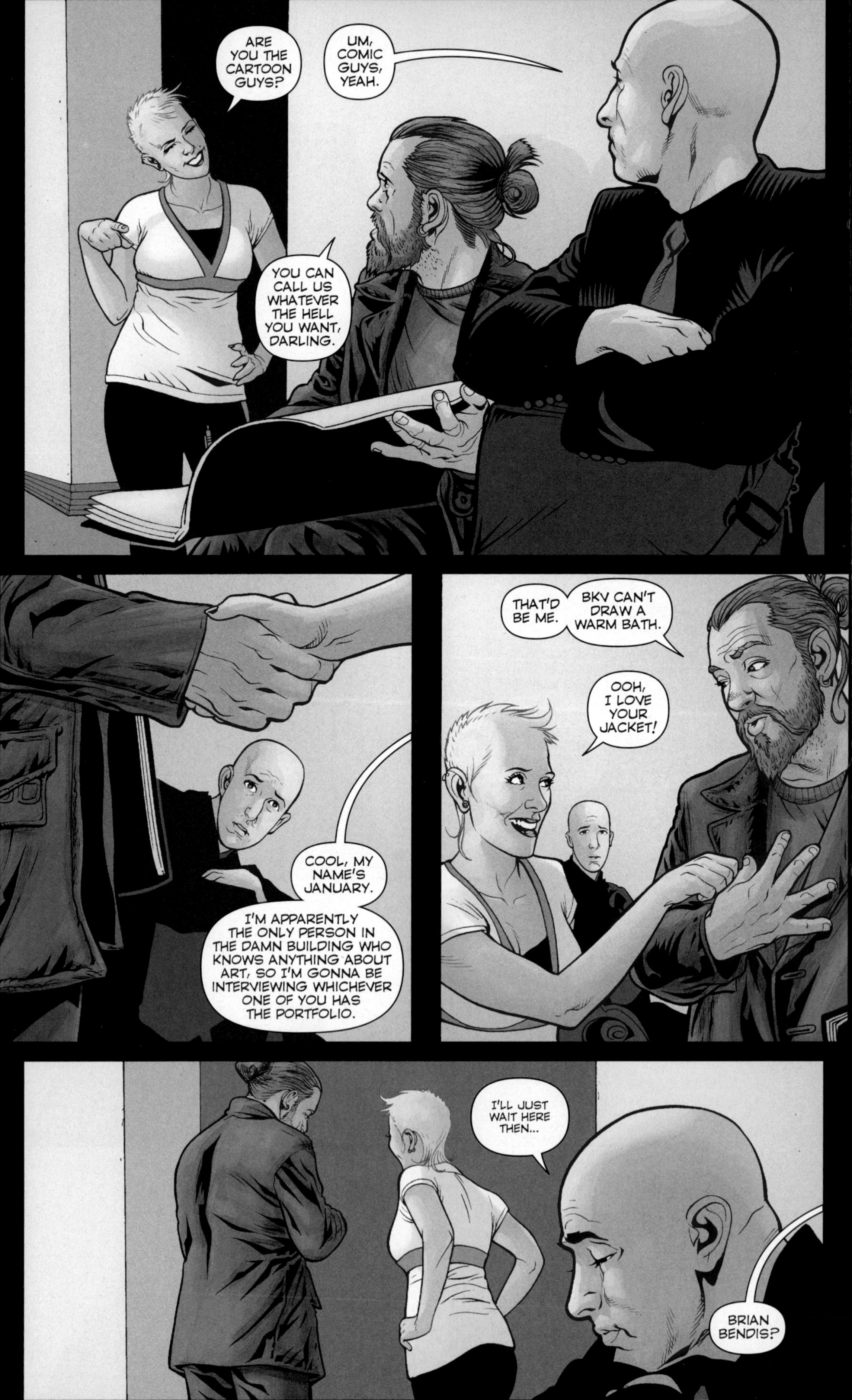
ARE YOU THE CARTOON GUYS?
UM, COMIC GUYS, YEAH.
YOU CAN CALL US WHATEVER THE HELL YOU WANT, DARLING.
COOL, MY NAME'S JANUARY.
I'M APPARENTLY THE ONLY PERSON IN THE DAMN BUILDING WHO KNOWS ANYTHING ABOUT ART, SO I'M GONNA BE INTERVIEWING WHICHEVER ONE OF YOU HAS THE PORTFOLIO.
THAT'D BE ME.
BKV CAN'T DRAW A WARM BATH.
OOH, I LOVE YOUR JACKET!
I'LL JUST WAIT HERE THEN...
BRIAN BENDIS?

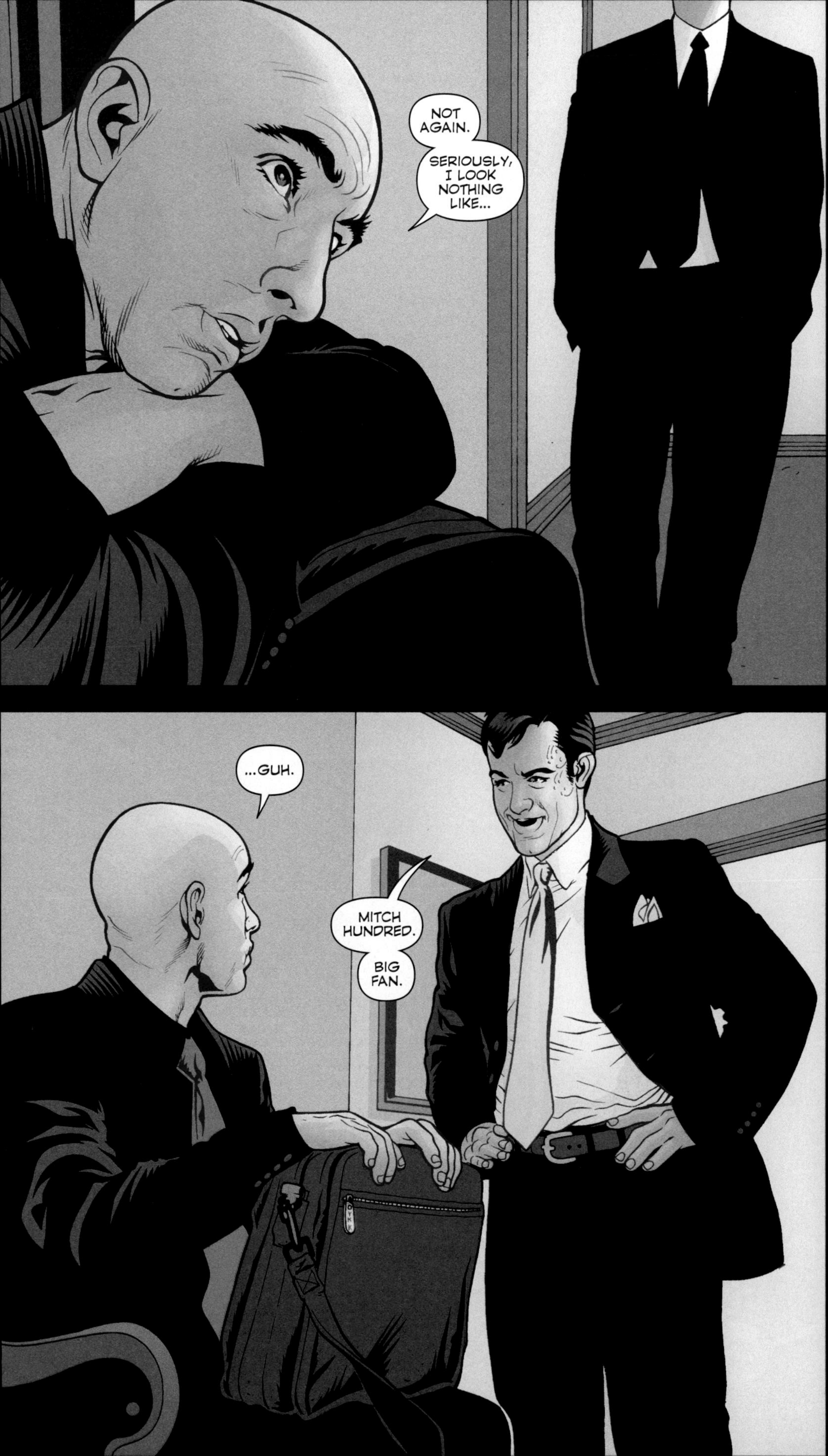
NOT AGAIN.
SERIOUSLY, I LOOK NOTHING LIKE...
...GUH.
MITCH HUNDRED.
BIG FAN.

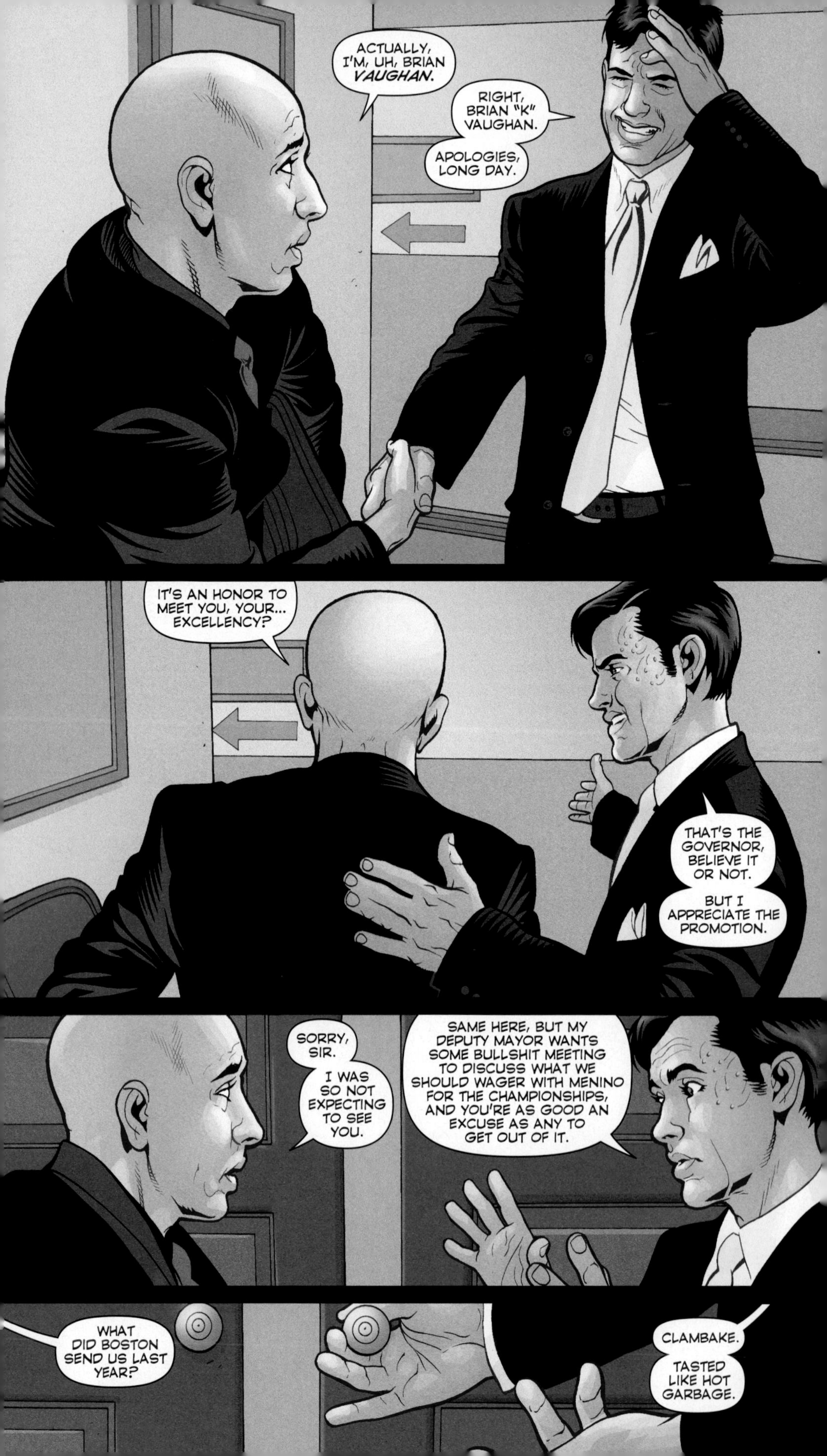

ACTUALLY, I'M, UH, BRIAN *VAUGHAN.*
RIGHT, BRIAN "K" VAUGHAN.
APOLOGIES, LONG DAY.
IT'S AN HONOR TO MEET YOU, YOUR... EXCELLENCY?
THAT'S THE GOVERNOR, BELIEVE IT OR NOT.
BUT I APPRECIATE THE PROMOTION.
SORRY, SIR.
I WAS SO NOT EXPECTING TO SEE YOU.
SAME HERE, BUT MY DEPUTY MAYOR WANTS SOME BULLSHIT MEETING TO DISCUSS WHAT WE SHOULD WAGER WITH MENINO FOR THE CHAMPIONSHIPS, AND YOU'RE AS GOOD AN EXCUSE AS ANY TO GET OUT OF IT.
WHAT DID BOSTON SEND US LAST YEAR?
CLAMBAKE.
TASTED LIKE HOT GARBAGE.

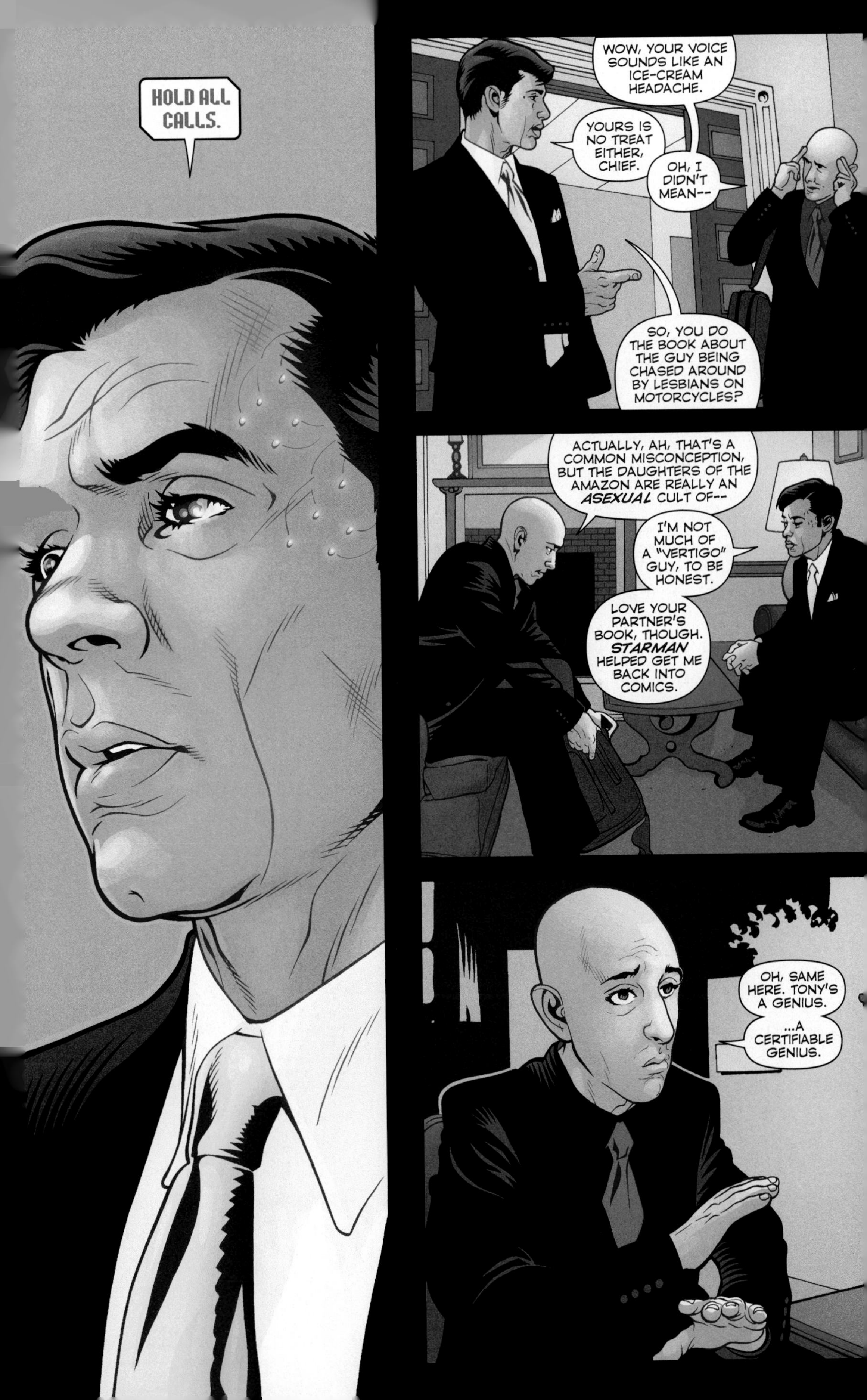
HOLD ALL CALLS.
WOW, YOUR VOICE SOUNDS LIKE AN ICE-CREAM HEADACHE.
YOURS IS NO TREAT EITHER, CHIEF.
OH, I DIDN'T MEAN--
SO, YOU DO THE BOOK ABOUT THE GUY BEING CHASED AROUND BY LESBIANS ON MOTORCYCLES?
ACTUALLY, AH, THAT'S A COMMON MISCONCEPTION, BUT THE DAUGHTERS OF THE AMAZON ARE REALLY AN *ASEXUAL* CULT OF--
I'M NOT MUCH OF A "VERTIGO" GUY, TO BE HONEST.
LOVE YOUR PARTNER'S BOOK, THOUGH. *STARMAN* HELPED GET ME BACK INTO COMICS.
OH, SAME HERE. TONY'S A GENIUS.
...A CERTIFIABLE GENIUS.

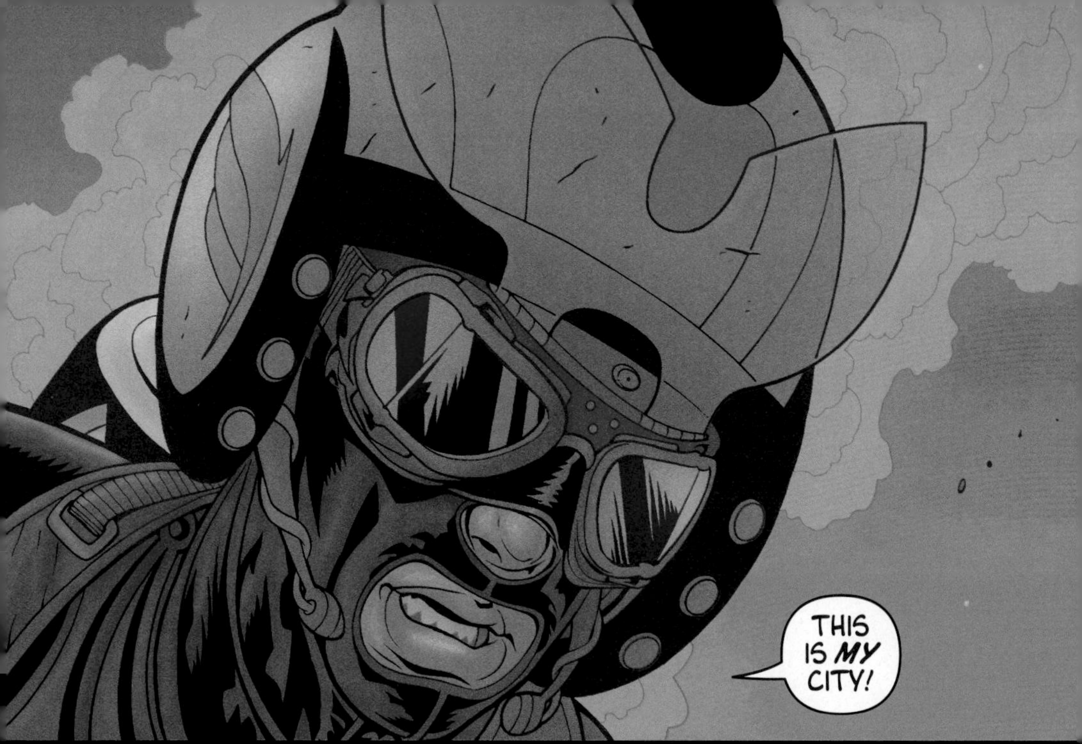
THIS IS MY CITY!

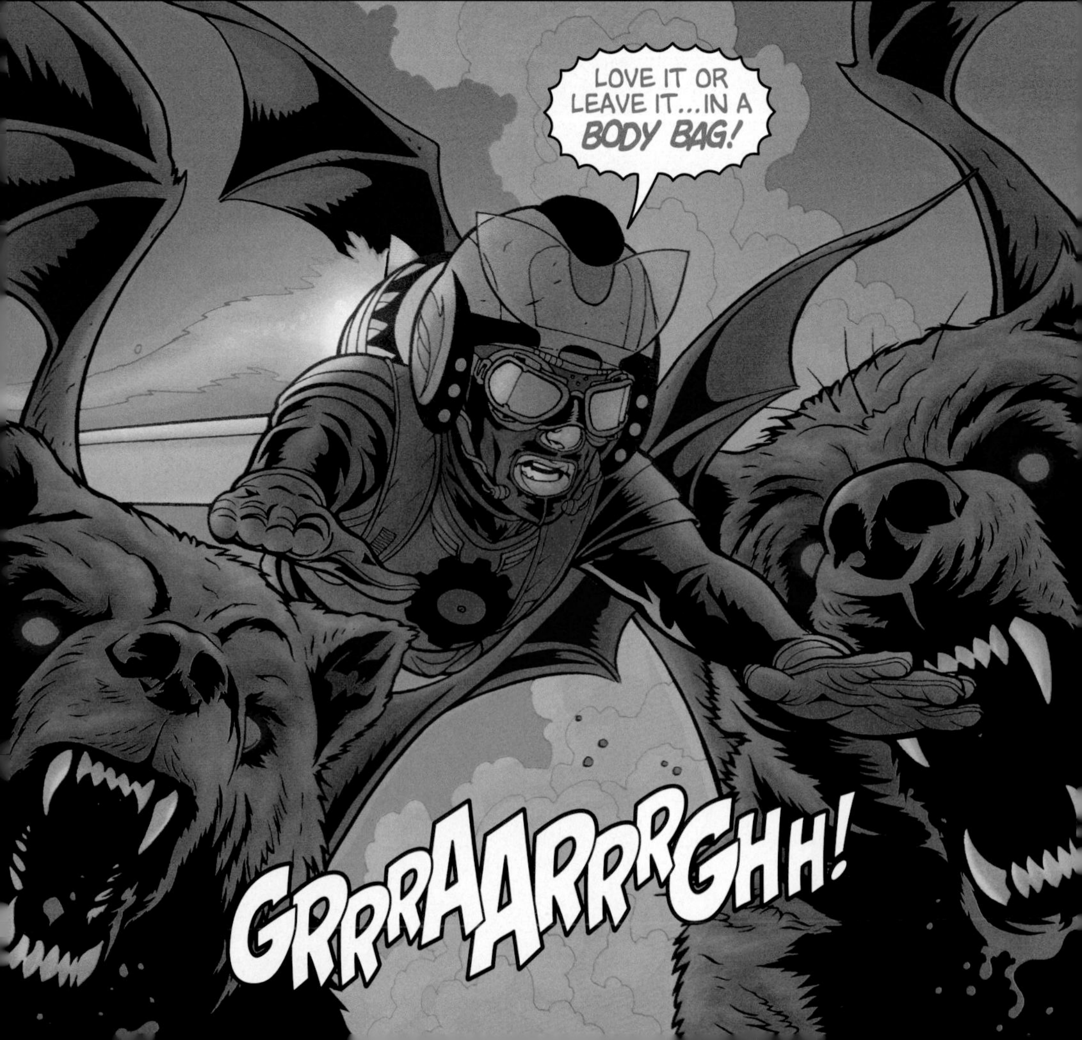
LOVE IT OR LEAVE IT...IN A BODY BAG!
GRRRRAARRRRGHH!

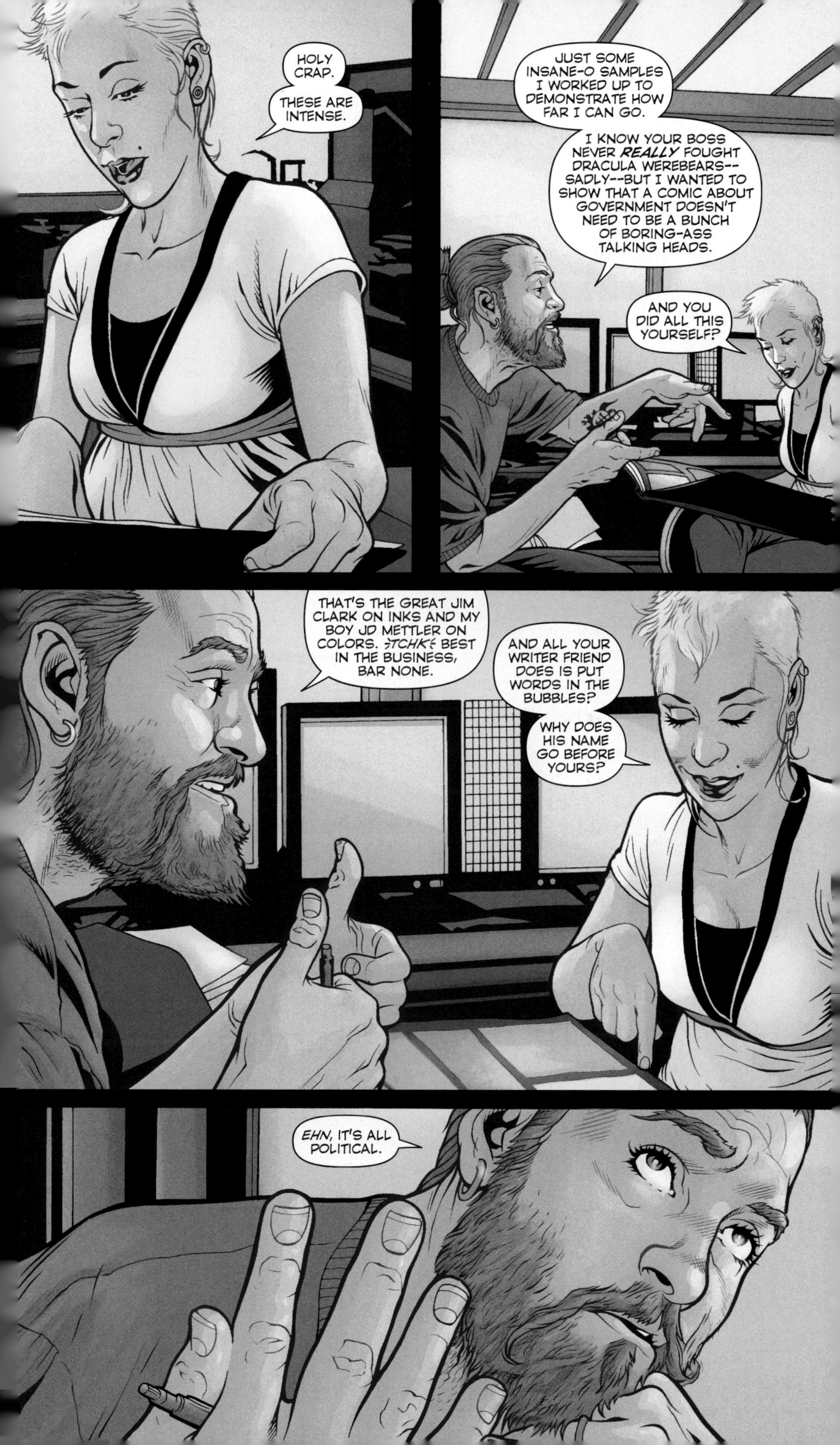
HOLY CRAP.
THESE ARE INTENSE.
JUST SOME INSANE-O SAMPLES I WORKED UP TO DEMONSTRATE HOW FAR I CAN GO.
I KNOW YOUR BOSS NEVER *REALLY* FOUGHT DRACULA WEREBEARS--SADLY--BUT I WANTED TO SHOW THAT A COMIC ABOUT GOVERNMENT DOESN'T NEED TO BE A BUNCH OF BORING-ASS TALKING HEADS.
AND YOU DID ALL THIS YOURSELF?
THAT'S THE GREAT JIM CLARK ON INKS AND MY BOY JD METTLER ON COLORS. *TCHK* BEST IN THE BUSINESS, BAR NONE.
AND ALL YOUR WRITER FRIEND DOES IS PUT WORDS IN THE BUBBLES?
WHY DOES HIS NAME GO BEFORE YOURS?
EHN, IT'S ALL POLITICAL.

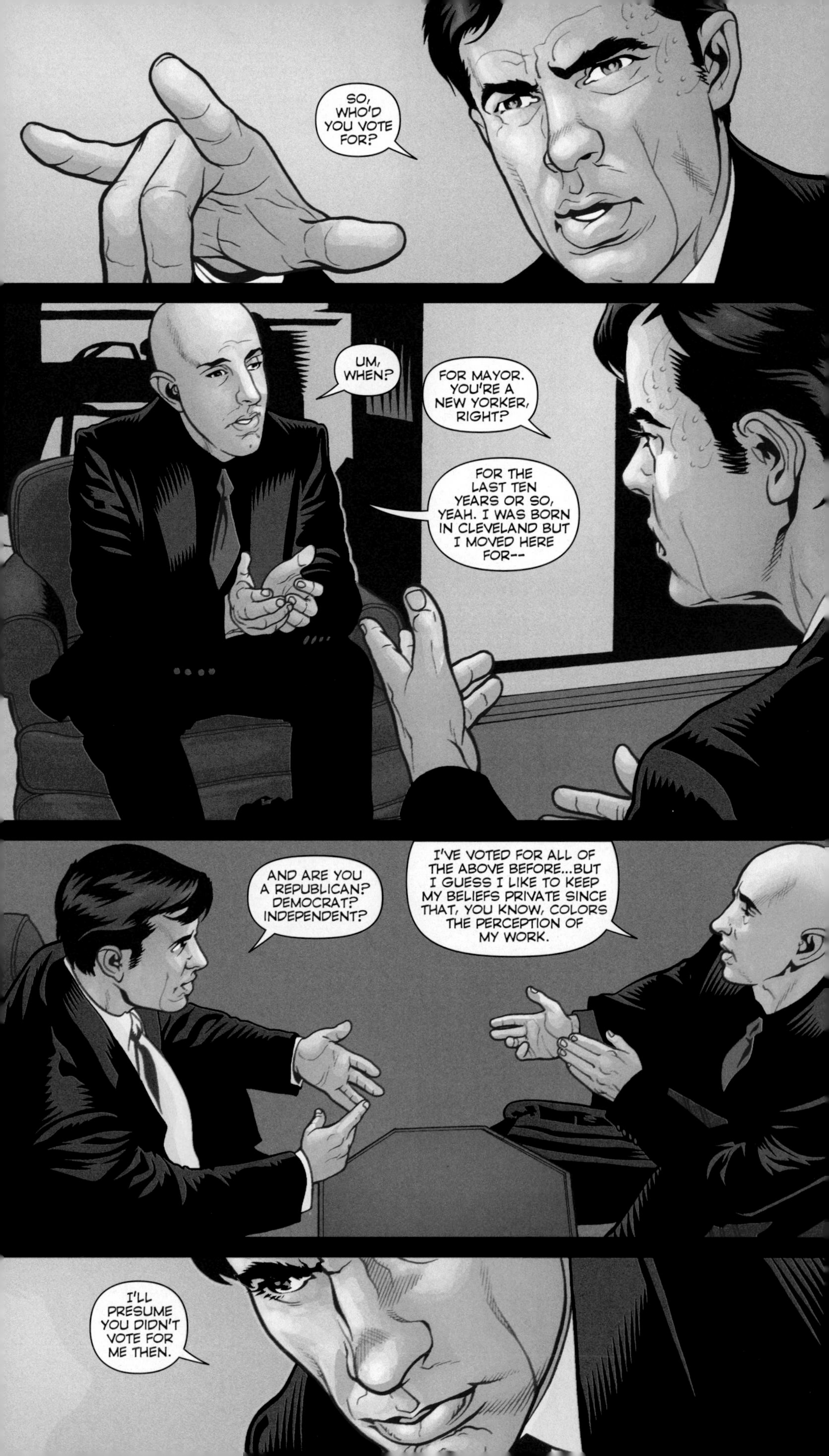
SO, WHO'D YOU VOTE FOR?
UM, WHEN?
FOR MAYOR. YOU'RE A NEW YORKER, RIGHT?
FOR THE LAST TEN YEARS OR SO, YEAH. I WAS BORN IN CLEVELAND BUT I MOVED HERE FOR--
AND ARE YOU A REPUBLICAN? DEMOCRAT? INDEPENDENT?
I'VE VOTED FOR ALL OF THE ABOVE BEFORE...BUT I GUESS I LIKE TO KEEP MY BELIEFS PRIVATE SINCE THAT, YOU KNOW, COLORS THE PERCEPTION OF MY WORK.
I'LL PRESUME YOU DIDN'T VOTE FOR ME THEN.

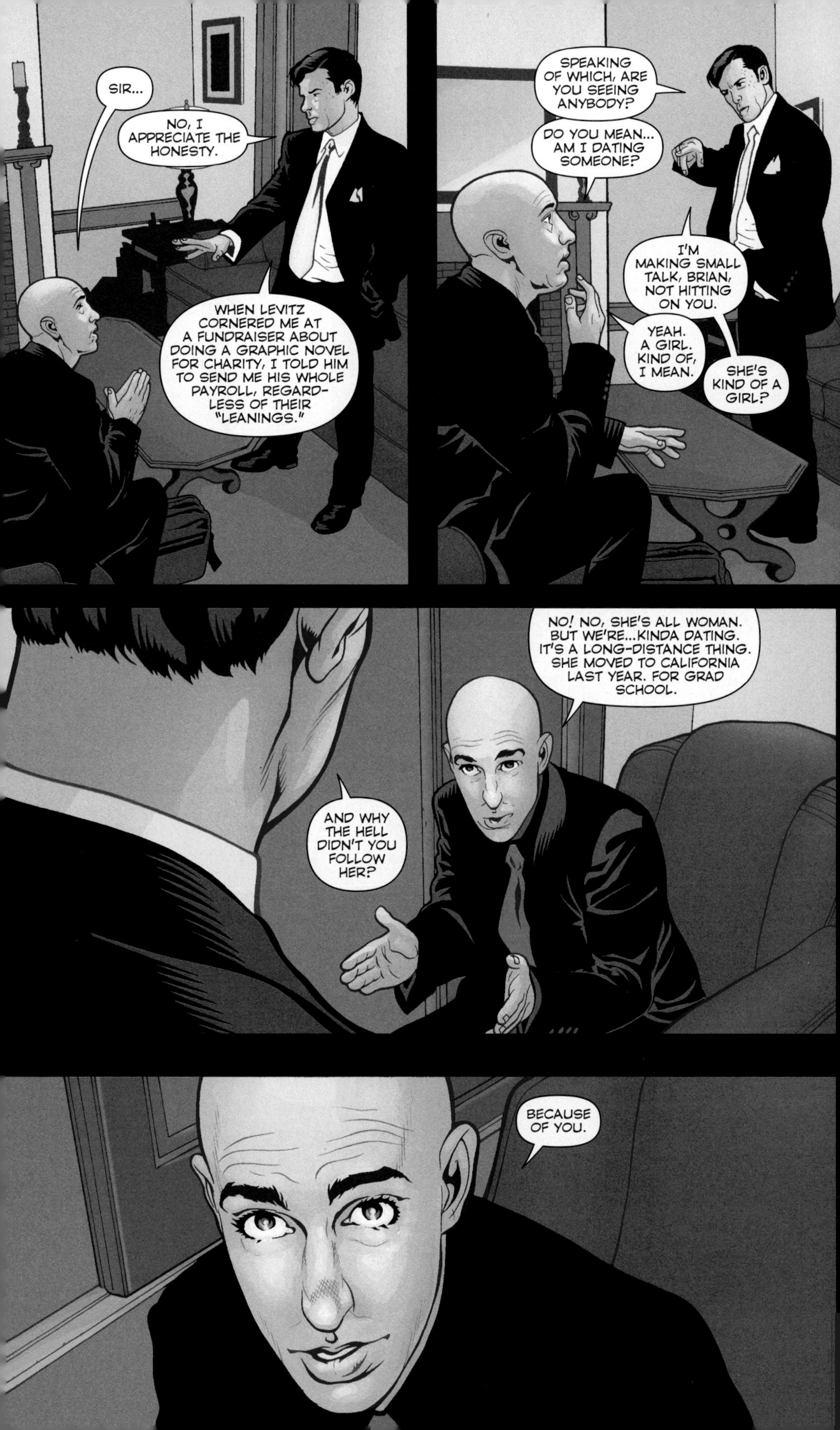
SIR...
NO, I APPRECIATE THE HONESTY.
WHEN LEVITZ CORNERED ME AT A FUNDRAISER ABOUT DOING A GRAPHIC NOVEL FOR CHARITY, I TOLD HIM TO SEND ME HIS WHOLE PAYROLL, REGARDLESS OF THEIR "LEANINGS."
SPEAKING OF WHICH, ARE YOU SEEING ANYBODY?
DO YOU MEAN... AM I DATING SOMEONE?
I'M MAKING SMALL TALK, BRIAN, NOT HITTING ON YOU.
YEAH. A GIRL. KIND OF, I MEAN.
SHE'S KIND OF A GIRL?
NO! NO, SHE'S ALL WOMAN. BUT WE'RE...KINDA DATING. IT'S A LONG-DISTANCE THING. SHE MOVED TO CALIFORNIA LAST YEAR. FOR GRAD SCHOOL.
AND WHY THE HELL DIDN'T YOU FOLLOW HER?
BECAUSE OF YOU.

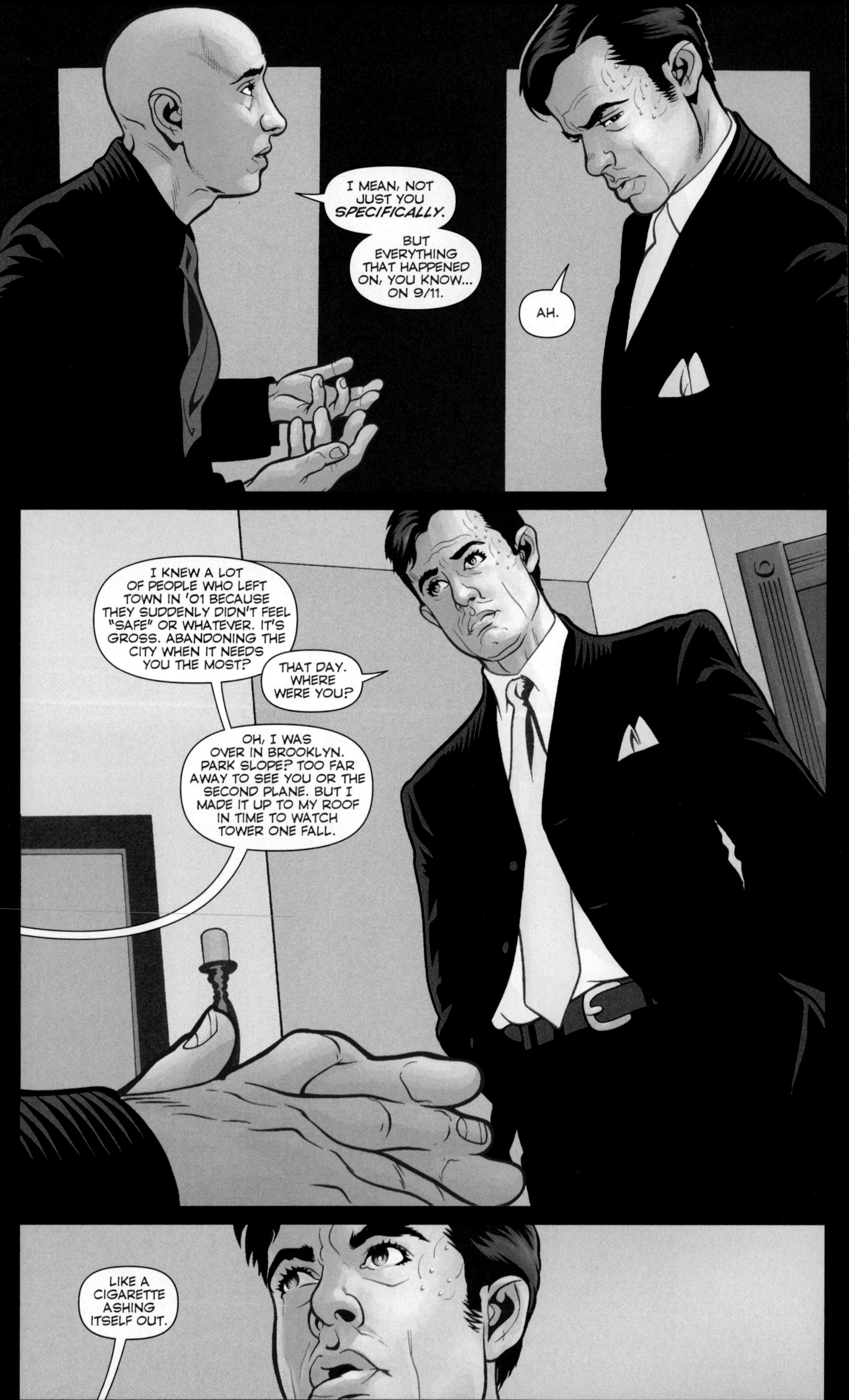
I MEAN, NOT JUST YOU SPECIFICALLY.
BUT EVERYTHING THAT HAPPENED ON, YOU KNOW... ON 9/11.
AH.
I KNEW A LOT OF PEOPLE WHO LEFT TOWN IN '01 BECAUSE THEY SUDDENLY DIDN'T FEEL "SAFE" OR WHATEVER. IT'S GROSS. ABANDONING THE CITY WHEN IT NEEDS YOU THE MOST?
THAT DAY. WHERE WERE YOU?
OH, I WAS OVER IN BROOKLYN. PARK SLOPE? TOO FAR AWAY TO SEE YOU OR THE SECOND PLANE. BUT I MADE IT UP TO MY ROOF IN TIME TO WATCH TOWER ONE FALL.
LIKE A CIGARETTE ASHING ITSELF OUT.

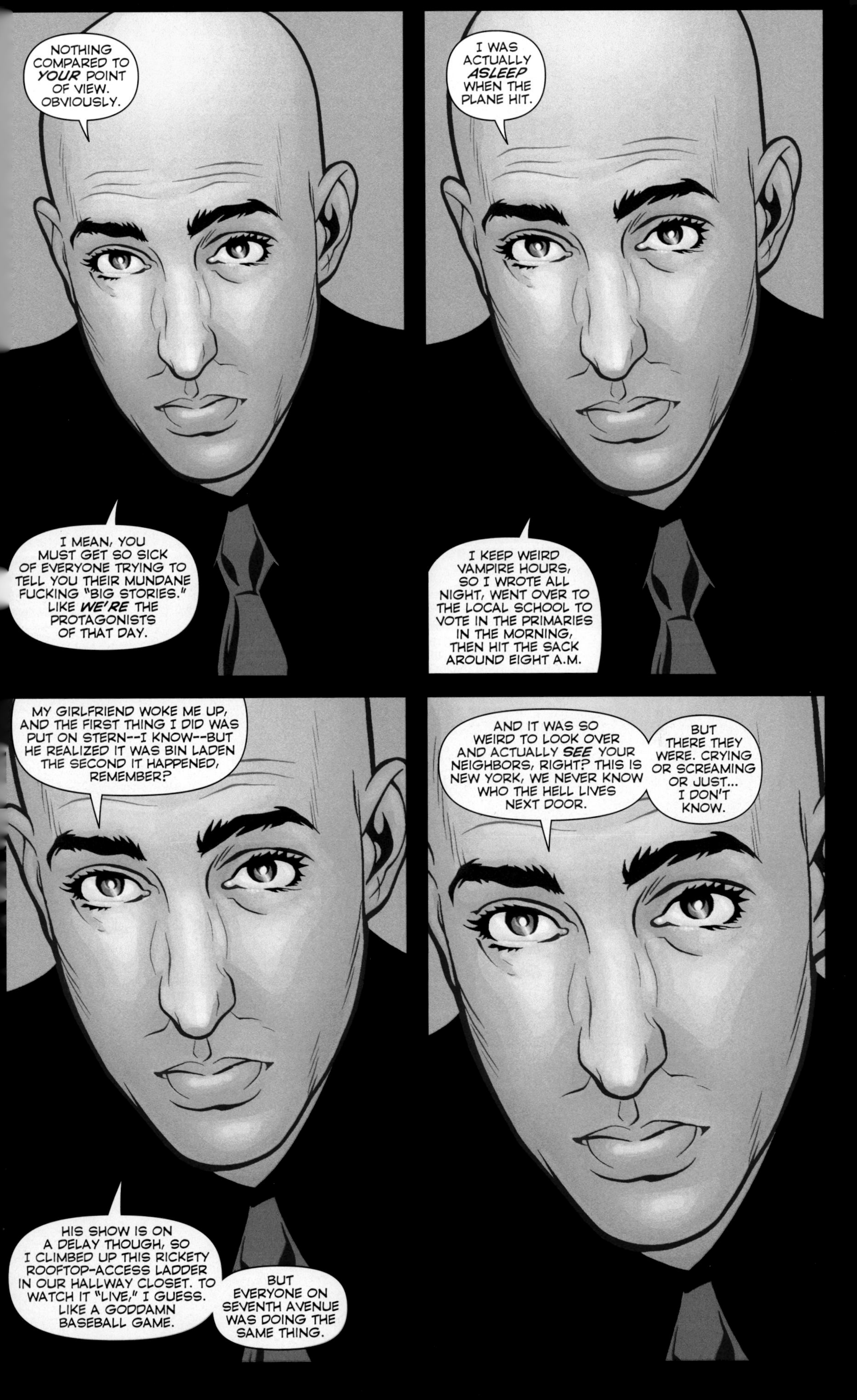
NOTHING COMPARED TO YOUR POINT OF VIEW. OBVIOUSLY.
I MEAN, YOU MUST GET SO SICK OF EVERYONE TRYING TO TELL YOU THEIR MUNDANE FUCKING "BIG STORIES." LIKE WE'RE THE PROTAGONISTS OF THAT DAY.
I WAS ACTUALLY ASLEEP WHEN THE PLANE HIT.
I KEEP WEIRD VAMPIRE HOURS, SO I WROTE ALL NIGHT, WENT OVER TO THE LOCAL SCHOOL TO VOTE IN THE PRIMARIES IN THE MORNING, THEN HIT THE SACK AROUND EIGHT A.M.
MY GIRLFRIEND WOKE ME UP, AND THE FIRST THING I DID WAS PUT ON STERN--I KNOW--BUT HE REALIZED IT WAS BIN LADEN THE SECOND IT HAPPENED, REMEMBER?
HIS SHOW IS ON A DELAY THOUGH, SO I CLIMBED UP THIS RICKETY ROOFTOP-ACCESS LADDER IN OUR HALLWAY CLOSET. TO WATCH IT "LIVE," I GUESS. LIKE A GODDAMN BASEBALL GAME.
BUT EVERYONE ON SEVENTH AVENUE WAS DOING THE SAME THING.
AND IT WAS SO WEIRD TO LOOK OVER AND ACTUALLY SEE YOUR NEIGHBORS, RIGHT? THIS IS NEW YORK, WE NEVER KNOW WHO THE HELL LIVES NEXT DOOR.
BUT THERE THEY WERE. CRYING OR SCREAMING OR JUST... I DON'T KNOW.

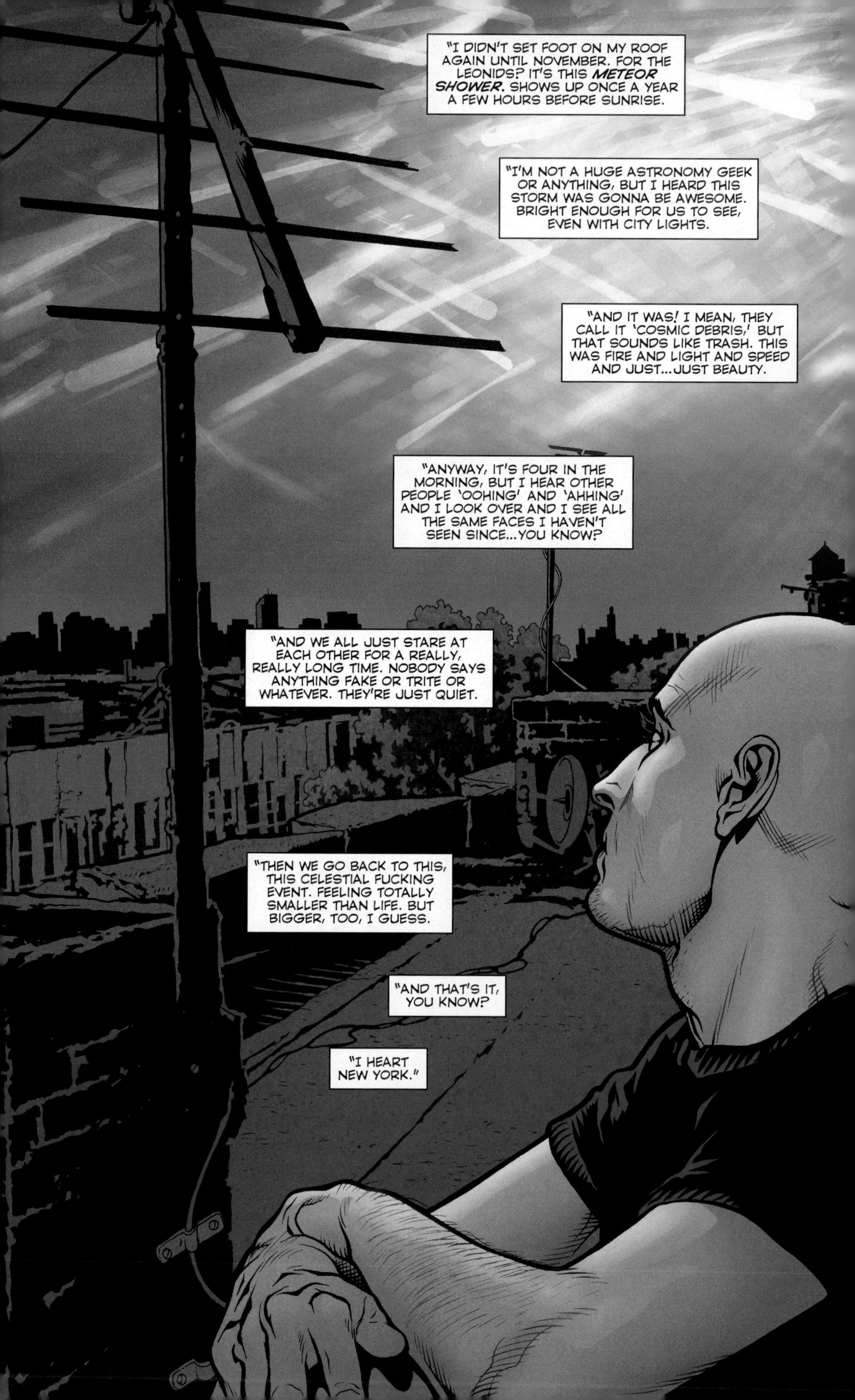
"I DIDN'T SET FOOT ON MY ROOF AGAIN UNTIL NOVEMBER. FOR THE LEONIDS? IT'S THIS METEOR SHOWER. SHOWS UP ONCE A YEAR A FEW HOURS BEFORE SUNRISE.
"I'M NOT A HUGE ASTRONOMY GEEK OR ANYTHING, BUT I HEARD THIS STORM WAS GONNA BE AWESOME. BRIGHT ENOUGH FOR US TO SEE, EVEN WITH CITY LIGHTS.
"AND IT WAS! I MEAN, THEY CALL IT 'COSMIC DEBRIS,' BUT THAT SOUNDS LIKE TRASH. THIS WAS FIRE AND LIGHT AND SPEED AND JUST...JUST BEAUTY.
"ANYWAY, IT'S FOUR IN THE MORNING, BUT I HEAR OTHER PEOPLE 'OOHING' AND 'AHHING' AND I LOOK OVER AND I SEE ALL THE SAME FACES I HAVEN'T SEEN SINCE...YOU KNOW?
"AND WE ALL JUST STARE AT EACH OTHER FOR A REALLY, REALLY LONG TIME. NOBODY SAYS ANYTHING FAKE OR TRITE OR WHATEVER. THEY'RE JUST QUIET.
"THEN WE GO BACK TO THIS, THIS CELESTIAL FUCKING EVENT. FEELING TOTALLY SMALLER THAN LIFE. BUT BIGGER, TOO, I GUESS.
"AND THAT'S IT, YOU KNOW?
"I HEART NEW YORK."

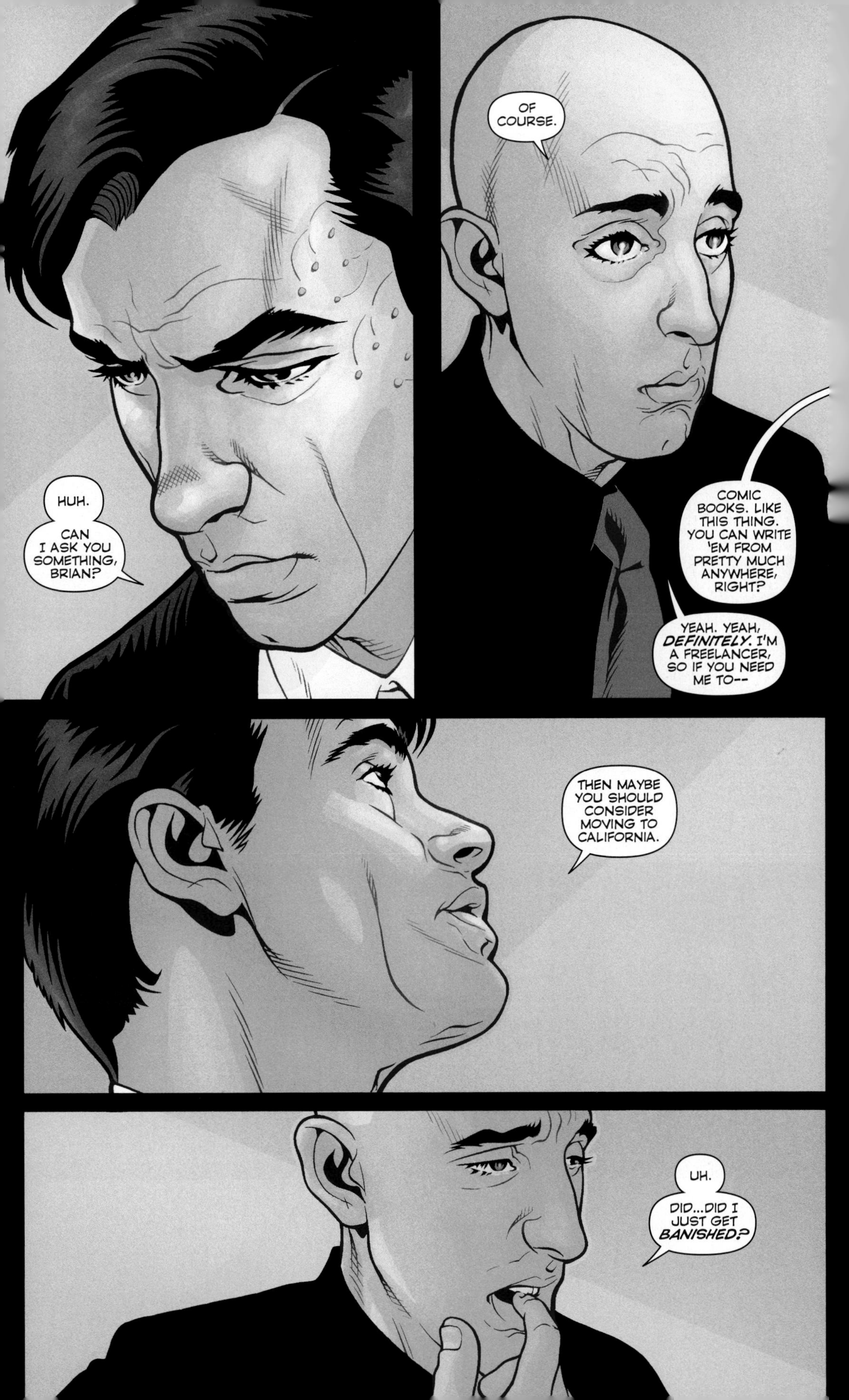

OF COURSE.
HUH.
CAN I ASK YOU SOMETHING, BRIAN?
COMIC BOOKS. LIKE THIS THING. YOU CAN WRITE 'EM FROM PRETTY MUCH ANYWHERE, RIGHT?
YEAH. YEAH, DEFINITELY. I'M A FREELANCER, SO IF YOU NEED ME TO--
THEN MAYBE YOU SHOULD CONSIDER MOVING TO CALIFORNIA.
UH.
DID...DID I JUST GET BANISHED?

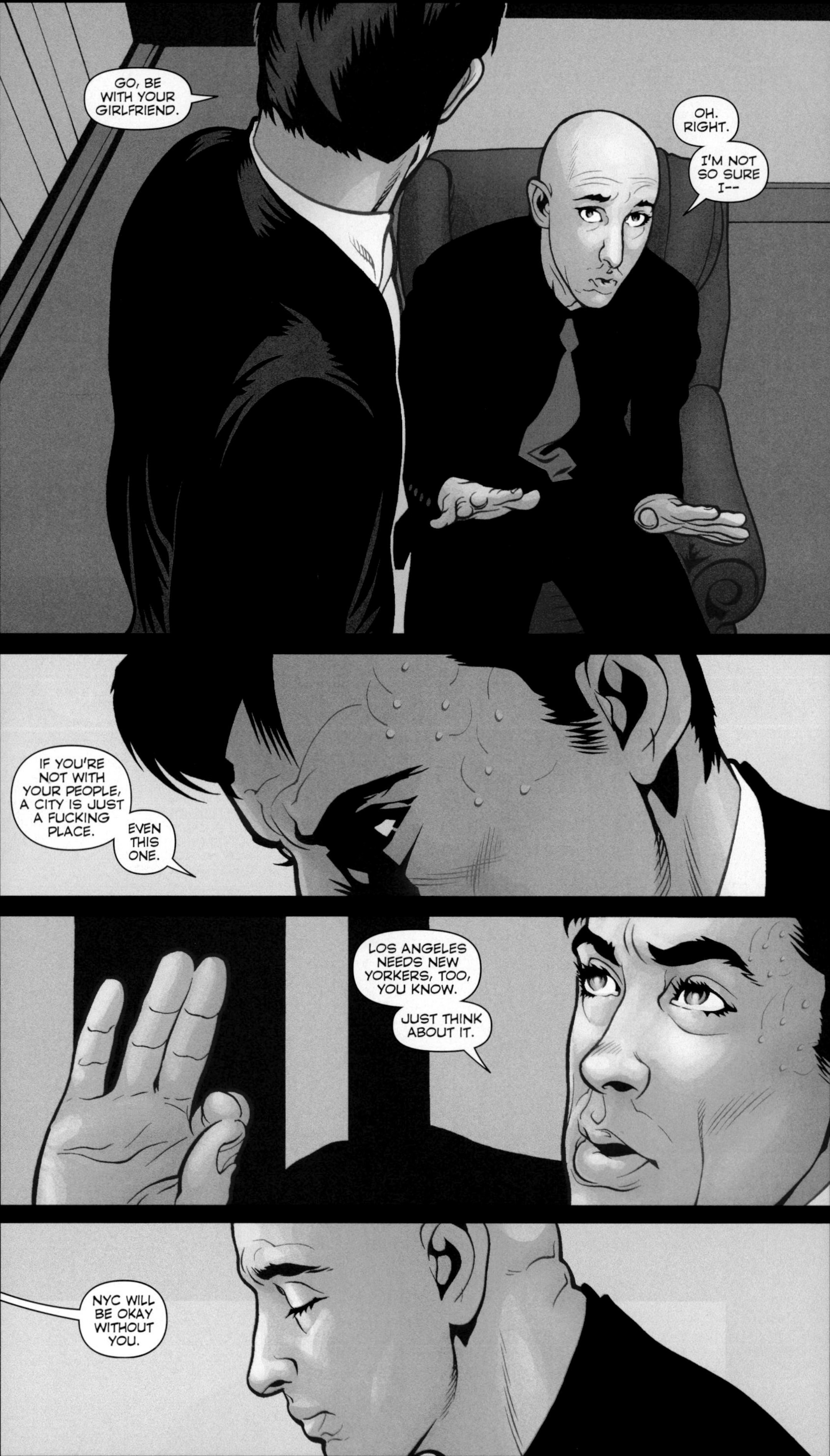
GO, BE WITH YOUR GIRLFRIEND.
OH. RIGHT.
I'M NOT SO SURE I--
IF YOU'RE NOT WITH YOUR PEOPLE, A CITY IS JUST A FUCKING PLACE.
EVEN THIS ONE.
LOS ANGELES NEEDS NEW YORKERS, TOO, YOU KNOW.
JUST THINK ABOUT IT.
NYC WILL BE OKAY WITHOUT YOU.

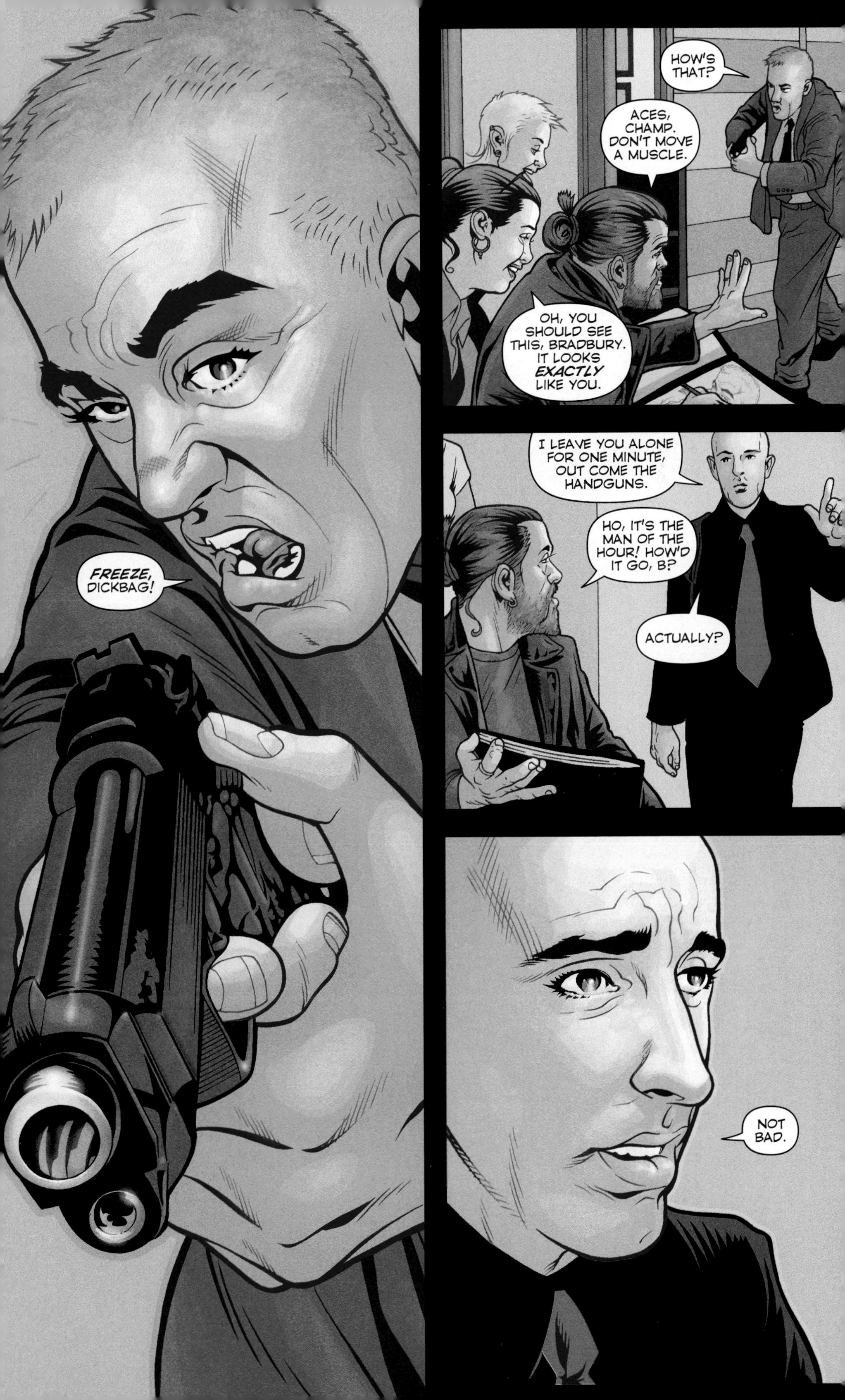
FREEZE, DICKBAG!
HOW'S THAT?
ACES, CHAMP. DON'T MOVE A MUSCLE.
OH, YOU SHOULD SEE THIS, BRADBURY. IT LOOKS EXACTLY LIKE YOU.
I LEAVE YOU ALONE FOR ONE MINUTE, OUT COME THE HANDGUNS.
HO, IT'S THE MAN OF THE HOUR! HOW'D IT GO, B?
ACTUALLY?
NOT BAD.

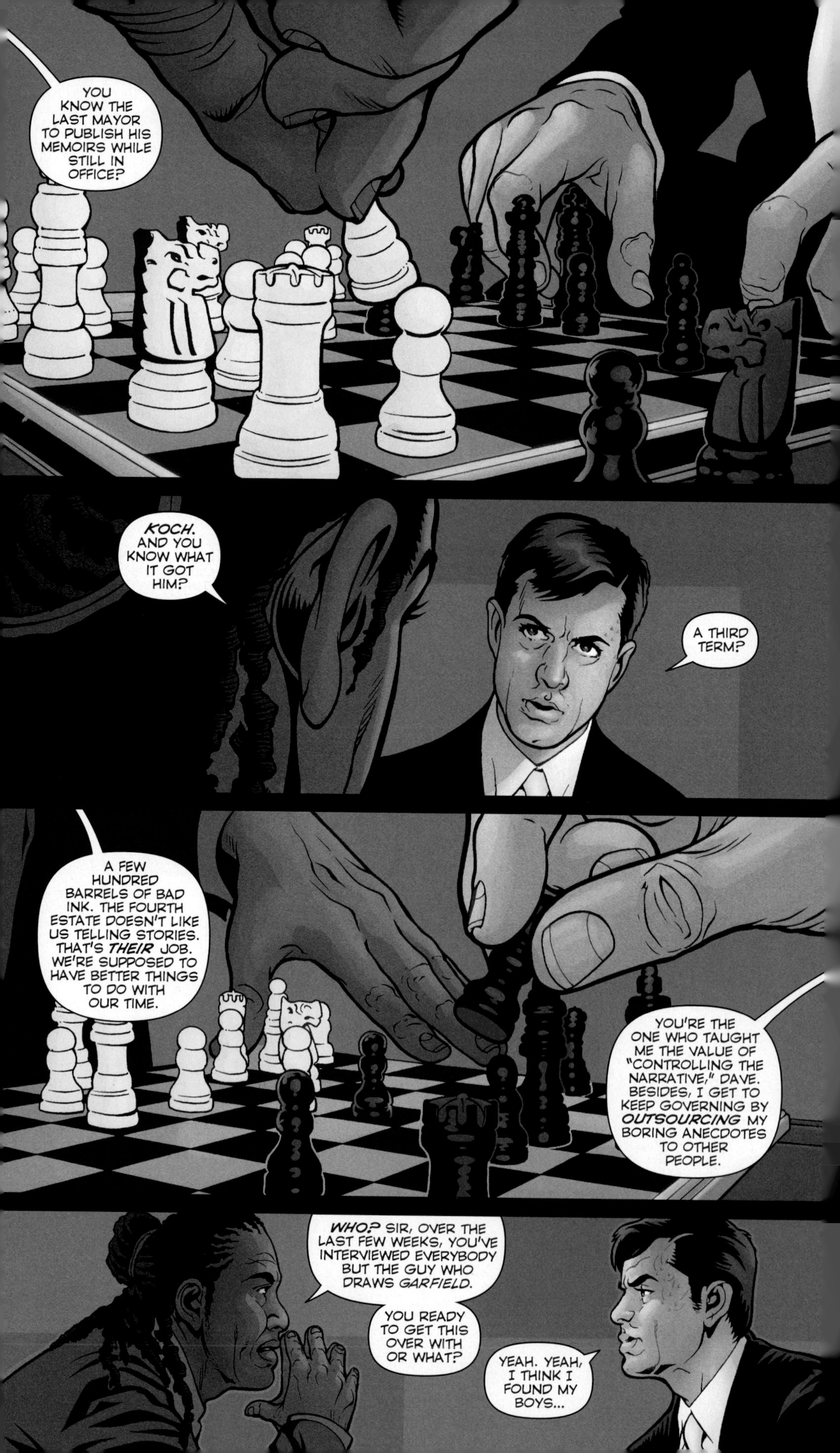
YOU KNOW THE LAST MAYOR TO PUBLISH HIS MEMOIRS WHILE STILL IN OFFICE?
KOCH. AND YOU KNOW WHAT IT GOT HIM?
A THIRD TERM?
A FEW HUNDRED BARRELS OF BAD INK. THE FOURTH ESTATE DOESN'T LIKE US TELLING STORIES. THAT'S THEIR JOB. WE'RE SUPPOSED TO HAVE BETTER THINGS TO DO WITH OUR TIME.
YOU'RE THE ONE WHO TAUGHT ME THE VALUE OF "CONTROLLING THE NARRATIVE," DAVE. BESIDES, I GET TO KEEP GOVERNING BY OUTSOURCING MY BORING ANECDOTES TO OTHER PEOPLE.
WHO? SIR, OVER THE LAST FEW WEEKS, YOU'VE INTERVIEWED EVERYBODY BUT THE GUY WHO DRAWS GARFIELD.
YOU READY TO GET THIS OVER WITH OR WHAT?
YEAH. YEAH, I THINK I FOUND MY BOYS...

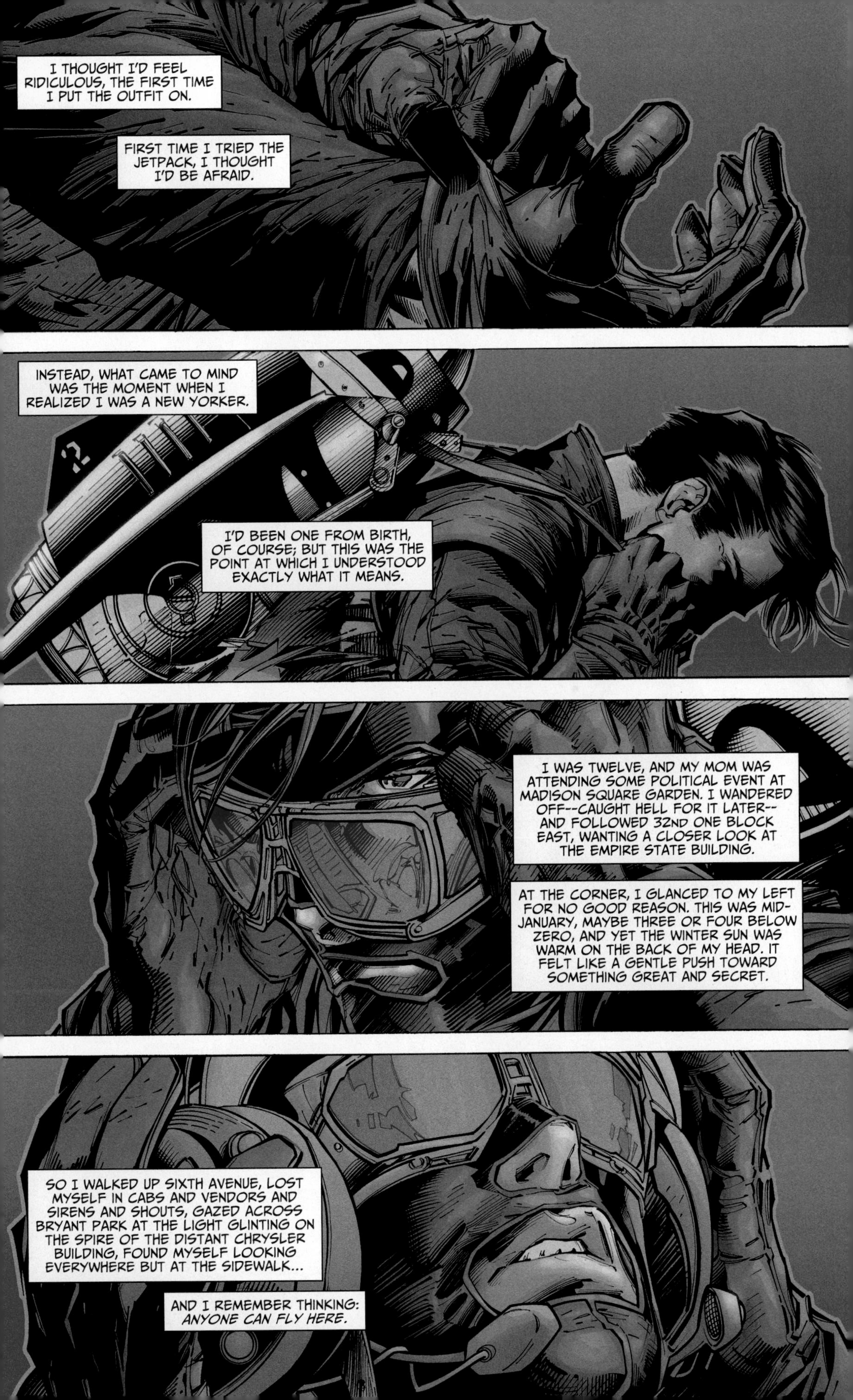
I THOUGHT I'D FEEL RIDICULOUS, THE FIRST TIME I PUT THE OUTFIT ON.
FIRST TIME I TRIED THE JETPACK, I THOUGHT I'D BE AFRAID.
INSTEAD, WHAT CAME TO MIND WAS THE MOMENT WHEN I REALIZED I WAS A NEW YORKER.
I'D BEEN ONE FROM BIRTH, OF COURSE; BUT THIS WAS THE POINT AT WHICH I UNDERSTOOD EXACTLY WHAT IT MEANS.
I WAS TWELVE, AND MY MOM WAS ATTENDING SOME POLITICAL EVENT AT MADISON SQUARE GARDEN. I WANDERED OFF--CAUGHT HELL FOR IT LATER--AND FOLLOWED 32ND ONE BLOCK EAST, WANTING A CLOSER LOOK AT THE EMPIRE STATE BUILDING.
AT THE CORNER, I GLANCED TO MY LEFT FOR NO GOOD REASON. THIS WAS MID-JANUARY, MAYBE THREE OR FOUR BELOW ZERO, AND YET THE WINTER SUN WAS WARM ON THE BACK OF MY HEAD. IT FELT LIKE A GENTLE PUSH TOWARD SOMETHING GREAT AND SECRET.
SO I WALKED UP SIXTH AVENUE, LOST MYSELF IN CABS AND VENDORS AND SIRENS AND SHOUTS, GAZED ACROSS BRYANT PARK AT THE LIGHT GLINTING ON THE SPIRE OF THE DISTANT CHRYSLER BUILDING, FOUND MYSELF LOOKING EVERYWHERE BUT AT THE SIDEWALK...
AND I REMEMBER THINKING: *ANYONE CAN FLY HERE.*

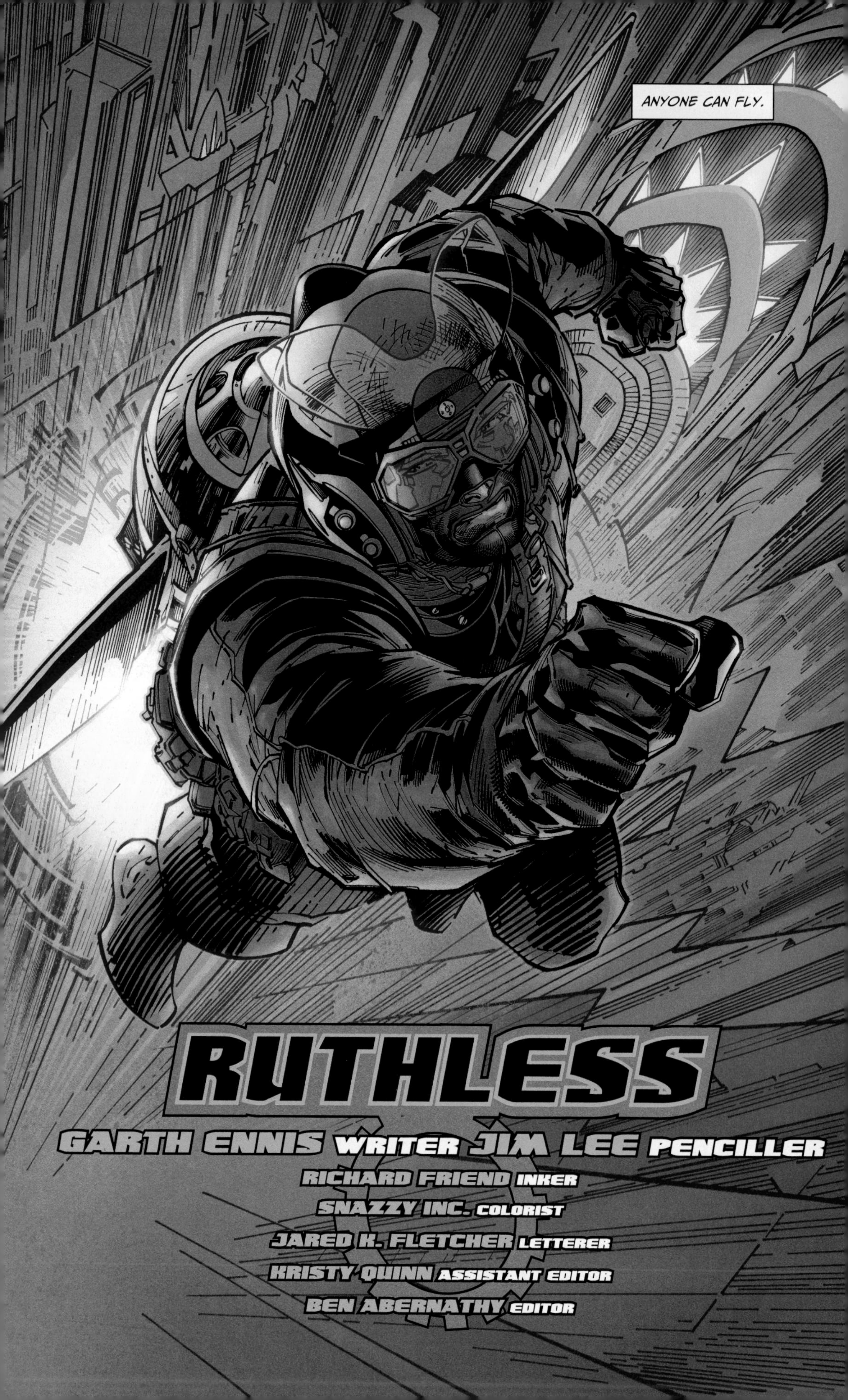
ANYONE CAN FLY.
RUTHLESS
GARTH ENNIS WRITER JIM LEE PENCILLER
RICHARD FRIEND INKER
SNAZZY INC. COLORIST
JARED K. FLETCHER LETTERER
KRISTY QUINN ASSISTANT EDITOR
BEN ABERNATHY EDITOR

COVER GALLERY

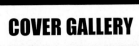

Editor's Note: since we've been depriving you of the chance to enjoy Tony's gorgeous covers for the series, we're beginning to rectify that here. Don't worry if your favorite isn't represented—we'll continue in Book Five!

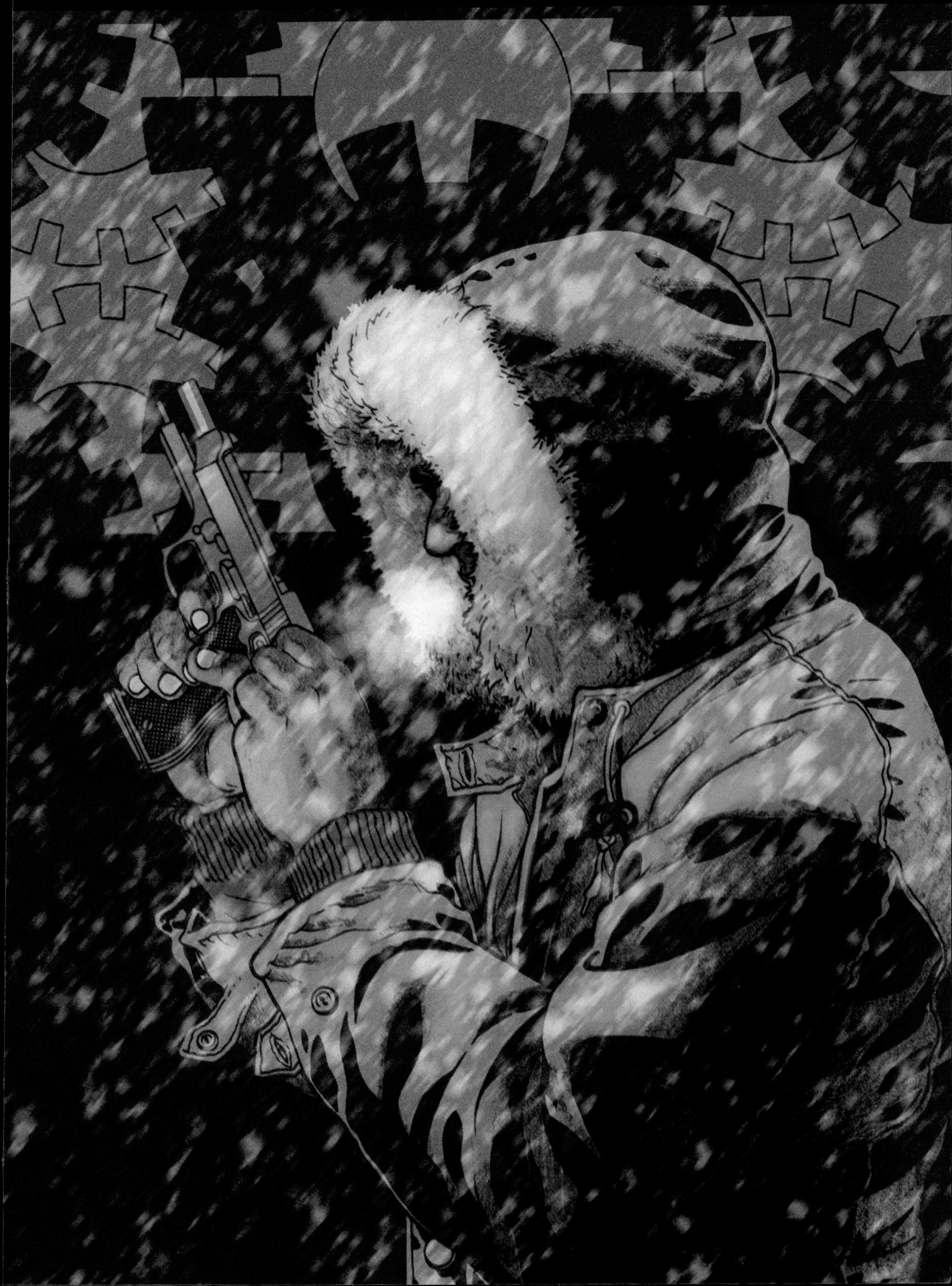

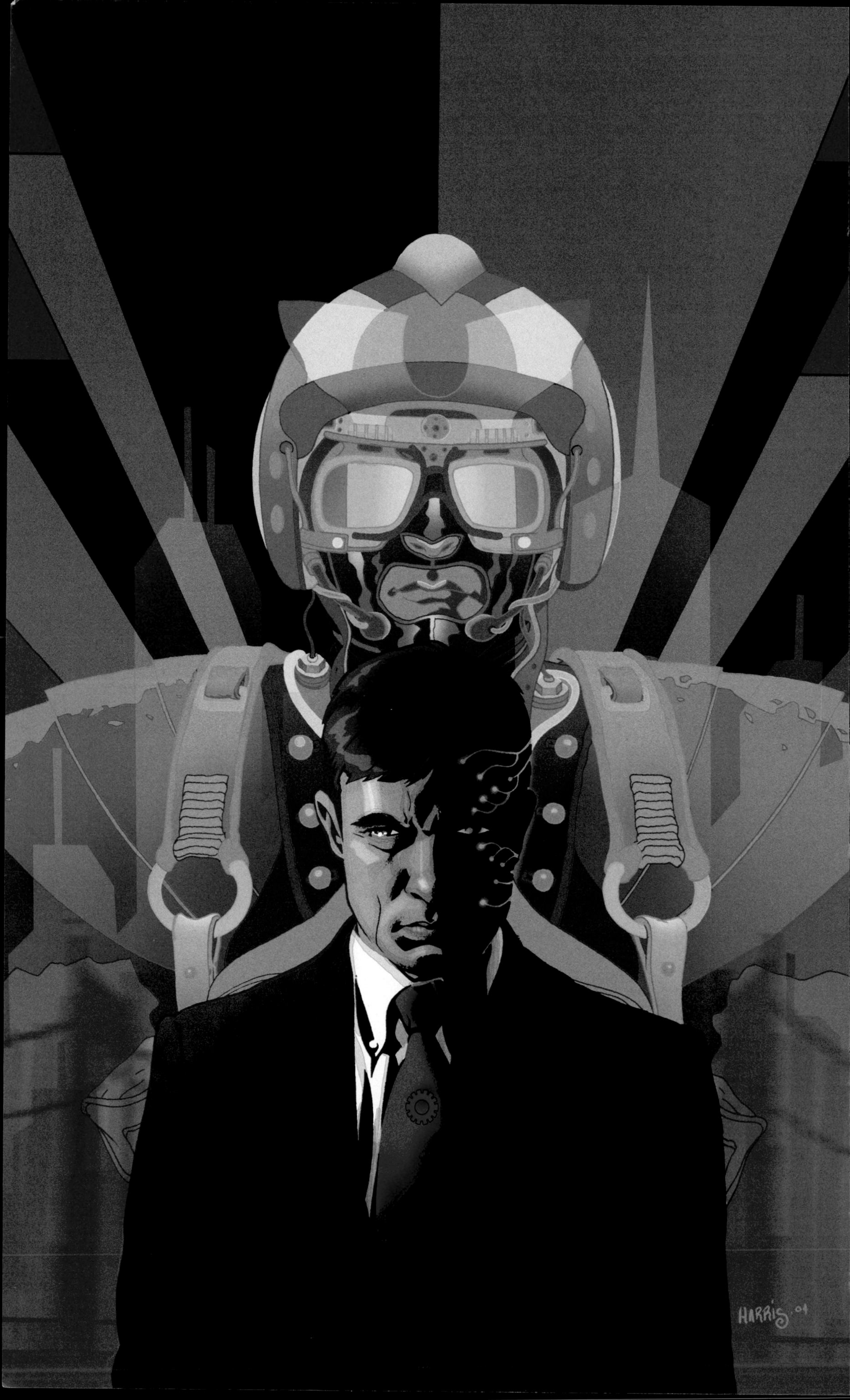
HARRIS '04

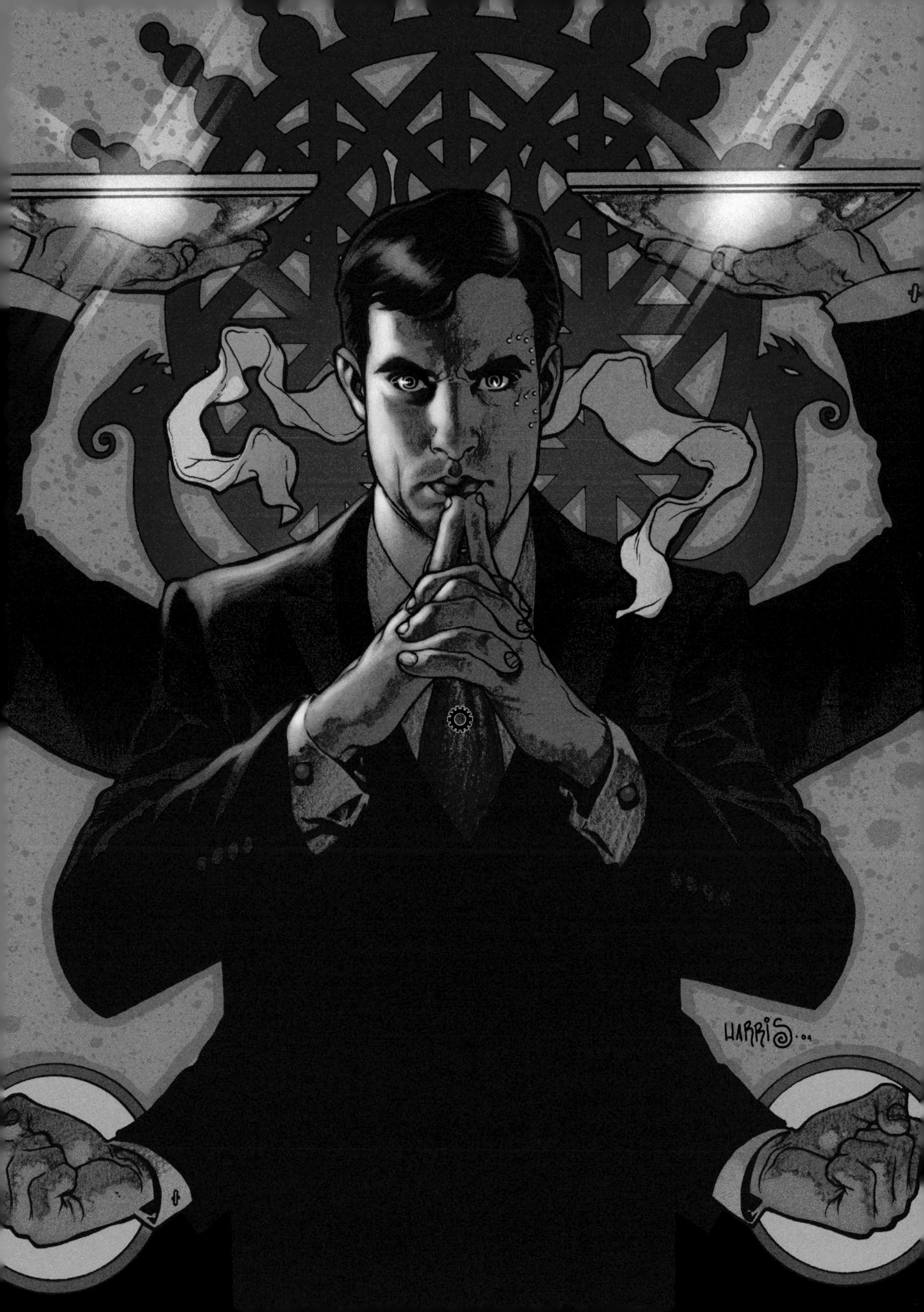
HARRIS.04

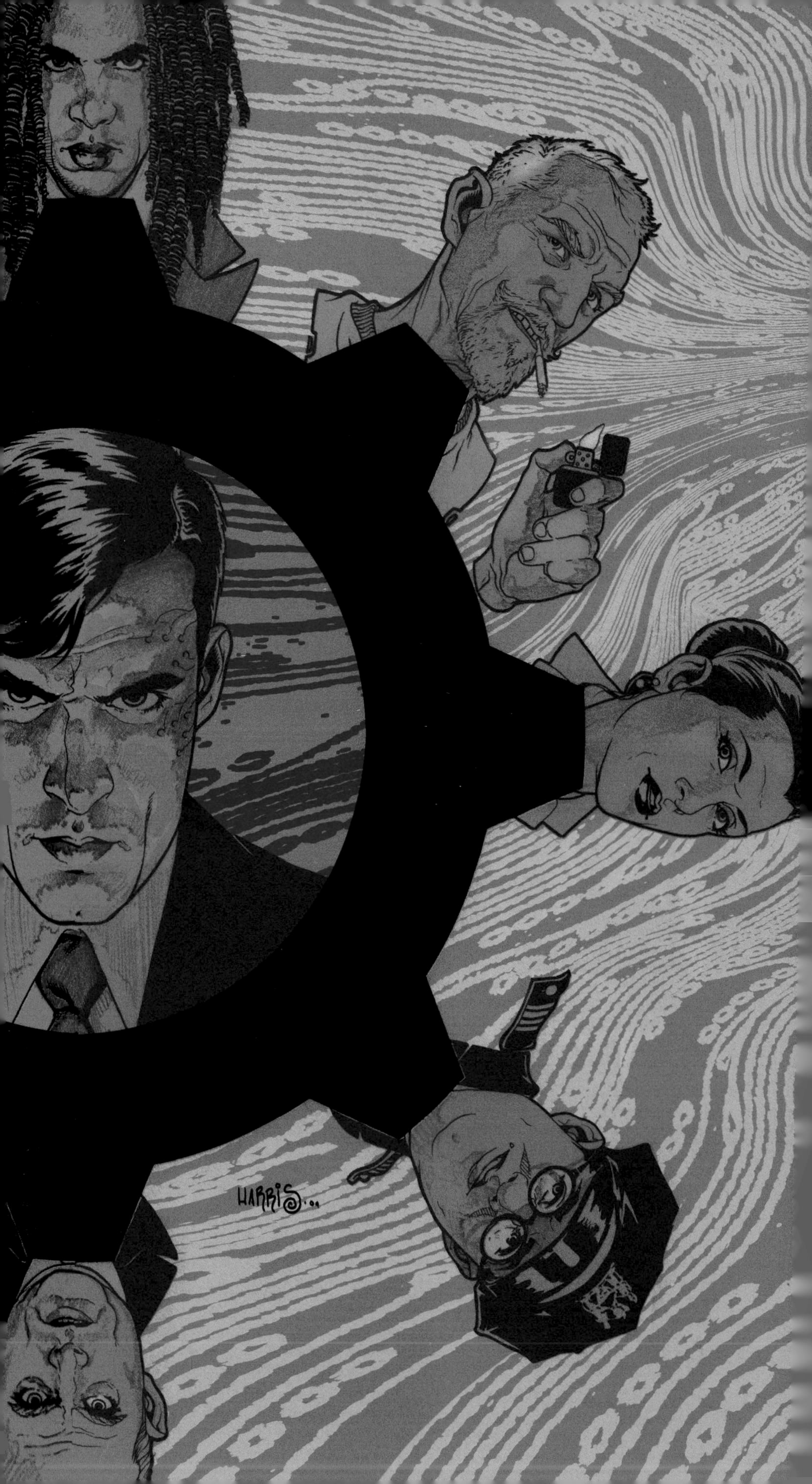
HARRIS

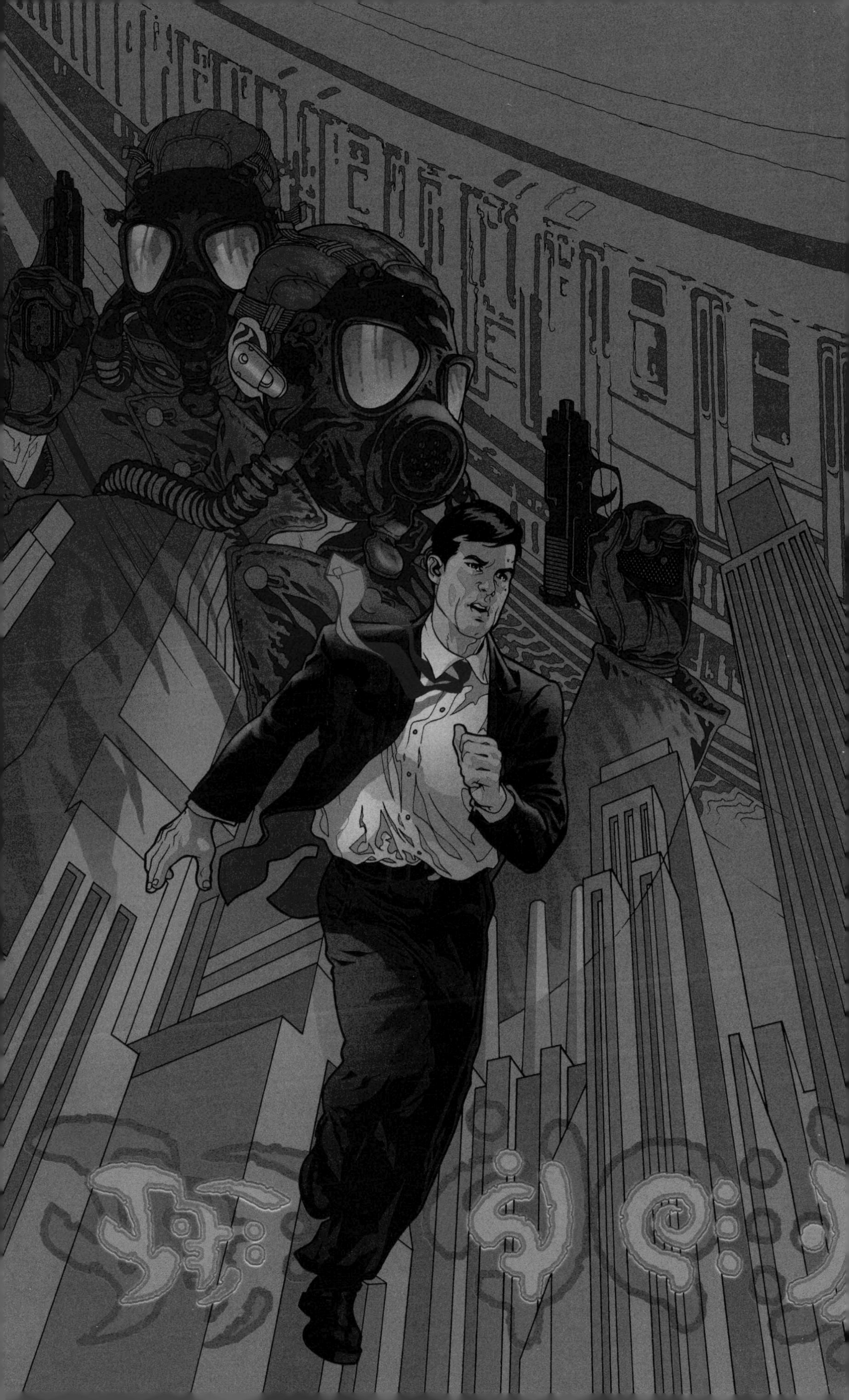

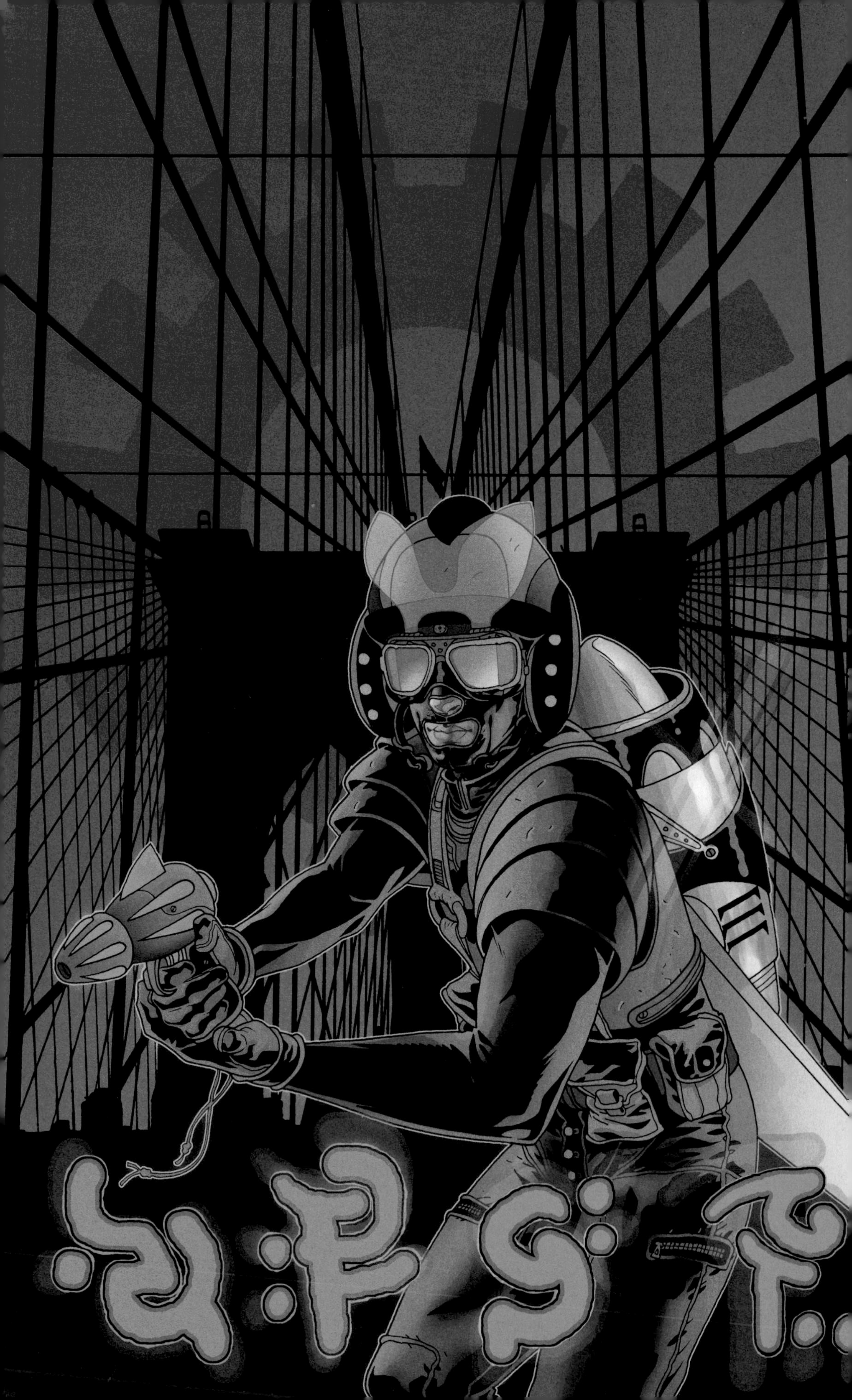

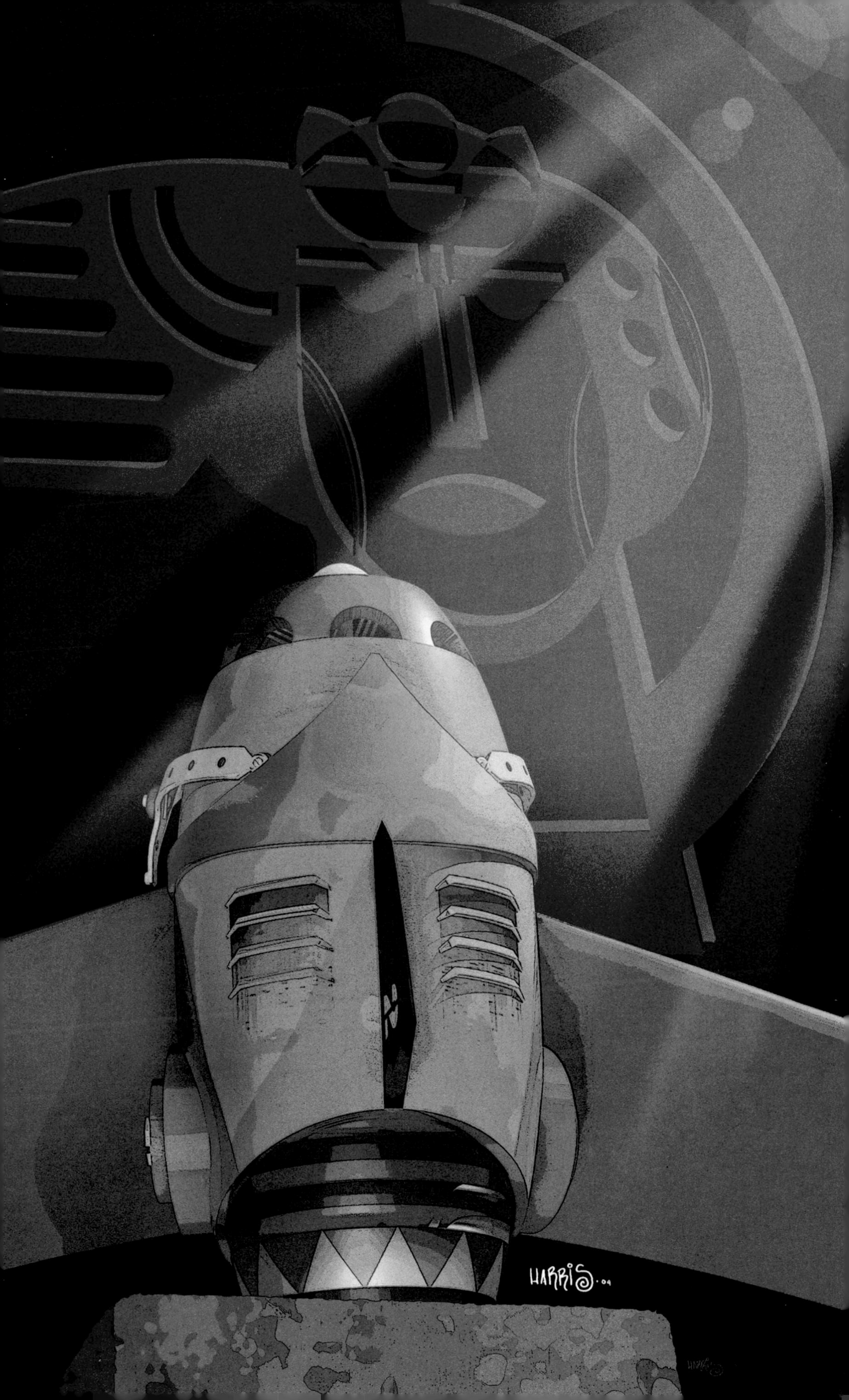
HARRIS .04

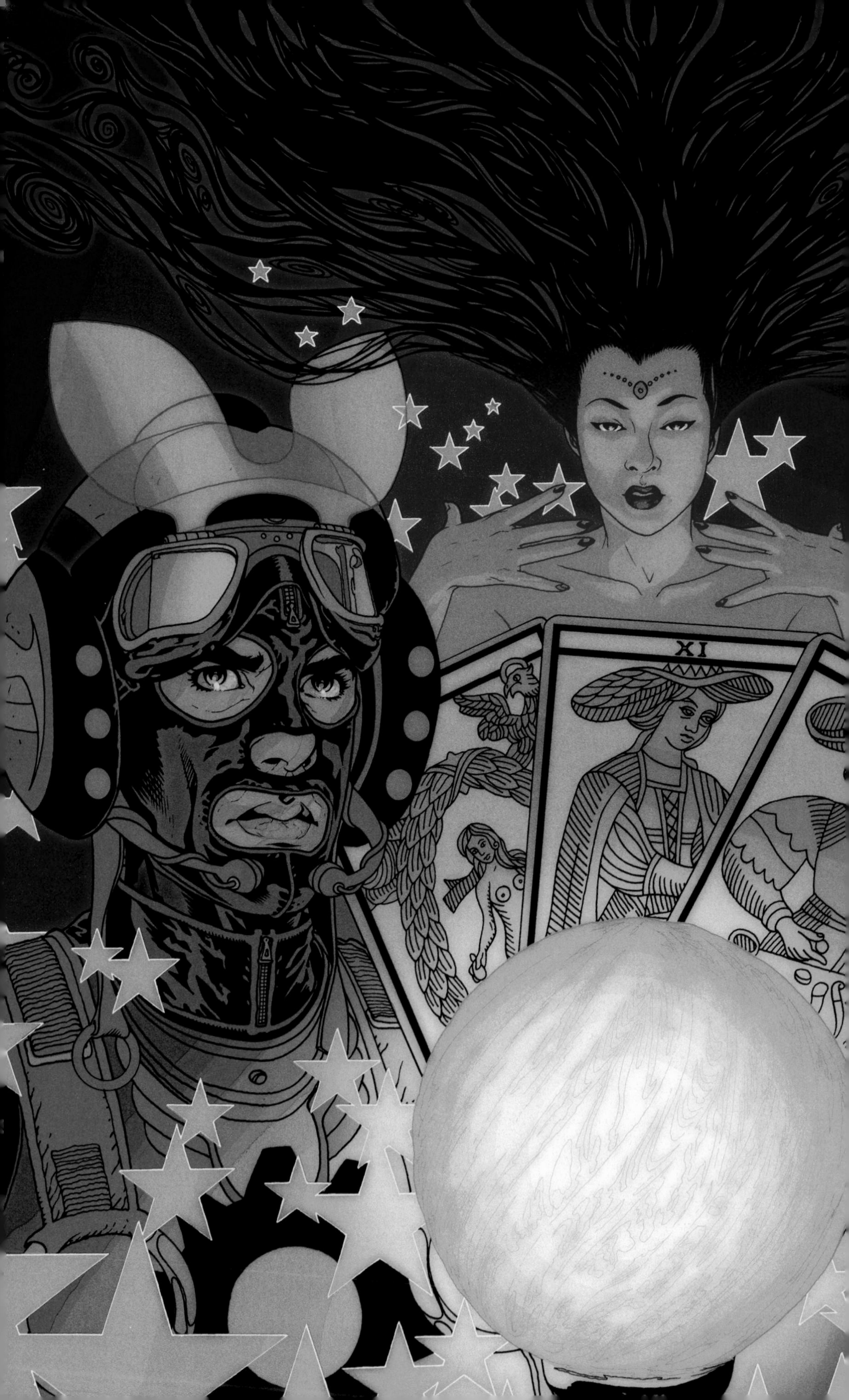

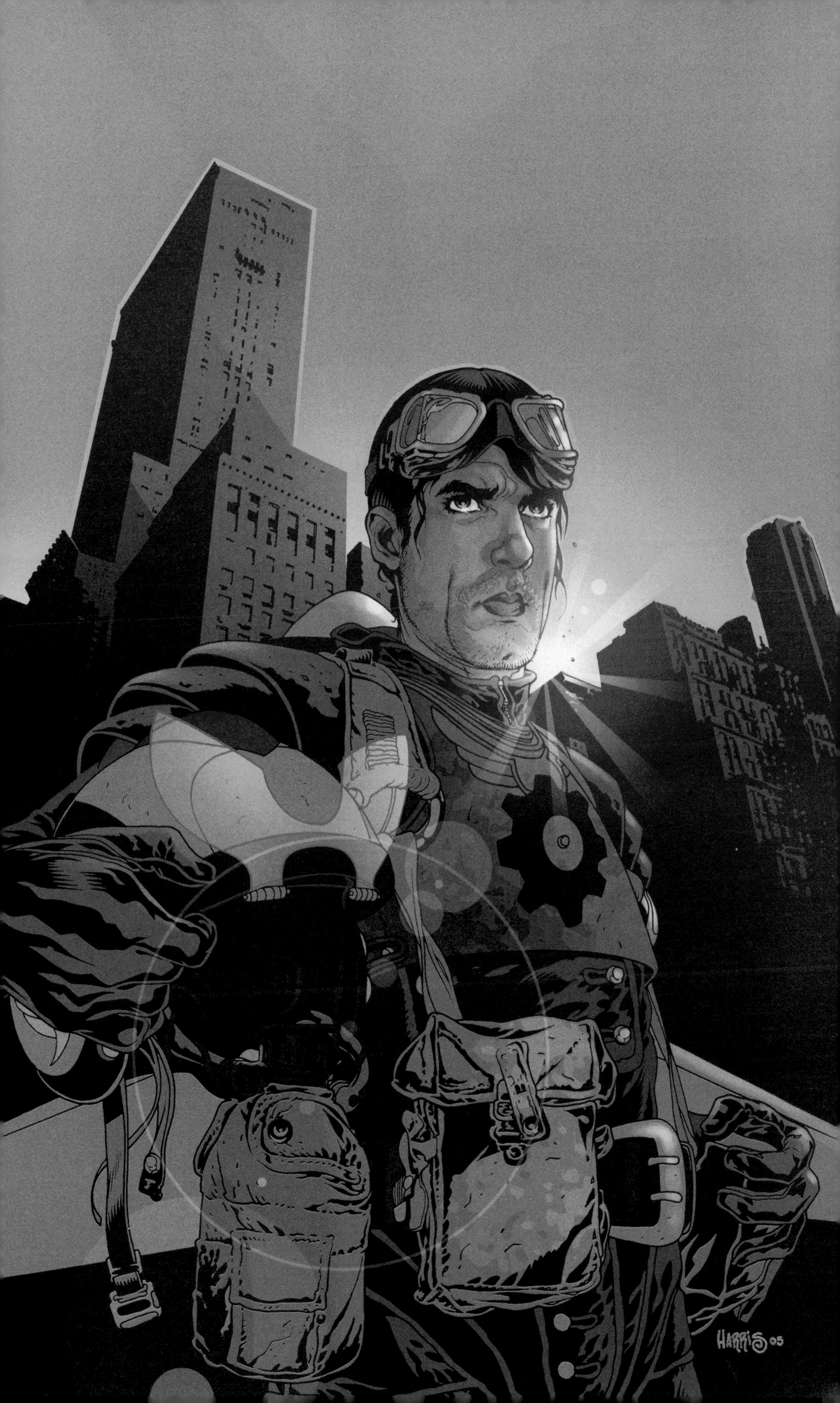
HARRIS 05

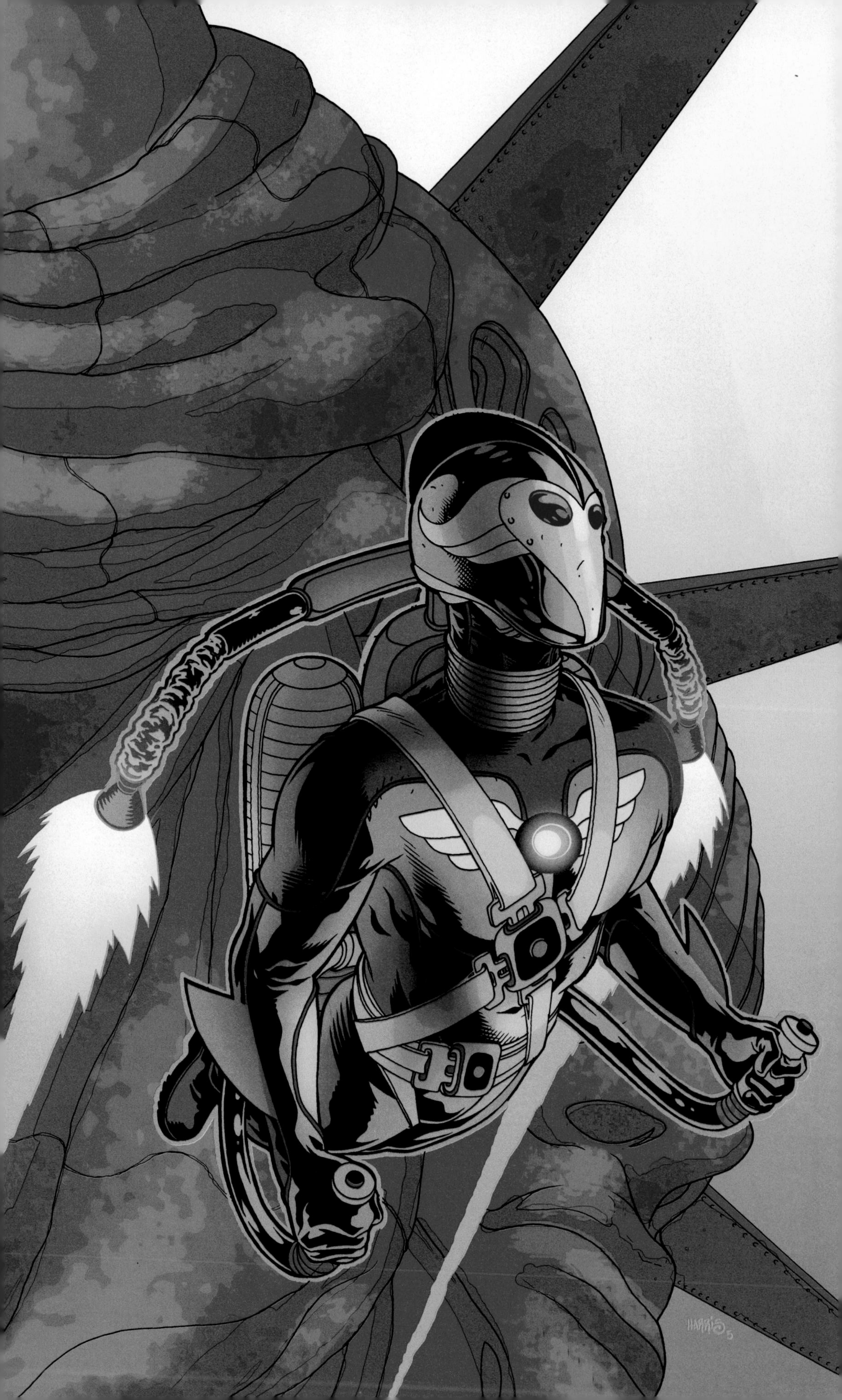
HARRIS

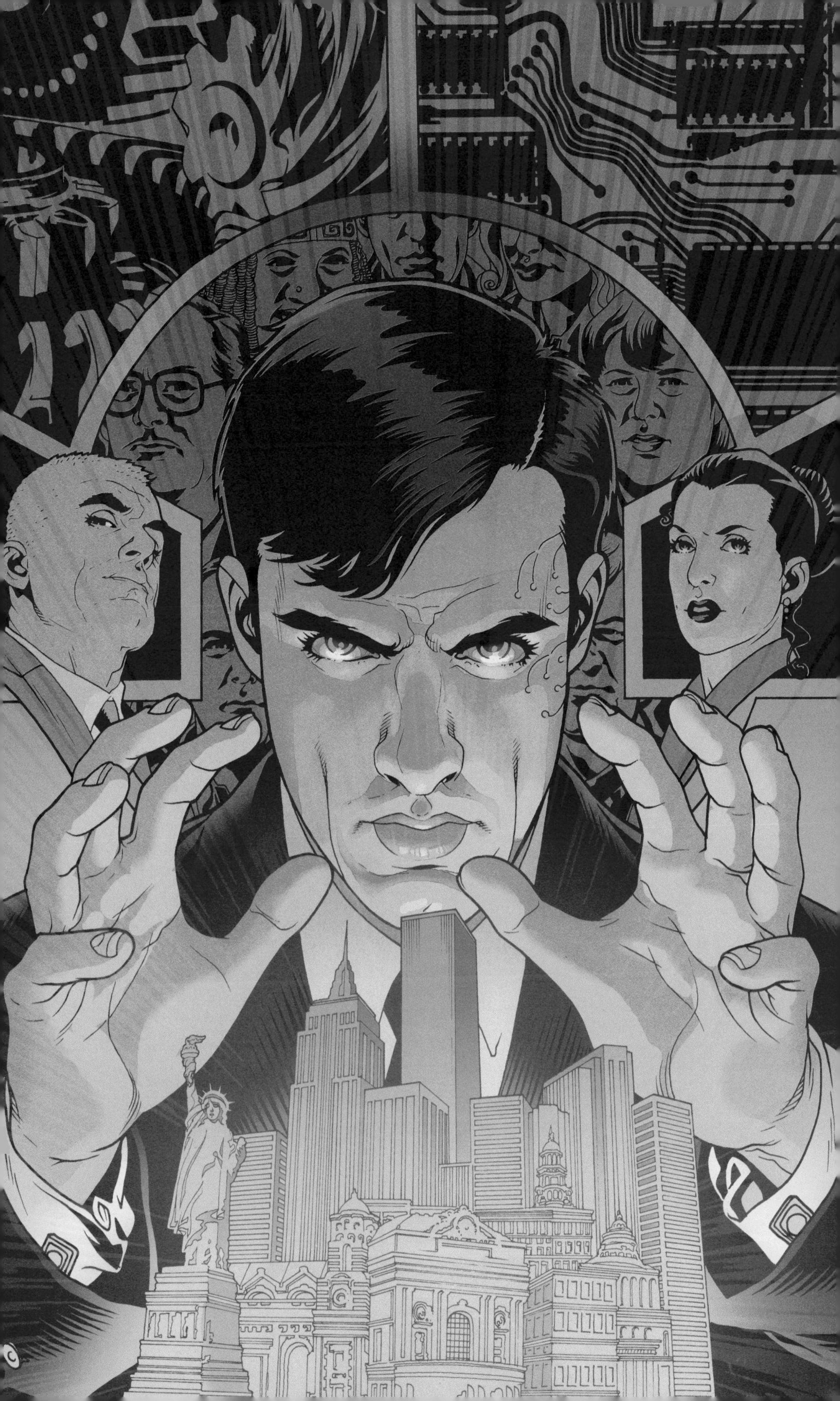

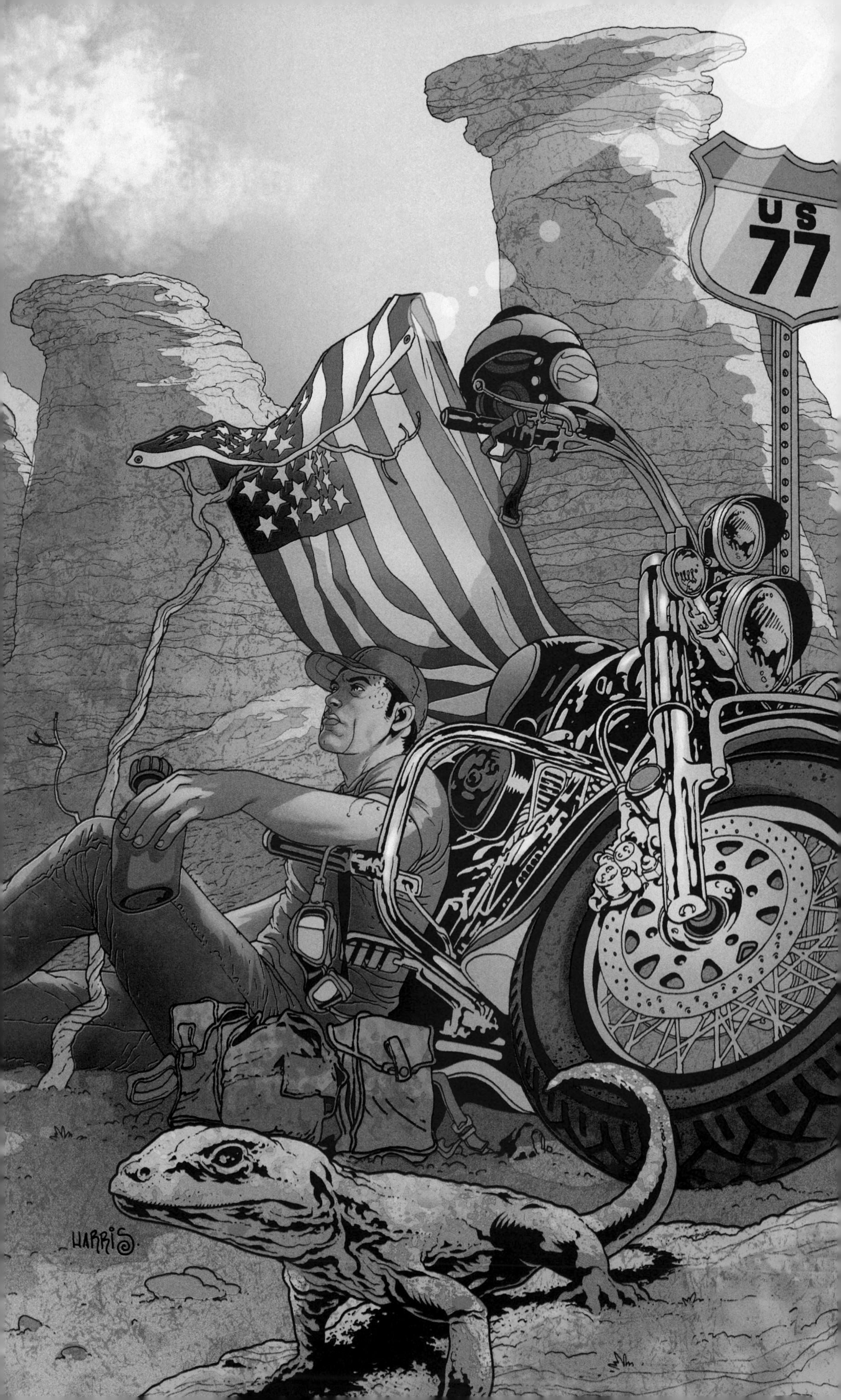
US
77
HARRIS

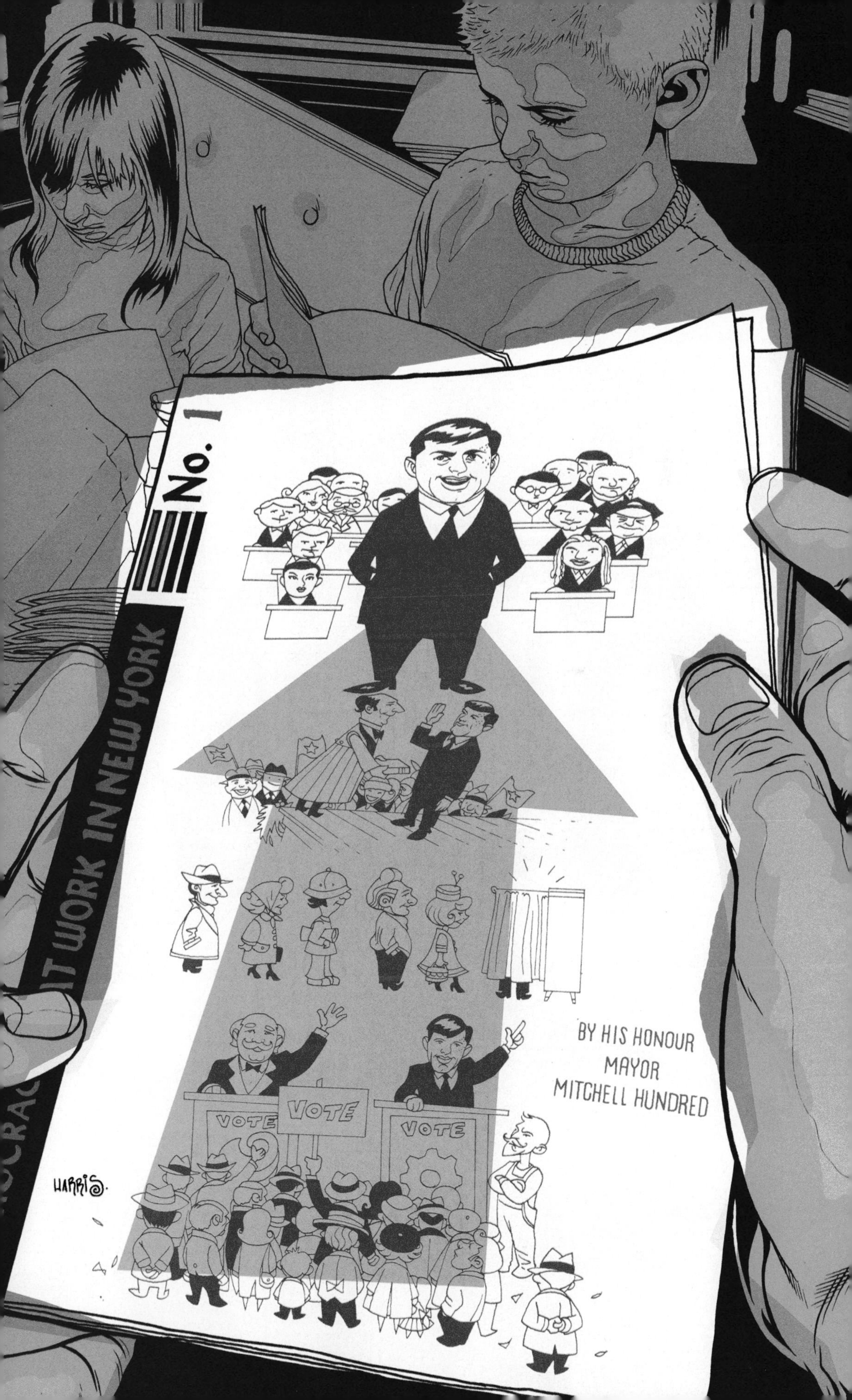
No. 1
T WORK IN NEW YORK
VOTE
VOTE
VOTE
BY HIS HONOUR
MAYOR
MITCHELL HUNDRED
HARRIS.

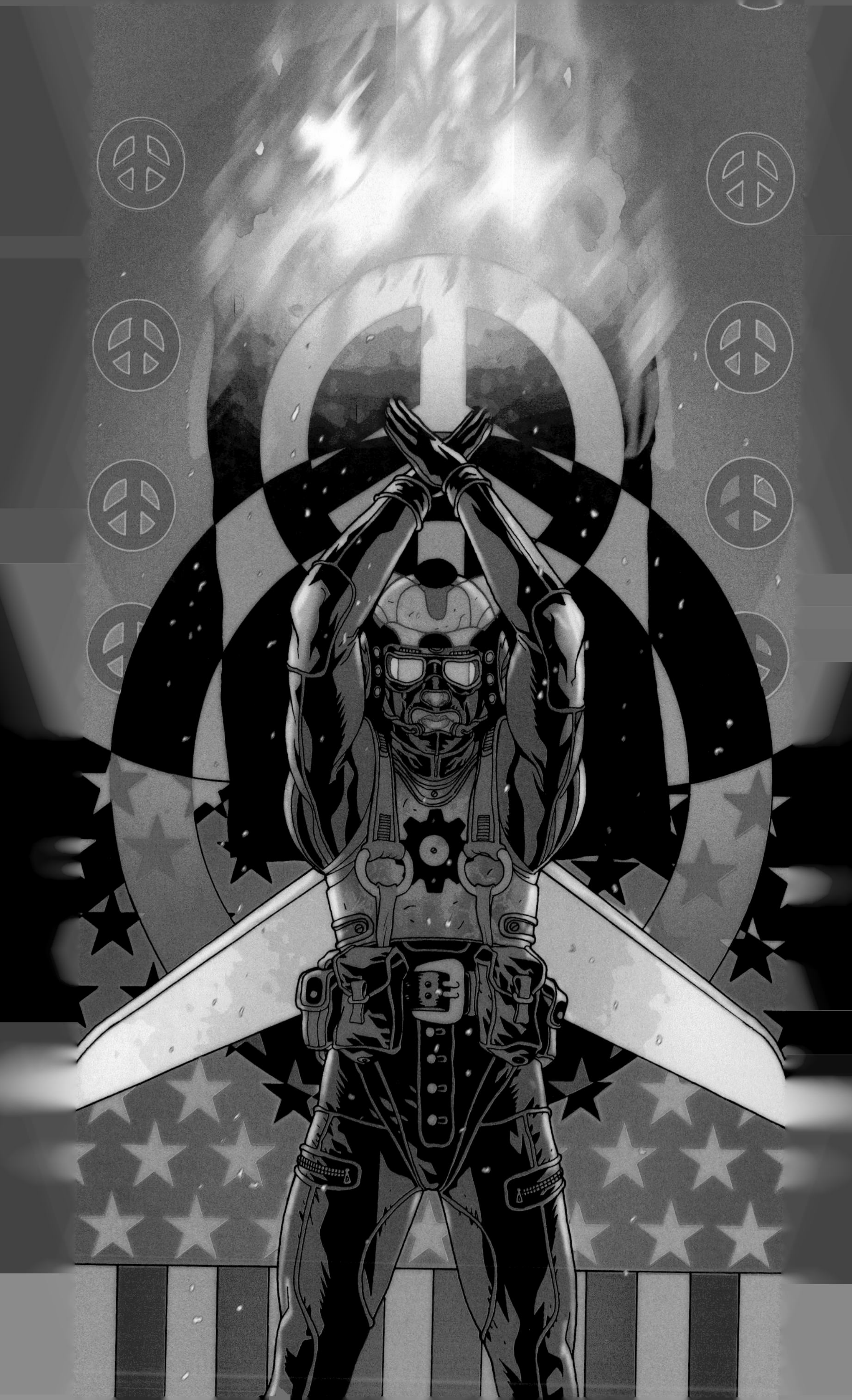

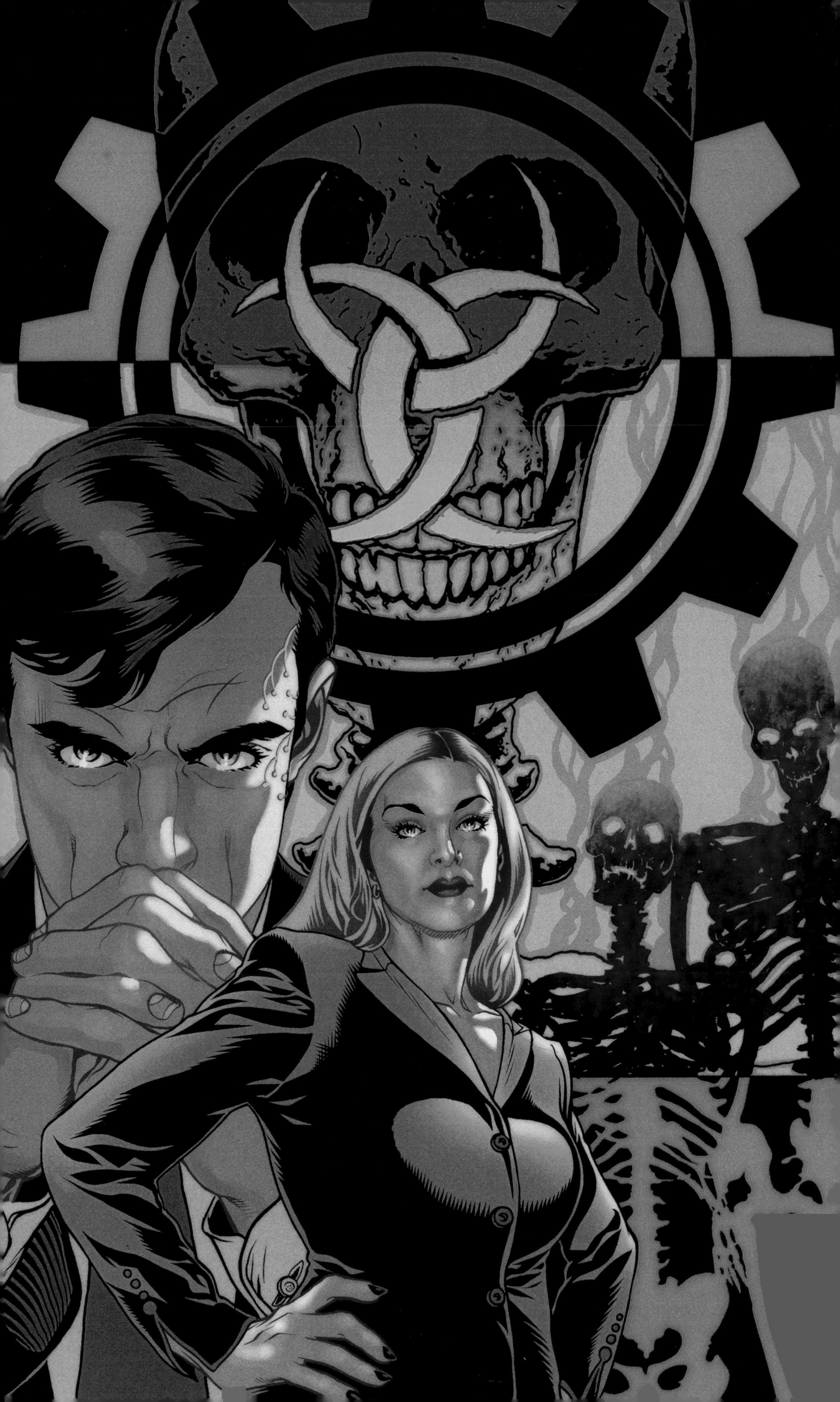

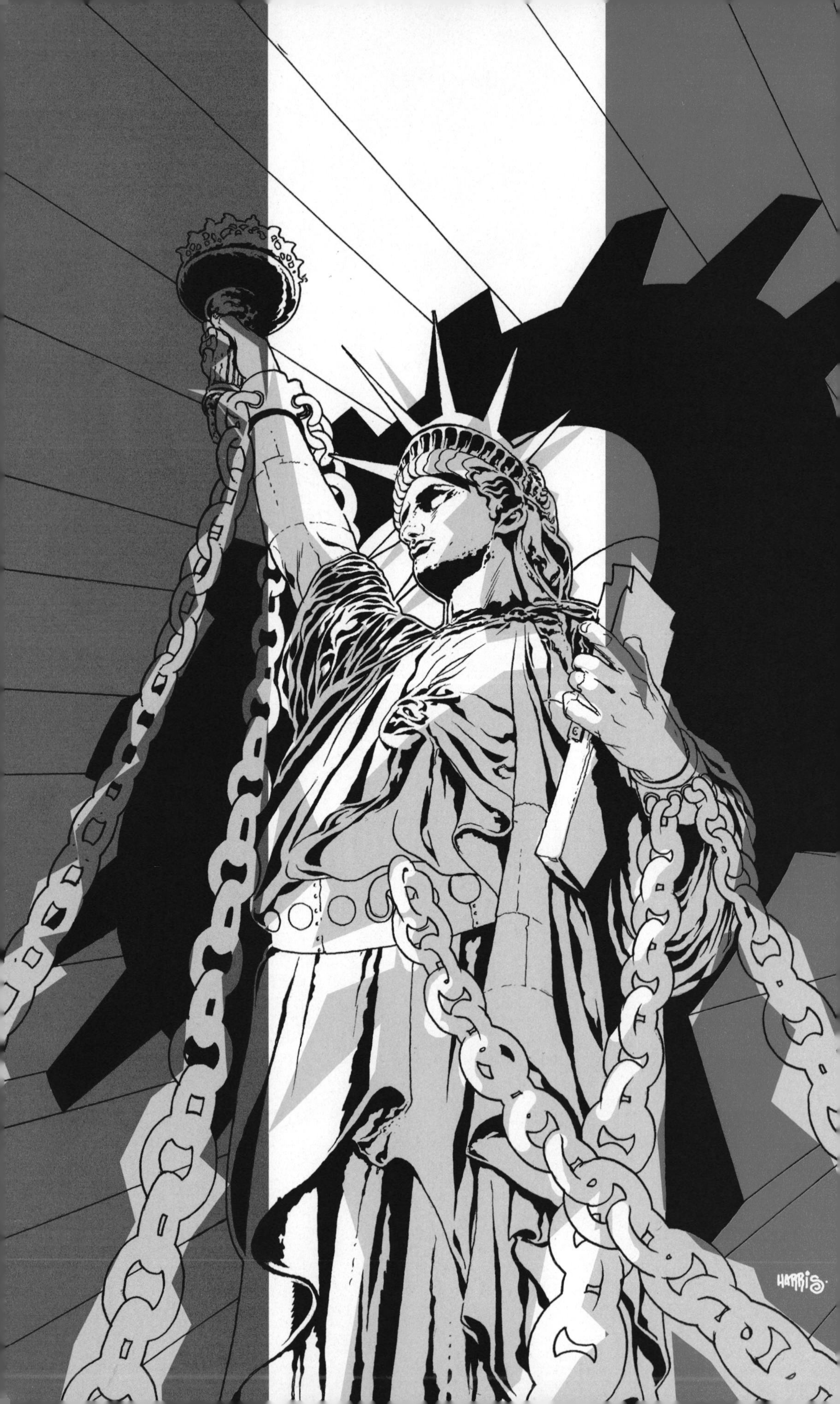
HARRIS

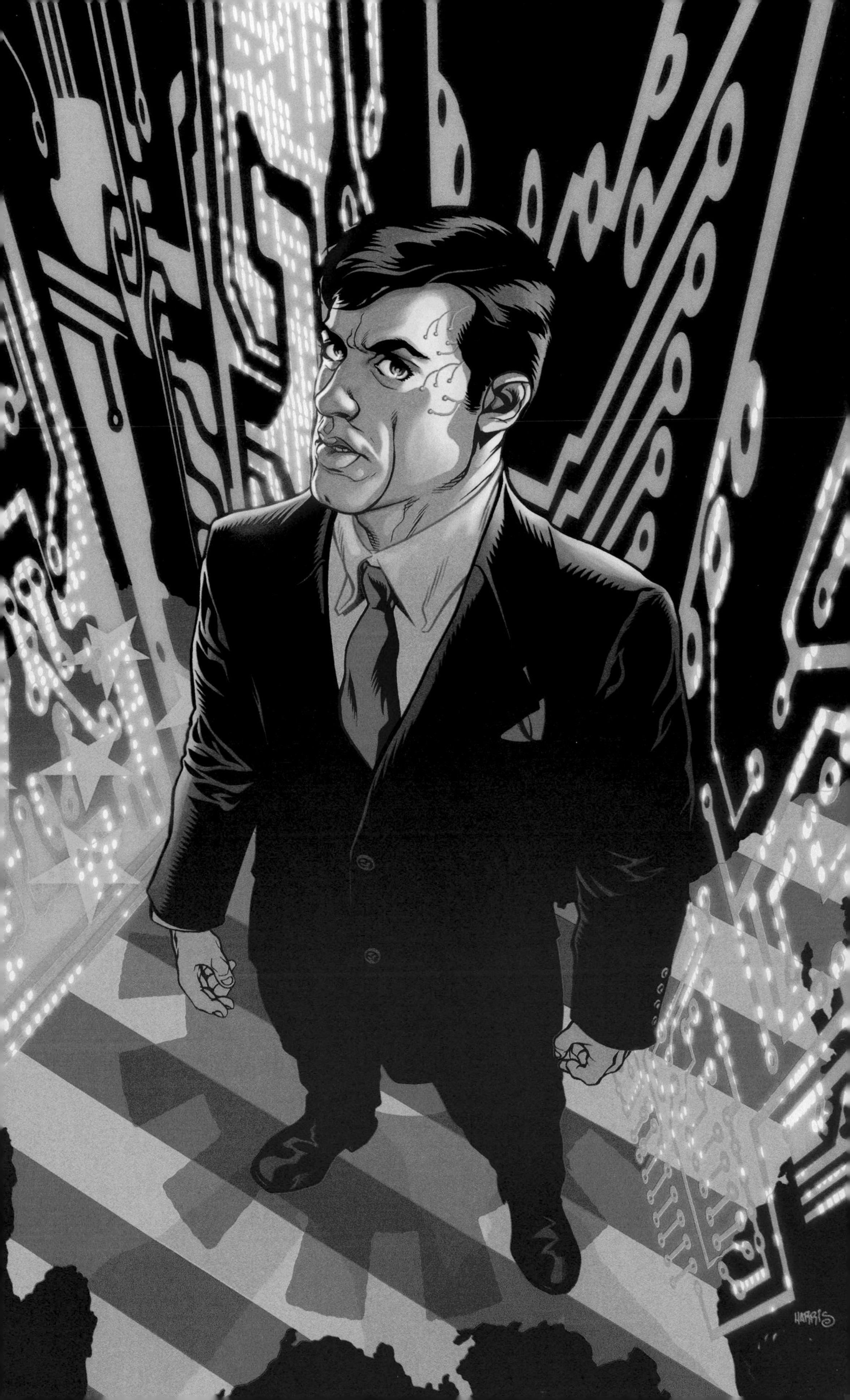

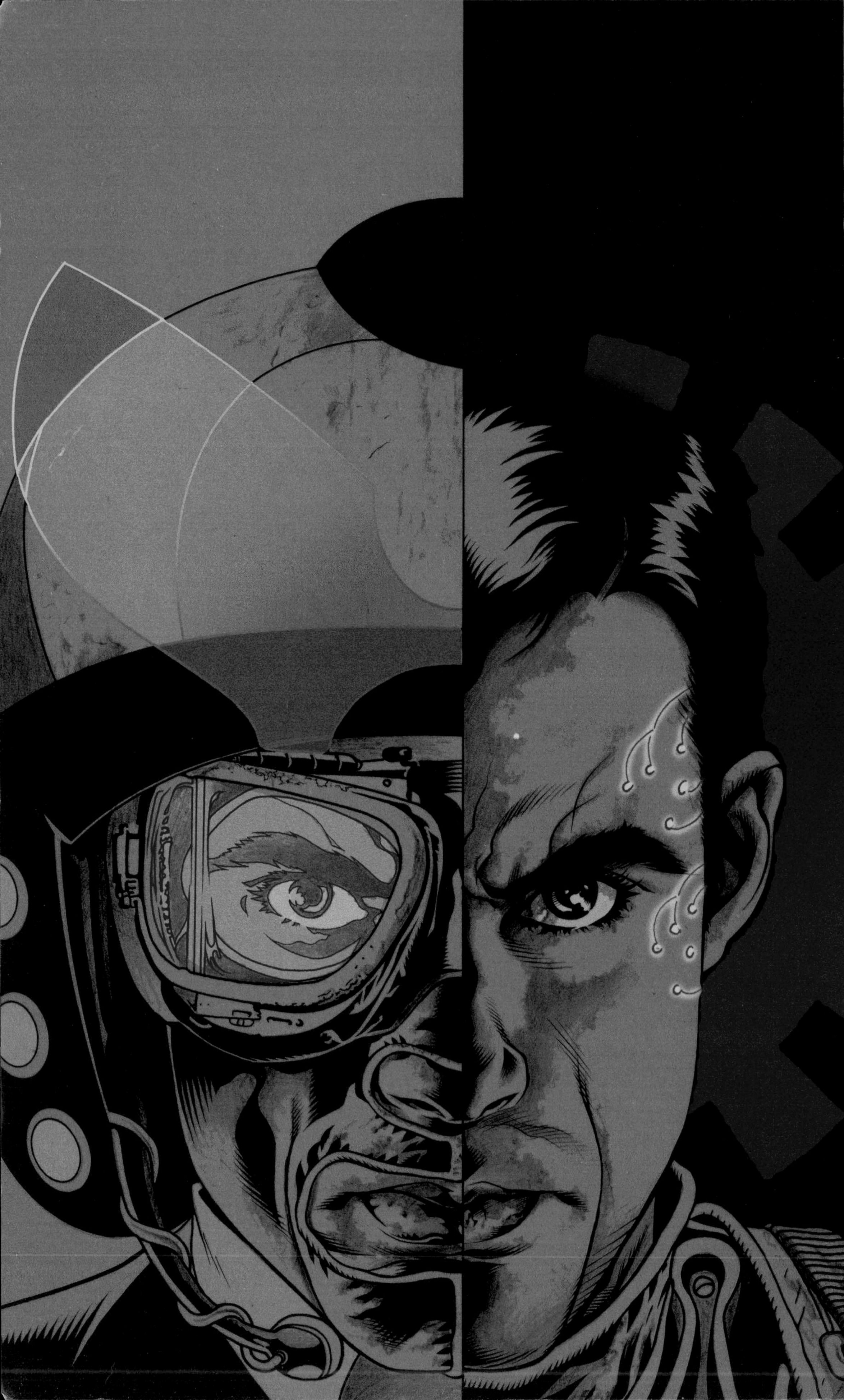

DAILY WIRE

New York's Most Respected Newspaper

★ EXCLUSIVE ★

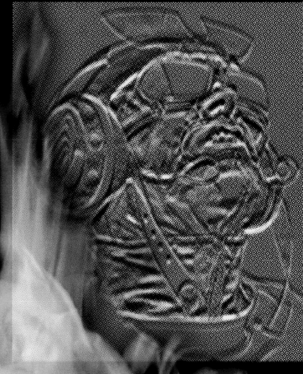

FIREFIGHTER THIEF STRIKES!

Sources at the N.Y.P.D. say that a man is posing as a New York City FireFighter and under that guise then enters peoples homes and robs them. He is allegedly targeting the upscale residents in the Soho area. Police are sorting through hundreds of leads, and phone calls from New Yorkers saying the (page 2)

NYC LOCAL 2507 HONORS MACHINE!

Sunday evening the Uniformed E.MT.'s and Paramedics of the Local 2507 will Honor The Great Machine and his efforts to save Tower 2 on 9/11. The ceremony will include a Banquet followed by the Unveiling of a relief plaque featuring a stunning likeness of The Great Machine. The Banquet is expected (page 6)

SPRAY IN THE STALL! TIDY BOWL KILLER STRIKES AGA

WILDSTORM.COM   MACHINACOMICS.CO

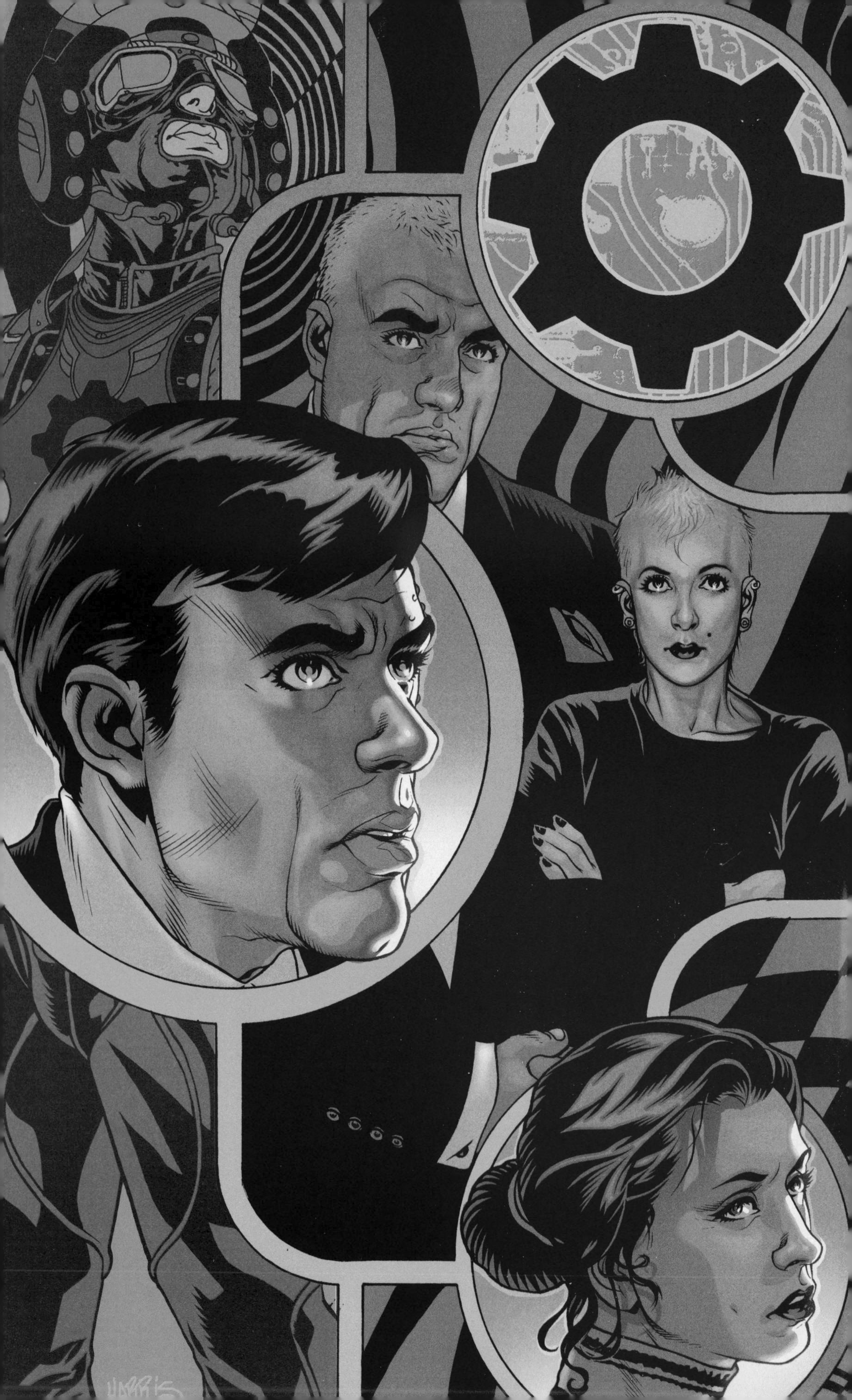